ROUTLEDGE HANDBOOK OF ENVIRONMENTAL ACCOUNTING

This handbook showcases the broad spectrum of diverse approaches to environmental accounting which have developed during the last 30 years across the globe.

The volume covers a range of physical issues such as water, carbon and biodiversity, as well as specific accounting matters such as management control, finance and audit. Moreover, seven chapters present environmental accounting issues that arise in the regions of Africa, Asia, Europe, MENA, North America, the Pacific and South America. The handbook also highlights future challenges in all the topic areas addressed as well as introducing new topics, such as links between environmental accounting and the circular economy, and the issues associated with animal rights. Edited by leading scholars in the area and with key contributions from across the discipline, and covering a diverse range of perspectives and locations, the volume is divided into five key parts:

- Part 1: Framing the issues
- Part 2: Financial accounting and reporting
- Part 3: Management accounting
- Part 4: Global and local perspectives
- Part 5: Thematic topics in environmental accounting

This handbook will act as a significant publication in drawing together the history of the field and important reference points in its future development, and will serve as a vital resource for students and scholars of environmental accounting and environmental economics.

Jan Bebbington is the Rubin professor of sustainability in business and Director of the Pentland Centre at the University of Lancaster, UK.

Carlos Larrinaga is a professor of accounting at the University of Burgos, Spain.

Brendan O'Dwyer is a professor of accounting at the Alliance Manchester Business School, UK, and the University of Amsterdam Business School, the Netherlands.

Ian Thomson is a professor of accounting and sustainability at Birmingham Business School, UK, and the director of the Lloyds Banking Group Centre for Responsible Business.

"This long-awaited handbook provides a comprehensive insight and overview of environmental accounting, written by some of the most distinguished researchers in the field. It is a helpful resource for students, lecturers and practitioners who wish to understand accounting theories, methods and approaches to analyse and antagonise global environmental crisis."

– *Tobias Viere, Professor at the Institute for Industrial Ecology, Pforzheim University Business School, Germany*

"Humanity affects the natural environment in ways that threaten its own existence and well-being. The incentives embedded in our systems of organization and governance, supported by accountants, perpetuate and exaggerate these effects. This important book, authored and edited by the who's who of environmental accounting, examines these issues and is a must-read for scholars, students, practitioners, and policymakers who are interested in forming a better understanding and making a difference."

– *Charl de Villiers, Professor of Accounting, The University of Auckland, New Zealand*

"Finally, a comprehensive account of environmental accounting at an organizational level! This handbook covers its history, lessons learned, current practices on all continents, and future challenges."

– *Ståle Navrud, Professor of Environmental Economics, School of Economics and Business, Norwegian University of Life Sciences, Norway*

ROUTLEDGE HANDBOOK OF ENVIRONMENTAL ACCOUNTING

Edited by Jan Bebbington, Carlos Larrinaga, Brendan O'Dwyer and Ian Thomson

Routledge
Taylor & Francis Group
LONDON AND NEW YORK
earthscan
from Routledge

First published 2021
by Routledge
2 Park Square, Milton Park, Abingdon, Oxon OX14 4RN

and by Routledge
52 Vanderbilt Avenue, New York, NY 10017

Routledge is an imprint of the Taylor & Francis Group, an informa business

British Library Cataloguing-in-Publication Data
A catalogue record for this book is available from the British Library

Library of Congress Cataloging-in-Publication Data
Names: Bebbington, Jan (Professor of accountancy and sustainable development), editor. | Larrinaga, Carlos, 1967– editor. | O'Dwyer, Brendan, 1968– editor. | Thomson, Ian, 1962– editor.
Title: Routledge handbook of environmental accounting / edited by Jan Bebbington, Carlos Larrinaga, Brendan O'Dwyer and Ian Thomson.
Description: Milton Park, Abingdon, Oxon; New York, NY: Routledge, 2021. | Includes bibliographical references and index.
Identifiers: LCCN 2020044183 (print) | LCCN 2020044184 (ebook)
Subjects: LCSH: Sustainable development reporting. | Social accounting. | Environmental auditing.
Classification: LCC HD60.3 .R68 2021 (print) | LCC HD60.3 (ebook) | DDC 658.4/083–dc23
LC record available at https://lccn.loc.gov/2020044183
LC ebook record available at https://lccn.loc.gov/2020044184

ISBN: 978-0-367-15233-8 (hbk)
ISBN: 978-0-367-72490-0 (pbk)
ISBN: 978-0-367-15236-9 (ebk)

Typeset in Bembo
by Newgen Publishing UK

This handbook is dedicated to the memory of Rob Gray (1952–2020) and Jeffrey Unerman (1960–2020), in recognition of their inspiring intellectual contributions to environmental accounting scholarship and to the creation of institutions that sustain the field as well as being dear friends and collaborators who enriched our lives in so many ways.

CONTENTS

List of figures *x*
List of tables *xi*
List of contributors *xiii*
Preface *xxi*
Rob Gray and David Owen

PART 1
Framing the issues **1**

1 Curating environmental accounting knowledge 3
Jan Bebbington, Carlos Larrinaga and Ian Thomson

2 The foundations of environmental accounting 17
Jan Bebbington

3 Theorising environmental accounting and reporting 29
Brendan O'Dwyer

4 Before research methods comes "methodising": Implications for environmental accounting research 46
Ian Thomson

5 The accounting profession's environmental accounting and reporting thought leadership 65
Jeffrey Unerman

6 Environmental accounting and 21st-century sustainability governance 78
Carlos Larrinaga

PART 2
Financial accounting and reporting **93**

7 Financial accounting and the natural environment 95
Thereza Raquel Sales de Aguiar and Jan Bebbington

8 Stand-alone and integrated reporting 108
Helen Tregidga and Matias Laine

9 Assurance services for sustainability reporting and beyond 125
Charika Channuntapipat

10 Norm development in environmental reporting 137
Carlos Larrinaga and Juliette Senn

11 Shareholder activism and the environment 151
Michelle Rodrigue and Giovanna Michelon

12 Financial markets and environmental information 165
Giovanna Michelon

PART 3
Management accounting **179**

13 Strategic environmental management accounting 181
Delphine Gibassier

14 Designing eco-controls for multi-objective organizations 194
Lies Bouten and Sophie Hoozée

15 Materials and energy accounting 207
Roger Burritt, Katherine Christ and Stefan Schaltegger

16 Externalities and decision-making 224
Nicolas Antheaume and Jan Bebbington

17 Designing environmental impact-valuation assemblages for sustainable decision-making 236
Ian Thomson

18 Accounting for circularity 251
Lucy Wishart and Nicolas Antheaume

PART 4
Global and local perspectives **263**

19 Africa, from the past to the present: Moving the critical environmental accounting research on Africa forward 265
Mercy Denedo and Osamuyimen Egbon

20 Environmental accounting and reporting practices in Asian countries 276
Tiffany Cheng-Han Leung

21 Europe 288
Thomas Riise Johansen

22 Environmental accounting and reporting: Evidence from the MENA region 300
Radhi Al-Hamadeen

23 The North American environmental accounting research landscape 315
Stacy L. Chavez and Andrea M. Romi

24 The Pacific region 328
Matthew Scobie, Matthew Sorola and Glenn Finau

25 Towards an accounting of socio-environmental conflicts in South America 339
Mauricio Gómez-Villegas

PART 5
Thematic topics in environmental accounting **351**

26 Carbon 353
Robert Charnock, Matthew Brander and Thomas Schneider

27 Water 365
Shona Russell

28 Biodiversity 377
Jan Bebbington, Thomas Cuckston and Clément Feger

29 Accounting for animal rights 388
Eija Vinnari and Markus Vinnari

Index *399*

FIGURES

4.1	Visualising SDG connections	49
4.2	Original rewilding mind map	51
4.3	Main stages of Resilience Assessment Framework	58
9.1	Overview of sustainability report assurance practice	127
10.1	Dynamics of norms	146
14.1	Eco-control subsystem	198
14.2	Two management control subsystems as a system in hybrid organizations	200
15.1	Sustainability accounting systems	209
15.2	Materials and energy accounting systems	209
16.1	The unflattering effect of externalities accounting	230
17.1	Socio-ecological systems assessment	242
17.2	Examples of the output of the Sustainability Assessment Model	245
18.1	Boundaries of the study	258

TABLES

2.1	Some resources and retrospectives on (social and) environmental accounting	19
4.1	Overview of methodising	47
4.2	Rewilding method possibilities partial list	53
4.3	Resource scenario examples	54
4.4	Methodising summary sheet	55
4.5	Examples of resilience assessment worksheets	59
5.1	2019 relative size of the Big Four accountancy/professional services firms globally	67
6.1	Corporate governance versus sustainability governance	83
7.1	Qualitative characteristics of financial information	96
7.2	Key financial statements	97
7.3	Environmental issues in financial statements	100
7.4	IFRIC 3 accounting for emissions rights summary	103
8.1	Characteristics of environmental reporting	113
8.2	Overview of key environmental reporting frameworks	114
9.1	Development of sustainability report assurance standards	131
10.1	Environmental regulation in Europe	140
10.2	Main standards in environmental reporting	142
10.3	The role of actors in the normativity process	143
11.1	Percentage of shareholder support for activist proposals	157
12.1	Financial impacts of climate risks and opportunities	173
14.1	Schematic representation of the different types of motivation within self-determination theory	195
15.1	Illustrative materials and energy accounting tools	213
15.2	Goals and information foci of different types of managers	215
16.1	Accounting for externalities in the 1970s and 1980s – a selection of landmark proposals	226

16.2 Accounting for externalities in the 1990s – a presentation of some landmark experiments 227
16.3 Accounting for externalities in the 2000s – a presentation of some landmark experiments 229
17.1 Examples of appropriable environmental impact techniques 238
18.1 A selection of indicators related to the circular economy 256
20.1 Comparison of environmental reporting practices in five Asian countries 283
22.1 Key demographical, economic and environmental characteristics of MENA region 301
22.2 Key and sub-thematic research ideas on EAR in the MENA region 303
23.1 Overview of regulatory environment 317
27.1 Challenges emerging from trends in the world's water resources 367
28.1 Strategic goals for biodiversity 379
29.1 Hierarchical approach to accounting for animal rights 393

CONTRIBUTORS

Radhi Al-Hamadeen is an associate professor and director of International Relations Office at the Princess Sumaya University for Technology, Amman, Jordan. Radhi's PhD was on the topic of assurance statements attached to "stand-alone" reports and he has also published on financial accounting topics such as dividends policy, determinants of corporate social responsibility, corporate disclosure, and mergers and acquisitions. These topics have focused on the context in Jordan as well as other national contexts. He has also published work on higher education policy in Jordan.

Nicolas Antheaume is a professor in management at the University of Nantes's School of Economics and Management, France and researches topics relating to science-based environmental accounting. He has recently been involved in such projects as the economic and environmental evaluation of recycling in mining industries, public works, quarries and agriculture. He has been involved in research projects with organisations such as EDF, Schneider Electric, the French Ministry of Transport, the French Agency for the Environment and Energy Management.

Jan Bebbington is the Rubin professor of sustainability in business and Director of the Pentland Centre in Sustainability in Business at the University of Lancaster and focuses on how sustainability has been understood by organisations and what activities have been undertaken by them to support its pursuit. Jan has been associated with the Centre for Social and Environmental Accounting Research since its inception, including being a co-editor of the *Social and Environmental Accountability Journal* (from 2008 to 2011).

Lies Bouten is an associate professor of Accounting at IESEG School of Management Lille-Paris (France) and member of LEM-CNRS 9221 (France). Her research focuses on the interface between external sustainability reporting, management accounting and external assurance. Lies is an editorial board member of *Social and Environmental Accountability Journal*, *Accounting and the Public Interest* and *Accounting Forum*. She is also a member of the CSR steering committee of IESEG School of Management Lille-Paris.

Matthew Brander is a senior lecturer in carbon accounting at the University of Edinburgh's Business School. His current research focuses on the development of methods for corporate, product (life cycle assessment), project and policy-level greenhouse gas accounting. Matthew has served as a member of several technical working groups for the Greenhouse Gas Protocol and the International Organisation for Standardisation (ISO).

Roger Burritt is an honorary professor at Fenner School of Environment and Society, Australian National University, Canberra, Australia and a Visiting Professor of Sustainability Business Metrics at the Centre for Sustainability Management, Leuphana Universität Lüneburg, Germany. Roger's research focuses on sustainability accounting and environmental management accounting. He is a fellow of CPA Australia and Chartered Accountants in Australia and New Zealand, a member of the Chartered Institute of Bankers and member of the Environment Institute of Australia and New Zealand.

Charika Channuntapipat is a lecturer at the University of Birmingham, UK. Her research interest focuses on the broad areas of sustainability governance and accountability; and the role of accounting profession in sustainable development, with a focus on non-financial reporting and assurance practices continues. Charika was also involved in research to explore the current status of the targets and indicators relating finance and trade under the Goal 17, funded by Thailand Science Research and Innovation.

Robert Charnock is a lecturer at the University of Birmingham, UK, focusing on the roles of accounting and finance in driving the transition to zero-carbon economies. His interdisciplinary research draws on insights from across sociology, regulation, strategy and accounting. Robert has engaged with global financial regulators and professional associations on matters of carbon finance, transition risks and climate performance metrics, and also served as a technical working group member on a United Nations and Greenhouse Gas Protocol standard-setting project.

Stacy L. Chavez is a PhD candidate in the School of Accounting at Texas Tech University's Rawls College of Business. Her current research focuses on accounting in various settings related to social issues, including research on gender, feminist social movements, pollinators and the cannabis industry. Stacy is a member of the Centre for Social and Environmental Accounting Research. Her previous experience includes positions at a Big Four accounting firm, and in other corporate settings, where she focused on international and technical accounting areas.

Katherine Christ is a lecturer at the University of South Australia and her research interests include sustainability accounting, environmental management accounting, water accounting and the management and reporting of modern slavery risk in corporate supply chains. Katherine is committed to undertaking research with real-world impact and regularly engages with business on areas related to sustainability management and performance.

Thomas Cuckston is a senior lecturer in accounting at the University of Birmingham and his research focuses on explaining how humanity can create societies that are capable of pursuing sustainable development while ensuring conservation of Earth's biosphere. To further this aim, he examines how different kinds of calculative devices can contribute to creating conditions in which people and organisations are collectively able to achieve agency – i.e. the capacity to act – such that the pursuit of sustainable development within societies becomes possible.

Mercy Denedo is an assistant professor in accounting at Durham University Business School. Underlining Mercy's research is an interest in social and environmental issues that affect people's everyday realities. She has conducted interdisciplinary qualitative and interpretive studies on social housing, public sector, social audit for home-grown school feeding programme; sustainability, human rights, accountability and governance research within a conflict and environmentally polluted arena, counter accounting and stakeholders' engagement and NGOs accountability.

Osamuyimen Egbon is a lecturer in accounting at the Essex Business School, University of Essex, UK. His research emerges from the intersection of organisations, sustainability and society and he explores the topics of accountability, social and environmental reporting, NGO accountability and community engagement, corporate social responsibility, and sustainability (including the Sustainable Development Goals). His recent works have focused on the accountability relations of multinational corporations and host communities in developing economy context.

Clément Feger is an associate professor in strategic environmental management analysis and ecological accounting at AgroParisTech and a researcher at the University of Montpellier (MRM Lab). His research focuses on developing accounting theory, frameworks and tools for the collective management of biodiversity and ecosystems, at the crossroads between qualitative accounting research and conservation science. He also works on the development of new business models for biodiversity as well as on context diagnostic methods in support of the strategic management and multi-stakeholders' governance of ecological landscapes (e.g. biodiversity corridors).

Glenn Finau is a lecturer at the University of Tasmania in Australia. Glenn previously worked at the University of the South Pacific based in Suva, Fiji and before that he was an auditor with Ernst & Young (Fiji). Glenn's current research focuses on the interface between accounting, customary land and Indigenous peoples in post-colonial states in the Pacific. His other areas of interests include accounting and sport, social media and governance, and the adoption of ICT innovations by organisations in the Pacific.

Delphine Gibassier is an associate professor of accounting for sustainable development at Audencia, director of the International Research Centre "Multi-Capital Integrated Performance" and academic director of the MBA Chief Value Officer. Her research, which mainly uses intervention research methods, focuses on carbon, water and biodiversity accounts, as well as multi-capital and integrated accountability systems. She is an associate editor of *Sustainability, Accounting, Management and Policy Journal.*

Mauricio Gómez-Villegas is an associate professor in the Management and Public Accountancy School at Universidad Nacional de Colombia. His research focuses on socio-environmental accounting, accounting theory, critical accounting and public sector accounting. Mauricio is an editorial board member of Public Money and Management (CIPFA), Contabilidad y Auditoría (Universidad de Buenos Aires), and Contaduría Universidad de Antioquia (Colombia). He was the chief editor of *Innovar Journal* (2014–2018).

Sophie Hoozée is an associate professor of management accounting and control at Ghent University in Belgium. Her research focuses on the design of costing systems and management control systems, as well as on social and environmental accounting. Sophie is an editorial board member of *Social and Environmental Accountability Journal* and acts as a jury member on the judging panel for the Best Belgian Sustainability Report Award. Sophie is also responsible for embedding sustainability in the business economics programme at Ghent University.

Thomas Riise Johansen is a professor in financial reporting and auditing at the Copenhagen Business School, Denmark. His research has focused on social and environmental accounting and accountability processes, including the role of stakeholders and institutional arrangements. He has also focused on financial and non-financial disclosures in annual reports and the way in which such disclosures are shaped by interactions between managers, users and auditors. In addition, his work explores the role of regulation, regulators, oversight and enforcement in accounting and auditing.

Matias Laine is an academy research fellow and an associate professor in accounting at Tampere University, Finland. In his research, Matias seeks to understand the interface of business, societies and the natural environment, and to use his privileged position to critically explore the roles sustainability accounting, accountability and reporting can play in the pursuit of a less unsustainable world. Matias has served both the European Accounting Association and the Centre for Social and Environmental Accounting Research in various roles for a number of years.

Carlos Larrinaga is a professor of accounting at the University of Burgos, Spain. He is interested in the potential of environmental accounting to mobilise change in the direction to a more sustainable society. He has addressed this concern through research engagements, surveys and theoretical studies in issues such as carbon accounting, reporting boundaries or environmental reporting regulation. Carlos has been a member of the Centre for Social and Environmental Accounting Research since 1994 and served as the co-editor of the *Social and Environmental Accountability Journal* from 2014 to 2017.

Tiffany Cheng-Han Leung is an assistant professor in the Faulty of Business at the City University of Macau. Her research interests include social and environmental accounting and governance, corporate social responsibility, creating shared value, controversial industries and business ethics. Tiffany is the coordinator in the Centre for Social and Environmental Accounting Research North Asia Satellite Office in Hong Kong and Macau. She is also a board member of *Accounting Forum*.

Giovanna Michelon is a professor of accounting at the University of Bristol. Her publications focused on the governance process and systems that underpin corporate actions and accountability on sustainability issues, as well as on the role that sustainability information plays in capital markets. Giovanna is currently the co-editor of *Accounting Forum*, editor-in-chief of the *European Accounting Association Resource Centre*, a council member of the Centre for Social and Environmental Accounting Research and chair of the ACCA Global Forum for Governance, Risk and Performance.

Brendan O'Dwyer is a professor of accounting at the Alliance Manchester Business School and the University of Amsterdam Business School and is a fellow of Chartered Accountants Ireland. Brendan's research and public policy work examines the role of accounting and assurance practices in making the complex social and environmental impacts of organisational activities visible. His recent work focuses on how new voluntary and mandatory non-financial reporting models are initiated, evolve and become embedded in corporate practice.

Michelle Rodrigue is a professor of accounting in the School of Accounting at Université Laval (Québec, Canada). Her research interests include the multiple forms of sustainability-related challenges raised by stakeholders to corporations and the role that accounting and reporting play in shaping and dealing with these challenges. She is the joint editor of the *Social and Environmental Accountability Journal*, a council member of the Centre for Social and Environmental Accounting Research and a member of the Centre for Research on Accounting and Sustainability (Université Laval).

Andrea M. Romi is an associate professor of accounting in the School of Accounting, Rawls College of Business, Texas Tech University and conducts research on the role of accounting in the social and environmental phenomena facing the world. She has worked with the Sustainability Consortium, to develop uniform, industry-wide sustainability measurements and assurance standards. Andrea also has experience within both non-governmental organisations and regulatory institutions (e.g. Coalition of Environmentally Responsible Economies [CERES], American Institute of Certified Public Accountants [AICPA] and Securities and Exchange Commission [SEC]) to gain practical experience concerning policy strategy as it relates to sustainability.

Shona Russell is a senior lecturer in knowledge and practice at the School of Management, University of St Andrews. Over the past 15 years, she has been researching accounting, accountability and governance that arise at the intersection of organisations, society and the natural environment. She regularly undertakes and reflects upon collaborative and interdisciplinary knowledge production to support sustainability. Her research is situated within the Centre for Social and Environmental Accounting Research, of which she is a co-director.

Thereza Raquel Sales de Aguiar is a senior lecturer in accountancy at the University of Aberdeen. Previously, she worked at the University of Glasgow and Herriot-Watt University as a lecturer in accountancy. Her research interests include corporate social responsibility, accountability, carbon accounting and gender. She has published her work in international and interdisciplinary journals, such as *Accounting, Auditing and Accountability Journal* and *Accounting Forum*.

Stefan Schaltegger is a professor and head of the Centre for Sustainability Management at Leuphana University Lüneburg, Germany. His research focuses on corporate sustainability management, including sustainability accounting and management control, performance measurement and management, concepts and tools of sustainability management, sustainable entrepreneurship and stakeholder theory. Stefan Schaltegger has served in various academic functions, including as vice-president research of Leuphana University Lüneburg (2006–2011), associate editor or member of the editorial board of 16 international academic journals.

Thomas Schneider is an associate professor of accounting at the Ted Rogers School of Management, Ryerson University, Toronto, Canada. His research is focused on environmental accounting, particularly in the natural resource sector. Thomas is a member of the United Nations Expert Group on Resource Management and has worked to develop the guidelines on social and environmental considerations for the United Nations Framework Classification for resources.

Matthew Scobie is a lecturer in organisational accountability at Te Whare Wānanga o Waitaha/University of Canterbury in Aotearoa, New Zealand. Matthew's research interests are broadly around exploring ways to hold organisations, businesses and governments accountable for their social, environmental, cultural and economic impacts, including a focus on Indigenous development and decolonisation, corporate social responsibility and social environmental accounting/accountability.

Juliette Senn is a postdoctoral researcher at the Universidad de Burgos, Spain, having graduated with a PhD from the University of Montpellier, France. Her research interests include social and environmental accounting, corporate reporting and governance systems. She has publications in *Accounting, Auditing and Accountability Journal* and *Advances in Environmental Accounting & Management* on these topics.

Matthew Sorola obtained his PhD from Victoria University of Wellington, New Zealand, and currently teaches management accounting in Toulouse Business School, France. Matthew is actively engaged in both critical and interpretive accounting research and is interested in the intersection between politics and accounting. More specifically, Matthew's research aims to surface alternative and marginalised perspectives to foster critically pluralist and reflexive understandings.

Ian Thomson is a professor in accounting and sustainability at the University of Birmingham's Business School, director of the Lloyds Banking Group Centre for Responsible Business and convenor of the Centre for Social and Environmental Accounting Research. His research has included studies on implementing cleaner technology, establishing industrial ecologies, effective stakeholder engagement, risk governance in water and salmon farming, sustainable development indicators, government policymaking, climate change, effective pedagogy, use of accounting by activists, human rights, international development programmes and climate change.

Helen Tregidga is a professor in accounting at Royal Holloway, University of London, whose work focuses on social and environmental accounting, accountability and reporting with a particular interest in corporate discourses on sustainability. Helen is a joint editor of the *Social and Environmental Accountability Journal* and an active member of the Centre for Social and Environmental Accounting Research, and is currently serving on the Executive Council.

Jeffrey Unerman was a professor in sustainability accounting in the Department of Accounting and Finance at Lancaster University Management School. He was a long-standing contributor to sustainability accounting, having researched in this area since the mid-1990s. He also actively engaged with the accounting profession in their development of sustainability accounting initiatives.

Eija Vinnari is a professor of public financial management at Tampere University, Finland. Her recent research has focused on non-human animals as a marginalised constituency and she has published on counter-accounts produced by animal rights activists; the incorporation of animal rights considerations in the definition of sustainability; sustainability matrices employed in decision-making related to the food sector; as well as the potential of agonistic democracy and critical dialogic accounting for facilitating a transition towards a more sustainable world characterised by inter-species justice.

Markus Vinnari is a senior lecturer of food economics at the University of Helsinki, Finland and an adjunct professor in economic sociology at the University of Turku, Finland. His recent research has focused on developing methods to accelerate food system transition towards de-animalisation. He has also developed sustainability frameworks to take into consideration both animal welfare and animal rights. His current work focuses on indicator systems to both monitor and advance the rights of non-human animals as well as the use of expert knowledge in decision-making.

Lucy Wishart is an associate lecturer in management at the University of St Andrews in Fife, Scotland and researches the governance of waste and sustainability. She is particularly interested in how the materiality of waste directs practices of organising at individual, organisational and national scales. She has experience of working with both commercial and community-led environmental organisations. Prior to working in academia, she trained as a lawyer specialising in environmental and planning law, and she is a qualified Scottish solicitor.

PREFACE

Accounts of humanity's relationship with the natural environment

It seems to be a truism that humans have always constructed and communicated accounts of the natural environment, whether those accounts were creation myths, advice on where to obtain the best honey, how to foretell the weather or places to avoid when the rains come. These accounts helped our ancestors navigate their relationship(s) with nature, whether those relationships were exploitive, harmonious or, indeed, something of both. It appears to be widely accepted that those relationships began to change immeasurably with the emergence of modernity. Inevitably, it seems, humanity's accounts of the environment also began to change. Broadly, modernity has encouraged a separation of humanity and nature: a separation that seems to get greater the more "advanced" our economies and societies. This separation has important implications for what we now understand as accounts of the environment.

Recognition of the serious consequences of humanity's separation from nature is often identified with accounts such as Aldo Leopold's *A Sand Country Almanac* (first published in 1949) and Rachel Carson's *Silent Spring* (first published in 1962). Modern humanity now has less direct experience of nature and consequently such accounts as exist seem to be less important to the sense of self and to society at large. Humanity has less understanding of nature – other than as a thing to be exploited – and accounts of the environment come to supplement – or even supplant – our own experiential accounts of nature. We now seem to have reached a point where our environmental accounts are, in many cases, not accounts of nature at all. Rather, they are accounts of humanity's increasingly detrimental impact upon aspects of the natural environment. We still have accounts of nature, of course, and these – like, for example, the WWF's *Living Planet Reports* or the UN's *Millennium Ecosystem Assessment* – are crucial in providing us with a global context within which we might try to understand our place in the natural environment. But even these accounts are inevitably partial, focussed as they are upon some categorised aspect(s) of the natural environment and mankind's interaction with it. In fact, it is arguable that a full, holistic account of nature may well be entirely beyond human capacity: whether this should concern us or not is quite another matter.

The sorts of accounts which tend to dominate what we now know as environmental accounting (and which largely dominate the chapters in this text) tend to be accounts based on organisations: companies, public sector bodies, third-sector organisations, governments and so on (see Part 5 of this handbook for a broader perspective). And, much like mainstream accounting itself, they broadly tend towards accounts for use either within the organisations (the equivalent of what accountants would know as management accounts) or designed for consumption by stakeholders external to the organisation (the equivalent of what accountants would know as financial accounts and reporting). Now, while this distinction is somewhat arbitrary, it does help highlight some of the strengths, limitations and possibilities that will be explored throughout the following chapters.

Environmental accounts designed for use by management are intended to help the organisation exploit eco-efficiencies and to enjoy those win-win opportunities which (like, say, energy usage) may lead to reduced costs and benefit to the natural environment. The crucial point about such accounts is that they are intended to be transformative. That is, they work with organisations in order to reduce the impact of the organisation on the environment in the (often implicit) assumption that organisational reform may eventually reach the point where organisational environmental impact is neutral, or even positive. However, as Walley and Whitehead so seminally demonstrated (in the *Harvard Business Review* as early as 1994), there are real limits to that transformation. Under current ways of organising, there has to be severe doubts about whether an organisation can become, say, entirely environmentally benign, no matter how excellent the environmental accounts.

Environmental accounts intended for external use can be thought of as comprising two sorts. First, environmental financial accounting seeks to incorporate aspects of the organisation's environmental interactions into the conventional financial accounting practices so that, notably, shareholders might be better informed as to the environmental risks and opportunities that are embedded in their investment. The exposure of, for example, environmental liabilities and the appeal to, for example, socially responsible investment offered great hope for further transformative power of environmental accounting through the operation of financial markets. That is, investors would recognise that the risks arising from suboptimal environmental performance were undesirable and capital would, accordingly, move from the more environmentally malign organisation to the more environmentally benign organisation. Once again, however, there were arguably limits to the extent to which such a reform was possible and the extent to which environmental concern could overcome more pressing financial exigencies.

Of perhaps more potential, however, was the development of environmental, as well as social and sustainability, reporting. This involved the production of (typically non-financial) accounts which sought to represent organisational environmental performance for a wider group of stakeholders: not only for investors and management but also for employees, customers and the local community, for example. On the face of it, such external environmental reports offer a low-cost, risk-free opportunity for stakeholders to learn fully about the environmental implications of organisational behaviour and, consequently, offer the opportunity for society to hold organisations to account for their interactions with nature. Whether they have come close to fulfilling this considerable potential remains a moot point.

The potential for environmental (and, indeed, social and sustainability) accounting is enormous and, as the text will demonstrate, considerable progress has been achieved as a result of experimentation, research and voluntary initiatives in the field. However, this potential remains muted: why might that be?

The simple answer is that environmental accounting is an essentially political act. The early attempts at environmental accounting attracted considerable criticism from liberals, Marxists, feminists, post-modernists and, perhaps most disturbingly, from deep ecologists precisely because they failed to recognise this. Examined carefully, environmental accounting essentially questions the extent to which the sacred cows of advanced financial capitalism – growth, profit, expansion, consumption, economic efficiency, separation of ownership and control and so on – are genuinely compatible with an active concern for the natural world. Indeed, the global evidence suggested, at least *a priori,* that it might actually be the very success of international financial capitalism that is among the principal reasons for the parlous state of the natural world. (Similar concerns might be voiced regarding social well-being.) Such a potential challenge will not sit easily with the vested interest and, more especially, offers a substantive challenge to what most of us take for granted, what universities and the professions teach, what accountants, economists and business practice and, disturbingly, what most scholars influence and re-enforce through research. No wonder environmental accounting has considerable serious political implications and why, as far as one can see, its adoption and use has been so limited. Modernity and capitalism have not been willing to embrace this potential conflict.

This political dimension, however, reflects deeper issues. Humanity has always created accounts of its environment and those accounts seem to reflect the changing relationship between humanity and nature, including, inevitably, our own, "human" nature. There is something spiritually and philosophically challenging about the idea that it might be apposite to understand nature – which is, after all, the very basis of all life – as only relevant through a lens of the economic or as a contributor to growth or profit. At a minimum, such views must be contentious. More especially, though, to only allow any discussion of nature as long as it does not challenge a very narrow notion of enterprise and financial economy is potentially absurd. Such a view is fundamentally flawed: without life there is no human and without humans there is no economics. Ultimately, absurdly placing an economic limit on nature may well have the effect that, eventually, there will be no life.

To consider any account of the environment (or indeed, any account of humanity's exploitation of nature) calls for a deep understanding that there may well be fundamental conflicts between, on the one hand, the principles of how humanity should live with nature and, on the other hand, the disciplines of modernity that we embrace. This is not to say that they are fundamentally in conflict (although we do believe them to be) but, rather, to emphasise that there is enough serious and persuasive evidence to demand that such matters are addressed fairly and carefully. We can only commend this present collection to you in the light of this most pressing problematique.

It is these deeply challenging conundrums that lie at the heart of any sensible study of environmental accounting and they lead to a realisation that to understand environmental accounting, we must first understand humanity and our place (if any) in the world.

Rob Gray and David Owen

PART 1

Framing the issues

1

CURATING ENVIRONMENTAL ACCOUNTING KNOWLEDGE

Jan Bebbington, Carlos Larrinaga and Ian Thomson

Introduction

In this handbook, we date the start of a distinctive field of academic inquiry into the "hybrid" of accounting and the natural environment to Gray (1990). Thirty years on, it is a suitable time to present chapters dedicated to elements of the field as well as to identify challenges that remain. We are indebted to the large team of writers who contributed chapters for this handbook and who responded in a positive way to our deadlines and editorial suggestions. This substantive piece of work was only possible because of the network of authors who have been working on this material for the last 18 months and we thank them all.

We approached this handbook as a "knowledge project" and in gathering this material together we thought of ourselves as curators of a variety of perspectives and insights. At the same time, we hope the synergy created by virtue of having these contributions in one place (and edited by a common team) might also generate overarching insights into environmental accounting. With these hopes in mind, this chapter undertakes several tasks, namely, it:

- describes the nature of the problem that environmental accounting seeks to address (including a consideration of the social aspects of environmental change);
- outlines the practice and other academic partners who have strengthened environmental accounting research;
- considers how future accountants might become ecologically literate, focusing on the role of accounting education (in universities and professional training/continuing education); and
- provides some reflections that emerge from having read the handbook as a whole and which may provide a glimpse into some of the contours of future environmental accounting.

Before moving onto these various topic areas, we also wished to provide some personal reflections on environmental accounting (see also Bebbington, Russell and Thomson 2017).

We all started our careers around 1990 and hence were part of the "first generation" of scholars who had the opportunity to dedicate themselves to researching environmental accounting. This opportunity was afforded to us by the leadership of the pioneers of the field including Rob

Gray, James Guthrie, Richard Laughlin, Reg Matthews, Keith Maunders, Dave Owen and Lee Parker. This handbook is possible because of their vision and leadership over many decades. Moreover, this group of scholars (along with the "first generation") engaged in institutional building that created, sustained, expanded and legitimated environmental accounting scholarship and practice. Elements of this process included the adoption of the pre-existing *Social Accounting Monitor* (which eventually became the *Social and Environmental Accountability Journal*) and the founding of the Centre for Social and Environmental Accounting Research (CSEAR) and the development of a series of specialist conferences to support scholars in the area (of which more will be discussed later).

Part of the excitement of being around at the start of an academic field was that we experienced its development first-hand rather than trying to piece the field together from academic literature. As a result, the handbook has sought to shed light on the (sometimes hidden and/or forgotten) foundations of environmental accounting (see especially Chapter 2). At the same time, a retrospective should also seek to identify missed opportunities, false turns, dead ends as well as a foundation from which to look forward as to what practice, policy and scholarship might emerge in the future. These desires shaped the structure and content of the handbook: some chapters deal with material that is still in embryonic form (e.g. accounting for circularity in Chapter 18 and accounting for animal rights in Chapter 29) while others deal with as yet unresolved issues of long-standing concern (such as "stand-alone" reporting in Chapter 8). That being said, most of the chapters reflect on the origins, current status and future shape of their respective topics.

In commissioning the chapters (and in conceptualising this handbook as a knowledge project), we also wanted diversity in the author set. We deliberately invited scholars who might be described as "second generation" environmental accounting researchers to contribute their perspectives. These colleagues will have the responsibility of shaping environmental accounting in the next 20–30 years through their research, supervision of PhD students, editing of journals and through the influence they will exert on policy and professional processes in their respective countries and regions.

In addition, and as with any academic field, the development of environmental accounting reflects a number of privileges and biases. These biases include gender, race, language, culture and geographical dimensions. We integrated these concerns in our commissioning process so that we could create a space for voices that are less often heard within the field. Intellectually, fostering diversity also supports addressing the globally connected nature of the natural environment (this is one hallmark of sustainability science – see Bebbington and Larrinaga 2014). There are also contemporary reasons for this strategy. The implications of the Black Lives Matter movement, the recognition of white privilege, the dominance of male voices/perspectives and the ongoing struggles of indigenous peoples against colonisation are issues for accounting scholars. The environmental accounting literature (in our view) currently suffers from a concentration on Western concerns and contexts as well as from being communicated primarily in English (see Chapter 25 for an explicit consideration of this problem). We accept that this handbook does not perfectly address the biases we identify, but we have sought to dilute them by drawing from a diverse author field as well as including a dedicated section on regional perspectives.

Taken together, this handbook is intended to mark a transition in environmental accounting: a transition that respects the past, present and future scholars involved in the collective co-production of environmental accounting theory, evidence, policy and practice. The inclusion of different voices from different places enables new insights to be drawn, while reducing the risk of finding in one study inadvertently oppressing those in another domain. Given that we curated (rather than orchestrated) this process, there remain areas of contradiction, contestation and friction between the materials presented. We did not seek to hide these tensions, but rather see this as evidence of an active, authentic research field that is struggling to make sense of our, often abusive, relationship with nature. It is to the outcomes of that relationship that attention now turns.

Defining the problem arena

Environment and accounting linkages

Bebbington and Thomson (2013, p. 281) highlighted that accounting seeks to respond to concerns "that economic systems (embedded in systems of cultural expectations) create outcomes that undermine the ecological systems on which human (and other species) prosperity rests". Any concern with the(a) state of the environment is therefore also a concern about the economic and social systems that co-created these challenges. It is also the case that science (as one possible knowledge system) has been narrating the myriad ways in which individual and collective human actions have affected the functioning of the environment, including phenomena such as: global climate change; biodiversity loss; the translocation of organisms; disruption to water, nitrogen and phosphorus cycles; the mass movement of materials within natural systems; and the creation of novel materials which have no parallel in nature. The extent and complexity of specific environmental changes have led to the current time being characterised as the Anthropocene: denoting an era where human actions are a perceptible driver of earth system processes (see Bebbington et al. 2020 for an introduction). Taken together there are concerns that this process will lead to simplified and less robust ecosystems (Nyström et al. 2019) and to the breaching of "planetary boundaries" (Rockstrom et al. 2009), beyond which all living beings will be threatened. It is within the context of these concerns that environmental accounting seeks to intervene.

At its core, environmental accounting focuses on processes that exert control over the impacts of organisations such that these diverse adverse effects are addressed or minimised (see, e.g., in this handbook, Chapter 14 on management control and Chapter 15 that addresses material and energy accounting). At other times, accounting techniques are used to demonstrate effects that are not experienced by or managed by organisations themselves: see Chapter 16 on externalities. In addition, environmental accounting scholars have examined how external accounts produced by organisations have provided (or not) visibility of these environmental effects in traditional accounting (see Chapter 7) or other reporting formats (see Chapter 8). Likewise, assuring this information (see Chapter 8), understanding why it has become normal (see Chapter 9) and the impact information provision has had on financial markets (see Chapter 12) is within the domain of environmental accounting. In all these examples, accounting functions are central, with environmental aspects of their functionality being highlighted.

In contrast, other scholarship starts with an element of the environment (in the case of this handbook: greenhouse gas emissions, water and biodiversity in chapters 26, 27 and 28, respectively) and assembles accounting "technologies" around that element in order to address environmental concerns. This approach to environmental accounting has relatively recently developed and also cross-fertilised with accounting subject domains (such as control systems, performance reporting, auditing and assurance activities and standard setting processes). This is a different way in which to link accounting and the environment but one that is gaining in salience. Moreover, it would be possible to imagine an "accounting for the total environment" from an account for a single entity that incorporated greenhouse gas emissions, water and biodiversity impacts and which would like to address issues of accounting for nature (for an introduction, see Russell, Milne and Dey 2017). This is an area of environmental accounting that is likely to develop considerably in the future.

At the same time, the commission to create a handbook specifically on ***environmental*** accounting (rather than social and environmental accounting or accounting for sustainable development) caused us concern. Here we seek to narrate how we have sought to deal with the particular challenge of delineating environmental accounting in a research and practice landscape that has not always separated social and environmental concerns.

Social dimensions of environmental change

Critically, it should be noted that environmental matters are always social. For example, those who are most likely to suffer environmental harm are often also the poorest in society (see, e.g., chapters 19, 24 and 25 where this case is powerfully articulated). This means that a focus on environmental concerns should also entail a concern with social issues. At the same time, environmental accounting itself has also had closer and more distant relationships with social issues and changes in these connections are now outlined.

First, as accounting was emerging as an academic area of research in the 1970s (see also Chapter 2), social accounting was not easily separated from environmental accounting, as illustrated by the label that was then used for the field: corporate social reporting (Gray et al. 1988) or social accounting, which was defined as dealing with "the social and economic effects of an institution on society" as well as concerns relating to "[p]hysical resources and environmental contributions" (Epstein et al. 1976, pp. 24 and 25, respectively). Social concerns gained particular salience in Europe in the 1970s when workers and unions were powerful in political and corporate governance and discussions about social dialogue and/or industrial democracy flourished. In this political climate, the value-added statement in countries such as the France, Germany, Spain and the UK (Reichmann and Lange 1981; Larrinaga 2001; Burchell et al. 1985) and the *bilan social* in France (Gond et al. 2013) were conceived as accounting instruments that could display the commonality of purpose of labour and capital within the corporation. However, as the political climate changed (particularly in the Anglo-Saxon world with the Thatcher–Reagan conservative revolution of the 1980) interest in the regulation of and research about the social aspects of accounting faded away.

Second, in the 1980s and 1990s, environmental accounting gained prominence at the cost of the social. The concern for the environment was not new, but it certainly grew in political salience (for more details, see Chapter 2). In accounting research, Gray (1992) was trying to bring the environment to a central position in the area. By the end of this period, however, there was a sense that the balance had moved too strongly towards the environment and leading authors argued for a renewal of interest in social accounting, without reducing attention given to environmental issues (Mathews 1997). This recovery of the social was perhaps more visibly enacted when Gray (2002) provided a definition for the field with his notion of the "social accounting project", based on the idea of challenging conventional accounting. The social accounting project did not just recover the social but what Gray (2002) reflected was the metamorphosis of the object of social and environmental accounting, which from then on went well beyond the limits of corporate disclosures to the employees and environmental reporting, to cover any aspect that challenges the implication of organisations in the social and environmental problems of our time (from forced labour to climate change and from animal welfare to coloniality). These ideas were reflected in other processes, for example, they underpinned and reflected the Global

Reporting Initiative guidelines and their desire to integrate economic, environmental and social indicators in sustainability reports (more information is available in chapters 8 and 10).

Third, although the debates since the end of the 1990s put the social back in the centre of the stage, it is the debate about planetary boundaries that created a new impetus for the integration between social and environment categories. As developed in more detail in Chapter 6, Rockström et al. (2009) identified nine boundaries whose transgression would strike at the foundations of socio-ecological systems, with evidence signalling that various processes are outside of the safe space for humanity (i.e, threatening the survival of human societies). The other side of the coin is how human activities are impacting the earth system itself, something that is captured by the debates about the Anthropocene (Bebbington et al. 2020). It is now evident is that the social cannot be easily separated from the ecological (Lade et al. 2020) and that any sustainable future will need the partnership between natural and social science (Bebbington and Larrinaga 2014).

Socio-ecological systems and planetary boundaries are also closely linked to the development of an awareness of globalisation (Martens and Rotmans 2005). A final point we wish to make concerning the recovery of a social focus in environmental accounting is the extent to which, contrasting with the globalisation of natural systems, the social structures of globalisation have privileged some perspectives above others (Chakrabarty 2000; Ibarra-Colado 2006). Indeed, global sustainability is not possible without equity in the access to economic and environmental resources (something that is reflected in the construction of the Sustainable Development Goals – Bebbington and Unerman 2018, 2020). An inclusive and global perspective of environmental accounting will need to explore perspectives on the environment coming from indigenous communities and the global South, which have been marginalised within the literature to date (see Chapter 25 in detail and also chapters 19, 22 and 24 which include traces of this concern). Just as environmental accounting cannot be formally separated from society and the economy, neither can academic activities be considered separate from accounting practice and policies that focus on both. It is to the consilience between practice and research that attention now turns.

Professional accounting and research partners

While we have pinned Gray (1990) as the starting point of the field, the reality is a little more nuanced. The notion that one might be concerned with the intersection of accounting and the natural environment has a long academic history (see Hopwood, 1979) as well as being reflected in accounting practice/policy making for an extended period of time (see Accounting Standards Steering Committee 1975; American Accounting Association 1972, 1973, 1974, 1975, 1976; American Institute of Chartered Public Accountants 1977). It is the case, however, that the dedicated focus on the accounting–environment hybrid accelerated after 1990 and drew in several communities of practice who supported the development of the field: it takes a research and practice "village" to raise an academic "child".

The accounting profession has championed environmental accounting, even if the support from any one body has shifted as the particular body's priorities have evolved (for a contemporary summary, see Chapter 5 and Collison and Slomp 2000 for an analysis of the role of the Fédération des Experts Comptables Européens – hereafter FEE). While professional accounting bodies funded research projects in selected topics, they were also influential because they published material aimed at informing their members of environmental matters (e.g., ICAEW Environment Research Group 1992; Canadian Institute of Chartered Accountants 1993a; FEE 1998). In addition, the profession was active in considering core financial accounting issues (e.g., see Canadian Institute of Chartered Accountants 1993b; Gray et al. 1998; FEE 1999a as well as Chapter 7) and financial audit (e.g., see Canadian Institute of Chartered Accountants 1992, 1994; FEE 1993, 1995; Collison, Gray and Innes 1996; Kamp-Roelands 1999 as well as Chapter 9). The role of the profession as carriers and amplifiers of ideas has been important in general (see also Chapter 10) and was particularly influential in terms of championing the development of environmental reporting, as a precursor to "sustainability reporting" (e.g., FEE 1999b as well as Chapter 8). Likewise, the role of umbrella bodies such as FEE (in 2016 this body become Accountancy Europe, whose members include 51 professional associations from 35 countries) promoted the ideas of environmental accounting across a wider geography as does the United Nations Conference for Trade and Development, International Standards of Accounting and Reporting (this is the United Nations focal point on accounting and corporate governance that was established by the United Nations Economic and Social Council in 1982). Finally, and critically, many professional accounting bodies have committees that shape their own responses to environmental challenges and public engagement (see also Chapter 5 that frames this activity as "thought leadership"). This activity is in addition to committees that oversee professional training, continuing professional development and which shape university accounting curriculums. In summary, academic environmental accounting has been intimately connected to professional body activities and has had its work funded and amplified by said bodies as well.

At the same time, there has also been support for environmental accounting from other parts of academia. For example, "mainstream" accounting colleagues (perhaps more so in Europe than elsewhere) have been welcoming of environmental accounting insights in conferences and journals such as *British Accounting Review* and *European Accounting Review* (in general and through special issues). At the same time, interpretative and critical accounting scholars have engaged in environmental accounting topic areas and, crucially, have strengthened the field through challenging environmental accountants to "do better" in their scholarship. At the same time, as environmental accounting scholarship has matured, these communities have been a productive source of underpinning theories and have thereby supporting conceptual development. This community also provided places where environmental accounting scholarship could be presented and refined (through, e.g., the Asia Pacific Interdisciplinary Perspectives on Accounting [APIRA], the Critical Perspectives on Accounting [CPA] and the Interdisciplinary Perspectives on Accounting [IPA] conferences). Likewise, journal such as *Accounting, Organizations and Society* and *Critical Perspectives on Accounting* complemented the work of *Accounting Auditing and Accountability Journal* and *Accounting Forum*. Various "public interest" networks (such as the Academy of Management and the American Accounting Association) also contain "fellow travellers" in tackling environmental challenges. It is also the case that specialist research networks have provided "safe" places where ideas could be developed and have been especially critical for colleagues who did not have an active and/or a supportive community of scholars around them. Of particular relevance is the Environmental and Sustainability Management Accounting Network (EMAN) and the CSEAR – along with its "house" journal *Social and Environmental Accountability Journal*). While these various activities speak about supporting academic research, there is also a need for future accountants to be able to support organisations as they seek to deal with their environmental dependencies and impacts.

Ecological literacy of future accountants

Critically, accounting education plays a constitutive role in creating environmentally (ir)responsible accounting professionals and citizens. This constitutive role can be either positive or negative, depending on how and what "accountants" are taught about the environment and environmental accounting in the context of their wider primary, secondary, tertiary and professional education (Thomson and Bebbington 2004; Gray 2013; Owen 2013; Contrafatto et al. 2015; Deegan 2017; Boulianne et al. 2018; Boulianne and Keddie 2018; Egan and Tweedie 2018). Whilst this handbook is primarily designed to inform future research projects and practice, it has the potential to play a major role in informing and reforming environmental accounting education. At the very least it provides part of the evolving answer to the question asked by Gray and Collison (2002) – what do accountants need to know about the environment?

Concerns over the limited inclusion of the environment in accounting programmes were expressed in the 1990s (Lewis et al., 1992 and Humphrey et al., 1996) and continue to be a cause for concern. While researchers report a gradual increase and innovation in environmental content (see, e.g., Wydner et al. 2013; Garcia and Thomson 2018), Deegan (2017 , p. 85) argued that:

> The reality, sadly, is that most accounting programs throughout the world have probably not really changed that much in the last 25 years in terms of fixating on financial performance and related measures, and ignoring the role that "accounting" can play in both creating social and environmental problems, as well as in addressing them. Social and environmental accounting and related issues typically get no more than a few weeks consideration across an accounting degree.

Similar concerns also exist about the inclusion of the environment in professional accounting exam syllabi (Lewis et al. 1992; Boulianne et al. 2018; Boulianne and Keddie 2018). There are, however, examples of good practice. For example, the 2021 Institute of Chartered Accountants of England and Wales (ICAEW) syllabus includes a learning and development objective for students to be able to identify ethical issues including public interest and sustainability issues in a scenario. Another pertinent example can be seen in the Association of Chartered Certified Accountants (ACCA), F5 Performance Management paper which includes as learning outcomes the ability to discuss the issues that businesses face in the management of environmental costs and describe the different methods a business may use to account for its environmental costs. The argument that environmental accounting does not form any part of professional accounting educational programme is difficult to sustain. In addition, the notion that it is not possible to justify the inclusion of environmental accounting from professional accounting syllabi or accreditation requirements is somewhat outdated. However, there remains questions about the scope/depth/coverage of this material and its relationship with the rest of the professional syllabi.

Despite the rising importance of environmental issues, the growth of research and teaching material (for an example of debates in this area, see Contrafatto 2013; Gray 2013) and increasing examples of professional practice in the area, challenges remain. Many readers will have experienced how quickly discussions on environmental accounting education highlight the problems of institutional resistance or indifference to anything other than the environment as an add-on to curricula.

In the development of this handbook, we had accounting education in mind and sought to design the handbook so that it could support accounting educational practices (i.e., we hope the handbook has "dip-ability", i.e., that single chapters can be used to support teaching programmes). For example, the presentation of research in different geographic regions, in Part 4, challenges the hidden European, business-oriented curricula of past environmental accounting research (Thomson and Bebbington 2004). This geographic perspective (Part 4) alongside the thematic perspectives (Part 5) sought to create closer alignment between research and the existential realities, oppressions and priorities in different parts of the world. That is, the handbook structure was designed to improve the ability to connect accounting research with local "manifestations" of environmental imperatives and conflicts. This increases the probability of making environmental accounting appear more real in different institutional fields and to emerging environmental challenges. Likewise, we sought to provide multiple chapters on environmental accounting fields that map onto structural elements of accounting programmes, thereby offering greater prospects of assimilation. For example, there are chapters that can inform more theoretical critical modules (Part 1), financial reporting (Part 2), management accounting (Part 3), global and local issues (Part 4) or emerging or contemporary issues (Part 5). We also hope that the material on methods in Chapter 4 will provide inspirations for projects or dissertations in environmental accounting topics. While these aspirations are content driven, how education is approached is also important.

Thomson and Bebbington (2004) utilised the work of Freire to explore the role of conventional accounting education in creating and sustaining environmental oppression and the potential of dialogic accounting education to move environmental accounting beyond its oppressive limit situation. This work is based on three interconnected concepts. First, education plays a constitutive role in that it creates an authoritative narrative about what we know about the world. Second, education can be used to maintain existing power differentials and to keep people in their place. Third, education can enable the co-creation of different narratives of what the world could be as the inspiration for transformation.

Reforming accounting educational programmes is critical to any transformation of individual action, collective values, norms or what constitutes legitimate conduct (Illich 1971). When we educate, we must be conscious that we are not only teaching accounting tools and techniques but we are reinforcing implicit assumptions about accountants' and social scientists' roles in perpetuating social and ecological risks and injustices (for an insightful work in this vein, see Ferguson, Collison, Power and Stevenson 2009). Environmental accounting education has the potential to form part of the process of exposing these risks and injustices, creating the capacity for change and enabling transformative action. Education should form part of what Freire describes as "the action and reflection of men and women upon their world in order to transform it" (Freire 1996, p. 60). Environmental accounting education should strive to co-investigate the realities of social-environmental relationships, leading to the problematisation of hidden or mystified knowledge that underpins the production and interpretation of all accounts. This involves both asking questions and calling into question and developing a challenging attitude, which should be an essential attribute of a professional accountant.

In our role as educators, we suggest that readers could use the material in this handbook to:

- critically evaluate the content of any educational programme they are involved in;
- reflect on any problematic hidden curriculum underpinning educational materials (e.g., the existence of managerialism, neoliberal assumptions or utopian theories of change);
- identify educational content that may be unintentionally alien or alienating to students' experiences or agency;
- identify any misalignment between what is "taught" and what is "assessed";
- identify the extent to which students are able to contribute their knowledge and experience of environmental problems or solutions;
- identify the extent to which students can inform the design and delivery of the educative material; and

- reflect on the appropriateness of the overall blend of these educational processes, in particular, how they relate to the past, present and future agency and transformative potential of the students.

We would encourage opening up the education "black box" to understand how your educational practices could allow accountants to engage effectively with resolving complex environmental problems. Gray (2013), Schaltegger (2013), Contrafatto (2013), Laine (2013) and Larrinaga (2013) all concur on the positive impact of integrating sustainability and environmental management into accounting education. For example, Schaltegger (2013) argues for the redesign of accounting education to support "change agents for sustainability" commenting on the value of case studies in exploring possible solutions to environmental and social problems. This handbook contains many examples of case studies that are suitable for this type of dialogic environmental accounting engagement. Larrinaga (2013) noted how positive attitudes in students emerged from educational experiences that critically engaged with environmental concepts and practices, but did qualify this with calls for further research into what constitutes effective environmental and sustainable accounting educational programmes, as well as consideration of the organisational contexts in which they will work. We support the desire for all accounting educators to reflect on their power and agency, and wherever possible act to help create environmentally responsible accounting professionals and citizens.

A glimpse to the future

It would be virtually impossible to synthesise from the contents of this handbook what the future of environmental accounting might entail because of the multitude of topics covered, the contexts in which any accounting might play out and the inherent uncertainty in such a task. That being said, we do have views of three areas where the field of environmental accounting might benefit from closer reflection (noting that these views reflect our particular perspectives at this point in time). These areas relate to:

- the ways in which accountability (as the assumed purpose of environmental accounting) might be understood and updated for current environmental challenges (this is also discussed in Chapter 2);
- the assumed objects of analysis for environmental accounting (shifting focus from external reporting of listed for-profit companies); and
- the need to bring greater ecological literacy to our research endeavours.

Each of these themes will be explored in more detail here, noting that these are not areas which are easily resolved, that others have raised similar concerns to us in each of these areas, and that we have intentionally been more provocative than we might actually feel in order to stimulate responses.

The framing of what duties/responsibilities organisations owe to significant others (most usually construed as being owners and other providers of capital) as determined by legal (and sometimes social contract) responsibilities is central to a relatively "thin" conception of accountability that pervades environmental accounting. Such a constrained view flies in the face of considerable literature elsewhere, including scholarship that problematises corporate responsibility and sketches a more expansive conception of responsibility. For example, Mansell, Ferguson, Gindis and Pasternak (2019) outline the context for these questions and assemble an array of valuable papers in their *Journal of Business Ethics* special issue on "Rethinking Corporate Agency in Business, Philosophy, and Law". This special issue provides one possible "jumping off" point for environmental accounting to become more theoretically sophisticated in its conception of corporate agency and responsibility. Conceiving of a responsibility to non-human animals (see, e.g., Chapter 29) as well as the rights of nature also expands discussions of responsibility from a more eco-centric view point. At the same time (and Chapter 2 highlights this), it might be the time to re-configure the notion of stewardship in accounting to move away from a narrow focus on financial stewardship to one that might reflect the driving role that organisations have across global eco-systems and the earth system as a whole. This proposal is grounded in the paper by Folke et al. (2019) who identified that 189 companies (focused on mining, fossil fuels, agriculture and forestry, seafood and agrochemicals) collectively move these key resources around the globe. From detailed work conducted on some of the seafood firms in this sample (Bebbington et al. 2020), it is possible to imagine working alongside these "keystone" actors to explore what it might mean to be "biosphere stewards". This work prompts the second concern that we have as it relates to the question of suitable objects of analysis for environmental accountants.

Given the mainstream accounting research preoccupation with for-profit, listed companies and a research bias towards understanding these organisations through what they say externally (with data being collated in research databases on aspects of this reporting), it should be no surprise that environmental accounting scholarship has taken a strong interest in the listed company-reporting nexus (for a discussion of this, see Chapter 23 and Gendron and Rodrigue in press for a wider perspective). While there is nothing inherently "wrong" with this approach (listed companies are powerful shapers of the landscape in which other organisations operate as well as conditioners of expectations about the nature and role of business), this has created some weaknesses in the field. First, this approach has lacked a sophisticated articulation of why organisations report, leading to a reliance on a relatively underspecified version of legitimacy theory (see also Chapter 3) as well as an uncertainty (and lack of a robust evidence base) as to whether reporting is related to performance (for a more in-depth consideration, see Chapter 8). A comparative lack of academic/research engagement with organisations themselves has also impoverished our collective understanding of why reporting has increased and how this reflects/affects organisational operations. A change in research approach towards more intimate research approaches (i.e., actually talking to and engaging closely with organisational participants) might deepen environmental accounting understandings of the phenomena of reporting as would a synthesis between qualitative and quantitative study findings. The second problem we wish to highlight in this context is the lack of strong ties in reporting research to wider considerations of transparency. This notion has been explored in depth, for example, by political scientists who link transparency (including corporate transparency) to particular approaches to governing (see Mol 2006 for an introduction). Linking these conceptual discussions about the shape of "globalised modernity" (Mol 2010, p. 132) and the extent to which corporate reporting might constitute "tamed transparency" (Dingwerth and Eichinger 2010, p. 74) will be critical for increasing the depth of sophistication that we might bring to reporting studies. This is a step-change from the current mainstream approach of regressing proxies that may well lack any underlying basis in organisational reality, as well as a movement beyond simple recourse to framing reporting as promotional "fluff". A deepening of perspectives is sorely needed in environmental reporting scholarship.

The final provocation we offer links to the encouragement in Chapter 4 to undertake "pre-study" seriously when constructing environmental accounting topics. This provocation also links to the previous point made that the norms of accounting scholarship have narrowed our understanding of the world-as-it-is and can-be and that we have tended to be self-contained in our use of insights from other fields. As we have highlighted in the preceding two provocations, political scientists, philosophers and legal researchers can bring valuable insight to environmental accounting. At the same time, greater ecological (and social) literacy would also strengthen accounting scholarship (see, e.g., Chapter 27 where this point is made in the case of water accounting). This point is developed in Bebbington and Larrinaga (2014) where we argue for sustainability science motifs to infuse accounting research and in Bebbington et al. (2020) where we suggest that an ecological framing would draw out different research samples than what has previously been the case. The aim of both of these papers has been to draw accounting closer to ecological thinking and scholars (see Österblom et al. 2020 for a complementary proposal: a discussion of how science and industry can work together). Bebbington and Unerman (2020) also highlight this point and note that there are practice-based initiatives (in the form of the Science-Based Targets Initiative as well as the World Benchmarking Alliance SDG2000 company benchmark) that provide points of translation between organisations and ecological salience. This is an area where we anticipate that environmental accounting will move in the future, drawing from insights drawn out in accounting for nature/biodiversity (see Chapter 28) as well as in carbon accounting (see Chapter 26).

Conclusion

A 30-year retrospective begs questions about what the next 30 years might entail. If 2020 has taught us anything, it is that the shape of the future can change in an instant in ways that were unimaginable just a few weeks earlier. That being said, there is an appeal to try to imagine what 2050 will look like and to wonder about the shape of environmental accounting scholarship (see also Chapter 2). While the detail of the 2050 state of the natural environment, and what impact this state will have had on human and more-than-human populations, is unknown, it seems likely that the situation will be worse than it is presently (see chapters 26, 27 and 28 alongside any serious policy analysis of various environmental challenges). By the middle of this century, global climate change is predicted (even under best-outcome scenarios using the most optimistic mitigation pathways) to have accelerated and widespread adaptation will be the norm. The knock-on effect of climate change on the living world will be substantial, with a changing distribution of food production systems, water stress, biodiversity disruption and movement of human populations across the globe. In this (granted dystopian) world, information from accountants to support organisations as they navigate the complexity of the Anthropocene and insights from academia will be required. Taking the combined insights from this handbook (and the work that will emerge in the next 30 years) we will as a scholarly community have a role to play: we hope it will be a transformational and positive one.

References

Accounting Standards Steering Committee, 1975. *The Corporate Report*. London: Institute of Chartered Accountants in England and Wales.

American Accounting Association, 1972. Committee on Measures of Effectiveness for Social Programs. *The supplement to the Accounting Review*, 47, 336–396.

American Accounting Association, 1973. Committee on Environmental Effects of Organization Behaviour. *The Supplement to the Accounting Review*, 47, 72–119.

American Accounting Association, 1974. Committee on Measurement of Social Costs. *The supplement to the Accounting Review*, 48, 98–113.

American Accounting Association, 1975. Committee on Social Costs. *The Supplement to the Accounting Review*, 49, 50–89.

American Accounting Association, 1976. Committee on Accounting for Social Performance. *The Supplement to the Accounting Review*, 50, 38–69.

American Institute of Chartered Public Accountants, 1977. *The Measurement of Corporate Social Performance.* New York: American Institute of Chartered Public Accountants.

Bebbington, J. and Larrinaga, C., 2014. Accounting and sustainable development: An exploration. *Accounting, Organizations and Society*, 39(6), 395–413.

Bebbington, J., Österblom, H., Crona, B., Jouffray, J.-B., Larrinaga, C., Russell, S. and Scholtens, B., 2020. Accounting and accountability in the Anthropocene. *Accounting, Auditing & Accountability Journal,* 33(1), 152–177.

Bebbington, J., Russell, S. and Thomson, I., 2017. Accounting and sustainable development: reflections and propositions. *Critical Perspectives on Accounting*, 48(1), 21–34.

Bebbington, J. and Thomson, I., 2013. Sustainable development, management and accounting: boundary crossing. *Management Accounting Research*, 24(4), 277–283.

Bebbington J. and Unerman, J., 2018. Achieving the United Nations sustainable development goals: an enabling role of accounting research. *Accounting, Auditing and Accountability Journal*, 31(1), 2–24.

Bebbington J. and Unerman, J., 2020. Advancing research into accounting and the UN sustainable development goals. *Accounting, Auditing and Accountability Journal*, 33(7), 1657-1670.

Boulianne, E. and Keddie, L., 2018. Where is sustainability within the Canadian CPA Education Program. *Advances in Environmental Accounting and Management*, Volume 7, Bingley: Emerald Publishing.

Boulianne, E., Keddie, L. and Postaire, M., 2018. (Non) coverage of sustainability within the French professional accounting education program. *Sustainability Accounting, Management and Policy Journal*, 9(3), 313–335.

Burchell, S., Clubb, C. and Hopwood, A. G. 1985. Accounting in its social context: towards a history of value added in the United Kingdom. *Accounting, Organizations and Society*, 10(4), 381–413.

Canadian Institute of Chartered Accountants, 1992. *Environmental Auditing and the Role of the Accounting Profession.* Toronto: Canadian Institute of Chartered Accountants.

Canadian Institute of Chartered Accountants, 1993a. *Environmental Stewardship: Management, Accountability and the Role of Chartered Accountants.* Toronto: Canadian Institute of Chartered Accountants.

Canadian Institute of Chartered Accountants, 1993b. *Environmental Costs and Liabilities: Accounting and Financial Reporting Issues.* Toronto: Canadian Institute of Chartered Accountants.

Canadian Institute of Chartered Accountants, 1994. *Audit of Financial Statements Affected by Environmental Matters.* Toronto: Canadian Institute of Chartered Accountants.

Chakrabarty, D., 2000. *Provincializing Europe: Postcolonial thought and historical difference.* Princeton, NJ: Princeton University Press.

Chua, W. F., 1986. Radical developments in accounting thought. *The Accounting Review*, LXI(4), 601–632.

Collison, D. J., Gray, R. H. and Innes, J., 1996. *The Financial Auditor and the Environment.* London: ICAEW

Collison, D. and Slomp, S., 2000. Environmental accounting, auditing and reporting in Europe: the role of FEE. *European Accounting Review*, 9(1), 111–129.

Contrafatto, M. 2013. "Utopia" and "passion": a commentary on "Sustainability and Accounting Education: the Elephant in the Classroom'. *Accounting Education: An International Journal*, 22(4), 336–339.

Contrafatto, M., Thomson, I. and Monks, L., 2015. Peru, Mountains and El Ninos: dialogic action, accounting and sustainable transformation. *Critical Perspectives on Accounting*, 15, 117–136.

Coulson, A. and Thomson, I., 2006. Accounting and sustainability, encouraging a dialogical approach; integrating learning activities, delivery mechanisms and assessment strategies. *Accounting Education: An International Journal*, 15(3), 261–273.

Deegan, C., 2017. Twenty five years of social and environmental accounting research within critical perspectives of accounting: hits, misses and ways forward. *Critical Perspectives on Accounting*, 43(2017), 65–87.

Dingwerth, K. and Eichinger, M., 2010. Tamed transparency: how information disclosure under the global reporting initiative fails to empower. *Global Environmental Politics*, 10(3), 74–96.

Egan, M. and Tweedie, D., 2018. A "green" accountant is difficult to find: can accountants contribute to sustainability management initiatives? *Accounting, Auditing and Accountability Journal*, 31(6), 1749–1773.

Epstein, M., Flamholtz, E. and McDonough, J. J., 1976. Corporate social accounting in the United States of America: state of the art and future prospects. *Accounting, Organizations and Society,* 1(1), 23–42.

FEE, 1993. *Environmental Accounting and Auditing: Survey of Current Activities and Developments.* FEE: Brussels.

FEE, 1995. *Environmental Accounting, Reporting and Auditing: Survey of Current Activities and Developments within the Accountancy Profession.* FEE: Brussels.

FEE, 1998. *European Accountancy Profession Unites on Environmental Issues*, FEE Information Sheet. FEE: Brussels.

FEE, 1999a. *Review of International Accounting Standards for Environmental Issues*, FEE Memorandum. FEE: Brussels.

FEE, 1999b. *Towards a Generally Accepted Framework for Environmental Reporting*, Discussion Paper. FEE: Brussels.

Ferguson, J., Collison, D., Power, D. and Stevenson, L., 2009. Constructing meaning in the service of power: an analysis of the typical modes of ideology in accounting textbooks. *Critical Perspectives on Accounting*, 20(8), 896–909.

Folke, C., Österblom, H., Jouffray, J.-B., Lambin, E., Adger, N., Scheffer, M., Crona, B., Nyström, M., Levin, S., Carpenter, S., Anderies, J., Chapin, S., Crépin, A.-S., Dauriach, A., Galaz, V., Gordon, L., Katutsky, N., Walker, B., Watson, J., Wilen, J. & de Zeeuw, A. (2019). Transnational corporations and the challenge of biosphere stewardship. *Nature Ecology & Evolution*, 3, 1396–1403.

Freire P., 1996. *Pedagogy of the Oppressed*. London: Pelican.

Garcia, S. and Thomson, I., 2018. The case of Assabi: expanding the learning on sustainability through an experiential qualitative multi-criteria decision making activity. *Social and Environmental Accountability Journal*, 38(3) 197–217.

Gendron, Y. and Rodrigue, M., (in press). On the centrality of peripheral research and the dangers of tight boundary gatekeeping. *Critical Perspectives on Accounting*. Retrieved from https://www.sciencedirect.com/science/article/pii/S1045235419300152

Gond, J., Igalens, J. and Brès, L., 2013. Rendre compte du social: L'art du compromis performatif. *Revue Française De Gestion*, 237, 201–226.

Gray, R., 1990. *The Greening of Accountancy: The Profession after Pearce*. London: Chartered Association of Certified Accountants.

Gray, R., 1992. Accounting and environmentalism: an exploration of the challenge of gently accounting for accountability, transparency and sustainability. *Accounting Organisations and Society*, 17(5), 399–425.

Gray, R., 2002. The social accounting project and accounting organizations and society privileging engagement, imaginings, new accountings and pragmatism over critique? *Accounting, Organizations and Society*, 27(7), 687–708.

Gray, R., 2013. Sustainability + accounting education: the elephant in the classroom. *Accounting Education: An International Journal*, 22(4), 308–332.

Gray, R., Bebbington, J. and Gray, S., 2010. *Social and Environmental Accounting* (Vols I–IV). London: Sage.

Gray, R., Bebbington, J., Collison, D., Kouhy, R., Lyon, B., Reid, C., Russell A. and Stevenson, L., 1998. *The Valuation of Assets and Liabilities: Environmental Law and the Impact of the Environmental Agenda for Business*. Edinburgh: Institute of Chartered Accountants of Scotland.

Gray, R. and Collison, D., 2002. Can't see the wood for the trees, can't see the trees for the numbers? Accounting education, sustainability and the public interest. *Critical Perspectives on Accounting*, 13, 797–836.

Gray R., Owen, D. and Maunders, K., 1987. *Corporate Social Reporting: Accounting and Accountability*. Hemel Hempstead: Prentice Hall.

Gray, R., Owen, D. and Maunders, K., 1988. Corporate social reporting: emerging trends in accountability and the social contract. *Accounting, Auditing & Accountability Journal*, 1(1), 6–20.

Gray, R. and Laughlin, R., 2012. It was 20 years ago today: Sgt Pepper, accounting, auditing & accountability journal, green accounting and the Blue Meanies. *Accounting, Auditing & Accountability Journal*, 25(2), 228–255.

Hopwood, A.G., 1979. Editorial, Accounting Organizations and Society. *Accounting Organizations and Society*, 4(3), 145–147.

Humphrey, C., Lewis, L. and Owen, D., 1996. Still too distant voices? Conversations and reflection on the social relevance of accounting education. *Critical Perspectives on Accounting*, 7(1/2), 77–99.

Ibarra-Colado, E., 2006. Organization studies and epistemic coloniality in Latin America: thinking otherness from the margins. *Organization*, 13(4), 463–488.

ICAEW Environment Research Group, Macve, R. and Carey, A. (eds)., 1992. *Business, Accountancy and the Environment: A Policy and Research Agenda*. London: Institute of Chartered Accountants of England and Wales.

Illich, I., 1971. *Deschooling Society*. London: Calder & Boyars.

Kamp-Roelands, N., 1999. *Audits of Environmental Reports*. Amsterdam: Royal NIVRA.

Lade, S. J., et al., 2020. Human impacts on planetary boundaries amplified by earth system interactions. *Nature Sustainability*, 3(2), 119–128.

Laine, M., 2013. A commentary on "sustainability and accounting education: the elephant in the classroom". *Accounting Education: An International Journal*, 22(4), 333–335.

Larrinaga, C., 2001. Aspectos sociales y políticos del estado de valor añadido. *Revista de contabilidad*, 4(8), 35–62.

Larrinaga, C., 2013. A commentary on 'Rhetoric or Reality? do accounting education and experience increase weighting on environmental performance in a balanced scorecard?' *Accounting Education: An International Journal*, 22(4), 366–381.

Lewis, L., Humphrey, C. and Owen D., 1992. Accounting and the social: a pedagogic perspective. *British Accounting Review*, 24(3), 219–233.

Mansell, S., Ferguson, J., Gindis, D. and Pasternak, A., 2019. Rethinking corporate agency in business, philosophy, and law. *Journal of Business Ethics*, 154(4), 893–899.

Martens, P. and Rotmans, J., 2005. Transitions in a globalising world. *Futures*, 37(10), 1133–1144.

Mathews, M., 1997. Twenty-five years of social and environmental accounting research: Is there a silver jubilee to celebrate? *Accounting, Auditing & Accountability Journal,* 10(4), 481–531.

Meyer, J., 1986. Social environments and organizational accounting. *Accounting, Organizations and Society*, 11(4/5), 345–356.

Mol, A., 2006. Environmental governance in the Information Age: the emergence of informational governance. *Environment and Planning C: Government and Policy*, 24(4), 497–514.

Mol, A., 2010. The future of transparency: power, pitfalls and promises. *Global Environmental Politics*, 10(3), 132–143.

Nyström, M., Jouffray, J.-B, Norström, A., Crona, B., Søgaard Jøgensen, P., Carpenter, S., Bodin, Ö., Galaz, V. and Folke, C., 2019. Anatomy and resilience of the global production system. *Nature*, 575, 98–108.

Österblom, H., Cvitanovic, C., van Putten, L., Addison, P., Bebbington, J., Hall, J., Ison, S., Jouffray, J.-B., LeBris, A., Mynott, S., Reid, D. and Sugimoto, A., 2020. Science-industry collaboration – sideways or highways to ocean sustainability? *One Earth*, 3(1), 79–88.

Reichmann, T. and Lange, C., 1981. The value added statement as part of corporate social reporting. *Management International Review,* 21(4), 17–22.

Rockström, J., Steffen, W., Noone, K., Persson, A., Chapin, F. and Lambin, E., 2009. A safe operating space for humanity. *Nature,* 461(7263), 472–475.

Russell, S., Milne, M. and Dey, C., 2017. Accounts of nature and the nature of accounts: critical reflections on environmental accounting and propositions for ecologically informed accounting. *Accounting, Auditing & Accountability Journal*, 30(7), 1426–1458.

Schaltegger, S., 2013. Sustainability education and accounting experience. What motivates higher valuation of environmental performance? *Accounting Education: An International Journal*, 22(4), 385–387.

Thomson, I. and Bebbington, J., 2004. It doesn't matter what you teach? *Critical Perspectives on Accounting*, 15(4/5), 609–628.

Wynder, M., Wellner, K. and Wynder, K., 2013. Rhetoric or reality? Do accounting education and experience increase weighting on environmental performance in a balanced scorecard? *Accounting Education: An International Journal*, 22(4), 366–381.

2
THE FOUNDATIONS OF ENVIRONMENTAL ACCOUNTING

Jan Bebbington

Introduction[1]

Other chapters in this handbook delve into the activities that emerge in particular environmental accounting and reporting topic areas, including a description of the background to specific innovations in those domains. In contrast, this chapter takes an overarching view of environmental accounting and will address three topics. First, it explores the conditions that made accounting for the environment possible in a practice sense and thinkable in a conceptual sense. Second, the chapter will characterise the foundations that underpin environmental accounting. The final section will look to the future and suggest how environmental accounting (now intertwined with sustainability concerns) might/could/should evolve in the future.

Environmental accounting: the start of the field

At least three elements came together to create the conditions for environmental accounting to emerge. First, from the late 1960s there had been debate within the accounting profession about how accounting might provide insight into the negative social and environmental effects of corporate behaviour (see, e.g., Accounting Standards Steering Committee 1975; American Accounting Association 1972, 1973, 1974, 1975, 1976; American Institute of Chartered Public Accountants 1977). The debates taking place in the professional space echoed wider debates about the responsibility of organisations (see Narver 1971 for a seminal paper[2] and Estes 1976 for an accounting equivalent). These debates had underpinned the field of social accounting (see especially Gray, Owen and Maunders 1987) and it was logical that as environmental issues gained greater salience (see more below), scholarly work would also seek to address the external environmental effects of organisational action. This also explains why key social accounting scholars (such as Rob Gray, James Guthrie, Reg Matthews, Keith Maunders, David Owen and Lee Parker) would become key instigators and contributors to environmental accounting.

At the same time, a second trend was evident: specifically, the emergence of a self-conscious and changing perception of accounting scholarship (noting also that accounting was a relatively newcomer to universities in the 1960s, at least in the United Kingdom). The mainstream conception of accounting was that it should focus on economic matters that could be translated into financial terms and that accounting was a neutral technical activity. In contrast, there had been a growing understanding of accounting as a social and institutional practice (Hopwood 1976, 1983; Burchell et al. 1980) with widespread effects (see, e.g., Tinker 1985 but also Solomons 1991 for a contestation of this view). This understanding opened up what could be seen as valid topics for an accountant to research as well as approaches to that activity (Chua 1986 and Tinker, Merino and Neimark 1982). An interpretative and socially constructionist approach supported the belief that accounting could create visibility around environmental harm (Hines 1988) and that accounting could and should be brought to bear on addressing that harm.

The third element that made environmental accounting possible was a greater science, policy and political awareness of problems associated with ensuring the integrity of environmental systems (see Bebbington 2001 and Warde, Robin and Sörlin 2018 for a political overview). For example, the *Brundtland Report* (United Nations World Commission on Environment and Development 1987) had recently been published; the United Nations Intergovernmental Panel on Climate Change was founded (in 1988) and research initiatives (such as the International Geosphere-Biosphere Programme, with a focus on studying the phenomenon of global change) commenced in 1987. These elements had knock-on effects in domestic politics and knowledge production system (see Warde, Robin and Sörlin 2018). For example, in the United Kingdom, the government of the time had commissioned a report to lay out their response to the *Brundtland Report*, resulting in the publication of what was known as the *Pearce Report* (Pearce, Markandya and Barbier 1989), which attempted to describe the "blue print for a green economy" (the subtitle of the report).

This rise of environmental awareness in the late 1980s and its salience for policy-making built on even earlier foundations. For example, a seminal contribution to this changing context was the publication of *Silent Spring* in 1962, which documented the hitherto underappreciated effects of pesticides (Carson 1962). At the same time, the 1960s saw the post-World War II generation become adults and champion new social movements such as civil rights in the United States of America, indigenous rights across the globe, decolonisation (e.g., many countries gaining independence from the British "Empire" in the 1960s), championing peace and opposing the Vietnam War, and opposing nuclear energy. The first "green" parties contested elections in 1972 in Australasia and political parties founded on peace and environmental values subsequently emerged across the world, gradually taking more prominent roles in governments (the West Germany Green Party, Die Grünen, being perhaps the most successful of these). In a more formal context, legislation was also passed to address systemic environmental problems (e.g., the Clean Air Act in the United States of America was passed in 1963 and the precursor to the European Union published its first environmental action plan in 1973).

It was against this background, and into this mix, that the first formal document to address environmental accounting emerged (Gray 1990), with the subtitle of "the profession after Pearce". This report was sponsored by the Association of Chartered Certified Accountants, with Roger Adams being an influential champion of environmental accounting and reporting within the association and the accounting profession more widely. The following years witnessed the first special issues dedicated to environmental accounting in journals that have become long-standing supporters of this line of work (especially *Accounting, Auditing and Accountability Journal* and *Accounting, Organizations and Society* in 1991 and 1992, respectively). Table 2.1 outlines additional resources that shed light on the history of and reflections upon environmental accounting (alongside social accounting). In addition, the table notes the founding of the *Centre for Social and Environmental Accounting Research*, a body that has been pivotal for the field (see also Chapter 1 of this handbook).

Table 2.1 Some resources and retrospectives on (social and) environmental accounting

Collection of 80 key articles in social and environmental accounting, arranged thematically into four volumes (Gray, Bebbington and Gray 2010): • Vol I: Laying the foundations • Vol II: Developing the field • Vol III: Controversies and conflicts • Vol IV: Practices, initiatives and possibilities for the future
Reflections on the field by selected authors: • Matthews (1997) – a reflection on how social and environmental accounting has developed since 1971 • Owen (2008) – a personal reflection on the current state of, and future prospects for, social and environmental accounting research • Gray and Laughlin (2012) – a retrospective some 20 years after the first special issue in environmental accounting in *Accounting, Auditing and Accountability Journal* in 1991 • Bebbington and Thomson (2013) – examining issues in management accounting specifically • Guthrie and Parker (2017) – this 30-year retrospective is from the founding editors of *Accounting, Auditing and Accountability Journal* • Bebbington, Russell and Thomson (2017) – personal reflections on motivations and understanding of how social/environmental accounting • Adams and Larrinaga (2019) – analysis of papers that focus on engagement focused research themes and trends
The Centre for Social and Environmental Accounting Research (see www.st-andrews.ac.uk/csear/) functions as a learned society through its journal (the *Social and Environmental Accountability Journal*) as well as supporting conferences in the field world-wide. The Centre was founded in 1992 by Rob Gray who also produced a number of seminal works in the field. Milestones in terms of reports, books and papers produced by him (and co-authors) include the following: Gray, Owen and Maunders (1987); Gray (1990); Gray (1992); Gray, Owen and Adams (1996); Gray (2002); Gray (2010); and Gray, Adams and Owen (2014).

Underpinning elements of environmental accounting

The elements that underpinned Gray (1990) are threefold and relate to:

- the nature and functionality of the system from which environmental effects are generated and on which it is hoped that environmental accounting interventions might have an effect;
- the grounds for assigning responsibility for effects to organisations and the way in which such responsibilities could be governed and could be said to have been discharged; and
- a deeper set of assumptions about the ethical and moral context in which human–nature relations might be understood.

Gray (1990) draws on general systems theory as a way to characterise the exchanges that arise between organisations and their environment (in its broadest sense). The version of systems theory used (von Bertalanffy 1956; Ackoff 1960; and Lovelock 1982) is drawn from biological sciences and contains ideas about emergent properties from systems that are subject to feedback loops that seek to bring a system back into some, possibly steady, state. If one knows what drives a system and how feedback loops operate, then it is possible to think about intervening in systems to achieve a desired state (Meadows 1999). In using this framing for accounting, Gray (1990) believed systems theory concepts had resonance in social domains and can be used to identify effects that arise from organisational action and suggest what a feedback mechanism would be. For example, in the case of organisationally generated externalities, we might hypothesise that a lack of "good" regulation and/or a lack of consumer knowledge about the link between organisations and their externalities might be remedied by the provision of information about externalities. The aim of such information provision would be to provide a basis to argue for "better" regulation and/or to inform consumer boycotts of organisations or products creating externalities (it might also be used for an organisation to better inform itself about its wider impacts and change those effects in response to that information).

Cognate with this systems conception of organisational impacts was a social contract informed framing of how responsibility for such impacts is determined (Gray, Owens and Maunders 1988; Gray 1992, as inspired by the work of John Rawls). Specifically, environmental accounting (as with social accounting before it) was founded on the idea that organisations and society have mutually constitutive effects on each other. Organisations are granted rights by society (e.g., to have legal personhood and limited liability) and society expects goods/services in return as well as behaviour that underpins sound societal functioning (lobbying for corporate self-interests, e.g., would not fit with this conception of a social contract). Given the power differences between organisations and society, the law provides a minimum set of responsibilities for organisations and mechanisms to monitor if the law is complied with along with sanctions should it not be (these elements are present to varying degrees, depending on the issue in question).

This framing is consistent with the focus of environmental accounting on the provision of information from organisations to wider relevant publics about organisational actions and impacts. It is assumed that information provision will support the sound functioning of a democratic society (Gray et al. 1987). These beliefs also underpin the idea of accountability: that organisations owe both a duty to act in certain ways and to provide information about their actions (the latter being transparency). In combination, the delineation of responsibilities, enforced by some governing process, coupled with information provision to interested and active persons provides the driving force for environmental accounting.

How environmental accounting might achieve the ambitions outlined above also reflected its close association with the fundamentals of the accounting craft. For example, environmental accounting maintained a focus on discrete economic entities as being the object for accounting/reporting activities. Likewise, there is a preference for some form of financial measurement/reporting as a way to articulate actions and their impacts. Moreover, the practice of reporting has been central to empirical investigations in the field (influenced by the dual themes of decision usefulness and information inductance – see Prakash and Rappaport 1977). To these, the notion that organisations owed a duty of accountability to stakeholders for the maintenance of legitimacy became the central organising principle of the field (with stakeholder theory drawing from the wider field of corporate social responsibility). In this way, accountability became the normative basis for environmental accounting and especially environmental reporting.

This position was contested from both those for whom environmental accounting breached the norms of accounting practice and those who sought more radical and critical responses to the problems facing society (the best example of the latter stream of works is Tinker, Lehman and Neimark 1991). It could be argued that the earlier critique (that environmental accounting is not accounting) has lost ground as policy and practice has recognised environmental protection as a mainstream position. On the other hand, the criticism that environmental accounting does not pay sufficient attention to achieving more critical societal ambitions is reflected in the disappointments expressed about what has not been achieved that have emerged from the founders of the field (see, e.g., Owen 2008; Gray 2010; Gray and Milne 2018) and remains a potent disciplining effect for the field as a whole (see Bebbington et al. 2017). Indeed, if you wished to gain a sense of how the hopes for environmental accounting have changed over time, Gray (1992, 2002 and 2010) provides a powerful run-through of the various issues at stake. Underlying worries about the achievements of environmental accounting are questions about the relative power of organisations to order society to suit themselves (rather than being held accountable) as well as deeper questions about the relationship between nature and human culture.

At the outset of environmental accounting, there was explicit attention paid to the conception of "nature" and what kind of relationship individuals and society might have with the natural world (see Gray 1992; Maunders and Burritt 1991; Birkin 1996; Milne and Gray 2013; Russell, Milne and Dey 2017 as well as Chapter 28 of this handbook). Concerns about the colonisation of the "environment" by the modes and values of accounting was also part of the early critiques of environmental accounting (Cooper 1992) and remain a potent source of reflection. There is no way to "resolve" these concerns, but they do remind us that the issues that environmental accounting seeks to address have resonance with much deeper questions that are debated in environmental philosophy and ethics.

Indeed, philosophy (and particularly environmental ethics) can help us to better understand our own underlying values and beliefs (Andrew 2000) in the context of seeking to develop environmental accounting as a scholarly area of activity as well as how values and beliefs drive personal commitment and activism (Carson 1962; Cafaro 2013). Environmental ethics provides ways of exploring the issues and consequences of human actions and is underpinned by multiple and broad ethical perspectives (e.g., human, animal or life-centred; "rights for rocks"; or ecological holism). Ethical issues from an environmental accounting perspective can be based within frames of utility (cost–benefit analysis or ethical protection); rights (human rights or animal rights – see also Chapter 29 of the handbook) or contract (legal frames and theories of justice). The different frames are linked to contrasting values and form the deeper underpinning and rationale of a commitment to environmental accounting.

While noting the complexity and nuance in environmental ethics, most approaches are pluralistic and encompass varying philosophical perspectives and orientations (Cafaro 2011). The writings of Leopold (1949) and Callicott (1979), for example, articulate the principles of such an approach whereby humans extend their sense of moral concern and vision to include soils, water and non-human animals and "value" these aspects in ways that are different from the more usual economic or instrumental conception of value. Rather, and as articulated by Rolston (1975), values inherent in nature are independent of human valuing agents and extend to all individual living things: this perspective has been extended to ecosystems as a whole as well. There is insufficient space to develop these arguments further here, but it is worth noting key sources which include deep ecology (Naess 1973), environmental pragmatism and anthropocentrism (Norton 1984) and ecofeminism, gender and inequality (Plumwood 1993; Warren 1990; Shiva 1989). Furthermore, Sandel (2012) provides a moral justice framework for market-based ethical issues. An introductory overview to this field as a whole can be found in Attfield (2018), while the edited collection of Gardiner and Thompson (2017) provides a comprehensive view. A specific review of environmental ethics for social and environmental accounting can be found in Andrew (2000) and the rights of non-human nature can be found in Barrett, Watene and McNicholas (2020).

Taken together, this section has sought to illuminate the founding principles of environmental accounting: principles that are not evident if one only examines more recent published work. At the same time, conceptions of the nature and functionality of the system from which environmental effects are generated, changing perceptions of organisational responsibilities (and associated accountability relationships) as well as beliefs about the ethical and moral context in which human–nature relations might be understood continue to evolve and will be considered later on in this chapter. Before this, however, attention will turn to "what happened next".

What happened next?

A great number of "things" happened in the 30 years since Gray (1990) and the various chapters of this handbook describe these happenings as well as evaluating their successes, shortcomings and possible futures. What is most interesting is that a myriad of "things" did happen, both in the internal accounting/management routines of organisations and in how organisations used accounting and reporting techniques to present their actions and outcomes to wider audiences. Indeed, it is clear from the last 30 years that environmental accounting scholarship and activism created novel forms of accounting and reporting, some of which have become the mainstay of organisational activity. This is, as far as I can tell, relatively unusual in accounting terms. While different forms of accounting have arisen from time to time (with the value-added statement being one such example – Burchell, Clubb and Hopwood 1985), they have not been sustained over time and have not become institutionalised to the degree that environmental accounting and reporting has been.

Likewise, academic activism/engagement with practice seeded a significant change in (especially) reporting practices. Critical to this was the partnership between Roger Adams, Rob Gray and David Owen who together "hatched" the idea of encouraging environmental reporting by way of an awards scheme. This approach was pivotal in creating, sustaining and formalising practices (awards schemes have been noted as being carriers of reporting practices – Amran and Haniffa 2011; Bebbington, Kirk and Larrinaga 2012) and the eventual formalisation of reporting norms into the Global Reporting Initiative in 1999 (see Levy, Brown and de Jong 2010 for an analysis of this process). Firms of accountants, in their consultancy roles and also as assurers, further encouraged reporting practices (Etzion and Ferraro 2010) as well as "carrying" environmental accounting practices to organisations they advised. While there are considerable doubts about the functionality of such reporting (see Chapter 8), it was by no means guaranteed that it would have emerged or would have become a legal requirement in some countries (e.g., see Chapter 21 of this handbook that traces this process in Europe). The outcome has been that reporting on environmental impacts has become de facto compulsory for many larger and environmentally sensitive companies: a process described in more detail in Chapter 10 of this handbook.

All this does not mean that environmental accounting has been "successful" against its original ambitions of enhancing transparency, discharging accountability, contributing to broader democratic processes and addressing environmental problems. Indeed, despite the proliferation of reporting practices there is widespread concern that reporting is used for isomorphic and/or reputational reasons in comparison to being about demonstrating operational impacts (Laine 2009). In addition, environmental accounting scholarship has been dominated by North America and the United Kingdom perspectives, priorities and publishing norms which have constrained the field. For an example of these concerns, see Patten (2013), Roberts and Wallace (2015) and Roberts (2018): Part 4 of this handbook seeks to address this problem, at least to some extent. Of course, the counterfactual of what "the world" would look like had environmental accounting and reporting had not become a widespread practice is unknown. At the same time, if we return to the foundations of the field, it is evident that these need to be updated in the context of the current moment as well as by 30 years of scholarship in related foundational fields.

Lessons from the past and looking to the future

The purpose of this chapter was to provide insights into the foundation of environmental accounting. This section will extend this work to describe current understandings of the nature and functionality of the earth system (the perceived "state of the environment" is the underpinning to any accounting for the environment). Here the news is nearly universally negative. In the last 30 years, the state of the natural environment has continued to deteriorate, including in the core areas of climate change, water resources and biodiversity (see chapters 26, 27 and 28 of this handbook). Moreover, the simultaneous breaching of planetary boundaries has moved humanity beyond a "safe operating space" (for accounting ramifications of this, see Chapter 6 of this handbook) and has brought global society to a realisation that we may be exiting the Holocene and entering the Anthropocene (see Bebbington et al. 2020 for an in-depth exposition). At the same time, global policy processes continue to adapt and evolve, with the Sustainable Development Goals being the most current incarnation of these concerns (see Bebbington and Unerman 2018, 2020).

Thinking about how the earth system is driven by a combination of social and economic forces (and vice versa) has also evolved from the general systems theory used by Gray (1990) to complex adaptive systems theory. Just as general systems theory was pivotal to the foundation of environmental accounting, more recent conceptions of how the earth system operates become relevant to future environmental accounting. The motifs of complex adaptive systems is that the system has emergent properties that are more complex than its parts and creates nonlinear systems dynamics. The "adaptive" element refers to the observation that collective behaviour mutates due to pressures and elements of self-organisation create new dynamics (Levin et al. 2012).

This understanding of systems function requires new approaches to accounting scholarship that take full cognisance of the "wickedness" of the problems that environmental accounting (often, now in the guise of sustainability accounting) is seeking to address. This is the context in which environmental accounting and accountants are called to operate in and responses are likely to require a sustainability science response (Bebbington and Larrinaga, 2014) and a further enlarged conception of accounting as well as the entities for which accounts might usefully be developed. Accounting will be called to also provide input to "super wicked" problems (defined by Levin et al. 2012, as consisting of four features, namely, that "time is running out; those who cause the problem also seek to provide a solution; the central authority needed to address it is weak or non-existent; and, partly as a result, policy responses discount the future irrationally" p. 124). It is discomforting to recognise that accounting scholars fit within the characterisation of those that seek to provide a solution are also the cause of the problem.

If we are living in a complex and adaptive world, further analysis of disclosure of a subset of economic actors (listed companies) is unlikely to be the most productive way forward (even while acknowledging the relevance of being informed about disclosure patterns to the extent to which they demonstrate changed operations and/or achievements). The shape of future environmental accounting scholarship that is fit for purpose remains unclear. Discussions within business and management scholars are a little more advanced and they might provide fruitful avenues for accountants to investigate (see, e.g., Whiteman, Walker and Perego 2013; Williams et al. 2017; Williams, Whiteman and Kennedy 2019).

The final theme that this chapter will consider is the extent to which the foundational normative basis for environmental accounting might also need to evolve in the circumstances in which we find ourselves. At the most fundamental level (that of conceptualising the "deal" between society and organisations), there have been doubts expressed outside the accounting literature about the adequacy of a social contract framing for corporate social responsibility. In particular, the context in which social contract theory is founded upon (Rawls 1971, 2001) has changed substantially and global society now faces qualitatively different challenges: namely, breaching ecological limits and persistent and structural inequality. Within political and philosophy scholarship, a "capabilities" approach has emerged as a successor to the social contract approach (see Nussbaum 2011 in particular, building on Sen 1999 and 2009 and sometimes described as a cosmopolitan approach – see Dobson 2006) and this approach has found favour in some sustainable development settings. Given this, it may be that environmental accounting would benefit from a revisiting of its social contract commitments.

In brief, the capabilities approach bases its view of what is "appropriately" due to people on a set of non-negotiable entitlements that are deemed to be necessary in order to have the capacity to flourish, in whatever way makes sense to those seeking to flourish. While this means that there can be a wide set of capacities, there is also an underpinning set of capabilities that are similar to basic human rights entitlements. This approach also differs from that of the social contract, where what individuals are entitled to arises from some societal deal. The capabilities approach has been influential in debates around human development as well as in "flourishing" frameworks that have an inclusive (and strongly ecologically informed) vision of well-being (see Chapter 6 of this handbook and Raworth 2017). Taking this material as a guide, it may be possible to examine human entitlements and explore the extent to which organisations support or impinge upon them, either directly or indirectly. While such thoughts might appear to be a long way from accounting scholarship, there are links between the basic idea of capabilities for flourishing to accounting-based explorations of, for example, animal rights (see Chapter 29 of this handbook); the rights of nature (see also Barrett, Watene and McNicholas 2020); accounting's engagement with notions of the common good (Killian and O'Regan 2020) and economic democracy (Bebbington and Campbell 2015). The proposition that the social contract basis for environmental accounting (alongside social and sustainability accounting) needs to be revisited is more an intuition than a well-formed hypothesis, the resolution of which awaits an academic year with time for reading and slow reflection.

In conclusion, this chapter has sought to illuminate the foundational principles on which environmental accounting was forged, which themselves may have faded from conscious collective memory. The ideals that motivated the field were focused on the provision of information about "things" for which organisations were (or could be held to be) responsible for. If this process operated effectively, organisations could be held accountable for their impacts and could be made to behave in ways that satisfied the social contract between organisations and society. Of course, this ambition has only been partially fulfilled and the multiple ways in which accounting has been implicated in this process makes up the contents of this handbook. At the same time, a revisiting of foundations required a reconsideration of the context in which environmental accounting is seeking to effect. As the Anthropocene becomes a reality, and as the cumulative effects of breaching various planetary boundaries come to the fore, it might be that how we seek to hold organisations accountable needs to be updated in practice and also in conceptual underpinnings. One proposition for re-envisioning the goals of environmental accounting sees a return to an earlier core accounting notion: that of stewardship of more than financial resources (see, e.g., Contrafatto and Bebbington 2013 and Bebbington et al. 2020). A focus on organisations and biosphere stewardship is also gaining consideration in the sustainability science context (see Folke et al. 2019). How stewardship and environmental accounting might "mesh" is something that might be the subject to take forward into the next 30 years of the field.

Notes

1 The author thanks Bisola Joloko for the helpful insights provided on an earlier version of this chapter and for input from Jane Gibbon on environmental ethics.
2 The author thanks Tom Schneider for identifying this neglected paper. Issues of the social responsibility of business began much earlier (Bowen 1953), but from an accounting/reporting perspective debates about the appropriate form of any additional reporting in this arena emerged a little later.

References

Accounting Standards Steering Committee, 1975. *The Corporate Report*. London: Institute of Chartered Accountants in England and Wales.

Ackoff R., 1960. Systems, organisations and interdisciplinary research. *General Systems Theory Yearbook*, 5, 1–8. Washington: Society for General Systems Research.

Adams, C. and Larrinaga, C., 2019. Progress: engaging with organisations in pursuit of improved sustainability accounting and performance. *Accounting, Auditing & Accountability Journal*, 32(8), 2367–2394

American Accounting Association, 1972. Committee on Measures of Effectiveness For Social Programs. *The Supplement to the Accounting Review*, 47, 336–396.

American Accounting Association, 1973. Committee on Environmental Effects of Organization Behaviour. *The Supplement to the Accounting Review*, 47, 72–119.

American Accounting Association, 1974. Committee on Measurement of Social Costs. *The supplement to The Accounting Review*, 48, 98–113.

American Accounting Association, 1975. Committee on Social Costs. *The Supplement to the Accounting Review*, 49, 50–89.

American Accounting Association, 1976. Committee on Accounting for Social Performance. *The Supplement to the Accounting Review*, 50, 38–69.

American Institute of Chartered Public Accountants, 1977. *The Measurement of Corporate Social Performance*. New York: American Institute of Chartered Public Accountants.

Amran, A. and Haniffa, R., 2011. Evidence in development of sustainability reporting: a case of a developing country. *Business Strategy and the Environment*, 20(3), 141–156.

Andrew, J., 2000. The accounting craft and the environmental crisis: reconsidering environmental ethics. *Accounting Forum*, 24, 197–222.

Attfield, R., 2018. *Environmental Ethics: A Very Short Introduction*. Oxford: Oxford University Press.

Barrett, M., Watene, K. and McNicholas, P., 2020. Legal personality in Aotearoa New Zealand: an example of integrated thinking on sustainable development. *Accounting, Auditing & Accountability Journal*, 33(7), 1705–1730.

Bebbington, J., 2001. Sustainable development: a review of the international development, business and accounting literature. *Accounting Forum*, 25(2), 128–157.

Bebbington, J. and Campbell, D., 2015. Economic democracy: exploring the ramifications for social and environmental accountants. *Social and Environmental Accountability Journal*, 35(2), 77–85.

Bebbington, J., Kirk, E. and Larrinaga-Gonzalez, C., 2012. The production of normativity: a comparison of reporting regimes in Spain and the UK. *Accounting, Organizations and Society*, 37(2), 78–94.

Bebbington, J. and Larrinaga, C., 2014. Accounting and sustainable development: an exploration. *Accounting, Organizations and Society*, 39(6), 395–413.

Bebbington, J., Österblom, H., Crona, B., Jouffray, J.-B., Larrinaga, C., Russell, S. and Scholtens, B., 2020. Accounting and accountability in the Anthropocene. *Accounting, Auditing and Accountability Journal*, 33(1), 152–177.

Bebbington, J., Russell, S. and Thomson, I., 2017. Accounting and sustainable development: reflections and propositions. *Critical Perspectives on Accounting*, 48(1), 21–34.

Bebbington, J. and Thomson, I., 2013. Sustainable development, management and accounting: boundary crossing. *Management Accounting Research*, 24(4), 277–283.
Bebbington J. and Unerman, J., 2018. Achieving the United Nations Sustainable Development Goals: an enabling role of accounting research. *Accounting, Auditing and Accountability Journal*, 31(1), 2–24.
Bebbington J. and Unerman, J., 2020. Advancing research into accounting and the UN sustainable development goals. *Accounting, Auditing and Accountability Journal*, 33(7), 1657–1670.
Birkin, F., 1996. The ecological accountant: from the cogito to thinking like a mountain. *Critical Perspectives on Accounting*, 7(3), 231–257.
Bowen, H., 1953. *Social Responsibilities of the Businessman*. New York: Harper and Row.
Burchell, S., Clubb, C. and Hopwood, A., 1985. Accounting in its social context: towards a history of value added in the United Kingdom. *Accounting, Auditing and Accountability Journal*, 10(4), 381–413.
Burchell, S., Clubb, C., Hopwood, A.G., Hughes, J. and Nahapiet, J., 1980. The roles of accounting in organizations and society. *Accounting, Organizations and Society*, 5(1), 5–27.
Cafaro, P., 2011. Taming growth and articulating a sustainable future: the way forward for environmental ethics. *Ethics and the Environment*, 16(1), 1–22.
Cafaro, P., 2013. Rachel Carson's environmental ethics. In: Rozzi R., Pickett S., Palmer C., Armesto J. and Callicott J. (eds.), *Linking Ecology and Ethics for a Changing World. Ecology and Ethics*. Dordrecht: Springer, pp. 163-171.
Callicott, J., 1979. Elements of an environmental ethic: moral considerability and the biotic community. *Environmental Ethics*, 1, 71–81.
Carson, R., 1962. *Silent Spring*. Boston, MA: Houghton Mifflin Company.
Chua, W. F., 1986. Radical developments in accounting thought. *The Accounting Review*, LXI(4), 601–632.
Contrafatto, M. and Bebbington, J., 2013. Developing techniques for stewardship: a Scottish study. In: Mook L. (ed.), *Accounting for Social Value*. Toronto: University of Toronto Press.
Cooper, C., 1992. The non and nom of accounting for (m)other nature. *Accounting, Auditing and Accountability Journal*, 6(3), 16–39.
Dobson, A., 2006. Thick cosmopolitanism. *Political Studies*, 54(1), 165–184.
Estes. R., 1976. *Corporate Social Accounting*. New York: John Wiley & Sons.
Etzion, D. and Ferraro, F., 2010. The role of analogy in the institutionalization of sustainability reporting. *Organization Science*, 21(5), 1092–1107.
Folke, C., Österblom, H., Jouffray, J.-B., Lambin, E., Adger, N., Scheffer, M., Crona, B., Nyström, M., Levin, S., Carpenter, S., Anderies, J., Chapin, S., Crépin, A.-S., Dauriach, A., Galaz, V., Gordon, L., Katutsky, N., Walker, B., Watson, J., Wilen, J. and de Zeeuw, A., 2019. Transnational corporations and the challenge of biosphere stewardship. *Nature Ecology & Evolution*, 3, 1396–1403.
Gardiner, S. and Thompson, A. (eds)., 2017. *Oxford Handbook of Environmental Ethics*. Oxford: Oxford University Press.
Gray, R., 1990. *The Greening of Accountancy: The Profession after Pearce*. London: Chartered Association of Certified Accountants.
Gray, R., 1992. Accounting and environmentalism: an exploration of the challenge of gently accounting for accountability, transparency and sustainability. *Accounting Organisations and Society*, 17(5), 399–425.
Gray, R., 2002. The social accounting project and Accounting Organizations and Society. Privileging engagement, imaginings, new accountings and pragmatism over critique? *Accounting Organisations and Society*, 27(7), 687–708.
Gray, R., 2010. Is accounting for sustainability actually accounting for sustainability… and how would we know? An exploration of narratives of organisations and the planet. *Accounting Organisations and Society*, 35(1), 47–62.
Gray, R., Adams, C. and Owen, D., 2014. *Accountability, Social Responsibility and Sustainability: Accounting for Society and the Environment*. London: Pearson.
Gray, R., Bebbington, J. and Gray, S., 2010. *Social and Environmental Accounting* (Vols I–IV). London: Sage.
Gray, R. and Laughlin, R., 2012. It was 20 years ago today: Sgt Pepper, accounting, auditing & accountability journal, green accounting and the Blue meanies. *Accounting, Auditing and Accountability Journal*, 25(2), 228–255.
Gray, R. and Milne, M., 2018. Perhaps the Dodo should have accounted for human beings? Accounts of humanity and (its) extinction. *Accounting, Auditing & Accountability Journal*, 31(3), 826–848.
Gray, R., Owen, D. and Maunders, K., 1987. *Corporate Social Reporting: Accounting and Accountability*. Prentice Hall: Hemel Hempstead.

Gray, R., Owen, D. and Maunders, K., 1988. Corporate social reporting: emerging trends in accountability and the social contract. *Accounting, Auditing & Accountability Journal*, 1(1), 6–20.
Gray, R., Owen, D. and Adams, C., 1996. *Accounting and Accountability*. Hemel Hempstead: Prentice Hall.
Guthrie, J. and Parker, L., 2017. Reflections and projections: 30 years of the interdisciplinary accounting, auditing and accountability search for a fairer society. *Accounting, Auditing & Accountability Journal*, 30(1), 2–17.
Hines, R., 1988. Financial accounting: in communicating reality, we construct reality. *Accounting, Organizations and Society*, 13(3), 343–361.
Hopwood, A., 1976. Editorial: the path ahead. *Accounting, Organizations and Society*, 1(1), 104.
Hopwood, A., 1983. On trying to study accounting in the contexts in which it operates. *Accounting, Organizations and Society*, 8(2–3), 287–305.
Killian, S. and O'Regan, P., 2020. Accounting, the public interest and the common good. *Critical Perspectives on Accounting*, 67–68, 102144.
Laine, M., 2009. Ensuring legitimacy through rhetorical changes?: a longitudinal interpretation of the environmental disclosures of a leading Finnish chemical company. *Accounting, Auditing & Accountability Journal*, 22(7), 1029–1054.
Leopold, A., 1949. *A Sand County Almanac: And Sketches Here and There*. New York: Oxford University Press.
Levin, K., Cashore, B., Bernstein, S. and Auld. G., 2012. Overcoming the tragedy of super wicked problems: constraining our future selves to ameliorate global climate change. *Policy Science*, 45, 123–152.
Levy, D. L., Brown, H. and de Jong, M., 2010. The contested politics of corporate governance: the case of the global reporting initiative. *Business and Society*, 49(1), 88–115.
Lovelock, J., 1982. *Gaia: A New Look at Life on Earth*. Oxford: Oxford University Press.
Mathews, M., 1997. Twenty-five years of social and environmental accounting research: is there a silver jubilee to celebrate? *Accounting, Auditing & Accountability Journal*, 10(4), 481–531.
Maunders, K. and Burritt, R., 1991. Accounting and ecological crisis. *Accounting, Auditing and Accountability Journal*, 4(3), 9–26.
Meadows, D., 1999. *Leverage points: Places to Intervene in a System*. The Sustainability Institute: Hartland.
Milne, M. and Gray, R., 2013. W(h)ither ecology? The triple bottom line, the global reporting initiative, and corporate sustainability reporting. *Journal of Business Ethics*, 118, 13–29.
Naess, A., 1973. The shallow and the deep: long-range ecology movements. *Inquiry*, 16, 95–100.
Narver, J., 1971. Rational management responses to external effects. *Academy of Management Journal*, 14(1), 99–115.
Norton, B., 1984. Environmental ethics and weak anthropocentrism. *Environmental Ethics*, 6(2), 131–148.
Nussbaum, M., 2011. *Creating Capabilities: The Human Development Approach*. Cambridge, MA: Belknap Press.
Owen, D., 2008. Chronicles of wasted time? A personal reflection on the current state of, and future prospects for, social and environmental accounting research. *Accounting, Auditing & Accountability Journal*, 21(2), 240–267.
Patten, D., 2013. Lessons from the third wave: a reflection on the rediscovery of corporate social responsibility by the mainstream accounting research community. *Financial Reporting*, 2(2), 9–26.
Pearce, D., Markandya, A. and Barbier, E., 1989. *Blueprint for a Green Economy*. London: Earthscan.
Plumwood, V., 1993. *Feminism and the Mastery of Nature*. London: Routledge.
Prakash, P. and Rappaport, A. 1977. Information inductance and its significance for accounting. *Accounting, Organizations and Society*, 2(1), 29–38.
Rawls, J., 1971. *A Theory of Justice*. Oxford: Oxford University Press.
Rawls, J., 2001. *Justice as Fairness*. Delhi: Universal Law Publishing.
Raworth, K., 2017. *Doughnut Economics: Seven Ways to Think Like a 21st-Century Economist*. Hartford: Chelsea Green Publishing.
Roberts, R., 2018. We can do so much better: reflections on reading "Signaling effects of scholarly profiles – the editorial teams of the North American Accounting Association Journals". *Critical Perspectives on Accounting*, 51, 70–77.
Roberts, R. and Wallace, D., 2015. Sustaining diversity in social and environmental accounting research. *Critical Perspective on Accounting*, 32, 78–87.
Rolston, H., 1975. Is there an ecological ethic? *Ethics*, 85, 93–109.
Russell, S., Milne, M. and Dey, C., 2017. Accounts of nature and the nature of accounts: critical reflections on environmental accounting and propositions for ecologically informed accounting. *Accounting, Auditing & Accountability Journal*, 30(7), 1426–1458.

Sandel, S., 2012. *What Money Can't Buy: The Moral Limit of Markets*. London: Penguin.
Sen, A., 1999. *Development as Freedom*. Oxford: Oxford University Press.
Sen, A., 2009. *The Idea of Justice*. London: Allen Lane.
Shiva, V., 1989. *Staying Alive: Women, Ecology and Development*. London: Zed Books.
Solomons, D., 1991. Accounting and social change: a neutralist view. *Accounting Organizations and Society*, 16(3), 287–295.
Tinker, A., 1985. *Paper Prophets: A Social Critique of Accounting*. Eastbourne: Holt Saunders.
Tinker, A., Lehman, C. and Neimark, M., 1991. Falling down the hole in the middle of the road: political quietism in corporate social reporting. *Accounting, Auditing and Accountability Journal*, 4(2), 28–54.
Tinker, A., Merino, B. and Neimark, M., 1982. The normative origins of positive theories: ideology and accounting thought. *Accounting Organizations and Society*, 7(2), 167–200.
United Nations World Commission on Environment and Development, 1987. *Our Common Future (The Brundtland Report)*. Oxford: Oxford University Press.
von Bertalanffy L., 1956 General Systems Theory. *General Systems Yearbook*, 1, 1-10.
von Bertalanffy, L., 1971. *General Systems Theory: Foundations, Development, Applications*. Harmondsworth: Penguin.
Warde, P., Robin, L. and Sörlin, S., 2018. *The Environment: A History of the Idea*. Baltimore, MD: Johns Hopkins University Press.
Warren, K., 1990. The power and promise of ecological feminism. *Environmental Ethics*, 12(2), 125–146.
Whiteman, G., Walker, B. and Perego, P., 2013. Planetary boundaries: ecological foundations for corporate sustainability. *Journal of Management Studies*, 50, 307–336.
Williams, A., Kennedy, S., Philipp, F. and Whiteman, G., 2017. Systems thinking: a review of sustainability management research. *Journal of Cleaner Production*, 148, 866–881.
Williams, A., Whiteman, G. and Kennedy, S., 2021 Cross-scale systemic resilience: implications for organization studies. *Business & Society*, 60(1), 95-124.

3
THEORISING ENVIRONMENTAL ACCOUNTING AND REPORTING

Brendan O'Dwyer

Introduction

Environmental accounting and reporting is a vast field of study embracing a variety of research topics and methods. In the past 30 years it has also evolved to embrace increasingly sophisticated theorisations of practice. This chapter reviews a selection of these efforts at theorising environmental accounting and reporting.

Theory can be defined as "a framework of concepts that help to structure our observations and then our understandings of these observed elements of the world, and to communicate this understanding" (Unerman and Chapman 2014, p. 389). Theory is the outcome of theorising (Swedberg 2014, 2016), a process which enables us to make sense of the world given that randomly accumulated data only offer an array of descriptive material "waiting for a theory, or a fire" (Coase 1988, p. 230, cited in Suddaby 2014, p. 408). Theorising consists of "activities like abstracting, generalizing, relating, selecting, explaining, synthesising and idealizing" (Weick 1995, p. 389). At its core it is a sense-making exercise (Chua and Mahama 2012) that, perhaps paradoxically, draws on an informing theory (Swedberg 2014, 2016), albeit not always (Eisenhardt and Graebner 2007; Suddaby 2014, 2006). In this chapter I embrace Weick's (1995) conception of theory: not as a way to label an ultimate triumph but to label the interim struggles to explain and understand – "to make sense of" – environmental accounting and reporting. Hence, the sections that follow synthesise assorted struggles to make sense of environmental accounting and reporting. I examine seven broad themes representing central foci of theorising in this domain.[1] These themes encompass the following: framing the emergence of environmental reporting, theorising the *why* of environmental reporting, theorising the *how* of environmental accounting and reporting, theorising the role of environmental accounting in organisational level change, theorising field-level change in environmental reporting, theorising stakeholder engagement around environmental reporting and theorising the role of language in environmental reporting.

Framing the emergence of environmental reporting

In response to concerns that social and environmental reporting (SER) lacked any underlying paradigm, Gray et al. (1988) theorised SER as a mechanism through which organisations could be compelled to discharge their accountability to "the wider society". They argued that a social contract existed between the organisation and society which *demanded* the discharge of accountability (p. 9) and SER was a way of realising this. A systems-oriented view was evoked in which entities were both affected by and affected key aspects of society (see also Gray et al. 1996, 2014). Gray et al. (1988) felt that their framework would enable the study of SER practice to "develop coherently after 15 years of gawky adolescence" (p. 14). Their framing attracted considerable critique as several scholars dismissed what they saw as its naïve, "middle of the road" leanings that downplayed political realities and structural inequities (see Tinker et al. 1991; Everett and Neu 2000; Puxty 1986). Lehman (1999) questioned the framework's tendency to "defer to instrumental criteria" (Lehman 1999, p. 218). Drawing on communitarian theory, he argued that its "strict liberal accountability" (p. 218) leanings bolstered the status quo "by simply providing additional information to stakeholders without investigating what corporations *[we] re doing* to the natural environment" (Lehman 1999, p. 218, emphasis added). He questioned whether corporations could be transformed and made accountable, and contended that Gray et al.'s (1988) framing needed to be developed to evaluate the need for institutions in both civil society and the state that could tackle the globalisation of capitalism.

Gray (1992) developed the ideas in Gray et al. (1988) when contemplating how a "deep green" position and the guiding principles of environmentalism might be articulated within accounting. He offered a more refined theorisation of accounting's potential to contribute to accountability and transparency in a participative democracy with the aim of provoking reflection on "how we might account for sustainability" (Gray 1992, p. 401). Gray (2010) later auto-critiqued the "essence" of accounting for sustainability as it had evolved through the 1990s and early 2000s and concluded that conventional accounting had lost relevance when seeking to account for sustainability. Bebbington and Larrinaga (2014) advanced Gray's (2010) "relevance lost" thesis when calling for the introduction of theories of sustainability science into the accounting for sustainability literature. They demonstrated how sustainability science and its underlying theorising could influence the practice and evaluation of full cost accounting. If scholars started theorising from a sustainability science perspective, they maintained that areas where accounting might play a more prominent role in contributing to sustainable development could be more readily identified. These efforts to frame a high-level understanding of SER evolved in parallel with a range of theoretical explorations of the practice of SER, to which I now turn my attention.

Theorising the *why* of environmental reporting

The early genesis of environmental reporting was characterised by positivist studies of disclosure practice and quests for associations with size, profitability and other variables (Bowman and Haire 1976; Cowen et al. 1987; Dierkes and Antal 1985; Ingram and Frazier 1980; Shane and Spicer 1983). The "progressive acquisition of knowledge" pervaded these efforts but a lack of systematic theorising was seen by many as stunting understanding of environmental reporting (see Ullmann 1985; Mathews 1987). Gray et al. (1995a) suggested that three core theories underlined why environmental disclosure might be undertaken: decision usefulness theory, economic theory and social and political theory. Decision usefulness and economic theory viewed disclosure as a response to the needs of financial market participants and responses to agency problems. Evidence here was, however, mixed and much of this theorisation seemed overly speculative. After an initial wave of interest in decision useful theory in the 1980s, its popularity waned before experiencing a renaissance in the major North American accounting journals in the past decade (see Dhaliwal et al. 2011; Elliott et al. 2014, 2017; Griffin et al. 2017; Martin and Moser 2016; Patten 2015; Roberts and Wallace 2015).

Gray et al.'s (1995a) summary of social and political theory explanations for environmental disclosure spurred a series of subsequent studies. They outlined a combination of complementary stakeholder theory, legitimacy theory and political economy theory explanations for disclosure. Variants of stakeholder theory and legitimacy theory emerged as the central theoretical crutches adopted to explain the growing evidence of disclosure. Instrumental stakeholder theory viewed environmental disclosure as a corporate response to managing key stakeholders. Roberts' (1992) work was influential here as he had earlier used Ullman's (1985) framework for predicting corporate social activity to empirically test the ability of stakeholder theory to explain social responsibility disclosure. Legitimacy theory viewed disclosure as part of a suite of organisational strategies aimed at convincing "relevant publics" to assign legitimacy to an organisation. A working paper from Lindblom (1994), much cited but seldom seen, theorised four possible legitimation strategies and became highly influential. A series of studies subsequently emerged advancing the initial work of Patten (1991, 1992) and Guthrie and Parker (1989) seeking to associate environmental disclosure with a range of legitimacy-oriented variables.

Legitimacy theory and its variants offered a launching pad for scholars who were concerned that their environmental disclosure data lacked theoretical import (Patten 1991, 1992). Its trajectory is ably analysed by Deegan (2002, 2019) who sketched how the theory evolved, the advances to understanding it proffered and its enduring problems. It is intriguing how the theory was popularised despite one of the first papers to adopt it to explain (social) disclosure offering no support for its explanatory power (Guthrie and Parker 1989). As its popularity soared, the theory and the way it was interpreted attracted considerable criticism. Accusations of an absence of nuance, insufficient contextual sensitivity and an ignorance of the theory's origins abounded (O'Dwyer et al. 2011; Parker 2005; Spence et al. 2010; Unerman and Chapman 2014). Some of these concerns surfaced in Deegan's (2002) special issue of *Accounting, Auditing and Accountability Journal* where the legitimation motives assigned to environmental reporting were challenged using direct managerial perceptions. A layer of sophistication was added which paved the way for work nuancing a perceived prevalence of narrow theorisations (see O'Dwyer et al. 2011). O'Dwyer (2002) emphasised the need to distinguish between legitimacy as a *state* and a *process* while contesting some of the prior presumptions surrounding legitimation motives. He suggested that *non-disclosure* could just as plausibly be motivated by legitimacy concerns (Belal and Cooper 2011), especially as target audiences differed in their responses to disclosure given the context being examined. Archel et al. (2009) maintained that legitimacy theory was too focused on the role of disclosure in managing relations between firms and their stakeholders, thereby ignoring the role of state support, or "ideological alignment with the state" (p. 1284) in legitimation strategies driving environmental disclosure. They called for more theorising around the nature of the *targets* of environmental disclosure and how this might shift legitimating motives. Neu et al. (1998) were rare in having addressed some of these concerns when demonstrating how disclosure was partially dependent on a *relevant public's influence* and a desire to manage the impressions of those publics (see also Solomon et al. 2013 in the unique context of private environmental reporting between investors and investees).[2]

Buhr (2002) extended legitimacy theorisations by embedding Lindblom's four legitimation strategies in her mobilisation of structuration theory to investigate the initiation of environmental reports in two Canadian pulp companies. She offered deeper insights into the legitimation and signification dimensions of structuration. Rahaman et al. (2004) combined components of institutional theory with Habermasian legitimation theory to reveal how environmental reporting *did not* produce legitimacy but actually stimulated *a crisis* of legitimation. Spence (2007) offered a rare route out of the legitimacy straitjacket when mobilising Laclau and Mouffe's discourse theory and placing it in the context of Gramscian thought. He maintained that "through the metaphor of balance, SER attempt[ed] to present the interests of business as largely congruent with social and environmental wellbeing" (p. 874). His case demonstrated how all motives for SER fell into some sort of hegemonic business case, thereby implying that the accountability ambitions of Gray et al. (1988) were unlikely to reflect emerging SER practice.

Bebbington et al. (2008a) argued that reputation risk management (RRM) could enhance legitimacy explanations for disclosure by operating as "an augmentation theory" that would allow for a more fine-grained analysis of disclosures. Adams (2008) robustly rebuffed their suggestion, asserting that RRM merely advanced a new labelling of legitimacy and therefore represented an "unnecessary diversion". Bebbington et al. (2008b) retorted by querying if "the legitimacy thesis [even] deserve[d] to be called a theory" (p. 372). They viewed legitimacy theory as a contested terrain in need of significant refining through reframing it in broader institutional or resource-based conceptions of corporations. While rejecting Adams' (2008) perceived attempt at theoretical closure, they argued for an "opening out" of theorising by embracing the possibilities offered by institutional theory, contingency theory, regime theory and structuration theory.[3]

More recently, social movement theory-inspired explanations for environmental reporting have emerged. O'Sullivan and O'Dwyer (2015) and Islam and Van Staden (2018) theorised social movements' impacts on disclosure, while Michelon et al. (2020) examined the role of *shareholder* activism in instigating disclosure. These studies implicitly re-embrace instrumental stakeholder theory explanations for environmental reporting and, in the case of O'Sullivan and O'Dwyer (2015), advance neo-institutional explanations of escalating disclosure by theorising how fields build around environmental issues to stimulate disclosure. In common with Islam and Van Staden's (2018) use of collaboration theory, O'Sullivan and O'Dwyer (2015) theorised the role of corporation-social movement *collaboration* as opposed to contestation in motivating disclosure. Cho et al. (2015) enhanced these stakeholder-focused theorisations, albeit indirectly, by mobilising the concepts of organised hypocrisy and organisational façades to theorise why companies may make certain disclosures (see also She and Michelon 2019). They highlighted how the prevailing economic system and conflicting stakeholder demands constrained the disclosure choices of individual corporations (see also She and Michelon 2019). These constraints are also evident in Rodrigue's (2014) partial use of a strategic accountability framing to explain the informational dynamics taking place between a firm and its stakeholders through its environmental reporting. Cho et al. (2015) offered an updated theorisation of the reasons for the "contrasting realities" of companies and stakeholders unveiled by Rodrigue (2014). Both of these studies significantly developed stakeholder theory interpretations of motives which simply view environmental reporting as a response to stakeholder demands (Liesen et al. 2015).

Theorising the *how* of environmental accounting and reporting

A related stream of research has theorised the processes underpinning the production of environmental reporting and the interactions within and around the organisations producing it. Adams (2002) entered organisations with the aim of better understanding these processes. However, she offered no explicit theorisation of her observations, simply stating that her findings "support[ed] all the theories of social reporting to various degrees" (p. 245) while bemoaning their limited explanatory power (see also Adams and Whelan 2009). Bebbington et al. (2009) offered more specificity in their theorising of underlying processes in their study of sustainability reporting champions. They mobilised neo-institutional theory to delve deeper into how the social context influences the choice of managers to initiate sustainability reporting. By de-emphasising the prevailing legitimacy theory focus on rationality they offered a subtler, more theoretically complex interpretation of the process (and the motives) through which sustainability reporting is embedded within organisations. Their paper was unique in posing questions about how and why sustainability reporting might become more widely institutionalised by demonstrating how organisational field-organisation dynamics underpinned evolutions in sustainability reporting. This focus on dynamics in a broader institutional framing fostered a welcome shift in the theoretical sophistication with which the evolution of sustainability reporting was interpreted.

Several variants of neo-institutional theory have surfaced to explain how environmental reporting is initiated within organisations. Qian et al. (2011) found that institutional theory and contingency theory helped to explain the development of environmental management accounting (EMA) in local governments in New South Wales while Higgins et al. (2014) used poetic analytics to illustrate how the sensemaking activities of early integrated reporting adopters contributed to its wider institutionalisation. As part of a growing trend researching the rise of EMA, Imtiaz Ferdous et al. (2019) combined the notions of reflexive isomorphism and institutional logics to investigate whether and how organisations actively engaged in shaping the legitimacy of the water supply field. They theorised how organisations in this emergent field reflexively shaped the emerging logics of the field. Using an institutional work framing, Farooq and De Villiers (2019) depicted a four-stage process of organisational transitioning with sustainability reporting within 30 Australian and New Zealand organisations. Related work adopted concepts such as loose coupling (Laine et al. 2017) and traditional agency theory (Sundin and Brown 2017) to examine the evolution of MCS seeking to integrate environmental issues and the production and substance of financial environmental information.

Theorising the role of environmental accounting in organisational level change

An extension of efforts to theorise the *how* of environmental accounting and reporting is a focus on how organisational change is engendered by environmental accounting. Laughlin's (1991) theoretical model of organisational change was initially popular among researchers starting to delve inside organisations. Laughlin (1991) conceived of organisations as a combination of subsystems (tangible elements such as buildings, behaviours and persons), design archetypes (intangible structures such as information systems) and interpretive schemes (metaphors, beliefs, values, riles and mission statements). He argued that organisations are normally balanced and coherent but that the balance between its components can be changed by environmental disturbances which engender what he refers to as first- and second-order change. Laughlin (1991) outlined different responses to and types of change in a series of change pathways, ranging from minimal to major change. Gray et al. (1995b) drew on this theorisation to study how environmental accounting might instigate different levels of organisational change. Larrinaga-Gonzalez et al. (2001) mapped organisational change in nine Spanish firms using Laughlin's (1991) key change elements of inertia, reorientation, colonisation and evolution. Their work was advanced by Bouten and Hoezée's (2013) study of four Belgian companies which showed how a range of different factors affected the interaction between environmental disturbances, environmental reporting and EMA systems. Bouten and Hoezée (2013) unveiled how similar environmental disturbances followed different change pathways, albeit none illustrated Laughlin's (1991) more fundamental second-order change (see also Narayanan and Adams 2017).

Laughlin's (1991) framework has continued to exert influence, albeit sporadically, in seeking to understand how and if variants of environmental reporting lead to different levels of organisational change (see also Fraser 2012; Powell and Tilt 2017; Stubbs and Higgins 2014). Given the process-oriented nature of Laughlin's framing, it is surprising that it has been primarily used in a static, categorising manner focused on labelling levels of change. Other than the original efforts by Gray et al. (1995b), there is little research which extends or develops Laughlin's (1991) framing which has led to a tendency to "draw insights from" Laughlin (1991) as opposed to developing his theorisation in the context of environmental accounting and organisational change. This is puzzling given that the nature of organisational forms has changed significantly since Laughlin's (1991) initial theorisation. It would, for example, be fascinating to see how his conceptualisation extends to "platform" organisations.

The theme of organisational change was a core feature of a special issue of *Management Accounting Research* edited by Bebbington and Thomson (2013). Laughlin's framing was revisited in two papers (Bouten and Hoezée 2013; Contrafatto and Burns 2013), while others engaged with common framings derived from the management accounting literature. Arjaliès and Mundy (2013) used Simon's levers of control (LOC) framework to explain how management control systems stimulate change towards sustainable development. Rodrigue et al. (2013) drew on the LOC framing to show how environmental performance indicators were used as interactive and diagnostic controls by an extractive company, and how stakeholders' perspectives were integrated into a corporation through its beliefs system. Moore (2013) re-embraced structuration theory, albeit in the context of wider institutional theorising, when seeking to explain how internal sustainable accounting processes become decoupled from external political discourses.

Adams and McNicholas (2007) introduced the action research method to offer insights into the potential for sustainability reporting academics to instigate organisational change. They used Lewin's (1947) field theory, group dynamics and three-step model to analyse and assist them in steering change within a state-owned organisation by helping it to adopt a sustainability reporting framework and integrate sustainability issues into planning and decision-making. It is intriguing to consider this effort in the context of Bebbington and Gray's (2001) efforts to develop full cost accounting at Landcare in New Zealand. This brave experiment also fits in the realm of action research and could have been theorised by depicting a process model of *failed* organisational change. Moreover, given Bebbington and Larrinaga's (2014) aforementioned exploration of how insights from sustainability science can contribute to developing full cost accounting, it seems evident that theorisation drawing on sustainability science would have enabled Bebbington and Gray (2001) to enhance our theoretical understanding of the possibilities of full cost accounting.

Ball and Craig (2010) theorised organisational change in two local government authorities using the "institutional toolkit" notion. They enriched our understanding of the changes these organisations make in response to environmental issues while simultaneously offering a perspective on the role organisations *should take* in addressing environmental challenges. Contrafatto (2014) later developed a related neo-institutional theory explanation in his study of the processes and stages through which environmental reporting became embedded in a multinational company. Leong and Hazelton (2019), however, cautioned against theorising organisational change in isolation of the *constraints* placed on organisations by their institutional environments,[4] something the institutional work literature is sensitive to.

A fascinating stream of research has adopted variants of governmentality theory to seek an understanding of organisational change dynamics in the realm of sustainability accounting. Similar to Leong and Hazelton (2019), Thomson et al. (2014) connected the institutional and organisational levels in their study of efforts at changing two public sector organisations' engagement with sustainable development. They linked wider programmes of government with the core technologies mobilised to enable these programmes in order to study the role of accounting in shaping and reshaping sustainability practices. They developed a holistic framework which is used to analyse the governing and mediating roles of accounting-sustainability hybrids. Spence and Rinaldi (2014) used four analytics of government (fields of visibility, techne, episteme and identity formation) to understand how accounting practices, operating in the context of a new sustainability regime, sought to shape the governance of a supply chain in a supermarket. Given the explosion of new accounting practices in the realm of sustainability in the past decade, it is surprising how this form of theorising has not gained greater traction, especially given key scholars' devotion to its potential to connect aspirational programmatic commitments to sustainability with core accounting technologies such as sustainable development indicators (Bebbington, Russell and Thomson 2017; Russell and Thomson 2009; Tregidga 2013).

Another emerging source of theorisation of organisational change draws on concepts from actor network theory (ANT). Georg and Justesen (2017) shifted attention away from a focus on how environmental accounting may *inform* management decisions towards how environmental accounting *forms* management decisions. They illuminated the performative role of environmental accounting in a study of "environmental accounting in the making" (p. 1066). Drawing on the notions of framing and overflowing they showed how environmental accounting was framed and, in turn, helped shape the design of a new green, zero energy building by helping to produce "new insights, visions and constellations of possible building designs" (p. 1067). A unique aspect of their theorising was its ability to reveal how environmental accounting can help *enact* the future, a departure from the prevalence of research which studies environmental accounting as a *representation* of past performance. Egan (2014) also drew on aspects of ANT to examine how distinct forms of accountability for water changed within an Australian university. He focused in particular on the role of non-human actants – such as water meters, spreadsheets, information systems and policy documents – in shaping a focus on water efficiency in the university.

Theorising field-level change in environmental reporting

Neo-institutional theory framings have permeated efforts to understand field-level developments in environmental accounting and reporting. O'Sullivan and O'Dwyer (2015) traced the rise of a field focused on banks' reporting on Equator Principles compliance using the notion of an issue-based field. They traced the dynamics underpinning the field's formation in a process model showing how the issue-based field formed and evolved by drawing on and extending the institutional infrastructure of a mature project finance field. Humphrey et al. (2017) theorised the field level rise of integrated reporting by combining institutional work-inspired theories of institutional change with the boundary work notion to demonstrate how integrated reporting's aim to reconfigure the corporate reporting field was contingent on its ability to reconfigure the institutional investment field. Rowbottom and Locke (2016) traced the early emergence of integrated reporting by drawing on the ANT concepts of detour, affordance and laboratory. These framing devices enabled the authors to highlight the way the core features of integrated reporting were shaped and remained continuously unstable in the face of competing pressures.

Clune and O'Dwyer (2020) examined the evolution of environmental reporting in the Dutch investment field by assimilating insights from institutional work, social movement theory and the notion of organising dissonance. They uncovered how dissensus was managed constructively by a diverse movement of actors that formed to foster enhanced environmental reporting within the Dutch investment field. Their study offers theoretical insights demonstrating how incremental change in environmental reporting is shaped by complex but carefully managed interactions at the field level which can eventually lead to norms of environmental reporting emerging in fields that are traditionally hostile to such reporting. Retaining the focus on reporting norms, Bebbington et al. (2012) examined how norms develop around environmental reporting practices, which determine how and whether these practices gain traction in a field. They theorised the construction of normativity around environmental reporting – how norms around environmental reporting were produced – and offered a complementary focus to neo-institutional approaches to norm diffusion by unveiling how shared beliefs around the legitimacy of norms emerge independent of formal legal enforcement. Their framing explained the production of normativity in the two contrasting cases of Spain and the UK, where environmental reporting had developed differently. Three internal conditions were uncovered, which contributed to the legitimacy of norms around environmental reporting: congruence with the underlying values of previous norms; the perceived integration of the rules in a coherent normative framework, and whether the rules are perceived to offer clarity (p. 89).

Van Bommel (2014) summoned Bolthanski and Thevenot's (2006) sociology of worth framework to explain efforts to legitimise integrated reporting in the Dutch reporting field. He showed how integrated reporting combined different domains of industrial, market, civic and green orders of worth which were reconciled to enable it to gain legitimacy. In a broader "how" vein, Russell et al. (2017) suggested using the orders of worth framing as a potentially useful way of advancing scholarship in the area of accounting and socio-ecological change, encapsulated in the term "ecological accounts" (see also Birkin 1996). They offered persuasive sophisticated arguments illustrating how this framing could help to broaden and open out accounts of human–nature relations. Vinnari and Laine (2013) conceived of environmental reporting as a managerial innovation and adopted Abrahamson's (1991) typology of innovation to theorise the diffusion and decline of environmental reporting practices in the Finnish water sector. They uncovered the role of "fad and fashion" in initiating environmental reporting and traced its eventual decline to internal organisational factors and the absence of persistent external pressures.

Examinations of field-level advances have also embraced Pierre Bourdieu's oeuvre. In seeking to understand how accountants can contribute to field and organisational level sustainability reforms, Egan and Tweedie (2018) marshalled the dynamic interactions between the concepts of habitus, capital and fields to offer "a multi-dimensional narrative of how firms can engage - or fail to engage - in sustainability initiatives" (pp. 1750–1751). They illuminated obstacles to engagement across individual, organisational and institutional levels. In a similar vein, Lodhia and Jacobs (2013) asserted that Bourdieu's work offered "a powerful set of tools to explore *how and why* environmental reporting occurs" (p. 600, emphasis added). Their analysis showed how environmental reporting was the result of strategic choices by internal champions in a field who were motivated by a desire to acquire different forms of cultural capital or more generalised forms of economic and social capital. Whether environmental reporting was considered legitimate or not was worked out in a struggle between different actors striving to gain different types of capital. Despite the field-level focus of Bourdieu's concepts, the authors focused their analysis on the importance of the internal context of two departments in the Australian commonwealth public sector in explaining environmental reporting practices.

Theorising stakeholder engagement around environmental reporting

Several scholars have theorised external stakeholder engagement with companies around environmental reporting. Thomson and Bebbington (2005) viewed the provision of environmental accounts as being akin to a process of education and thus amenable to pedagogic evaluation. They used Paolo Freire's distinction between banking and dialogic education as a heuristic enabling them to reflect on and understand the processes that generate environmental reports. Drawing on their experiences of stakeholder engagement exercises, they criticised the tendency for these processes to exhibit a narrow form of banking education in which stakeholder influence and the nature of mutual learning were inadequate (see also Bebbington 1997). They argued for an interactive two-way dialogic education process as an ideal for company–stakeholder interactions around environmental reports. Bebbington et al. (2007) extended this work when drawing on wider variants of dialogic theory to advance theorising, which could shape, guide and support engagements around environmental accounting. A dialogic-informed engagement approach to environmental accounting theory and praxis was presented, which augmented Thomson and Bebbington's (2005) engagement with Freire's work by mobilising a number of related theorists (such as Bakhtin and Giroux). Consistent with Thomson and Bebbington (2005), Bebbington et al. (2007) focused on mutual learning within accountability relationships between stakeholders and entities – "dialogic processes of accountability" (Bebbington et al. 2007, p. 358) – aimed at advancing substantive emancipatory change (see also Contrafatto et al. 2015). Their theorisation conceived of fluid principal–agent relationships with an enhanced voice for non-financial stakeholders and greater agency in defining accountabilities.

Unerman and Bennett (2004) enrolled Habermas's ideal speech situation to assess the extent to which Shell's internet stakeholder dialogue forum conformed with the theoretical consensus building discourse ethics criteria of an ideal speech situation. Consistent with Bebbington et al. (2007) they theorised processes leading to mutual understanding and enabling debate that offered the prospect of reaching agreement or some form of moral consensus through democratic dialogue among different stakeholder groups. Cooper and Owen (2007) also used Habermas' ideal speech situation as an evaluative mechanism to ascertain if UK stakeholder accountability practice enabled stakeholders to enter into "discourse, discussion and dialogue with corporate management and government" (p. 653). They were especially concerned to comprehend how power differentials between accountors and accountees could be mitigated in these circumstances. They concluded that environmental disclosure processes offered little opportunity for facilitating action on the part of organisational stakeholders, and questioned their role as mechanisms of accountability. Archel et al.'s (2011) critical neo-institutionalist framing similarly studied how social movement engagement with dominant institutional arrangements in Spain led to the reinforcement of the status quo. They theorised the discursive orientation of the institutionalisation process and the power dynamics which influenced it. In a more descriptive vein, Kaur and Lodhia (2018) drew on the notion of stakeholder salience to theorise how stakeholder engagement around sustainability accounting evolved in three Australian local councils, while Solomon et al. (2013) used the work of Erving Goffman to theorise the stakeholder engagement setting of private SER in interactions between investors and investees. They revealed how frontstage ritualistic impression management in private SER was inconsistent with backstage activities within financial institutions where private financial reporting was prioritised (see also Solomon and Solomon 2006) and concluded that private SER was mainly a "cosmetic, theatrical and empty exercise" (Solomon et al. 2013, p. 195).

Brown (2009) argued that social and environmental accounting was inadequately theorised to cope with difference and diversity in dialogical processes, despite claims to embracing plurality. She argued for a shift from consensus-oriented theorisations of engagement towards an agonistic form of theorising that placed ideological conflicts and domination and denial of voice at its core (see also Brown and Dillard 2013, 2014). In an extension of this critique, Brown and Tregidga (2017) "re-examined" Unerman and Bennett's (2004) study using Ranciere's theoretical insights. Along with a related stream of social and environmental accounting research, Unerman and Bennett's (2004) work was rendered naive as their proposed ideal speech situation was considered "conceptually impossible" (p.12). According to Brown and Tregidga (2017), its privileging of consensus failed to recognise that stakeholder engagement does not pay sufficient attention to the deprivation of voice (p. 11) and severely underestimates the challenges facing those who want to present non-hegemonic arguments (see Brown and Dillard 2013 for similar arguments). This is an intriguing theoretical paper and forms part of a trend in social and environmental accounting research where critical theorists denounce consensus-oriented theorisations (see Tinker et al. 1991). A puzzling feature of Brown and Tregidga's (2017) work was its failure to acknowledge Bebbington et al.'s (2007) prior work, co-authored by Brown, which addressed many of their "political" concerns from a dialogic education perspective.

While Alawatage and Fernando (2017) saw much to commend in Brown's (2009) political theorisation of SER, they missed consideration of the "postcolonial periphery". They proposed a theorisation of SER in postcolonial social spaces to explain how "a new hegemonic order is constructed through [SER] discourses" (p. 2). They used a discourse analysis of interviews with corporate managers and their published sustainability information to show how western SER was culturally reproduced in peripheral countries, thereby recreating a postcolonial hegemonic order. Homi Bhabha's postcolonial theory underpinned their theorisation. Their attention to how local managers used global SER discourse to reimagine their organisations advanced a stream of research theorising the role of language in environmental reporting.[5]

Theorising the role of language in environmental reporting

Studies of environmental reporting have regularly drawn on discourse theory to investigate how organisations *represent themselves* in relation to sustainable development. These studies focus on the role of language in shaping a wider understanding of environmental issues *vis-a-vis* business (Ferguson et al. 2016, p. 281). Tregidga et al. (2014) used Laclau and Mouffe's conceptualisations of discourse, identity and group formation and their theory of hegemony to interpret the emergence of corporate reporting on sustainable development from 1992 to 2010 in a sample of New Zealand organisations (see also Spence 2007). They uncovered three distinct organisational identities represented in these reports: environmentally responsible and compliant organisations, leaders in sustainability and strategically "good" organisations. In earlier work, both authors theorised how broader discourses of sustainable development influenced how companies constructed the concept of sustainable development in their reporting (Milne et al. 2009; Tregidga and Milne 2006). Discourse studies by Laine (2009) and Spence (2007) argued that corporate disclosure on sustainability is ideological as it constitutes meaning in the service of power by representing the corporation as a liberating and protecting force that can assist in the survival of the human race while serving its own economic interests (see also Brennan and Merkl-Davies 2014).

Milne et al. (2006) mobilised the notion of "the journey metaphor" to theorise linguistic strategies in corporate communication surrounding sustainability issues, while illustrating that the destination of the journey is rarely articulated in this "story" (see O'Dochartaigh 2019). They uncovered a linguistic strategy which reinforced business as usual. Ferguson et al. (2016) extended discourse-oriented studies by employing Thompson's depth-hermeneutic framework to emphasise the wider context in which texts are produced. This framework offered them a typology of linguistic strategies to inform their analysis of corporate texts related to climate change in conjunction with a conceptual framework enabling a wider socio-historical analysis. This facilitated their theorisation of "the historical and social factors that [lay] beyond the texts[s] [analysed]" (Ferguson et al. 2016, p. 281) through which they demonstrated how companies' communicative practices helped to constitute and reproduce the structure of the field in which they operated. Busco et al. (2018) subsequently shifted the focus away from studies of corporate communications to analyse the discourses concerning sustainability and the initiatives for embedding sustainability into accounting and reporting practices that emerged in a large international oil and gas company. They used the notion of "discursive concepts" to interpret sustainability "as being an empty category with no fixed meaning, through which individuals try to make sense of different aspects of organisational performance" (Busco et al. 2018, p. 2219).

Conclusion

In a review paper published in 2002, the late Rob Gray (2002) bemoaned social (and environmental) accounting scholars' inability to theorise. As this chapter hopefully demonstrates, Rob's pessimism has proven unfounded. The range of theorisations depicted above bear testament to a field of study that has been sharpening its theoretical tools for the past three decades. In fact, the concern may now be with the sheer range of theorisations being mobilised to understand similar phenomena. Nevertheless, a fascinating feature of these developments is how theoretical frames from outside the accounting and management fields, such as sustainability science, are now being adopted to inform developing work in areas like ecological accounting. In the future, I hope more scholars gain the confidence to extend and challenge existing theory as well as drawing inspiration from grounded theory methods in order to offer unique theorisations of underlying processes of environmental reporting and accounting (Langley 1999; Langley et al. 2013). "Making sense" of emerging developments through "abstracting, generalizing, relating, selecting, explaining, synthesising and idealizing" (Weick 1995, p. 389) all aspects of environmental accounting and reporting is an endeavour worth pursuing, not just for intellectual advancement, but for its role in assisting in the creation of the "new realities" that many scholars aspire to.

Notes

1 These themes are not exhaustive but they are designed to offer a flavour of the vast range of theorising evident in the literature. For example, I do not delve into theorising around assurance on environmental reporting (see Canning et al. 2019; O'Dwyer et al. 2011; O'Dwyer 2011). I also do not delve into the emerging work on ecological accounting and extinction accounting which offers a range of alternative theorisations.

2 Ball (2007) theorised the motives for introducing environmental accounting in a Canadian City Council as a form of "workplace activism" in which employees sought to build a genuine organisational response to environmental issues. Thoradeniya et al. (2015) introduced the theory of planned behaviour to uncover psychological factors that induced managers to engage in environmental disclosure.

3 Subsequent research indirectly tested Bebbington et al.'s (2008a) additional theorisation by presenting results consistent with companies engaging in environmental disclosure to offset the potential reputational effects of poor environmental performance (Cho et al. 2012).

4 See Adams and Larrinaga (2019, pp. 2380–2382) for a review of theorisations of engagement-based social accounting more generally.

5 For another perspective on how environmental accounting might be theorised in non-western contexts, see Gallhofer et al. (2000) which consider how environmental accounting might be theorised using insights from indigenous cultures.

References

Abrahamson, E., 1991. Managerial fads and fashions: the diffusion and rejection of innovations, *Academy of Management Review*, 16, 586-612.

Adams, C., 2002. Internal organisational factors influencing corporate social and ethical reporting: beyond current theorising. *Accounting, Auditing & Accountability*, 15 (2), 223–250.

Adams, C., 2008. A commentary on: corporate social responsibility reporting and reputation risk management. *Accounting, Auditing & Accountability Journal*, 21 (3), 365–370.

Adams, C. and Larrinaga, C., 2019. Progress: engaging with organisations in pursuit of improved sustainability accounting and performance. *Accounting, Auditing & Accountability Journal*, 32 (8), 2367–2394.

Adams, C. and McNicholas, P., 2007. Making a difference: sustainability reporting, accountability and organisational change. *Accounting, Auditing & Accountability Journal*, 20 (3), 382–402.

Adams, C. and Whelan, G., 2009. Conceptualising future change in corporate sustainability reporting. *Accounting, Auditing & Accountability Journal*, 22 (1), 118–143.

Alawattage, C. and Fernando, S., 2017. Postcoloniality in corporate social and environmental accountability. *Accounting, Organizations and Society*, 60, 1–20.

Archel, P., Husillos, J., Larrinaga, C. and Spence, C., 2009. Social disclosure, legitimacy theory and the role of the state. *Accounting, Auditing & Accountability Journal*, 22 (8), 1284–1307.

Archel, P., Husillos, J. and Spence, C., 2011. The institutionalisation of unaccountability: loading the dice of corporate social responsibility discourse. *Accounting, Organizations and Society*, 36 (6), 327–343.

Arjaliès, D. and Mundy, J., 2013. The use of management control systems to manage CSR strategy: a levers of control perspective. *Management Accounting Research*, 24 (4), 284–300.

Ball, A., 2007. Environmental accounting as workplace activism. *Critical Perspectives on Accounting*, 18, 759–778.

Ball, A. and Craig, R., 2010. Using neo-institutionalism to advance social and environmental accounting. *Critical Perspectives on Accounting*, 21, 283–293.

Bebbington, J., 1997. Engagement, education and sustainability: a review essay on environmental accounting. *Accounting, Auditing & Accountability Journal*, 10 (3), 365–381.

Bebbington, J. and Gray, R., 2001. An account of sustainability: failure, success and a reconceptualization. *Critical Perspectives on Accounting*, 12, 557–587.

Bebbington, J., Brown, J., Frame, B. and Thomson, I., 2007. Theorising engagement: the potential of a critical dialogic approach. *Accounting, Auditing & Accountability Journal*, 20 (3), 356–381.

Bebbington, J., Higgins, C. and Frame, B. 2009. Initiating sustainable development reporting: evidence from New Zealand. *Accounting, Auditing & Accountability Journal*, 22, (4), 588–625.

Bebbington, J., Kirk, E. and Larrinaga, C., 2012. The production of normativity: a comparison of reporting regimes in Spain and the UK. *Accounting, Organizations and Society*, 37 (2), 78–94.

Bebbington, J. and Larrinaga, C., 2014. Accounting and sustainable development: an exploration. *Accounting, Organizations and Society*, 39 (6), 395–413.

Bebbington, J. and Thomson, I., 2013. Sustainable development, management and accounting: boundary crossing. *Management Accounting Research*, 24 (4), 277–283.

Bebbington, J., Larrinaga, C. and Moneva, J., 2008a. Corporate social reporting and reputation risk management. *Accounting, Auditing & Accountability Journal*, 21 (3), 337–361.

Bebbington, J., Larrinaga-González, C. and Moneva-Abadía, J., 2008b. Legitimating reputation/the reputation of legitimacy theory. *Accounting, Auditing & Accountability Journal*, 21 (3), 371–374.

Bebbington, J., Russell, S. and Thomson, I., 2017. Accounting and sustainable development: reflections and propositions. *Critical Perspectives on Accounting*, 48 (1), 21–34.

Belal, A. and Cooper, S., 2011. The absence of corporate social responsibility reporting in Bangladesh. *Critical Perspectives on Accounting*, 22 (7), 654–667.

Bellucci, M. and Manetti, G., 2017. Facebook as a tool for supporting dialogic accounting? Evidence from large philanthropic foundations in the United States. *Accounting, Auditing & Accountability Journal*, 30 (4), 874–905.

Birkin, F., 1996. The ecological accountant: from the cogito to thinking like a mountain. *Critical Perspectives on Accounting*, 7, 231–257.

Boltanski, L. and Thévenot, L., 2006. *On Justification: Economies of Worth*. Princeton University Press, Princeton, NJ.

Bouten, L. and Hoozée, S., 2013. On the interplay between environmental reporting and management accounting change. *Management Accounting Research*, 24 (33), 333–348.

Bowman, E. H. and Haire, M., 1976. Social impact disclosure and corporate annual reports. *Accounting, Organizations and Society*, 1 (1), 11–21.
Brennan, N. and Merkl-Davies, D., 2014. Rhetoric and argument in social and environmental reporting: the Dirty Laundry case. *Accounting, Auditing & Accountability Journal*, 27 (4), 602–633.
Brown, J., 2009. Democracy, sustainability and dialogic accounting technologies: taking pluralism seriously. *Critical Perspectives on Accounting*, 20, 313–342.
Brown, J. and Dillard, J., 2013. Agonizing over engagement: SEA and the "death of environmentalism" debates. *Critical Perspectives on Accounting*, 24 (1), 1–18.
Brown, J. and Tregigda, H., 2017. Re-politicizing social and environmental accounting through Rancière: on the value of dissensus. *Accounting, Organizations and Society*, 61, 1–21.
Buhr, N., 2002. A structuration view on the initiation of environmental reports. *Critical Perspectives on Accounting*, 13, 17–38.
Burchell, S., Clubb, C. and Hopwood, A., 1985. Accounting in its social context: towards a history of value added in the United Kingdom. *Accounting, Organizations and Society*, 10 (4), 381–413.
Busco, C., Giovannoni, E., Granà, F. and Izzo, M. F., 2018. Making sustainability meaningful: aspirations, discourses and reporting practices. *Accounting, Auditing & Accountability Journal*, 31 (8), 2218–2246.
Canning, M., O'Dwyer, B. and Georgakopoulos, G., 2019. Processes of auditability in sustainability assurance – the case of materiality construction. *Accounting and Business Research*, 49 (1), 1–27.
Clune, C. and O'Dwyer, B., 2020. Organizing dissonance through institutional work: the embedding of social and environmental accountability in an investment field. *Accounting, Organizations and Society*. Forthcoming.
Chen, Y., Hung, M. and Wang, Y., 2018. The effect of mandatory CSR disclosure on firm profitability and social externalities: evidence from China. *Journal of Accounting and Economics*, 65 (1), 169–190.
Cho, C., Guidry, R., Hageman, A. and Patten, D., 2012. Do actions speak louder than words? An empirical investigation of corporate environmental reputation. *Accounting, Organizations and Society*, 37 (1), 14–25.
Cho, C., Laine, M., Roberts, R. and Rodrigue, M., 2015. Organized hypocrisy, organizational façades, and sustainability reporting. *Accounting, Organizations and Society*, 40, 78–94.
Cho, C. and Patten, D., 2007. The role of environmental disclosures as tools of legitimacy: a research note. *Accounting, Organizations and Society*, 32 (7–8), 639–647.
Cho, C., Roberts, R. and Patten, D., 2010. The language of US corporate environmental disclosure. *Accounting, Organizations and Society*, 35 (4) 431–443.
Chua, W. and Mahama, H., 2012. On theory as a "deliverable" and its relevance in "policy" arenas. *Critical Perspectives on Accounting*, 23 (1), 78–82.
Contrafatto, M., 2014. The institutionalization of social and environmental reporting: an Italian narrative. *Accounting, Organizations and Society*, 39 (6), 414–432.
Contrafatto, M. and Burns, J., 2013. Social and environmental accounting, organisational change and management accounting: a processual view. *Management Accounting Research*, 24 (4), 349–365.
Contrafatto, M., Costa, E. and Pesci, C., 2019. Examining the dynamics of SER evolution: an institutional understanding. *Accounting, Auditing & Accountability Journal*, 32 (6), 1771–1800.
Contrafatto, M., Thomson, I. and Monk, E., 2015. Peru, mountains and los niños: dialogic action, accounting and sustainable transformation. *Critical Perspectives on Accounting*, 33, 117–136.
Cooper, S. and Owen, D., 2007. Corporate social reporting and stakeholder accountability: the missing link. *Accounting, Organizations and Society*, 32, (7–8), 649–667.
Cowen, S., Ferreri, L. and Parker, L., 1987. The impact of corporate characteristics on social responsibility disclosure: a typology and frequency-based analysis. *Accounting, Organizations and Society*, 12 (2), 111–122.
De Villiers, C. and Alexander, D., 2014. The institutionalisation of corporate social responsibility reporting. *The British Accounting Review*, 46 (2), 198–212.
Deegan, C., 2002. Introduction: the legitimising effect of social and environmental disclosures - a theoretical foundation. *Accounting, Auditing & Accountability Journal*, 15 (3), 282–311.
Deegan, C., 2019. Legitimacy theory: despite its enduring popularity and contribution, time is right for a necessary makeover. *Accounting, Auditing & Accountability Journal*, 32 (8), 2307–2309.
Dhaliwal, D., Li, O., Tsang, A. and Yang Y., 2011. Voluntary nonfinancial disclosure and the cost of equity capital: the initiation of corporate social responsibility reporting. *The Accounting Review*, 86 (1), 59–100.
Dierkes, M. and Antal, A., 1985. The usefulness and use of social reporting information. *Accounting, Organizations and Society*, 10 (1), 29–34.

Egan, M., 2014. Making water count: water accountability change within an Australian university. *Accounting, Auditing & Accountability Journal*, 27 (2), 259–282.

Egan, M. and Tweedie, D., 2018. A "green" accountant is difficult to find: can accountants contribute to sustainability management initiatives? *Accounting, Auditing & Accountability Journal*, 31 (6), 1749–1773.

Everett, J. and Neu, D., 2000. Ecological modernization and the limits of environmental accounting? *Accounting Forum*, 24 (1), 5–29.

Elliott, W., Grant, S. and Rennekamp, K., 2017. How disclosure features of corporate social responsibility reports interact with investor numeracy to influence investor judgments. *Contemporary Accounting Research*, 34 (3), 1596–1621.

Elliott, W., Jackson, K., Peecher, M. and White, B., 2014. The unintended effect of corporate social responsibility performance on investors' estimates of fundamental value. *The Accounting Review*, 89 (1), 275–302.

Eisenhardt, K. and Graebner, M., 2007. Theory building from cases: opportunities and challenges. *Academy of Management Journal*, 50, 25–32.

Farooq, M. and De Villiers, C., 2019. How sustainability assurance engagement scopes are determined, and its impact on capture and credibility enhancement. *Accounting, Auditing & Accountability Journal*, 33 (2), 417–445.

Ferguson, J., Sales de Aguiar, T. R. and Fearfull, A., 2016. Corporate response to climate change: language, power and symbolic construction. *Accounting, Auditing & Accountability Journal*, 29 (2), 278–304.

Fraser, M., 2012. "Fleshing out" an engagement with a social accounting technology. *Accounting, Auditing & Accountability Journal*, 25 (3), 508–534.

Freire, P., 2005. *The Pedagogy of the Oppressed*. New York, NY: Continuum.

Georg, S. and Justesen, L., 2017. Counting to zero: accounting for a green building. *Accounting, Auditing & Accountability Journal*, 30 (5), 1065–1081.

Gray, R., 1992. Accounting and environmentalism: an exploration of the challenge of gently accounting for accountability, transparency and sustainability. *Accounting, Organizations and Society*, 17 (5), 399–425.

Gray, R., 1998. Imagination: a bowl of petunias and social accounting. *Critical Perspectives on Accounting*, 9, 205–216.

Gray, R., 2002. The social accounting project and accounting organizations and society privileging engagement, imaginings, new accountings and pragmatism over critique? *Accounting, Organizations and Society*, 27 (7), 687–708.

Gray, R., 2010. Is accounting for sustainability actually accounting for sustainability … and how would we know? An exploration of narratives of organisations and the planet. *Accounting, Organizations and Society*, 35 (1), 47–62.

Gray, R., Adams, C. and Owen, D., 2014. *Accountability. Social Responsibility and Sustainability*. London: Pearson Education.

Gray, R., Kouhy, R. and Lavers, S., 1995a. Constructing a research database of social and environmental reporting by UK companies. *Accounting, Auditing & Accountability Journal*, 8 (2), 78–101.

Gray, R., Owen, D. and Adams, C., 1996. *Accounting and Accountability: Changes and Challenges in Corporate Social and Environmental Reporting*. London: Prentice Hall.

Gray, R., Owen, D. and Maunders, K., 1987. *Corporate Social Reporting*. Hemel Hempstead and London: Prentice-Hall.

Gray, R., Owen, D. and Maunders, K., 1988. Corporate social reporting: emerging trends in accountability and the social contract. *Accounting, Auditing & Accountability Journal*, 1 (1), 6–20.

Gray, R., Walters, D., Bebbington, J. and Thomson, I., 1995b. The greening of enterprise: an exploration of the (non) role of environmental accounting and environmental accountants in organizational change. *Critical Perspectives on Accounting*, 6, 211–239.

Griffin, P., Lont, D. and Sun, E., 2017. The relevance to investors of greenhouse gas emission disclosures. *Contemporary Accounting Research*, 34 (2), 1265–1297.

Guthrie, J. and Parker, L. D., 1989. Corporate social reporting: a rebuttal of legitimacy theory. *Accounting and Business Research*, 19 (6), 343–352.

Humphrey, C., O'Dwyer, B. and Unerman, J., 2017. Re-theorising the configuration of organizational fields: the IIRC and the pursuit of "enlightened" corporate reporting. *Accounting and Business Research*, 47 (1), 30–63.

Imtiaz Ferdous, M., Adams, C. and Boyce, G., 2019. Institutional drivers of environmental management accounting adoption in public sector water organisations. *Accounting, Auditing & Accountability Journal*, 32 (4), 984–1012.

Ingram, R. and Frazier, K., 1980. Environmental performance and corporate disclosure. *Journal of Accounting Research*, 18 (2), 614–622.
Islam, M. and van Staden, C., 2018. Social movement NGOs and the comprehensiveness of conflict mineral disclosures: evidence from global companies. *Accounting, Organizations and Society*, 65, 1–19.
Kaur, A. and Lodhia, S., 2018. Stakeholder engagement in sustainability accounting and reporting: a study of Australian local councils. *Accounting, Auditing & Accountability Journal*, 31 (1), 338–368.
Laine, M., 2005. Meanings of the term "sustainable development" in Finnish corporate disclosures. *Accounting Forum*, 29 (4), 395–413.
Laine, M., 2009. Ensuring legitimacy through rhetorical changes? A longitudinal interpretation of the environmental disclosures of a leading Finnish chemical company. *Accounting, Auditing & Accountability Journal*, 22 (7), 1029–1054.
Laine, M., J. Järvinen, T., Hyvönen, T. and Kantola, H., 2017. Ambiguity of financial environmental information: a case study of a Finnish energy company. *Accounting, Auditing & Accountability Journal*, 30 (3), 593–619.
Langley, A., 1999. Strategies for theorising from process data. *Academy of Management Journal*, 24, 691–710.
Langley, A., Smallman, C., Tsoukas, H. and Van de Ven, A., 2013. Process studies of change in organization and management: unveiling temporality, activity and flow. *Academy of Management Journal*, 56 (1), 1–13.
Larringa-Gonzalez, C. and Bebbington, J., 2001. Accounting change or institutional appropriation? A case study of the implementation of environmental accounting. *Critical Perspectives on Accounting*, 12, 269–292.
Laughlin, R., 1991. Environmental disturbances and organizational transitions and transformations: some alternative models. *Organization Studies*, 12 (2), 209–232.
Lehman, G., 1999. Disclosing new worlds: a role for social and environmental accounting and auditing. *Accounting, Organizations and Society*, 24 (3), 217–241.
Leong, S. and Hazelton, J., 2019. Under what conditions is mandatory disclosure most likely to cause organisational change? *Accounting, Auditing & Accountability Journal*, 32 (3), 811–835.
Liesen, A., Hoepner, A., Patten, D. and Figge, F., 2015. Does stakeholder pressure influence corporate GHG emissions reporting? Empirical evidence from Europe. *Accounting, Auditing & Accountability Journal*, 28 (7), 1047–1074.
Lindblom, C., 1994. The implications of organizational legitimacy for corporate social performance and disclosure, paper presented at Critical Perspectives on Accounting Conference, New York, NY.
Lodhia, S. and Jacobs, K., 2013. The practice turn in environmental reporting: A study into current practices in two Australian commonwealth departments. *Accounting, Auditing & Accountability Journal*, 26 (4), 595–615.
Martin, P. and Moser, D., 2016. "Managers" green investment disclosures and investors' reaction. *Journal of Accounting and Economics*, 61 (1), 239–254.
Michelon G., Rodrigue, M. and Trevisan, E., 2020. The marketization of a social movement: activists, shareholders and CSR disclosure. *Accounting, Organizations and Society*, 80.
Milne, M., Walton, S. and Tregidga, H., 2009. Words not actions! The ideological role of sustainable development reporting. *Accounting, Auditing & Accountability Journal*, 22 (8), 1211–1257.
Narayanan V. and Adams C.A., 2017. Transformative change towards sustainability: the interaction between organisational discourses and organisational practices. *Accounting and Business Research* 47(3), 344-368
Neu, D., Warsame, H. and Pedwell, K., 1998. Managing pubic impressions: environmental disclosure in annual reports. *Accounting, Organizations and Society*, 23 (3), 265–282.
O'Dochartaigh, A., 2019. No more fairytales: a quest for alternative narratives of sustainable business. *Accounting, Auditing & Accountability Journal*, 32 (5), 1384–1413.
O'Dwyer, B., 2002. Managerial perceptions of corporate social disclosure: an Irish story. *Accounting, Auditing & Accountability Journal*, 15 (3), 406–436.
O'Dwyer, B., 2011. The case of sustainability assurance: constructing a new assurance service. *Contemporary Accounting Research*, 28 (4), 1230–1266.
O'Dwyer, B., Owen, D. and Unerman, J., 2011. Seeking legitimacy for new assurance forms: the case of assurance on sustainability reporting. *Accounting, Organizations and Society*, 36 (1), 31–52.
O'Sullivan, N., & O'Dwyer, B., 2015. The structuration of issue-based fields: Social accountability, social movements and the Equator Principles issue-based field. *Accounting, Organizations and Society*, 21, 33-55
Owen, D., 2008. Chronicles of wasted time? A personal reflection on the current state of, and future prospects for social and environmental accounting research. *Accounting, Auditing & Accountability Journal*, 21 (2), 240–267.

Parker, L., 2005. Social and environmental accountability research: a view from the commentary box. *Accounting, Auditing & Accountability Journal*, 18 (6), 842–860.
Patten, D., 1991. Exposure, legitimacy, and social disclosure. *Journal of Accounting and Public Policy*, 10 (4), 297–308.
Patten, D., 1992. Intra-industry environmental disclosures in response to the Alaskan oil spill: a note on legitimacy theory. *Accounting, Organizations and Society*, 17 (5), 471–475.
Patten, D. M., 2002. The relation between environmental performance and environmental disclosure: a research note. *Accounting, Organizations and Society*, 27 (8), 763–773.
Patten, D. M., 2015. An insider's reflection on quantitative research in the social and environmental disclosure domain. *Critical Perspectives on Accounting*, 32, 45–50.
Powell, L. and Tilt, C., 2017. The examination of power and politics in a conservation organisation. *Accounting, Auditing & Accountability Journal*, 30 (3), 482–509.
Puxty, A., 1986. Social accounting as immanent legitimation: a critique of a technist ideology. *Advances in Public Interest Accounting*, 1, 95–112.
Puxty, A., 1991. Social accountability and universal pragmatics. *Advances in Public Interest Accounting*, 4, 35–46.
Qian, W., Burritt, R. and Monroe, G., 2011. Environmental management accounting in local government: a case of waste management. *Accounting, Auditing & Accountability Journal*, 24 (1), 93–128.
Rahaman, A., Lawrence, S. and Roper, J., 2004. Social and environmental reporting at the VRA: institutionalised legitimacy or legitimation crisis? *Critical Perspectives on Accounting*, 15, 35–56.
Roberts, R. W., 1992. Determinants of corporate social responsibility disclosure: an application of stakeholder theory. *Accounting, Organizations and Society*, 17 (6), 595–612.
Roberts, R. W. and Wallace, D., 2015. Sustaining diversity in social and environmental accounting research. *Critical Perspectives on Accounting*, 32, 78–87.
Rodrigue, M., 2014. Contrasting realities: corporate environmental disclosure and stakeholder-released information. *Accounting, Auditing & Accountability Journal*, 27 (1), 119–149
Rodrigue, M., Magnan, M. and Boulianne, E., 2013. Stakeholders' influence on environmental strategy and performance indicators: a managerial perspective. *Management Accounting Research*, 24 (4), 301–316.
Russell, S. L. and Thomson, I., 2009. Analysing the role of sustainable development indicators in accounting for and constructing a sustainable Scotland. *Accounting Forum*, 33 (3), 225–244.
Russell, S., Milne, M. J. and Dey, C., 2017. Accounts of nature and the nature of accounts: critical reflections on environmental accounting and propositions for ecologically informed accounting. *Accounting, Auditing & Accountability Journal*, 30 (7), 1426–1458.
Shane, P. and Spicer, B., 1983. Market response to environmental information produced outside the firm. *The Accounting Review*, July, 521–538.
She, C. and Michelon, G., 2019. Managing stakeholder perceptions: organized hypocrisy in CSR disclosures on Facebook. *Critical Perspectives on Accounting*, 61, 54–76.
Solomon, A. and Solomon, J., 2006. Private social, ethical and environmental disclosures. *Accounting, Auditing & Accountability Journal*, 19 (4), 564–591.
Solomon, J., Solomon, A., Norton, S. and Joseph, N., 2011. Private climate change reporting: an emerging discourse of risk and opportunity? *Accounting, Auditing & Accountability Journal*, 24 (8), 1119–1149.
Solomon, J., Solomon, A., Joseph, N. and Norton, S., 2013. Impression management, myth creation and fabrication in private social and environmental reporting: insights from Erving Goffman. *Accounting, Organizations and Society*, 38 (3), 195–213.
Spence, C., 2007. Social and environmental reporting and hegemonic discourse. *Accounting, Auditing & Accountability Journal*, 20 (6), 855–882.
Spence, C., 2009. Social accounting's emancipatory potential: a Gramscian critique. *Critical Perspectives on Accounting*, 20 (2), 205–227.
Spence, C., Husillos, J. and Correa-Ruiz, C., 2010. Cargo cult science and the death of politics: a critical review of social and environmental accounting research. *Critical Perspectives on Accounting*, 21, 76–78.
Spence, L. and Rinaldi, L., 2014. Governmentality in accounting and accountability: a case study of embedding sustainability in a supply chain. *Accounting, Organizations and Society*, 39 (6), 433–452.
Stubbs, W. and Higgins, C., 2014. Integrated reporting and internal mechanisms of change. *Accounting, Auditing & Accountability Journal*, 27 (7), 1068–1089.
Suddaby, R., 2014. Editor's comments; Why theory? *Academy of Management Review*, 39 (4), 407–411.
Sundin, H. and Brown, D.A. (2017), "Greening the black box: integrating the environment and management control systems", *Accounting, Auditing & Accountability Journal*, 30(3) 620-642.

Swedberg, R., 2014. *The Art of Social Theory*. Princeton, NJ: Princeton University Press.
Swedberg, R., 2016. Before theory comes theorising or how to make social science more interesting. *The British Journal of Sociology*, 67 (1), 5–22.
Tashakor, S., Appuhami, R. and Munir, R., 2019. Environmental management accounting practices in Australian cotton farming: the use of the theory of planned behaviour. *Accounting, Auditing & Accountability Journal*, 32 (4), 1175–1202.
Thomson, I., Grubnic, S. and Georgakopoulos, G., 2014. Exploring accounting sustainability hybridisation in the UK public sector. *Accounting, Organizations and Society*, 39 (6), 453–476.
Thomson, I. and Bebbington, J., 2005. Social and environmental reporting in the UK: a pedagogic evaluation. *Critical Perspectives on Accounting*, 16, 507–533.
Tinker, A., Lehman, C. and Niemark, M., 1991. Falling down the hole in the middle of the road: political quietism in corporate social reporting. *Accounting, Auditing and Accountability Journal*, 4 (1), 8–54.
Tregidga, H., 2013. Biodiversity offsetting: problematisation of an emerging governance regime. *Accounting, Auditing & Accountability Journal*, 26 (5), 806–832.
Tregidga, H. and Milne, M., 2006. From sustainable management to sustainable development: a longitudinal analysis of a leading New Zealand environmental reporter. *Business Strategy and the Environment*, 15 (4), 219–241.
Tregidga, H., M. Milne, M., and Kearins, K. (2014) (Re)presenting 'sustainable organizations' *Accounting, Organizations and Society,* 39 (6), 477-494
Ullmann, A. E., 1985. Data in search of a theory: a critical examination of the relationships among social performance, social disclosure and economic performance of US firms. *Academy of Management Review*, 10 (3), 540–557.
Unerman, J. and Bennett, M., 2004. Increased stakeholder dialogue and the internet: towards greater corporate accountability or reinforcing capitalist hegemony? *Accounting, Organizations and Society*, 29, 685–707.
Unerman, J. and Chapman, C., 2014. Academic contributions to accounting for sustainable development. *Accounting, Organizations and Society*, 39 (6), 385–394.
Van Bommel, K., 2014. Towards a legitimate compromise? An exploration of integrated reporting in the Netherlands. *Accounting, Auditing & Accountability Journal*, 27 (7), 1157–1189.
Vinnari, E. and Laine, M., 2013. Just a passing fad?: The diffusion and decline of environmental reporting in the Finnish water sector*Accounting, Auditing & Accountability Journal*, 26 (7), 1107–1134.
Weick, K., 1995. What theory is not, theorising is. *Administrative Science Quarterly*, 40 (3), 385–390.

4

BEFORE RESEARCH METHODS COMES "METHODISING"

Implications for environmental accounting research

Ian Thomson

Introduction

The research method sections in journal articles present an after-the-fact version of the research methods, all shiny, idealised and logical, co-produced and honed between researcher, editors and reviewer, designed to justify and scientifically legitimate the paper. This account of research methods serves an important function in the communication of research findings, but bears no resemblance to the reactive, fraught, stressful, sometimes joyful, attempts to capture sufficient, compelling and meaningful evidence in a project that unfolds in unexpected directions.

Research methods are often reified as a set of codified, prescriptive set of commandments that if followed will produce high-quality research. If these rules are broken or creatively interpreted, then you risk your findings being unpublishable or rejected. Designing research projects is portrayed as searching for the perfect, generally applicable research method, then looking for applicable problems (Humphrey and Lee 2004). However, in the context of discovery, this is not how things work, particularly in the environmental accounting. Environmental accounting practice or research does not fit into neat boxes and exists in the boundaries and intersections of different social worlds, expertise and epistemologies. Environmental accounting is a set of emerging hybrid practices, assembled from fragments of techniques, disciplines, institutional norms and existential risks (Thomson et al. 2014).

Environmental accounting exists in ill-defined, dynamic problem spaces embedded in complex adaptive systems (Bebbington et al. 2017). It engages, often simultaneously, with different dimensions of sustainability science, policies, governance and practice. These are problem spaces without a foundational research discipline with the need for creating adaptive, hybrid research methods, borrowing and blending from other disciplines (Oswick et al. 2011; Swedberg 2016).

At the risk of disappointing readers before they begin, this chapter will not provide a definitive answer as to which method to use in different contexts or the relative strengths and weaknesses of different research methods. The starting assumption is that all research methods are potentially insightful and relevant to environmental accounting (Thomson 2007, 2014). Researchers are referred to a number of excellent methods texts that provide essential inputs into methodising work (see Appendix 1). As part of methodising, researchers must imagine and create a compelling case for what and how they are problematising, proposing to change or contributing to future research. Methodising draws on Swedberg's (2016) distinction between theorising and theory. Theorising is a creative process that emerges in the discovery stage of research. This is contrasted with theory as a noun in the context of justification.

This chapter will make visible some of the invisible work involved with bundling together and adapting research methods during the discovery phase, rather at the justification phase. It will emphasise the twists, turns, dead ends and messy work associated with research in practice (see Humphrey and Lee 2004; Law 2004; Swedberg 2016). It will do this by outlining important aspects of methodising (see Table 4.1) that may help guide the creative and adaptive work in bundling together an appropriate research design to address meaningful environmental accounting research questions.

Why methodising? Emulation rather than replication

Research papers incorporate methods for the purpose of justification and typically use discursive strategies of compliance with ideal versions. Despite the rhetoric attached to normal science processes, replication is rarely possible or rewarded in environmental accounting due to the dynamic problem spaces in which it is embedded (Humphrey and Lee 2004). Creative emulation of research you admire and find inspiring is a much better strategy than replication. Very few seminal environmental accounting papers are replication studies, rather they are based on innovative, adaptive methods, borrowing and blending to construct unique methods that can radically transform our understanding of accounting. However, methodising will always involve risk and judgement, but these risks are not necessarily mitigated by replication.

Table 4.1 lists the key stages of methodising. Although there is an implied order in Table 4.1, it is possible to start anywhere and move round the stages following your own preferred thought processes. However, whatever order chosen, you should try to cover all stages at least once, preferably more than once.

Purpose and imagination

"Speculation is the soul of the social sciences" (Lave and March 1993, p. 3).

Good social science requires speculating, guessing, imagining and coming up with new or surprising ideas (Swedberg 2016). Researchers need to learn how to assemble and reassemble their own method bundles before and during the process of discovery. Research methodising is therefore immanent and future oriented, as it occurs before action. Methodising requires imagining what our research project might be, why we are about to engage in what will be

Table 4.1 Overview of methodising

Imagining research project and purpose
Pre-study of domain
Creative representation of project
Scoping methods, theories and evidence
Building method bundles
Multi-perspective bundle evaluation
Method bundling, pathways and contingencies
Start, stop and think, share and reflect.

a challenging, sometimes tedious, frustrating piece of work, that may fail to produce anything useful to anyone. Spending time in this imaginary space will be productive, rather than rushing to replication. In this space, ask yourself:

- What is the "new" you want to create?
- What is your underlying intuition as to what might emerge from your research?
- Who do you imagine benefiting (or suffering) from your research?
- What changes do you imagine your work will lead to?
- What will be the most surprising or provocative finding?
- Who do you want to read it?

As accounting researchers, we often deny the importance of imagination and creative thought in research methods. We are silent as to the influence of "non-scientific", "irrational" sources, such as passion, compassion, anger and closing our minds to their power in shaping research. A critical aspect of methodising is to become receptive to all insights, emotions and sources of knowledge. Draw on past observations, readings, music, art, inspiring work of others or experience of problems that need to be solved. It is not possible or necessary to generalise here as we all have different ways of imagining.

Colleagues have recounted different inspirations for their research. These include hill walking, sailing, painting, music, meditation, dance, drama, museums, films, TV, playing with children or enjoying the craic with friends.

This chapter will use a methodising example of an imagined environmental accounting project that was initially triggered by a criticism from business leaders that our research was setting the bar too low and locking ecosystems in its damaged state. We were challenged on the absence of environmental accounting research that would enhance nature. During the next 18 months I kept coming back to this criticism at unexpected times and activities imagining how (or whether) accounting could be involved in rewilding projects that enhance ecosystems.

These included the following:

- cycling to work,
- hiking in a reserve where beavers had been reintroduced,
- weekend retreat to a wolf rescue centre,
- a wildlife photography exhibit,
- chatting with a friend finishing a dissertation on the carnage in Scottish hunting estates,
- watching nature documentaries,
- listening to Out of Doors[1] on Radio Scotland.

At this stage the only physical manifestations of these imaginary "research projects" are hastily scribbled indecipherable diagrams in a notebook full of indecipherable plans for projects that went nowhere. To start to move beyond this immanent stage, it was useful to think of the potential purposes of these imaginary research projects.

One useful visual thinking exercise to help flesh out purpose involves printing off and cutting out each Sustainable Development Goal[2], then dividing a flat surface into four spaces. These spaces represent possible impacts of your research: *positive contribution, negative contribution, no impact* and *don't know*. You then recall a version of your research idea picking up each SDG in turn and placing it in one of the four spaces based on your imagined outcomes (see Figure 4.1). You then step back and look at the profile of imagined impacts matching it to

Figure 4.1 Visualising SDG connections.

your imagined purpose of the research idea. Then you shuffle the SDGs around until you are happy with it.

This apparently simple visual and manual exercise maps out a comprehensive sustainability purpose of your imagined research and a starting point as to why you might want to take this project further. If you find your research idea results in 17 SDGs in the *don't know, no impact* or *negative contribution*, then you may want to rethink the idea or ditch it!

It is also possible to work this exercise in reverse. Think about what SDGs you want to make a *positive contribution* and lay them out in that space. Place all other SDGs in the *don't know* space for just now. Then start to imagine environmental accounting project that may achieve these goals. As your thoughts emerge, start thinking about the impact on other SDGs and move them from the *don't know* space as appropriate. Keep going reflecting on what is emerging in your head until you have dealt with all 17 SDGs and are happy with the outcomes. Note that you do not have to use the SDGs. This exercise works just as well with cards of criteria that are important to you and your imagined future world. Other variants could include Planetary Boundaries,[3] OXFAM Donut[4] and Future Fit.[5]

Pre-study of domain

As a colleague, teacher, reviewer and reader I am continually surprised at the lack of domain knowledge exhibited in proposals, papers or presentations, manifesting in irrelevant or inappropriate research methods. How can we design meaningful environmental accounting research projects without some consideration of what we are researching? How can we account for things without knowing about that thing?

Imagine if Atkins and Atkins (2016) designed their research on bees without a pre-study of bees. Imagine if Dey and Russell (2014) undertook their research on River Garry with no knowledge of that river. Imagine if Bebbington's innovative collaboration with SeaBOS[6] was restricted to the domain knowledge of sustainability reports of fishery companies published in English.

It is possible for papers that are functionally ignorant of the domain to get published. However, these papers often fail to make a meaningful contribution or impact after publication. Understanding the domain prevents false results or meaningless research. I remember a seminar where an excited researcher presented his findings as to how to beat the United Kingdom (UK) bookmakers. His data set, model and results were indeed compelling, noting the statistical significance of the gender and age of the horse in spotting "abnormal odds". While most of the audience started opening online gambling accounts, an older academic with extensive domain knowledge in losing money to the bookies asked about the races that formed the sample. The presenter reeled of the races that included high-profile races exclusively for female horses, or for horses under a certain age – important facts that he was unaware of. The public realisation of a serious, but easily avoidable, flaw in his methods as his post-study domain knowledge increased has stayed with me for decades.

Things are always more complex than represented in research papers, which are extremely poor sources of domain knowledge. Environmental accounting research should build from "*the environment*", recognising that the presence of "*the environment*" is limited in environmental accounting research publications. The impact of domain knowledge on research methods is significant. I can recall substantive changes in research design by my colleague (see Georgakopoulos and Thomson 2005; Georgakopoulos and Thomson 2008) after he visited salmon farms, talked informally to farmers, regulators, aquaculture scientists, politicians, fishmongers and chefs. This despite the existence of a well-developed research proposal, well-constructed research questions built on his prior training in agronomy and finance.

Environmental accounting methodising must include a non-scientific pre-study of your immanent project. A pre-study is a quick, but broad and deep dive into the subject domain. Pre-study should be inquisitive, instinctive, intuitive and unscientific. You should experience the domain from multiple perspectives, observing, listening, watching or seeking out insights from non-conventional sources. Swedberg (2016) recommends actively avoiding being methodical, as you are trying to find something new. He suggests movies, poetry, dreams, graffiti and newspaper articles as possible sources. To this list you can include folk tales, music, art, documentaries, activist videos, citizen journalism, social media, museums, oral histories and photographs. Use your imagination, passion and enthusiasm to keep the pre-study going until you feel comfortable in that domain. Try to remember when or why you were surprised, shocked, inspired or angered. You should reflect on the contribution to your understanding of the different sources. What sources changed your understanding, how things were connected, where power lies and the different thinking within the domain. You should also reflect on what you still don't know about the domain and what you would like to know about. These reflections are important in assembling your research methods.

Creative representation of project

When methodising it is important to find a way to capture elements of your pre-study that works for you. Don't get too precious with this process, as you are the main audience for this and it is unlikely to make it into a journal – so let many flowers bloom. Colleagues who have shared these initial representations have successfully used different techniques. These include a scrap book of photos, drawings, newspaper articles, cartoons, lines from books, poems and songs; a multimedia collage on their living room wall; and an animated PowerPoint presentation. Lacking any artistic talent, I prefer whiteboards or mindmaps. Due to developments in digital technologies, my approach is to "draw" a starter map (see Figure 4.2), photograph it, upload into a graphic app, then annotate, change, colour or rework in any way that makes sense to me.

What is important at this stage is to keep away from writing prose. Prose writing is a wonderful skill and highly effective in the context of justification and knowledge sharing, but is

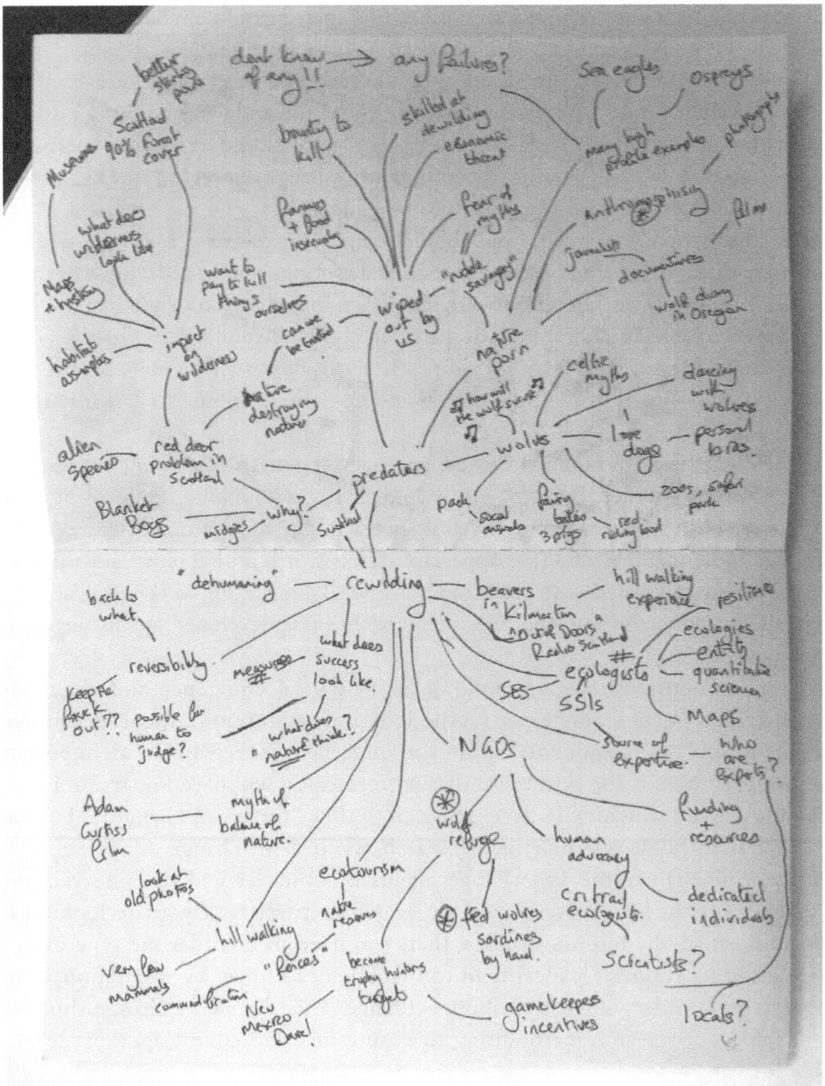

Figure 4.2 Original rewilding mind map. (Source: Author's own work.)

extremely limited in the early stages of methodising. This is due to writing's linear structure, grammatical disciplines and glottographic domination (Bassnet et al. 2018) that privilege slow thinking mechanisms (Kahneman 2012). Don't worry; there are plenty of opportunities for writing later!

Scoping methods, theories and evidence

While scoping there is no need for a deep knowledge of every research method. It is critical, however, to scope out what is out there (Hughes 1984). Research method books help in sensitising the researcher to the exotic land of research methods (see Appendix 1 for an illustrative list of books). Research method texts are much more useful sources than research methods sections in papers. The book format allows contributors to spend more time evaluating methods, exploring variants and reflecting on their experiences in applying methods in the discovery stages (Humphrey and Lee 2004; Law 2004; Cassells et al. 2018). It is important to emphasise that you are sensitising, not immersing yourself in a deep study of everything. Scoping involves looking at content pages, skim reading chapter introductions, noting possibilities, alignment with purpose and any surprising methods. You should not discount expertise or knowledge in your chosen discipline, but it is recommended that you revert to this knowledge at the end of the scoping process so as to be open to new ideas.

To help with this scoping exercise, you should consider exploring research methods associated with your domain pre-study, paying particular attention to your reflections of influential sources, connections, power, knowledge sets, ignorance and what you would like to know. Revisiting your creative representation of the domain can also be helpful in this process. Given environmental accounting is an emerging, hybrid practice, it is important to consider the usefulness of research methods used in the different disciplines that contribute to "environment" as well as "accounting".

For example, referring back to Figure 4.2, there appears to be merit in scoping out research method texts in Cultural Studies, Ecology, Geography, Systems Thinking, Political Science, Development Studies, History, Cartography, Psychology, Sociology and Natural Science. As you are flicking through these method texts (see Appendix 1), it is worth noting down any theories, evidence sources that are associated with these methods (see Table 4.2 for workings relating to an emerging rewilding project). Note that it is deliberately underdeveloped at this stage, just lists of ideas and possibilities.

At this stage it is important to start thinking about logical coherence and alignment between your imagined purpose, methods, methodological assumptions, theories and evidence. Identifying possible misalignments before you undertake the research is an important part of methodising. If there is the possibility that your research will have impact on policy or practice, then it may be worthwhile developing an outline "theory of change"[7] (Funnell and Rogers 2011) as to how your imagined research could drive change. Mapping out a theory of change will identify the key change agents or obstacles and the interventions or evidence that is likely to help drive change or overcome barriers. If you are looking to change the decisions made by business leaders, then you need to consider the type of evidence they will listen to. Business leaders tend to be convinced to act by inspirational case studies and storytelling underpinned by robust evidence. This theory of change thinking should be built into your research methodising to ensure that you collect appropriate evidence in usable format.

Table 4.2 Rewilding method possibilities partial list

Methods	*Source*	*Theories*	*Evidence*
Resilience Assessment Framework	Socio-ecological systems	Complex adaptive system	Prior science studies, Environmental regulators, national statistics
Public Participative Online Mapping, satellite imagery	Geography/urban studies/development studies	Multiple	Online maps, citizen science projects
Netography	Online search	Networks, social media studies, communication	Social media publicly available
Elite expert interviews with naturalists	Sociology	Suitable for many	Qualitative, deep insights
Ethnography	Anthropology	Cultural studies, suitable for many	Experiential emerging over time
...			

Building method bundles

Hopefully, you have now gathered some thoughts on purpose, theory of change, domain knowledge and sensitised yourself to interdisciplinary research methods, theories as well as evidential possibilities. This will allow you to begin experimenting with different research configurations of purpose, questions and research methods, including the possibility of borrowing and blending from different sciences (similar to that described by Oswick et al. 2011). This can be particularly relevant if you are considering importing theories, insights and evidence from these different literatures as part of your project. Using theories and methods from other disciplines may enable your future work to travel and make legitimate contributions in other research literatures.

Method borrowing and blending strategies are an integral part of interdisciplinary research into complex problems (Funtowicz and Ravetz 1993; Frame et al. 2009) including environmental accounting. However, this does require understanding and respecting the methodological underpinning of other disciplinary research methods in order to ensure a coherent research design. For example, if you are looking to apply an interpretative approach to climate change accounting practices, you need to take care if you are motivating your research on hard quantitative "facts" from research from positivistic climate scientists or engineers.

It is important to recognise that research involves social, organisational and political work that takes place in resource-constrained institutions. There is a need to reflect on your objectives for undertaking this research, taking account of your project of self, institutional context, short- and long-term career milestones, societal opportunities to act and work–life balance. An important consideration in this reflection is the time commitment and resources you have, either individually or collectively, in your communities of practice. This requires considering the degrees of freedom and constraints internally and externally imposed on any imagined

Table 4.3 Resource scenario examples

Scenario 1 – Rewilding	
Working title	The role of accounting in evaluating rewilding project (success or failure)
Resource scenarios and timeline	Just me and 12 months version
Problem boundaries	Focus on single local case – look for a success or failure
Theory?	Adaptive accountability for resilience in socio-ecological systems
Tools?	Reinterpreting documented local case study augmented with limited set of interviews with key actors (form of alternative accounting) – think about methods of interpretation Working with someone else on a project in progress – possibility of coming back in future
Evidence?	Published data from multiple sources and primary interview data, key issue is searching for candidates for case study
Scenario 2 – Rewilding	
Working title	Remediating, restoring, rewilding or repressing: the role of accounting in re-engineering nature
Resource scenarios and timeline	Interdisciplinary research team working on an ongoing project – likely to be medium term project (3–5 years)
Problem boundaries	Measuring and accounting for changes to ecosystem, impact on local communities, eco-tourism possibilities, policy evaluation.
Theory?	To be determined by interdisciplinary team
Tools?	Ecosystem mapping, scientific measurement indicators, emerging case study, visualisation, social network monitoring, use of GIS, visual imagining, extensive interviews and focus groups
Evidence?	Rich set of different evidence sources, but problem with storage, sharing, alignment and interpretation

project. This will allow the construction of a range of feasible, but desirable configurations based on resource and time commitment scenario assumptions (see Table 4.3).

Although publications are a critical part of sharing your findings and legitimating your research, they must not dominate the choice of methods, particularly in wicked problem spaces and practices such as environmental accounting. If, institutionally, you need to target specific journals, it is worth mapping out the legitimate research methods associated with these journals. However, you should not rely on received wisdom, war stories from gnarled researchers or gossip. Research the journals yourself, look for changes in editors, the composition of an editorial board, special issues and calls for papers. Journals and the peer review process are conservative in nature, but they do change. You should think about your project lead time. For example, it may be that this project won't result in a submitted paper for 5 years; therefore, you need to predict what the legitimate research methods will be then, not now. However, you should not fall into the trap of conflating a research project with a single research publication or commit to a single publication, but rather consider an interdisciplinary portfolio of outlets relevant to the underlying purposes of the research project.

At this stage it is useful to assembling existing research methods into bundles, rather than trying to design from scratch. This may require following up on some of the method sources used earlier. Once you have constructed these method bundles and preferred scenarios, they need to be subjected to deeper scrutiny before crafting them into a more coherent set of methods.

Multi-perspective bundle evaluation

At this stage the researcher should look to consider potential challenges to their bundle of research methods, for example:

- Are there any weaknesses or gaps that may need to be filled?
- Any resistance from established researchers in the field?
- Any criticism from those invested in specific research method traditions?
- Any challenges to disciplinary (or interdisciplinary) paradigms or epistemology?
- Any misalignment with possible theorising strategies?
- Appropriateness to potential dissemination strategies, pathways to impact or key change agents?

To do this it is worth considering drawing up a Methodising Summary Sheet (Table 4.4). This is a structured approach designed to quickly capture the essence of future research project in a way

Table 4.4 Methodising summary sheet[a]

Working title	Remediating, restoring, rewilding or repressing: the role of accounting in re-engineering nature
Inspiration	Image of wolves roaming wild in Scottish Highlands with golden eagles soaring overhead, reclaiming imagined historic rugged grandeur of my homeland. Urgent and compelling need to stop this and reverse trends of biodiversity loss. Shifting from reducing business negative impact on nature to positive enhancement of nature in the Anthropocene. However, there is an unanswered question as to "is rewilding simply a romantic project that will simply perpetuate the problem?"
How will this make the world more sustainable	Answering the question "is authentic rewilding possible, desirable" and if it is "by designing rewilding accounting and accountability processes"
Three arguments against this project	• Too broad in scope and complexity to make a meaningful contribution • Based on a utopian view of the ability of humans to positively intervene in natural systems • Ignores the real-politick and power dynamics
SDGs	**Positively impacted** Directly – 6, 14, 15, 16, 17; Indirectly – 3, 4, 9, 11, 13 **Negatively impacted** Worst-case scenario 2, 8, 12 **Neutral impact** 1, 2, 5, 7, 10

(continued)

Table 4.4 Cont.

Theory of change – assumptions	By developing a holistic evaluation framework for rewilding; possible critique of rewilding governance and performance metrics; critique and design of appropriate rewilding accounts and accountability; feed into appropriate policy forum to reform existing projects and/or new initiatives; evidential support to mobilise resources to improve our natural environment.
Winners and losers	**Losers –** existing land users, other species, business whose supply chain depends on land, investors in future stranded natural assets, groups of employees and communities, tax payers. **Winners** – communities associated with nature tourism, specific species, specific ecosystems, NGOs.
Pre-study of domain – key findings	Humans have continually interacted, positively and negatively, with nature, attempting to extract value and disrupting adaptive natural dynamics. Main ecosystems are now dependent on human intervention, but our interventions are incapable of even maintaining necessary ecosystem services. How effective would rewilding be, particularly the reintroduction of high level mammals, in enhancing natural systems. How could these projects be promoted, legitimated, success measured or monitored and attract investments/funding?
Possible theories and disciplines?	Adaptive Accountability – accountability Governance – politics; sociology Resilience – socio-ecological systems Dialogics – pedagogy
Possible method bundles	Case studies of rewilding initiatives Keystone actor/regulations analysis Dialogic encounter sessions – series of interviews Ecological system mapping Social media analysis Video/photographic analysis
Resource scenario assumption	This project is based on attracting funding for a 5-year project, which would allow for 5 annual iterations and continued internal institution support for this project.
Risks	Complexity and access to ecosystem mapping and measurement expertise Continued funding of underlying projects Escalation in conflict – sabotage Climate change or other ecological events
Dissemination strategy	Book; ongoing blogs/podcasts; workshops/forums; policy briefs; social and mass media articles; academic journals (to be confirmed later)
Readership – who to provoke; sources of support or resistance	**Provoke** – conventional business/accounting audience; those who argue nothing can be done – it is all too late **Resistors** – Neo-libs, deep greens, critical scholars, single disciplinary purists, reviewers and journal editors **Supporters** – Middle of road SEAR scholars, interdisciplinary enthusiasts; SES; regulators and conservationists

[a] This methodising form was adapted from the Research Pitch Form developed by Professor Robert Faff (http://pitchingresearch.com/guide.html).

that allows it to be the subject of meaningful discussions before committing to a full written proposal and closing down the design work.

Now it's time for the detailed evaluation of the most likely assemblage of research methods that leads to the construction of an idealised research process. This is where you begin to really flesh out the research design in a way that is appropriate to the contexts of discovery and justification. This will require researching, extensive reading and robust methodological considerations. This stage is often considered as the starting point of consideration of research methods, rather than what is an intermediate stage in methodising.

Research method texts really come into their own at this stage, as you draw on the experts in different fields. Don't be afraid to contact these experts directly if you are not sure about the applicability of their methods to your problem. However, ensure that you are familiar with all their recent works in this area before contacting them. There is nothing more embarrassing than being told that this issue is addressed in an article by Dr. Banana in 1995 or a number of projects that have already been published.

Swedberg recommends Peirce's (1997) simple but effective method of writing down all the arguments and counter-arguments in favour of a method. Address it from different perspectives and repeat until you convince yourself of the merits of a particular bundle of research methods. During this process you can begin to hone the methods in different bundles and possibilities.

It is also worthwhile to share these lists with peers, mentors, friends, stakeholders or anyone who will listen. This will allow a sense checking as to whether others think you are on the right path. As mentioned, methodising is a creative, subjective process and it is unlikely that there will be consensus from all those you talk to. Be prepared to receive mixed feedback and puzzled looks. Do not automatically accept or reject this feedback, but rather reflect on the logic that underpins their comments and integrate this into your evaluations.

Example of method bundle, pathways and contingencies

This section will provide an example of an environmental accounting rewilding project, based on the resilience assessment framework (Resilience Alliance 2010). Resilience assessment methods draw on research insights from complex adaptive systems (Carpenter et al. 2001; Walker et al. 2004), and integrate a set of key concepts that provide alternative ways of thinking about and practising natural resource management informed by the dynamics of change in social-ecological systems (Chapin et al. 2009). This interdisciplinary framework was developed by a coalition of world's leading research centres and is well established in ecological research (Anderies et al. 2004), fits with the research domain (Folke et al. 2005), appropriate for interdisciplinary publications and policy impact (Milkoreit et al. 2015; Thiel et al. 2015). The resilience assessment framework is methodologically consistent with a substantive body of environmental accounting research, theories and methods (such as stakeholder engagement, accountability and governance). It also offers the possibility of exploring interconnectedness, critical thresholds, impact measurement and system-level resilience into environmental accounting. In contrast to conventional environmental accounting with its embedded notions of controlling natural resources for stable or maximum production for economic gain, resilience seeks to maintain sustainable long-term delivery of environmental benefits linked to human well-being. There is a normative assumption that resolving specific environmental governance issues must not damage the integrity of the system as a whole. This research strategy appears to be highly appropriate for exploring the role of accounting (if any) in rewilding projects. This research design is reflexive and allows for domain-specific adaptability and innovations.

The decision was taken to go for a longitudinal, episodic research design based on a single case study over a 5-year period. The episodic nature of the study allows the possibility of interim outputs, adaptable design that co-evolves with the project that can cope with domain-level uncertainty and change.[8] The long timescale and longitudinal dimension enable the possibility of meaningful measurement of impacts at an ecosystem level. This also informed the choice of an ongoing rewilding project involving the reintroduction of European Beavers in Knapdale, Scotland.[9] This project started in 2009 with clear observable impacts in the landscape over the first 10 years.

The physical location is easily accessible to visitors and from a research point of view does not involve significant amount of resource for travel and subsistence. As this is a high-profile controversial project, it has been subject to significant levels of media coverage, scientific studies and government reports. It is unusual in a UK context as it did not involve the reintroduction of a high-level predator or raptor species, but it does have significant physical impact on the land and associated eco-systems. Currently, there are calls for this project to be replicated across rural Scotland, with contested opinions as to the merits of this. This gives this research a potential policy impact (Figure 4.3).

The Resilience Assessment Framework is comprehensive in nature and involves five main stages. The research methods are intended to be reflexive and iterative, rather than applied in a serial fashion. It is imagined that the initial stage will involve constructing a conceptual

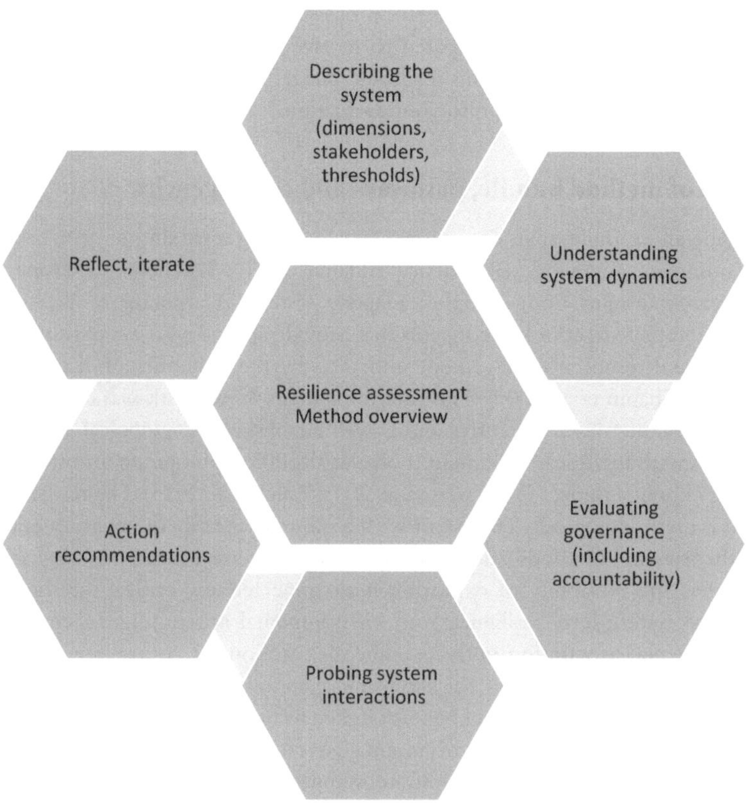

Figure 4.3 Main stages of Resilience Assessment Framework (Source: Resilience Assessment 2010).

model of the social-ecological system that represents the Beavers@Knapdale including natural resources, governance and accountability infrastructure, stakeholders, institutions, conflicts and system dimensions. This will be followed by a process of identifying potential thresholds that represent breakpoints between two alternative system states, *unwilded* and *rewilded,* in order to reveal what is contributing to or eroding system resilience.

Different sources and research methods will form the basis of the initial imagined research stages based on the worksheets (see Table 4.5) from the Practitioners' workbook (Resilience Assessment 2010). These include:

Table 4.5 Examples of resilience assessment worksheets

Worksheet 4.1

<table>
<tr><td colspan="5">Key formal and informal institutions</td></tr>
<tr><td></td><td>List of institutions</td><td colspan="2">Enhance flexibility (Yes/No)</td><td>Restrain flexibility (Yes/No)</td></tr>
<tr><td>Main issue 1</td><td></td><td colspan="2"></td><td></td></tr>
<tr><td>Main issue 2</td><td></td><td colspan="2"></td><td></td></tr>
<tr><td>Overarching</td><td></td><td colspan="2"></td><td></td></tr>
<tr><td colspan="5">Level of decision-making</td></tr>
<tr><td></td><td>Local, municipal, provincial, national, regional</td><td colspan="2">Appropriate given ecological processes? (Yes/No)</td><td>Suggested improvements</td></tr>
<tr><td>Main issue 1</td><td></td><td colspan="2"></td><td></td></tr>
<tr><td>Main issue 2</td><td></td><td colspan="2"></td><td></td></tr>
<tr><td colspan="5">Rule enforcement and compliance</td></tr>
<tr><td></td><td>Is it effective? (Yes/No)</td><td colspan="3">Suggested improvements</td></tr>
<tr><td>Main issue 1</td><td></td><td colspan="3"></td></tr>
<tr><td>Main issue 2</td><td></td><td colspan="3"></td></tr>
<tr><td colspan="5">Mapping power relations and conflicts</td></tr>
<tr><td>List of stakeholders</td><td>Formal power (strong, intermediate, weak)</td><td>Informal power (strong, intermediate, weak)</td><td>Conflicts with other stakeholders? Specify.</td><td>Conflict resolution mechanisms in place?</td></tr>
<tr><td></td><td></td><td></td><td></td><td></td></tr>
</table>

Table 4.5 Cont.

Worksheet 1.2 Direct and indirect uses of key natural resources supplied by the system and the stakeholder that rely on them.

Natural resource uses	*Stakeholders*
Direct uses	Inside focal system
Indirect uses	Outside focal system

Worksheet 1.3 Summary of focal system disturbances and their attributes.

Disturbance (past or present)	*Pulse or press*	*Frequency of occurrence*	*Time for recovery between occurrences*	*Components most affected*	*Magnitude of impact (minor to severe)*	*Any change in past years or decades?*
Future disturbances						

Worksheet 1.4 Social and ecological dimensions of systems at larger and smaller scales that interact with the focal system.

	Social dimensions that influence the focal system	*Ecological dimensions that influence the focal system*
Larger-scale systems		
Focal System		
Smaller-scale systems		

Table 4.5 Cont.

Worksheet 3.2 Thresholds of slow variables and potential interactions.

	Smaller-scale system(s) ←——— *Focal system* ———→ *Larger-scale system(s)*
Social	
Ecological	

Worksheet 1.1 Summary of main issues of concern for the assessment and of valued attributes of the system.

Issues	*Main issue(s) of concern for the assessment*	*Valued attributes of the system*
Issue 1		
Issue 2		
Issue 3		

- Documentary review of scientific and policy papers associated with this intervention, including press coverage and social media analysis to complete worksheets 1.1, 1.2, 1.3, 1.4, 3.2, 4.1.
- Gather mapping data and satellite imagery.
- Begin monitoring press and social media.
- Undertake initial formal site visit to get sense of physical scale and begin photographic surveys (repeat visits every 3 months to build an image database).
- Interview project teams at Royal Zoological Society, Wildlife Scotland and Rangers at Knapdale.
- Establish project governance structure and accountability processes, formal and informal.
- Non-participant observation at public meeting, governance meetings.

- Construct multiple criterion model of existing formal and informal performance and impact measurement processes.
- Map out original implied theories of change. (Look to revisit over time.)
- Identify stakeholders and areas of conflict.
- Interview and gather data from stakeholders in series of interviews, focus groups and citizen juries.
- Initial identification of critical system dimensions and range of critical thresholds.
- Prepare initial map of system, evaluation of dynamics, performance relative to goals, governance and accountability mechanisms.
- Present to participants with recommendations.

This process will be repeated at least three times in the five-year period, following a period of review and reflection after each iteration or new opportunities to engage.

However, while you may feel that you have solved all possible problems and created your perfect research method, you need to be sensitive to the risks, unpredictability and messiness of field work. The only thing that you can be sure of is that it will not work the way you designed it. You need to build in alternatives, in particular, recognising your dependencies on the cooperation of others. Experienced environmental accounting researchers can recount how despite their best laid plans, they had to adjust their timelines, develop strategies to deal with unavailability of sources or other contingencies. What is important in more linear research assemblages is to design in alternative pathways, key milestones, must-have evidence, nested or contingent evidence gathering strategies.

In the Beavers@Knapdale example above, the research method is intrinsically reflexive and capable of dealing with accessibility of key actors, etc. However, there are still a number of potential risks and obstacles. The main risks are in being unable to access the "backstage" elements of formal governance structures, policy setting or the historic data and reliable accounts of the original opposition/support for their reintroduction. It is highly dependent on cooperation from key stakeholders; however, the pre-study did identify a high level of information in different formats in the public domain. Given the high-profile, contested nature of this project, there is reasonable confidence in completing the first iteration. It is anticipated that this first iteration will provide more opportunities for others to engage with the emerging research project. After that who knows, but that is the joy of research!

Start, stop and think, share and reflect

At this stage you could go around the houses again, but best advice is to get out there and start collecting evidence. Involving others in your methodising is really valuable, as research is a collective exercise. Present regularly at internal seminars, workshops and conferences. Talk to people about your emerging research project and listen carefully.

Conclusion

This chapter has tried to fill in some of the gaps of the invisible, often silenced work associated with research methods and tried to illustrate some of the ways to fill in these gaps. It has introduced the verb "methodising" in the context of discovery to complement the noun "methods" in the context of justification. Hopefully, it has opened up the black box enough to allow readers to avoid some of the trials and tribulations the environmental accounting community have experienced in the past.

Notes

1 https://www.bbc.co.uk/programmes/b0074hjr/episodes/player
2 www.un.org/sustainabledevelopment/sustainable-development-goals/
3 www.stockholmresilience.org/research/planetary-boundaries/planetary-boundaries/about-the-research/the-nine-planetary-boundaries.html
4 https://policy-practice.oxfam.org.uk/publications/the-uk-doughnut-a-framework-for-environmental-sustainability-and-social-justice-344550
5 https://futurefitbusiness.org/explore-the-benchmark/
6 https://keystonedialogues.earth/
7 Theory of change maps out the "missing middle" between what a change initiative does (its activities or interventions) and how these lead to desired goals being achieved. www.theoryofchange.org/what-is-theory-of-change/
8 There is also an element of emulation in this research design, which relates to one of my favourite series of research papers relating to the long-running Caterpillar study by Peter Miller and Ted O'Leary.
9 https://scottishwildlifetrust.org.uk/our-work/our-projects/scottish-beavers/ See the earlier comment about visiting this site on a number of occasions for pleasure and curiosity.

References

Anderies, J., Janssen, M. and Ostrom, E., 2004. A framework to analyze the robustness of social-ecological systems from an institutional perspective. *Ecology and Society*, 9(1), 18.

Atkins, J. and Atkins, B., 2016. *The Business of Bees: An Integrated Approach to Bee Decline and Corporate Responsibility*. Abington: Routledge.

Bassnett, A., Frandsen, A. and Hoskin, K., 2018. The unspeakable truth of accounting: on the genesis and consequences of the first "non-glottographic" statement form. *Accounting, Auditing & Accountability Journal*, 31(7): 2083–2107.

Bebbington, J., Russell, S. and Thomson, I., 2017. Accounting and sustainable development: reflections and propositions. *Critical Perspectives on Accounting*, 48: 21–34.

Carpenter, S., Walker, B., Anderies, J. and Abel, N., 2001. From metaphor to measurement: resilience of what to what? *Ecosystems*, 4, 765–781.

Chapin, F., Kofinas, G. and Folke, C. (eds.), 2009. *Principles of Ecosystem Stewardship: Resilience-Based Natural Resource Management in a Changing World*. New York: Springer.

Dey, C. and Russell, S., 2014. Who speaks for the river? Exploring biodiversity accounting using an arena approach. In: Jones, M. (ed.), *Accounting for Biodiversity*. London: Routledge, pp. 245–266.

Ernstson, H., Sörlin, S. and Elmqvist, T., 2008. Social movements and ecosystem services–the role of social network structure in protecting and managing urban green areas in Stockholm. *Ecology and Society*, 13(2), 39.

Folke, C. et al., 2005. Regime shifts, resilience and biodiversity in ecosystem management. *Annual Review of Ecology Evolution and Systematics*, 35, 557–581.

Frame, R., Gordon, R. and Mortimer, C., 2009. Hatched: the capacity for sustainable development, Landcare research, available at www.landcareresearch.co.nz/__data/assets/pdf_file/0003/28263/hatched_ebook_entire_web.pdf (accessed 19th February 2021).

Funtowicz, S. and Ravetz, R., 1993. Science for the post-normal age. *Futures*, 25, 739–755.

Georgakopoulos, G. and Thomson, I., 2005. Organic Salmon farming: risk perceptions, decision heuristics and the absence of environmental accounting. *Accounting Forum*, 29(1): 49–75.

Georgakopoulos, G. and Thomson, I., 2008. Social reporting, engagements, controversies and conflict in Scottish Salmon farming. *Accounting, Auditing and Accountability Journal*, 21(8): 1116–1143.

Hughes, E., 1984. *The Sociological Eye: Selected Papers*. New Brunswick: Transaction Press.

Humphrey, C. and Lee, B., (eds.), 2004. *The Real Life Guide to Accounting Research: A Behind-the-Scenes View of Using Qualitative Research Methods*, Oxford: Elsevier.

Kahneman, D., 2012. *Thinking, Fast and Slow*. London: Penguin.

Lave, C. and March, J., 1993. *An Introduction to Models in the Social Sciences*. New York: University Press.

Milkoreit, M. et al., 2015. Resilience scientists as change-makers: growing the middle ground between science and advocacy? *Environmental Science and Policy*, 53, 87–95.

Oswick, C., Fleming, P. and Hanlon, G., 2011. From borrowing to blending: rethinking the processes of organizational theory building. *Academy of Management Review*, 36(2), 318–337.

Peirce, C., 1997. *Pragmatism as a Principle and Method of Right Thinking*. Albany, NY: State University of New York Press.

Resilience Alliance., 2010. Assessing resilience in social-ecological systems: Workbook for practitioners. Version 2.0. Available at www.resiliencealliance.org/3871.php (accessed 19th February 2021).

Swedberg, R., 2016. Before theory comes theorizing or how to make social science more interesting. *British Journal of Sociology*, 67(1), 5–22.

Thiel, A., Mukhtarov, F. and Zikos, D., 2015. Crafting or designing? Science and politics for purposeful institutional change in Social–Ecological Systems. *Environmental Science and Policy*, 5 (3), 81–86.

Thomson, I., 2007. Accounting and sustainability: mapping the terrain. In Bebbington, J., O'Dwyer, B. and Unerman, J. (eds.), *Sustainable Accounting and Accountability*. Abington: Routledge.

Thomson, I., 2014. Accounting and sustainability: mapping the new research topology. In Bebbington, J., O'Dwyer, B., and Unerman, J. (eds.), *Sustainable Accounting and Accountability,* 2nd edn. Abington: Routledge.

Thomson, I., Georgakopoulos, G., and Grubnic. S., 2014. Exploring accounting sustainability hybridisation in the UK public sector. *Accounting, Organisations and Society*, 39, 453–476.

Walker, B., Holling, C., Carpenter, S. and Kinzig, A., 2004. Resilience, adaptability and transformability in social–ecological systems. *Ecology and Society*, 9(2), 5.

Appendix 1 – Useful Research Method Texts

Atkinson, P., Delamont, S., Hardy, M. and Williams, M., 2008. *SAGE Encyclopedia of Research Methods*. Thousand Oaks, CA: Sage.

Cassell, C., Cunliffe, C. and Grandy, G., 2018). *The SAGE Handbook of Qualitative Business and Management Research Methods: Methods and Challenges*. London: Sage.

Creswell, J. and Clark, V., 2017. *Designing and Conducting Mixed Methods Research*. Thousand Oaks, CA: Sage.

Funnell, S. and Rogers, P., 2011. *Purposeful Program Theory: Effective Use of Theories of Change and Logic Models (Research Methods for the Social Sciences)*. California: John Wiley and Co.

Hay, I., 2016. *Qualitative Research Methods in Human Geography*. Oxford: Oxford University Press.

Hill, D. et al., 2005. *Handbook of Biodiversity Methods: Survey, Evaluation and Monitoring*. Cambridge: Cambridge University Press.

Hoque, Z., Parker, L., Covaleski, M. and Haynes, K., 2017. *The Routledge Companion to Qualitative Accounting Research Methods*. London: Routledge.

Kanazawa, M., 2017. *Research Methods for Environmental Studies*, London: Routledge.

Kara, H., 2015. *Creative research methods in the social sciences: A Practical Guide*. Bristol: Policy Press.

Law, J., 2004. After Method: Mess in Social Science Research. *International Library of Sociology*.

Nash, C. and Browne, K., 2016. *Queer Methods and Methodologies: Intersecting Queer Theories and Social Science Research*. London: Routledge.

Smith, R. and McConnell, L., 2018. *Research Methods in Human Rights*. London: Routledge.

Snee, H. and Hine, C., 2016. *Digital Methods for Social Science*. Basingstoke: Palgrave Mcmillan.

Steinberg, S. and Steinberg, S., 2015. *GIS Research Methods: Incorporating Spatial Perspectives*. Redlands, CA: Esri.

Teddlie, C. and Tashakkori, A., 2008. *Foundations of Mixed Methods Research: Integrating Quantitative and Qualitative Approaches in the Social and Behavioral Sciences*. Thousand Oaks, CA: Sage.

Tight, M., 2019. *Documentary Research in the Social Sciences*. London: Sage.

5
THE ACCOUNTING PROFESSION'S ENVIRONMENTAL ACCOUNTING AND REPORTING THOUGHT LEADERSHIP

Jeffrey Unerman

Introduction

Effective thought leadership, defined as "intellectual influence; innovative or pioneering thinking" (OED 2020), can be a crucial factor in advancing any field of human endeavour. Other chapters in this handbook demonstrate how academic research in environmental accounting has provided such thought leadership through a range of insights and constructive critiques that have advanced accounting and reporting policies and practices. In addition, and based on the definition of a thought leader as "an influential or innovative thinker; a person with intellectual influence over a society or group" (OED 2020), a wide range of individuals and institutions outside academia have also been thought leaders in environmental accounting. This chapter explores some of the accounting profession's current thought leadership initiatives in this field.

Understanding the accounting profession's influence is important as it has the potential to make a significant contribution to developments in environmental accounting and reporting policies and practices. As earlier chapters have demonstrated, past thought leadership interventions from the accounting profession have indeed been influential in the development of environmental accounting.

While some current and past contributions from the profession might have been informed by insights from academic research, others do not always have an obvious link to academic research outputs. Regardless, initiatives from the profession have exerted considerable influence upon the shape of environmental accounting and reporting – with potential for considerably more direct influence than academic research – given the extensive networks of policy and practice within which the accounting profession is embedded and their acknowledged expertise in accounting and reporting matters.

This potential for strong influence and impact from the accounting profession's thought leadership is intensified through the profession's apparently greater agility than many in the academic community to engage rapidly with, and drive, major shifts in the context for environmental accounting and reporting that lead to widely adopted innovations in practice. For example, Bebbington and Unerman (2018), O'Dwyer and Unerman (2020) and Bebbington and Unerman (2020) have all observed novel areas of sustainability policy where there have been developments in transformative and innovative forms of sustainability accounting and reporting, but where these new forms of practice have taken a long time to be picked up by academic researchers. From this perspective, there is considerable potential for the accounting profession's thought leadership to identify novel and impactful new areas for environmental accounting academic research. By engaging with the accounting profession, research then has the potential to provide high-quality evidence and critique to improve the effectiveness of the practices we study. A symbiotic relationship can thereby be developed between the contributions of both academics and the accounting profession in continually improving environmental accounting and reporting. This provides a compelling reason for academics to engage with the accounting profession.

This chapter explores some of the accounting profession's current major environmental accounting and reporting thought leadership initiatives, with a focus on such initiatives from the "Big Four" global accountancy/professional service firms and the large professional accounting bodies.

The next section of the chapter will outline how the accounting profession can be and is influential in developing and embedding new environmental accounting and reporting practices, distinguishing between the strong potential for influence from both the Big Four global firms and professional bodies. This is followed by a section that identifies the Big Four's apparent top-level commitments to advancing environmental accounting and reporting, with the subsequent section exploring these issues for a sample of large professional accountancy bodies. A further section explains some of the more enduring and influential collaborative projects that have drawn from environmental accounting expertise across the accounting profession. The final section draws some conclusions.

Potential influence of the accounting profession

Professionally qualified accountants undertake an extensive range of strategic and operational functions across many different sectors and organisational types in the private, public and third sectors. Given the importance of sound financial management to the viability of all organisations, accountants can be found among the senior executives of many. Other accountants working for professional accountancy (or professional services) firms provide a range of advisory services that are relied upon by many of their clients, both large and small, across all sectors. Through this widespread embedding of professional accountants in the decision-making processes of many organisations, policy insights generated and promoted by the accounting profession can have considerable influence.

As a core function of accounting is to provide information that will aid decision-making, professional accountants also have a role to play in providing and evaluating information that aids organisational environmental decisions. Some large environmentally impactful businesses employ teams of sustainability experts. These can include environmental accountants, who may also contribute insights and expertise to environmental accounting policy bodies and networks of which their business is a member. However, many smaller and/or less environmentally impactful (or aware) businesses are likely to lack the resources to have dedicated expertise in this area. Environmental accounting thought leadership insights generated and disseminated by professional accountancy firms, professional bodies and specialist sustainability accounting networks/policymakers will be important in raising the awareness of these businesses about the significance and potential of environmental accounting for enhancing their environmental and financial performance. This awareness raising can be a key factor in generating growing interest in, and commitments to, environmental accounting.

The potential for "Big Four" influence

Professional accountancy firms range in size from sole practitioners through to the Big Four. Sole practitioners may focus on providing a range of accountancy-related services to their clients or may specialise in one or a narrow range of advisory services and/or sectors. In either case, most small firms are unlikely to have the resources that larger practices have to contribute significantly to policy development activities. Conversely, the scale of the Big Four global accountancy firms, as shown in Table 5.1, is substantial, equivalent to the world's largest multinational corporations. They are therefore more likely than smaller firms to have resources to put into substantive thought leadership initiatives in areas commensurate with the nature of their advisory businesses.

Compared to the Fortune Global 500 rankings of the world's largest multinationals (Fortune Media 2020), Deloitte had slightly higher 2019 revenues than the world's 243rd largest multinational (China Shipbuilding Industry with US$46.1 billion revenue), while KPMG was slightly ahead of the 421st largest (Arrow Electronics with US$29.7 billion revenues). In terms of workforce, Deloitte had a slightly larger global workforce than the 42nd largest global corporation by workforce (Bank of China with 310,000 employees) while KPMG's global workforce was around the same size as the 83rd largest global employer (Finatis of France with 219,000 employees).

As all of the Big Four firms have revenues on a par with the world's largest 500 multinational corporations, and workforces on a par with the largest 100 multinationals, even though they do not have external shareholders (instead legally being networks of member firms) they are likely to be subject to many of the types of social contractual pressures that other very large intellectually based multinationals experience. The motivations of these Big Four global firms to put resources into environmental accounting and reporting initiatives are therefore likely to reflect

Table 5.1 2019 relative size of the Big Four accountancy/professional services firms globally

Firm[a]	*2019 Global revenue (US$ billion)*	*2019 Global workforce (thousands)*
Deloitte	46.2	312
EY	36.4	284
KPMG	29.8	219
PwC	42.4	276
Total Big Four	154.8	1,091
Average Big Four	38.7	273
Average Fortune 500 (US-headquartered) companies in 2019	*27.4*	*57*
Average for Fortune Global 500 companies in 2019	*65.4*	*139*

[a] Data are drawn from Deloitte (2020), EY (2020), KPMG (2020) and PwC (2019a).

the complex array of motives underlying any multinational's decisions to devote resources to environmental initiatives. These could be a complex combination of one of more of:

- *Ethical reasoning*, with senior executives of the firms recognising a moral duty to provide leadership in helping the transformation towards zero-carbon sustainable economies;
- *Business case reasoning* recognising a broad range of potential direct and indirect financial benefits flowing from supporting environmental sustainability; and/or
- *A possible desire to deflect attention* from aspects of their operations that attract public disapproval. For large accountancy firms these could include issues such as audit failure, helping large businesses arrange their operations in such a way as to legally avoid paying substantive amounts of taxation, and/or working with clients that may have a high profile for other environmentally and socially unsustainable operations.

As the focus of this chapter is on the provision of insights into some of the accounting profession's current environmental accounting thought leadership initiatives, analysis of possible motives for Big Four firms to champion these initiatives (or a broader critique of the profession) is beyond its scope. However, we should recognise that nowadays in large complex organisations, including the Big Four, narrow financial benefits are unlikely to be a sole motivator to engage in pro-environmental activities.

Public interest remit and influence of professional accounting bodies

In contrast to the substantial size of the Big Four, professional accounting bodies have much lower revenues and numbers of employees. They are largely non-profit organisations whose thought leadership influence is exerted through the size and range of their membership and the policy networks of which they themselves are members. The International Federation of Accountants (IFAC) is the main global representative organisation for professional accounting bodies. At the end of 2019, it had 175 member bodies from 130 jurisdictions, with a combined individual membership of approximately 3 million accountants (IFAC 2020), giving an average of approximately 17,000 members per professional body. However, some of the IFAC member bodies are considerably larger than this.[1]

In deciding which aspects of public policy they seek to influence through their membership base (and through the networks in which they are embedded) by drawing on their thought leadership work, non-profit professional bodies will have regard to the interests of their members in conjunction with the wide public interest. Indeed, many professional accounting bodies have a formal requirement to undertake their activities in the public interest. For example, the Association of International Certified Public Accountants' (AICPA) mission includes "protecting the evolving public interest" (AICPA 2020). Similarly, ACCA's "purpose and values" include "act[ing] in the public interest" (ACCA 2020). ICAEW has a mission of "creating a world of strong economies together" (ICAEW 2020b) rooted in an enduring obligation from their Royal Charter to act in the public interest (ICAEW 2020a).

Thus, while supporting an accounting profession many of whose members seek to generate (large) financial returns for their employers and clients, professional accounting bodies themselves can be both non-profit membership organisations and required to advance the public interest. Where they see the longer-term interests of the accounting profession (and therefore the interests of their members) and the broader public interest as being served by the development of environmental accounting, they have the scope to engage in thought leadership in this area. They also have potentially significant influence through disseminating this thought leadership via their members who are in influential positions in many businesses, policymakers and professional accountancy firms.

Cross-profession collaborative environmental accounting projects

A further channel of influence for the accounting profession's environmental accounting thought leadership initiatives include projects that draw on expertise and insights from across the profession. The Prince of Wales's Accounting for Sustainability Project (A4S) is probably the most enduring and influential of such collaborative bodies that focus exclusively on sustainability accounting. Accountancy Europe is another enduring collaborative project, where sustainability is one of several strands of its activities.

Accounting profession's track record

Overall, the accounting profession, including the Big Four firms, has a long but patchy history of resourcing thought leadership in environmental accounting and reporting. For example, as highlighted in the introductory chapter (Chapter 1) to this book and Chapter 2 on the foundations of environmental accounting, the ACCA was instrumental in the emergence of environmental accounting as a subfield within accounting research over 30 years ago when they sponsored Professor Rob Gray's report *The Greening of Accountancy: The Profession After Pearce* (Gray 1990). The profession's support for this visionary thought leadership from a pioneering academic working with the profession was largely due to ACCA's Technical Director at the time, Roger Adams, who also established the ACCA's *Environmental Reporting Awards* in 1991 (Bruce 2015). However, this innovative leadership on environmental accounting was not followed with substantive initiatives from other professional bodies or Big Four firms at the time:

> … [D]espite the reactions of professional accounting bodies which, with some exceptions, have ignored the area, individual reporting entities have developed new forms of reporting. Although social accounting has been downplayed in the overall research agenda for several years, an examination of the annual reports of the larger corporations would reveal many disclosures recognizable as social accounting information. Similarly, larger organizations are also producing environmental reports, despite the lack of interest in these developments by most of the professional accounting bodies.
>
> *(Mathews 1997, p. 502)*

In face of this prevalent indifference towards environmental accounting from the accounting profession, there was some recognition in the 1990s that greater thought leadership was needed from the profession in this area:

> The environment is an opportunity for the accounting profession to demonstrate that it is on top of contemporary issues and that the profession can grasp new opportunities and run with modern issues. The environment will be a challenge, but it is a challenge that accountants are well able to deal with, well able to run with, and well able to demonstrate that it is an issue that they can truly grasp. Accountants have a key role to play in the environmental debate, so that they too can turn around in the future and say "we have made a difference to the world we live in".
>
> *(Medley 1997, pp. 599–600)*

In more recent years, some professional accounting bodies and the Big Four firms have become much more active in environmental accounting and reporting initiatives. As indicated earlier in this chapter, thought leadership in this area from the profession often now addresses contemporary issues that academics have yet to address substantively. Rather than chart the awakening and upsurge of the accounting profession's interest in thought leadership on environmental accounting and reporting (noting that some initiatives over the years are reflected in other chapters in this handbook), the remainder of this chapter will explore some of the main environmental accounting initiatives from the profession that are current at the time of writing.

The most recent annual reviews (or similar documents) of each of the professional bodies featured in this section and the Big Four firms have been reviewed to identify their key environmental accounting and reporting thought leadership initiatives. An important context in which these annual reviews were written was 2019's substantial growth in societal concerns about environmental sustainability, with a rapid expansion of mass protest movements (Hook 2019a, 2019b) amid declarations of a climate and planetary emergency (The Club of Rome 2019).

Although the professional accounting bodies and Big Four are likely to engage in a wider range of environmental accounting and reporting initiatives than disclosed in their annual reviews, materiality judgements in deciding which issues to cover in a limited length annual review are a filter that can indicate which initiatives an entity considers to be its most significant. The next section of this chapter will explore these environment-related initiatives of the Big Four firms, with the subsequent section reviewing professional bodies' commitments, followed by a section outlining some of the initiatives championed by A4S and Accountancy Europe.

Key "Big Four" global environmental accounting activities

The 2019 global annual reviews of each of the Big Four articulate the role the firms can and do play in helping their clients identify and address sustainability challenges. KPMG has the most prominent commitments in this regard, in disclosing them in the introductory *Leadership* Reflections section of its 2019 Global Review and explaining them in the context of 2019's rising of environmental consciousness:

> 2019 has been a year of significant volatility — social, political and environmental. We have seen some of the most dramatic climate-related disasters with an unwelcome frequency. It has also been a year in which new generations are stepping forward to make their voices heard and demand changes to our environmental practices. Businesses are taking a lead, innovating in areas including packaging, water stewardship and climate change reduction … KPMG remains committed to helping each of our clients in addressing the Sustainable Development Goals.
>
> *(KPMG 2020, p. 4)*

Other firms similarly recognised their roles in helping clients in these areas, albeit not disclosing them in such a prominent location in their annual reviews. For example, while also recognising the importance of these issues for its own operations, for Deloitte:

> Climate change, water scarcity, supply chain risks, waste and recycling are challenging the limits of traditional processes and technologies and demanding greater attention from business. As a result, environmental sustainability has moved from being a niche area overseen by specialists to becoming a [board level] priority. Environmental sustainability is now often a consideration in Deloitte client engagements and is increasingly

> a critical component of Deloitte's own operations, strategic initiatives and senior-level agendas.
>
> *(Deloitte 2020, p. 26)*

In support of this, a number a number of Deloitte services are outlined that aim to build the environmental management and accounting capabilities of Deloitte clients in the areas of "strategy, resource productivity, risk mitigation, attest services and supply chain" across "energy [including renewables], water, greenhouse gas emissions, plastics, circular economy and supply chain" (Deloitte 2020, p. 26).

Ernst and Young place developments in these types of services firmly in the context of arguments for social justice:

> When we look at the world today, we see a huge opportunity to use our skills, knowledge and experience to address some of the toughest challenges of our time – from inequality to climate change to tech-led job displacement – and drive sustainable, inclusive growth.
>
> *(EY 2020, p. 25)*

> Wherever they occur around the world, climate shocks hit the poorest in society hardest. The World Bank has estimated that, if global temperature rises continue unabated, it could result in 100 million more people living in extreme poverty by 2030. … EY remains committed to driving purposeful action that minimizes the negative impacts of businesses' activities on the environment. EY Climate Change and Sustainability Services teams help clients understand and act on the risks and opportunities arising from climate change, innovating in areas such as climate resilience, the circular economy, renewable energy, water accounting and alternative waste treatment. Working with clients to understand the sustainability issues that matter most to their businesses, we evaluate supply chains, conduct materiality assessments, create sustainability strategies, and more – ultimately helping clients reduce costs while unlocking sustainable business opportunities.
>
> *(EY 2020, p. 28)*

The 2019 annual reviews of the Big Four also mention a small number of specific environmental accounting thought leadership initiatives sponsored by the firms. These include, for example:

- An EY report that identified business opportunities in addressing the substantial level of greenhouse gases generated and water consumed by world agriculture at a time when levels of obesity are growing – and the market changes this could lead to;
- KPMG's advisory role to the Task Force on Climate-related Financial Disclosures (TCFD) to help "develop voluntary, consistent climate-related financial risk disclosures for use by companies in providing information to investors, lenders, insurers, and other stakeholders" (KPMG 2020, p. 4);
- KPMG's work reducing the climate impact of the fashion industry through a joint initiative *Sustainable Fashion: Committing to a Sustainable Future through the Fashion Industry Charter for Climate Action*;
- KPMG's Work on a number of World Business Council for Sustainable Development projects, including those related to the circular economy and using "KPMG's proprietary Dynamic Risk Assessment tool to enrich understanding of the severity,

likelihood, velocity and interconnectedness of environmental, social and governance risks in the food industry" (KPMG 2020, p. 45);
- PwC's Collaboration with the World Economic Forum on researching and writing its guide *How should corporate boards respond to climate change?*;
- PWC's collection of evidence "around carbon pricing and what's needed to achieve the Paris Agreement" (PwC 2019b, p. 2).

Environmental accounting thought leadership from the larger professional accounting bodies

Analysing contents of the 2019 annual reviews (or equivalents) of four large professional accounting bodies (the two largest Certified Accountancy bodies: AICPA (incorporating CIMA) and ACCA; and the two largest Chartered Accountancy bodies: ICAI and ICAEW) identified relatively few significant environmental accounting thought leadership activities other than from ICAEW. Commitments to some of the SDGs, including the environmentally focused SDG 13 (Climate Action), were mentioned briefly by ACCA and across two pages in AICPA's review; however, ICAEW discussed a broad range of substantive environmental sustainability initiatives in addition to its actions in support of the SDGs. As it appears from the material issues discussed in the 2019 integrated reports or annual reports/reviews of these large professional accounting bodies that ICAEW is taking a clear leadership role among them in advancing environmental sustainability, its contemporary initiatives in this area are the focus of this section as an example of how professional accounting bodies can help to advance these issues.[2]

ICAEW's 2019 Annual Review contains extensive discussion of the importance of the accounting profession recognising and taking meaningful action on environmental challenges, along with a broader range of social sustainability and responsibility issues. The environmental commitments are encapsulated in the statements that:

> We want to strengthen economies and build prosperity in ways that will last long into the future. There continues to be an increasing need for business and economic activity to be sustainable for the long term. … We recognise that business success is interdependent with both environmental and social responsibility. In that vein, we want to play our part in changing behaviour across the economy to live within its means.
>
> *(ICAEW 2020a, p. 18)*

> As a professional membership organisation, we represent a common voice for our members and the profession. We believe that the successful business of the future will be a sustainable business. As a profession we support economic development and prosperity, and as an organisation our vision is to have a net positive impact on the economy, society and environment. … we recognise that business has a significant impact on the environment, and although ICAEW does not operate in a business sector which causes significant pollution, we aim to promote and follow good environmental practices and reduce the negative impacts of our activities. On an international scale, we convene the debate on natural capital policy in government forums and financial institutions. This includes hosting the Capitals Coalition.
>
> *(ICAEW 2020a, p. 29)*

Environmental sustainability was a topic mentioned in four of the nine thought leadership programmes outlined in the report (the "sustainability", "public policy", "one young world" and the "more than a number" programmes, with issues of social sustainability also covered in several of these programmes).

Key environmental initiatives disclosed as part of ICAEW's sustainability thought leadership programme include (ICAEW 2020a, p. 18) the following:

- Linking ICAEW's vision of *A World of Strong Economies* to the SDGs through regarding the SDGs as a clear articulation of the global public interest. In this regard, ICAEW was at the vanguard of the profession's actions on sustainability when, in 2016, it embedded its strategy in sustainability through the SDGs. In recognising its Royal Charter obligation to always act in the public interest, ICAEW declared that the SDGs represented a broad global consensus on what the "public interest" meant. As such, since 2016, ICAEW's understanding and strategies towards acting in the public interest have been guided by the need to support achievement of the SDGs. This can be regarded as transformative thought leadership initiative and commitment, providing an exemplar to many other organisations globally.
- Working to position ICAEW as a contributor to the necessary transitioning to a socially and ecologically sustainable economy.
- Hosting the *Natural Capital Coalition* – "a global collaboration of 300 organisations who promote the importance of natural capital, and work to conserve and enhance it" (ICAEW 2020a, p. 18).
- A request from ICAEW's governing Council "for a plan to make ICAEW carbon-neutral and to build on measures already in place to further reduce our carbon footprint" (ICAEW 2020a, p. 18).
- Launching, with Deloitte, a video-based training programme on climate change aimed at a range of finance professionals.

Among the environmental accounting issues addressed in the other thought leadership programmes were:

- Focusing on accounting and climate change at ICAEW events in the "One Young World" summit held in London in October 2019, an event that convenes a large number of young leaders from many fields across the globe. During the event, ICAEW also hosted an SDG themed dinner for One Young World delegates, spotlighting the profession's key roles in contributing to achievement of the SDGs.
- As part of ICAEW's *More Than a Number* podcast series (with a reach of approximately 7.9 million), an episode featuring the Deputy Leader of the UK Green Party discussing "the financial impact of climate change and how well companies are prepared for it" (ICAEW 2020a, p. 21)
- Confronting leading politicians on sustainability issues during the 2019 UK General Election campaign as one of the major challenges that the future government would have to grapple with.

It is clear from the above sample of substantive and innovative environmental accounting initiatives that ICAEW regards positive environmental action as being a key part of the public interest remit of professional accounting bodies. While the other large professional accounting bodies whose annual reviews were analysed for this section provided varying levels of support for environmental accounting initiatives, few of these initiatives were considered significant enough by these bodies to be disclosed in their annual reviews. It will be interesting to see whether, and if so how, future increasing levels of public concern over environmental degradation lead to environmental accounting becoming a key priority for these other large professional bodies to the extent it has for ICAEW. This section has only provided a partial picture of these issues as it has not analysed the environmental accounting in initiatives of the many other professional accounting bodies. Readers interested in developing a deeper understanding of the public interest environmental accounting actions of any professional body should be able to find this information readily accessible on the websites of those bodies active in this space.

Enduring collaborative professional thought leadership projects

As noted earlier, over the years there have been a number of collaborative environmental accounting projects drawing on a broad range of expertise from across the accounting profession. This section outlines some of the initiatives currently promoted on the websites of two of the most enduring of these projects: A4S and Accountancy Europe.

A4S

Since the Prince of Wales launched his accounting for sustainability project in 2004, it has drawn on expertise from across the accounting profession to help advance social and environmental sustainability accounting. Given the nature of members of its networks, it is clear that A4S has considerable convening power to influence the development and adoption of pro-environmental accounting practices.

The aims of A4S are (A4S 2020a):

To inspire action by finance leaders to drive a fundamental shift towards resilient business models and a sustainable economy. To do this, A4S has three core aims that underpin everything we do:

- Inspire finance leaders to adopt sustainable and resilient business models
- Transform financial decision-making to enable an integrated approach, reflective of the opportunities and risks posed by environmental and social issues
- Scale up action across the global finance and accounting community.

They have five main communities with whom they work to deliver these aims (A4S 2020a):

- Chief Financial Officers (CFOs) and finance teams
- The accounting community
- Investors, capital markets and the wider finance community
- Governments, regulators and policymakers
- Business schools and academia.

There is a wealth of environmental accounting resources available on the A4S website to support the above communities in addressing A4S's aims. For detailed information, see www.accountingforsustainability.org/en/index.html. At the time of writing this chapter, the current initiatives listed on A4S's website included:

- Eleven projects focusing on different aspects of sustainability accounting, with participation from leading organisations. These were categorised into four overarching themes (A4S 2020b):

- Lead the way
    - Transform your decisions
    - Measure what matters
    - Access finance.
- A statement of support for achieving net-zero carbon, signed by Chief Financial Officers (CFOs) of 36 major organisations
- Nine practical guides from the A4S leadership network to help organisations engage in sustainability accounting practices. Many of these can also be very helpful to students of environmental accounting as teaching and learning resources. See www.accountingforsustainability.org/en/activities/a4s-essential-guide-series.html
- A knowledge hub providing access to many more social and environmental accounting resources.

Accountancy Europe

Accountancy Europe (formerly known as Fédération des Experts-comptables Européens or FEE) provides a collaborative space for 51 of the professional accounting bodies in Europe to work together on projects where their 1 million members are likely to benefit from such cross-profession cooperation. Sustainable finance is among the issues in which it is active.

Its website lists nine publications from 2018, 2019 and 2020 related to sustainable finance (Accountancy Europe 2020). These cover topics ranging from the increasing importance of sustainability for SMEs through to issues around corporate governance, regulation and reporting standards.

Conclusions

This chapter has explored the role of the accounting profession in providing thought leadership supporting the development environmental accounting and reporting. While ACCA played a crucial and visionary role in supporting the early development of environmental accounting and reporting, commitments and leadership from other sections of the accounting profession mostly came later (while the ACCA's role has ironically declined).

Today, as we face a planetary climate and environmental emergency, this chapter has provided insights into some of the accounting profession's current commitments to playing a major role in developing environmental accounting and reporting policies and practices. Activities range from helping a range of organisations use accounting to help identify and manage the risks associated with the outcomes of climate and environmental change, while managing the risks and realising the opportunities associated with a transition to a zero-carbon economy.

The Big Four global accountancy/professional services firms are influential in these endeavours both as exemplars (being among the largest global commercial organisations) and through the influence they exert on many businesses and governments in their advisory work. The professional accounting bodies are influential through the size and range of their membership bases and through their recognised commitment to act in the public interest.

In some innovative areas, thought leadership of accounting academics appears to lag behind thought leadership provided by the accounting profession. As our skills and expertise as academics position us strongly to provide in-depth reliable evidence to support effective thought leadership, there are many opportunities for academic researchers to work collaboratively with the profession to provide even more impactful thought leadership in improving the functioning of accounting policies and practices for a more environmentally sustainable world.

Notes

1 For example: The Association of International Certified Public Accountants (AICPA), incorporating the American Institute of Certified Public Accountants and the Charted Institute of Management Accountants (CIMA), has the largest membership of such bodies globally, with over 431,000 members across 130 jurisdictions (AICPA 2020). This gives it considerable reach compared to the size of its revenues (which in 2019 were US$319 million) and its workforce (1,211 employees in 2019). Another large certified accountancy professional body, the Association of Chartered Certified Accountants (ACCA), had 219,000 members worldwide and generated £206m revenue (approximately US$254 million) in its year ended 31 March 2019. Among the largest chartered accountancy bodies are the Institute of Chartered Accountants of India (ICAI) with over 291,000 members and revenue of ₹8,937 million (approximately US$111 million) for its year ended 31 March 2019 (ICAI 2019), and the Institute of Chartered Accountants in England and Wales (ICAEW) with approximately 154,000 members globally and £105 million revenue (approximately US$130 million) with 777 employees for its year ended 31 December 2019 (ICAEW 2020a).

2 I have to declare a potential conflict of interest here. My role as a co-opted member of ICAEW's governing Council from 2014 to 2021 might have affected my positive view of ICAEW's environmental accounting commitments and initiatives. I have, however, sought to be dispassionate in my writing of this section which is based on environmental accounting issues disclosed in the integrated reports or annual reviews/reports of the four bodies covered. I have also only used publicly available information on ICAEW to avoid risking disclosing any confidential information I have from my role in ICAEW Council.

References

A4S, 2020a. A4S Aims, Available from: www.accountingforsustainability.org/en/about-us/overview.html [Accessed 11 August 2020].

A4S, 2020b. Projects, Available from: www.accountingforsustainability.org/en/activities/projects.html [Accessed 11 August 2020].

ACCA, 2020. Our purpose and values, Available from: www.accaglobal.com/gb/en/about-us/our-mission-and-values.html [Accessed 22 June 2020].

Accountancy Europe, 2020, Sustainable Finance: Publications, Available from: www.accountancyeurope.eu/tag/sustainable-finance/?type=publications [Accessed 20 August 2020].

AICPA., 2020. AICPA Mission and History, Available from: www.aicpa.org/about/missionandhistory.html [Accessed 26 June 2020].

Bebbington, J., and Unerman, J., 2018. Achieving the United Nations sustainable development goals: an enabling role for accounting research, *Accounting, Auditing & Accountability Journal*, 31 (1), 2–24.

Bebbington, J., and Unerman, J., 2020. Advancing research into accounting and the UN sustainable development goals, *Accounting, Auditing and Accountability Journal,* 33() 1657-1670.

Bruce, R., 2015. Sustainability reporting: from acorn to mighty oak, *Accounting and Business*. April.

Deloitte, 2020. *Connect for impact: 2019 Global Impact Report*, Deloitte Touche Tohmatsu Limited.

EY, 2020. *How can we create long-term value for a better working world? EY Global Review 2019*, EY.

Fortune Media, 2020. Global 500, Available from: https://fortune.com/global500/ (Accessed 22 April 2020).

Gray, R. H., 1990. *The Greening of Accountancy: The Profession After Pearce*, Chartered Association of Certified Accountants, London.

Hook, L., 2019a. Donations pour in as Extinction Rebellion goes global, *Financial Times,* 11 October 2019. Online edition. Available from: www.ft.com/content/321f4402-ec31–11e9–85f4-d00e5018f061 [Accessed 3 July 2020].

Hook, L., 2019b. Millions of demonstrators join largest climate protest in history, *Financial Times,* 20 September 2019. Online edition, Available from: www.ft.com/content/d1b401d6-dbc1–11e9–8f9b–77216ebe1f17 [Accessed 3 July 2020].

ICAEW, 2020a. *Institute of Chartered Accountants in England and Wales Annual Review and Financial Statements*, ICAEW, London. Available from: www.icaew.com/-/media/corporate/files/about-icaew/who-we-are/annual-review/2019/annual-review–2019.ashx?la=en. [Accessed 18 March 2020].

ICAEW, 2020b. An overview of ICAEW, Available from: www.icaew.com/about-icaew/who-we-are/icaew-overview [Accessed 22 June 2020].

ICAI, 2019. *The Institute of Chartered Accountants of India 70th Annual Report (for year ended 31 March 2019)*, ICAI, New Delhi, 30 September 2019.

IFAC, 2020. *2019 Financial Statements*, International Federation of Accountants, New York, Available from: www.ifac.org/system/files/publications/files/IFAC–2019-Financial-Statements.pdf. [Accessed 20 April 2020].

KPMG, 2020. *People. Perspectives. Possibilities. 2019 KPMG Global Review*, KPMG International Cooperative.

Mathews, M. R., 1997. Twenty-five years of social and environmental accounting research: Is there a silver jubilee to celebrate?, *Accounting, Auditing & Accountability Journal,* 10 (4), 481–531.

Medley, P., 1997. Environmental accounting - what does it mean to professional accountants?, *Accounting, Auditing & Accountability Journal,* 10 (4), 594–600.

O'Dwyer, B., and Unerman, J., 2020. Shifting the focus of sustainability accounting from impacts to risks and dependencies: researching the transformative potential of TCFD reporting, *Accounting, Auditing & Accountability Journal,* 33 (5), 1113–1141.

OED, 2020. Thought leadership and thought leader, in *Oxford English Dictionary*. Oxford University Press, Oxford.

PwC, 2019a. *New world: Transforming talent and trust, 2019 Global Annual Review*, Available from: www.pwc.com/gx/en/about/global-annual-review–2019.html [Accessed 22 June 2020].

PwC, 2019b. *Our impact on society: PwC's Global Annual Review 2019*, PwC, Available from: www.pwc.com/gx/en/about-pwc/global-annual-review–2019/downloads/impact-on-society.pdf.[Accessed 22 June 2020].

The Club of Rome, 2019. *Planetary Emergency Plan: Securing a New Deal for People, Nature and Climate*, The Club of Rome, Winterthur, Switzerland, September 2019, Available from: https://clubofrome.org/wp-content/uploads/2020/02/PlanetaryEmergencyPlan_CoR–4.pdf.[Accessed 3 July 2020].

6

ENVIRONMENTAL ACCOUNTING AND 21ST-CENTURY SUSTAINABILITY GOVERNANCE

Carlos Larrinaga

Introduction

There is increasing evidence that global environmental problems have more far-reaching ramifications that have been previously appreciated. The proposition that there are planetary boundaries (Rockström et al. 2009) for human flourishing and of how the humanity is producing transformations at a geological scale (Davies 2016) provides a challenge to the integrity of socio-ecological systems (Lade et al. 2020). This framing has recently come to transform the representation of ecological problems and thereafter the demands for accounting scholarship that explores environmental accounting (see also Chapter 2 in this handbook). This chapter focuses on how environmental accounting can contribute to the governance of socio-ecological systems towards the safe operating space for humanity (itself the task of 21st century sustainability governance). I will inquire as to what type of accounting can assist the transformation of the relationship between organisations and the biosphere. To that end, I review the different understandings of sustainability governance that are found in the environmental accounting literature, illustrating the unfruitfulness of a corporate governance approach, and exploring the role of environmental accounting in adaptive and transformative forms of sustainability governance.

Anthropocene

We do not live in the Holocene anymore, but in a new epoch, the Anthropocene, characterised by the geological agency of the human being (Davies 2016; Bebbington et al. 2020a). Human actions are not just "the main driver of global environmental change" (Rockström et al. 2009, p. 472), but they also have an impact that could be observable in the future (by some form of future intelligence) in the form of geological markers (for an exploration, see Weisman 2007). Although humanity could be extinct in a geological distant future, it is paradoxical that being geological agents, we humans lack the skills to govern the consequences of our powers (Hamilton et al. 2015).

This paradox has motivated researchers to explore ways to connect biophysical sciences with business, economics and social science to study the dynamics of global society and biophysical processes (Österblom et al. 2015) in what is called coupled human–environment systems or socio-ecological systems (Young et al. 2006). Specifically, biophysical processes are characterised by the existence of "planetary boundaries", that is, thresholds beyond which the alterations generated in the Earth-system processes could have devastating consequences for humanity (Rockström et al. 2009; Steffen et al. 2015). Rockström et al. (2009) reviewed the expert-estimated boundaries for nine of such processes, with climate change and biosphere integrity (genetic and functional diversity) being considered as the core boundaries, considering their importance for the Earth system. In addition, this framework seeks to assess the aggregated interference of global society in biophysical processes (Lade et al. 2020) to reach a conclusion on the sustainability of the planetary socio-ecological system. For example, one of the variables accounting for biosphere integrity is extinction rate, as the unique genetic material determines the potential resilience for the biosphere (Steffen et al. 2015). The boundary proposed by scientists for this process is less than ten extinct species per million species-year, but the pressure of human activities is estimated to cause this factor to be between 100 and 1,000, well beyond the proposed boundary (Steffen et al. 2015).

Rockström et al. (2009) also proposed the notion of the "safe operating space for humanity", which has been defined by Lade et al. (2020) "as those combinations of human impacts on the planetary boundaries that cause no planetary boundary to be transgressed" (p. 122). Different analyses (Rockström et al. 2009; Steffen et al. 2015; Lade et al. 2020) concluded that the variables measuring the state of the different Earth processes indicate that socio-ecological systems are operating outside the safe operating space. To this framing, Raworth (2017) added social minimums to come up with a "safe and just" operating space for humanity.

Navigating back towards a safe (and just) operating space

Considering that humanity is beyond the safe operating space, as well as our limited capacity to transform planetary boundaries, the only part of the equation on which humanity can make a difference is on our own impact on Earth processes. This prompts the question of whether and how the capacity to govern the dynamics of the Anthropocene can be built.

Lade et al. (2020) invited for a trajectory leading "towards the safe operating space and a Holocene-like state of the Earth system" (p. 122), something they call "sustainability governance". This is the notion of sustainability governance that informs this chapter and, therefore, it concerns the governance of human impact on the nine Earth processes identified in the planetary boundaries framework, that is, climate change, biological integrity (genetic diversity and functional diversity), land-system change, freshwater use, biochemical flows (phosphorus and nitrogen), ocean acidification, atmospheric aerosol loading, stratospheric ozone depletion and novel entities (Steffen et al. 2015). Chapters in Part 5 of this handbook address how environmental accounting is developing in response to the challenges of climate change, biodiversity and freshwater availability.

Despite the biophysical relevance of the processes mentioned above, to be meaningful in social terms, they need to be translated in terms of human activities. For example, Gerten et al. (2020) have estimated the capacity of the global food system to feed humanity, finding that it could currently support 3.4 billion people respecting strictly the planetary boundaries. This scenario is obviously not providing a safe operating space because it is unable to feed all the world population. However, they demonstrate how specific sustainable forms of production and consumption could lead the food system to the safe operating space (feeding up to 10.2 billion people). For more information and proposals to support healthy diets in a safe operating space, see the EAT–Lancet Commission (Willett et al. 2019).

Sustainability governance could be framed in terms of robust scientific structures addressing one (e.g. the Convention on Biological Diversity) or more (e.g. the United Nations' Sustainable Development Goals – SDGs) critical Earth System processes (Bebbington and Unerman 2018; Dahlmann et al. 2019; Folke et al. 2019). Those structures provide a reference point for the objectives of sustainability governance and the trajectory towards a safe operating space, based on scientific research. For example, SDGs include 17 goals, developed into 169 targets and 232 indicators (Bebbington and Unerman 2018), covering the most important challenges from a socio-ecological systems perspective.

While the handbook's focus on environmental accounting centres a concern with ecological matters, sustainability governance can and is being mobilised to address issues of justice. Apart from the integration of social aspects into SDGs themselves, the recent Regulation 2017/821 of the European Union concerning due diligence obligations for importers of some raw materials originating from conflict-affected and high-risk areas is an example of fighting structural human right abuses (European Union 2017). National examples include the United Kingdom Modern Slavery Act or the French Corporate Duty ofVigilance Law (Folke et al. 2019).

Organisations and the Anthropocene

Sustainability governance is framed in terms of robust scientific and/or ethical structures inherent within trajectories towards the safe operating space for humanity (Lade et al. 2020). The question that concerns this chapter is the role of accounting in sustainability governance. More specifically, what kind of environmental accounting can identify where organisations are challenging the integrity of socio-ecological systems and what accounting techniques/tools can assist the transformation of the relationship between organisations and the biosphere to promote the desired global sustainable change? At a very initial level, it could be said that sustainability governance requires reliable information on Earth systems processes from the agents (often, but not solely organisations) that create these impacts. This may require some kind of mandatory and structured reporting requirements for certain "keystone" actors (see Österblom et al. 2015 and below). Notwithstanding the importance of those logics, the Anthropocene adds different layers of complexity to the understanding of environmental accounting (Bebbington et al. 2020a).

First, although in Modernity we tend to think about nature and society as two different ontological entities (Hamilton 2015), the Anthropocene has evidenced the coupled and dynamic nature of social and biophysical systems (Chaffin et al. 2016). The Anthropocene requires the integration of science and society. While social activities collectively alter Earth systems, the dynamics, resilience and feedback loops of Earth systems make their future trajectories uncertain in some cases, and unknown in others. For example, Österblom et al. (2015) showed how the increasing demand of seafood production is shaping marine ecosystems, while at the same time Steffen et al. (2015) reported how appropriate variables are not available for measuring changes in biosphere integrity. Steffen et al. used instead a less appropriate measure (extinction rate), but are still unable to reduce uncertainty in the ranges of proposed scientific boundaries (1–100) and current value (100–1,000). Bebbington et al. (2020a) contended that accounting information needs to incorporate this complexity (uncertainty) and will need to be more "tightly linked to global environmental change, although the source of these impacts might be obscured" (Bebbington et al. 2020a, p. 160).

Second, organisations are central actors of the Anthropocene. In particular, multinational corporations (MNCs) are a major force shaping socio-ecological systems and critical processes of the biosphere (Whiteman et al. 2013; Folke et al. 2019).

> [MNCS] have become a defining feature of the interconnected planet of people and nature, with humans as a hyper-dominant species in the biosphere affecting global patterns of ecological change.
>
> *(Folke et al. 2019, p. 1)*

For example, Österblom et al. (2015) studied MNCs as global marine socio-ecosystem's keystone actors, that is, actors with a disproportionate agency to influence the seafood production industry. Industries such as agriculture, forestry, seafood, cement, minerals and fossil energy are also of particular importance (Folke et al. 2019) for key biophysical Earth processes. Apart from MNCs, Bebbington and Larrinaga (2014) highlighted the role of other entities (see also Bebbington and Unerman 2018; Rinaldi 2019), including a broader set of socio-economic arrangements, such as public sector organisations and resource governance pools (Thomson et al. 2014) or certification regimes (Tregidga et al. 2019).

Although organisations are *already* part of the biosphere, modernity has led to conceive them (as part of the society) as separate entities; organisations conventionally saw the environment as "out there" (Hopwood 2009; Russell et al. 2017). However, what the Anthropocene teaches us is the artificiality of such a distinction. Considering the importance of organisations in the Anthropocene, a trajectory towards the safe operating space requires to rebuild their connections with Earth systems (Bebbington et al. 2020a). However, accounting is not providing the appropriate information about the interaction between corporate activities and the global ecological processes. For example, the scope of indicators is usually limited to the accounting entity defined by financial control (Antonini and Larrinaga 2017). Likewise, accounting is contributing to assign positive values to carbon reserves that, according to science and global climate change governance processes, will not be combusted (Bebbington et al. 2020b).

In summary, Anthropocene is characterised by complex tightly coupled social and natural systems, with organisations being a central driving force in these couplings. Likewise, there is a need (if we are to operate within planetary boundaries) to articulate and reenvision the connections between organisations and the biosphere. Building on these two points, the chapter now moves to consider how accounting fits within a plurality of understandings of sustainability governance.

Sustainability governance

I proposed above a working definition of sustainability governance that was framed in terms of scientific or ethical robust structures that supported organisational trajectories towards a safe and just operating space for humanity. This proposal, however, has to be contrasted with current understandings of sustainability governance. Rinaldi (2019) identified different streams of accounting research that seek to address sustainability governance, from those self-centred in the conventional objectives of the organisation (strategic aims, risks and administrative structure), to those that are more closely aligned with the perspective presented here (i.e. focused on the governance of social and environmental challenges).

This plurality of understandings of sustainability governance is generated by the interplay between sustainability and corporate social responsibility, the evolution of corporate governance (Elkington 2006; Rodrigue et al. 2013; Peters and Romi 2015; Adams 2017; Elsayed and Ammar

2020) and broader scale adaptative and transformative sustainability governance (Chaffin et al. 2016; Folke et al. 2019; Bebbington et al. 2020a). In the following sections, I outline the plurality of understandings of sustainability governance, from pristine and reformist formulations of corporate governance to adaptive and transformative sustainability governance.

Corporate governance

As the trajectory towards the safe and just operating space requires structural shifts in the relationship between organisations (specially MNCs) and the biosphere, researchers have turned their attention to the position where key corporate decisions are made (i.e. the board of directors) and the mechanisms of corporate governance that steer organisations. As different authors stress the importance of a reform of corporate governance to include sustainability issues (Elkington 2006; Adams 2017), it is important to review the dominant model of corporate governance (Rinaldi 2019), at least to understand the implications for sustainability governance.

Corporate governance (see Table 6.1) responds to the dysfunctionality created by the pursuit of self-interest in the context of separation between control and ownership of capital that characterises large corporations, in such a way that self-interested managers could lack incentives to maximise the value of capital for its owners (shareholders). Corporate governance research has focused on analysing the mechanisms that align the interests of the managers with those of capital (Bushman and Smith 2001).

> Two hundred years of work in economics and finance implies that in the absence of externalities and monopoly (and when all goods are priced), social welfare is maximized when each firm in an economy maximises its total market value.
>
> *(Jensen 2001. p. 297)*

Jensen explains how stakeholder theory and corporate social responsibility are flawed because the corporation cannot maximise simultaneously different objectives and those theories do not specify how a trade-off between different objectives can be made. Under this lack of theoretical specification, Jensen argues, self-interested stakeholders can influence managers to allocate resources to satisfy their ends, while legitimating managers to please their own appetites, everything at the cost of making society worse-off.

> With the widespread failure of centrally planned socialist and communist economies, those who wish to use non-market forces to reallocate wealth find great solace in the playing field that stakeholder theory opens to them.
>
> *(Jensen 2001 p. 306)*

This model of corporate governance that has dominated mainstream accounting research provides very little space for environmental accounting. For example, the fact that the European accounting regulation "derived from a tradition which recognized the *social* (…) and the role of the State in enabling and facilitating rather than transcending market processes" (Hopwood 1994, p. 250; my emphasis)[1] is considered as a politicisation of accounting in processes in which labour unions and other stakeholders are represented, increasing the agency cost of monitoring managers (Ball et al. 2000).

In summary, environmental accounting's place in this pristine version of corporate governance is as a diversion of management attention from their fiduciary duty to maximise shareholder value and an unethical practice draining social welfare. Despite the evidence reviewed above, this pristine version is more common than it might appear.

A reform: enlightened corporate governance

Despite his criticism of stakeholder theory and corporate social responsibility, Jensen (2001) conceded that the maximisation of shareholder value requires the organisation to be on good terms with important stakeholders. It is what this author names "enlightened stakeholder theory" or what I prefer to describe as "enlightened corporate governance".

Enlightened corporate governance (see Table 6.1) has become extremely popular, particularly in the corporate social responsibility literature (Elkington 2006; Gimenez and Sierra 2013),

Table 6.1 Corporate governance versus sustainability governance

	Pristine corporate governance	*Enlightened corporate governance*	*Adaptative sustainability governance*	*Transformative sustainability governance*
Ends promoted by governance	Maximisation of shareholder value	Maximisation of shareholder value	Mitigating and adapting to socio-ecological change	Regime shift towards the safe operating space
Scope	Limited corporation	Limited corporation	Socio-ecological systems	Socio-ecological systems
Focus	Agency problem	Agency problem License to operate	Relation between society and the biosphere	Relation between society and the biosphere
Structures that enable governance	Market, board of directors Corporate law	Market, board of directors Corporate law	Self-governed and self-organised institutions	Problematisations
Mechanisms that create governance	Contracts between managers and shareholders Monitoring by the board of directors	Contracts and monitoring (including monitoring of risk and opportunities created by stakeholders)	Rules Scientific engagement Support by external actors	New visibilities
Logic	Self-interest	Self-interest Risk and opportunities	Collective action Enlightened self-interest	Common good Power
Governance output	Management alignment with shareholder value maximisation	Stakeholders and managers aligned with shareholder value creation	New information considered Fiduciary duties adapted	Radical and systemic changes
Putative governance outcomes	Sound allocation of resources	Sound allocation of resources	Steady flow of ecosystem services	New organisational designs Social transformation

(continued)

Table 6.1 Cont.

	Pristine corporate governance	*Enlightened corporate governance*	*Adaptative sustainability governance*	*Transformative sustainability governance*
Limitations of governance	Disruption by other objectives; stakeholder theory	Socio-ecological systems	Might not be sufficient given the pace of ecological change	Resistance Politically undesirable
Governance functions performed by environmental accounting	Destroys good governance	Good relations with stakeholders	Connecting, mediating	Creating visibilities, problematising
Scope of environmental accounts	Greenwashing	Stakeholders' interests	Connection with ecosystems and planetary boundaries	Alternative accounts Engagements with science
Structures and mechanisms that enable environmental accounts	Not applicable	Legitimacy Reputation	Science Non-financial reporting regulation SDGs	Science New information technologies (Folke)
Environmental accounting outputs	Irrelevant	Voluntary sustainability reports	Dialogues Mandated indicators crossing scales	Counter accounts?

as it is increasingly evident that supply chain ethics, human rights, corruption or climate change are a source of risks and opportunities that determine corporate success (Adams 2017).

The environmental accounting literature interested in corporate governance has focused on one specific control mechanism, that is, monitoring by the board of directors (Haniffa and Cooke 2005; Michelon and Parbonetti 2012; Rodrigue et al. 2013; Peters and Romi 2015; Adams 2017). Directors' responsibilities include providing the leadership for, and supervising, the ethical conduct of the corporation and the responsibility with regard to stakeholders' demands, including societal environmental expectations (Rodrigue et al. 2013). Therefore, studies within this perspective typically hypothesise that specific configurations of governance mechanisms could create higher environmental consciousness in the organisation, helping to better identify, address and disclose corporate risks and opportunities. The presence of non-executive directors, gender diversity, the existence of an environmental committee, the appointment of an environmental officer as well as their specialised knowledge are governance mechanisms that have been tested in the environmental accounting literature.

Independent and more gender-diverse boards of directors are expected to bring a broader set of experiences and opinions that better represent the diverse interests of stakeholders and, therefore, would be more inclined to sponsor environmental disclosure. The results of empirical studies, however, are inconclusive (Haniffa and Cooke 2005; Michelon and Parbonetti 2012; Liao et al. 2015). Likewise, environmental committees and environmental officers, especially skilful ones, can enhance the identification and disclosure of environmental risks. Here, again, studies report conflicting results (Michelon and Parbonetti 2012; Liao et al. 2015; Peters and Romi 2015) excepted for the positive influence of specialised knowledge (Peters and Romi 2015; Adams 2017). Moreover, those mechanisms do not seem to be associated with corporate environmental performance (Rodrigue et al. 2013).

In particular, Rodrigue et al. (2013) contended that environmental governance mechanisms are not associated with changes in environmental performance but are used to fabricate congruence with stakeholders' expectations. This is consistent with Jensen's (2001) arguments:

> [I]t is obvious that we cannot maximise the long-term market value of an organisation if we ignore or mistreat any important constituency. We cannot create value without good relations with customers, employees, financial backers, suppliers, regulators, communities, and so on. But having said that, we can now use the [shareholder] value criterion for choosing among those competing interests.
>
> *(p. 309)*

There is now abundant environmental reporting research observing how managers voluntarily disclose positive environmental information to improve their position considering the proprietary costs of disclosure (Clarkson et al. 2008), to gain or maintain legitimacy and access to valuable social resources (Deegan 2002; Cho and Patten 2007; Elsayed and Ammar 2020) or to manage the reputation of the firm (Bebbington et al. 2008; Cho et al. 2012).

As we can see, on the one hand, enlightened corporate governance boils always down to the fiduciary duty to maximise shareholder value. Enlightened corporate governance is a good descriptive approach of the behaviour of corporations *outside* the safe operating space, acting and making decisions as if we were not in the Anthropocene. But this perspective neglects the dynamics of socio-ecological systems, considers that appropriate information is available to make decisions and ignores most externalities as well as unequal distribution of power.

On the other hand, the consideration of environmental issues in boardrooms discussions is still essential for producing substantive change in corporate practices, disclosure and performance (Adams 2017). Adams (2017) found that different approaches in corporate governance between Australian and South African companies (the latter being more enlightened) were explained by the national context, showing that there is nothing immanent to corporate governance, or to the relationship between shareholder value and sustainability. Instead, governance can be seen as an adaptive instrument that performs different functions in different institutional contexts. Considering pragmatically that corporations will still need to be governed in the trajectory towards the safe and just operating space, it is important to think of corporate governance instrumentally.

Adaptive sustainability governance

The oil and gas industry is not inactive in terms of the genre of corporate governance described above. For example, Elsayed and Ammar (2020) described how BP's corporate governance reacted and evolved in the aftermath of the Gulf of Mexico Deepwater Horizon oil spill in an effort to maintain legitimacy. Moreover, the oil and gas industry featured in 2017 as the top industry in terms of corporate social responsibility reporting (KPMG 2017). However, in a planetary boundaries framework it would be relevant to question whether a 30% increase in oil production and a 126% increase in gas production, between 1990 and 2015[2], conform to expectations for a safe operating space for humanity: climate change is a core planetary boundary (see also Bebbington et al. 2020b). Similar trajectories can be observed, for example, in the use of the ocean across various industries and activities (Jouffray et al. 2020). In these contexts, planetary boundaries have already been transgressed and the question is how to navigate back towards a safe operating space. Conventional corporate governance does not seem to contribute to this task, rather the opposite (Gray 2006). Shifting this trajectory requires governing sustainability at a broader scale.

Sustainability governance, therefore, is the process of both the assessment of the state of socio-ecological systems (based on robust scientific and ethical structures) and the ensuing set of rules, norms and normativity production systems (including enforcement mechanisms) that regulate socio-economic arrangements such that we might craft a trajectory towards a safe and just operating space for humanity. In this task, sustainability governance can adopt two different approaches: adaptive and transformative. Adaptive sustainability governance has emerged with the objective of preventing, mitigating or adapting to unpredictable and sudden changes in the configuration of local and global socio-ecological systems, to ensure a continuous "stream of ecosystem services including raw materials, food and other ecosystem functions such as water purification and nutrient cycling" (Chaffin et al. 2016, p. 401).

Adaptive governance is associated with the perceived failure of two major alternative governance structures, that is, market and centralised bureaucracies, in dealing with socio-ecological challenges (Steelman 2016). As socio-ecological changes can neither be planned by central bureaucracies nor be captured by the market, adaptive governance is inspired by self-organised and self-governed institutions (Ostrom 1990) and hence needs to be polycentric, experimental and continuously monitored (Jacob et al. 2019).

Adaptive sustainability governance seeks to maintain a desired configuration of socio-ecological systems that allows a steady flow of ecosystem services. It often emerges in wicked-problem contexts, where scientific expertise cannot deliver technical solutions, but the definition of both problems and courses of actions need to be negotiated with those affected (Bebbington and Larrinaga 2014). It is often found in small-scale self-organised users of natural resources, with the support of national agencies, and non-governmental organisations, in response to environmental crisis (Chaffin et al. 2016). Effective self-governing institutions cannot be prescribed but are to be constructed locally (Steelman 2016).

Although adaptive governance is associated with local users of natural resources, Folke et al. (2019) observed how, at a larger scale, progressive corporations are supplementing the market and environmental regulation and engaging in substantive sustainability efforts. Considering that those large corporations "have become a defining feature of the interconnected planet of people and nature" (p. 1), they propose to expand the focus from corporate social responsibility to corporate biosphere stewardship.

Adaptive governance, in contrast with corporate governance, problematises scale. In fact, never-ending growth seems to be a prerequisite for shareholder value creation. However, safeguarding the resilience of the biosphere requires considering the planetary boundaries and, therefore, that eco-efficiency or improvements by individual companies are not enough (Dahlmann et al. 2019), because in default of collective action structures (Ostrom 1990) marginal improvements would be offset by a free rider.

Following an adaptive framing, Österblom et al. (2017) have led an initiative (and natural experiment) with the worldwide largest corporations in the seafood production industry to stimulate adaptive governance and ocean stewardship. The SeaBOS initiative is a science–business engagement, trying to influence future collective action in the industry to foster the resilience of declining marine ecosystems and to ensure a continuous stream of ecosystem services (see also Österblom et al. 2020). There is an emerging literature exploring the role of environmental accounting in this form of governance pointing towards different areas requiring research.

First, sustainability-relevant environmental accounting needs to consider issues of scale (Gray and Milne 2004; Gray 2010), with the integration of global goals in corporate management and accounting being problematic (Antonini and Larrinaga 2017; Bebbington et al. 2020b). It has been proposed that SDG indicators can perform this role (Bebbington and Unerman 2018; Dahlmann et al. 2019; Folke et al. 2019). The integration of corporate performance within broader objectives will require accounting researchers to engage both with wider (inter-disciplinary) discussions about sustainable development (Bebbington and Larrinaga 2014) and with (trans-disciplinary) socio-economic arrangements affecting, and affected by, planetary boundaries (Bebbington et al. 2020a; Jouffray et al. 2020).

Second, environmental accounting researchers will need to reconsider the topics of relevance for research. Bebbington and Larrinaga (2014) proposed an applied sustainability science approach focusing on specific problems, which would allow to gain a nuanced understanding of the specific issues and contexts (see also Bebbington et al. 2017). For example, in the case of oceans, the economic expansion has produced what Jouffray et al. (2020) call the "Blue Acceleration", that is, an unprecedented anthropogenic pressure on the ocean that requires urgent attention. Further relevant areas include climate change (Chapter 26 in this handbook), water (Chapter 27) and biodiversity (Chapter 28). The Carbon Disclosure Project (CDP) and the Task Force on Climate-related Financial Disclosures (TCFD) could be seen as efforts by corporations and investors to use carbon disclosures to mitigate or adapt to climate change.

Third, further research needs to broaden the scope of studied organisations (usually large listed corporations) to embrace other socio-economic arrangements (Bebbington and Larrinaga 2014; Bebbington and Unerman 2018; Bebbington et al. 2020a) or ecosystems (Cuckston 2017; Russell et al. 2017) where environmental accounting could be performing a role.

Fourth, environmental accounting can contribute to adaptive governance debates by further theorising notions of accountability, stewardship, corporate boundaries and regulation (Bebbington et al. 2017). For example, the consequences for accountability of increasing transparency (Folke et al. 2019; Nyström et al. 2019) will need to be explored, as well as the interplay between accountability and stewardship (Bebbington et al. 2020a). Likewise, the distinction between public and private environmental accounting regulation will need to be relaxed to cope with adaptive sustainability governance (see Chapter 10).

Finally, environmental accounting will need to explore its relationship with science. Sustainability governance needs to connect robust scientific structures with action (Folke et al. 2019). Here, an initiative deserving attention is the World Benchmarking Alliance, which has identified 2,000 global keystone companies in terms of meeting the SDGs (see Österblom et al. 2015 for the concept of keystone).

Transformative corporate governance

Transformative corporate governance reflects the theme of the human limitations to cope with the Anthropocene. Central to this notion is the fact that adaptive governance might not be sufficient to navigate back towards the safe operating space for humanity because our current societies are fundamentally framed along unsustainable institutional designs. In this regard, adaptation and mitigation alone are unlikely to yield a desired socio-ecological configuration (Chaffin et al. 2016).

> The rapid trajectory of global change is likely outpacing societal abilities to preserve desirable regimes in many [social-ecological systems] nested within a global system.
>
> *(Chaffin et al. 2016, p. 405)*

Addressing ecological problems is likely, therefore, to require radical and systemic changes in the socio-ecological systems, involving values, patterns of behaviour and governance.

Following Chaffin et al. (2016), transformative sustainability governance is a point of departure from adaptive governance: conserving the latter's structures but adding additional capacities to produce new socio-ecological systems when the existing systems are unsustainable. Three aspects need to be considered in this context. First, unsustainable socio-ecological configurations can remain taken for granted and alternatives to it are unconceivable. Transformative governance is about framing sustainability issues as problematic and identifying "acceptable solutions spaces" (Meadowcroft 2011, p. 73). Second, Jacob et al. (2019) contended that transformative changes are likely to emerge in niches and diffuse in bottom-up dynamics. However, Chaffin et al. (2016) observed that self-organised approaches can often be insufficient to govern transformations, with formal regulation and enforcement playing increasing roles over time. Finally, as sustainability is normative, defining the direction of transformative sustainability, governance and the solutions envisaged are an inherently political activity (Meadowcroft 2011; Chaffin et al. 2016). For example, changing the focus away from shareholder maximisation and GDP growth, patterns of mass consumption, mass tourism or automobile personal mobility would require substantive political resources.

The role of environmental accounting in transformative sustainability governance has yet to be fully articulated. However, the governmentality literature can provide some insight to explore how accounting can problematise socio-ecological configurations and define the potential area of solutions. Accounting, in general, has been viewed as a calculative device rendering specific realities visible and amenable to intervention (Miller and Napier 1993; Miller and Power 2013). Accounting has, thus, the capacity to introduce new elements to socio-ecological systems, give new significance to existing ones, as well as reshape the relations between them. For example, Jensen et al. (2017) studied how calculative practices created the conditions for the transformation of urban cycling in the 1900–2015 period from a safety problem to a transport mode. Thomson et al. (2014) studied how accounting devices created the opportunity to produce sustainability transformations in a public sector organisation. Bebbington et al. (2020b) problematised the valuation of unburnable carbon. Likewise, experiments such as the *Common Good Balance Sheet* (Jacob et al. 2019), focusing on sufficiency and absolute reduction, provide stimulation for experimentation.

More generally, environmental accounting needs to explore the extent to which interdisciplinary work with scientists, as well as the scientific evidence provided, can facilitate problematisations and the identification of solution spaces in the sense suggested by Folke et al. (2019), triggering transformations. Initiatives and debates about science-based targets demand the attention of environmental accounting researchers (Walenta 2020).

In summary, given the current operation of society outside the safe operating space, the dominance of large corporations and the shrinking window of opportunity to transform socio-ecological systems (Folke et al. 2019), research on how environmental accounting can problematise current configurations is vital.

Conclusion

Sustainability governance aims to regulate and imagine socio-economic arrangements for a trajectory towards the safe operating space for humanity. Although the accounting literature has referred to corporate governance as a mechanism producing movement in a sustainability direction, it is very unlikely that a set of practices devised to ensure the sole objective of producing value for shareholders will produce the level of required change. Explanations of environmental accounting in relation to corporate governance are familiar, ranging from protecting against shareholders extracting excess value from organisations and the natural environment to practices that are symbolic from an environmental perspective.

This chapter proposed two additional, and more substantive, forms of sustainability governance. Adaptive governance strives to mitigate and adapt to changes in the configuration of socio-ecological systems to ensure a steady flow of ecosystem services. Associated environmental accounting will need to reconnect different scales (e.g. organisations with planetary boundaries); deal with specific issues in a wide array of contexts including, and beyond, the corporation; and reconsider established theories, such as accountability.

Adaptive governance, however, might not be sufficient, given the pace of transformation experimented by socio-ecological systems. Transformative governance problematises current configurations and seeks a regime shift that is inherently political. Although there is limited research on correlated environmental accounting, some governmentality ideas as well as engagement with science can provide insight for further research in this area.

Notes

1 According to the widespread and popular version in the corporate governance literature, this tradition is deterministically characteristic of the so-called code-law countries, and derives from the Romano-Germanic legal tradition (La Porta et al. 1998).

2 Data retrieved from Data and Statistics (www.iea.org/data-and-statistics) by the International Energy Agency.

References

Adams, C.A. 2017. Conceptualising the contemporary corporate value creation process. *Accounting, Auditing & Accountability Journal,* 30(4), 906–931.

Antonini, C. and Larrinaga, C. 2017. Planetary boundaries and sustainability indicators. A survey of corporate reporting boundaries. *Sustainable Development,* 25(2), 123–137.

Ball, R., Kothari, S. P. and Robin, A. 2000. The effect of international institutional factors on properties of accounting earnings. *Journal of Accounting and Economics,* 29(1), 1–51.

Bebbington, J. and Larrinaga, C. 2014. Accounting and sustainable development: an exploration. *Accounting, Organizations and Society,* 39(6), 395–413.

Bebbington, J. and Unerman, J. 2018. Achieving the United Nations sustainable development goals: an enabling role for accounting research. *Accounting, Auditing & Accountability Journal,* 31(1), 2–24.

Bebbington, J., et al. 2020a. Accounting and accountability in the Anthropocene. *Accounting, Auditing & Accountability Journal,* 33(1), 152–177.

Bebbington, J., et al. 2020b. Fossil fuel reserves and resources reporting and unburnable carbon: investigating conflicting accounts. *Critical Perspectives on Accounting,* 66, 102083.

Bebbington, J., Larrinaga, C. and Moneva, J. M. 2008. Corporate social reporting and reputation risk management. *Accounting, Auditing & Accountability Journal,* 21(3), 337–361.

Bebbington, J., Russell, S. and Thomson, I. 2017. Accounting and sustainable development: reflections and propositions. *Critical Perspectives on Accounting,* 48, 21–34.

Bushman, R. M. and Smith, A. J. 2001. Financial accounting information and corporate governance. *Journal of Accounting and Economics,* 32(1–3), 237–333.

Chaffin, B. C., et al. 2016. Transformative environmental governance. *Annual Review of Environment and Resources,* 41(1), 399–423.

Cho, C. H. and Patten, D. M. 2007. The role of environmental disclosures as tools of legitimacy: a research note. *Accounting, Organizations and Society,* 32(7–8), 639–647.

Cho, C. H., et al. 2012. Do actions speak louder than words? An empirical investigation of corporate environmental reputation. *Accounting, Organizations and Society,* 37(1), 14–25.

Clarkson, P. M., et al. 2008. Revisiting the relation between environmental performance and environmental disclosure: an empirical analysis. *Accounting, Organizations and Society,* 33(4–5), 303–327.

Cuckston, T. 2017. Ecology-centred accounting for biodiversity in the production of a blanket bog. *Accounting, Auditing & Accountability Journal,* 30(7), 1537–1567.

Dahlmann, F. et al. 2019. Corporate actors, the UN sustainable development goals and earth system governance: a research agenda. *The Anthropocene Review,* 6(1–2), 167–176.

Davies, J., 2016. *The Birth of the Anthropocene.* Oakland, CA: University of California Press.

Deegan, C. 2002. The legitimising effect of social and environmental disclosures – a theoretical foundation. *Accounting, Auditing & Accountability Journal,* 15(3), 282–311.

Elkington, J. 2006. Governance for sustainability. *Corporate Governance: An International Review,* 14(6), 522–529.

Elsayed, N. and Ammar, S. 2020. Sustainability governance and legitimisation processes: Gulf of Mexico oil spill. *Sustainability Accounting, Management and Policy Journal,* 11(1), 253–278.

European Union, 2017. Regulation (EU) 2017/821 of the European Parliament and of the Council of 17 May 2017 laying down supply chain due diligence obligations for Union importers of tin, tantalum and tungsten, their ores, and gold originating from conflict-affected and high-risk areas. http://data.europa.eu/eli/reg/2017/821/oj.

Folke, C., et al. 2019. Transnational corporations and the challenge of biosphere stewardship. *Nature Ecology & Evolution,* 3(10), 1396–1403.

Gerten, D., et al. 2020. Feeding ten billion people is possible within four terrestrial planetary boundaries. *Nature Sustainability,* 3(3), 200–208.

Gimenez, C. and Sierra, V. 2013. Sustainable supply chains: governance mechanisms to greening suppliers. *Journal of Business Ethics,* 116(1), 189–203.

Gray, R. 2006. Social, environmental and sustainability reporting and organisational value creation?: Whose value? Whose creation? *Accounting, Auditing & Accountability Journal,* 19(6), 793–819.

Gray, R. 2010. Is accounting for sustainability actually accounting for sustainability…and how would we know? An exploration of narratives of organisations and the planet. *Accounting, Organizations and Society,* 35(1), 47–62.

Gray, R. and Milne, M. 2004. Towards reporting on the triple bottom line: mirages, methods and myths. In: Henriques, A. (ed.), *Triple Bottom Line: Does It All Add up?: Assessing the Sustainability of Business and CSR.* London: Earthscan Publications.

Hamilton, C., 2015. Human destiny in the Anthropocene. In: Hamilton, C., Bonneuil, C. and Gemenne, F. (eds.), *The Anthropocene and the Global Environmental Crisis.* London: Routledge, pp. 32–43.

Hamilton, C., Bonneuil, C. and Gemenne, F., 2015. Thinking the Anthropocene. In: Hamilton, C., Bonneuil, C. and Gemenne, F. (eds.), *The Anthropocene and the Global Environmental Crisis.* London: Routledge, pp. 1–14.

Haniffa, R. M. and Cooke, T. E. 2005. The impact of culture and governance on corporate social reporting. *Journal of Accounting and Public Policy,* 24(5), 391–430.

Hopwood, A. G. 1994. Some reflections on 'The harmonization of accounting within the EU'. *European Accounting Review,* 3(2), 241–254.

Hopwood, A. G. 2009. Accounting and the environment. *Accounting, Organizations and Society,* 34 433–439.

Jacob, K. et al. 2019. Governance for the sustainable economy: Institutional innovation from the bottom up? *GAIA - Ecological Perspectives for Science and Society,* 28(1), 204–209.

Jensen, J. S., Cashmore, M. and Elle, M. 2017. Reinventing the bicycle: how calculative practices shape urban environmental governance. *Environmental Politics,* 26(3), 459–479.

Jensen, M. C. 2001. Value maximisation, stakeholder theory, and the corporate objective function. *Journal of Applied Corporate Finance,* 14(3), 8–21.

Jouffray, J.-B. et al. 2020. The blue acceleration: the trajectory of human expansion into the ocean. *One Earth,* 2(1), 43–54.

KPMG, 2017. *The Road Ahead. The KPMG Survey of Corporate Responsibility Reporting 2017.* KPMG, available at: www.kpmg.com/sustainability.

La Porta, R. et al. 1998. Law and finance. *Journal of Political Economy,* 106(6), 1113–1155.

Lade, S. J. et al. 2020. Human impacts on planetary boundaries amplified by Earth system interactions. *Nature Sustainability,* 3(2), 119–128.

Liao, L., Luo, L. and Tang, Q. 2015. Gender diversity, board independence, environmental committee and greenhouse gas disclosure. *The British Accounting Review,* 47(4), 409–424.

Meadowcroft, J. 2011. Engaging with the politics of sustainability transitions. *Environmental Innovation and Societal Transitions,* 1(1), 70–75.

Michelon, G. and Parbonetti, A. 2012. The effect of corporate governance on sustainability disclosure. *Journal of Management & Governance,* 16(3), 477–509.
Miller, P. and Napier, C. 1993. Genealogies of calculation. *Accounting, Organizations and Society,* 18(7–8), 631–647.
Miller, P. and Power, M. 2013. Accounting, organizing, and economizing: connecting accounting research and organization theory. *The Academy of Management Annals,* 7(1), 557–605.
Narver, J. C. 1971. Rational management responses to external effects. *Academy of Management Journal,* 14(1), 99–115.
Nyström, M. et al. 2019. Anatomy and resilience of the global production ecosystem. *Nature,* 575(7781), 98–108.
Österblom, H. et al. 2015. Transnational corporations as "keystone actors" in marine ecosystems. *PLoS ONE,* 10(5), e0127533.
Österblom, H. et al. 2017. Emergence of a global science–business initiative for ocean stewardship. *Proceedings of the National Academy of Sciences,* 114(34), 9038–9043.
Österblom, H., Cvitanovic, C., van Putten, L., Addison, P., Bebbington, J., Hall, J., Ison, S., Jouffray, J.-B., LeBris, A., Mynott, S., Reid, D. and Sugimoto, A. 2020. Science-industry collaboration – sideways or highways to ocean sustainability? *One Earth,* 3(1), 79-88.
Ostrom, E. 1990. *Governing the Commons. The Evolution of Institutions for Collective Action.* Cambridge, UK: Cambridge University Press.
Peters, G. F. and Romi, A. M. 2015. The association between sustainability governance characteristics and the assurance of corporate sustainability reports. *AUDITING: A Journal of Practice & Theory,* 34(1), 163–198.
Raworth, K. 2017. *Doughnut Economics: Seven Ways to Think Like a 21st-Century Economist.* Vermont: Chelsea Green Publishing.
Rinaldi, L. 2019. Accounting for sustainability governance: the enabling role of social and environmental accountability research. *Social and Environmental Accountability Journal,* 39(1), 1–22.
Rockström, J., et al. 2009. A safe operating space for humanity. *Nature,* 461(7263), 472–475.
Rodrigue, M., Magnan, M. and Cho, C. H. 2013. Is environmental governance substantive or symbolic? An empirical investigation. *Journal of Business Ethics,* 114(1), 107–129.
Russell, S., Milne Markus, J. and Dey, C. 2017. Accounts of nature and the nature of accounts: critical reflections on environmental accounting and propositions for ecologically informed accounting. *Accounting, Auditing & Accountability Journal,* 30(7), 1426–1458.
Steelman, T., 2016. Adaptive governance. In: Ansell, C. and Torfing, J. (eds.), *Handbook on Theories of Governance.* Cheltenham: Edward Elgar Publishing.
Steffen, W., et al. 2015. Planetary boundaries: guiding human development on a changing planet. *Science,* 347(6223), 1259855.
Thomson, I., Grubnic, S. and Georgakopoulos, G. 2014. Exploring accounting-sustainability hybridisation in the UK public sector. *Accounting, Organizations and Society,* 39(6), 453–476.
Tregidga, H., Kearins, K. and Collins, E. 2019. Towards transparency? Analysing the sustainability governance practices of ethical certification. *Social and Environmental Accountability Journal,* 39(1), 44–69.
Walenta, J. 2020. Climate risk assessments and science-based targets: a review of emerging private sector climate action tools. *WIREs Climate Change,* 11(2), e628.
Weisman, A., 2007. *The World without Us.* New York: Picador.
Whiteman, G., Walker, B. and Perego, P. 2013. Planetary boundaries: ecological foundations for corporate sustainability. *Journal of Management Studies,* 50(2), 307–336.
Willett, W., et al. 2019. Food in the Anthropocene: the EAT–Lancet Commission on healthy diets from sustainable food systems. *The Lancet,* 393(10170), 447–492.
Young, O. R., et al. 2006. The globalization of socio-ecological systems: an agenda for scientific research. *Global Environmental Change,* 16(3), 304–316.

PART 2

Financial accounting and reporting

7
FINANCIAL ACCOUNTING AND THE NATURAL ENVIRONMENT

Thereza Raquel Sales de Aguiar and Jan Bebbington

Introduction

This chapter provides insight into the challenges that environmental issues raise for financial accounting, focusing narrowly on the financial statements, along with associated notes to the accounts. This narrow focus, however, needs to be briefly dispensed with in order to place this chapter into a wider context and to demonstrate how an interest in financial accounting issues intersects with other chapters in this handbook. For example, this chapter should be read in conjunction with Chapter 2, which presents a review of the foundations of environmental accounting, as well as Chapter 5, where the contributions of the accounting profession are considered. Likewise, the various regional chapters (Part 4) will contain material that is relevant to financial accounting considerations. Finally, chapters 11 and 12 contain insights into what happens to financial accounting information when it encounters shareholders and capital markets, respectively.

From the outset of the environmental accounting field, there was the concern that financial statements mis-represented "reality" because they did not reflect the impact of organisations on the natural environment. Indeed, Gray (1990) questioned if a "true and fair view" of an organisation could be presented if its impact on the natural environment is not taken into account. Likewise, the annual report and accounts "package" was the first place where disclosures were made concerning organisations' environmental impacts (see, e.g., Gray et al. 1995; Gray et al. 2014; KPMG et al. 2016; KPMG 2017; Bebbington et al. 1994). As time progressed, some of what was previously disclosed within annual reports moved in "stand-alone" formats (see Chapter 8 where this form of accounting is further considered). Moreover, the audit function has also been enrolled in supporting the disclosure practices of organisations (see also Chapter 9). Given the proliferation of disclosure practices in other formats, what might need to be disclosed in the financial accounts narrowed and to understand the scope of this chapter a brief revisiting of the focus and purpose of financial accounting is necessary.

Financial accounting reporting: focus and purpose

The American Accounting Association (AAA) defines accounting as "the process of identifying, measuring and communicating economic information to permit informed judgements and decisions by users of the information"(American Accounting Association 1966, p. 1). In order to regulate this practice, account providers are governed by the need to make certain disclosures (mandated by national laws as well as stock exchange listing requirements) alongside requirements to apply particular measurement and classification practices (found in accounting standards). Parallel to these requirements, various national and international standard setting and guidance processes ensure that accounting professionals are able to implement these requirements with oversight provided by relevant authorities (in the United Kingdom, e.g., this is the Financial Reporting Council – hereafter FRC). All these bodies have a desire to ensure that financial statements show a "true and fair" view of the underlying "reality" of the firm, and what this might be is underpinned by the conceptual framework in which accounting sits. The most accepted conceptual framework is the Framework for Preparation and Presentation of Financial Statements issued by the International Accounting Standards Board (IASB) in 1989. This framework consists of eight chapters, which describe the main concepts in financial reporting. The following paragraphs provide a summary of these chapters, highlighting the main concepts in the IASB Conceptual Framework that are relevant for the purpose of this chapter.

Financial information should be produced in accordance with a set of qualitative characteristics. As illustrated in Table 7.1, the IASB Conceptual Framework adopts two fundamental and four enhancing qualitative characteristics (IFRS Foundation 2018). In addition to these characteristics, the conceptual framework also makes reference to prudence and "substance over form" to support the qualitative characteristics of financial information (ACCA 2018). Prudence refers to exercising "caution" when faced with uncertain circumstances in order to avoid optimistic considerations (ACCA 2018; IFRS Foundation 2018). "Substance over form" is applied to ensure that information provides a faithful representation of economic resources of an entity (ACCA 2018) and a faithful representation of economic situation should prevail over the established rules/standards for elaboration of financial statements (ACCA 2018; IFRS Foundation 2018).

Table 7.1 Qualitative characteristics of financial information

Characteristic type	*Qualitative characteristics*	*Description*
Fundamental	Relevant information	Information is relevant if users would make a different decision in the absence of it.
	Faithfull information	Faithfulness requires that information should be neutral and free from bias and errors.
Enhancing	Timeless	Information is timely if it enables users' decision-making.
	Understandability	Information should be clear and concise.
	Verifiability	If independent observers agree on the measurement and presentation of information, it can be said to be verifiable.
	Comparability	Information should enable the identification and understanding of similarities between organisations.

Source: IFRS Foundation (2018) and Grant Thornton (2018).

The IASB Conceptual Framework establishes the principles for financial reporting, with this information being provided for a reporting entity (establishing the boundaries of a reporting entity is a non-trivial task). The IASB defines a reporting entity as:

> [A]n entity that is required, or chooses, to prepare financial statements. A reporting entity can be a single entity or a portion of an entity or can comprise more than one entity. A reporting entity is not necessarily a legal entity.
>
> *(IFRS Foundation 2018, p. A33)*

In addition, the IASB Conceptual Framework also establishes norms with regard to the time period of financial information to be considered. Moreover, and critically, information should be produced assuming that the organisation is a going concern, that is, it will continue to operate in the future (IFRS Foundation 2018). The form of the accounts to be presented is also specified. Table 7.2 describes the types of financial statements specified by the IASB Conceptual Framework. The recognition (capturing for inclusion) of the elements of financial statement should be done in line with qualitative characteristics of financial reports explained above and derecognition (removal of items from financial statements) of these elements should represent faithfully changes in assets and liabilities (ACCA 2018; EY 2018; IFRS Foundation 2018).

The final element in financial accounting relates to measurement and requires the information of financial statements to be quantified in monetary terms. The process of monetisation should consider the relevance to representing the economic resources of an entity and be guided by the qualitative characteristics of financial information. In addition, there are two ways that monetisation can be achieved: the historical cost of the transaction or the current value of the item. Current value measurement basis can be made by considering the following: fair value, value in use or current cost of an item.

Table 7.2 Key financial statements

Type of statement	*Type of information*	*Definitions of elements*
Statement of Financial Position	Reports on the financial equation in which Equity = Assets – Liabilities	Assets is "a present economic resource controlled by the entity as a result of past events" and economic resource is "a right that has the potential to produce economic benefits". Liability is "a present obligation of the entity to transfer an economic resource as a result of past events" and obligation is "a duty of responsibility that an entity has no practical ability to avoid".
Statement of Financial Performance	Recognises expenses and income	Income corresponds to "increases in assets, or decreases in liabilities, that result in increases in equity, other than those relating to contributions from holders of equity claims". Expenses represent "decreases in assets, or increases in liabilities, that result in decreases in equity, other than those relating to distributions to holders of equity claims".

Source: IFRS Foundation (2018).

In summary, the IASB Conceptual Framework prescribes what information should be included in financial statements as well as the principles that must be applied to the financial accounting process. This creates a series of restrictions: a concentration on an individual entity, separate from its substantive environment; an emphasis on monetary expression of matters of interest; and an information created in specified formats, with a focus on the perceived desires of users. This means that the potential of financial statements to provide a "true and fair" representation of an entity's impact on the natural environment is limited. The next section describes those limitations followed by a section on how environmental matters have been incorporated into financial accounting despite these limitations.

The limits of financial accounting and reporting

Limitations of financial accounting and reporting have been discussed in the literature for more than 45 years. For example, Dieker and Preston (1977) and Benston (1982) argued that accounting information that does not include organisations' externalities (Coase 1960) so it is incomplete and creates a limited account of management actions. From this, they concluded that financial accounting has a limited role to play in communicating about corporate responsibility (Benston 1982). In addition, these authors identified issues with assigning responsibility for externalities to the entity itself and argued that this failure of financial accounting has serious consequences on organisational behaviour because it can prevent deeper political changes (Benston 1982). Chapter 16 of this handbook further considers externalities and decision-making.

Indeed, Tinker focused on the political nature of accounting, noting that the perception of its neutrality is influenced by accounting's close connection with neoclassical economics, arguing that economic reductionism is the hallmark of neoclassical economics (Tinker 1984; Tinker et al. 1982). Hines reinforced this observation and described the impact of such reductionism. Hines highlighted that accounting communicates about "things" (Hines 1988; Hines 1989) and this communication is based on a language that classifies, recognises and measures a limited array of information that might matter to organisations and stakeholders (Hines 1991b; Hines 1991a). Consequently, financial accounting cannot reflect a true, accurate and fair view of "reality": rather, it can only partially represent quantifiable reality, which ignores qualitative aspects of the world we live in (Morgan 1988; Maunders and Burritt 1991).

Moreover, Hines (1989) argued that accounting cannot provide an independent and neutral perspective of an organisation because accounting itself constructs the idea of a business. Hines further stressed that the IASB Conceptual Framework lacks a sound conceptual basis and that accounting knowledge is the result of a political process (Hines 1989). She challenged the tautology that capital is equal to assets less liabilities by questioning what is actually an asset, who defines the size of an organisation and what is exactly the boundaries of an entity. Hines also identified the arbitrariness of accounting concepts, standards and practices as a major concern with accounting (Hines 1989). Maunders and Burritt (1991) built on this point to describe the limits of financial accounting's ability to recognise ecological problems and argued that environmental issues cannot be "adapted" to the demands of financial accounting concepts. For example, they argued that conventional notions of going concern exclude environmental impacts; qualitative impacts of accruals are not communicated; notions of consistency cannot be applied to environmental issues and the impossibility of prudence to represent irreversible impacts caused by organisations. Thus, financial accounting can actually be the cause of environmental and social degradation if it is taken as the only and exclusive basis for financial and economic decisions (Maunders and Burritt 1991). Regardless, there have been numerous attempts to bring environmental concerns into the ambit of financial accounting.

Financial accounting and environmental disclosure

The accounting profession has a track record of sponsoring research that explored how financial accounting might accommodate environmental matters. For example, the Association of Chartered Certified Accountants (ACCA) sponsored work over many years that examined, among other things, asbestos and long-tail liabilities (Moerman and van der Laan 2013), the role of small- and medium-sized enterprises in the pursuit of sustainability (Spence et al. 2012), the characteristics of organisations that pursue environmental sustainability (Barter and Bebbington 2010) and work sponsored by other accounting bodies has also addressed issues such as the valuation of assets and liabilities (Gray et al. 1998).

At the same time, the profession has created guidance as to how the natural environment would affect existing financial accounting activities. An early (and comprehensive) example of this work is that of the Canadian Institute of Chartered Accountants (1993). Another material was published by the United Nations Conference on Trade and Development (UNCTAD 1998; UNCTAD 2002) and by the Institute of Chartered Accountants of England and Wales (ICAEW 2015; ICAEW and Environmental Agency 2009). Building on these works, as well as on an extensive literature review of key journals, the following paragraphs summarise the impact of environmental issues on financial statements (see also Table 7.3).

In the context of liabilities, the literature identifies problems in measuring a liability due to the lack of a stronger and comprehensive set of financial accounting rules in this area (Collison and Slomp 2000; Larrinaga et al. 2002; Negash and Lemma 2020). In addition, the short-term focus of financial accounting standards tends to focus on environmental accruals (i.e. expenses related to the period that had not been paid) rather than liabilities that might crystallise in the more distant future (Collison and Slomp 2000; Larrinaga et al. 2002; Negash and Lemma 2020).

The impetus for recognition of environmental liabilities first arose from obligations to clean up polluted sites in the United States of America (generated by the "superfund" legislation) and how to recognise liabilities in this context has featured heavily in the literature (Bath et al. 1997; Bath and McNichols 1994; Campbell et al. 1998). Accruals for these liabilities were difficult to estimate in terms of the extent of future costs and the timing of recognition. As a result, managers were left with discretion on the disclosure of costs in this area (Bath et al. 1997; Bath and McNichols 1994). In addition, firms were reluctant to disclose information on this issue due to at least two reasons: first, it was costly to produce this information and, second, disclosure of this information could cause negative capital market responses (Bath and McNichols 1994; Campbell et al. 1998). Moreover, the literature found that regulatory influence, such as the one produced in the United States of America by the Financial Accounting Standard Board and the Security and Exchange Commission, was essential to avoid firms' discretion to recognise and disclose provisions for cleaning up superfund sites (Bath et al. 1997). Canadian regulations on disclosure of clean-up of natural sites contaminated were also found to have influenced financial reporting positively (Li and McConom 1999).

Another setting in which these problems arise is that relating to the provision for decommissioning costs, for example, in the oil and gas sector or by nuclear power plants (Gray et al. 1997; Alciatore et al. 2004). With regard to decommissioning in oil and gas sector, the literature suggests that companies do not comply fully with financial reporting standards. Rather, they disclosure the minimum required with no explanatory notes to support readers to understand the information disclosed (Abdo et al. 2018). Companies justified this approach by saying that this information is demanded by the users of financial accounting and also claim that this information can increase public scrutiny, decrease competitive advantage and generate misinterpretations (Abdo et al. 2018). These observations are reflected more broadly. For

Table 7.3 Environmental issues in financial statements

Impact on financial statements	*Accounting treatment*	*Related environmental issues*	*Examples of IFRS-related standards*
Environmental costs	They should be capitalised if meet the criteria to be recognised as an assets (e.g. increasing future economic benefits) (UNCTAD 2002, p.18). If not an asset, they should be charged to the income statement (UNCTAD 2002, p.19).	Conserving the environment, treatment of waste products, clean-up costs and auditing.	IAS 16 – Property, plant and equipment IAS 38 – Intangible assets
Recovery and impairment[3]	"When an environmental cost is recognised as an asset is related to another asset, it should be included as an integral part of that asset and not recognised separately" (UNCTAD 2002, p. 22). "Environmental cost is capitalised and included as an integral part of another asset, the combined assets should be tested for impairment and where appropriated written down to its recoverable amount" (UNCTAD 2002, p. 22).	Emissions rights, soil and water contaminated.	IAS 36 – Impairment of assets
Environmental liabilities[4]	It is the obligation of the entity to incur a future environmental cost. This obligation can be legally enforced or not and it should be disclosed in either balance sheet or notes (UNCTAD 2002, pp. 23,34).	Fines and penalties, waste disposal, clean-up superfund sites,[5] decommissioning[6] and changes in technology/ regulations.[7]	IAS 37 – Provisions, contingent liabilities and contingent assets
Recognition of recoveries	Recoveries from third parties should not be netted against environmental liabilities unless there is a legal right to set off in which case gross amount should be disclosed for both – liability and recovery (UNCTAD 2002, p. 28).	Land reinstatements.	IAS 37 – Provisions, contingent liabilities and contingent assets.
Measurement of environmental liabilities	Estimations in notes should be provided in case of uncertainty to measure environmental liabilities.	Type of hazardous substance in a site and type of technology for remediation.	IAS 37 – Provisions, contingent liabilities and contingent assets

Source: UNCTAD (1998), UNCTAD (2002), ICAEW and Environmental Agency (2009) and ICAEW (2015).

example, environmental fines and penalties have been highlighted as having the potential to cause misinterpretation in financial statements, as they may be mixed up with costs for environmental improvements, such as research and development (Gray et al. 1997). Buccina et al. (2013) also found that financial accounting standard (e.g. US GAAP – United States Generally Accepted Accounting Principles) were not sufficiently detailed to create disclosure of the cost of litigation arising from oil spills.

In general, the transparency of environment-related disclosure is considered essential for the sound provision of financial information (ICAEW 2015; ICAEW and Environmental Agency 2009). One qualitative aspect of financial statements that can affect the financial presentation of environmental issues is relevance, more specifically those aspects that are related to materiality (ICAEW and Environmental Agency 2009). According to the IASB Conceptual Framework, information is material if its omission or mis-statement will influence decisions based on financial reports (IFRS Foundation 2018). The main issue with materiality is the fact that it should be measured according to the relevance and magnitude of a particular item in relation to each individual entity. Thus, an entity should decide on material aspects to disclose and the information can be presented in two ways: either separately or aggregated with large amounts, which approach is adopted affects the identification and transparency of environmental issues in financial statements (ICAEW 2015).

The problem arises, however, when the relevance of information can be perceived differently by reporters: as a result, the disclosure of environmental related financial information is not only a matter of technical materiality assessment but also subject of professional judgement (Laine et al. 2017) as well as regulatory scope (Senn and Spring 2020). For example, the literature suggests that non-disclosure of capital expenditures tends to be justified due to quantitative immaterial nature of such information (Patten 2005; Cho et al. 2012). Another example, from the French context, explains that decommissioning assets and liabilities are perceived by reporters as relevant financial information in terms of standards compliance because there is clear accounting guidance on how it should be treated (Senn and Spring 2020). In contrast, expenses are not perceived by reporters as useful/reliable disclosure because how these items are calculated is not specific enough and as a result it is not clear what information conveyed as "environmental expenses" actually entails (Senn and Spring 2020). Despite the (at times, seemingly) arbitrary nature of the environmental information disclosed, the authors assert that organisations dedicate resources to define accounting classifications and measurement rules (Laine et al. 2017). This is because environmental financial accounting information may not be material in quantitative terms but this information is still relevant to comply with regulations as well as to create a positive image of an organisation since financial information may represent a signal of an organisational commitment to the environment (Laine et al. 2017).

In summary, this section has provided a synthesis of the issues that arise for financial accounting, including measurement, classification and disclosure choices. These are generic issues for financial accounting. At the same time, aspects of environmental governance also create novel issues for financial accounting choices, namely, issues that arise related to climate change and financial reporting.

Novel financial accounting issues

Climate change is one of the most serious environmental issues of our generation and is considered in more detail in Chapter 26 of this handbook. In this section, two areas of particular concern that affect financial accounting are briefly highlighted: financial accounting issues emerging from of emissions rights and accounting for climate change-related risks and uncertainties. These issues come into play when emissions rights are gifted to organisations, rather than being paid for.

Emissions rights are given to organisations in the context of emissions trading schemes that seek to reduce greenhouse gas emissions (Bebbington and Larrinaga-Gonzalez 2008; Lovell 2014). Emissions trading works (normally) by setting a cap on an entity's emissions and then creating a market whereby organisations can decide to emit to the level they have the rights for, reduce their emissions (thereby creating emissions to sell) or exceed their emissions entitlement (and buy emissions rights in the market to cover the excess). Emissions trading gives economic value to a unit of emissions based on supply and demand and provides organisations with flexibility to set strategies according to their economic preferences. There are emissions markets operating in many countries,[1] with the European Union (EU) Emissions Trading Scheme (EU ETS) being both the first and largest emissions trading scheme in the world.

Emissions trading schemes (where rights were allocated for "free") created problems with respect to how to recognise and value those rights. As a result, in 2004, the IASB issued a guidance in this area through the International Financial Reporting Interpretation Committee 3 – Emissions right (hereafter IFRIC 3). IFRIC 3 was later withdrawn due to "accounting mismatches"[2]. Table 7.4 demonstrates that IFRIC 3 recommended that changes in the value of liabilities should be directly recognised in the income statement, in contrast to the case for changes in the value of assets (Lovell et al. 2013). Different recommendations in terms of measurements of assets and liabilities were also a concern. It was argued that these mismatches could cause value-relevant impacts on companies' financial results, if companies were operating in a volatile market (de Aguiar 2018). There is presently no standard on offer in this area and in its absence reporters have decided to recognise emissions rights in different ways, thereby compromising the comparability of financial information (PricewaterhouseCoopers – PwC and International Emissions Trading Association – IETA 2007; Lovell 2014; Lovell et al. 2013). There were several attempts to set new standards for emissions rights but with no success (de Aguiar 2018). This situation highlights the continued struggle that financial reporting has with incorporating environmental aspects in a way that reflects science/policy imperatives accurately (Ascui and Lovell 2011).

This illustration makes the case that aspects of the natural environment (even where they are subject to formal governance) still create problems in terms of financial accounting's ability to create accounts that reflect the underlying reality. This may explain why environmental matters can be found more readily in non-financial reporting formats (see also Chapter 8 of this handbook) rather than directly incorporated into financial statements. At the same time, failure to adequately account for environmental matters means that financial accounts do not show a "true and fair" view to capital market participants and other users. This is reflected in the provision of alternative sources of information, such as the Carbon Disclosure Project (CDP) and the more recent work of the Task Force on Climate-related Financial Disclosures (TCFD – see TCFD 2017b; TCFD 2017a). In particular, the TCFD has highlighted that disclosure on climate-related financial information is still insufficient to investors and that the impact of climate change on organisations is unclear, including financial impacts (TCFD 2019). This has to be an inappropriate position for the accounting profession to find itself in.

Conclusion

This chapter sought to demonstrate the issues at stake as financial accounting seeks to reflect the impacts of the natural environment on organisations. While financial accounting does (and

Table 7.4 IFRIC 3 accounting for emissions rights summary

IFRIC 3 – Emissions rights	
IAS 38 – Intangible assets	*IAS 37 – Provisions, contingent liabilities and contingent assets*
Treatment Allowances should be treated as intangible assets to recognise emissions rights allocated free of charge or purchased.	Treatment Liability to provide allowances should be treated as a "provision" and recognised as the emissions are produced.
Measurement • "When allowances are issued to a participant by government (or government agency) for less than their fair value, the difference between the amount paid (if any) and their fair value is a government grant that is accounted for in accordance IAS 20 Accounting for Government Grants and Disclosure of Government Assistance".[a] • The "Government Grant" should initially be classified as deferred income in the statement of financial position and as income over the compliance period.	Measurement • It should be measured at market value. • Revaluation should be recognised in income statement.

[a] www.iasplus.com/en/standards/ifric/ifric3.

Source: www.iasplus.com/en/standards/ifric/ifric3 and Lovell et al. (2013).

has) reflect(ed) aspects of environmental matters, the extent and robustness of these accounts have troubled the profession, standard setters and the academia over the last 30 years. As has been demonstrated, the constraining nature of the IASB Conceptual Framework has made recognition of environmental matter problematic, given the mismatch between the rules and norms of accounting versus the nature of environmental concerns. Even where governance and/or policy "makes" the environment evident (e.g. in carbon trading schemes), accounting has found it problematic to reflect these matters in accounting rules in such a way that robust and comparable information can be provided to decision-makers/information users. Likewise, given that materiality is an overarching principle on which the provision of accounting information rests, it is often the case that environmental related information does not cross this threshold. At the same time, and given the lack of representation of environmental matters, it is not always clear that this information is immaterial. As a result, the communication of an organisation's financial position may be flawed in ways that cannot be easily discerned (see also Chapter 12 that considers financial markets and environmental information).

More theoretically informed explanations exist to explain the problem of translating environmental matters into financial accounting. In particular, Bebbington et al. (2020) examined these themes in the case of "unburnable carbon". In this case, fossil fuel reserves are reflected in the notes to the accounts as well as (partially – in terms of prior capital expenditure to identify fossil fuel reserves) in the financial statements. At the same time, it can be demonstrated that if global climate change governance evolves to a scientifically robust position, a large proportion of these reserves will not be combusted and hence will have little economic value (in this case a material effect will be generated). In seeking to explain why there is no current financial accounting response to this issue, Bebbington et al. (2020), drawing from Miller and Power (2013), noted that there is a problem with the functions that underpin accounting's force. In the first instance, accounting finds it difficult to create "calculative spaces" (territorialising in the language used by Miller and Power 2013) that translate environmental matters into financial matters. This problem arises from the problems of recognition identified in this chapter as well as from the tendency for disclosures to be required/regulated while the measurement and classification rules that would support such disclosures remain weak and/or absent (this is a key insight from Senn and Spring 2020). If it is impossible to create calculations, then the second element of accounting's productive force (the ability for actors to use accounting information to interact with each other – mediating) cannot be achieved. Once these impediments are in place, other roles for accounting information, namely, adjudicating (the provision of information that allows activities to be evaluated) and subjectivising (the creation of contexts in which control can be achieved) are also lost. These insights also explain why other forms of accounting for the environment have developed (especially outside of the annual report and accounts package). Regardless, the need for financial accounting information to better reflect the environmental performance of organisations still exists and is still imperfectly realised.

Notes

1 For reports on different carbon markets, see: www.ieta.org/The-Worlds-Carbon-Markets.
2 www.iasplus.com/en/news/2005/June/news2147.
3 According to ACCA, "If an asset's carrying value exceeds the amount that could be received through use or selling the asset, then the asset is impaired and the standard requires a company to make provision for the impairment loss" (www.accaglobal.com/my/en/member/discover/cpd-articles/corporate-reporting/ias36-impairment.html).
4 Provision should be recognised when: "(i) an entity has a present obligation as a result of a past event; (ii) it is probable that a transfer of economic benefits will be required to settle the obligation; and (iii) a reliable estimate can be made of the amount of the obligation" (ICAEW 2015).
5 Sites polluted, for example, contaminated with hazardous substances.
6 Decommissioning means the dismantling and disposal of facilities. In oil and gas sector, it is common decommission of offshore platforms installations and pipelines. Another example is decommissioning of nuclear power plants.
7 For example, replacement of fuel cars with electric cars due to regulation requirements.

References

Abdo, H., Mangena, M., Needham, G. and Hunt, D. 2018. Disclosure of provisions for decommissioning costs in annual reports of oil and gas companies: A content analysis and stakeholder views. *Accounting Forum,* 42(4), 341–358.

ACCA 2018. The Conceptual Framework. Available from: www.grantthornton.global/globalassets/1.-member-firms/global/insights/article-pdfs/2018/ifrs-news---a-revised-conceptual-framework-for-financial-reporting.pdf [Accessed 26 January 2020].

Alciatore, M., Dee, C. C. and Easton, P. 2004. Changes in environmental regulation and reporting: The case of the petroleum industry from 1989 to 1998. *Journal of Accounting and Public Policy,* 23, 295–304.

American Accounting Association. 1966. A *Statement of Basic Accounting Theory.* Evanston, IL: American Accounting Association.

Ascui, F. and Lovell, H. 2011. As frames collide: Making sense of carbon accounting. *Accounting, Auditing & Accountability Journal,* 24, 978–999.

Barter, N. and Bebbington, J. 2010. Pursuing environmental sustainability. Available from: www.accaglobal.com/pk/en/technical-activities/technical-resources-search/2010/may/pursuing-environmental-sustainability.html [Accessed 21 July 2020].

Bath, M. E. and McNichols, M. F. 1994. Estimation and market valuation of environmental liabilities relating to superfund sites. *Journal of Accounting Research,* 32, 177–209.

Bath, M. E., McNichios, M. and Wilson, G. P. 1997. Factors influencing firms' disclosures about environmental liabilities. *Review of Accounting Studies,* 2, 35–64.

Bebbington, K. J., Gray, R. H., Thomson, I. and Walters, D. 1994. Accountants' attitudes and environmentally sensitive accounting. *Accounting & Business Research,* 54, 109–120.

Bebbington, J. and Larrinaga-Gonzalez, C. 2008. Carbon trading: Accounting and reporting issues. *European Accounting Review,* 17, 697–717.

Bebbington, J., Schneider, T., Stevenson, L. and Fox, A. 2020. Fossil fuel reserves and resources reporting and unburnable carbon: Investigating conflicting accounts. *Critical Perspectives on Accounting,* 66, 1–22.

Benston, G. 1982. An analysis of the role of accounting standards for enhancing corporate governance and social responsibility. *Journal of Accounting and Public Policy,* 1, 5–17.

Campbell, K., Sefcik, S. E. and Soderstrom, N. S. 1998. Site uncertainty, allocation uncertainty, and superfund liability valuation. *Journal of Accounting and Public Policy,* 17, 331–366.

Canadian Institute of Chartered Accountants. 1993. Environmental costs and liabilities: Accounting and financial reporting issues. Toronto: Canadian Institute of Chartered Accountants.

Cho, C. H., Freedman, M. and Patten, D. M. 2012. Corporate disclosure of environmental capital expenditures: A test of alternative theories. *Accounting, Auditing & Accountability Journal,* 25(3), 486–507.

Coase, R. H. 1960. The problem of social cost. *Journal of Law and Economics,* 3 (October), 1–44.

Collison, D. and Slomp, S. 2000. Environmental accounting, auditing and reporting in Europe: The role of FEE. *European Accounting Review,* 9(1), 111–129.

de Aguiar, T. 2018. Turning accounting for emissions rights inside out as well as upside down. *Environment and Planning C: Politics and Space,* 36(1), 139–159.

Dierker, M. and Preston, L. E. 1977. Corporate social accounting reporting for the physical environment: A critical review and implementation proposal *Accounting, Organizations and Society,* 2(3–22).

EY 2018. Applying IFRS: IASB issues revised conceptual framework for financial reporting. Available from: www.ey.com/Publication/vwLUAssets/ey-applying-conceptual-framework-april2018/$FILE/ey-applying-conceptual-framework-april2018.pdf [Accessed 26 January 2020].

FRC 2019. Key facts and trends in the accountancy professions. Available from: www.frc.org.uk/getattachment/109373d4-abc2-424f-84d0-b80c2cec861a/Key-Facts-and-Trends-2019.pdf [Accessed on 26 January 2020].

Grant Thornton. 2018. IFRS News - Special edition - A revised 'Conceptual Framework for Financial Reporting'. Available from: www.grantthornton.global/globalassets/1.-member-firms/global/insights/article-pdfs/2018/ifrs-news---a-revised-conceptual-framework-for-financial-reporting.pdf [Accessed 26 January 2020].

Gray, R., Adams, C. A. and Owen, D., 2014. *Accountability, Social Responsibility and Sustainability: Accounting for Society and the Environment.* Harlow: Pearson.

Gray, R., Bebbington, J., Collison, D., Kouhy, R., Lyon, B., Reid, C., A, R. and Stevenson, L. 1998. The valuation of assets and liabilities: Environmental law and the impact of the environmental agenda for business. Available from: www.icas.com/__data/assets/pdf_file/0018/10584/29-The-Valuation-of-Assets-and-Liabilities-ICAS.pdf [Accessed 21 July 2020].

Gray, R., Collison, D. and Bebbington, J. 1997. Environmental and social accounting & reporting. Available from: www.st-andrews.ac.uk/media/csear/discussion-papers/CSEAR_dps-socenv-socacc.pdf [Accessed 30 January 2020].

Gray, R., Kouhy, R. and Lavers, S. 1995. Corporate social and environmental reporting: A review of the literature and a longitudinal study of UK disclosure. *Accounting, Auditing & Accountability Journal,* 8(2), 47–77.

Gray, R. H. 1990. *The Greening of Accountancy: The Profession after Pearce.* London: Chartered Association of Certified Accountants.

Hines, R. D. 1988. Financial accounting: In communicating reality, we construct reality. *Accounting, Organisations and Society,* 13(3), 251–261.

Hines, R. D. 1989. Financial accounting knowledge, conceptual framework projects and the social construction of the accounting profession. *Accounting, Auditing & Accountability Journal,* 2(2), 313–332.

Hines, R. D. 1991a. The FAB's conceptual framework, financial accounting and the maintenance of the social world. *Accounting, Organisations and Society,* 16(4), 313–331.

Hines, R. D. 1991b. On valuing nature. *Accounting, Auditing & Accountability Journal,* 4(3), 27–29.

ICAEW 2015. Environmental issues and UK annual reporting: Sustainable business initiative – Turning questions into answers. Available from: www.icaew.com/-/media/corporate/files/technical/sustainability/tecpln12453-eiafr-annual-report–2nd-edition-final.ashx?la=en [Accessed 26 January 2020].

ICAEW and Environmental Agency. 2009. *Turning Questions into Answers: Environmental Issues and Annual Financial Reporting.* London: The Institute of Chartered Accountants in England.

IFRS Foundation. 2018. Conceptual Framework for Financial Reporting. Available from: www.ifrs.org/projects/2018/conceptual-framework/ [Accessed 20 June 2019].

KPMG. 2017. The road ahead: The KPMG survey on corporate responsibility report. Available from: https://assets.kpmg/content/dam/kpmg/be/pdf/2017/kpmg-survey-of-corporate-responsibility-reporting–2017.pdf [Accessed 27 January 2020].

KPMG, GRI, UNEP and Centre for Governance in Africa. 2016. Carrots & stick: Global trends in sustainability reporting regulation and policy. Available from: https://assets.kpmg/content/dam/kpmg/pdf/2016/05/carrots-and-sticks-may–2016.pdf [Accessed 27 January 2020].

Laine, M., Järvinen, J. T., Hyvönen, T. and Kantola, H. 2017. Ambiguity of financial environmental information. *Accounting, Auditing & Accountability Journal,* 30(3), 593–619.

Larrinaga, C., Carrasco, F., Correa, C., Llena, F. and Moneva, J. 2002. Accountability and accounting regulation: The case of the Spanish environmental disclosure standard. *European Accounting Review,* 11(4), 723–774.

Li, Y. and McConom, B. 1999. An empirical examination of factors affecting the timing of environmental accounting standard adoption and the impact on corporate valuation. *Journal of Accounting, Auditing & Finance,* 279–313.

Lovell, H. 2014. Climate change, markets and standards: The case of financial accounting. *Economy and Society,* 43(2), 260–284.

Lovell, H., Bebbington, J., Larrinaga, C. and de Aguiar, T. R. S. 2013. Putting carbon markets into practice: A case study of financial accounting in Europe. *Environment and Planning C: Government and Policy,* 31(4), 741–757.

Maunders, K. and Burritt, R. L. 1991. Accounting and ecological crisis. *Accounting, Auditing & Accountability Journal,* 4(1), 9–26.

Miller, P. and Power, M. 2013. Accounting, organizing, and economizing: Connecting accounting research and organization theory. *The Academy of Management Annals,* 7(1), 557–605.

Moerman, L. and van der Laan, S. 2013. Accounting and long-tail liabilities: The case of asbestos. Available from: www.accaglobal.com/pk/en/technical-activities/technical-resources-search/2013/march/the-case-of-asbestos.html [Accessed 21 July 2020].

Morgan, G. 1988. Accounting as reality construction: Towards a new epistemology for accounting practice. *Accounting, Organisations and Society,* 13(5), 477–485.

Negash, M. and Lemma, T. T. 2020. Institutional pressures and the accounting and reporting of environmental liabilities. *Business Strategy and the Environment,* 29(5), 1941–1960.

Patten, D. M. 2005. The accuracy of financial report projections of future environmental capital expenditures: A research note. *Accounting, Organizations and Society,* 30(5), 457–468.

PwC and IETA, 2007. *Trouble-Entry Accounting: Revisited.* London: PriceWaterhouse Coopers and the International Emissions Trading Association.

Senn, J. and Spring, S. 2020. The limits of environmental accounting disclosure: Enforcement of regulations, standards and interpretative strategies. *Accounting, Auditing & Accountability Journal,* 33(6), 1367–1393.

Spence, L. J., Agyemang, G. and Rinaldi, L. 2012. Environmental aspects of sustainability, SMEs and the role of accountant. Available from: www.accaglobal.com/pk/en/technical-activities/technical-resources-search/2012/july/environmental-aspects-sustainability-smes.html [Accessed 21 July 2020].

TCFD, 2017a. Implementing the recommendations of the task force on climate-related financial disclosures. Available from: www.fsb-tcfd.org/wp-content/uploads/2017/12/FINAL-TCFD-Annex-Amended–121517.pdf [Accessed 30 January 2020]..

TCFD, 2017b. Recommendations of the task force on climate-related financial disclosures. Available from: www.fsb-tcfd.org/wp-content/uploads/2017/06/FINAL–2017-TCFD-Report–11052018.pdf [Accessed 30 January 2020]. .

TCFD, 2019. Task force on climate-related financial disclosures: Status report. Available from: www.fsb.org/2019/06/task-force-on-climate-related-financial-disclosures–2019-status-report/ [Accessed 26 January 2020].

Tinker, A. M. 1984. Theories of the state and the state of accounting: Economic reductionism and political voluntarism in accounting regulation theory. *Journal of Accounting and Public Policy,* 3, 55–74.

Tinker, A. M., Merino, B. D. and Neimark, M. D. 1982. The normative origins of positive theory ideology and accounting thought. *Accounting, Organisations and Society*, 7(2), 167–200.
UNCTAD. 1998. Environmental financial accounting and reporting at the corporate level. Available from: https://unctad.org/en/Docs/c2isard2.en.pdf [Accessed 21 July 2020].
UNCTAD. 2002. Guidance manual: Accounting and financial reporting for environmental costs and liabilities. Available from: https://unctad.org/en/Docs/iteeds4_en.pdf [Accessed 19 June 2020].

8

STAND-ALONE AND INTEGRATED REPORTING

Helen Tregidga and Matias Laine

Introduction

Environmental reporting is the practice of an entity reporting on environmental matters. Environmental reporting can relate to an entity's priorities, policies and practices concerning environmental issues, the environmental performance of an entity and the environmental impacts the operations have. Environmental reporting can also, among other things, discuss how an entity is dependent on the environment and natural systems, the risks associated with environmental matters, as well as the entity's environmental responsibilities and accountabilities.

This chapter focuses on the various forms environmental reports published by organisations take. We discuss the common ways in which entities report on the environment, the characteristics of these reports and the most prominent frameworks that relate to the practice. To further contextualise and understand environmental reporting, we introduce some key issues and discussions surrounding the practice.

In line with the focus of this book, we refer in this chapter to environmental reporting. However, it is important to recognise that environmental reporting cannot be unproblematically separated from discussions of social and economic reporting. Furthermore, it is also important to recognise that environmental reporting can carry various labels, such as sustainability reporting, corporate social responsibility reporting and corporate citizenship reporting. While recognising that such labels are important (see Tregidga, Milne and Kearins 2014; Laine 2010), we do not distinguish between them here. Rather we discuss practices that, in general terms, fall under the remit of environmental reporting as we define it above.

There are several chapters which discuss various aspects of environmental reporting in this handbook. This chapter has been written with these in mind. Therefore, while we will at times refer to aspects of theory and research methods, they are covered elsewhere and will hence not be a key focus here. Likewise, in seeking to provide a broad contemporary and critical perspective to environmental reporting practice, it is inevitable that some historical insights are included. However, these are covered elsewhere (Chapter 2) so we direct the readers there for further discussion. And similarly, while we touch upon some norms and regulations as these are significant when looking into the reporting landscape, this handbook includes a chapter on this (Chapter 10).

We structure this chapter as follows. After a short background to current environmental reporting we begin with a discussion of the most popular forms environmental reporting takes. We then introduce some key characteristics of environmental reporting, which in many cases also provide a basis upon which the practice can be evaluated. We follow with a discussion of prominent frameworks which guide environmental reporting practice, as well as the institutions that develop and promote them. Thereafter we introduce some of the current and ongoing issues related to the practice of environmental reporting. The intent here is to introduce for reflection some broad questions relating to the role of environmental reporting in contemporary societies. We will conclude the chapter by discussing some areas for future research, especially those relevant for enhancing our collective knowledge of environmental reporting. Throughout the chapter we draw on both foundational and contemporary research to provide an overview of the current state of knowledge.

Background to current environmental reporting practice

Environmental reporting has developed into a mainstay feature in many organisations (especially large corporations) (see KPMG 2017)[1]. While a small number of pioneering organisations were providing some environmental information in the early 20th century (Guthrie and Parker, 1989), environmental reporting begun to gather more serious momentum in the 1990s (Gray and Bebbington 2001). Environmental reporting can now be seen as a fairly standard practice for large commercial organisations. It is also increasingly common practice in public sector organisations, small- and medium-sized enterprises (SMEs), non-government organisations (NGOs) and other entities such as cities, states and countries. Furthermore, while early reporting diffused more swiftly in countries like the United Kingdom (UK), Australia and France, environmental reporting is now established as a global practice, with a rapid growth in countries in Asia and South America in particular (KPMG 2017).[2]

It is worth noting from the outset that environmental reporting practices are not uniform. One of the reasons for this is that environmental reporting continues to be mostly a voluntary practice. While an increasing number of regulatory frameworks have emerged for some forms or aspects of such reporting, organisations can, for the most part, decide whether they want to engage in environmental reporting. This includes decisions on what information they include (and exclude), and how they present it. In this sense, environmental reporting differs from financial reporting for which there are often strict and detailed regulatory frameworks in each jurisdiction. There are, however, several frameworks for environmental reporting, which have been developed to help organisations produce environmental reports. We discuss these in more detail below.

Despite environmental reporting becoming common practice in many societies, discussions on the role and relevance of environmental reporting continue (Andrew and Baker 2020). To better understand how and why organisations publish environmental information, academic research has for many years analysed how things like organisational size, industry, geographical context, financial position and prior environmental performance, to name but a few, affect an entity's environmental reporting practices (for an early example, see Adams 2002). As environmental reports are mostly voluntary and there is no formal audit mechanism to verify the information, there continue to be concerns regarding the credibility of the reports and discussion whether they are primarily about greenwashing (Cho, Guidry, Hageman and Patten 2012; Diouf and Boiral 2017; Milne and Gray 2013). The investment community, especially in recent years, has shown interest in environmental performance and related environmental reporting (Michelon, Rodrigue and Trevisan 2020), and there are ongoing debates regarding whether environmental disclosures are useful for investors' decisions (see Cho, Laine, Roberts and Rodrigue 2015). In addition to external audiences, environmental reports have relevance inside the organisation. For example, management can use such reports in an attempt to develop organisational culture with regard to environmental issues (Adams and McNicholas 2007). So, while it remains unclear how widely environmental reports are read, there are various audiences for which there would appear to be some relevance.

Environmental reporting forms

In this section we discuss the various forms environmental reports can take. This helps understand the practice and the various ways in which organisations report on the environment to stakeholders.

Stand-alone environmental reports

In the early stages of the development of environmental reporting, it was common for the environmental report to be a separate stand-alone report, that is, prepared and published separately from the annual report containing an entity's financial reporting. Stand-alone environmental reporting often follows the same reporting cycle as the financial report, implying that the environmental report is published on an annual basis either alongside the financial report or afterwards with a minor delay. An annual environmental report usually focuses on the same time period as the financial report. Some organisations, however, prefer to publish their environmental report less frequently, such as every two years. While in the early stages environmental reports were often published only as paper versions, now organisations usually make the stand-alone environmental report available as pdf files on their website.

Despite the emergence of other forms of reporting introduced below, stand-alone reports are an attractive research site and continue to be the focus of much research in the area. While this is likely due to their long history and the advantages of them being produced on a regular basis, they also, for many companies, remain a major and arguably the most comprehensive source of environmental information for which the organisation has editorial control (Tregidga, Kearins and Milne 2013).

Integrated reports

More recently, and in light of an increasing recognition of the need for environmental reporting to be seen as important as financial reporting, there is an increasing trend towards what can be referred to as an integrated report – a report containing an entity's environmental and financial information (usually including social information). These can have some similarities to stand-alone reports, as they are, for example, usually prepared annually and often appear online as pdf files. However, the key difference relates to the attempt to integrate environmental, social and financial dimensions into one reporting format.

Integrated reporting is not without its challenges and the "best" way to report and how one might integrate the financial and non-financial reporting are ongoing issues. Integrated reports hence come in many forms, and the emphasis given to different types of information can vary substantially from one organisation to another. Integrated reports have also been the focus of research in the area. Increasingly research on integrated reporting has focused on the form promoted by the International Integrated Reporting Council (IIRC) discussed further below (see Rinaldi, Unerman and de Villiers 2018).

Web-based disclosure

In addition to stand-alone and integrated environmental reports, other forms of environmental reporting, which take place in the digital world, are popular. Web-based reporting refers to the broader spectrum of reporting beyond the pdf versions of environmental reports published on an organisation's website. While web-based reporting can be simply a replication of environmental information, which also appears in a pdf version, it can also include different or alternative information and make use of the technological advantages of the medium (Adams and Frost 2006). For example, web-based reporting allows for real-time communication with more immediate and frequently updated information. It also increases opportunities for stakeholder interaction (for an early example, see Unerman and Bennett 2004). There has been long-term interest in and analysis of web-based environmental reporting; however, it has not been as well researched as stand-alone and integrated reports.

Social media reporting

As the digital world becomes more dominant, environmental reporting using these platforms has evolved and many organisations now communicate and provide information through various social media channels on a frequent basis (She and Michelon 2019). As such, social media is another way in which organisations report on environmental matters. Environmental reporting through social media occurs at a faster pace, it can be targeted at specific stakeholders, and it offers opportunities for stakeholder engagement (Bellucci and Manetti 2017; Manetti and Bellucci 2016). Indeed, social media has the potential to reach a substantially different set of stakeholders from the other forms of reporting discussed. However, reporting on social media is not without challenges for an organisation. A single post can suddenly become viral, spreading unexpectedly to audiences well beyond the original target group, and also becoming potentially uncontrollable.

In essence, while more traditional forms of environmental reporting often focus on providing a more comprehensive and regular view of an organisation's environmental activities, reporting on social media tends to be focused on a more limited scale, such as particular actions, single incidents or otherwise temporally constrained events. Social media disclosures are potentially turning into an entirely different form of environmental reporting, complementing the more traditional forms and providing an opportunity to rethink understandings of environmental reporting and related accountability relationships. While being limited in research focus at present, it can be expected that research in this area will continue to grow (Arnaboldi, Busco and Cuganesan 2017; Saxton et al. 2018).

Summary

There are many different forms of environmental reporting. Stand-alone and integrated reporting continue to be the key practices with a regular reporting cycle, while the increasing use of websites and social media further extends and develops environmental reporting. While recognising these various forms, from this point on we focus on stand-alone and integrated reporting only. We focus our discussion so as to examine the characteristics of these forms of reporting and consider the context within which they are situated. We begin this discussion with a look at some of the key characteristics of stand-alone and integrated environmental reporting which assist us in further understanding this practice.

Key characteristics of environmental reporting

As noted, environmental reporting is largely a voluntary activity. Organisations have substantial freedom with regard to how they report. It is hence relevant to ask what characteristics might we expect a "good" environmental report to have, not only in relation to *how* information in a report is presented, but also *what* information the report includes. While in financial reporting most organisations are expected to produce their reports according to the same principles and templates, with environmental reports such uniformity does not exist. Furthermore, it might not even make as much sense. For instance, relevant environmental matters for a mining company are likely to be different from a food and beverage firm. Stakeholders also go beyond financial stakeholders, and as different organisations have different stakeholder responsibilities, this can further complicate things.

Despite these challenges, the content of an environmental report is closely related to three concepts: boundary, materiality and accountability. Reporting boundaries relate to the question of which operations are included in a report. In financial reporting boundaries are set based on ownership and control. There are often clear rules regarding how different types of entities are included in the financial report. In environmental reporting the boundaries and scope of the report are less clear (Antonini and Larrinaga 2017; Unerman, Bebbington and O'Dwyer 2018). For instance, an organisation's main environmental impacts may take place in an outsourced factory located upstream in the supply chain, as would be the case for many retailers selling fast fashion clothing. Alternatively, carbon dioxide emissions from oil production take place mostly downstream, as oil is, for instance, burned to power airplanes or cars. The question hence becomes how broad or narrow should the scope of an environmental report be.

The second key concept is materiality. Materiality refers to identifying the most relevant issues for environmental reporting and is closely related to reporting boundaries. Materiality is a complex concept as, for example, different issues can have very different levels of significance to different people, in different contexts, and at different points of time (Edgley, Jones and Atkins 2015; Puroila and Mäkelä 2019). It is therefore important to know how materiality is understood by a reporting organisation, including which criteria they have used to evaluate material items. Materiality is also an important consideration for researchers (Unerman and Zappettini 2014). As you will see below, the major environmental reporting frameworks have different approaches to materiality.

The third important concept is accountability. In simple terms, accountability relates to the duty to provide an account of the actions over which one is considered to have responsibility (Gray et al. 1996). For organisations, this would imply that they should provide information on their activities and the implications these activities may have had. The key thing to note here is that we are talking of duties going beyond the legal requirements. That is, while there might not be a legal duty for an organisation to provide information, there might nonetheless be a moral duty to do so. This is not that simple however. Different organisations, stakeholders and societies have different views, for instance, on what kind of responsibilities organisations have in societies, as well as on what kind of information, to whom and how should organisations then provide in addition to that required by law. In essence, accountability is a contested idea, with the key environmental reporting frameworks discussed below looking at it in different ways.

Still, it is a central concept in discussions regarding organisations' environmental reporting (see Dillard and Vinnari 2019).

Setting the reporting boundaries and identifying material issues as part of accountability relationships help in setting the scope of a report and deciding which items should be reported on, but they do not yet specify how the reporting should be done. For this, there are some common characteristics, which are often considered to be features of a high-quality environmental report (see Table 8.1). While some of these might feel self-evident, such as expectations regarding reliable, clear and comparable information, environmental reports are often found to be lagging in various ways (Diouf and Boiral 2017; Michelon, Pilonato and Ricceri 2015). Again, this is closely related to the fact that environmental reporting continues to be mostly a voluntary practice, with a reporting entity having substantial control over what is included in the report, how the information is presented, and which aspects might potentially be omitted altogether.

Table 8.1 Characteristics of environmental reporting

Concept	*Description*	*Points to consider*
Accuracy	Information in a report should be sufficiently accurate and detailed to allow readers to assess an organisation's performance.	Organisations are at times vague when presenting negative information. Are graphs and tables structured properly, or have they been skewed or distorted?
Balance	A report should include both positive and negative aspects so that users can assess the overall performance of the organisation.	Organisations often emphasise positive information. Frameworks and assurance practices hope to help in getting more balanced reports.
Clarity	Information in a report should be presented in a clear, understandable and accessible form.	User groups vary in their knowledge and ability to understand information. What is complex to some can be self-evident and simplistic to others.
Comparability	Information should be selected, compiled and reported consistently. It should allow analysing changes both over time and in relation to other organisations where possible.	Reporting frameworks can help by providing standard practices. Does the organisation provide information from previous years to allow reader to see trends and developments easily?
Reliability	Reported information should be based on reliable processes, which could also be subject to independent evaluation.	Implies that in addition to the reported information it is also relevant to discuss how the information has been collected.
Stakeholder inclusiveness	An organisation should identify and engage stakeholders, and discuss how it has responded to their expectations and interests.	Stakeholder groups can have very different expectations. Different forms of reporting have different audiences, who can have varying expectations.
Timeliness	Reports should be published on regular schedule and in a timely manner so that it allows the report users to make informed decisions.	Web-based reporting can often be more timely, but an annual and regular reporting cycle can have other advantages. Timeliness is not just about speed, but also regularity.

Overall, the characteristics listed above are not clear-cut. An organisation and its various stakeholders might, for instance, understand accuracy and balance in very different ways, and hence have different expectations regarding what should be reported on and how it should be reported (Rodrigue 2014; Diouf and Boiral 2017). It has been suggested that assurance might be a potential avenue to enhance the quality of environmental reporting, as such a third-party statement could give the readers more confidence in the reported information (see Chapter 9 for more details). Still, both the organisations preparing the reports and their stakeholders using the information keep looking for more standardised practices to emerge, as these would make both preparing and using environmental reports easier.

Environmental reporting frameworks

As environmental reporting has become more common, there have been various attempts to establish frameworks to promote and guide the practice. We discuss three frameworks here: the Global Reporting Initiative (GRI), published by the GRI; Integrated Reporting (<IR>), published by the IIRC; and the Sustainability Accounting Standards Board (SASB), published by the SASB. Other environmental reporting frameworks and initiatives exist, including the CDP, which focuses on collecting information on climate and water in particular (see Andrew and Cortese 2011; Ascui 2014), and the Task Force on Climate-Related Financial Disclosures (TCFD), which emphasises taking a financial perspective on climate and carbon issues (O'Dwyer and Unerman 2020). However, the three selected here for further discussion are arguably among the most widely recognised and influential, and they also represent three different approaches to stand-alone and integrated environmental reporting.[3]

Table 8.2 summarises key features of each framework before we discuss each in more detail, including some relevant insights from academic research. The stated missions show how each

Table 8.2 Overview of key environmental reporting frameworks

	Global Reporting Initiative (GRI)	*International Integrated Reporting Council <IR>*	*Sustainability Accounting Standards Board (SASB)*
Founded	1997	2010	2011
Aim	To empower decisions that create social, environmental and economic benefits for everyone.	Establish integrated reporting and thinking within mainstream business practice as the norm in the public and private sectors.	Establish industry-specific disclosure standards across environmental, social, and governance topics that facilitate communication between companies and investors about financially material, decision-useful information.
Main users of the report	Stakeholders at large	Mainly investors, but also others	Financial markets, investors
Key concepts	Materiality, accountability	Integrated thinking, value creation	Financial materiality, decision-usefulness, value relevance

framework conceptualises the role and function of environmental reporting in different ways. Moreover, both the primary audiences of the reports and the key concepts through which the frameworks are structured also differ, which leads to differences in how the reports look and how they are structured. The frameworks also influence what information is included in a report and relatedly, and perhaps more importantly, what information is excluded. Moreover, the frameworks also include guidelines and instructions on how particular issues are to be reported as well as on what kind of qualitative and quantitative indicators should be used.

The Global Reporting Initiative

The GRI has arguably been the most influential and widespread reporting framework for sustainability reporting. The GRI publishes standards and guidance documents, developed taking a multi-stakeholder approach, to promote and support the practice of sustainability reporting. Since the first set of guidelines were published in 2000, the GRI frameworks have developed through several iterations into their current format (Levy, Brown and de Jong 2010). Of the prominent environmental reporting frameworks, GRI provides the most detailed and structured guidelines for organisations to follow. A separate standard is provided for various environmental topics, such as material use, energy, water and climate. In each of these topics, there are several detailed disclosure standards providing guidance on how an organisation should report on the topic, how it should be assessed and what kind of qualitative and quantitative information should be provided. It needs to be noted however that organisations are not expected to include all the topics in their reports, but they should instead conduct a materiality assessment to identify the most significant ones.

In international surveys, it has been noted that within the largest private corporations across a range of countries, the GRI framework has been followed by more than half of the companies (KPMG 2017). In addition, a range of other types of organisations, such as universities, publicly held utilities and non-governmental organisations (NGOs), are known to prepare their reports following the GRI framework. The popularity of the GRI framework has helped facilitate the production of environmental reporting, as organisations have been able to report against a widely accepted framework, with guidance regarding how particular indicators should be measured, assessed and understood. Likewise, this development has most likely also made it easier for stakeholders to assess environmental information, since there is some similarity between how organisations provide their disclosures enabling some comparability.

Several key questions remain, however. Take, for instance, the materiality assessment mentioned above, which organisations should use to determine which topics should be discussed in their environmental reports. According to the materiality approach promoted by GRI, each reporting organisation should identify which aspects are producing the most significant environmental impacts, or might substantively influence the assessments of the organisation's stakeholders, and then focus on these in their reporting. While such an assessment is often represented as a fairly neutral and technical procedure, Puroila and Mäkelä (2019) highlighted how materiality can be seen as a political choice including value-laden judgments, and as such can have implications on the accountability relations as well as on how sustainability is seen and discussed in the organisational context.

As the GRI framework has in each iteration included a comprehensive list of indicators, researchers have used it as a basis to develop criteria for content analysis methodologies, which have been used to study, for instance, how environmental reporting practices have evolved over time and how practices differ across contexts or industries. At the same time, discussion continues with regard to whether or not the increased use of the GRI framework has enhanced the quality of environmental reporting (e.g. Milne and Gray 2013). While the GRI framework aspires to help organisations produce reliable and high-quality information, Diouf and Boiral (2017), for instance, pointed out how stakeholders using environmental reports produced according to GRI guidelines are sceptical of the reliability and quality of the information. Questions have also been presented on whether organisations actually comply with the reporting guidelines, and as a result of whether the environmental information provided is comparable or sufficiently unambiguous for evaluation and decision-making purposes (e.g. Michelon et al. 2015; Moneva, Archel and Correa 2006).

Despite its shortcomings, GRI continues to be the "go-to" choice for many reporting organisations. Moreover, while the other two prominent frameworks we discuss here, <IR> and SASB, are more focused on developing environmental reporting for the needs of the investors, GRI has a broader focus. It emphasises that environmental reports should be prepared for a broader group of stakeholders and also notes that these reports should function as an accountability mechanism, which does not only focus on the potential financial implications environmental issues can have for an organisation.

Integrated Reporting

When discussing environmental reporting practices, it is relevant to distinguish between integrated reporting in general, which refers to a reporting form where economic, social and environmental issues are included in a single report, and <IR>, which refers to specific reporting framework developed and promoted by the IIRC. It is the latter that we focus on here as it represents a key reporting framework.

<IR> has been a visible and broadly discussed initiative in the reporting sphere since it was established in 2010. The <IR> framework has as its key concepts six capitals (financial, manufactured, intellectual, human, social and relational and natural), integrated thinking and value creation (see IIRC, 2019). The underlying theme of <IR> is integrated thinking, which is used to describe a new way of seeing businesses and value creation processes. This includes highlighting that financial, social and environmental matters (represented through the six capitals) should be considered as intertwined rather than separate (a key critique of other approaches, including the GRI). <IR> takes a strategic and future orientation which also differentiates <IR> from usual reporting practices focusing more on past performance. In terms of guidance, however, the <IR> framework does not offer any specific guidance or template for reporting, and hence organisations have flexibility with regard to how they produce their report.

While it is often emphasised that the <IR> initiative should not be seen as a sustainability or corporate social responsibility (CSR) report, it is often discussed side-by-side with sustainability reporting frameworks such as GRI and may hence appear to be serving the same purpose. The initiative has also received active support from the big global accounting firms as well as other major commercial organisations (Rinaldi et al. 2018). The emergence of <IR> to the corporate reporting landscape, as well as its substantial promotion by powerful social actors, has arguably had an effect on how some organisations report on their environmental issues, how different stakeholder groups and society more broadly understand reporting, and how particular concepts, terms and expressions are used and understood.

Despite the prominence of <IR> in many arenas, the true essence of the <IR> initiative remains unclear (Brown and Dillard, 2014; Humphrey, O'Dwyer and Unerman, 2017). Organisations appear to be publishing <IR> in some contexts, like South Africa, Japan or the Netherlands, although at the same time many maintain that they are yet to see one (Gibassier, Rodrigue and Arjaliès 2018). The <IR> initiative speaks of enhancing our understanding of how different types of capital, including natural capital, are needed for an organisation to succeed, yet the implications of this type of reporting for stakeholders or the broader society remain unclear (Tweedie and Martinov-Bennie 2015; Flower 2015; Rinaldi et al. 2018). Similarly, it remains an open question whether this type of reporting has the potential to change our conceptualisation of value and value creation. As such, it is likely that scholarly discussion around integrated reporting will continue and provide us with more critical insights on this developing phenomenon.

Sustainability Accounting Standards Board

SASB is a US-based initiative launched in 2011, which seeks to establish a set of reporting standards for corporations. SASB explicitly aims at developing an environmental reporting practice that would be relevant for investors. This makes it closer to the approach of IIRC, which focuses on providers of financial capital, than GRI, which takes a much broader range of stakeholder views into account. This narrow stakeholder focus within SASB also means that the understanding of materiality is significantly different: the material aspects for each industrial sector get defined through the potential financial implications an environmental aspect can have for businesses in that sector. SASB's idea is to limit environmental reporting to a smaller number of aspects, allowing more concise reporting and hence keeping the reporting costs lower for both producers and users of the reported information.

It remains to be seen how SASB will eventually be received by organisations and the investment community. While draft frameworks have been available for some time, SASB published its reporting framework for 77 industries in November 2018. Current research on SASB and its potential implications is therefore still scarce. It appears, however, that in the financial markets there is considerable interest for concise and supposedly comparable environmental information. Indeed, the investment community appears to be seeking ways to better understand the potential significance of environmental issues for different firms and industries (Michelon et al. 2020).

Accounting researchers are also starting to employ SASB's framework in their studies. Scholars have, for instance, begun to analyse whether the materiality considerations presented by SASB would be value relevant for investors, and whether stock market reactions would be different when firms are disclosing CSR information falling into different categories on the SASB's materiality classification for a particular industry (Khan, Serafeim and Yoon 2016). These topics are significant also for SASB, which explicitly aims at enhancing the value relevance of CSR information for investors. Christensen, Hail and Leuz (2018) however pointed out in a broad literature review that the adoption of CSR standards will not by itself lead to harmonised CSR reporting practice, as firms are, for instance, able to use boilerplate language or otherwise provide vague information. Moreover, as suggested by Christensen et al. (2018), the position of SASB and its reporting framework in the United States (US) context is still unclear. The landscape of environmental reporting in the US in general and related to SASB in particular continue to develop, and as such early research evidence needs to be approached with caution (see Roberts 2018).

Summary

We have discussed three prominent frameworks for stand-alone and integrated environmental reporting. It is worth pointing out here that there are no separate frameworks or guidelines for web-based or social media reporting. These can obviously be informed by the frameworks discussed above, as many organisations may, for instance, simply reproduce in their social media disclosures some information prepared earlier for a stand-alone report.

In general, while the frameworks discussed approach aspects of environmental reporting from different perspectives and have varying priorities, they all arguably aspire to enhance both the quantity and quality of environmental reporting, to make it more comparable and useful for those using the reports, and also to aid those producing the reports. Taken together, it is reasonable to state that the frameworks have improved the amount of environmental reporting present in societies, as well as have made some progress in the content of those reports. At the same time, however, it is important to raise questions as to the role and value of environmental reporting for organisations in relation to improving performance, for broader society, and perhaps most importantly whether the reporting function assists organisations to address the underlying environmental challenges that such reports are often seen to relate to (Tregidga et al. 2014; Laine 2010; Gray 2010; Spence 2009).

Current and ongoing issues and questions related to environmental reporting

While environmental reporting has developed into a significant area of practice and research, plenty of ongoing debates and questions remain. Discussions are largely centred on how environmental reporting practices might continue to improve both the quantity and quality of reported environmental information. However, questions also remain as to whether or not reporting, at least in its current form, is useful in moving organisations towards greater accountability and sustainability in the first place. While these issues are numerous, here, due to space constraints, we discuss just a few of the key ones discussed in the literature.

Talk vs action

Despite what may be considered improvements in environmental reporting, a discrepancy between organisational talk and action continues to be a key concern to researchers. Environmental reports are often noted to represent the reporting organisation in a (overly) favourable light, rather than present a more balanced picture, a phenomenon often referred to as impression management (e.g. Brennan and Merkl-Davies 2014). It appears that the voluntary frameworks continue to leave space for organisations to use the reports as vehicles to improve their reputation – rather than provide a "warts and all" account of their performance. While some have argued that differences between organisational talk and action should be tolerated, as such aspirational talk could spur organisational development and thereby improve performance over time (e.g. Schoeneborn, Morsing and Crane 2019), others consider such a gap to be problematic, as it gives stakeholders a misleading picture of an organisation's impacts and performance (Cho, Michelon and Patten 2012).

Moreover, the existence of a performance-portrayal gap (Adams 2004), that is, the gap between an organisation's performance and the way in which it presents itself in the report, is also noteworthy from a research perspective. As the prominence of sustainability continues to grow in the business world and in wider society, the attention scholars give to this area has also increased substantially. Here, and related to quantitative mainstream accounting research in particular, there continues to be some tendency for scholars to use information about organisational environmental reporting as a proxy for environmental performance (Gray and Milne 2015; Roberts 2018; Roberts and Wallace 2015). The underlying reason might be that while data regarding environmental performance and organisational actions may be hard to collect, data on reporting practices or other types of aggregated information are more readily available on various databases. Using valid and rigorous constructs is a key element of producing reliable research findings, and it is worth asking how such conflation of talk and action affects the broader body of knowledge we have about environmental reporting and its societal implications (Laine, Scobie, Sorola and Tregidga 2020).

Regulation

To remedy the observed impression management and difference between talk and action, it has been suggested that stronger regulation should be introduced and enforced, or alternatively that independent third-party assurance would aid in enhancing the quality of the reported information. However, there is ongoing discussion regarding whether regulation in fact would help improve the reliability, quality and usefulness of environmental reporting, and if so, under which conditions this would occur. With regard to SASB, Christensen et al. (2018) have argued that regulation is unlikely to lead to major changes, unless it is strictly enforced and comes with a sufficiently strong assurance function. Similarly, research conducted in other contexts has noted that the introduction of new reporting requirements does not necessarily result in better information for various reasons. For example, organisations might not comply with requirements, there might be other unexpected implications, or the enforced disclosures might not be in line with what would be expected by stakeholders (Grewal, Riedl and Serafeim 2019; Situ and Tilt 2018; Fallan 2016; Bebbington, Kirk and Larrinaga 2012).

In this context, it is also significant to recognise how the proliferation of the various standard-setters, such as GRI, <IR> and SASB, potentially plays a role in a shift from traditional public governance towards a model of private governance in the area of environmental reporting (e.g. Eberlein 2019; Thistlethwaite and Paterson 2016). Obviously, these frameworks are just one of the factors affecting how environmental reporting takes shape and develops, but they are powerful. The power and influence of the various frameworks, or more specifically the institutions that develop and promote them, happen through multiple avenues. Reporting frameworks, for instance, affect the terms and concepts used in reports, thus influencing the tone of the reports as well as potentially impacting which aspects appear to be more set and taken-for-granted and which ones seem to be more open for discussion (see Tregidga, Milne and Kearins 2014). This takes place, for instance, through the materiality considerations used for deciding which topics organisations should include in their environmental reports (Puroila and Mäkelä 2019). Taken together, the reporting frameworks are arguably highly influential as they affect which environmental aspects are discussed in the reports and how, which stakeholders are prioritised or alternatively considered secondary, which type of accountability is being promoted and, on a broader level, which environmental issues and questions are framed as primary and perhaps governable (see Levy, Brown and de Jong 2010; Thomson, Grubnic and Georgakopoulos 2014; Rinaldi 2019).

Assurance

Ongoing discussions also relate to the potential effects of assurance in the area of environmental reporting (see also Chapter 9). The accountancy profession is increasingly interested in environmental matters (see also Chapter 5) and the major accounting firms provide assurance services, the use of which could serve in enhancing the quality of the reported environmental information. These assurance services are, however, fundamentally different from the financial audit function (O'Dwyer 2011). While the latter is strictly regulated and a mandatory element of the financial reporting system serving to reduce the information asymmetries between the owners and the management, in the context of environmental reporting the scope and type of assurance is set by management, which also has implications on the assurance report produced. As such, while often called for as a potential solution to improve the quality of reporting, it remains uncertain whether assurance does, at least in the current setting, have the potential to substantially change the features of environmental reporting (Michelon, Patten and Romi 2019).

Counter accounting

While the issues discussed above relate to how we might improve the practice of environmental reporting, there also remains an ongoing concern as to the ability of environmental reporting in general to serve accountability purposes or to assist in societies' broader transition towards sustainability. These concerns are related to the above issues and the ability of organisations to use such reports for their own purposes. For some, practices referred to as external accounting or counter accounting hold some potential. Counter accounting (sometimes also called external accounting) has been defined as "accounting for the other by the other" (Medawar 1976). That is, it is when an individual or group external to the organisation provides an account of its impacts and/or performance, often in response to no or inadequate reporting from the organisation itself. Such accounting can be seen as a means to highlight the perceived deficiencies in social and environmental accountability and reporting practices of organisations (Dey 2007) by creating new visibilities and representations (Dey, Russell and Thomson 2011), and are often noted as having emancipatory potential (e.g. Gallhofer, Haslam, Monk and Roberts 2006). In short, the practice of external and counter accounting is a potential way in which to consider the limits of current environmental reporting, perhaps limits that cannot be overcome through efforts to improve organisational environmental reporting due to the inherent context and system within which these accounts are prepared (e.g. Denedo, Thomson and Yonekura 2017; Tregidga 2017; Vinnari and Laine 2017).

Conclusion and notes on further research

We have discussed the forms that environmental reports take as well as the characteristics, frameworks and issues that surround stand-alone and integrated reports. As is hopefully clear, despite their relatively long history, and despite a lot of scholarly attention being focused on environmental reporting over a long period, there remains uncertainty as to the ideal form such reporting should take and also how we, as environmental accounting researchers, might assist in improving such practices. This includes whether or not our attention would be best served elsewhere in effort to enhance transparency and accountability (Laine et al. 2020; Milne and Gray 2013; Roberts 2018; Tregidga, Milne and Kearins 2018).

What should also be evident is that environmental reporting, and the various forms it takes whether stand-alone, integrated, web-based or social media, is an area where further research is required. For example, further research on the frameworks that guide such practices, and research on the institutions that govern it, would seem particularly pertinent. With more and more standards and frameworks being developed and promoted, all with different foci and agendas, research on this aspect of reporting, including the power and politics of their development as well as the impact and effect of the frameworks and standards on reporting, from multiple perspectives, is needed (see Eberlein 2019; O'Dwyer and Unerman 2020; Unerman et al. 2018).

We would also encourage a consideration of the need for further research at the intersection between environmental reporting forms and the topics of the other chapters in this handbook, such as extending theories and methods used to analyse stand-alone and integrated reporting, scrutinising the relationships between environmental reporting, assurance and the accounting profession, as well as discussing the complex interplay between corporate reports and external accounting. We would also note that research into the reporting aspect of each of the topics outlined in Part 5 of this book also provides a myriad of opportunities.

In concluding this chapter, we would like to urge researchers interested in environmental reporting to be reflexive in their approach and have a critical awareness of the potential, and limits, of such reporting in relation to the achievement of more sustainable organisations and societies.

Notes

1 KPMG has produced international surveys of corporate environmental reporting practices for almost three decades. The first edition was published in 1993, with updates every two or three years. These reports are a valuable source for an overview of the current state and historical development of corporate environmental reporting.

2 A more detailed discussion of the development of environmental reporting practices is presented in Chapter 2 (see also Buhr, Gray and Milne 2014; Gray and Bebbington 2001; Gray, Adams and Owen 2014).

3 It is worth noting that in November 2020 the SASB and the IIRC announced plans to merge and to become the Value Reporting Foundation, illustrating the shared goals and interests of these two institutions. This development highlights the continuous evolution of the reporting landscape.

References

Adams, C.A. 2002. Internal organisational factors influencing corporate social and ethical reporting: beyond current theorising. *Accounting, Auditing and Accountability Journal*, 15(2), 223–250.

Adams, C. A. 2004. The ethical, social and environmental reporting performance-portrayal gap. *Accounting, Auditing and Accountability Journal*, 17(5), 731–757.

Adams, C.A. and Frost, G.R. 2006. Accessibility and functionality of the corporate web site: implications for sustainability reporting. *Business Strategy and the Environment*, 15, 275–287.

Adams, C. and McNicholas, P. 2007. Making a difference: sustainability reporting, accountability and organisational change. *Accounting, Auditing and Accountability Journal*, 20(3), 382–402.

Andrew, J. and Baker, M. 2020. Corporate social responsibility reporting: the last 40 years and a path to sharing future insights. *Abacus*, 56(1), 35–65.

Andrew, J. and Cortese, C. 2011. Accounting for climate change and the self-regulation of carbon disclosures. *Accounting Forum*, 35(3), 130–138.

Antonini, C. and Larrinaga, C. 2017. Planetary boundaries and sustainability indicators. A survey of corporate reporting boundaries. *Sustainable Development*, 25, 123–137.

Arnaboldi, M., Busco, C. and Cuganesan, S. 2017. Accounting, accountability, social media and big data: revolution or hype? *Accounting, Auditing and Accountability Journal*, 30(4), 762–776.

Ascui, F. 2014. A review of carbon accounting in the social and environmental accounting literature: what can it contribute to the debate? *Social and Environmental Accountability Journal*, 34(1), 6–28.

Bebbington, J., Kirk, E.A. and Larrinaga, C. 2012. The production of normativity: A comparison of reporting regimes in Spain and the UK. *Accounting, Organizations and Society*, 37, 78–94.

Bellucci, M. and Manetti, G. 2017. Facebook as a tool for supporting dialogic accounting? Evidence from large philanthropic foundations in the United States. *Accounting, Auditing and Accountability Journal*, 30(4), 874–905.

Brennan, N.M. and Merkl-Davies, D.M. 2014. Rhetoric and argument in social and environmental reporting: the Dirty Laundry case. *Accounting, Auditing and Accountability Journal*, 27(4), 602–633.

Brown, J. and Dillard, J. 2014. Integrated reporting: on the need for broadening out and opening up. *Accounting, Auditing and Accountability Journal*, 27, 1120–1156.

Buhr, N., Gray, R. and Milne, M. 2014. Histories, rationales and future prospects for sustainability reporting. In Unerman, J., Bebbington, J. and O'Dwyer, B. (Eds.), *Sustainability Accounting and Accountability* (2nd ed.). London: Routledge, pp. 51–70.

Cho, C., Guidry, R., Hageman, A. and Patten, D. 2012. Do actions speak louder than words? An empirical investigation of corporate environmental reputation. *Accounting, Organizations and Society,* 37(1), 14–25.

Cho, C. H., Laine, M., Roberts, R.W. and Rodrigue, M. 2015. Organized hypocrisy, organizational façades, and sustainability reporting. *Accounting, Organizations and Society*, 40, 78–94.

Cho, C. H., Michelon, G. and Patten, D. M. 2012. Impression management in sustainability reports: an empirical investigation of the use of graphs. *Accounting and the Public Interest*, 12(1), 16–37.

Christensen, H. B., Hail, L. and Leuz, C. 2018. Economic analysis of widespread adoption of CSR and sustainability reporting standards. SSRN working paper. Available at SSRN: https://ssrn.com/abstract=3315673 or http://dx.doi.org/10.2139/ssrn.3315673.

Denedo, M., Thomson, I. and Yonekura, A. 2017. International advocacy NGOs, counter accounting, accountability and engagement. *Accounting, Auditing and Accountability Journal*, 30(6), 1309–1343.

Dey, C. (2007). Developing silent and shadow accounts. In Unerman, J., Bebbington, J. and O'Dwyer, B. (Eds.), *Sustainability Accounting and Accountability.* London: Routledge, pp. 307–326.

Dey, C., Russell, S. and Thomson, I. 2011. Exploring the potential of shadow accounts in problematizing institutional conduct. In Ball, A. and Osbourne, S. (Eds.), *Social Accounting and Public Management: Accountability for the Common Good*, London: Routledge, pp. 64–75.

Dillard, J. and Vinnari, E. 2019. Critical dialogical accountability: from accounting-based accountability to accountability-based accounting. *Critical Perspectives on Accounting*, 62, 16–38.

Diouf, D. and Boiral, O. 2017. The quality of sustainability reports and impression management: a stakeholder perspective. *Accounting, Auditing and Accountability Journal*, 30(3), 643–667.

Eberlein, B. 2019. Who fills the global governance gap? Rethinking the roles of business and government in global governance. *Organization Studies*, 40(8), 1125–1145.

Edgley, C. R., Jones, M. J. and Atkins, J. 2015. The adoption of the materiality concept in social and environmental reporting assurance: a field study approach. *British Accounting Review,* 47(1), 1–18.

Fallan, E. 2016. Environmental reporting regulations and reporting practices. *Social and Environmental Accountability Journal*, 36(1), 34–55.

Flower, J. 2015. The International Integrated Reporting Council: a story of failure. *Critical Perspectives on Accounting,* 27, 1–17.

Gallhofer, S., Haslam, J., Monk, E. and Roberts, C. 2006. The emancipatory potential of online reporting: the case of counter accounting. *Accounting, Auditing and Accountability Journal,* 19(5), 681–718.

Gibassier, D., Rodrigue, M. and Arjaliès, D.-L. 2018. "Integrated reporting is like God: no one has met Him, but everybody talks about Him": the power of myths in the adoption of management innovations. *Accounting, Auditing and Accountability Journal*, 31(5), 1349–1380.

Gray, R. 2010. A re-evaluation of social, environmental and sustainability accounting. *Sustainability Accounting, Management and Policy Journal,* 1(1), 11–32.

Gray, R., Adam, C. and Owens, D. 2014. *Accountability, social responsibility and sustainability: Accounting for society and the environment.* London: Pearson.

Gray, R. and Bebbington, J. 2001. *Accounting for the Environment.* London: Sage.

Gray, R. and Milne, M. 2015. It's not what you do, it's the way that you do it? Of method and madness. *Critical Perspectives on Accounting,* 32, 51–66.

Gray, R., Owen, D. and Adams, C. 1996. *Accounting and Accountability*. Hemel Hempstead: Prentice Hall.

Grewal, J., Riedl, E. and Serafeim, G. 2019. Market reaction to mandatory nonfinancial disclosure. *Management Science,* 65(7), 3061–3084.

Guthrie, J. and Parker, L. 1989. Corporate social reporting: a rebuttal of legitimacy theory. *Accounting and Business Research,* 19 (76), 343–352.

Humphrey, C., O'Dwyer, B. and Unerman, J. 2017. Re-theorizing the configuration of organizational fields: the IIRC and the pursuit of "Enlightened" corporate reporting. *Accounting and Business Research,* 47(1), 30–63.

IIRC. 2019. Integrated thinking and strategy. State of play report.

Khan, M., Serafeim, G. and Yoon, A. 2016. Corporate sustainability: first evidence on materiality. *The Accounting Review,* 91(6), 1697–1724.

KPMG. 2017. The road ahead: the KPMG survey of corporate responsibility reporting 2017. KPMG International.

Laine, M. 2010. Towards sustaining the status quo: business talk of sustainability in Finnish corporate disclosures 1987–2005. *European Accounting Review*, 19(2), 247–274.

Laine, M., Scobie, M., Sorola, M. and Tregidga, H. (2020). Special Issue Editorial: social and environmental account/ability 2020 and beyond. *Social and Environmental Accountability Journal*, 40(1), 1–23.

Levy, D. L., Brown, H. S., and de Jong, M. 2010. The contested politics of corporate governance the case of the global reporting initiative. *Business and Society*. 49(1), 88–115.

Manetti, G. and Bellucci, M. 2016. The use of social media for engaging stakeholders in sustainability reporting. *Accounting, Auditing and Accountability Journal*, 29(6), 985–1011.

Medawar, C. 1976. The social audit: a political view. *Accounting, Organizations and Society*, 15(3), 389–394.

Michelon, G., Patten, D. M. and Romi, A. M. 2019. Creating legitimacy for sustainability assurance practices: evidence from sustainability restatements. *European Accounting Review*, 28(2), 395–422.

Michelon, G., Pilonato, S. and Ricceri, F. 2015. CSR reporting practices and the quality of disclosure: an empirical analysis. *Critical Perspectives on Accounting*, 33, 59–78.

Michelon, G., Rodrigue, M. and Trevisan, E. 2020. The marketization of a social movement: activists, shareholders and CSR disclosure. *Accounting, Organizations and Society*, 80, 1–18.

Milne, M. J., and Gray, R. 2013. W(h)ither ecology? The triple bottom line, the global reporting initiative, and corporate sustainability reporting. *Journal of Business Ethics*, 118(1), 13–29.

Moneva, J., Archel, P. and Correa, C. 2006. GRI and the camouflaging of corporate unsustainability. *Accounting Forum*, 30(2), 121–137.

O'Dwyer, B. 2011. The case of sustainability assurance: constructing a new assurance service. *Contemporary Accounting Research*, 28(4), 1230–1266.

O'Dwyer, B. and Unerman, J. 2020. Shifting the focus of sustainability accounting from impacts to risks and dependencies: researching the transformative potential of TCFD reporting. *Accounting, Auditing and Accountability Journal*, 33(5), 1113–1141.

Puroila, J. and Mäkelä, H. 2019. Matter of opinion. *Accounting, Auditing and Accountability Journal*, 32(4), 1043–1072.

Rinaldi, L. 2019. Accounting for sustainability governance: the enabling role of social and environmental accountability research. *Social and Environmental Accountability Journal*, 39(1), 1–22.

Rinaldi, L., Unerman, J. and de Villiers, C. 2018. Evaluating the integrated reporting journey: insights, gaps and agendas for future research. *Accounting, Auditing and Accountability Journal*, 31(5), 1294–1318.

Roberts, R. W. 2018. We can do so much better: reflections on reading "Signaling effects of scholarly profiles—The editorial teams of North American accounting association journals". *Critical Perspectives on Accounting*, 51, 70–77.

Roberts, R. and Wallace, D. 2015. Sustaining diversity in social and environmental accounting research. *Critical Perspectives on Accounting*, 32, 78–87.

Rodrigue, M. 2014. Contrasting realities: corporate environmental disclosure and stakeholder-released information. *Accounting, Auditing and Accountability Journal*, 27(1), 119-149.

Saxton, G. D., Gomez, L., Ngoh, Z., Lin, Y.-P. and Dietrich, S. 2019. Do CSR messages resonate? Examining public reactions to firms' CSR efforts on social media. *Journal of Business Ethics*, 155, 359–377.

Schoeneborn, D., Morsing, M. and Crane, A. 2019. Formative perspectives on the relation between CSR communication and CSR practices: pathways for walking, talking, and t(w)alking. *Business and Society*.

She, C. and Michelon, G. 2019. Managing stakeholder perceptions: organized hypocrisy in CSR disclosures on Facebook. *Critical Perspectives on Accounting*, 61, 54–76.

Situ, H. and Tilt, C. 2018. Mandatory? Voluntary? A discussion of corporate environmental disclosure requirements in China. *Social and Environmental Accountability Journal*, 38(2), 131–144.

Spence, C. 2009. Social accounting's emancipatory potential: a Gramscian critique. *Critical Perspectives on Accounting*, 20(2), 205–227.

Thistlethwaite, J. and Paterson, M. 2016. Private governance and accounting for sustainability networks. *Environment and Planning C: Government and Policy*, 34(7), 1197–1221.

Thomson, I., Grubnic, S. and Georgakopoulos, G. 2014. Exploring accounting-sustainability hybridisation in the UK public sector. *Accounting, Organizations and Society*, 39(6), 453–476.

Tregidga, H. 2017. "Speaking truth to power": analysing shadow reporting as a form of shadow accounting. *Accounting, Auditing and Accountability Journal*, 30(3), 510–533.

Tregidga, H., Kearins, K. and Milne, M. 2013. The politics of knowing "organizational sustainable development". *Organization and Environment*. 26(1), 102–129.

Tregidga, H., Milne, M. and Kearins, K. 2014. (Re)presenting "sustainable organizations". *Accounting, Organizations and Society*, 39(6), 477–494.

Tregidga, H., Milne, M. and Kearins, K. 2018. Ramping up resistance: corporate sustainable development and academic research. *Business and Society*, 57, 292–334.

Tweedie, D. and Martinov-Bennie, N. 2015. Entitlements and time: integrated reporting's double-edged agenda. *Social and Environmental Accountability Journal*, 35(1), 49–61.

Unerman, J. and Zappettini, F. 2014. Incorporating materiality considerations into analyses of absence from sustainability reporting. *Social and Environmental Accountability Journal*, 34(3), 172–186.

Unerman, J. and Bennett, M. 2004. Increased stakeholder dialogue and the internet: towards greater corporate accountability or reinforcing capitalist hegemony? *Accounting, Organizations and Society*, 29(7), 685–707.

Unerman, J., Bebbington, J. and O'Dwyer, B. 2018. Corporate reporting and accounting for externalities. *Accounting and Business Research*, 48(5), 497–522.

Vinnari, E. and Laine, M. 2017. The moral mechanism of counter accounts: the case of industrial animal production. *Accounting, Organizations and Society*, 57, 1–17.

9

ASSURANCE SERVICES FOR SUSTAINABILITY REPORTING AND BEYOND

Charika Channuntapipat

Introduction

This chapter discusses issues relating to assurance[1] practice for the so-called sustainability reporting (sometimes called social or environmental reporting), which is one form of corporate non-financial reporting practice. The demand for non-financial information drives the growth of this type of corporate reporting. As sustainability reporting has become a norm and a legitimising tool for organisations, auditing and assurance are perceived to play an important role in enhancing the credibility of and trust in the reported information. Assurance of such information can be called sustainability report assurance, which is considered as one of the non-financial assurance practices (Manetti and Becatti 2009). The information in these reports may involve information relating to environmental, social and governance aspects of organisational activities. The term "assurance" is sometimes used interchangeably with terms such as "audit" and "verification" (O'Dwyer and Owen 2005). In this chapter, the term "sustainability report assurance" (hereafter SRA) will be used as an overarching term to refer also to related practices and services.

Although users of sustainability reports have expressed positive perceptions towards sustainability reports when they are accompanied by SRA statements, differences in the scopes and levels of assurance, as evidenced by a number of studies, limit the information value of assurance to the report users. Moreover, the plurality of reporting guidelines and assurance standards lead to diversity in the content of reports and difficulties in setting the scope and levels of assurance (Channuntapipat et al. 2019).

As the services relating to SRA practice are largely unregulated, there are therefore many different types of SRA service providers in the assurance market. Large accounting firms (or professional firms) are among those service providers who hold the majority of the market share (KPMG 2015). Accounting is a dominant profession that has the potential to transfer knowledge from the financial statement audit process to new areas of assurance and that possesses independence as a quality, adding value to the assurance process. However, one of the main issues for non-financial assurance services is the expertise of the assurance practitioners in specific subject matters relevant to a particular practice. This provides an opportunity for environmental consultancy firms and certification bodies, who argue that they have more expertise on such aspects and tend to emphasise stakeholder involvement in the assurance process, to participate in the market as SRA service providers. Still, the main aim of the assurance remains similar to that of financial assurance, which is to increase the relevance and reliability of the assured non-financial information. Figure 9.1 illustrates an overview of SRA practice, with the purpose of providing a brief understanding and introducing issues related to this practice (some of the elements included here are discussed in detail later in the chapter). The diagram outlines the rationales for sustainability reporting and assurance practice, related standards and guidelines, and the roles of SRA providers as well as posing questions about the stakeholders and users of the reports and assurance statements. At the top of the diagram, there are issues around perceived SRA quality, which is affected by various factors, including types of providers, assurance standard used, level and scope of the assurance engagement and the assurance opinion.

The purpose of this chapter is to address the following issues relevant to assurance practice: *why* reporting organisations engage with or commission SRA services, *which* bodies are qualified to conduct such assurance and *how* assurance engagements are structured (i.e. level and scope). The chapter also aims to critically evaluate the current trend and to comment on the future of SRA practice. By addressing these issues, the chapter elaborates on the purposes of SRA and the roles of assurance providers, the types of assurance providers and their (perceived) expertise, variability of assurance engagements and the concept of materiality used in the SRA context. The chapter is concluded by a reflection on the current practice and future development, including policy and future research recommendations.

Rationales and purposes of sustainability report assurance

There has been a considerable growth in SRA accompanying sustainability reports. KPMG, one of the Big Four accounting firms, has continuously conducted international surveys to record the trends in sustainability reporting and assurance (KPMG 2017; KPMG 2015; KPMG 2013; KPMG 2011; KPMG 2008; KPMG 2005). The most recent report in 2017 showed that around 67% of the world's 250 largest companies commission SRA for their sustainability-related data (KPMG 2017). The percentage of the surveyed companies having their sustainability reports assured has been increasing throughout the last decade, from 29% in 2002 to 67% in 2017 (KPMG 2017; KPMG 2013). The rate of SRA adoption has increased rapidly in countries where there is currently a high rate of sustainability reporting (KPMG 2017). In countries where sustainability reporting is still in its early development stage, such as Indonesia, Israel, Kazakhstan, Malaysia, Nigeria, Singapore and the UAE, there is a low rate of SRA commissioned for sustainability reports (KPMG 2013, p. 33). It is expected that the rate of SRA commissioning will increase in these countries as their sustainability reporting practice becomes more advanced and widespread (Park and Brorson 2005).

Jones and Solomon (2010) interviewed representatives from 20 United Kingdom (UK) companies regarding their views on SRA. The study provides managerial insights, highlighting that some representatives agreed that SRA could increase the credibility of reports, while others were uncertain about the benefits of this assurance. Besides these managerial perspectives, Wong and Millington (2014) explored the non-managerial demand for SRA engagements. They focused on three groups of stakeholders: investing professionals, local authorities and non-governmental organisations (NGOs). The results from 147 questionnaire surveys showed that only 56% of the respondents used SRA. The majority of the investing professionals and NGOs checked for the presence of SRA in corporate reports, while limited numbers of the local authorities used the SRA statements (Wong and Millington 2014). This shows that the users of sustainability reports might not be the same groups that use SRA statements, as depicted in Figure 9.1. Both studies mentioned above explored the demand (or user) side of the practice.

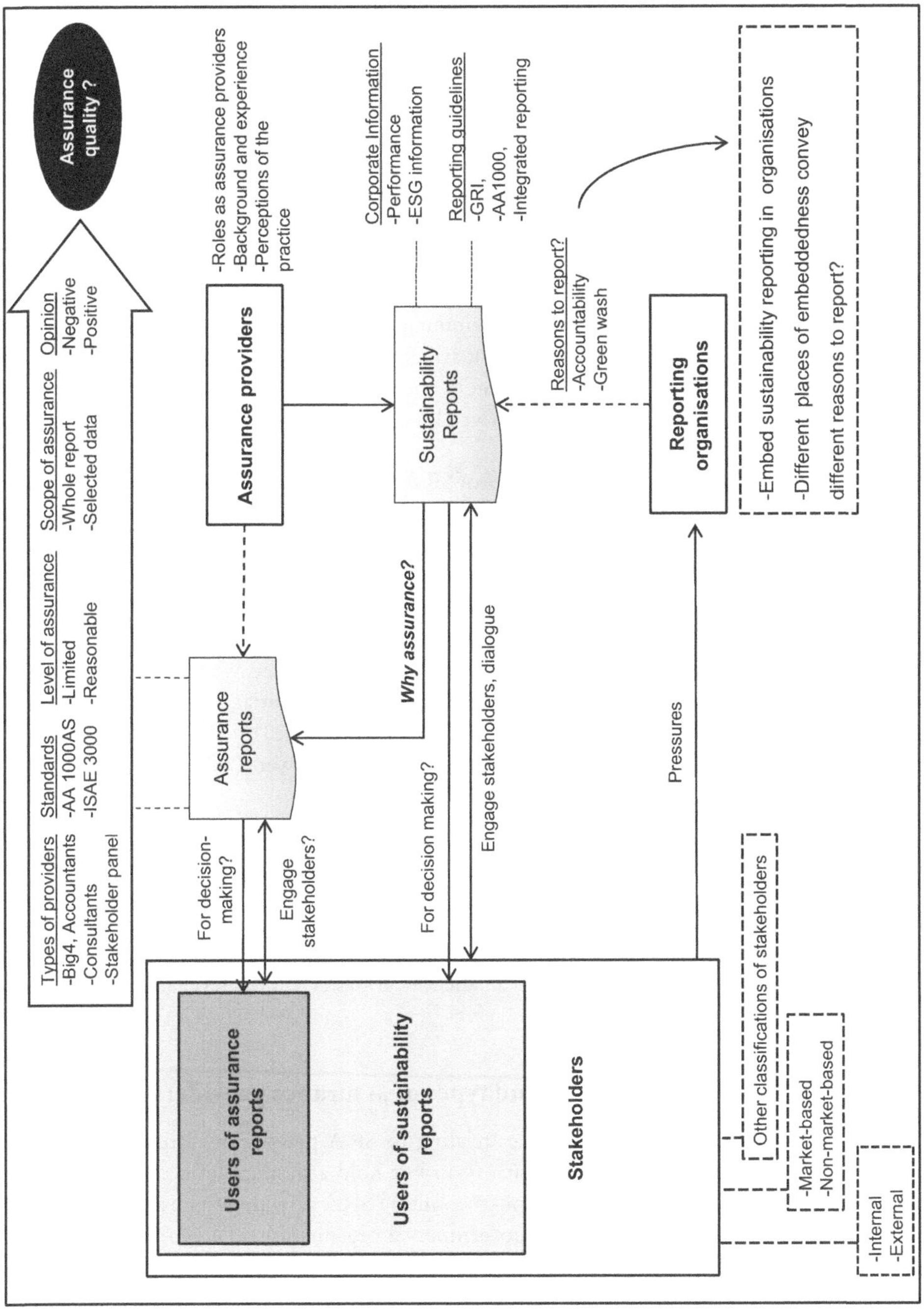

Figure 9.1 Overview of sustainability report assurance practice. (Source: Author's own work.)

They highlighted similar perceived benefits of the SRA, including its role as a monitoring tool to enhance the credibility of corporate information. Also, they emphasised concerns related to the necessity, value and quality of the assurance (Jones and Solomon 2010; Wong and Millington 2014). Another point added by Jones and Solomon (2010) is that the most basic form of SRA is internal assurance. SRA in this case is perceived by the management of reporting organisations as a managerial tool to enhance the internal efficiency of companies' operations, management control systems and corporate reports, rather than as an external accountability enhancing mechanism.

These different rationales for reporting organisations to commission SRA could be observed by how SRA providers problematise assurance practice. Channuntapipat (2018) discussed the problematisation of the practice by different SRA providers from the observation of narratives on the practice from providers' websites. The benefits provided by SRA include responding to the demand for credibility of reported information, improving internal efficiency and encouraging more sustainable corporate actions (Channuntapipat 2018), because SRA procedures can make related risks more observable for different stakeholders (Bebbington and Thomson 2007). Such rationales and benefits of SRA are consistent with Power and Terziovski's (2007) comment that the need for non-financial assurance is driven by either compliance purposes or continuous improvement in the assured organisations.

The issue of conflicting roles and identities of SRA providers could arise because of different perceptions of both the purposes of SRA practice and of their responsibility towards different stakeholder groups (Channuntapipat 2018; Power and Terziovski 2007). Ethical issues in SRA services relating to the client–provider relationship could arise as a result of these conflicting identities (Boiral et al. 2018), which could lead to the capture of SRA practice by managerial and professional interests (Smith et al. 2011). This issue of capture has been raised in a number of studies expressing concerns about the real function of assurance when current corporate governance structure places greater emphasis on managerial advantage over corporate transparency and accountability (see, e.g., Ball et al. 2000; Boiral et al. 2018; Dando and Swift 2003; Edgley et al. 2010; Jones and Solomon 2010; O'Dwyer and Owen 2005; Owen et al. 2000; Smith et al. 2011).

Different rationales and purposes of SRA could also be influenced by the conceptualisation of "sustainability" and "assurance" by different involved actors (Channuntapipat et al. 2019; Moneva et al. 2006). This conceptualisation depends on different factors, including the professional backgrounds of SRA providers. As highlighted by Channuntapipat et al. (2019), variation in SRA engagements can depend on the professional background of assurance providers and the underlying assurance standards, which can affect negotiation on the level and scope of SRA engagements.

The market for SRA and types of assurance providers

Unlike financial audit practice, the services relating to SRA practice are largely unregulated; therefore, accounting firms (or auditing firms) do not hold a monopoly in the SRA market. They operate alongside various kinds of non-accounting SRA providers, such as environmental and management consultancies and non-governmental organisations (Perego and Kolk 2012). The number of companies commissioning large accounting firms to assure their sustainability reports, according to KPMG market surveys, has increased from 58% in 2005 to 64% in the most recent year of survey (KPMG 2015; KPMG 2013; KPMG 2011; KPMG 2005). Although the accounting profession has gained the dominant brand position, non-accounting assurance providers are also important market players.

Empirical studies on types of assurance provider highlight that the type of provider affects how report users perceive the quality of assurance statements (see, e.g., Perego and Kolk 2012; Pflugrath et al. 2011; Perego 2009; Hodge et al. 2009; Zorio et al. 2013). Thus, there has been continuous debate and study regarding differences between SRA providers from different professional backgrounds. The aspects explored in the literature addressing types of SRA provider are mainly the independence, size advantage, expertise and approach of SRA providers in relation to the perceived quality of the assurance (Farooq and De Villiers 2019b). Thus, one professional group of SRA providers might have more competitive advantage in particular aspects compared to others (Channuntapipat et al. 2020).

One such competitive advantage could be assurance providers' degree of independence as perceived by report users (Wallage 2000). SRA delivered by accounting firms is perceived to have a higher quality and credibility (Hodge et al. 2009) because their perceived independence is greater due to their reputational capital and professional monitoring mechanism inherited from financial audit practice (Dixon et al. 2004; Simnett et al. 2009). Although the concept of independence has no fixed meaning (Dogui et al. 2013), a series of reassuring rationalisations of it by the accounting profession has gained strong support, as the independence attached to financial audit practice can be used to make sense of independence for SRA (Gendron and Spira 2010). In order to maintain this professional reputation, especially in terms of independence, the accounting profession therefore seems to focus its approach on data verifying activities (O'Dwyer and Owen 2005), rather than on providing recommendations on reporting or organisational activities, and potentially provides a clear distinction between the assurance and consulting functions that might be related to SRA engagements (Owen et al. 2000).

While SRA providers from the accounting profession have independence as a quality that adds value to their SRA services, non-accounting assurance providers bring their own social capital to the competition (Andon et al. 2015) and emphasise their expertise on related subject matters along with their useful recommendations that add value to the assured reports (Perego and Kolk 2012). Non-accounting practitioners tend to focus more on stakeholder engagement in the assurance process (Manetti and Toccafondi 2012). To some extent, they are also more likely to include within their assurance statements recommendations and comments on the sustainability reporting process (Perego and Kolk 2012). Such commentary on the reporting process could facilitate future assurance practice and help create an auditable environment for sustainability-related information (O'Dwyer 2011). However, this could weaken assurance providers' degree of independence and lead to conflicting roles for SRA providers (Channuntapipat et al. 2019; Channuntapipat 2018).

According to the extant literature, it seems that sustainability experts with a higher level of subject matter expertise tend to be non-accounting assurance providers (Huggins et al. 2011), while their accounting counterparts possess higher brand reputation to render a higher quality of assurance (Zorio et al. 2013). Martínez-Ferrero and García-Sánchez (2018) extended the understanding of such perceived brand premium and expertise by looking at industry specialisation in relation to quality of SRA. The results of their study indicate that the status of being Big Four SRA providers and that of having industry specialisation are the determinants of a higher level of assurance (Martínez-Ferrero and García-Sánchez 2018). However, a contrasting result regarding industry specialisation was reported by Ferguson and Pündrich (2015). There is weak evidence to suggest that changes in industry specialisation for non-financial assurance practice matter to the information users, as reflected through abnormal returns (Ferguson and Pündrich 2015). This could potentially be the case for SRA as one form of non-financial assurance practice.

Assurance providers from both professional groups have distinctive characteristics that could affect the perceived expertise and quality of assurance. Although accounting assurance providers are perceived to provide a higher quality of assurance due to their independence and more robust procedures, they need to demonstrate their subject matter expertise to some extent (i.e. using specialists from other departments, or specifically recruiting specialists to their teams). Here, assurance providers from non-accounting professions tend to attract clients by emphasising their expert knowledge of particular areas of reported information.

The dominance of accounting assurance professionals and accounting assurance standards

The dominance of SRA providers from the accounting profession has contributed to the development of assurance standards and vice versa. The efforts of the accounting profession to expand its professional work space beyond financial audits and assurance (Andon et al. 2015) include the creation of networks of support (Gendron and Barrett 2004) and of a link between the new area of practice and the more institutionalised financial assurance practice (Farooq and De Villiers 2019a; Manetti and Toccafondi 2012). This has managed to render accounting discourse as the core function of the business and to establish its claims of superior expertise and other characteristics (Power 1997). Establishing an accounting standard to guide this kind of non-financial assurance has been one part of the effort to show the intersection between financial audit technology and other areas of work (Andon et al. 2015).

The two primary assurance standards for SRA engagements are ISAE3000[2] and AA1000AS.[3] The professional affiliations of those standards are related to different types of standard setters. ISAE3000 comes from the accounting profession, while AA1000AS comes from an international sustainability consulting and standard-setting institution. The focuses of the two standards are different, although they have no methodological conflicts and can be used together (Iansen-Rogers and Oelschlaegel 2005). Table 9.1 shows the timeline for the development of these two assurance standards.

The ISAE3000, the assurance standard of the accounting profession, is driven by concepts from financial audits and assurance (Deegan et al. 2006). It is proposed as a principle-based standard, which can be applied to different kinds of subject matters. As this standard is affiliated to the accounting profession, accounting assurance providers are obliged to use it. Since the launch of ISAE3000 in 2003 (for use by accounting firms for all statements issued after 1 January 2005), its adoption in comparison to that of AA1000AS has been increasing (KPMG 2008). This trend towards the adoption of this accounting assurance standard for SRA engagements has been gaining much traction, especially after the revised version in 2013. This is due to the fact that the revised ISAE3000 (2013) officially allows "competent" non-accounting assurance providers to comply with the standard.

Unlike AA1000AS, ISAE3000 has been criticised for not being developed specifically for SRA engagements (Manetti and Becatti 2009) and for being constrained by the logic of financial assurance (Dillard 2011). However, Simnett (2012) argued that specific SRA standards might be difficult to develop conceptually; the risk-based approach is then used to develop ISAE3000. The ambiguity of the concepts of "sustainability" and "assurance", which can be interpreted and perceived differently by various actors (Channuntapipat et al. 2019; Moneva et al. 2006), could be one of the contributing factors for this principle-based standard covering the assurance for non-financial information.

This more or less shows the success of the accounting profession competing in the new arena of services by creating this link between their expertise in assurance procedures and

Table 9.1 Development of sustainability report assurance standards

	Period 2003-2019																
	03	*04*	*05*	*06*	*07*	*08*	*09*	*10*	*11*	*12*	*13*	*14*	*15*	*16*	*17*	*18*	*19*
ISAE3000			ISAE 3000			ISAE3000 (Revised)					ISAE3000 (Revised)						*
AA1000AS	AA1000AS (2003)					AA1000AS (2008)											**

Source: author's own work.
* There was a call for public comments on the related standard called Extended External Reporting Assurance.
** There was a call for public comments on the revised assurance standard.

the subject of sustainability. However, the practice might be influenced by the vocabularies and rationales inherited from financial accounting practice (Dillard 2011), which leads to the criticism of the accounting profession in terms of its understanding of the emerging assurance practices beyond financial auditing. Therefore, accounting assurance practitioners offering SRA services need to expand the traditional connotations associated with their assurance (Ballou et al. 2012).

Trends towards limited level and scope of assurance justified by materiality assessment

The diversity of the content of sustainability reports and corporate reports in general due to different reporting criteria (Hodge et al. 2009) could result in difficulties in defining the scope and level of SRA engagements (Manetti and Becatti 2009). Differences in the scope and level of SRA stated in assurance statements could potentially restrain the quality and the usefulness of assurance statements for users (Low and Boo 2012). This is especially so for the level of assurance, which might be judgmental (O'Dwyer and Owen 2005) and could confuse report users (Perego and Kolk 2012), as it is difficult to distinguish between limited and reasonable assurance levels (Simnett 2012). However, Low and Boo (2012) suggested that description of the nature of assurance performed and of the types of opinion given, along with the inclusion of contrasting statements, could clarify the level of assurance provided.[4]

The market surveys by KPMG show that around 50% of the 100 largest companies chose to assure the whole report, while the rest commissioned assurance only on specific indicators and/ or on particular chapters of their reports (KPMG 2015; KPMG 2013). The information on the level of assurance from the KPMG surveys also shows that the majority of SRA engagements were planned with a limited level of assurance, rather than reasonable assurance (i.e. high level of assurance) (KPMG 2013; KPMG 2008). Some companies decided to have a combination of assurance levels depending on the reported indicators. This trend towards limited scope (i.e. to assure parts of reports) and level is due to the negotiation between corporate management, who commission the assurance, and the assurance provider (Channuntapipat et al. 2019). This leads to the criticism that the practice is being captured by managerial and professional interests, as mentioned earlier (Smith et al. 2011).

In order to justify the chosen (limited) scope and level of SRA engagements, the importance of reported information from the stakeholders' perspective comes into question. With this, the notion of "materiality" and the materiality assessment procedure are helpful tools for justifying the level and scope of assurance engagements. Materiality assessment is a collaborative effort (Canning et al. 2018) between related actors influenced by different logics (Edgley et al. 2015). For example, traditionally the term "materiality" in the financial accounting domain has been driven by market and professional logics, while stakeholder logic is extensively involved in the domain of sustainability and non-financial reporting (Edgley et al. 2015). In addition, the meaning of "materiality" used in the domain of SRA might be different from its conventional meaning in financial audit practice, as reflected by the findings of Channuntapipat et al. (2019), in which the meaning of "materiality" is more a reflection of the qualitative perspective and refers to scope more than scale. In other words, materiality for the SRA context can help address what issues are important to include in the scope of the SRA engagement and are crucial enough to provide a high level of assurance. Still, the process of materiality assessment and utilisation of the concept are not straightforward. Materiality identification is a contested arena where meanings are constructed, and identification of material issues is negotiated (Unerman and Zappettini 2014). Thus, tensions can arise between different logics, stemming from different beliefs about, and conceptualisations of, SRA practice on the part of different actors (Channuntapipat et al. 2019; Edgley et al. 2015).

Reflecting on current practice and future development

Sustainability reporting and assurance is one kind of non-financial reporting and assurance practice. As the term "sustainability" is the overarching term that covers many aspects of corporate activities, sustainability-related disclosures can involve diverse issues, from information relating to carbon emission to information on modern slavery. The growing demand for and supply of non-financial disclosures as one of the elements of corporate accountability are contributing to the rise of an array of non-financial assurance practices, especially assurance on integrated reports.

Integrated reporting practice is one of the dominant emerging forms of non-financial corporate reporting, which leads, in turn, to further demand and pressure for the assurance provided for this type of reporting. Existing assurance standards and guidelines have not been intended to cover the integration of financial and non-financial information (Simnett and Huggins 2015), or of historical and forward-looking information, which are the characteristics of the information in integrated reports. Also, the important issues for the provision of this type of assurance work are assurance providers' independence and subject matter expertise, as well as the auditability of the underlying information.

There are some possible ways for different experts to contribute to the assurance of a report with an integrative nature, like sustainability or integrated reports (Manetti and Becatti 2009). Those are (1) a single assurance provider with undivided responsibility for a single assurance engagement, (2) shared responsibility of different experts or assurance providers for a single assurance engagement and (3) multiple experts or assurance providers with separate responsibility for separate assurance engagements (Manetti and Becatti 2009). While a particular approach might currently be more common than the others, the proposed revisions of related assurance standards by IAASB and AccountAbility could accommodate further developments of assurance practices on new forms of non-financial reporting practices that will emerge.

In addition to the revisions of existing assurance standards, regulatory requirements relating to the SRA and other non-financial assurance practices should be tightened. Interventions by relevant regulators are necessary to raise the level of corporate accountability which are expected from the assurance practice (Owen 2007). Recognising and understanding the diverse operationalisation of SRA could help regulators to place some requirements and regulations on specific types of assurance engagements (Channuntapipat et al. 2019). This could alleviate transparency issues, especially the problem that some assurance statements are not disclosed to the public (Ballou et al. 2012), and the potential expectation gap associated with assurance services. Although pressure from private institutions and the public could drive such accountability, authoritative intervention is necessary for the development of SRA and other types of non-financial assurance practices.

The discussion in this chapter opens up some future research directions. Firstly, future studies could explore further on how different individual assurance providers approach the operationalisation of SRA. Except one study by Channuntapipat et al. (2020), the previous literature has largely assumed the homogeneity of assurance providers in the same professional group (i.e. accounting and non-accounting) and has made overarching claims about their differences from mere observations of assurance statements. Exploring sub-groups of accounting providers (e.g. Big Four vs non-Big Four) and of non-accounting providers (e.g. environmental consultancy or certification body) could shed some light on practice variation.

Secondly, future research relating to SRA practice can potentially explore the influence of SRA process and SRA providers on the corporate decisions made by reporting organisations. The research on the use of management reports from the assurance process by reporting organisations could be explored by action research or interviews with the organisations' management and audit committees. This could provide more understanding on the value of SRA contributing to the development in sustainability reporting, and to more sustainable corporate decisions. Finally, as mentioned earlier, in the current era that corporate communication is not limited to corporate reports, it is important to explore assurance practices for sustainability-related disclosures beyond the assurance on particular non-financial reports. Such disclosures can include any kind of non-financial communication in different formats, such as information presented in websites or advertisements. Thus, the research on SRA can be expanded to sustainability "communication" assurance practices. The focus of future studies should not only be on the scope of the assurance itself, but also on the presentation of assured information and assurance opinions so that the expectation gap is minimised. There is a need for more innovative research and new theorisation of SRA and other forms of non-financial assurance practices, as this could possibly lead to developments in assurance practices (Tyson and Adams 2019).

Notes

1 An assurance engagement is defined as "an engagement in which a practitioner aims to obtain sufficient appropriate evidence in order to express a conclusion designed to enhance the degree of confidence of the intended users other than the responsible party about the subject matter information" (IAASB, 2013). ISAE 3000 (Revised), Assurance Engagements Other than Audits or Reviews of Historical Financial Information International Framework for Assurance Engagements and Related Conforming Amendments . This definition highlights the nature of the relationship among the three key parties: (1) the responsible party, (2) an assurance provider and (3) an intended user.

2 International Standard on Assurance Engagement 3000 (ISAE3000) was developed by the International Auditing and Assurance Standards Board (IAASB), an independent standard setting body of the International Federation of Accountants (IFAC).

3 AccountAbility 1000 Assurance Standard (AA1000AS) was developed by a non-profit organisation called AccountAbility, providing corporate responsibility and sustainability consultation.

4 When a lower level of assurance (limited assurance) is provided, a contrasting statement is used. Instead of providing positive wording in the assurance, negative wording is given in the assurance opinion (e.g. "Nothing has come to our attention that…").

References

Andon, P., Free, C. and O'Dwyer, B. 2015. Annexing new audit spaces: challenges and adaptations. *Accounting, Auditing & Accountability Journal,* 28(8), 1400–1430.

Ball, A., Owen, D. L. and Gray, R. 2000. External transparency or internal capture? The role of third-party statements in adding value to corporate environmental reports. *Business Strategy and the Environment,* 9(1), 1–23.

Ballou, B. et al. 2012. Exploring the strategic integration of sustainability initiatives: opportunities for accounting research. *Accounting Horizons,* 26(2), 265–288.

Bebbington, J. and Thomson, I. 2007. Social and environmental accounting, auditing, and reporting: a potential source of organisational risk governance? *Environment and Planning C: Government and Policy,* 25(1), 38–55.

Boiral, O., et al. 2018. Ethical issues in the assurance of sustainability reports: perspectives from assurance providers. *Journal of Business Ethics,* 159, 1111–1125

Canning, M., O'Dwyer, B. and Georgakopoulos, G. 2018. Processes of auditability in sustainability assurance – the case of materiality construction. *Accounting and Business Research,* 49(1), 1–27.

Channuntapipat, C. 2018. Problematising sustainability assurance practice: roles of sustainability assurance providers. In: Gal, G., Akisik, O. and Wooldridge, W. eds. *Sustainability and Social Responsibility: Regulation and Reporting*. Singapore: Springer Singapore, pp. 81–116.
Channuntapipat, C., Samsonova-Taddei, A. and Turley, S. 2019. Exploring diversity in sustainability assurance practice: evidence from assurance providers in the UK. *Accounting Auditing & Accountability Journal,* 32(2), 556–580.
Channuntapipat, C., Samsonova-Taddei, A. and Turley, S. 2020. Variation in sustainability assurance practice: an analysis of accounting versus non-accounting providers. *The British Accounting Review,* 52(2).
Dando, N. and Swift, T. 2003. Transparency and assurance minding the credibility gap. *Journal of Business Ethics,* 44(2–3), 195–200.
Deegan, C., Cooper, B. J. and Shelly, M. 2006. An investigation of TBL report assurance statements: UK and European evidence. *Managerial Auditing Journal,* 21(4), 329–371.
Dillard, J. 2011. Double loop learning; or, just another service to sell: a comment on "the case of sustainability assurance: constructing a new assurance service"*. *Contemporary Accounting Research,* 28(4), 1267–1277.
Dixon, R., Mousa, G. A. and Woodhead, A. D. 2004. The necessary characteristics of environmental auditors: a review of the contribution of the financial auditing profession. *Accounting Forum,* 28(2), 119–138.
Dogui, K., Boiral, O. and Gendron, Y. 2013. ISO auditing and the construction of trust in auditor independence. *Accounting, Auditing & Accountability Journal,* 26(8), 1279–1305.
Edgley, C., Jones, M. J. and Atkins, J. 2015. The adoption of the materiality concept in social and environmental reporting assurance: A field study approach. *The British Accounting Review,* 47(1), 1–18.
Edgley, C. R., Jones, M. J. and Solomon, J. F. 2010. Stakeholder inclusivity in social and environmental report assurance. *Accounting, Auditing & Accountability Journal,* 23(4), 532–557.
Farooq, M. B. and De Villiers, C. 2019a. The shaping of sustainability assurance through the competition between accounting and non-accounting providers. *Accounting, Auditing & Accountability Journal,* 32(1), 307–336.
Farooq, M. B. and De Villiers, C., 2019b. Sustainability assurance: who are the assurance providers and what do they do? In: Arvidsson, S. (ed.), *Challenges in Managing Sustainable Business: Reporting, Taxation, Ethics and Governance.* Cham: Springer International Publishing, pp. 137–154.
Ferguson, A. and Pündrich, G. 2015. Does industry specialist assurance of non-financial information matter to investors? *Auditing: A Journal of Practice & Theory,* 34(2), 121–146.
Gendron, Y. and Barrett, M. 2004. Professionalization in action: accountants' attempt at building a network of support for the webtrust seal of assurance. *Contemporary Accounting Research,* 21(3), 563–602.
Gendron, Y. and Spira, L. F. 2010. Identity narratives under threat: A study of former members of Arthur Andersen. *Accounting, Organizations and Society,* 35(3), 275–300.
Hodge, K., Subramaniam, N. and Stewart, J. 2009. Assurance of sustainability reports: impact on report users' confidence and perceptions of information credibility. *Australian Accounting Review,* 19(3), 178–194.
Huggins, A., Green, W. J. and Simnett, R. 2011. The competitive market for assurance engagements on greenhouse gas statements: is there a role for assurers from the accounting profession? *Current Issues in Auditing,* 5(2), A1–A12.
IAASB, 2013. ISAE 3000 (revised), assurance engagements other than audits or reviews of historical financial information international framework for assurance engagements and related conforming amendments. IFAC, New York. Available at https://www.iaasb.org/publications/international-standard-assurance-engagements-isae-3000-revised-assurance-engagements-other-audits-or-0.
Iansen-Rogers, J. and Oelschlaegel, J. 2005. *Assurance Standards Briefing. AA1000 Assurance Standards & ISAE3000.* AccountAbility in association with KPMG Sustainability, The Netherlands.
Jones, M. J. and Solomon, J. F. 2010. Social and environmental report assurance: some interview evidence. *Accounting Forum,* 34(1), 20–31.
KPMG. 2005. *KPMG International Survey of Corporate Responsibility Reporting 2005.* KPMG International, Switzerland.
KPMG. 2008. *KPMG International Survey of Corporate Responsibility Reporting 2008.* KPMG International, Switzerland.
KPMG. 2011. *KPMG International Survey of Corporate Responsibility Reporting 2011.* KPMG International, Switzerland.
KPMG. 2013. *The KPMG Survey of Corporate Responsibility Reporting 2013.* KPMG International, Switzerland.

KPMG. 2015. *The KPMG Survey of Corporate Responsibility Reporting 2015*. KPMG International, Switzerland.

KPMG. 2017. *The Road Ahead: The KPMG Survey of Corporate Responsibility Reporting 2017*. KPMG International, Switzerland.

Low, K.-Y. and Boo, E. F. 2012. Do contrasting statements improve users' understanding of different assurance levels conveyed in assurance reports? *International Journal of Auditing*, 16(1), 19–34.

Manetti, G. and Becatti, L. 2009. Assurance services for sustainability reports: standards and empirical evidence. *Journal of Business Ethics*, 87(1), 289–298.

Manetti, G. and Toccafondi, S. 2012. The role of stakeholders in sustainability reporting assurance. *Journal of Business Ethics*, 107(3), 363–377.

Martínez-Ferrero, J. and García-Sánchez, I.-M. 2018. The level of sustainability assurance: the effects of brand reputation and industry specialisation of assurance providers. *Journal of Business Ethics*, 150(4), 971–990.

Moneva, J. M., Archel, P. and Correa, C. 2006. GRI and the camouflaging of corporate unsustainability. *Accounting Forum*, 30(2), 121–137.

O'Dwyer, B. and Owen, D. L. 2005. Assurance statement practice in environmental, social and sustainability reporting: a critical evaluation. *The British Accounting Review*, 37(2), 205–229.

O'Dwyer, B. 2011. The case of sustainability assurance: constructing a new assurance service. *Contemporary Accounting Research*, 28(4), 1230–1266.

Owen, D., 2007. Assurance practice in sustainability reporting. In: Unerman, J., Bebbington, J. and O'Dwyer, B. (eds.), *Sustainability Accounting and Accountability*. Routledge, Switzerland.

Owen, D. L., et al. 2000. The new social audits: accountability, managerial capture or the agenda of social champions? *European Accounting Review*, 9(1), 81–98.

Park, J. and Brorson, T. 2005. Experiences of and views on third-party assurance of corporate environmental and sustainability reports. *Journal of Cleaner Production*, 13(10–11), 1095–1106.

Perego, P. 2009. Causes and consequences of choosing different assurance providers: an international study of sustainability reporting. *International Journal of Management*, 26(3), 412–425.

Perego, P. and Kolk, A. 2012. Multinationals' accountability on sustainability: the evolution of third-party assurance of sustainability reports. *Journal of Business Ethics*, 110(2), 173–190.

Pflugrath, G., Roebuck, P. and Simnett, R. 2011. Impact of assurance and assurer's professional affiliation on financial analysts' assessment of credibility of corporate social responsibility information. *Auditing: A Journal of Practice & Theory*, 30(3), 239–254.

Power, D. and Terziovski, M. 2007. Quality audit roles and skills: perceptions of non-financial auditors and their clients. *Journal of Operations Management*, 25(1), 126–147.

Power, M. 1997. Expertise and the construction of relevance: accountants and environmental audit. *Accounting, Organizations and Society*, 22(2), 123–146.

Simnett, R. 2012. Assurance of sustainability reports: revision of ISAE 3000 and associated research opportunities. *Sustainability Accounting, Management and Policy Journal*, 3(1), 89–98.

Simnett, R. and Huggins, A. 2015. Integrated reporting and assurance: where can research add value? *The Accounting Review*, 6(1), 29053.

Simnett, R., Vanstraelen, A. and Chua, W. F. 2009. Assurance on sustainability reports: an international comparison. *The Accounting Review*, 84(3), 937–967.

Smith, J., Haniffa, R. and Fairbrass, J. 2011. A conceptual framework for investigating 'capture' in corporate sustainability reporting assurance. *Journal of Business Ethics*, 99(3), 425–439.

Tyson, T. and Adams, C. 2019. Increasing the scope of assurance research: new lines of inquiry and novel theoretical perspectives. *Sustainability Accounting, Management and Policy Journal*, 11(2), 291–316.

Unerman, J. and Zappettini, F. 2014. Incorporating materiality considerations into analyses of absence from sustainability reporting. *Social and Environmental Accountability Journal*, 34(3), 172–186.

Wallage, P. 2000. Assurance on sustainability reporting: an auditor's view. *Auditing: A Journal of Practice & Theory*, 19(s–1), 53–65.

Wong, R. and Millington, A. 2014. Corporate social disclosures: a user perspective on assurance. *Accounting, Auditing & Accountability Journal*, 27(5), 863–887.

Zorio, A., García-Benau, M. A. and Sierra, L. 2013. Sustainability development and the quality of assurance reports: empirical evidence. *Business Strategy and the Environment*, 22(7), 484–500.

10
NORM DEVELOPMENT IN ENVIRONMENTAL REPORTING

Carlos Larrinaga and Juliette Senn

Introduction

Environmental reporting (ER) has evolved significantly in the past three decades. From a virtually non-existent activity, most large and medium-sized corporations are now involved in some form of environmental disclosure. This expansion arises from different proposals and assessments made by stakeholders interested in increasing corporate transparency, in such a way that a form of ER has become a norm for a given set of organizations. However, as discussed in Chapter 8 of this handbook (see also Gray 2010), despite its institutionalization, ER still seems ill suited to make a real impact on sustainable development and concerns with the quality of such information remain high (Boiral 2013). This chapter takes stock of the literature on environmental accounting normativity and regulation, drawing extensively on Bebbington et al. (2012), to explain how this activity becomes a norm, what is entailed by the interplay between norms and regulation, the process that norm development entails, the different forms of normativity production and the actors involved.

The rest of this chapter addresses, first, the effectiveness of environmental accounting regulation and whether regulation affects ER practice by developing the notion of norms. Second, it considers ER regulation as an attempt to transform ER norms. This distinction between norms and regulation provides the basis for understanding the complexity of normativity production, addressing in turn the different forms of regulation, the diversity of actors intervening in norm development, and the problematization of the authority to regulate. Third, this chapter addresses the dynamics of normativity production. Finally, it concludes with some implications and research perspectives for the future direction of norm development in ER.

Environmental reporting norms

The literature on ER has often differentiated between voluntary and mandatory ER (e.g. Deegan and Shelly 2014; Schneider et al. 2018, Situ and Tilt 2018). Voluntary ER consists of discretionary disclosures made by companies with a variety of motivations, including the demand of different stakeholders (see, e.g., Cho and Patten 2007; Rodrigue et al. 2013; Cho et al. 2015). Conversely, there is no discretion when it comes to mandatory ER requirements arising from state regulation (Peters and Romi 2013).

However, beyond the two archetypes of voluntary and mandatory reporting, the literature has found a grey area where (i) the law does not always affect corporate practices and is not fully applied by organizations (Freedman and Stagliano 1998; Larrinaga et al. 2002; Criado-Jiménez et al. 2008; Peters and Romi 2013; Chauvey et al. 2015; Depoers and Jérôme 2017); and (ii) progressive ER disclosure norms have emerged from practice and have produced a convergence of expectations and practices around a recognized pattern of behavior, regardless of the absence of a direct reporting mandate (Bebbington et al. 2012; Larrinaga et al. 2020). For example, as mentioned above, without regulation, ER has become a norm for a given set of organizations.

What these findings suggest is that there are some ER norms that question not only the presumed discretion of some "voluntary" practices (sustainability reporting), but also the compulsion of other regulated activities. Bebbington et al. (2012) tried to make sense of this situation by characterizing the notions of regulation and normativity. In this regard, the terms "law" and "norms" express distinct concepts, even if they are most often used interchangeably. The law is viewed as a set of formal rules (e.g. directives or laws) and coercive pressures which may be "found, defined and labelled" (Brunnee and Toope 1997, p. 22; Edelman and Stryker 2005). As these authors explain, formal rules can, in principle, exert compliance independently from the context in which they are introduced and are supposed to work.

In contrast, norms refer to a convergence of expectations about recognized patterns of behavior (Bebbington et al. 2012; Larrinaga et al. 2020). This notion resonates with insights drawn from institutional sociology, implying that organizational dynamics are the result of social norms and beliefs to which managers comply to ensure organizational legitimacy and survival (Meyer and Rowan 1977; DiMaggio and Powell 1983). Corporate practices are then embedded in cognitive and normative frameworks beyond formal rules (Hopwood and Miller 1994). The norms that emerge in this context are, to some extent, collectively enacted and enforced by the regulated actors themselves (Brunsson et al. 2012).

Bebbington et al. (2012) used these insights to explore the notion of normativity, that is, the degree to which actors understand rules as binding. In their view, norms are not necessarily under government monopoly: they argue that formal legislation must be perceived by actors as appropriate and legitimate in order to be successfully implemented; but at the same time, these same qualities can also institutionalize informal guidelines. For instance, in their comparative study, Bebbington et al. (2012) showed that a Spanish law achieved less compliance than a voluntary standard developed informally by a combination of actors, events and ideas in the United Kingdom (UK).

While rule-making is traditionally associated with the coercive power of the state, to develop the notion of normativity, Bebbington et al. (2012) drew on broader conceptions of regulation developed in the fields of transnational regulation (Djelic and Sahlin-Andersson 2006; Bulkeley et al. 2012), where the authority to produce regulation and enforcement is problematic and a plurality of actors such as non-governmental organizations (NGOs), professional associations, expert groups, corporations and transnational organizations (Djelic and Sahlin-Andersson 2006; Eberlein et al. 2014) are embedded in rule issuing and monitoring (Hedmo et al. 2006). The International Accounting Standards Board (IASB), for example, has been studied as an example of non-law regime for financial reporting (Botzem and Quack 2006). Likewise, the Global Reporting Initiative (GRI) is a central actor in the regulation of ER (Boiral 2013; Levy et al. 2010). According to this organization's annual report, 75% of the world's largest companies follow its guidelines to shape their sustainability reports[1]. Ehnert et al. (2016) reported that 87% of Forbes 250 companies worldwide publish a sustainability or responsibility report (with 55% explicitly following the GRI guidelines).

In summary, in absence of formal regulation produced and enforced by the state, there is still a flow of ideas, proposals and guidelines that have produced different regimes (environmental, sustainability and integrated reporting) where expectations converge around recognized patterns of ER in such a way that those practices acquire normativity.

Environmental reporting regulation

A growing body of research focuses on the distinction between law and non-law system of rules and their ability to produce normativity (Bebbington et al. 2012; Chelli et al. 2016). Notwithstanding this distinction, the regulation produced and enforced by the state is not disappearing from the ER landscape, but rather its role, deriving from the circumstances described above, is increasingly complex. Regulation has been seen, both in theory and praxis, as a possible instrument to transform ER norms (Deegan 2002; Mobus 2005). In particular, given the flaws of much current ER activity (see above and Chapter 8), some scholars have suggested that governmental regulation is needed to increase corporate environmental transparency, as well as to enhance the quality of such information.

There is a growing trend towards ER regulation. As Table 10.1 shows for the case of Europe (see also Chapter 21), an increasing number of regulations are mandating European companies to disclose a wide array of environmental informations. Such a trend is reflected in Directive 2014/95/EU requiring member states to legislate on a range of non-financial and diversity information disclosures in the annual reports of companies exceeding 500 employees. Applicable since 2017, the Directive has been anticipated by countries, such as France, Spain, Sweden, Denmark and the UK (Fallan 2016), where national laws were introduced before the EU Directive (see Table 10.1).

Different observations emerge when ER norms and ER regulation are viewed together. First, the mechanisms that produce normativity have differences that can be captured by the distinction between hard law and soft law. The second observation concerns the plurality of actors participating in the production of normativity. Governments and states still produce rules and represent the single most important source of authority. However, together with the state, an increasing number of actors are operating in the soft law field, producing rules with varying degrees of normativity. Third, the authority of different actors plays an important role in legitimizing and stabilizing norms (Botzem and Dobusch 2012), that is, in producing normativity. Finally, the observation of ER norms and regulation suggests that normativity production is better conceived as a process whereby some innovations are gradually adopted by relavant actors and finally produce the convergence of practices around a set of expectations. At some point of its lifecycle, the norms (or maybe the innovations) can be codified into state rules, providing further support to the production of normativity. These observations are explored in the rest of the chapter.

Hard and soft law

Consistent with the idea that normativity has many sources, modes of regulation and compliance mechanisms are also quite diverse. The most significant trend in this respect is the rise of self-regulation and soft law (Mörth 2004; Djelic and Sahlin-Andersson 2006). Indeed, as previously observed, the environmental governance arena has gradually moved in recent decades from a regulatory system characterized by formal rules and the strong coercive power of the state (hard law), to rules that are legally non-binding, induced by international bodies (Botzem and Quack 2006; Brunsson et al. 2012; Voegtlin and Scherer 2017). Soft law is,

Table 10.1 Environmental regulation in Europe

Country	*Name*	*Year*	*Organizations involved*	*Disclosure requirements*	*Compliance*
Europe	Directive 2014/95/EU of non-financial information (article L. 225-102-1)	2014	Companies exceeding 500 employees and whose turnover and balance sheet exceed a fixed amount	Four categories of social and environmental information: social consequences, environmental consequences, human rights (only for listed companies) and the fight against corruption (only for listed companies)	Comply or explain principle
France	Law on Energy Transition for Green Growth (no 2015-992, article 225-105)	2015	Companies exceeding 500 employees and whose turnover and balance sheet exceed a fixed amount	Disclosure of the financial risks linked to the climate change as well as the measures adopted to mitigate them	
	Grenelle 2 law (no 2010-788 article 225)	2010	Companies exceeding 500 employees and whose turnover and balance sheet exceed a fixed amount	Disclosure of social and environmental information (42 topics)	- No penalties for non-compliance - Report assurance by an independent third-party organization - Comply or explain principle
	NRE law (no 2001-420, article 116)	2001	Companies exceeding 500 employees and whose turnover and balance sheet exceed a fixed amount	Disclosure of social and environmental information	No penalties for non-compliance

Spain	Sustainability Economy Law (no 2/2011, article 39)	2011	Companies exceeding 1,000 employees	Disclosure of a sustainability report	Report assurance by an independent third-party organization recommended
Denmark	Danish Act (no 1403)	2008	Companies exceeding 250 employees and whose turnover and balance sheet exceed a fixed amount	Revision of the rules in 2012: companies need to report on human rights and climate issues	Comply or explain principle
United Kingdom	Climate Change Act 2008	2008	Listed companies	Disclosure of greenhouse gas emissions	
	Company Act 2006	2006		Environmental information and consequences of the firm's activity	
Sweden	Swedish guidelines	2007	State-owned companies (partially or totally)	Disclosure based on GRI guidelines	Comply or explain principle
	Swedish environmental code	1998	Environmentally sensitive industries	Disclosure of a sustainability report	

Table 10.2 Main standards in environmental reporting

Main standards	*Focus*
World Business Council for Sustainable Development (WBCSD) – 1995	Improvement of economic, social and environmental performance.
Global Reporting Initiative (GRI) – 1997	Guidance on content of environmental reports. The last version of the GRI guidelines (G4) was published in 2013.
Institute of Social and Ethical Accountability (AA1000) – 1999	Process of social and ethical accountability, auditing and reporting.
Greenhouse Gas (GHG) protocol – 2001	Measurement and report of GHG emissions.
International Integrated Reporting Council (IIRC) – 2010	Integrated information that gathers financial and environmental information.
International Organization for Standardization (ISO 26000) – 2010	How organizations can communicate regarding their environmental responsibilities.
Sustainability Accounting Standards Board (SASB) – 2011	Dissemination of accounting standards.

singularly, characteristic of ER, and takes different forms, typically with the proposal of a set of general principles, guidelines, directives or codes of conduct, which are presented to the regulated population to cover an alleged need. Most often, those instruments are coupled with soft non-compliance consequences. Different guidelines have been proposed since the 1990s to "softly" regulate environmental, sustainability and integrated reporting. Those developments are outlined in Chapter 8. The GRI reporting guidelines is one key example of soft law, consisting of a reporting framework that was made available to companies interested in producing sustainability reports. It is an internationally recognized system that has led most of the world's largest organizations to consider ER as an essential part of their reporting practices without a formal legal requirement. However, sustainability reporting is regularly and informally monitored by GRI and other organizations (e.g. KPMG surveys), providing incentives for companies to comply with this instantiation of soft law. Table 10.2 presents some of the existing initiatives with implications for ER.

For Mörth (2004), the difference between hard and soft law lies essentially in the fact that soft law lacks sanctions for non-compliance and, consequently, legally binding character. In particular, soft law reflects a complex production process where many different actors are involved at various levels and in different ways. In this context, international bodies of different sorts (such as the GRI and IASB) can be characterized as highly influential rule-makers that regulate through soft law (Jacobsson and Sahlin-Andersson 2006). But in addition to them, other actors have the ability to modify, interpret and edit the soft rules and contribute to their construction. Because soft law needs to gain normativity, it is in such interactions between actors that common understanding develops and rules can achieve a "quasi-binding" character over time (Botzem and Dobusch 2012).

In practice, however, it is often difficult to unambiguously identify different sources of normativity (Bebbington et al. 2012; Djelic and Sahlin-Andersson 2006). For example, states and intergovernmental bodies often use soft law mechanisms to issue new regulations (e.g. eco-management and audit scheme – EMAS) (Delbard 2008). This is particularly the case in the

European directive which promotes a "comply or explain" principle and thus links regulation with soft law instruments. Much of the ER regulation in Table 10.1 addresses the characteristics and content of such reporting only superficially, omitting the more technical elements and externalizing them to soft law mechanisms developed by non-state third parties. The following section will extend the discussion of the participation of some of these actors in the development of ER norms in a soft law context.

A plurality of regulatory actors: state and non-state actors

The understanding of ER norms beyond the dichotomy between voluntary and mandatory ER requires an exploration of the grey area that lies in between, where different ideas, proposals and guidelines flow and, eventually, can produce norms or soft law, through the participation of a plurality of actors.

Regulatory actors can be characterized as state and non-state actors. The state (the legislative and executive) is constitutionally entitled to codify rules in the law and enforce them coercively in its jurisdiction. However, one of the characteristics of sustainability and environmental problems is that many issues resist being governed solely within the national borders (e.g. climate change). The alternative to state regulation is the regulation of ER by non-state actors (Gulbrandsen 2008; Bozanic et al. 2012; Eberlein et al. 2014). The discussion of soft law has illustrated how a plurality of actors, mainly non-state actors, play a role in the production of ER norms. Non-sate actors do not enjoy constitutional legitimacy to enforce the law coercively. Instead, they play different roles in normativity production that allow them to build a sort of authority (see below).

Four groups of non-state actors can be identified (Djelic and Sahlin-Andersson 2006; Hedmo et al. 2006; Hardy and Maguire 2008; Aldrich 2011; Bebbington et al. 2012). The role of institutional entrepreneurs, epistemic communities, carriers, regulators and organizations themselves in ER norms production is discussed here. To illustrate the various roles in the normativity process, examples are shown in Table 10.3.

First, epistemic communities refer to networks of professionals retaining appropriate knowledge and expertise in a given area, common beliefs about the causality between practices and problems and a claim of authority recognized by all, together with a normative agenda (Haas 1992). These communities, which can include academics and experts, play a role in shaping the generation of new ideas about reporting norms, as well as about strategies to develop those norms.

Table 10.3 The role of actors in the normativity process

	Generate ideas	*Innovate, translate or resist to ideas*	*Diffuse practices*	*Stabilize and enable the inscription of norms*
Actors	Epistemic communities	Institutional entrepreneurs	Carriers	Regulators and reporters
Examples	Academic and experts, think tanks	International initiatives (e.g. GRI)	Consultants, auditors and professional associations	Government and organizations

Second, institutional entrepreneurs are key for the emergence of norms. They are strongly involved in institutional networks, sharing distinct ideas about and developing a certain understanding of ER practices. Entrepreneurship entails the construction and exercise of power, struggle between multiple actors and the negotiation of diverging interests (Djelic and Sahlin-Andersson 2006; O'Sullivan and O'Dwyer 2009, 2015; Archel et al. 2011). Successful institutional entrepreneurs engage in different strategies to influence their institutional field through, for example, the construction of coalitions, lobbying for regulation or discursive action. The GRI, for example, is portrayed as the successful institutional entrepreneur of sustainability reporting (Levy et al. 2010).

Third, carriers refer to actors in a professional environment, that is, auditors, professional associations or consultants (Perego 2009) that can disseminate and influence practices in the organizational field. Carriers participate in processes of innovation and diffusion, proposing practices and interpretations that can tailor the norms to different contexts, thereby contributing to the generalization of particular shapes of the norms (Sahlin-Andersson and Engwall 2002; Scott 2008). For example, consultants and assurance providers can shape ER through their interaction with colleagues and information preparers (Bebbington et al. 2012; Larrinaga et al. 2020). Carriers are not innocuous because they actively interpret and edit the ideas and the practices they transport.

And finally, both governments (regulators) and organizations themselves (reporters) play a role in the constitution of norms. On the one hand, despite the soft nature of the regulation, the formation and legitimization of norms are not completely detached from the state (Archel et al. 2009, 2011; Botzem and Hofmann 2010). For example, by formally or informally endorsing different bodies, or by recognizing a non-state effort in a regulation or in a policy, the state can play a role in the formalization and stabilization of norms. On the other hand, Bebbington et al. (2012) contend that reporters themselves can influence aspects of the regulation and use their position to determine what parts of the norms deserve compliance or otherwise (Senn and Giordano-Spring 2020). Through their reporting practice, by adhering to some rules and resisting others (Johansen and Plenborg 2018) and serving as models to other companies, they actively shape reporting expectations.

Authority

It has been argued that the authority of different actors plays an important role in the production of normativity. Authority provides legitimacy and helps to stabilize norms; it contributes to the pace of normativity production and to the convergence of expectations. In traditional forms of regulation, there is an authoritative center (the state) that produces rules and directives that organizations must follow. In contrast, in soft law contexts, the authority of non-sate actors is exposed and needs to be continuously built.

The literature interested in the production of normativity in this area has generally been more interested in the distribution of power among the different actors. For example, Archel et al. (2011) found in their study that while civic actors lacked the power to promote social responsibility reforms in Spain, the corporate sector could deploy discursive resources and align with the state to subvert the radical potential of this reform. Levy et al. (2010) argued that the GRI transformed sustainability reporting through the construction of a coalition with powerful actors to avoid a confrontation with the industry, at the cost of relegating the most challenging aspects. In contrast, in their study of the Equator Principles, O'Sullivan and O'Dwyer (2015) contended that a group of NGOs were able to draw attention to the social and environmental consequences of the financial industry, paving the ground for the emergence of accountability norms that, although not radically transforming the industry, have meant a progression in its accountability.

Notwithstanding the manifest importance of the authority of actors (rule-makers), other authors also paid attention to how the characteristics of norms and the processes by which they are formed are important element of normativity (Bebbington et al. 2012; Senn and Giordano-Spring 2020). Accordingly, ER rules are more likely to become norms if they have institutional support (Brunnee and Toope 2000); ER rules do not emerge in a vacuum, but they are associated with other rules and are the result of gradual processes whose understanding requires paying attention to the origin of specific ER practices (Berger and Luckmann 1994; Bourdieu 1977). Following Bebbington et al. (2012), the perceived integration of the rules in a coherent normative framework, the existence of previous similar practice that can provide analogies or patterns to develop practice and, finally, the clarity of the rules, all these conditions provide institutional support to ER norms.

First, the perceived integration within the values of higher-level norms provides accounting rules with predictability (Johansen and Plenborg 2018). Coherence with the values and ideas of prevailing standards of practice reduces the ambiguity of the requirements and is conducive to the adoption of the reform. The association of non-financial reporting with the reporting financial framework (with considerations such as the qualitative characteristics of information and the establishment of the entity, and hence associated entity boundaries) provides analogies for implementing, for example, performance indicators or sustainability assurance. In this regard, the analogy of the GRI guidelines with financial reporting might have been an incentive for providing environmental disclosure and signaling adherence to established institutional logics or rules (Chelli et al. 2016).

Second, the existence of previous similar practice provides a template for the new practices and facilitates compliance. In the most obvious case, new ER regulation could simply codify practices around which social expectations have already converged. The EU Directive provides an empirical context to explore whether regulations (as defined in different countries) codify existing ER practice and how this has determined the level of compliance. But often new proposals are built over previous similar practices. Such is the case of sustainability reporting, which followed (and to some extent replaced) the template offered by ER in the 1990s (e.g. following EMAS, Hillary 1995).

Finally, the legal literature argues that normativity depends on rules that are precise and intelligible. Bebbington et al. (2012) described how a convoluted framework for environmental financial accounting made the distinction between environmental expenditures and liabilities unclear and provided space for the regulated companies to interpret the rule in a way that avoided the need to disclose liabilities (Senn 2018; see also Luque-Vílchez and Larrinaga 2016 and Johansen and Plenborg 2018 for further perspectives in this area).

Dynamics of normativity production

The production of normativity is usually conceived as a linear process. Evidence in this context suggests that patterns of emergence, diffusion and eventual norm internalization of ideas representing ER in practice depend on the dynamic interplay between the various institutional forces that enable and constrain organizations' activities (Matten and Moon 2008; Bebbington et al. 2012). The notion of the lifecycle of norms has been proposed to investigate the dynamics of norms and the participation of different actors (Brunnee and Toope 1997; Finnemore and Sikkink 1998). This notion, conceived as a process, is illustrated in Figure 10.1 with three stages: emergence, cascade and internalization.

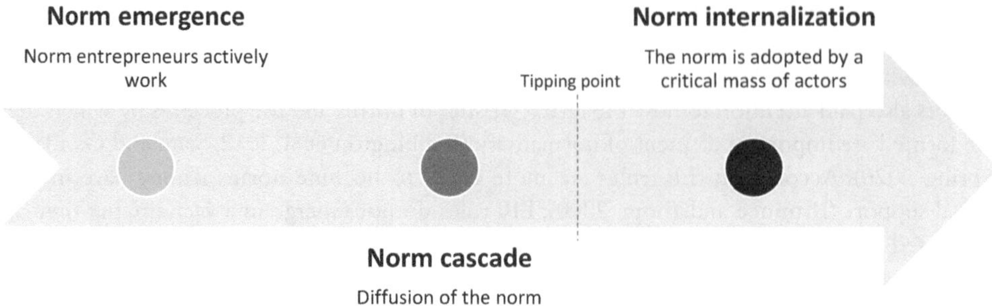

Figure 10.1 Dynamics of norms.

The early stages of the norm lifecycle are seen as a challenging process because new norms originate in a space characterized by innovation and by the assembly of shared meanings and understandings of emerging practices (Djelic and Quack 2008). Innovation is produced by the actions of institutional entrepreneurs advancing new ideas, solutions, and practices (Scott 2008, p. 126). This follows what Table 10.3 identified, that is, such actors innovate, translate or resist ideas and provide understanding about practices. In the case of the institutionalization of sustainability assurance, Larrinaga et al. (2020) have found that assurance providers without an accounting background have played a significant role in the earlier stages of the production of such norms.

Entrepreneurship is followed by the diffusion of the emerging practices, leading to a "tipping point" after which they "cascade" to a convergence toward defined structures and patterned practices (Djelic and Quack 2008). This perspective suggests that different pressures lead to the diffusion of these practices. Bebbington et al. (2012) found that the Association of Chartered Certified Accountants, through its ER awards, was conducive to the generalization of some ER practices in the UK in the 1990s. Larrinaga et al. (2020; see also O'Dwyer 2011 and Hummel et al. 2019 for further perspectives in this area) suggest that assurance providers play such a role in the institutionalization of sustainability assurance.

Finally, once a taken-for-granted status is attained, non-reporters feel a strong pressure to comply with the rules. The crucial change that takes place once the norm is internalized is that the practice depends less on external enforcement and incentives and more on beliefs over its legitimacy as discussed in the previous section (Finnemore and Sikkink 1998; Bebbington et al. 2012). This linear conception of a lifecycle might, however, portray a too simple model of normativity production. Considering the observations made in the previous sections about the institutional support of norms, Luque-Vílchez and Larrinaga (2016) studied a process of regulation in Spain that is more characteristic of the blurred space between voluntary and mandatory ER referred to earlier in this chapter.

The future of environmental reporting regulation

Regulation is asked, by both academics and practitioners, to transform ER, to enhance the quality of such information and to increase corporate transparency. Since the first calls for regulation, now, there is a clearer picture about what can voluntary and mandatory ER deliver. Any progressive proposal to regulate ER needs to bear in mind what we know about ER regulation.

A growing body of literature has studied different aspects of, and characterized, informal non-state ER norms. However, thick descriptions of the institutionalization process of, for example, sustainability reporting or integrated reporting are still missing. Likewise, the accomplishments of different initiatives and attempts to regulate (or influence) practice require further analysis. This includes those initiatives that are more invisible because they failed in their early stages and, consequently, did not produce any norm. Relatedly, it would be interesting to ascertain the reasons for, and the consequences of, the profusion of ER initiatives. Questions that arise in this context include the following: which is the role to play by the global accounting profession in the production/facilitation of normativity? To what extent the expansion of norms could lead to international/global homogeneity in terms of ER practices?

Although ER was the province of voluntary initiatives, this chapter showed how states are increasingly regulating this practice. State hard law is far from a natural phenomenon: it is the construction of a plurality of actors through a complex process. Although some students are exploring those processes to understand the normativity of hard law (again, it is important to remind the distinction between law and norms), further studies should investigate the diversity of these processes, with a view to make ER laws more progressive and more effective.

There is a profusion of voluntary initiatives and state regulations and, with them, an increasing grey area where it is increasingly difficult to ascertain whether a particular initiative conforms to the characteristics of hard or soft law; and whether it is produced by the state or non-state actors. For example, following the EU Directive 2014/95, different European countries have regulated non-financial reporting, relying on international guidelines (e.g. GRI) and on enforcement mechanisms (e.g. sustainability assurance) that are produced by non-state actors. The nature and consequences of this hybrid forms of ER regulation (see Hess 2008) are something that needs to be further researched.

Note

1 The data are from the GRI 2016–2017 annual report (p. 22). Available at : www.globalreporting.org/resourcelibrary/GRI%20Annual%20Report%2020162017.pdf.

References

Aldrich, H. E. 2011. Heroes, villains, and fools: Institutional entrepreneurship, NOT institutional entrepreneurs. *Entrepreneurship Research Journal*, 1(2), 1–6.

Archel, P., Husillos, J., Larrinaga, C., & Spence, C. 2009. Social disclosure, legitimacy theory and the role of the state. *Accounting, Auditing & Accountability Journal*, 22 (8), 1284–1307.

Archel, P., Husillos, J., & Spence, C. 2011. The institutionalisation of unaccountability: Loading the dice of corporate social responsibility discourse. *Accounting, Organizations and Society*, 36 (6), 327–343.

Bebbington, J., Kirk, E.A., & Larrinaga, C. 2012. The production of normativity: A comparison of reporting regimes in Spain and the UK. *Accounting, Organizations and Society*, 37 (2), 78–94.

Berger, P., & Luckmann, T. 1994. *La construcción social de la realidad*. (S. Zuleta, Trans.) Buenos Aires: Amorrortu Editores.

Boiral, O. 2013. Sustainability reports as simulacra? A counter-account of A and A+ GRI reports. *Accounting, Auditing & Accountability Journal*, 26 (7), 1036–1071.

Botzem, S., & Dobusch, L. 2012. Standardization cycles: A process perspective on the formation and diffusion of transnational standards. *Organization Studies*, 33 (5–6), 737–762.

Botzem, S., & Hofmann, J. 2010. Transnational governance spirals: The transformation of rule-making authority in Internet regulation and corporate financial reporting. *Critical Policy Studies*, 4 (1), 18–37.

Botzem, S., & Quack, S. 2006. Contested rules and shifting boundaries: international standard setting in accounting. In: Djelic M.L., Sahlin-Andersson K. (Eds.), *Transnational Governance: Institutional Dynamics of Regulation*. Cambridge: Cambridge University Press, pp. 266–286.

Bourdieu, P. 1977. *Outline of a Theory of Practice*. In: C. U. Press (Ed.). Cambridge, UK.

Bozanic, Z., Dirsmith, M.W., & Huddart, S. 2012. The social constitution of regulation: The endogenization of insider trading laws. *Accounting, Organizations and Society*, 37 (7), 461–481.

Brunnee, J., & Toope, S. J. 1997. Environmental security and freshwater resources: Ecosystem regime building. *The American Journal of International Law*, 91, 26–59.
Brunnee, J., & Toope, S. J. 2000. International law and constructivism: Elements of an interactional theory of international law. *Columbia Journal of Transnational Law*, 39, 19–74.
Brunsson, N., Rasche, A., & Seidl, D. 2012. The dynamics of standardization: Three perspectives on standards in organization studies. *Organization Studies*, 33 (5–6), 613–632.
Bulkeley, H., Andonova, L., Bäckstrand, K., Betsill, M., Compagnon, D., Duffy, R., ... VanDeveer, S. 2012. Governing climate change transnationally: Assessing the evidence from a database of sixty initiatives. *Environment and Planning C: Government and Policy*, 30 (4), 591–612.
Chauvey, J.-N., Giordano-Spring, S., Cho, C. H., & Patten, D. M. 2015. The normativity and legitimacy of CSR disclosure : Evidence from France. *Journal of Business Ethics*, 130 (4), 789–803.
Chelli, M., Durocher, S., & Fortin, A. 2016. Normativity in environmental reporting: A comparison of three regimes. *Journal of Business Ethics*, 1–27.
Cho, C. H., Michelon, G., Patten, D. M., & Roberts, R. W. 2015. CSR disclosure: The more things change...?. *Accounting, Auditing & Accountability Journal*, 28 (1), 14–35.
Cho, C. H., & Patten, D. M. 2007. The role of environmental disclosures as tools of legitimacy: A research note. *Accounting, Organizations and Society*, 32(7–8), 639–647.
Criado-Jiménez, I., Fernández-Chulián, M., Larrinaga-González, C., & Husillos-Carqués, F. J. 2008. Compliance with mandatory environmental reporting in financial statements: The case of Spain (2001–2003). *Journal of Business Ethics*, 79 (3), 245–262.
Deegan, C. 2002. Introduction: The legitimising effect of social and environmental disclosures – A theoretical foundation. *Accounting, Auditing & Accountability Journal*, 15 (3), 282–311.
Deegan, C., & Shelly, M. 2014. Corporate social responsibilities: Alternative perspectives about the need to legislate. *Journal of Business Ethics*, 121 (4), 499–526.
Delbard, O. 2008. CSR legislation in France and the European regulatory paradox: An analysis of EU CSR policy and sustainability reporting practice. *Corporate Governance*, 8 (4), 397–405.
Depoers, F., & Jérôme, T. 2017. Stratégies de publication des dépenses environnementales dans un cadre réglementaire. *Comptabilite Controle Audit*, 1 (23), 41–74.
De Villiers, C., & Van Staden, C. J. 2011. Where firms choose to disclose voluntary environmental information. *Journal of Accounting and Public Policy*, 30 (6), 504–525.
DiMaggio, P. J., & Powell, W. W. 1983. The Iron Cage revisited: Institutional isomorphism and collective rationality in organizational fields. *American Sociological Review*, 48 (2), 147–160.
Djelic, M. L., & Quack, S. 2008. Institutions and transnationalization. In: Greenwood R., Oliver C., Suddaby R. and Sahlin K. (Eds.), *Organizational Institutionalism*, London: Sage Publications, pp. 299–324.
Djelic, M.L., & Sahlin-Andersson, K. 2006. Introduction: A world of governance: The rise of transnational regulation. In: Djelic M.L. and Sahlin-Andersson, K. (Eds.), Transnational governance: Institutional dynamics of regulation, pp. 1–28. Cambridge: Cambridge University Press.
Eberlein, B., Abbott, K. W., Black, J., Meidinger, E., & Wood, S. 2014. Transnational business governance interactions: Conceptualization and framework for analysis. *Regulation and Governance*, 8 (1), 1–21.
Edelman, L. B., & Stryker, R. 2005. A sociological approach to law and the economy. In: Smelser N. and Swedberg R. (Eds.), *The Handbook of Economic Sociology*, 2nd edn., pp. 527–551. Princeton, NJ: Princeton University Press.
Ehnert, I., Parsa, S., Roper, I., Wagner, M., & Muller-Camen, M. 2016. Reporting on sustainability and HRM: A comparative study of sustainability reporting practices by the world's largest companies. *The International Journal of Human Resource Management*, 27 (1), 88–108.
Fallan, E. 2016. Environmental reporting regulations and reporting practices. *Social and Environmental Accountability Journal*, 36 (1), 34–55.
Finnemore, M., & Sikkink, K. 1998. International norm dynamics and political change. *International Organization*, 52 (4), 887–917.
Freedman, M., & Stagliano, A. J. 1998. Political pressure and environmental disclosure: The case of EPA and the Superfund. *Research on Accounting Ethics*, 4, 211–224.
Gray, R. 2010. Is accounting for sustainability actually accounting for sustainability...and how would we know? An exploration of narratives of organisations and the planet. *Accounting, Organizations and Society*, 35 (1), 47–62.
Gulbrandsen, L. H. 2008. Accountability arrangements in non-state standards organizations: Instrumental design and imitation. *Organization*, 15 (4), 563–583.

Haas, P. 1992. Introduction: Epistemic communities in international policy coordination. *International Organization*, 46, 1–35.
Hardy, C., & Maguire, S. 2008. Institutional entrepreneurship. In: Greenwood, R., Oliver, C., Sahlin, K. & Suddaby, R. (Eds.), *The SAGE Handbook of Organizational Institutionalism* (pp. 198–218). Greenwood: SAGE.
Hedmo, T., Sahlin-Andersson, K., & Wedlin, L. 2006. The emergence of a European regulatory field of management education. In: Djelic M.L. and Sahlin-Andersson, K. (Eds.), *Transnational Governance: Institutional Dynamics of Regulation* (pp. 308–328). Cambridge: Cambridge University Press
Hess, D. 2008. The three pillars of corporate social reporting as new governance regulation: Disclosure, dialogue, and development. *Business Ethics Quarterly*, 18 (4), 447–482.
Hillary, R. 1995. Environmental reporting requirements under the EU: Eco-management and audit scheme (EMAS). *Environmentalist*, 15 (4), 293–299.
Hopwood, A. G., & Miller, P. 1994. *Accounting as Social and Institutional Practice*. Cambridge: Cambridge University Press.
Hummel, K., Schlick, C., & Fifka, M. 2019. The role of sustainability performance and accounting assurors in sustainability assurance engagements. *Journal of Business Ethics*, 154 (3), 733–757.
Jacobsson, B., & Sahlin-Andersson, K. 2006. Dynamics of soft regulations. In: Djelic M.L. and Sahlin-Andersson, K. (Eds.), *Transnational governance: Institutional dynamics of regulation*. (pp. 247–265) Cambridge: Cambridge University Press
Johansen, T. R. 2016. EU regulation of corporate social and environmental reporting. *Social and Environmental Accountability Journal*, 36 (1), 1–9.
Johansen, T. R., & Plenborg, T. 2018. Company responses to demands for annual report changes. *Accounting, Auditing & Accountability Journal*, 31 (6), 1593–1617.
Larrinaga, C., & Bebbington, J. 2019. The institutionalization of sustainability reporting. Working paper.
Larrinaga, C., Carrasco, F., Correa, C., Llena, F., & Moneva, J. M. 2002. Accountability and accounting regulation: The case of the Spanish environmental disclosure standard. *European Accounting Review*, 11 (4), 723–740.
Larrinaga, C., Rossi, A., Luque-Vilchez, M., & Núñez-Nickel, M. 2020. Institutionalization of the contents of sustainability assurance services: A comparison between Italy and United States. *Journal of Business Ethics*, 163 (1), 67–83..
Luque-Vílchez, M., & Larrinaga, C. 2016. Reporting models do not translate well: Failing to regulate CSR reporting in Spain. *Social and Environmental Accountability Journal*, 36 (1), 56–75.
Levy, D. L., Szejnwald Brown, H., & de Jong, M. 2010. The contested politics of corporate governance: The case of the Global Reporting Initiative. *Business and Society*, 49 (1), 88–115.
Matten, D., & Moon, J. 2008. "Implicit" and "explicit" CSR: A conceptual framework for a comparative understanding of corporate social responsibility. *Academy of Management Review*, 33 (2), 404–424.
Meyer, J. W., & Rowan, B. 1977. Institutionalized organizations: Formal structure as myth and ceremony. *American Journal of Sociology*, 83 (2), 340–363.
Mobus, J. L. 2005. Mandatory environmental disclosures in a legitimacy theory context. *Accounting, Auditing & Accountability Journal*, 18 (4), 492–517.
Mörth, U. 2004. *Soft law in Governance and Regulation: An Interdisciplinary Analysis*. Cheltenham: Edward Elgar Publishing.
O'Dwyer, B. 2011. The case of sustainability assurance: Constructing a new assurance service. *Contemporary Accounting Research*, 28 (4), 1230–1266.
O'Sullivan, N., & O'Dwyer, B. 2009. Stakeholder perspectives on a financial sector legitimation process: The case of NGOs and the equator principles. *Accounting, Auditing and Accountability Journal*, 22 (4), 553–587.
O'Sullivan, N., & O'Dwyer, B. 2015. The structuration of issue-based fields: Social accountability, social movements and the Equator Principles issue-based field. *Accounting, Organizations and Society*, 43, 33–55.
Perego, P. 2009. Causes and consequences of choosing different assurance providers: An international study of sustainability reporting. *International Journal of Management*, 26 (3), 412–425.
Peters, G. F., & Romi, A. M. 2013. Discretionary compliance with mandatory environmental disclosures: Evidence from SEC filings. *Journal of Accounting and Public Policy*, 32 (4), 213–236.
Rodrigue, M., Magnan, M., & Boulianne, E. 2013. Stakeholders' influence on environmental strategy and performance indicators: A managerial perspective. *Management Accounting Research*, 24 (4), 301–316.

Sahlin-Andersson, K., & Engwall, L. 2002. *The Expansion of Management Knowledge: Carriers, Flows, and Sources*. Stanford, California: Stanford University Press. .

Schneider, T., Michelon, G., & Paananen, M. 2018. Environmental and social matters in mandatory corporate reporting: An academic note. *Accounting Perspectives*, 17 (2), 275–305.

Scott, W. R. 2008. *Institutions and Organizations: Ideas and Interests*. Los Angeles, CA: Sage Publications.

Senn, J. 2018. "Comply or explain" if you do not disclose environmental accounting information: Does new French regulation work? *Advances in Environmental Accounting & Management*, 7, 113–133.

Senn, J., & Giordano-Spring, S. 2020. The limits of environmental accounting disclosure: Enforcement of regulations, standards and interpretative strategies. *Accounting, Auditing and Accountability Journal*, 33(6), 1367–1393.

Situ, H., & Tilt, C. 2018. Mandatory? Voluntary? A discussion of corporate environmental disclosure requirements in China. *Social and Environmental Accountability Journal*, 38(2), 131–144.

Voegtlin, C., & Scherer, A. G. 2017. Responsible innovation and the innovation of responsibility: Governing sustainable development in a globalized world. *Journal of Business Ethics*, 143 (2), 227–243.

11
SHAREHOLDER ACTIVISM AND THE ENVIRONMENT

Michelle Rodrigue and Giovanna Michelon

Introduction

Headlines such as "Investors push Exxon to list emission targets in annual reports" (Financial Times, 16 December 2018) and "Investors push power companies to end coal use by 2030" (Financial Times, 20 December 2018) are now common currency in newspapers and on social media. They represent vivid examples of shareholder activism on environmental issues, our focus of interest for this chapter. Through activism, shareholders voice to managers and boards their preferences and concerns with respect to environmental issues and rely on the power of their ownership status to generate change in corporate activities. More formally, shareholder activism can be defined as "actions taken by shareholders with the explicit intention of influencing corporations' policies and practices" (Goranova and Ryan 2014, p. 1233). Through dialogue and engagement with companies, filing of shareholder proposals or/and discussions at the annual general meeting (AGM), activist shareholders take on a proactive role (as opposed to simply selling their shares) to stimulate transformations into environmental practices (Sjöström 2008). This chapter aims to offer a portrayal of shareholder activism on environmental issues,[1] in terms of its nature, history and current developments, and will end with some reflexions arising from our integration of academic research and trends in practice.

A brief history of shareholder activism[2]

Shareholder activism on environmental issues (and on social issues more broadly) emerged in the United States (US) in the 1960s and 1970s. At that time, individual investors (often called corporate gadflies), advocacy groups and religious organisations mobilised their small ownership into major corporations to request changes with respect to the major social and environmental issues of the time (Marens 2002). This movement contributed to underline the premise that "by investing in a company, one was indirectly supporting that company's actions" (King and Gish 2015, p. 715) and emphasised the possibility for shareholders to proactively voice their concerns over company's actions when they are at odds with their expectations and to pressure the companies for change.

In the 1980s and 1990s, in order to keep the momentum of their pressures on corporations, activist shareholders started seeking support from other large investors, such as pension funds and asset management firms (Proffitt and Spicer 2006; Lee and Lounsbury 2011). Religious institutions remained the most active shareholders until the early 2000s, where investment and pension funds took centre stage (Michelon and Rodrigue 2015). Institutional investors and socially responsible investment (SRI) firms now dominate the environmental shareholder activism landscape (King and Gish 2015). This transformation of the field has also been accompanied by an increased professionalisation of activist investors. Shareholder groups coordinate, strategise, fill and track proposals through networks such as the "Aiming for A" Coalition, the Interfaith Center on Corporate Responsibility and the Ceres Investor Network. Within those networks, members are invited to collaborate in order to promote "leading investment practices, corporate engagement strategies and policy solutions" (Ceres 2019).

The significance of shareholder activism on (social and) environmental issues has also grown in importance over the years. While occurrences of all types of activism tactics cannot be fully documented, descriptive evidence on shareholder proposals (or resolutions) offers an evocative portrayal. In recent years, social and environmental proposals account for 50% or more of submitted requests in the US, with environmental concerns dominating the agenda (Copland and O'Keefe 2016, 2017), against about 20% documented in the early 2000s (Thomas and Cotter 2007). While support for these proposals rarely reaches the majority,[3] a noticeable increase in the number of shareholders in favour of environmental proposals has been observed (Copland and O'Keefe 2016). While the phenomenon is prevalent in the US, shareholder activism on social and environmental issues is also on the rise in other regions. In Canada, for instance (see Serret and Berthelot 2013), shareholder activism emerged in the 1980s through advocacy groups. Shareholders became more active in the late 1990s, when the possibility to submit social proposals was facilitated by federal court, with the years 2000–2013 noting a significant increase in (social and) environmental resolutions among activist shareholders. On the other side, European companies are less likely to be targeted by proposals on environmental (or social) issues (Cziraki et al. 2010), mainly due to institutional, cultural and regulatory factors (Horster and Papadopoulos 2019).

Environmental shareholder activism literature: a multilevel approach

In order to provide an overview of the literature on environmental shareholder activism, we adopt a multilevel model addressing the antecedents, the process and the outcomes of the phenomenon (Goranova and Ryan 2014). While the antecedents portray the actors involved, the process opens a window into the tactics adopted by shareholders as well as into the conceptual lenses used to make sense of the phenomenon, and the outcomes summarise the impacts attributed to environmental shareholder activism.

Antecedents: who are the actors in play?

The historical account described above identifies many types of shareholders involved in activism. Broadly speaking, they can be grouped into two categories: special interest groups and mainstream investors. *Special interest groups* are said to be driven by a wider social purpose (principle or value based), and thus engaging in activism due to their environmental, ethical and social justice concerns (Sjöström 2008). We find among their ranks religious institutions and advocacy groups. They are activists becoming shareholders, in that their share ownership is just one of many mechanisms they mobilise to influence organisations (King and Gish 2015). The Dominican Sisters of Caldwell are an example of this type of activists, being particularly focused on the adoption of green practices. *Mainstream investors*, on the other hand, are shareholders becoming activists. They are mainly institutional investors and socially responsible investment firms that engage with organisations on environmental issues, most likely out of financial concerns including risk management, returns and reputation (Sjöström 2008; King and Gish 2015). While their engagement may also be inspired by ethical values or principles, financial motives are likely to take precedence over environmental issues (Solomon et al. 2013), owing to their nature as traditional investors. Trillium Asset Management, for instance, petitioned the Chipotle restaurant chain to report on its contribution to pesticide reduction within its supply chain, in light of the criticality of pesticide use for the company's brand.

Regardless of the nature of shareholders' motivations, firms are typically more likely to be targeted by environmental shareholder activism when they hold greater "potential" for impact or change into environmental policies and practices (Goranova and Ryan 2014). Large and/or visible firms constitute relevant targets, as their status gives visibility to the activist campaign and attracts greater attention to the environmental matter at hand (Rehbein et al. 2004; Lenox and Eesley 2009). High polluters or firms in environmentally sensitive industries also attract activists' attention due to the significant consequences of their activities and hence the greater need for intervention (Rehbein et al. 2004; Lenox and Eesley 2009). Profitable firms are also under activists' radar, as their financial health is interpreted as a signal of resource availability to respond to shareholder environmental requests (Lenox and Eesley 2009).

The process: what are shareholders' tactics? How do we make sense of them?

Tactics

Shareholders may use different tactics in their attempt to stimulate change in corporate environmental practices. The nature of engagement with corporations varies significantly depending on the tactic adopted. When they choose to initiate *dialogue* with their target organisation, shareholders embark on a private engagement tactic aiming to negotiate some form of change with regard to the environmental issue at stake. While in its simplest form, dialogue could be limited to the exchange of information on environmental practices between both parties (Solomon and Solomon 2006), usually this dialogue requires ongoing, often long-term, communications between shareholders and corporations to secure an agreement (Logsdon and Van Buren 2009). In spirit, this agreement should enable shareholders and corporations to share common principles and find solutions that meet the interest of both parties (Rehbein et al. 2013). As the dialogue represents solely an opportunity to encourage change rather than a guarantee change will happen (Logsdon and Van Buren 2009), the agreement reached behind closed doors will then require further monitoring by shareholders to assess whether managers stay true to their word.

Shareholders can also decide to engage publicly with corporations through the filing of *proposals* for discussion and vote at the AGM, where their proposals are for all stakeholders to see. In these situations, the environmental campaign attracts visibility since it generates media attention and public discussion around the environmental issue at the AGM (and potentially on other tribunes as well). Such tactic is very common in the US, whereas it is less diffused elsewhere. Prior research suggests that the upmost value of proposals is not found in their short-term voting results. Since they expose problematic corporate activities to multiple stakeholder groups (Clark and Crawford 2012), they could represent a long-term engagement strategy to bring about changes in corporate policies and practices (Tkac 2006), pressure corporations to re-assess the challenged activities (Clark and Crawford 2012) and even generate changes within non-targeted firms (Reid and Toffel 2009). In some situations, proposals will ultimately lead to *dialogue* with targeted corporations.

Divesting is also considered to be part of the arsenal of tactics at shareholders' disposal. For example, more and more investors pledge to divest from fossil fuel companies.[4] Here, traditional economic arguments are mobilised to explain this tactic as the ultimate signal of shareholders' discontent which they express through selling their shares of the company, severing their ties with the environmental issue they condemn. Unfortunately, there is not much academic evidence as to whether this tactic actually drives a change in the underlying environmental practice of concern (or whether a systematic divestment from certain industries or products has gained sufficient momentum to trigger a strategic change in corporate operations). Furthermore, in instances where activist shareholders own a very small proportion of shares within a company, the economic signal sent by divestment is not likely to be perceived. This is where political motives for divestment may come into play. Indeed, religious organisations were shown to combine their divestment in targeted firms with public statements, in order to maintain the focus on the issue of concern and to keep on engaging with the corporation as stakeholders, transforming their "exit" strategy into an engagement strategy (Goodman et al. 2014).

Conceptualisations

Social movement and stakeholder theories stand out as prominent conceptual underpinnings to make sense of the (social and) environmental shareholder activism phenomenon (Goranova and Ryan 2014).

Social movement theory offers "insights into the process by which actors translate shared interests into collective action" (Davis and Thompson 1994, p. 152). It conceptualises environmental shareholder activism as a social movement, that is, a public, collective and organised action aiming to generate change – in this case shareholders mobilising to influence corporate environmental management and reporting. The theory is helpful to identify which *mechanisms* social movements may draw upon to influence the outcomes of collective actions (King 2008; Lee and Lounsbury 2011). *Routine disruption* aims at creating significant enough unease among managers to make them direct their attention towards the environmental issue at stake (Proffitt and Spicer 2006). *Resources and constituencies building* endeavours to gather support beyond social movement members, to add credibility to the movement and fuel its actions (Scheinberg and Lounsbury 2007). *Political opportunities* are "opportunities for mobilization imposed by the larger [social] movement environment" (King 2008, p. 29). When tied to the social movement's objectives, these opportunities reinforce the legitimacy of the movement and offer a springboard for action. Altogether, these mechanisms are conceptualised by social movement theory to potentially contribute to the success of the shareholder environmental movement (Reid and Toffel 2009; Lee and Lounsbury 2011).

Stakeholder theory is mobilised to explain the context in which firms would be responsive to activist shareholders' claims. Stakeholder salience and its attributes of power, legitimacy and urgency (Mitchell et al. 1997) are drawn upon to decompose the characteristics of the activist shareholders that are most likely to spur firms into actions (David et al. 2007). Stakeholder theory is also used in combination with social movement theory to explain which firms are likely to be targeted by shareholder activism (Rehbein et al. 2004). This view suggests that shareholders may be motivated to target certain firms to protect their interests and generate certain benefits, such as high returns or better risk management, and/or to define or affirm their identity as environmentally responsible shareholders (Rowley and Moldoveanu 2003).

Outcomes: are shareholders successful? What is "success"?

The purpose of environmental shareholder activism is to influence corporations to change their policies, practices and disclosures in order to better protect the natural environment. The explicit outcomes of such activism are thus framed in terms of corporate environmental management. Academic work offers evidence that shareholders achieve some transformation in this respect. Proposals on environmental issues have been shown to encourage participation in the Carbon Disclosure Project (Reid and Toffel 2009) and to improve environmental performance (Lee and Lounsbury 2011). However, firms targeted by environmental proposals are perceived to be riskier than their non-targeted counterparts, which negatively affects their financial performance (Vasi and King 2012). According to Logsdon and Van Buren (2009), dialogue between shareholders and investors represent the best way to secure change in corporations, although they are careful to categorise this change as incremental. Some instances of dialogue between companies and investors were reported to be useful for companies to improve their reporting practices (Solomon and Solomon 2006). Others portrayed dialogue as symbolic engagements with little underlying commitment on environmental matters (Solomon et al. 2013) or overly focused on discourses of risk and opportunities for investors and companies, casting aside environmental considerations for their own sake (Solomon et al. 2011). Altogether, knowledge regarding the environmental impacts of shareholder activism remains equivocal.

Many shareholders see value in their environmental activism beyond the explicit outcomes tied to the nature of their request. When public, shareholder activism raises awareness about or direct attention to problematic environmental issues both at the firm level (Rehbein et al. 2004) and among a broad range of stakeholders (Clark and Crawford 2012), which accentuate the legitimacy of their requests and campaigns. It can also have spillover effects, as some firms may proactively adapt their practices when witnessing their competitors being the targets of shareholder activism (Reid and Toffel 2009). Ultimately, some shareholder activists may have broader goals in mind than the explicit requests of their current campaign (King and Gish 2015). For example, shareholders engaging with corporations for increased transparency on greenhouse gas emissions might ultimately aim for encouraging a transition to a low-carbon business model. In this sense, different forms of activism might be woven together into a long-term influence strategy (Goodman et al. 2014). From this perspective, success in shareholder activism can be defined quite broadly, composed of various intangible effects that are hard to assess entirely (Tkac 2006). Some will even say that an activist shareholder's work is never done, as when an issue is "resolved", it is time to address the next issue (Goodman et al. 2014).

Shareholder activism in the US and Europe: setting, topics and actions pursued in practice

This section is dedicated to providing an overview of which environmental topics and corporate actions are being publicly pursued by activist shareholders in recent years.

In the US, shareholder activism via submission of proposals is particularly common. Here, it is relatively easy and cheap for shareholders to advance their requests using proposals: any shareholder that has held shares in a publicly traded corporation valued at $2,000 or more for at least a year can introduce a proposal for consideration (SEC rule 14a-8[5]). This official written demand is, potentially, up for discussion and vote at the AGM. It is important to note that submitted proposals may not be included in the proxy statement. Instead, targeted firms can decide to petition the SEC to be granted permission to omit the proposal from its proxy statement, thereby indisputably indicating their non-responsiveness to the issue raised (Clark and Crawford 2012).

On the contrary, once a proposal is submitted, management could decide to engage with the sponsoring shareholders before the AGM and negotiate a course of action for their requests. Upon agreement, the shareholders will withdraw the proposal (David et al. 2007; Logsdon and Van Buren 2009). It is typically assumed that withdrawals are a signal that the company is more responsive to the issue at stake than when it allows a vote at the AGM (Tkac 2006; Clark and Crawford 2012). However, as explained above, discussion at the AGM grants visibility to the issue of concern and attracts the attention of all stakeholders.

If included in the proxy statement, all the shareholders will read the proposal and vote on it. Voted proposals, however, do not bind management into implementing the requested changes, even when they get a majority of votes. Regardless, as explained above, the ultimate goal of these proposals may not be the short-term voting outcome, but rather maintain the pressure high, gain support among the shareholder basis and keep management's attention on specific topics. Box 11.1 illustrates a case where the environmental issue of concern was not considered by the company, yet it generated increasing support among the shareholder basis and accentuated the pressure on the company.

Box 11.1 Activist shareholders on hydraulic fracturing: a short story of persistence and hostility

Hydraulic fracturing is a relatively recent method to extract oil and gas from low-permeability formations, such as shale and sandstone. By injecting a mix of water, sand and chemicals at a very high pressure, it creates small fractures in a formation and thus allows the oil and gas to flow through the fractures and up the production well to the surface, where they are collected and managed. Despite granting substantial access to oil and gas reserves, hydraulic fracturing remains controversial because of its potential ecological impacts (Howarth et al. 2011).

The first proposal on reporting about hydraulic fracturing appeared in the US proxy season 2010, targeting most of oil and gas companies, among which was ExxonMobil. The proposal was filed by a *coalition* of shareholders (pension funds, socially responsible investment funds and advocacy groups) dedicated to the aid and support of education, public broadcasting, environment and other selected areas of interest.

> Fracturing operations can have significant impacts on surrounding communities including the potential for increased incidents of toxic spills, impacts to local water quantity and quality, and degradation of air quality. Government officials in Ohio, Pennsylvania and Colorado have documented methane gas linked to fracturing operations in drinking water. In Wyoming, the US Environmental Protection Agency (EPA) recently found a chemical known to be used in fracturing in at least three wells adjacent to drilling operations.
>
> There is virtually no public disclosure of chemicals used at fracturing locations. The Energy Policy Act of 2005 stripped EPA of its authority to regulate fracturing under the Safe Drinking Water Act and state regulation is uneven and limited. But recently, some new federal and state regulations have been proposed. (… .)

> Media attention has increased exponentially. (...)
>
> In the proponents' opinion, emerging technologies to track "chemical signatures" from drilling activities increase the potential for reputational damage and vulnerability to litigation. Furthermore, we believe uneven regulatory controls and reported contamination incidents compel companies to protect their long-term financial interests by taking measures beyond regulatory requirements to reduce environmental hazards.
>
> Therefore be it resolved,
>
> Shareholders request that the Board of Directors prepare a report by October 1, 2010, at reasonable cost and omitting proprietary information, summarizing 1. the environmental impact of fracturing operations of ExxonMobil; 2. potential policies for the company to adopt, above and beyond regulatory requirements, to reduce or eliminate hazards to air, water, and soil quality from fracturing.

By reading through the proposal, we gain some insights into how shareholders bring forward their arguments and frame their issues. The proposal starts off reflecting on the environmental and health impacts of fracturing on the surrounding communities, and the lack of mandatory disclosure on fracturing chemicals. It recalls the public exposure of the issue in the media and the potential reputational damage and litigation risk. Thus, the shareholders formally request that the company issues a report discussing the environmental impact of fracturing operations and potential policies to minimise hazards. The recommendation of Exxon's board is to vote *against* the proposal, essentially on the grounds that the company is complying with all regulation and any additional information would not be necessary.

The coalition of shareholders keeps pressure high by submitting the proposal for the following three years. Although the prominence of the proposal continues to grow, it never reaches the majority of votes (see Table 11.1). The board continues to recommend voting against the proposal in all years. In 2011 and 2012, Exxon even petitioned the SEC to omit the proposal from the AGM arguing – once again – that information was widely available in mandatory disclosures, that is, that the proposal was already "implemented".

Shareholders mobilise also outside the AGM. For example, in 2013, a shareholder advisory group (As You Sow) and an investment advisory firm (Boston Common Asset Management), which also sponsored the proposals, issued a "transparency" ranking for companies operating with hydraulic

Table 11.1 Percentage of shareholder support for activist proposals

Year	*Sponsor* *	*Status*	*% support*
2010	As You Sow	Voted	26.3
2011	Park Foundation	Voted	28.2
2012	Park Foundation	Voted	29.6
2013	New York City Pension Funds	Voted	30.2
2014	New York City Pension Funds	Withdrawn	--
2015	As You Sow	Voted	24.9
2016	Park Foundation	Voted	24.5
2017	Park Foundation	Voted	38.7

* On behalf of several co-filers.

fracturing, entitled "Disclosing the Facts" (http://disclosingthefacts.org/). In this ranking, Exxon performed poorly, lying at the bottom of the ranking (discloses 2 items out of 32).

A change of direction occurred on 3 April 2014: the coalition announced that it will withdraw the most recent proposal from discussion at the AGM due to an agreement reached with the company (with the help of other external constituents). Unfortunately, six months afterwards, on September 30, the Washington Post reported that the disclosures provided by the firm do not report the information the firm and shareholders agreed upon. "Exxon continues to discuss generalized practices but provides no concrete data on whether it is actually reducing risks and impacts at each of the plays in which it is conducting fracking" are the reported words of Danielle Fugere, President of As You Sow.

In 2015, the shareholder proposal campaign is reactivated. Exxon transparency score is still among the lowest in the 2015 Disclosing the Facts Report and the proposal was debated and voted for in the 2015 AGM. Despite gaining relatively lower votes than in 2013 (see Table 11.1), the proposal still attracts considerable support with its all-time highest proportion in 2017, when the coalition changed the focus of the proposal from hydraulic fracturing per se to "reporting on methane emission". Regardless, ExxonMobil continues to seek to exclude the proposal from voting or recommends voting against it.

Although this example is a case of "no change" (we are not aware that ExxonMobil has – at the time of writing – satisfied shareholder requests), it illustrates that shareholders are persistent in their requests for more transparency, despite the hostile responses from the firm. It also narrates a story of organised actions, where the campaign is not only addressing the corporation publicly during the AGM, but also through other mechanisms, such as the production of transparency rankings, aimed at publicly shaming opaque corporations. Furthermore, it tells us that shareholders closely monitor if and how companies implement the requests, even after reaching an agreement.

There have not been resolutions on hydraulic fracturing (or methane emissions) targeting Exxon in most recent years. However, the coalition of shareholders continues to provide annual transparency scores on hydraulic fracturing. ExxonMobil's transparency score continues to be low (even in 2019), but the industry seems to be slowly improving, as the average transparency score is increasing.

References and useful sources

Howarth, R. W., Ingrafea, A. and Engelder, T. 2011. Should fracking stop? Extracting gas from shale increases the availability of this resource, but the health and environmental risks may be too high. *Nature*, 477(7364), 271.

The text of shareholder proposals can be retrieved in the proxy statements (form DEF 14A) through the SEC EDGAR file (www.sec.gov/edgar/searchedgar/companysearch.html).

A search in the ISS/IRRC (Institutional Shareholder Services/Investor Responsibility Research Center) database in the period 2015–2017 reveals a total of 465 proposals submitted to 224 US companies on environmental issues (representing about 20% of all submitted proposals), quite evenly distributed in the three years. On average, in each year companies are targeted by 1.3 proposals, but there are few notable exceptions. For example, three companies in the oil industry (Chevron, Dominion Energy and ExxonMobil) are targeted with more than 13 proposals each over the period considered. Interestingly, about half (n = 222) contain requests aiming at improving *reporting and disclosure* of environmental issues. Other types of requests include *action on business operations* (n = 160), and changes in *policy or governance structure* (n = 83). Among the most common environmental reporting requests are proposals asking companies to produce a sustainability report, report on policies addressing climate change and climate change risk, as well as reporting information about corporate greenhouse gas emissions. Few other proposals encourage companies to disclose information about recycling policies, or other more industry-specific items such as use of pesticides, hydraulic fracturing, deforestation, palm oil and renewable energy. Most of the proposals that require adoption of policies or changes in business operations focus on reducing greenhouse gas emissions, adopting (or producing) renewable energy and taking action to tackle climate change impacts of corporate operations. Governance-related proposals generally ask to establish a board committee to tackle environmental responsibilities, link management remuneration to environmental criteria and appoint a director with environmental expertise. Overall, climate change and carbon risk feature highly among activist shareholders' priorities.

Michelon and Rodrigue (2015) noted that, up to 2009, proposals demanding action on business operations were more likely to be omitted from discussion at the AGM, suggesting that these types of proposals typically do not trigger a positive response from companies. However, proposals that focus on reporting and disclosure were more likely to be voted for and less likely to be omitted. Similarly, in the period 2015–2017, 2.7% (6.9%) of proposals asking for reporting (actions) were omitted, and 68% (51.2%) were voted, leaving 29.3% (41.9%) proposals to be withdrawn. On average, voted proposals have 22.63% of votes in support, with proposals asking for reporting obtaining the highest support (27%).

Shareholder proposals are less common in Europe than in the US, mainly due to the institutional features of European markets and regulations,[6] as well as due to the different nature of the shareholder basis (Renneboog and Szilagyi 2013). Not least, European companies are leaders in sustainability reporting (KPMG 2017), compared to the US counterparts, and generally more engaged on sustainability, in line with the different regulatory developments and political commitments of the European Union (Renneboog and Szilagyi 2015; Horster and Papadopoulos 2019). This does not imply that shareholders do not engage with companies. Rather, they are more likely to voice their concerns through shareholder dissent over management proposals, that is, shareholder votes cast in opposition to the board's voting recommendation (Cziraki et al. 2010; Sauerald et al. 2016).

Cziraki et al. (2010) documented only 290 proposals submitted by shareholders in Europe over the period 1998–2008, with only 21 of them being on social and environmental issues. Renneboog and Szilagyi (2015) however also reported that over the period 2005–2010, the management themselves put up for vote a total of 439 proposals, mostly related to charitable donations and political expenditures. A search in the Minerva database suggests that in the period 2015–2017, only 15 proposals were submitted by shareholders on environmental issues, seven of which asking for specific environmental information, and eight to adopt specific policies or change business operations to tackle issues related to climate change, renewable energies and strategic resilience in the transition to a low carbon economy. This last campaign goes beyond European boarders as it was launched by a coalition of investors that targeted companies worldwide. Box 11.2 illustrates this campaign.

Box 11.2 Climate change and strategic resilience

In December 2014, concern grew among shareholders that the oil and gas sector was not adequately preparing itself for the transition to a low carbon economy and the related necessary industrial changes. Despite the fact that shareholder proposals are rare in the UK market – and if anything – more common in the context of proxy fights (where shareholders are seeking a change of management), a group of shareholders known as the "Aiming for A" coalition filed a resolution at BP Plc (United Kingdom) and Royal Dutch Shell Plc (The Netherlands).

The "Aiming for A" coalition includes the Local Authority Pension Fund Forum, a number of UK and international pension funds, the UK Church Investors Group as well as US and Canadian faith investors. The coalition was convened by CCLA Investment Management in 2011/2012, to support extractives and utilities companies in preparation for the low-carbon transition. Ultimately, the proposals called for increased disclosures on the assessment and management of systemic risks that unmitigated temperature rises pose for the global economy and therefore to the companies' short-, medium- and long-term commercial resilience, in terms of business models and capital expenditure plans in the context of the shift to a low-carbon energy mix:

> That in order to address our interest in the longer term success of the Company, given the recognised risks and opportunities associated with climate change, we as shareholders of the Company direct that routine annual reporting from 2017 includes further information about: ongoing operational emissions management; asset portfolio resilience to the International Energy Agency's (IEA's) scenarios; low-carbon energy research and development (R&D) and investment strategies; relevant strategic key performance indicators (KPIs) and executive incentives; and public policy positions relating to climate change. This additional ongoing annual reporting could build on the disclosures already made to CDP (formerly the Carbon Disclosure Project) and/or those already made within the Company's Annual Report and Sustainable Development Report.

The management of both Shell and BP recommended shareholder support to the resolutions, as being in the best interests of the company and its shareholders and the resolutions passed with 98.8% and 98.3% in Shell and BP, respectively.

The following year (2016), the US members of the "Aiming for A" coalition submitted to Chevron and ExxonMobil the same proposals. Both companies petition the SEC to omit the proposal but were not successful, and despite the vote against recommendation put forward by both boards, the proposals received 40.8% and 38.1% of votes in support at Chevron and ExxonMobil, respectively.

Following the relatively high support received on the proposal, in March 2017 Chevron published its first "Managing climate change risks" report, and this led the coalition to withdraw their proposal from the 2017 proxy season, illustrating that strong votes (albeit not a majority) can lead to company action.

On the contrary, ExxonMobil maintained its hostile response to the initiative, trying to omit again the proposal from the AGM but unsuccessfully. Some 62% of shareholders voted for the resolutions, against the board recommendation (The Guardian, 31 May 2017).

Companies like ExxonMobil seem to be generally resistant to requests to disclose information about its management of climate risk or other environmental issues. In its 2014 report "Energy &

Carbon – Managing the Risks", the company stated that a 2°C scenario does not merit examination because it is "not reasonably likely to occur" (2017 Investor Climate Compass) Shareholders maintain pressure on Exxon in recent years, with nine shareholder resolutions on climate change from 2014 to 2019. The Securities and Exchange Commission (SEC) has also increased scrutiny on Exxon's climate risk reporting.

This box illustrates not only that shareholder activism on the environment is a global phenomenon, with coalitions of shareholders spreading across national borders, but also speaks to the increasing importance that investors put on environmental risk, and in particular climate change. It also narrates that corporate response varies across different countries, and that some companies are more likely to engage and listen to shareholders than others. Furthermore, it suggests that shareholder attention on certain issues may attract scrutiny by different stakeholders, including regulators.

References and useful resources

Full information about members of the "Aiming for A" coalition can be found at: www.ap4.se/globalassets/dokument/rapportarkiv/2015/institutional-cofiling-group-bp-and-shell-2015.pdf

The full text of the resolution can be downloaded at: www.iccr.org/special-resolution-strategic-resilience-2035-and-beyond.

The Guardian: www.theguardian.com/business/2017/may/31/exxonmobil-climate-change-cost-shareholders

2017 Investor Climate Compass: www.eenews.net/assets/2017/05/15/document_cw_01.pdf

Conclusion

Our overview of environmental shareholder activism offers some rays of hope. It shows that some shareholders are concerned about environmental issues (with climate change at the top of their list) and endeavour to leverage their ownership to pressure corporations into change. The tenacity of some shareholders on the matter is noticeable and some accomplishment cannot be denied. But our overview also underlines some causes for concerns. The fact that US shareholder proposals focus on requesting additional environmental information rather than changes in operations harming the environment is troubling, as it is likely to lead to incremental rather than substantive changes (if any) and to direct managers' attention towards reporting rather than action (Gold & Heikkurinen 2018). More broadly, the co-existence of two motivations for activism, the principle-based motivation of special interest groups and the financial motivation of mainstream investors, is disquieting, since the dominance of the latter in the investment world could be a threat to the legitimacy of the former (Michelon et al. 2020).

Ultimately, this chapter generally highlights how environmental shareholder activism represents a fertile ground for research. In some respect, environmental shareholder activism remains a "black box", as the inner workings of activism campaigns have not been explored yet. We know little about how investors view and approach activism, how they mobilise – and whether it matters for securing change and what type of change. For example, as the tactic of dialogue occurs behind closed doors, access is challenging for academics. Given that dialogue is viewed as one of the most effective tactic (Logsdon and Van Burren 2009), undertaking scholarly work on the matter may lead to useful insights. Similarly, while the tactic of divestment has been adopted for some time, the effectiveness of the approach in transforming the problematic activities remains to be assessed. Paying attention to how shareholders' motivations shape their tactics and strategy is also of importance. Additionally, as presented in Boxes 11.1 and 11.2, corporate responses to activism vary in many respects and deserve further attention. Of particular interest is the impact of shareholders' motivation (principles or profit) on both the recognition and response to their request.

Altogether, these questions point towards one of the most challenging – and also one of the most significant – avenues of research on shareholder activism: the way success is defined, shaped and assessed. Not only academic research on the explicit outcomes of environmental shareholder activism is ambiguous, but the broader consequences of activism are also the basis of various speculations (and hopes) with little accompanying evidence. Our exploration into practice suggests that persistence could play a role in securing and maintaining some changes. Among the many questions to pursue, we encourage reflecting about the following: on what grounds can we affirm that environmental activism is successful? Successful for whom? Is it enough for activism to meet shareholders' (performance) expectations? Only once we better understand what success is and how it is shaped will we know whether environmental shareholder activism can play a significant role in tackling the enormous environmental challenges of our time.

Notes

1 Broadly speaking, there are two streams of shareholder activism: (1) financial shareholder activism, focusing, for example, on governance, executive compensation, etc.; and (2) social shareholder activism focusing on societal considerations such as environmental protection, labour conditions, etc. (Goranova and Ryan 2014). This chapter concentrates on a subset of the latter, namely, environmental activism, although it will refer to social activism more generally when appropriate.
2 Our brief historical account covers shareholder activism on social and environmental issues altogether as both types of activism share similar roots.
3 Box 11.2 features an exceptional case where proposals received majority support.
4 https://gofossilfree.org/divestment/commitments/.
5 www.ecfr.gov/cgi-bin/text-idx?SID=797d170e7970e40bfe223dfe9b8e0bbf&mc=true&node=se17.4.240_114a_68&rgn=div8
6 High ownership requirements make it difficult to file proposals in most markets (especially for individual investors) – https://corpgov.law.harvard.edu/2019/01/07/climate-change-and-proxy-voting-in-the-u-s-and-europe/.

References

Ceres, 2019. Ceres Investor Network on Climate Risk and Sustainability. Available from: www.ceres.org/networks/ceres-investor-network [Accessed 11 June 2019].
Clark, C.E. and Crawford. E.P., 2012. Influencing climate change policy: The effect of shareholder pressure and firm environmental performance. *Business & Society*, 51(1), 148–175.
Copland, J. and O'Keefe, M.M., 2016. *Proxy Monitor: A Report on Corporate Governance and Shareholder Activism*. New York: Manhattan Institute.
Copland, J., and O'Keefe, M.M., 2017. *Proxy Monitor: A Report on Corporate Governance and Shareholder Activism*. New York: Manhattan Institute.
Cziraki, P., Renneboog, L., and Szilagyi, P.G., 2010. Shareholder activism through proxy proposals: The European perspective. *European Financial Management*, 5, 738–777.
David, P., Bloom, M., and Hillman, A.J., 2007. Investor activism, managerial responsiveness, and corporate social performance. *Strategic Management Journal*, 28(1), 91–100.
Davis, G.F., and Thompson, T.A., 1994. A social movement perspective on corporate control. *Administrative Science Quarterly*, 39(1), 141–173.
Gold, S., and Heikkurinen, P., 2018. Transparency fallacy: Unintended consequences of stakeholder claims on responsibility in supply chains. *Accounting, Auditing & Accountability Journal*, 31(1), 318–337.

Goodman, J., Louche, C., van Cranenburgh, K.C., and Arenas, D., 2014. Social shareholder engagement: The dynamics of voice and exit. *Journal of Business Ethics,* 125(2), 193–210.
Goranova, M., and Ryan, L.V., 2014. Shareholder activism: A multidisciplinary review. *Journal of Management,* 40(5), 1230–1268.
Horster, M., and Papadopoulos, K., 2019. Climate change and proxy voting in the U.S. and Europe. *Harvard Law School Forum on Corporate Governance and Financial Regulation.* Available from: https://corpgov.law.harvard.edu/2019/01/07/climate-change-and-proxy-voting-in-the-u-s-and-europe/ [Accessed 22 June 2019].
King, B.G., 2008. A social movement perspective of stakeholder collective action and influence. *Business & Society,* 47(1), 21–49.
King, L., and Gish, E., 2015. Marketizing social change: Social shareholder activism and responsible investing. *Sociological Perspectives*, 58(4), 711–730.
KPMG, 2017. *The KPMG Survey of Corporate Responsibility Reporting 2017.* Available from: https://assets.kpmg/content/dam/kpmg/be/pdf/2017/kpmg-survey-of-corporate-responsibility-reporting–2017.pdf [Accessed 12 July 2019].
Lee, M.D.P., and Lounsbury, M., 2011. Domesticating radical rant and rage: An exploration of the consequences of environmental shareholder resolutions on corporate environmental performance. *Business & Society*, 50(1), 155–188.
Lenox, M.J., and Eesley, C.E., 2009. Private environmental activism and the selection and response of firm targets. *Journal of Economics & Management Strategy*, 18(1), 45–73.
Logsdon, J., and Van Buren, H. III., 2009. Beyond the proxy vote: Dialogues between shareholder activists and corporations. *Journal of Business Ethics,* 87(1 Supplement April), 353–365.
Marens, R., 2002. Inventing corporate governance: The mid-century emergence of shareholder activism. *Journal of Business and Management,* 8(4), 365–389.
Michelon G., and Rodrigue, M., 2015. Demand for CSR: Insights from shareholders proposals. *Social and Environmental Accountability Journal*, 35(3), 157–175.
Michelon, G., Rodrigue, M., and Trevisan, E., 2020. The marketization of a social movement: Activists, shareholders and CSR disclosure. *Accounting, Organizations and Society*, Change for *80*, 101074. doi: https://doi.org/10.1016/j.aos.2019.101074
Mitchell, R.K., Agle, B.R., and Wood, D.J., 1997. Toward a theory of stakeholder identification and salience: Defining the principle of who and what really counts. *Academy of Management Review,* 22(4), 853–885.
Proffitt, W.T., and Spicer. A., 2006. Shaping the shareholder activism agenda: Institutional investors and global social issues. *Strategic Organization*, 4(2), 165–190.
Reid, E.M., and Toffel, M.W., 2009. Responding to public and private politics: Corporate disclosure of climate change strategies. *Strategic Management Journal*, 30(11), 1157–1178.
Rehbein, K., Waddock, S., and Graves, S.B., 2004. Understanding shareholder activism: Which corporations are targeted? *Business & Society*, 43(3), 239–267.
Rehbein, K., Logsdon, J.M., and Van Buren, H.J., 2013. Corporate responses to shareholder activists: Considering the dialogue alternative. *Journal of Business Ethics,* 112(1), 137–154.
Renneboog, L., & Szilagyi, P.G. 2013. Shareholder engagement at European general meeting. In Belcredin M., & Ferrarini, G. (eds). *Boards and Shareholders in European listed companies*: 315-364. Cambridge.
Renneboog, L., and Szilagi, P.G., 2011. The role of shareholder proposals in corporate governance. *Journal of Corporate Finance*, 17(1), 167–188.
Rowley, T.J., and Moldoveanu, M., 2003. When will stakeholder groups act? An interest- and identity-based model of stakeholder group mobilization. *Academy of Management Review*, 28(2), 204–219.
Sauerwald, S., Van Oosterhout, J.H., and Van Essen, M., 2016. Expressive shareholder democracy: A multilevel study of shareholder dissent in 15 Western European countries. *Journal of Management Studies*, 53(4), 520–551.
Schneiberg, M., and Lounsbury, M., 2007. Social movements and institutional analysis. In: R. Greenwood, C. Oliver, R. Suddaby, and K. Sahlin (eds.), *The SAGE Handbook of Organizational Institutionalism.* London: Sage, pp. 650–673.
Serret, V., and Berthelot, S. 2013. Activisme actionnarial et responsabilité sociétale des entreprises au canada analyse des résolutions soumises par les actionnaires entre 2000 et 2013. *Revue de l'organisation responsable*, 8(1), 17–32.
Sjöström, E., 2008. Shareholder activism for corporate social responsibility: What do we know? *Sustainable Development,* 16(3), 141–154.

Solomon, J.F., and Solomon, A., 2006. Private social, ethical and environmental disclosure. *Accounting, Auditing & Accountability Journal*, 19(4), 564–591.

Solomon, J.F., Solomon, A., Joseph, N.L., and Norton, S.D., 2013. Impression management, myth creation and fabrication in private social and environmental reporting: Insights from Erving Goffman. *Accounting, Organizations and Society*, 38(3), 195–213.

Solomon, J.F., Solomon, A., Norton, S.D., and Joseph, N.L., 2011. Private climate change reporting: An emerging discourse of risk and opportunity? *Accounting, Auditing & Accountability Journal*, 24(8), 1119–1148.

Thomas, R.S., and Cotter., J.F., 2007. Shareholder proposals in the new millennium: Shareholder support, board response, and market reaction. *Journal of Corporate Finance*, 13, 368–391.

Tkac, P., 2006. One proxy at a time: Pursuing social change through shareholder proposals. *Economic Review of the Federal Reserve Bank of Atlanta*, 91 (Third Quarter), 1–20.

Vasi, I.B., and King, B.G., 2012. Social movements, risk perceptions, and economic outcomes: The effect of primary and secondary stakeholder activism on firms' perceived environmental risk and financial performance. *American Sociological Review*, 77(4), 573–596.

12

FINANCIAL MARKETS AND ENVIRONMENTAL INFORMATION

Giovanna Michelon

Introduction

> Human drivers are judged extremely likely to have been the dominant cause of global warming since the mid-20th century. While natural fluctuations may mask it temporarily, the underlying human-induced warming trend of two-tenths of a degree per decade has continued unabated since the 1970s.

Whose words may these be? An earth scientist? A climate change activist? A member of the Green Party? This quote is part of a speech entitled "Breaking the Tragedy of the Horizon – climate change and financial stability" that economist Mark Carney, Governor of the Bank of England (and Chairman of the Financial Stability Board), gave at Lloyd's of London on 29 September 2015[1]. In this speech, Carney describes climate change as the "Tragedy of the Horizon", comparing it with the well-known economic problem of the tragedy of the commons[2]. Impacts of climate change are likely to be felt beyond "the traditional horizons of most actors" including that adopted by central banks to set policies for financial stability. "In other words, once climate change becomes a defining issue for financial stability, it may already be too late". These introductory quotes intuitively reveal that environmental issues, such as carbon emissions and climate change, can have wide impact on the functioning of financial markets.

While the attention of the financial community on environmental matters is relatively recent, accounting academics have since long focused on the role of corporate environmental disclosures in financial markets. An overview of this literature is provided in the next section, which covers both research that employs statistical methods to investigate the relationship between environmental disclosure and market outcomes, and experiments and survey studies that are useful to understand investment decisions and investor preferences.

This chapter further presents recent institutional initiatives on environmental reporting, specifically around climate change issues, which have become important for the financial industry and markets in the aftermath of the Paris Agreement. It concludes by reflecting upon the public interest function of environmental reporting *vis-à-vis* its role for financial market participants, highlighting potential risks and challenges.

An overview of the academic literature

The role of corporate reporting, broadly defined, in financial markets is twofold (Beyer et al. 2010).[3] Investors need information to evaluate the potential return of investment opportunities. Therefore, corporate reporting is deemed to provide information that is relevant and useful for investment decisions. Furthermore, reporting also serves the purpose of shareholder protection, in that it allows investors to monitor the use of the capital, once it has been committed. While these notions have been developed primarily for accounting information and financial reporting, they apply also to environmental information and reporting, under two assumptions (Berthelot et al. 2003; Christensen et al. 2019). First, corporate environmental activities and their impacts have some relation with the underlying financial performance of companies (i.e. have financial impacts, whether positive or negative) and therefore are relevant for investors to understand business operations, risks and opportunities and assess future cash flows. Second, environmental disclosure should be costly, as inherently it would bear a credible signal that investors can rely upon. Costs of disclosures are not only direct costs sustained to produce the information, such as the gathering of relevant data and implementation of information systems, but also indirect costs such as litigation risk, reputational and proprietary costs (i.e. costs arising when the information provided to the markets can also be used by other parties like competitors, regulators, labour unions, etc.).

Most of the research on the effects of environmental information on financial markets is rooted in two alternative theoretical frames (see Theoretical views) and uses archival data and statistical methods to find associations between environmental reporting (see Characteristics of disclosure) and market outcomes (see Effects on financial markets and investors use of environmental information). Despite the abundance of this type of research, perhaps not surprisingly, the literature provides contrasting and mixed evidence.[4] Further insights on the role of environmental information in financial markets are provided by experiments (which are useful to understand investment decisions) and surveys (that allow to investigate investors' information needs and preferences), discussed in Experimental research and survey studies. Overall, this overview will be useful to understand why research has produced mixed evidence.

Theoretical views

There are two competing, although not necessarily mutually exclusive, theories that give explanations as to why companies disclose information about environmental activities (Cho et al. 2015; Cho and Patten 2007; Clarkson et al. 2008; Heflin and Wallace 2017). These theories are key to the understanding of financial market consequences as they relate the reporting strategy of a firm to its underlying performance.

Voluntary disclosure theory, rooted in neo-classical economics, posits that firms with good environmental performance have incentives to use disclosure to signal their type to investors, given that most of corporate environmental strategies and policies are not observable by external stakeholders (Berthelot et al. 2003; Clarkson et al. 2008). If environmental disclosures are a credible sign and inform about the underlying environmental performance of a firm, they reduce *estimation risk*, by decreasing the total risk in owning shares, and/or they reduce *information asymmetries* between firms and investors (Richardson and Welker 2001). Such decrease in risk and information asymmetries is then reflected in share prices. This theoretical approach implicitly recognises that firms' optimal levels of disclosures are based on the trade-off between costs and benefits, and that ultimately the quality of the information provided to the markets also depends on the underlying reporting incentives, including issues of managerial opportunism (Beyer et al. 2010).

Another stream of literature, rooted in the sociopolitical approach, instead posits the opposite: firms that perform poorly on the environment use disclosure as a tool of legitimacy (Lindblom 2010). Disclosure helps managing the perceptions that relevant publics have about firms' environmental performance, possibly even deflecting attention from issues of concerns or emphasising accomplishments (Cho and Patten 2007; Deegan and Rankin 1996; Neu et al. 1998; Patten 2002). Since environmental disclosure is driven by exposure to legitimacy factors (e.g., operating in an environmentally sensitive business or the visibility of the firm) and not to provide investors with meaningful information to lower information asymmetries or reduce estimation risk, its value relevance for investment decision would be very modest (Cho et al. 2015; Guidry and Patten 2012). However, supporters of this view do recognise that when firms are exposed to regulatory and political pressure, environmental disclosure can mitigate negative financial market reactions in the presence of exogenous environmental accidents (Blacconiere and Patten 1994; Patten 1991, 1992; Patten and Nance 1998). For example, Heflin and Wallace (2017) find that oil and gas firms with more expansive environmental disclosure suffer less negative stock price declines following the BP oil spill in the Gulf of Mexico. Firms with lower pre-spill environmental performance are more likely to increase the environmental disclosure in the aftermath of the accident, as legitimacy theory would predict, and also to improve their environmental performance. Hence, their findings are not completely consistent with the idea that the increase in disclosure post-spill is solely explained by legitimacy purposes and provide support also for the voluntary disclosure theory perspective.

Ultimately, when determining its environmental disclosure strategy, a firm's management is likely to face a tension between responding to the information needs of financial markets and maintaining its legitimacy within other stakeholders, so it is not surprising that the literature has found empirical evidence for both theories. A paper that reconciles the two views is Cormier and Magnan (2015). They find that a firm's environmental disclosure enhances the analysts information context, leading them to provide better forecasts, and, at the same time, also positively affects how stakeholders perceive the firm legitimacy (proxied by favourable news in the media). Legitimacy further reduces the information uncertainty faced by financial analysts.

Regardless of the theoretical approach, a key concern in the literature that estimates the market outcomes of environmental reporting is that whatever causes firms to report on environmental issues also affects firm value (Christensen et al. 2019). For example, the decision to undertake environmental initiatives and report about them could be related to growth opportunities or management reputation, which are not observable or easy to measure. If these unobservable factors are not accounted for in the statistical model, they may induce a bias in the estimation of financial market effects (i.e. one could incorrectly attribute to disclosure the economic effect when instead is driven by the "unobservable" factor). This implies that most studies that find statistical associations between environmental disclosure and financial market outcomes can hardly claim a causal relationship, unless the research design is able to correct for this bias.

Characteristics of disclosure

Having discussed the theoretical frameworks that explain the motives behind environmental disclosures, we now consider the characteristics of environmental disclosures that have been considered in capital market research. For our purposes, we consider environmental information as any disclosure about firms' environmental activities and impacts, as well as the "financial implications from a firm's environmental management decision or action" (Berthelot et al. 2003, p. 2).

Environmental disclosures include financial information about the firm's corporate environmental impacts embedded in financial statements. This is the case, for example, for firms operating in natural resource industries, as they are required to account for any future decommissioning, clean-up and other environmental costs (environmental liabilities). Off-balance sheet environmental liabilities have been shown to affect equity value (Barth and McNichols 1994; Clarkson et al. 2004; Cormier and Magnan 1997) and also bond pricing (Schneider 2011). However, Schneider et al. (2017) are unable to document that the on-balance sheet liabilities are value relevant in the pricing model. Two interpretations of the null finding are possible: either equity investors do not consider environmental liabilities to be relevant in firm valuation, or the reported amounts are not accurate reflections of the underlying liabilities. They call for further research to investigate the relation between firm value and environmental liabilities, as well as on the accounting behind their estimation.

Other industrial firms may also account for, and disclose, capital expenditure for pollution control and abatement. The literature finds that regulatory environmental capital expenditures are negatively associated with future abnormal earnings and share price, in line with the prediction that capital expenditure incurred to comply with environmental regulations represents negative present value projects (Johnston 2005). However, research has also shown that the financial market reacts positively to new voluntary capital expenditure announcements when projects are expected to experience long delays in obtaining environmental regulatory approval, ascribing the positive effect to firm learning and first mover advantages (Wirth et al. 2013).

A large stream of research has focused on narrative disclosures (Beattie 2014). Often firms use both qualitative accounts describing policies and strategies and quantitative indicators that inform about the environmental performance, that is, the outcome of the firm's environmental policies and initiatives (Cho et al. 2010; Michelon et al. 2015; Muslu et al. 2019). Textual characteristics of narrative disclosures are particularly important for research investigating the effects on the financial markets (Lewis and Young 2019). Papers in the literature have adopted a variety of different approaches, making it difficult to understand which disclosures and which characteristics of disclosures matter the most. On one side, studies that take a broad, comprehensive approach to measurement of environmental disclosure typically employ a disclosure framework (i.e. list of information items) covering a variety of topics (e.g. general environmental strategies and policies, energy use, biodiversity preservation, waste production and recycling) (Blacconiere and Patten 1994; Cormier and Magnan 2007; Ingram and Frazier 1980). These indexes assess the extent (presence or absence of the disclosure with respect to the items in the disclosure framework) or quantity (how many pieces of information are reported for each item, e.g., in terms of number of sentences, or words, etc.) of disclosure. Researchers can either collect these data themselves or rely on third-party providers, such as, for example, Bloomberg. Other studies focus on the disclosure of specific environmental issues (among the most common is surely greenhouse gas (GHG) and carbon emissions), but it is hard to disentangle whether the effect on capital market is determined by disclosure *vis-à-vis* the underlying environmental performance that is being reported.

Research has also attempted to measure the "quality" of narrative environmental disclosure by considering the presence of soft or hard information (soft being qualitative statements, whereas hard information is quantitative or financial) (Clarkson et al. 2008; Plumlee et al. 2015), the nature of the news being communicated (positive, negative or neutral) (Deegan and Rankin 1996; Wang et al. 2019), the orientation (forward looking vs. backward looking) (Michelon et al. 2015; Muslu et al. 2019), its tone (optimism) and readability (complexity and certainty of the language used) (Cho et al. 2010; Melloni et al. 2017; Muslu et al. 2019). Such nuances in analysing disclosure are fundamental because they are able to capture the degree to which environmental information is being manipulated (or not) to manage impressions. For example, firms may provide positive information, and omit to disclose negative news; or may use complex language to obfuscate negative performance. It is important to note that the less sophisticated the variable used to proxy for the "quality" of disclosure, the more likely is that any documented effect on capital markets is related to some other factor that is not being accounted for properly. For example, Dhaliwal et al. (2011) consider a very coarse measure for reporting, that is, the presence or absence of a stand-alone CSR or sustainability report and document that firms adopting the report for the first time experience a reduction in the cost of capital. However, once they split the sample according to the underlying CSR performance, the reduction in the cost of capital holds only for good performers, suggesting that it is not the reporting per se that drives the market effect, but the underlying CSR activities. This result however was not new. Guidry and Patten (2010) had already documented that it is the quality, rather than the adoption, of a sustainability report that drives positive market reactions (in terms of cumulative abnormal accruals in the three days period around the release of the report).

Financial markets participants will broadly rely on information available through a variety of channels for reporting (e.g. the financial statements, the management discussion and analysis in the annual report, corporate websites or sustainability and other stand-alone reports) (Cho et al. 2009; Lodhia 2014; Wanderley et al. 2008). Assuming market efficiency, it should not matter where information is reported. However, a recent paper by Christensen et al. (2017) exploits a regulatory change that requires SEC-registered companies to include information regarding mine-safety performance in the financial reports (Section 1503 of the Dodd-Frank Act). This information was already available to the public, via the US Mine Safety and Health Administration website. Hence, the regulatory change only adds a reporting channel for (rather than content to) this information. Christensen et al. (2017) document a more negative market reaction to the disclosure of safety accidents when these are also reported in the financial report. These results suggest that the reporting channel affects the visibility of information and raise the question for further research about whether the reporting channel matters for investors' decisions, and why firms choose different channels when they are allowed to do so.

Finally, one last key aspect related to the reporting channel is the distinction between voluntary and mandatory disclosures. However, nowadays there is a blurred line between what is mandatory and what is voluntary (Schneider et al. 2018). Most regulations in this area may mandate the reporting on certain environmental items, but the mandate itself only sets the minimum that should be reported, or provides very broad requirements, leaving managerial discretion with respect to the actual content of environmental disclosures, how to craft it, which specific issues to report about and how to report about them. Hence, especially narrative information, whether mandatory or voluntary, is discretionary and the reporting practice will reflect the underlying reporting incentives of the firm (Christensen et al. 2019; Leuz and Wysocki 2016). Not least, voluntary and mandatory disclosures are likely to affect the market jointly; so as environmental disclosure regulation increases, studies will need to consider the interaction between mandatory and voluntary disclosures. Two papers that tackle how mandatory and voluntary disclosures interact are, for example, Peters and Romi (2013) and Wegener and Labelle (2017). Peters and Romi (2013) studied the compliance to SEC-mandated disclosures of environmental sanctions and found that voluntary disclosure incentives impact compliance with the mandatory requirements (in other words, there is greater compliance for firms that have greater incentives to provide voluntary environmental information). They call for more research to focus on deviation from mandatory disclosure, especially in light of the increase in investors' interest in environmental performance. Wegener and Label (2017) investigated the value relevance of environmental provisions pre- and post-International Financial Reporting Standards (IFRS) adoption. Their results suggest that environmental provisions act as liabilities for oil and gas firms that also have a sustainability report. For firms in the oil and gas industry that do not have sustainability reports, provisions are interpreted by the market as a costly signal about future growth and this information is associated with higher market values. Both of these studies suggest the need to better understand how mandatory and voluntary disclosures interact and how the market perceives them.

Effects on financial markets and investors use of environmental information

Having discussed the key characteristics of disclosure that have been considered in financial markets research, we proceed with discussing the financial markets effects of environmental disclosure. As mentioned, most of these findings are obtained through archival studies, which rely on secondary data sets and investigate the existence of statistical associations between environmental disclosure and a certain market outcome (e.g. firm's value). However, academics have also used experiments to investigate investors' preferences and investment decisions, and survey studies that provide direct evidence on the use of environmental information by financial market participants. We will discuss these in Experimental research and survey studies on the following page.

Disclosure literature based in neo-classical economics hypothesizes that better corporate reporting mitigates information asymmetries, improves liquidity and is associated with other capital market effects: reduction of the cost-of-capital, improved value relevance, stock returns effects (Leuz and Wysocki 2016). Theoretically, environmental disclosures would help assessing the financial impact of potential regulatory actions and the risks associated with future compliance requirements (Blacconiere and Patten 1994). Furthermore, as environmental disclosures provide information about firms' environmental policies (Clarkson et al. 2011), in turn it would improve investors' information base and reduce a firm's cost of capital (Lambert et al. 2007). However, the empirical literature has found mixed evidence.

Moneva and Cuellar (2009) provided evidence that *financial* environmental disclosures (investments, costs and contingencies) are value-relevant, but non-financial ones are not. Furthermore, their evidence corroborates the increase of the value relevance of compulsory environmental information. Clarkson et al. (2013) found that voluntary environmental disclosure has more explanatory power than current environmental performance (i.e. the toxic release inventory) for firm market value but not for firm cost of capital. Plumlee et al. (2015) found a positive association between environmental disclosure and firm value after controlling for environmental performance, but no association was found between environmental disclosure and cost of capital. However, when they classified the sample based on whether the information disclosed is soft/hard and positive/neutral/negative, they found that soft/positive environmental disclosures are associated with a lower cost of capital, whereas soft/negative environmental disclosures are associated with a higher cost of capital. Hence, these findings show value relevance of the quality of a firm's voluntary environmental disclosures, with the corresponding effect working through both the cost of equity capital and through the expected future cash flow channels.

A specific stream of literature has focused on disclosure of GHG and carbon emissions. This stream of research is particularly important in light of the climate emergency and the wave of regulatory actions calling for disclosure about how firms contribute to, and are affected by, climate change. Prior literature shows that GHG emissions are value relevant (Baboukardos 2017; Chapple et al. 2013; Clarkson et al. 2015; Griffin et al. 2017; Matsumura et al. 2013) and easily integrated by investors into valuation models (Eccles et al. 2011). Furthermore, the inclusion of emission information in an environmental report increases the precision of environmental disclosure because it provides quantitative and verifiable information about a firm's environmental performance (Clarkson et al. 2008; Plumlee et al. 2015). Recently, Liesen et al. (2017) showed that GHG emissions disclosures and, to a lesser extent, carbon performance are value relevant: portfolios made of firms with (complete) GHG emissions disclosure and good corporate climate change performance in terms of GHG efficiency are shown to lead to abnormal risk-adjusted returns of up to 13.05% annually. This abnormal return suggests that financial markets are inefficient in pricing publicly available information on carbon disclosure and calls for mandatory and standardised information on carbon performance to increase market efficiency and improve allocation of capital.

Overall, while research points to the relevance of environmental information for financial markets, future research will need to address two major limitations. First, the identification of causal effects is often challenging, as there may be several concurrent events or unobservable factors that bias the estimations. Second, the documented statistical associations are unsuitable to provide any economic cost–benefit analysis to policymakers and regulators because the estimated coefficients may be biased.

Experimental research and survey studies

Experimental research is useful to understand how environmental information affects investment decisions. Chan and Milne (1999) examined whether disclosure of positive or negative environmental information affects investment decisions for a sample of accountants and investment analysts. While positive information is found to have little impact, the release of negative information reduces investment levels. Milne and Patten (2002) complemented this finding by showing that positive environmental disclosure is able to mitigate the impact of negative environmental performance, attesting to the legitimising role of environmental disclosure. However, these results are not univocal, and in most recent years experiments have provided alternative evidence. In the experiment run by Holm and Rikhardsson (2008), positive environmental performance disclosure positively influences investment choice across both differing investment time horizons and the experience level of the investor. Rikhardsson and Holm (2008) further documented that qualitative environmental information affects short-term allocation decisions, indicating a risk reduction potential of environmental information. Somewhat surprisingly, quantitative environmental information was found to mitigate, rather than extend, the effect of qualitative information. More recently, Martin and Moser (2016) used an experimental setting in which green investments have no impact on the firm's future cash flows by design. They find that investors respond favorably when managers make and disclose a green investment, and document that this response is even more favorable when the disclosure emphasises societal benefits rather than the cost to the company. Rivière-Giordano et al. (2018) instead focused on whether different levels of assurance statements of environmental disclosures affect investment recommendations. While they found that generally environmental disclosure has a positive impact on investment recommendations, recommendations are less favourable when environmental information is provided with low-level assurance than for a company with no assurance statement at all. Their study documented the relevance to increase the level of requested assurance for environmental disclosure.

The main limitation of this approach is that often investors are proxied by students in accounting or business degrees, therefore not having the same level of expertise and abilities (and social context) of real market players (Libby et al. 2002). Furthermore, experiments typically make use of limited investment amounts and it is not clear whether the magnitude of the underlying investment decision affects the investment strategy itself.

Survey evidence is important in that it allows us to understand directly how investors and other market participants use environmental disclosure. However, such stream of research is relatively scant. Diouf and Boiral (2017) interviewed a range of corporate stakeholders, including fund managers and analysts, to assess their perceptions of firm sustainability reports. Interestingly, their evidence suggest that investors are aware of firms' use of impression management strategies aimed at highlighting positive aspects of their performance and obfuscating negative outcomes. Slack and Tsalavoutas (2018) surveyed sell-side equity analysts and fund managers and provided a similar view of the usefulness of International Integrated Reporting (<IR>) Framework, which includes issues related to the environment. However, investors surveyed by Stubbs and Higgins (2018) would support the adoption of mandatory <IR> because, in their view, other, voluntary forms of sustainability reporting have not led to substantive disclosures or increased the quality of reporting. A recent study by Amel-Zadeh and Serafeim (2018) surveyed mainstream investment firms about their use of and reliance upon environmental, social and governance (ESG) information. The findings suggest that ESG information is relevant to investment performance, but its use is also driven by client demand, product strategy and ethical considerations. Respondents also emphasise the lack of established reporting standards for such disclosures, which makes them hardly comparable.

While in surveys there is always the possibility that participants will not be completely sincere, given the documented scepticism described above, future surveys could be used to understand which specific characteristics, or channels, of disclosure investors would deem most appropriate and useful.

Recent institutional developments

The overview presented above suggests that environmental information does play a role in financial markets, and it is relevant and useful for investors. However, results are not always consistent, partly because various studies have different research designs (e.g. they operationalise differently environmental disclosure), partly because the institutional contexts may be different (e.g. mandatory settings may include different enforcement rules). However, the years ahead will likely generate more research in this area, given the growing number of regulations and guidance documents on environmental (and social) reporting.

One key aspect of this new regulatory wave is the effort to involve more predominantly the financial community (investors, banks and shareholders), as well as the emphasis on the use of environmental (and social) disclosures for the benefits of investors, rather than broader stakeholder groups.

In 2015 the UN 2030 Agenda for Sustainable Development Goals (SDGs) and the Paris Climate Agreement created the conditions for subsequent regulatory actions aimed at aligning financial flows and allocations with the transition to a low-carbon economy and a climate-resilient economic development. The Sustainable Finance Initiative[5] prompted by the EU Commission recognises that the financial sector has a key role to play in reaching the SDGs, as it has the potential to reorient investments towards more sustainable technologies and businesses, finance growth in a sustainable manner over the long term and contribute to the creation of a low-carbon, climate-resilient and circular economy. The Commission set up a technical expert group (TEG) on sustainable finance to support the development of a unified classification system for sustainable economic activities, an EU green bond standard, methodologies for low-carbon indices and metrics for climate-related disclosure (TEG 2019).

A great deal of attention within environmental issues is given to climate-related information. In December 2015, few months after the speech given by Mark Carney on climate change and financial stability, the Financial Stability Board announced the establishment of an industry-led disclosure task force to develop "voluntary, consistent climate-related disclosures of the sort that would be useful to lenders, insurers, investors and other stakeholders in understanding material risks".[6] In June 2017, the task force released a set of recommendations for climate-related financial disclosures (TCFD 2017). These recommendations are meant to be a foundation to improve investors' ability to appropriately assess and price climate-related risks and opportunities. The guidance of the TCFD recommends not only to identify risks and opportunities, but also to assess the financial impacts (see Table 12.1). Furthermore, given the uncertainty in the timing and magnitude of the financial impacts of climate change, it recommends utilising scenario analysis for developing strategic plans that can adjust to a range of plausible future scenarios.

Table 12.1 Financial impacts of climate risks and opportunities

Income statement	*Balance sheet*
Revenues. Transition and physical risks may affect demand for products and services. Organisations should consider the potential impact on revenues and identify potential opportunities for enhancing or developing new revenues. In particular, given the emergence and likely growth of carbon pricing as a mechanism to regulate emissions, it is important for affected industries to consider the potential impacts of such pricing on business revenues. **Expenditures.** An organisation's response to climate-related risks and opportunities may depend, in part, on the organisation's cost tructure. Lower-cost suppliers may be more resilient to changes in cost resulting from climate-related issues and more flexible in their ability to address such issues. By providing an indication of their cost structure and flexibility to adapt, organisations can better inform investors about their investment potential. It is also helpful for investors to understand capital expenditure plans and the level of debt or equity needed to fund these plans. The resilience of such plans should be considered bearing in mind organisations' flexibility to shift capital and the willingness of capital markets to fund organisations exposed to significant levels of climate-related risks. Transparency of these plans may provide greater access to capital markets or improved financing terms.	**Assets and liabilities.** Supply and demand changes from changes in policies, technology, and market dynamics related to climate change could affect the valuation of organisations' assets and liabilities. Use of long-lived assets and, where relevant, reserves may be particularly affected by climate-related issues. It is important for organisations to provide an indication of the potential climate-related impact on their assets and liabilities, particularly long-lived assets. This should focus on existing and committed future activities and decisions requiring new investment, restructuring, write- downs or impairment. **Capital and financing.** Climate-related risks and opportunities may change the profile of an organisation's debt and equity structure, either by increasing debt levels to compensate for reduced operating cash flows or for new capital expenditures or R&D. It may also affect the ability to raise new debt or refinance existing debt, or reduce the tenor of borrowing available to the organisation. There could also be changes to capital and reserves from operating losses, asset write-downs, or the need to raise new equity to meet investment.

Source: TCFD (2017).

The EU Commission also released supplemental guidance on climate-related disclosures (European Commission 2019). An important message contained in the document is the idea that materiality in the context of environmental information is twofold, something that academic research has only limitedly investigated (Canning et al. 2019; Humphrey et al. 2017; Unerman and Zappettini 2014). Climate-related information should be reported if it is necessary to understand the external environmental impacts of corporate activities (environmental materiality). This perspective is of interest mainly for non-financial stakeholders, including regulators and policymakers. However, climate-related information also refers to how climate change may affect the value of the company. Such a perspective is central for investors (financial materiality). While the materiality perspective embedded in the Non-Financial Reporting Directive 2014/95/EU covers both financial materiality and environmental (and social) materiality, the TCFD adopts a financial materiality perspective only. This distinction is also key when comparing other reporting guidance. For example, the GRI framework recommends extensive stakeholder engagement in the definition and identification of social and environmental matters that are to be deemed as material, whereas the Sustainability Accounting Standard Board identifies which items are material by industry in terms of their potential effects on firm's performance (SASB 2016).

While the two approaches can be complementary, it is important to note that there is a trade-off between the two. There is a risk that items that do not necessarily have (short-term) financial implications for capital markets, do have an impact for other stakeholders (i.e. negative externalities) and until these potential negative impacts become a risk for the firm (whether legal, operational or reputational), they may go unaccounted for and their impacts on financial markets unknown and hard to estimate. In other words, an excessive focus on financial materiality of environmental issues bears implicitly the risk that environmental disclosure may be incomplete. A potential solution to this problem is proposed in a recent paper by Unerman et al. (2018). Sustainability reporting often includes issues that "are not captured in, or are external to, the financial dimensions of transactions and events as communicated in financial reporting" (p. 498). These "externalities" arise from the corporate activities, but are borne by others, and therefore do not bear implications for the short-term financial performance (although they may have long-term effects). However, if these externalities are recognised as financial risks or opportunities, firms may voluntarily internalise them. Despite the challenges in quantifying these externalities, the ultimate argument in this paper is that in order to communicate the financial impacts of externalities, the "silos" between domains of financial reporting and sustainability reporting should be broken down.

Overall, recent regulatory developments represent an interesting setting to better understand the role of financial information for financial markets and market-wide effects of regulation, as well as whether and how information released for the benefits of financial markets will be able to drive the change towards a low-carbon economy, as auspicated by policymakers in recent years.

Conclusion

The chapter has provided an overview of the academic research on the role of environmental information for financial markets. As discussed, empirical evidence is mixed, and research is not always able to provide evidence for causal effects. Furthermore, as the regulatory environment is changing rapidly and the financial community is being urged to take an active role in tackling global issues such as climate change, there will be numerous opportunities for future research that have been highlighted throughout the chapter.

One key aspect that will be important for all of us to understand is whether the involvement of the financial community and the proliferation of environmental reporting guidelines conceived to fulfill investors' information needs will also serve a public interest function, and assist policymakers and civil society to achieve theSDGs. Surely, there seems to be a momentum for environmental information in helping investors assess the risks and opportunities of their investment. It could be that efficient markets incorporate these risks and will drive the allocation of financial resources to those firms that are able to best mitigate their impact on the environment. However, if disclosure remains discretionary, and weakly enforced, there is a possibility that companies will continue to selectively report on those aspects that put them in the best light, providing therefore a biased picture of their environmental commitment. Finally, even in contexts where environmental reporting is mandated and enforced, the risk is that excessive focus on investors needs may create blind spots and lead companies to provide information that is unable to inform public policy and regulatory actions, for example, because limited to short-term financial implications rather than broader environmental impacts that may have long-term effects. A challenge for future research on financial markets will be to address and consider this trade-off in order to properly inform public policy and regulators.

Notes

1 The full speech is available at: www.bankofengland.co.uk/speech/2015/breaking-the-tragedy-of-the-horizon-climate-change-and-financial-stability. (accessed on 17/01/2020)

2 The tragedy of the commons describes an economic problem in which a common-pool (scarce) resource is overconsumed and ultimately depleted by individual users, who act independently and according to their own self-interest, rather than considering the optimal level of consumption for the common good.

3 It is important to note that these two roles for reporting assume a very narrow view of accountability that only considers investors as addressees of corporate information.

4 We performed a search of academic literature on Scopus with a Boolean approach searching keywords "environmental reporting" OR "environmental disclosure" OR "sustainability reporting" AND one of the following keywords associated with financial market effects: analyst, capital market, cost of capital, financial market, financial performance, firm value, information asymmetry, investment decisions, investor, liquidity, stock market and Tobin Q. This search resulted in 154 papers published since the early 1980s across disciplines. Using my own academic judgement, the discussion provided in this chapter summarises the most relevant insights, as well as highlights venues for future research. I gratefully acknowledge the research assistance of Chaoyuan She.

5 https://ec.europa.eu/info/business-economy-euro/banking-and-finance/sustainable-finance_en. (accessed on 17/01/2020)

6 www.fsb-tcfd.org/wp-content/uploads/2016/01/12-4-2015-Climate-change-task-force-press-release.pdf. (accessed on 17/01/2020)

References

Amel-Zadeh, A., and Serafeim, G., 2018. Why and how investors use ESG information: Evidence from a global survey. *Financial Analysts Journal*, 74(3), 87–103.

Baboukardos, D., 2017. Market valuation of greenhouse gas emissions under a mandatory reporting regime: Evidence from the UK. *Accounting Forum*, 41(3), 221–233.

Barth, M.E., and McNichols, M.F., 1994. Estimation and market valuation of environmental liabilities relating to superfund sites. *Journal of Accounting Research*, 32, 177–209.

Beattie, V., 2014. Accounting narratives and the narrative turn in accounting research: Issues, theory, methodology, methods and a research framework. *The British Accounting Review*, 46(2), 111–134.

Berthelot, S., Cormier, D., and Magnan, M., 2003. Environmental disclosure research: Review and synthesis. *Journal of Accounting Literature, 22*, 1–44.

Beyer, A., Cohen, D.A., Lys, T.Z., and Walther, B.R., 2010. The financial reporting environment: Review of the recent literature. *Journal of Accounting and Economics*, 50(2), 296–343.

Blacconiere, W.G., and Patten, D.M., 1994. Environmental disclosures, regulatory costs, and changes in firm value. *Journal of Accounting and Economics,* 18(3), 357–377.
Canning, M., O'Dwyer, B., and Georgakopoulos, G., 2019. Processes of auditability in sustainability assurance – The case of materiality construction. *Accounting and Business Research,* 49(1), 1–27.
Chan, C.C., and Milne, M.J., 1999. Investor reactions to corporate environmental saints and sinners: An experimental analysis. *Accounting and Business Research,* 29(4), 265–279.
Chapple, L., Clarkson, P.M., and Gold, D.L., 2013. The cost of carbon: Capital market effects of the proposed emission trading scheme (ETS). *Abacus,* 49(1), 1–33.
Cho, C.H., Michelon, G., Patten, D.M., and Roberts, R.W., 2015. CSR disclosure: The more things change…? *Accounting, Auditing & Accountability Journal,* 28(1), 14–35.
Cho, C.H., and Patten, D.M., 2007. The role of environmental disclosures as tools of legitimacy: A research note. *Accounting, Organizations and Society,* 32(7–8), 639–647.
Cho, C.H., Phillips, J.R., Hageman, A.M., and Patten, D.M., 2009. Media richness, user trust, and perceptions of corporate social responsibility: An experimental investigation of visual web site disclosures. *Accounting, Auditing & Accountability Journal,* 22(6), 933–952.
Cho, C.H., Roberts, R.W., and Patten, D.M., 2010. The language of US corporate environmental disclosure. *Accounting, Organizations and Society,* 35(4), 431–443.
Christensen, H.B., Floyd, E., Liu, L.Y., and Maffett, M., 2017. The real effects of mandated information on social responsibility in financial reports: Evidence from mine-safety records. *Journal of Accounting and Economics,* 64(2), 284–304.
Christensen, H.B., Hail, L., and Leuz, C., 2019. Economic analysis of widespread adoption of CSR and sustainability reporting standards. *SSRN Working Paper no. 3315673.* Available at https://papers.ssrn.com/sol3/papers.cfm?abstract_id=3315673. (accessed on 17 January 2020)
Clarkson, P.M., Fang, X., Li, Y., and Richardson, G., 2013. The relevance of environmental disclosures: Are such disclosures incrementally informative? *Journal of Accounting and Public Policy,* 32(5), 410–431.
Clarkson, P.M., Li, Y., Pinnuck, M., and Richardson, G.D., 2015. The valuation relevance of greenhouse gas emissions under the European Union Carbon Emissions Trading Scheme. *European Accounting Review,* 24(3), 551–580.
Clarkson, P.M., Li, Y., and Richardson, G.D., 2004. The market valuation of environmental capital expenditures by pulp and paper companies. *The Accounting Review,* 79(2), 329–353.
Clarkson, P.M., Li, Y., Richardson, G.D., and Vasvari, F.P., 2008. Revisiting the relation between environmental performance and environmental disclosure: An empirical analysis. *Accounting, Organizations and Society,* 33(4–5), 303–327.
Clarkson, P.M., Li, Y., Richardson, G.D., and Vasvari, F.P., 2011. Does it really pay to be green? Determinants and consequences of proactive environmental strategies. *Journal of Accounting and Public Policy,* 30(2), 122–144.
Cormier, D., and Magnan, M., 1997. Investors' assessment of implicit environmental liabilities: An empirical investigation. *Journal of Accounting and Public Policy,* 16(2), 215–241.
Cormier, D., and Magnan, M., 2007. The revisited contribution of environmental reporting to investors' valuation of a firm's earnings: An international perspective. *Ecological Economics,* 62(3–4), 613–626.
Cormier, D., and Magnan, M., 2015. The economic relevance of environmental disclosure and its impact on corporate legitimacy: An empirical investigation. *Business Strategy and the Environment,* 24(6), 431–450.
Deegan, B., and Rankin, M., 1996. Do Australian companies report environmental news objectively?: An analysis of environmental disclosures by firms prosecuted successfully by the Environmental Protection Authority. *Accounting, Auditing & Accountability Journal,* 9(2), 50–67.
Dhaliwal, D.S., Li, O.Z., Tsang, A., and Yang, Y.G., 2011. Voluntary nonfinancial disclosure and the cost of equity capital: The initiation of corporate social responsibility reporting. *The Accounting Review,* 86(1), 59–100.
Diouf, D., and Boiral, O., 2017. The quality of sustainability reports and impression management: A stakeholder perspective. *Accounting, Auditing & Accountability Journal,* 30(3), 643–667.
Dyer, T., Lang, M., and Stice-Lawrence, L., 2017. The evolution of 10-K textual disclosure: Evidence from latent Dirichlet allocation. *Journal of Accounting and Economics,* 64(2), 221–245.
Eccles, R.G., Serafeim, G., and Krzus, M.P., 2011. Market interest in nonfinancial information. *Journal of Applied Corporate Finance,* 23(4), 113–127.
European Commission, 2019. *Guidelines on reporting climate-related information.* Directorate-general for financial stability, financial services and capital markets union, European Commission, Brussels, Belgium.

Griffin, P.A., Lont, D.H., and Sun, E.Y., 2017. The relevance to investors of greenhouse gas emission disclosures. *Contemporary Accounting Research,* 34(2), 1265–1297.

Guidry, R.P., and Patten, D.M., 2010. Market reactions to the first-time issuance of corporate sustainability reports. *Sustainability Accounting, Management and Policy Journal,* 1(1), 33–50.

Guidry, R.P., and Patten, D.M., 2012. Voluntary disclosure theory and financial control variables: An assessment of recent environmental disclosure research. *Accounting Forum,* 36(2), 81–90.

Heflin, F., and Wallace, D., 2017. The BP oil spill: Shareholder wealth effects and environmental disclosures. *Journal of Business Finance & Accounting,* 44(3–4), 337–374.

Holm, C., and Rikhardsson, P., 2008. Experienced and novice investors: Does environmental information influence investment allocation decisions? *European Accounting Review,* 17(3), 537–557.

Humphrey, C., O'Dwyer, B., and Unerman, J., 2017. Re-theorizing the configuration of organizational fields: The IIRC and the pursuit of "Enlightened" corporate reporting. *Accounting and Business Research,* 47(1), 30–63.

Ingram, R.W., and Frazier, K.B., 1980. Environmental performance and corporate disclosure. *Journal of Accounting Research,* 18(2), 614–622.

Johnston, D., 2005. An investigation of regulatory and voluntary environmental capital expenditures. *Journal of Accounting and Public Policy,* 24(3), 175–206.

Lambert, R., Leuz, C., and Verrecchia, R.E., 2007. Accounting information, disclosure, and the cost of capital. *Journal of Accounting Research,* 45(2), 385–420.

Leuz, C., and Wysocki, P.D., 2016. The economics of disclosure and financial reporting regulation: Evidence and suggestions for future research. *Journal of Accounting Research,* 54(2), 525–622.

Lewis, C., and Young, S., 2019. Fad or future? Automated analysis of financial text and its implications for corporate reporting. *Accounting and Business Research,* 49(5), 587–615.

Libby, R., Bloomfield, R., and Nelson, M.W., 2002. Experimental research in financial accounting. *Accounting, Organizations and Society,* 27(8), 775–810.

Liesen, A., Figge, F., Hoepner, A., and Patten, D.M., 2017. Climate change and asset prices: Are corporate carbon disclosure and performance priced appropriately? *Journal of Business Finance & Accounting,* 44(1–2), 35–62.

Lindblom, C.K., 2010. The implications of organizational legitimacy for corporate social performance and disclosure. In: Gray, R., Bebbington, J., Gray, S. (Eds.), *Social and Environmental Accounting.* Los Angeles, CA: Sage.

Lodhia, S., 2014. Factors influencing the use of the World Wide Web for sustainability communication: An Australian mining perspective. *Journal of Cleaner Production,* 84, 142–154.

Martin, P.R., and Moser, D.V., 2016. Managers' green investment disclosures and investors' reaction. *Journal of Accounting and Economics,* 61(1), 239–254.

Matsumura, E.M., Prakash, R., and Vera-Muñoz, S.C., 2013. Firm-value effects of carbon emissions and carbon disclosures. *The Accounting Review,* 89(2), 695–724.

Melloni, G., Caglio, A., and Perego, P., 2017. Saying more with less? Disclosure conciseness, completeness and balance in integrated reports. *Journal of Accounting and Public Policy,* 36(3), 220–238.

Michelon, G., Pilonato, S., and Ricceri, F., 2015. CSR reporting practices and the quality of disclosure: An empirical analysis. *Critical Perspectives on Accounting,* 33, 59–78.

Milne, M.J., and Patten, D.M., 2002. Securing organizational legitimacy: An experimental decision case examining the impact of environmental disclosures. *Accounting, Auditing & Accountability Journal,* 15(3), 372–405.

Moneva, J.M., and Cuellar, B., 2009. The value relevance of financial and non-financial environmental reporting. *Environmental and Resource Economics,* 44(3), 441–456.

Muslu, V., Mutlu, S., Radhakrishnan, S., and Tsang, A., 2019. Corporate social responsibility report narratives and analyst forecast accuracy. *Journal of Business Ethics,* 154(4), 1119–1142.

Neu, D., Warsame, H., and Pedwell, K., 1998. Managing public impressions: Environmental disclosures in annual reports. *Accounting, Organizations and Society,* 23(3), 265–282.

Patten, D.M., 1991. Exposure, legitimacy, and social disclosure. *Journal of Accounting and Public Policy,* 10(4), 297–308.

Patten, D.M., 1992. Intra-industry environmental disclosures in response to the Alaskan oil spill: A note on legitimacy theory. *Accounting, Organizations and Society,* 17(5), 471–475.

Patten, D.M., 2002. The relation between environmental performance and environmental disclosure: A research note. *Accounting, Organizations and Society,* 27(8), 763–773.

Patten, D.M., and Nance, J.R., 1998. Regulatory cost effects in a good news environment: The intra-industry reaction to the Alaskan oil spill. *Journal of Accounting and Public Policy,* 17(4–5), 409–429.
Peters, G.F., and Romi, A.M., 2013. Discretionary compliance with mandatory environmental disclosures: Evidence from SEC filings. *Journal of Accounting and Public Policy,* 32(4), 213–236.
Plumlee, M., Brown, D., Hayes, R.M., and Marshall, R.S., 2015. Voluntary environmental disclosure quality and firm value: Further evidence. *Journal of Accounting and Public Policy,* 34(4), 336–361.
Richardson, A.J., and Welker, M., 2001. Social disclosure, financial disclosure and the cost of equity capital. *Accounting, Organizations and Society,* 26(7), 597–616.
Rikhardsson, P., and Holm, C., 2008. The effect of environmental information on investment allocation decisions–an experimental study. *Business Strategy and the Environment,* 17(6), 382–397.
Rivière-Giordano, G., Giordano-Spring, S., and Cho, C.H., 2018. Does the level of assurance statement on environmental disclosure affect investor assessment? An experimental study. *Sustainability Accounting, Management and Policy Journal,* 9(3), 336–360.
SASB, 2016. *Climate Risk – Technical Bulleting.* Available at https://library.sasb.org/climate-risk-technical-bulletin/. (accessed on 17 January 2020)
Schneider, T.E., 2011. Is environmental performance a determinant of bond pricing? Evidence from the U.s. pulp and paper and chemical industries. *Contemporary Accounting Research,* 28(5), 1537–1561.
Schneider, T.E., Michelon, G., and Maier, M., 2017. Environmental liabilities and diversity in practice under international financial reporting standards. *Accounting, Auditing & Accountability Journal,* 30(2), 378–403.
Schneider, T.E., Michelon, G., and Paananen, M., 2018. Environmental and social matters in mandatory corporate reporting: An academic note. *Accounting Perspectives,* 17(2), 275–305.
Slack, R., and Tsalavoutas, I., 2018. Integrated reporting decision usefulness: Mainstream equity market views. *Accounting Forum,* 42(2), 184–198.
Stubbs, W., and Higgins, C., 2018. Stakeholders' perspectives on the role of regulatory reform in integrated reporting. *Journal of Business Ethics,* 147(3), 489–508.
TCFD, 2017. *Recommendation of Task Force on Climate-Related Financial Disclosures.* Available at www.fsb-tcfd.org/wp-content/uploads/2017/06/FINAL-TCFD-Report-062817.pdf. (accessed on 17 January 2020)
TEG, 2019. *Report on Climate-related Disclosures.* Available at https://ec.europa.eu/info/sites/info/files/business_economy_euro/banking_and_finance/documents/190110-sustainable-finance-teg-report-climate-related-disclosures_en.pdf. (accessed on 17 January 2020)
Unerman, J., Bebbington, J., and O'Dwyer, B., 2018. Corporate reporting and accounting for externalities. *Accounting and Business Research,* 48(5), 497–522.
Unerman, J., and Zappettini, F., 2014. Incorporating materiality considerations into analyses of absence from sustainability reporting. *Social and Environmental Accountability Journal,* 34(3), 172–186.
Wanderley, L.S.O., Lucian, R., Farache, F., and de Sousa Filho, J.M., 2008. CSR information disclosure on the web: A context-based approach analysing the influence of country of origin and industry sector. *Journal of Business Ethics,* 82(2), 369–378.
Wang, Y., Delgado, M.S., Khanna, N., and Bogan, V.L., 2019. Good news for environmental self-regulation? Finding the right link. *Journal of Environmental Economics and Management,* 94, 217–235.
Wegener, M., and Labelle, R., 2017. Value relevance of environmental provisions pre-and post-IFRS. *Accounting Perspectives,* 16(3), 139–168.
Wirth, C., Chi, J., and Young, M., 2013. The economic impact of capital expenditures: Environmental regulatory delay as a source of competitive advantage? *Journal of Business Finance & Accounting,* 40(1–2), 115–141.

PART 3

Management accounting

13
STRATEGIC ENVIRONMENTAL MANAGEMENT ACCOUNTING

Delphine Gibassier

Introduction and outline of the field

Strategic management accounting (SMA) is defined as "the provision and analysis of information about a business and its competitors for use in developing and monitoring the business strategy" (Simmonds 1981, p. 26), thereby bringing accountants into "corporate strategic decision-making processes" (Cadez and Guilding 2008, p. 838.) SMA assumes that organisations are more likely to be successful if they adopt a long-term strategic orientation to attaining organisational goals and outcomes. Activities that sit within the domain of SMA include strategic business unit identification, strategic cost analysis, strategic market analysis and strategy evaluation (Govindarajan and Shank 1992; Dixon and Smith 1993; Langfield-Smith 2008) as well as benchmarking and multidimensional performance measures (Kaplan and Norton 1992; Lord 1996; Roslender and Hart 2002; Busco and Quattrone 2015).

A 2001 United Nations Report defined environmental management accounting as "the identification, collection, estimation, analysis, internal reporting, and use of physical flow information (i.e., materials, water, and energy flows), *environmental cost information*, and other monetary information for both conventional and environmental decision-making within an organization" (United Nations, 2001, p. 4, emphasis added). Gond et al. (2012) extended this definition, noting that "because management control systems (MCSs) support strategy, they can, if used appropriately, push organizations in the direction of sustainability. MCSs are central to strategy-making, as they shape the process of strategy emergence and support the implementation of deliberate strategies" (Gond et al. 2012, p. 206).

SMA is predicated on the need for accounting information to support strategic management, with some accounting techniques being better suited to this purpose. SMA techniques can be seen as a response to those who argue that management accounting techniques are short term, financially fixated, inward looking and controlling. As a result, SMA techniques incorporate non-financial dimensions, external factors, a range of expertise, measures of effectiveness and long-term goal-oriented thinking. SMA alters the role of management accountants from controllers to strategic business partners (Siegel et al. 2003) or guardians of strategy (Roslender and Hart 2002).

SMA research is typically concerned with problems with the alignment of strategy, management control systems and other contextual variables (Govindarajan and Shank 1992;

Langfield-Smith 2008) and offers the possibility for the inclusion of environmental strategy, environmental strategic goals, external environmental factors or environmental management control systems (Pondeville et al. 2013). There is a high degree of commonality between SMA, environmental management and environmental accounting. These include a concern with consequences over different timescales, aligning functions within organisations, concern with outcomes rather than efficiency, long-term orientation and monitoring of external contexts. For example, both SMA and environmental accounting systems incorporate life cycle costing techniques. Henri et al. (2016) reported on how life cycle assessment, originating as an environmental cost control mechanism, was integrated into SMA to help achieve environmental objectives. Another example is the development of Balanced Scorecards (Kaplan and Norton, 1992) into Sustainability Balanced Scorecards (Figge et al. 2002) as a way to incorporate the environment into SMA systems. Despite criticisms, Busco and Quattrone (2015) reported on the balanced scorecard's potential as a tool for strategy diffusion and control.

SMA openness for interdisciplinary integration within businesses (Roslender and Hart 2003) offers potential for the inclusion of the environment in strategic management processes. Indeed, Riccaboni and Leone (2010) examined how P&G made trade-offs between environmental decisions and market appeal of greener products, something that can be observed in Solvay and L'Oréal's current practices.

SMA research also exhibits an openness in terms of disciplinary and theoretical integration. For example, the work of Simons (1987, 1995, 2000) has greatly influenced SMA and a number of environmental management accounting research papers have analysed sustainability controls through this theoretical lens (Gond et al. 2012; Arjaliès and Mundy 2013; Renaud 2013; Wijethilake 2017 and see also Chapter 14 of this handbook). While diagnostic control systems helped achieve organisation's intended strategies, interactive control systems stimulated "emergent strategies in response to opportunities and/or threats within an organization's operating environment" (Caputo et al. 2017, p.5). Gond et al. (2012[BIB-029], p. 206) emphasised that interactive controls must also be developed as strategic levers "to focus actors' attention on key goals and support changes aligned with higher strategic objectives".

The integration of environmental accounting and SMA has created what is often labelled Strategic Environmental Management Accounting (SEMA). SEMA occurs when environmental elements penetrate SMA practices and tools. According to Gond et al. (2012), SEMA should not be an autonomous tool, but should inform formal management control mechanisms in order to "contribute to an effective integration of sustainability within strategy'" (Gond et al. 2012, p. 206). Formal controls elucidate strategic uncertainties and reveal strategic risks (a key topic for current environmental issues such as climate change, according to the Taskforce on Climate-related Financial Disclosures, see O'Dwyer and Unerman 2020). Moreover, the integration of environment into formal SMA will minimise organisation threats, and potentially allow environmental opportunities to be embraced (Gond et al. 2012). Johnstone (2019) noted that environmental control systems exist at the interface between strategy and operations, where they seek to improve environmental performance outcomes.

A strategic management perspective on environmental accounting surfaces a number of insights and areas of interest. They include:

- Exploration of the emergence and implementation of environmental strategy in organisational contexts
- Improving environmental decision-making and innovation
- Extending the timescale and factors to be incorporated in strategic decision-making

- Evaluating the effectiveness of formal and informal strategic decision and related performance measurement processes
- Reflexive relationships between SEMA and different stakeholders
- Changing role of management accountants – from controllers to strategic partners for the environment
- Challenging assumptions as to appropriate management accounting entities or cost objects
- How to stimulate environmental accounting innovations and the emergence of new strategic environmental accounting tools in relation to
  - Ranking and benchmarking
  - Structural cost management
  - Sustainable scorecards
  - Product footprinting
  - Life cycle costing
  - Environmental capex tools.

This chapter will proceed to review prior research in these areas in order to draw out areas of further research.

Key questions developed in the SEMA literature

According to the literature, SEMA supports three SMA goals: the emergence and implementation of strategies (Chung and Parker 2008; Perego and Hartman 2009; Solovida and Latan 2017); improvement of decision-making processes (Vesty et al. 2015); and stimulation of innovation in search of new strategic opportunities (Renaud 2013). Each of these aspects will now be considered.

Emergence and implementation of strategy

One of the main SMA and SEMA research topics has been the discussion of how firms adapt control systems to strategy, and vice versa: how performance control systems provide the channels to formalise emerging strategy (Simons 2000; Langfield-Smith 2005). Environmental strategy has been defined by Banerjee (2002, p. 181) as "the organization-wide recognition of the legitimacy and importance of the biophysical environment in the formulation of organization strategy, and the integration of environmental issues into the strategic process". In practice, this is achieved through a "set of initiatives that can reduce the impact of activities on the natural environment through a company's products, processes and policies, such as reducing energy consumption and waste, using sustainable ecological resources, and implementing environmental management systems" (Bansal and Roth 2000, p.717). The recent literature on environmental management systems (EMS) suggests that they have "a potential role in supporting top management's implementation of a proactive sustainability strategy by disseminating sustainability core values and measuring sustainability performance but also by minimizing sustainability strategic risks and avoiding uncertainties associated with sustainability strategies" (Wijethilake 2017, p. 570)

Solovida and Latan (2017) have, for example, tested if a company's environmental strategy had a positive influence on the use of EMA, through "providing information on their operational activities" (p. 613). Chung and Parker (2008) make similar conclusions in the case of the hotel industry, where environmental strategies could be effectively implemented with the support of environmentally efficient resourcing. Moreover, this study found links between both environmental and financial outcomes through the achievement of operational enhancement, that is, the associated cost savings that come with a net reduction in environmental impacts. Chung and Parker concluded that there was the possibility to seek long-term, not just short-term ad hoc, benefits "through a strategic management approach to environment that includes a full spectrum of dimensions, from organizational philosophy to environmental and financial outcomes" (p. 283).

Perego and Harmann (2009) also sought to understand the link between the strategic stance of an organisation and the environmental performance measures used. Overall, a more proactive environmental strategy appears to be associated with the use of environmental performance measures. More specifically, the links between strategy and management accounting systems operated indirectly through a greater focus on "environmental information quantified in financial terms" (Perego and Hartmann 2009, p. 417). The link between proactive environmental strategy and the use of environmental management control systems was also found by Wijethilake (2017) in a study of Sri Lankan companies.

It would appear that these links also arise in reverse. For example, Epstein and Roy (2001, p. 600) outlined how environmental management control systems provide "feedback information on potential environmental and social impacts, sustainability performance (at all organizational levels), sustainability initiatives, stakeholder reactions and corporate financial performance". Similarly, Riccaboni and Leone (2010) explored how management control systems have a role in implementation and translation of strategies, seeing benefit in the combined effects of formal and informal controls.

Improving decision-making processes

Strategy alignment requires tools that better motivate employees to make the right decisions. Norris and O'Dwyer (2004) specified three components of strategic decision-making: objectives, performance measure systems and reward systems. They explored the motives and internal processes of managers that were taking "socially responsive decisions" linked to the informal control system of the company and documented cognitive dissonance and frustration arising from the lack of alignment of their actions with formal controls. In order to address such problems, Dutta et al. (2013) designed what they defined as a "proper" reward system: that is, a system that aligns strategic sustainability objectives with the environmental strategy. To do this they introduced a new metric, the "sustainability variance", which is "the externalities present in the organization's resource use" (p. 457). This data is then used to incentivise managers to reduce the variance (the cost to society), and to reduce deviance from social optimality (see also Chapter 16 of this handbook).

Stimulation of innovation

Sustainable decision-making has also been identified as being enhanced by the use of product environmental footprinting and the use of environmental indicators that act as "hurdles" during product innovation (Riccaboni and Leone 2010; Gibassier 2014). Environmentally sound decision-making can also be developed through new capital investment accounts, such as the ones described by Vesty et al. (2015) and the "green capex" scheme of Danone (Gibassier 2014).

Renaud (2013) argued that "unlike diagnostic control, which is concerned with the smooth running of the organizational routine, interactive control can stimulate innovation and the search for new strategic opportunities" (p. 3). Interactive control has also been found to offer the possibility for the development of new ideas and initiatives that focus on strategic uncertainties, and emerging threats and opportunities (Rodrigue et al. 2013). Renaud (2013, p. 3) further developed the idea that interactive controls are particularly suitable for environmental topics given the strategic uncertainties characterising the practice. Interactive controls have the potential to support green innovation given their focus on multiple interactions with stakeholders. This work also proposed four organisational archetypes that used interactive controls for radical or incremental green innovations. Eco-designers and eco-institutionalists both used interactive controls with high external dialogue with stakeholders, with the aim to develop radical green innovations. On the contrary, eco-managers and eco-educators both used interactive controls for tactical improvements (incremental innovations) and education of external stakeholders to environmental solutions. Arjaliès and Mundy (2013) studied French CAC 40 companies' reports and similarly found that interactive controls such as communities of practices and recurrent meetings between operational managers and senior managers were used "to reveal and debate emergent strategies and identify opportunities for innovation in relation to CSR activities" (p. 296).

SEMA and links to environmental strategy

While SEMA research has developed in the last 15 years around traditional SMA themes, it has also addressed questions around integration (with financial control systems), stakeholders' role in designing key performance indicators and the role played by informal controls in furthering SEMA. The three following topics pertain to the specificities of dealing with environmental strategy in opposition to traditional business strategy.

Integration of sustainability into strategy

The first specific topic developed in the SEMA literature is the question of integration between non-financial and financial control systems. Gond et al. (2012) defined integration as "the interplay of these systems with regular management control" (p. 209). Caputo et al. (2017, p. 5) argued that if environmental control systems "remain peripheral and decoupled from core business activities, they fail to reshape organizational strategy to integrate sustainability". Proactive corporations are more likely to integrate sustainability control systems with traditional systems (Ditillo and Lisi 2016).

Gond et al. (2012) and Caputo et al. (2017) claimed that integration encompasses three dimensions: technical, organisational and cognitive. Technical integration is achieved when, for example, common calculability infrastructure allows information to be gathered for both the financial and environmental performance. For example, the System Applications and Products (SAP) system that gathers both financial and climate change accounts at Danone (Gibassier 2014) transforms them into a common source of information for different performance measurement purposes.

Organisational integration occurs when environmental accountability resides in an organisation and system design allows the dissemination of information to facilitate analysis and discussion of environmental topics. This could manifest in new teams such as the "finance for sustainability" at Olam, or the ESG accounting team at Orsted (see Egan and Tweedie 2018 and Johnstone 2019) or innovations in institutional roles such as "Chief Value Officers" (King and Atkins 2016).

Finally, cognitive integration refers to knowledge exchanged and assimilated on the environment. While accountant's environmental knowledge is often acquired though practice (Caron and Fortin 2014), there are calls for integration within accountancy curriculum (Boulianne et al. 2018). These calls have also been made by others in the context of environmental accounting (Gray 2013; Wyner, Wellner and Wynder 2013).

The three types of integrative dimensions can coexist in the same organisation compensating and/or reinforcing each other as bridges between traditional MCS and sustainability-orientated control systems (Gond et al. 2012). This could take the form of integrating environmental variables in performance measurement and compensation (Dutta et al. 2013) or the development of green market-oriented products (Riccaboni and Leone 2010). Multidimensional environmental integration can also be integral to organisational systems, such as the one from Proctor and Gamble, that allows global sustainability targets to be broken down into objectives for each country, team and individual, mirroring traditional performance systems (Riccaboni and Leone 2010).

Gond et al. (2012) theorised eight integration configurations, which range from a dormant decoupled strategy, where systems operate in parallel and neither are mobilised to deploy any kind of strategy to an integrated sustainability strategy. In an integrated sustainability configuration, the business strategy and sustainability strategy overlap completely, with interactive control systems that fully support strategy making. While at the time of their research this last ideal type was rare, it could become more common with the advancement of integrated environmental performance systems and new roles such as "sustainability accountants" and Chief Value Officers. However, other studies of integration warn that "strong cognitive (and organisational) barriers have gradually stifled the cognitive enablers and have not enabled sustainability to be fully integrated into the organisational strategy" (Battaglia et al. 2016, p. 213).

SEMA and stakeholder interactions

Traditional management control systems usually evaluate performance in line with the interest of shareholders and are not well equipped to integrate environmental or social metrics (Bonacchi and Rinaldi 2007). However, interactive controls are particularly well suited to extending interactions "beyond the organization, focusing attention and initiating dialogues" (Rodrigue et al. 2013, p. 303). Pondeville et al. (2013) demonstrated that stakeholder pressure positively influences both the degree of corporate environmental proactivity, but also the development of informal environmental management control systems. Notably, Pondeville et al. (2013) emphasised the role of employees in supporting a proactive environmental strategy, concluding that companies "should ensure employees' involvement, perhaps by rewarding environmental improvements in their day-to-day activities" (p. 328). Formal controls were influenced mainly by market stakeholders, with regulatory stakeholders tending to influence environmental information systems (Pondeville et al. 2013).

The diverse needs of stakeholders are not always easy to design into SEMA tools, regardless of the benefits that such integration generates. Mir and Rahaman (2011) concluded that in their case organisation, the choices of environmental indicators satisfied some stakeholders (management and regulatory authorities) while leaving unresolved conflicts related to other stakeholder needs. This issue was also addressed by Bonacchi and Rinaldi (2007) who proposed a "dart board" for integrating stakeholders needs. In their work, they argued (following the Rawlsian concept of justice) that "the loss of utility suffered by one stakeholder cannot be justified by a gain of utility achieved by another stakeholder" (p. 464).

Finally, organisations could influence their network of stakeholders towards more sustainable futures, whether it is through leadership in ratings, influencing industry norms, participating in business "clubs" (Bebbington et al. 2020), or influencing consumption patterns through activism (e.g. in the case of Patagonia). This offers the potential of SEMA to become influential in the broader fields of sustainable governance (Gibassier and Alcouffe 2018; Rinaldi 2019) or sustainable stewardship (Bebbington et al. 2020).

The role of informal controls

Informal controls can be broadly defined as norms and values, beliefs and traditions that guide behaviours (Norris and O'Dwyer 2014; Johnstone 2018). For example, Riccaboni and Leone (2010) described the progressive inclusion of sustainability principles into the organisational culture of P&G through ad hoc initiatives, leadership commitment and internal communications through their sustainability newsletter. According to Norris and O'Dwyer, informal controls work well when they are congruent with formal controls, that is, when both encourage similar behaviours (Norris and O'Dwyer 2004). To the contrary, informal controls can trigger cognitive dissonance and become detrimental when they strongly support social objectives, while formal controls reward based on profit and turnover, consequently relaying mixed messages (Norris and O'Dwyer 2004). Moreover, formal environmental controls that align with informal controls would need to include enabling design features that motivate employees (Johnstone 2019), reflecting employees' individual values.

SEMA tools

Cadez and Guilding (2008) provided a list of SEMA techniques, which they distinguished from conventional EMA tools. They identified the characteristics they expected such tools to possess: namely, they assumed that SEMA tools will have a strategic orientation (implying a long-term future-oriented time frame) and an external focus. These tools are further considered here.

Strategic environmental cost management

Parker (2000) emphasised the potential contribution management accountants could make through environmental costing. With clear organisational "green strategies", accountants would have the necessary templates to design relevant costing systems. The more proactive green strategy, the more integrated the environmental costing could be. Costing not only includes financial costing of environmental impacts already present in financial accounts, but also highlights potential attempts at "full costing" (see also Chapter 16 of this handbook), and monetisation of environmental impacts for capital appraisal. Full costing entails attempts to estimate probable future costs, calculating future valuations, and contingent liabilities.

In 2016, Henri et al. distinguished between executional cost management and structural cost management when analysing the association between environmental costs and financial performance. Both executional (e.g. short-term tactics such as cost reductions) and structural cost management (e.g. re-engineering of the value chains) are considered necessary if strategic cost management is to optimise strategic performance. In their paper, Henri et al. (2016) considered environmental cost tracking as "the identification and accumulation of specific internal costs related to the protection of the environment" (p. 271) which formed part of the implementation of environmental initiatives to master operational control over activities that have an impact on the environment. Their results demonstrate the indirect association between tracking environmental costs (that helps reduce costs for the strategy) with financial performance, and the direct association of environmental initiatives with financial performance. Their paper however ignored externalities (full cost) and the possibility of enhancing environmental performance in its own right.

Sustainability balanced scorecard

The balanced scorecard is an emblematic SMA tool that has been used to coordinate the translation of business strategy, provide a long-term focus and bridge the gap between operational and strategic planning (Kaplan and Norton 1992; Busco and Quattrone 2015). These functions are achieved through the translation of the strategy into four perspectives, namely, financial, customer, business process and learning (Figge et al. 2002). The balanced scorecard is believed to be particularly well suited for integrating economic, social and environmental business goals by integrating the (so-called) "soft factors" such as environmental and social objectives into the core of management systems instead of being "add-ons" (Figge et al. 2002).

A sustainability balanced scorecard can take three different forms: a specific environmental and/or social scorecard, the extended model with the addition of an extra perspective into conventional scorecards, or the integration of social and environmental objectives within the four existing scorecard perspectives (Figge et al. 2002). A recent literature review of these different forms confirmed that these variants of balanced scorecard remain relevant, but that in profit-driven businesses, the extended model is preferred (Hansen and Schaltegger 2016). A significant challenge with the design of sustainability balanced scorecards is the integration and commensuration of its different dimensions into a performance system designed to achieve all strategic objectives of the organisation.

However, given that balanced scorecards are typically composed of leading and lagged performances, this offers some useful insights for strategically accounting for environmental impacts. Epstein and Wisner (2001) proposed that a facility's emissions were a lagged measure of process efficiency, and a leading indicator of environmental costs (drawing from a case study with Bristol-Meyers). They also found that balanced scorecards are consistent with the learning perspective inherent in ISO 14001 certifications and product life cycle reviews, aligned with internal business process improvements and makes visible the financial benefits of investing in remediation and prevention projects.

Product footprinting for strategic decision-making

Since the 1970s, one of the main environmental accounting tools has been product life cycle assessment (Gibassier 2017; see also chapters 15 and 17). For example, this tool has been used to account for a single environmental impact, such as product carbon footprinting (Gibassier and Schaltegger 2015), or through product labelling (Berquier 2017). Riccaboni and Leone (2010) reported how the "Product Sustainability Assessment Tool" provided the necessary data to take decisions on sustainable product development through greater visibility of each proposed innovation's financial, social and environmental consequences. This tool was used by an internal multi-stakeholder team from finance, health, safety and the environment and external relations to evaluate the results from different viewpoints (Riccaboni and Leone 2010). It was noted that despite the greater visibility and granularity of information there remained difficulties in evaluating different combinations of effects and trade-offs.

Environmental capital expenditure tools

Since the 1990s many organisations have attempted to develop ways to "green" their capital investment decisions often through including full cost assessment tools (Gibassier 2014). Modifying capex approaches have been identified as a critical component of green finance

(A4S 2017). For example, Vesty et al. (2015) worked on the implementation of a "green capex" tool within an organisation in Australia and demonstrated how a representation of carbon (by way of monetised greenhouse gas emissions) became a pivotal actor in the organisation through its integration in the investment decision-making process. By integrating emissions avoided through management initiatives, environmental leadership could be quantified and linked to long-term management. The use of environmental capital expenditure tools were also part of the SEMA developed at Danone, 'green capex' criteria included tonnes of CO_2 saved per million of Euros of investment and a CO_2 payback period using a calculated saving of 15 euros per tonne (Gibassier 2014).

Rankings and benchmarking

A key development in SEMA has been the emergence of rating agencies that seek to benchmark the environmental, social and sustainability performance of organisations. For example, the World Benchmarking Alliance[1] has developed benchmarks for key transformative systems to track the achievement of the Sustainable Development Goals. Concerns over the expansion of rating agencies prompted the consulting agency SustainAbility to produce their *Rate the Raters to* analyse these approaches and produce confidence scores in the ratings produced (SustainAbility 2020). This analysis identified that rating agencies use different methodologies of inclusion, exclusion, declared performance or solicited performance to assign performance categories.

Prior to this study, Chelli and Gendron (2013, p. 200) observed that ratings alter the "conceptions, attitudes and behaviours of companies in terms of sustainable development" and also adopt rationales that reflected the interests of the financial industry and focused on financial materiality (Déjean et al. 2004). Any rating or rankings are substantially affected by the methodology used and biased by any privileged perspectives. Examples exist regarding organisations using elements of these rating methodologies to frame "good" environmental performance or use their rankings as a way to advertise their credentials. While rankings and benchmarking might form part of SEMA, the ways in which they do so are not entirely evident and an area of further research.

The environmental accountant as strategic business partner for the environment

This chapter has concerned itself with the role of management accountants as supporters of organisations' strategies with respect to the natural environment. There is some evidence that accountants may need support to fulfil this role effectively. For example, Schaltegger and Zvedov (2015) and Egan and Tweedie (2018) explored the role of accountants within organisations and expressed concern about the ability of environmental accountants to become strategic business partners. For example, Egan and Tweedie (2018) suggested that accountants' professional habitus, and the necessity to maintain distinctive professional expertise, impairs their engagements in sustainability. At the same time, Egan and Tweedie (2018) were hopeful that "given sufficient investment in material and symbolic capital over time, alongside sufficient organisational support to engage with other professionals" (p. 1768), accountants might play a greater strategic role in the future.

In this vein, Johnstone (2019) raised the idea of accountants as boundary spanners, who with sufficient autonomy and empowered with their personal sustainability knowledge could participate in facilitating sharing experience and strategic intent with others inside an organisation. These accountants can be seen as change agents able to play the role of facilitator, catalyst or activist (Johnstone 2019). Indeed, a recent study of "sustainability CFOs" (IMA 2018) demonstrated how some companies have created a specific strategic role to integrate finance with sustainability, which supports the boundary spanner role noted by Johnstone (2019). Similarly, King and Atkins (2016) called for a Chief Value Officer, a strategic role recently embraced by the International Federation of Accountants (IFAC) and the International Integrated Reporting Council (IIRC) (2019) and defined on the IIRC's website as "ensuring that all relevant aspects of value creation and destruction are accounted for and communicated to boards, management, and external stakeholders". Collectively these new accounting roles share common ground with the SMA aspiration of the accountant as a strategic business partner. However, this is empirically underdeveloped in the SEMA literature.

Conclusion

In this chapter various important themes for environmentally focused SMA have been considered. It has been argued that SEMA is well placed for encouraging long-term environmental thinking within the strategic performance system of organisations (Arjaliès and Mundy 2013). SEMA can be seen as extending beyond organisational boundaries by reaching out to competitors (Chelli and Gendron 2013) and through life cycle footprinting to consumers (Berquier 2017). It also demonstrated that SEMA primarily relied on interactive controls with internal stakeholders while having some connection to external stakeholders (Renaud 2013; Rodrigue et al. 2013). In many ways, SEMA has co-evolved alongside knowledge of sustainable development (Gibassier and Alcouffe 2018). A stronger integration of planetary boundaries (Schaltegger 2018) and intergenerational equity could help bring SEMA even closer to a strategic integration of sustainable development. This chapter has outlined research on the link between environmental/sustainability strategy and controls, and the integration of financial and non-financial controls in organisational strategy.

There are, however, further avenues for research in SEMA. First, Crutzen et al. (2017) opened an avenue for research into the extent to which the connection of both formal and informal management controls could better support organisations achieve their environmental objectives. Second, it is also puzzling why, despite the environment being a good candidate for interactive control (Renaud 2013), there is relative lack of practice in that area. Third, further research is also warranted into the decoupling of financial management control systems and environmental control systems: a phenomenon that Riccaboni and Leone (2010) have suggested arises through the contextual nature of environmental goals that require a decentralised structure of management control systems. Johnstone (2019) further suggests that system design needs to be flexible and malleable to adapt to environmental performance outcomes, specifically because they extend over time (and generations) and physical space (which can be different from organisational space). She also emphasises the need for further research into how "bottom-up" development of environmental control systems might emerge in dynamic environments which may (in turn) allow environmental control systems to respond better to organisational needs. An employee-driven strategic environmental control system could also play the role of developing competence in environmentally sound behaviours and solutions (Wijethilake 2017). Finally, further research in the role of "sustainability accountants" as business partners could further help understand the cognitive barriers that accountants have to be effective actors in this space (Battaglia et al. 2016; Egan and Tweedie 2018).

Note

1 https://sdg2000.worldbenchmarkingalliance.org/.

References

A4S, 2017. *Capex Deep Dive Integrating Social and Environmental Factors into Capital Investment Decision Making*. London: Accounting for Sustainability.
Arjalies, D.-L. and Mundy, J., 2013. The use of management control systems to manage CSR strategy: A levers of control perspective. *Management Accounting Research*, 24, 284–300.
Bannerjee, S.B., 2002. Corporate environmentalism: The construct and its measurement. *Journal of Business Research*, 55 (3), 177–191.
Bansal, P. and Roth, K., 2002. Why companies go green: A model of ecological responsiveness. *Academy of Management Journal*, 43(4), 717–736.
Battaglia, M., Passetti E., Bianchi L. and Frey, M., 2016. Managing for integration: A longitudinal analysis of management control for sustainability. *Journal of Cleaner Production*, 136, 213–225.
Bebbington, J., Österblom, H., Crona, B., Jouffray, J.-B., Larrinaga, C., Russell, S. and Scholtens, B., 2020. Accounting and accountability in the Anthropocene. *Accounting, Auditing & Accountability Journal*, 33 (1), 152–177.
Berquier, R., 2017. *La participation des entreprises aux travaux de standardisation de la comptabilité environnementale: le cas de la comptabilité environnementale des produits*. PhD Thesis. Toulouse School of Management.
Bonacchi, M. and Rinaldi, L., 2007. Dart boards and clovers as new tools in sustainability planning and control. *Business, Strategy and the Environment*, 16, 461–473.
Boulianne, E., Keddie, L.S. and Postaire, M., 2018. (Non) coverage of sustainability within the French professional accounting education program. *Sustainability Accounting, Management and Policy Journal*, 9 (3), 313–335.
Busco, C. and Quattrone, P., 2015. Exploring how the balanced scorecard engages and unfolds: Articulating the visual power of accounting inscriptions. *Contemporary Accounting Research*, 32 (3), 1236–1262.
Cadez, S. and Guilding, C., 2008. An exploratory investigation of an integrated contingency model of strategic management accounting. *Accounting, Organizations and Society*, 33, 836–863.
Caputo, F., Veltri, S. and Venturelli, A., 2017. Sustainability strategy and management control systems in family firms. Evidence from a case study. *Sustainability*. 9, 1–23.
Caron, M.-A. and Fortin, A., 2014. Accountants' construction of CSR competencies and commitment. *Sustainability Accounting, Management and Policy Journal*, 5 (2), 172–196.
Chelli, M. and Gendron, Y., 2013. Sustainability ratings and the disciplinary power of the ideology of numbers. *Journal of Business Ethics*, 112, 187–203.
Chung, L.H. and Parker, L.D., 2008. Integrating hotel environmental strategies with management control: A structuration approach. *Business Strategy and the Environment*, 17, 272–286.
Crutzen, N., Zvezdov, D. and Schaltegger, S., 2017. Sustainability and management control. Exploring and theorizing control patterns in large European firms. *Journal of Cleaner Production*, 143, 1291–1301.
Déjean, F., Gond, J.-P. and Leca, B., 2004. Measuring the unmeasured: An institutional entrepreneur strategy in an emerging industry. *Human Relations*, 57 (6), 741–764.
Ditillo, A. and Lisi, I.E., 2016. Exploring sustainability control systems' integration: The relevance of sustainability orientation. *Journal of Management Accounting Research*, 28 (2), 125–148.
Dixon, R. and Smith, D., 1993. Strategic management accounting. *Omega*, 21 (6), 605–618.
Dutta, S.K., Lawson, R.A. and Marcinko, D.J., 2013. Alignment of performance measurement to sustainability objectives: A variance-based framework. *Journal of Accounting and Public Policy*, 32, 456–474.
Egan, M. and Tweedie, D., 2018. A "green" accountant is difficult to find: Can accountants contribute to sustainability management initiatives? *Accounting, Auditing & Accountability Journal*, 31 (6), 1749–1773.
Epstein, M.J. and Roy, M., 2001. Sustainability in action: Identifying and measuring the key performance drivers. *Long Range Planning*, 1 (34), 585–604.
Epstein, M. and Wisner, P.S., 2001. Using a balanced scorecard to implement sustainability. *Environmental Quality Management*, 11 (2), 1–10.
Figge, F., Hahn, T., Schaltegger, S. and Wagner, M., 2002. The sustainability balanced scorecard: Linking sustainability management to business strategy. *Business Strategy and the Environment*, 11, 269–284.

Gibassier, D., 2014. *Environmental Management Accounting Development in France: Institutionalization, Adoption and Practice*. PhD Thesis. HEC Paris.

Gibassier, D. and Schaltegger, S., 2015. Carbon management accounting and reporting in practice. *Sustainability Accounting, Management and Policy Journal*, 6 (3), 340–365.

Gibassier, D. and Alcouffe, S., 2018. Environmental management accounting: The missing link to sustainability? *Social and Environmental Accountability Journal*, 38 (1), 1–18.

Gibassier, D., 2017. From écobilan to LCA: The elite's institutional work in the creation of an environmental management accounting tool. *Critical Perspectives on Accounting*, 43, 36–58.

Gond, J.P., Grubnic, S., Herzig, C. and Moon, J., 2012. Configuring management control systems: Theorizing the integration of strategy and sustainability. *Management Accounting Research*, 23, 205–223.

Govindarajan, V. and Shank, J.K., 1992. Strategic cost management: Tailoring controls to strategies. *Journal of Cost Management*, Fall 1992, 14–24.

Gray, R., 2013. Sustainability + accounting education: The elephant in the classroom. *Accounting Education: An International Journal*, 22(4), 308–332.

Hansen, E.G. and Schaltegger, S., 2016. The sustainability balanced scorecard: A systematic review of architectures. *Journal of Business Ethics*, 133, 193–221.

Henri, J.F., Boiral, O. and Roy, M.J., 2016. Strategic cost management and performance: The case of environmental costs. *The British Accounting Review*, 48, 269–282.

IFAC and IIRC, 2019. Accounting for value creation and encouraging the rise of the chief value officer. Available from: https://integratedreporting.org/news/accounting-for-value-creation-and-encouraging-the-rise-of-the-chief-value-officer/. 7 November 2020.

IMA, 2018. *Sustainability CFO: The CFO of the Future?* Montvale, NJ: Institute of Management Accountants .

Johnstone, L., 2018. Theorising and modelling social control in environmental management accounting research. *Social and Environmental Accountability Journal*, 38 (1), 30–48.

Johnstone, L., 2019. Theorising and conceptualising the sustainability control system for effective sustainability management. *Journal of Management Control*, 30, 25–64.

Kaplan, R.S. and Norton, D.P., 1992. The balanced scorecard—Measures that drive performance. *Harvard Business Review*, 70(1), 71–79.

King, M. and Atkins, J., 2016. *The Chief Value Officer. Accountants Can Save the Planet*. Saltaire: Greenleaf.

Langfield-Smith, K., 2005. What do we know about management control systems and strategy. In: C. Chapman (Ed.), *Controlling Strategy: Management, Accounting, and Performance Measurement*. New York, NY: Oxford University Press, pp. 62–85.

Langfield-Smith, K., 2008. Strategic management accounting: How far have we come in 25 years? *Accounting, Auditing and Accountability Journal*, 21 (2), 204–228.

Lord, B., 1996. Strategic management accounting: The emperor's new clothes? *Management Accounting Research*, 7 (3), 347–366.

Mir, M.Z. and Rahaman, A.S., 2011. In pursuit of environmental excellence: A stakeholder analysis of the environmental management strategies and performance of an Australian energy company. *Accounting, Auditing & Accountability Journal*, 24 (7), 848–878.

Norris, G. and O'Dwyer, B., 2004. Motivating socially responsive decision making: The operation of management controls in a socially responsive organisation. *The British Accounting Review*, 36, 173–196.

O'Dwyer, B. and Unerman, J., 2020. Shifting the focus of sustainability accounting from impacts to risks and dependencies: Researching the transformative potential of TCFD reporting. *Accounting, Auditing & Accountability Journal*, 33 (5), 1113–1141.

Parker, L.D., 2000. Green strategy costing: Early days. *Australian Accounting Review*, 10 (1), 46–55.

Perego, P. and Hartmann, F., 2009. Aligning performance measurement systems with strategy: The case of environmental strategy. *Abacus*, 45 (4), 397–428.

Pondeville, S., Swaen, V. and De Rongé, Y., 2013. Environmental management control systems: The role of contextual and strategic factors. *Management Accounting Research*, 24, 317–332.

Renaud, A., 2013. Configurations of the interactive use of environmental management control. *Comptabilité-Contrôle-Audit*, 19 (2), 101–132.

Riccaboni, A. and Leone, E.L., 2010. Implementing strategies through management control systems: The case of sustainability. *International Journal of Productivity and Performance Management*, 59, 130–144.

Rinaldi, L., 2019. Accounting for sustainability governance: The enabling role of social and environmental accountability research. *Social and Environmental Accountability Journal*, 39 (1), 1–22.

Rodrigue, M., Magnan, M. and Boulianne, E., 2013. Stakeholders' influence on environmental strategy and performance indicators: A managerial perspective. *Management Accounting Research*, 24, 301–316.
Roslender, R. and Hart, S.J., 2002. Integrating management accounting and marketing in the pursuit of competitive advantage: The case for strategic management accounting. *Critical Perspectives on Accounting*, 13 (2), 255–277.
Roslender, R. and Hart, S.J., 2003. In search of strategic management accounting: Theoretical and field study perspectives. *Management Accounting Research*, 14 (3), 255–279.
Schaltegger, S., 2018. Linking environmental management accounting. A reflection on (missing) links to sustainability and planetary boundaries. *Social and Environmental Accountability Journal*, 38 (1), 19–29.
Schaltegger, S. and Zvezdov, D., 2015. Gatekeepers of sustainability information: Exploring the roles of accountants. *Journal of Accounting & Organizational Change*, 11 (3), 333–361.
Siegel, G., Sorensen, J.E. and Richtermeyer, S.R., 2003. Becoming a business partner. *Strategic Finance*, 85 (4), 37.
Simmonds, K., 1981. Strategic management accounting. *Management Accounting*, 59 (4), 26–30.
Simons, R., 1987. Accounting control systems and business strategy: An empirical analysis. *Accounting, Organizations and Society*, 12 (4), 357–374.
Simons, R., 1995. *Levers of Control*. Boston, MA: Harvard Business School Press.
Simons, R., 2000. *Performance Measurement and Control Systems for Implementing Strategy*. Upper Saddle River, NJ: Prentice Hall.
Solovida, G.T. and Latan, H., 2017. Linking environmental strategy to environmental performance: Mediation role of environmental management accounting. *Sustainability Accounting, Management and Policy Journal*, 8 (5), 595–619.
SustainAbility, 2020. *Rate the Raters 2020: Investor Survey and Interview Results*. London: SustainAbility.
United Nations, 2001. *Environmental Management Accounting: Policies and Linkages*. New York, NY: United Nations.
Vesty, G.M., Telgenkamp, A. and Roscoe, P., 2015. Creating numbers: Carbon and capital investment. *Accounting, Auditing and Accountability Journal*, 28, 302–324.
Wijethilake, C., 2017. Proactive sustainability strategy and corporate sustainability performance: The mediating effect of sustainability control systems. *Journal of Environmental Management*, 196, 569–582.
Wynder, M., Wellner, K. and Wynder, K., 2013. Rhetoric or reality? Do accounting education and experience increase weighting on environmental performance in a balanced scorecard? *Accounting Education: An International Journal*, 22(4), 366–381.

14

DESIGNING ECO-CONTROLS FOR MULTI-OBJECTIVE ORGANIZATIONS[1]

Lies Bouten and Sophie Hoozée

Introduction

Internal accounting information serves two primary roles (e.g. Demski and Feltham 1976; Zimmerman 2017). The first role refers to the use of accounting information to support decision-making. In particular, environmental management accounting encompasses the provision of information to manage environmental performance (e.g. Burritt and Schaltegger 2010). This was the focus of Chapter 13. The second role, the decision-influencing or control role of accounting information, is covered in this chapter.

Management controls are designed "to ensure that the behaviour of employees is consistent with the organization's objectives and strategy" (Malmi and Brown 2008, p. 290). In the context of the environment, we view environmental controls or *eco-controls* as mechanisms used to direct organizational members as well as other stakeholders such that they perform activities that contribute to the achievement of organizations' environmental objectives and the implementation of their related strategies.

The objective of this chapter is to provide an overview of prior research on eco-control practices and to offer critical reflections and avenues for future work. To categorize eco-control practices, we will rely on the framework of Malmi and Brown (2008).

Eco-control types

Environmental planning controls

Environmental planning may support ex-ante decision-making (e.g. Heggen 2019) when it is used to decide on future goals and actions for the long run (long-range or strategic planning) as well as for the immediate future (action planning). However, for environmental planning to operate as a control and thus create goal congruence, employees need to be involved in environmental planning activities (cf. Malmi and Brown 2008). They may, for instance, participate in the prioritization of environmental issues (cf. Baker et al. 2012). Employee participation in planning activities creates buy-in by encouraging the internalization of organizational objectives, which fosters their autonomous motivation to achieve these objectives (cf. De Baerdemaeker and Bruggeman 2015).

Cybernetic environmental controls

As explained in Chapter 13, more refined allocation of environmental overheads can enhance decision-making (e.g. Burritt and Schaltegger 2001; Henri et al. 2014, 2016). However, costing information may also be used as a control to modify employee behaviour. In particular, cybernetic controls establish standards of performance or targets to be met, evaluate actual performance against those predetermined levels and provide feedback on unwanted variances (Green and Welsh 1988). For instance, environmental budgeting involves the setting of detailed goals for environmental revenues, costs and investments (Henri and Journeault 2010). Allowable levels of consumption of environmental resources may be expressed in monetary (or financial) units, but organizations may also use physical (or non-financial) environmental performance indicators (EPIs) to execute their environmental strategies (e.g. Burritt et al. 2002; Lisi 2015; Perego and Hartmann 2009). Hybrid environmental performance measurement systems are scorecards that contain both financial and non-financial EPIs (e.g. Epstein and Wisner 2001; Figge et al. 2002).

Environmental reward and compensation controls

Rewards and compensation may be linked to the achievement of environmental targets. Although monetary incentives may be used to focus employee efforts on tasks contributing to environmental performance (Henri and Journeault 2010; Journeault 2016), alternative reward and compensation schemes, such as getting time off for volunteer work on environmental projects, may also be considered (Dutta and Lawson 2009).

Assuming that external regulation (e.g. monetary incentives) motivates agents to exert effort, agency theorists advocate pay-for-performance. Motivational psychologists argue, however, that extrinsic motivation is not a unitary concept. In particular, self-determination theory (Deci and Ryan 2000; Ryan and Deci 2017; see Table 14.1) distinguishes different types of extrinsic motivation, with some of them being more controlled (external regulation and introjected regulation)

Table 14.1 Schematic representation of the different types of motivation within self-determination theory (adapted from Vansteenkiste et al. 2008, 2018)

Extrinsic motivation			*Intrinsic motivation*
Punishment, rewards, expectation	Shame, guilt, self-worth	Personal relevance, meaningful	Pleasure, passion, interest
External regulation	*Introjected regulation*	*Identified regulation*	*Intrinsic regulation*
Lack of internalization	Partial internalization	Full internalization	Internalization not required
CONTROLLED MOTIVATION "Having to"		AUTONOMOUS MOTIVATION "Wanting to"	

Why do you cycle to work?

"because my employer pays me to do so"	*"because I need to show to my colleagues I care for the environment"*	*"I choose to come by bike to limit my ecological footprint"*	*"because I truly love to ride my bike"*

and others being more autonomous (identified regulation). In contrast, intrinsic motivation refers to doing an activity for its own sake because it is interesting and enjoyable. Consider recycling or reducing one's ecological footprint (Aitken et al. 2016). These activities are typically not inherently enjoyable and thus not intrinsically motivated. Self-determination theory suggests, however, that when people identify with the value of these extrinsically motivated activities and accept or integrate them as personally relevant (i.e. when they internalize them), they will take more personal responsibility for their behaviour (Vansteenkiste et al. 2018). When internalized, extrinsically motivated behaviour is experienced as volitional and autonomous, thereby entailing a more enduring enactment of the required activities (e.g. Gagné and Deci 2005). As such, autonomous motivation is self-determined and results from "wanting to" (either pure intrinsic motivation or resulting from internalization). In contrast, under controlled motivation employees engage in activities because they "have to".

In line with self-determination theory, control systems can lead to both autonomous or controlled types of motivation, depending on the extent to which they satisfy people's inherent psychological needs for autonomy (i.e. experience of volition), belongingness (i.e. experience of connection) and competence (i.e. experience of effectiveness). A number of recent management control studies have considered autonomous motivation in the design and implementation of control systems for financial objectives (e.g. De Baerdemaeker and Bruggeman 2015; Chen et al. 2020; Groen et al. 2017; Kunz 2015; Pfister and Lukka 2019; Wong-On-Wing et al. 2010). Examples of autonomy-supportive control systems include bottom-up establishment of performance indicators, interactive use of performance reports, participative team processes for strategy development and implementation and constructive feedback on performance data.

It is important to note that people may also pursue extrinsic and intrinsic life goals. Examples of extrinsic life goals include amassing wealth, creating an attractive image and having power over others. Intrinsic goals refer to aspirations such as personal development, physical health, caring, community contribution and sustainability. In contrast to extrinsic goals, intrinsic goals are directly linked to the satisfaction of people's inherent psychological needs for autonomy, belongingness and competence and, as such, to their psychological well-being (Vansteenkiste et al. 2008). As monetary (extrinsic) rewards can crowd out intrinsic motivation (Frey 1997) by thwarting basic psychological need satisfaction, they may be less effective (Sharma 2000), and therefore less used (e.g. Arjaliès and Mundy 2013; Crutzen et al. 2017; Lueg and Radlach 2016) for stimulating environmentally conscious behaviour. In fact, as humans are innately motivated by altruistic perspectives, the development of autonomy-supportive control systems can be expected to operate as a natural lever towards achieving broader societal objectives. Interestingly, a recent study by Parmar et al. (2019) suggests that altruistic employees may even self-select into organizations that create value for multiple stakeholders due to the higher psychological need satisfaction this entails.

Administrative environmental controls

Administrative control devices include (1) organizational structure (i.e. how tasks are grouped to control within the organization), (2) governance structure (i.e. who is made accountable and for what) and (3) policies and procedures (Malmi and Brown 2008). First, the degree of centralization of the environmental function within the organizational chart may influence employee behaviour (cf. Epstein and Buhovac 2010). Second, systems may be in place to ensure vertical and horizontal coordination between the activities of environmental specialists and other organizational members (Ditillo and Lisi 2014). Third, environmental policies and procedures represent formal statements regarding environmental rules as well as codes of conduct that prescribe the behaviour and actions that must be used or avoided by employees (Journeault 2016), such as the integration of environmental considerations within procurement or capital expenditure approval procedures (Ditillo and Lisi 2014).

Cultural environmental controls

Although organizational culture may be a contingency beyond managerial control (Chenhall 2003), organizations can also use cultural controls such as values, symbols or rituals to craft organizational culture (Malmi and Brown 2008). The impact of values on behaviour works on three levels. First, employees may be selected based on their environmental values (intrinsic regulation). Second, they may act in line with them because they have internalized them (identified regulation). When organizations try to control employees' mindsets, this is referred to as socio-ideological control (Alvesson and Kärreman 2004). Third, employees may feel forced to act in line with organizational values (introjected regulation, external regulation). Values may be conveyed through belief systems, such as environmental mission statements (Journeault 2016). Examples of symbols and rituals in the context of the environment include the use of nudges, "exemplary team of the month" posters and the daily routine of unplugging one's own electronic devices and double-checking those of colleagues before leaving the office.

Overlapping eco-control types

It should be noted that a particular practice can sometimes be categorized into multiple control types of Malmi and Brown's typology. Consider the example of environmental management systems such as the European Commission's Eco-Management and Audit Scheme (EMAS) and the International Standard ISO 14001. Since these environmental management systems entail a commitment to the continuous improvement of environmental performance as well as regular audits, they can operate as cybernetic and administrative environmental controls. Alternatively, by enabling the internalization of environmental values (Albelda 2011; Albelda Pérez et al. 2007; Lueg and Radlach 2016), they can also act as a cultural control since certification may symbolize organizations' environmental commitment.

Eco-controls beyond organizational boundaries

Stakeholder pressures may influence organizations' EPI selection and accompanying target setting (Rodrigue et al. 2013). However, EPIs do not automatically operate as control mechanisms. Indeed, when environmental practices are merely undertaken to manage stakeholders (Tucker and Parker 2015; Wijethilake et al. 2017) or comply with legal requirements (e.g. Hubbard 2009), they are typically a "hodge-podge" (Porter and Kramer 2006, p. 83) that runs parallel to corporate strategy (cf. Gond et al. 2012). According to Kaplan (2009), in such instances, stakeholders should not "feature on the scorecard" (p. 1260). In fact, environmental practices that are decoupled from corporate strategy are merely a solution to a legitimacy problem rather than to a control problem (Brunsson 1990). As such, they should not be labelled as control practices. Alternatively, when corporate strategy is altered to accommodate stakeholder pressures, these pressures play out in control practices that motivate environmentally conscious behaviour. As such, stakeholder pressures can be an important contingency factor in the context of eco-controls (Henri and Journeault 2010; Pondeville et al. 2013; Rodrigue et al. 2013).

When apart from employee actions, actions from external stakeholders are also required to achieve environmental objectives, eco-controls may be used to motivate behaviour beyond organizational boundaries (Baker et al. 2018). For example, eco-controls may transcend organizational boundaries when suppliers' formal consent to a joint code of conduct is required (cf. Lueg et al. 2015) or when incentives are developed for customers to contribute to environmental performance.

Designing a control package to cope with multiple objectives

As shown in Figure 14.1, individual eco-control practices do not operate in isolation; they are interrelated and combined into an *eco-control subsystem* that is aligned with the organization's environmental objectives (cf. Malmi and Brown 2008). Interrelations between eco-control practices (i.e. elements of an eco-control subsystem) may be complementary or substitutive: two control practices are complementary (substitutive) when one control practice increases (decreases) the effectiveness of the other (Grabner and Moers 2013). Several researchers have emphasized the importance of a more holistic approach that acknowledges interactions between eco-control practices (e.g. Burritt 2004; Ditillo and Lisi 2014; Epstein and Buhovac 2010; Guenther et al. 2016; Lueg and Radlach 2016; Sundin and Brown 2017). Research on those interactions is, however, still in its infancy. Assuming complementarity, Journeault (2016) has found some first evidence of the overall effect of simultaneously used eco-control practices. Relatedly, a number of studies have suggested that successful implementation of corporate social responsibility strategies requires informal controls to complement formal controls (e.g. Baker et al. 2012; Crutzen et al. 2017; Epstein and Buhovac 2010). In contrast, Balakrishnan et al. (2011) argued that selecting employees who believe that giving to charity is important may act as a cultural control substituting for costly accounting-based reward systems and controls.

Prior research has typically established a positive relationship between environmental and financial performance (Kim and Matsumura 2017). A recent meta-analysis by Vishwanathan et al.

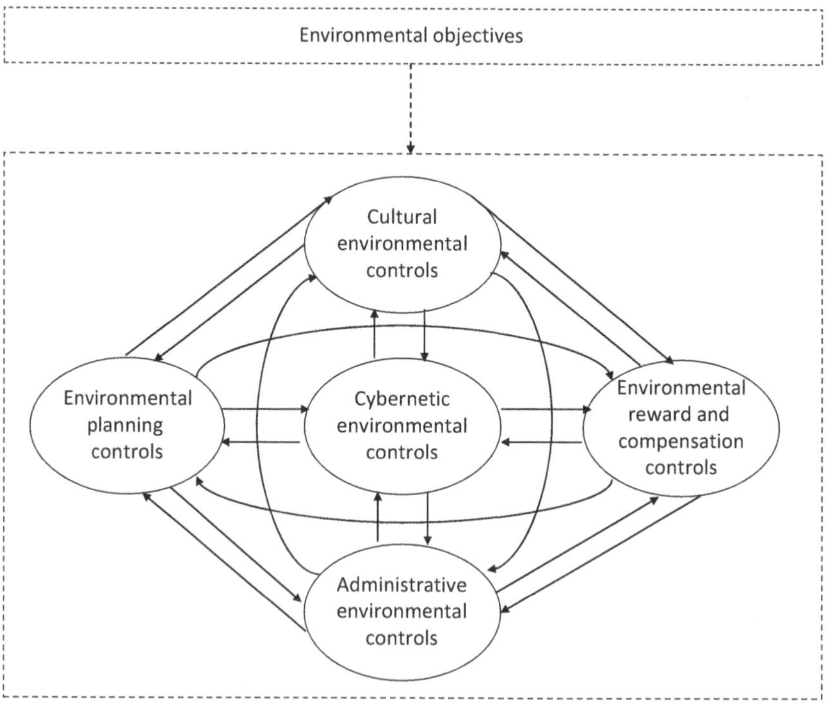

Figure 14.1 Eco-control subsystem. (Source: Authors' own work.)

(2020) ascribed this positive effect to enhanced firm reputation, stakeholder reciprocation, risk mitigation and improved innovation capacity. In a similar vein, studies on eco-controls have viewed environmental performance as an intermediate level of performance, that is, eco-controls influence financial performance indirectly through environmental performance (Lisi 2015). Based on a survey in Canadian manufacturing firms, Journeault (2016) found that the positive association between eco-controls and environmental performance operates, in turn, through the development of environmental capabilities. Moreover, the indirect effect of eco-controls on financial performance through environmental performance was found to be greater for firms operating in more polluting industries, public firms, firms indicating higher integration of environmental issues into their strategic planning process and larger firms (Henri and Journeault 2010).

When environmental objectives are viewed as secondary objectives (i.e. a means to achieve a business end; Soderstrom et al. 2017), the environment is integrated into the profit-seeking corporate strategy and elements of the environmental agenda that are not perceived as directly supporting the business case are disregarded (Arjaliès and Mundy 2013). Eco-control practices are subsumed into the overall control system[2] designed to maximize shareholder value. Strategy maps may help to translate corporate strategy by expressing causal links between environmental success factors, other non-financial success factors and financial success factors (e.g. Figge et al. 2002; Islam 2019; Kaplan 2009). Organizations may also use a balanced scorecard to operationalize their critical success factors into measures (i.e. key performance indicators – KPIs), assign targets to their KPIs and assess the evolution against those targets. EPIs (i.e. KPIs related to environment) may then either be contained in a separate environmental perspective (e.g. Atkinson et al. 1997; Epstein and Wisner 2001; Hubbard 2009) or, alternatively, they may be subsumed under the four standard perspectives of the balanced scorecard (e.g. Epstein and Wisner 2001; Figge et al. 2002), that is, the financial perspective, the customer perspective, the internal business perspective and the innovation and learning perspective (Kaplan and Norton 1992, 1996).

Instead of viewing environmental objectives as subordinate means to maximize shareholder value, environmental and financial objectives may also co-exist (e.g. Chenhall 2003; Otley 2008). Organizations that do not single out one objective as the dominant one are called hybrid organizations (e.g. Battilana and Dorado 2010; Pache and Santos 2013). This shift towards a more stakeholder-oriented model of the organization implies that controls need to be designed to ensure that the organization will be effective in satisfying multiple stakeholder objectives (Sundin and Brown 2017; Sundin et al. 2010). Given that there are interrelations not only between the eco-subsystem (aligned with environmental objectives) and the traditional subsystem (aligned with financial objectives), but also within the elements of each subsystem (see Figure 14.2), the question arises as to how to integrate both subsystems into one overall system to implement hybrid organizations' multi-objective corporate strategy. In addition, although co-existing objectives may be complementary to some extent (as in the case of eco-efficiency), it would be naive to assume that there are no tensions between the multiple objectives (Crane et al. 2014; Vallaster et al. forthcoming). This further complicates the design of the overall control package. Some researchers (e.g. Atkinson et al. 1997; Dutta and Lawson 2009; Hales et al. 2016) have proposed to assign weights to the different performance dimensions (which may vary between corporate and operating divisions; Sundin and Brown 2017). A study of Carlsson-Wall et al. (2016) in a hybrid football organization demonstrated, however, that the prioritization of objectives may be situational, which makes the feasibility of ex-ante fixation of weights questionable.

In the context of social objectives, Norris and O'Dwyer (2004) offer a potential way forward. They examined an internationally operating United Kingdom (UK) retailer that used structurally differentiated controls (Carlsson-Wall et al. 2016), that is, formal controls (performance evaluation and performance-based rewards) were used for financial imperatives and

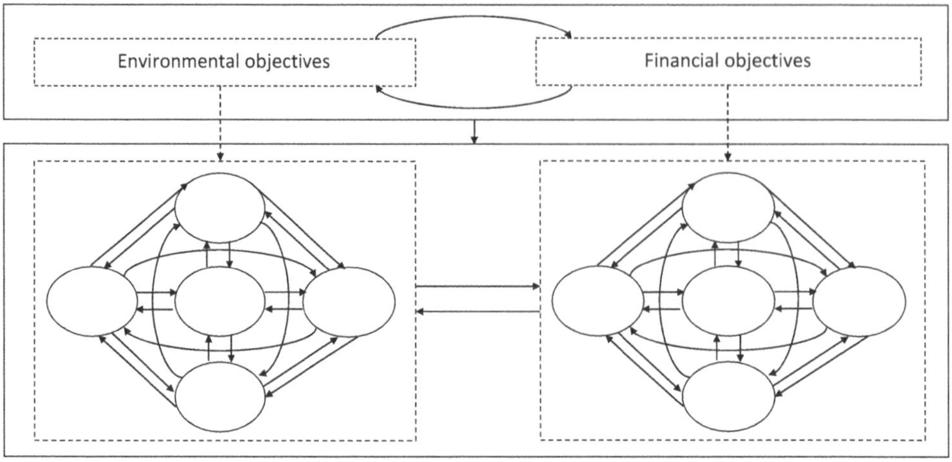

Figure 14.2 Two management control subsystems as a system in hybrid organizations. (Source: Authors' own work.)

Note: to not overload the figure, the ovals referring to the elements of the eco-subsystem (left) and the traditional subsystem (right) have not been labelled.

informal controls (employee [self-] selection and socialization to internalize social values) for social imperatives (see also Epstein et al. 2015). In case of a "clash" between formal and informal controls, managers were so motivated by cultural controls that they ignored the formal controls, taking decisions in line with social imperatives that harmed their personal financial performance-based evaluations and rewards. This resonates with Parker and Chung's (2018) study in the hotel sector, where employees were so committed to the environment that they creatively evoked financial controls to achieve social and environmental performance (for instance, by slicing resource demands to make environmental investments more palatable to senior management). Taken together, these two studies suggest that cultural controls have a strong potential to orientate employees in prioritizing sustainability-related objectives when tensions occur and that the power of values to steer the organization in the direction of these objectives should not be underestimated. Conversely, Durden's (2008) case study of a New Zealand food manufacturing company describes a failure story. Neither formal nor informal controls were effective in guiding socially responsible behaviour. This ineffectiveness could be ascribed to a lack of clearly defined social responsibility goals by top management. Indeed, as argued by Epstein and Buhovac (2010), leadership is important, as leaders may articulate trade-offs and thus help employees to deal with tensions present in hybrid organizations.

Instead of using structurally differentiated control subsystems to achieve multiple competing objectives or using cultural controls to automatically prioritize sustainability-related objectives, control practices may also be used in a dynamic way to manage conflicting objectives without explicitly prioritizing them (Sundin and Brown 2017). Sundin et al. (2010) offer one particular example of such a balancing control practice. In their case study of a state-owned electricity company with multiple and equally important objectives, the balanced scorecard was used to communicate that the overarching objective was continuously balancing the objectives given the constraints. A satisficing approach was employed to ensure that all stakeholders were satisfied to some minimum level. This is related to the boundary perspective of Epstein et al. (2015), which refers to minimum boundaries for social and environmental performance regardless of the financial payoff. In contrast, concerns for sustainability of the business may also result in maximum boundaries for social and environmental performance (Parker and Chung 2018).

Concluding reflections and future research directions

Prior work suggests that when eco-control practices are driven by enlightened self-interest (e.g. eco-efficiency, improved reputation, etc.), they are integrated into an overall control package with the unitary aim of maximizing shareholder value. In contrast, in hybrid organizations, which do not hierarchically rank their multiple objectives, ecological responsibility figures as a goal in itself, such that eco-controls are *not* simply "a specific application of management control systems" (Henri and Journeault 2010, p. 63). Although Contrafatto and Burns (2013) warn that controls may be limited in their ability to incorporate the interests of a broad range of stakeholders other than shareholders, in line with Ball and Milne (2005), we argue that the jeopardy does not lie in the controls as such but rather in the purpose for which they have been designed.

We argue that, in hybrid organizations, controls may foster the simultaneous pursuit of co-existing objectives and influence employees' as well as other stakeholders' behaviour, both within and outside organizational boundaries. Hence, in contemporary hybrid organizations populated by individuals who pursue multiple life goals, the aim of management control is to autonomously motivate employees *as well as other stakeholders* to internalize the organization's multi-objective corporate strategy such that they will perform activities that contribute to its implementation. The effectiveness of a management control configuration should then be assessed against the multi-dimensional performance envisioned by the organization (cf. Malmi and Brown 2008; Otley 1980). Due to the situational prioritization of organizational objectives, the answer to the control problem in hybrid organizations is, however, not straightforward.

As the control problem in hybrid organizations differs from the control problem in organizations that single out one objective as the dominant one, we encourage researchers to be explicit about the assumptions and beliefs that reign in the organizations that they study (see also Malmi and Granlund 2009). Apart from this general advice, we offer a number of areas that merit future research attention.

First, in response to the increasing societal demand to limit environmentally detrimental impacts, hybrid organizations are mushrooming (e.g. Vallaster et al. forthcoming). To better understand how control systems may help to achieve the at times conflicting objectives in hybrid organizations, we should search for cases where trade-offs are successfully made (cf. Burritt 2004). In particular, we need more insight into how structural differentiation and/or situational compromises work in practice at all organizational levels, as well as the conditions under which each solution is most effective. Powerful examples of control tools may assist managers in driving multiple objectives through their organizations. Researchers interested in hybrid organizations could find inspiration in the recent management literature (see, for instance, Vallaster et al. forthcoming).

Second, given the complexity involved in the measurement of environmental performance (Virtanen et al. 2013) and given that extrinsic rewards may crowd out people's inherent motivation to pursue intrinsic goals related to sustainability, the question arises whether other controls may operate as substitutes for extrinsic rewards when striving for broader societal objectives. Indeed, the transition to sustainability implies attention to how people are motivated at work (Ball and Milne 2005) rather than simply assuming that they are endlessly motivated by money. We advise researchers interested in employee motivation and well-being to keep up to date with the motivational psychology literature.

Third, more work on changes in the role of the management accountant is needed. The advocacy of a business partner role (e.g. CIMA 2009; ICAEW 2009) is being extended beyond organizational boundaries by professional management accounting bodies (IMA 2019). For example, one of the objectives in a sustainable financial organization may be that their lending activity results in reducing the ecological footprint of a particular region. In determining these boundary-transcending objectives and measuring the progress towards them, dialogue with various stakeholders is indispensable. Management accountants could act as interlocutors in this respect. They may also have a pivotal role to play in explicating trade-offs between conflicting objectives (Bonacchi and Rinaldi 2007). Multi-disciplinary knowledge of engineering, psychology and finance can enable them to fulfil this role. Hence, the question arises whether or under which conditions the management accounting function should be centralized (cf. Gibassier and Alcouffe 2018).

Fourth, although some studies have investigated the proactiveness of environmental strategies (Ditillo and Lisi 2016; Perego and Hartmann 2009), perceived ecological environmental uncertainty (Pondeville et al. 2013) and stakeholder pressure (Henri and Journeault 2010; Pondeville et al. 2013; Rodrigue et al. 2013) as contingency factors in the design of eco-controls, more work on additional contingency factors is needed. Apart from limited insight into the fit of eco-control systems with their context, there is also a lack of in-depth understanding of the interplay between elements of eco-controls subsystems (cf. Lueg and Radlach 2016).

Fifth, while there are certainly interactions between environmental management accounting and control practices and external reporting (e.g. Bouten and Hoozée 2013), deep understanding of control configurations of multi-objective organizations requires engagement with these organizations and their stakeholders. Indeed, as some control information is confidential, examining external disclosures will only offer partial insights. More insight is also needed on the institutional effects *of* rather than *on* management accounting and control practices (cf. Modell 2014), given that in the context of wider societal objectives, management accounting and control practices surpass organizational boundaries.

Finally, while in this chapter we focus on dual-objective organizations, all of the above suggestions may also be extended to the social domain. In addition, the list of topics worthy of attention will continue to evolve. We hope that our chapter will inspire scholars to take up the challenges inherent in studying multi-objective organizations and their stakeholders. Although such studies will only be small steps, we wish that, together, they may form a giant leap in levering the transformational potential of management control.

Notes

1 We thank David Brown, Teemu Malmi and Maarten Vansteenkiste for friendly comments on this chapter.

2 If all controls are designed jointly, this is referred to as a control system instead of a package (Grabner and Moers 2013; Malmi and Brown 2008).

References

Aitken, N.M., Pelletier, L.G., and Baxter, D.E., 2016. Doing the difficult stuff: influence of self-determined motivation toward the environment on transportation proenvironmental behavior. *Ecopsychology*, 8 (2), 153–162.

Albelda, E., 2011. The role of management accounting practices as facilitators of the environmental management: evidence from EMAS organisations. *Sustainability Accounting, Management and Policy Journal*, 2 (1), 76–100.

Albelda Pérez, E., Correa Ruiz, C., and Carrasco Fenech, F., 2007. Environmental management systems as an embedding mechanism: a research note. *Accounting, Auditing & Accountability Journal*, 20 (3), 403–422.
Alvesson, M., and Kärreman, D., 2004. Interfaces of control. Technocratic and socio-ideological control in a global management consultancy firm. *Accounting, Organizations and Society*, 29 (3–4), 423–444.
Arjaliès, D.-L., and Mundy, J., 2013. The use of management control systems to manage CSR strategy: a levers of control perspective. *Management Accounting Research*, 24 (4), 284–300.
Atkinson, A.A., Waterhouse, J.H., and Wells, R.B., 1997. A stakeholder approach to strategic performance measurement. *Sloan Management Review*, 38 (3), 25–37.
Baker, C.R., Cohanier, B., and Gibassier, D., 2018. Environmental management controls at Michelin - How do they link to sustainability? *Social and Environmental Accountability Journal*, 38 (1), 75–96.
Baker, M.L., Brown, D.A., and Malmi, T., 2012. An integrated package of environmental management control systems. In: G.N. Gregoriou and N. Finch, eds. *Best Practices in Management Accounting*. London, UK: Palgrave Macmillan, pp. 115–129.
Balakrishnan, R., Sprinkle, G.B., and Williamson, M.G., 2011. Contracting benefits of corporate giving: an experimental investigation. *The Accounting Review*, 86 (6), 1887–1907.
Ball, A., and Milne, M.J., 2005. Sustainability and management control. In: D. Otley, J. Broadbent and T. Berry, eds. *Management Control*. 2nd edn. Houndmills, UK: Palgrave Macmillan, pp. 314–337.
Battilana, J., and Dorado, S., 2010. Building sustainable hybrid organizations: the case of commercial microfinance organizations. *Academy of Management Journal*, 53 (6), 1419–1440.
Bonacchi, M., and Rinaldi, L., 2007. DartBoards and Clovers as new tools in sustainability planning and control. *Business Strategy and the Environment*, 16 (7), 461–473.
Bouten, L., and Hoozée, S., 2013. On the interplay between environmental reporting and management accounting change. *Management Accounting Research*, 24 (4), 333–348.
Brunsson, N., 1990. Deciding for responsibility and legitimation: alternative interpretations of organizational decision-making. *Accounting, Organizations and Society*, 15 (1–2), 47–59.
Burritt, R.L., 2004. Environmental management accounting: roadblocks on the way to the green and pleasant land. *Business Strategy and the Environment*, 13 (1), 13–32.
Burritt, R.L., Hahn, T., and Schaltegger, S., 2002. Towards a comprehensive framework for environmental management accounting - Links between business actors and environmental management accounting tools. *Australian Accounting Review*, 12 (2), 39–50.
Burritt, R. and Schaltegger, S., 2001. Eco-efficiency in corporate budgeting. *Environmental Management and Health*, 12 (2), 158–174.
Burritt, R., and Schaltegger, S., 2010. Sustainability accounting and reporting: fad or trend? *Accounting, Auditing & Accountability Journal*, 23 (7), 829–846.
Carlsson-Wall, M., Kraus, K., and Messner, M., 2016. Performance measurement systems and the enactment of different institutional logics: insights from a football organization. *Management Accounting Research*, 32, 45–61.
Chen, C.X., Lill, J.B., and Vance, T.W., 2020. Management control system design and employees' autonomous motivation. *Journal of Management Accounting Research*, 32(3), 71–91.
Chenhall, R.H., 2003. Management control systems design within its organizational context: findings from contingency-based research and directions for the future. *Accounting, Organizations and Society*, 28 (2–3), 127–168.
CIMA, 2009. *Finance Transformation: The Evolution to Value Creation*. London, UK: Chartered Institute of Management Accountants.
Contrafatto, M., and Burns, J., 2013. Social and environmental accounting, organisational change and management accounting: a processual view. *Management Accounting Research*, 24 (4), 349–365.
Crane, A., Palazzo, G., Spence, L.J., and Matten, D., 2014. Contesting the value of "creating shared value". *California Management Review*, 56 (2), 130–153.
Crutzen, N., Zvezdov, D., and Schaltegger, S., 2017. Sustainability and management control. Exploring and theorizing control patterns in large European firms. *Journal of Cleaner Production*, 143, 1291–1301.
De Baerdemaeker, J., and Bruggeman, W., 2015. The impact of participation in strategic planning on managers' creation of budgetary slack: the mediating role of autonomous motivation and affective organisational commitment. *Management Accounting Research*, 29, 1–12.
Deci, E.L., and Ryan, R.M., 2000. The "what" and "why" of goal pursuits: human needs and the self-determination of behavior. *Psychological Inquiry*, 11 (4), 227–268.
Demski, J.S., and Feltham, G.A., 1976. *Cost Determination: A Conceptual Approach*. Ames, IA: Iowa State University Press.

Ditillo, A., and Lisi, I.E., 2014. Towards a more comprehensive framework for sustainability control systems research. In: M. Freedman and B. Jaggi, eds. *Accounting for the Environment: More Talk and Little Progress* (Advances in Environmental Accounting & Management, Volume 5). Bingley, UK: Emerald Group Publishing Limited, pp. 23–47.

Ditillo, A., and Lisi, I.E., 2016. Exploring sustainability control systems' integration: the relevance of sustainability orientation. *Journal of Management Accounting Research*, 28 (2), 125–148.

Durden, C., 2008. Towards a socially responsible management control system. *Accounting, Auditing & Accountability Journal*, 21 (5), 671–694.

Dutta, S.K., and Lawson, R.A., 2009. Aligning performance evaluation and reward systems with corporate sustainability goals. *Cost Management*, 23 (6), 15–23.

Epstein, M.J. and Buhovac, A.R., 2010. Solving the sustainability implementation challenge. *Organizational Dynamics*, 39 (4), 306–315.

Epstein, M.J., Buhovac, A.R., and Yuthas, K., 2015. Managing social, environmental and financial performance simultaneously. *Long Range Planning*, 48 (1), 35–45.

Epstein, M.J. and Wisner, P.S., 2001. Using a balanced scorecard to implement sustainability. *Environmental Quality Management*, 11 (2), 1–10.

Figge, F., Hahn, T., Schaltegger, S., and Wagner, M., 2002. The sustainability balanced scorecard - Linking sustainability management to business strategy. *Business Strategy and the Environment*, 11 (5), 269–284.

Frey, B.S., 1997. *Not just for the Money: An Economic Theory of Human Motivation*. Brookfield, VT: Edward Elgar Publishers.

Gagné, M., and Deci, E.L., 2005. Self-determination theory and work motivation. *Journal of Organizational Behavior*, 26 (4), 331–362.

Gibassier, D., and Alcouffe, S., 2018. Environmental management accounting: the missing link to sustainability? *Social and Environmental Accountability Journal*, 38 (1), 1–18.

Gond, J.-P., Grubnic, S., Herzig, C., and Moon, J., 2012. Configuring management control systems: theorizing the integration of strategy and sustainability. *Management Accounting Research*, 23 (3), 205–223.

Grabner, I., and Moers, F., 2013. Management control as a system or a package? Conceptual and empirical issues. *Accounting, Organizations and Society*, 38 (6–7), 407–419.

Green, S., and Welsh, M., 1988. Cybernetics and dependence: reframing the control concept. *Academy of Management Review*, 13 (2), 287–301.

Groen, B.A.C., Wouters, M.J.F., and Wilderom, C.P.M., 2017. Employee participation, performance metrics, and job performance: a survey study based on self-determination theory. *Management Accounting Research*, 36, 51–66.

Guenther, E., Endrikat, J., and Guenther, T.W., 2016. Environmental management control systems: a conceptualization and a review of the empirical evidence. *Journal of Cleaner Production*, 136, 147–171.

Hales, J., Matsumura, E.M., Moser, D.V., and Payne, R., 2016. Becoming sustainable: a rational decision based on sound information and effective processes. *Journal of Management Accounting Research*, 28 (2), 13–28.

Heggen, C., 2019. The role of value systems in translating environmental planning into performance. *British Accounting Review*, 51 (2), 130–147.

Henri, J.-F., Boiral, O., and Roy, M.-J., 2014. The tracking of environmental costs: motivations and impacts. *European Accounting Review*, 23 (4), 647–669.

Henri, J.-F., Boiral, O., and Roy, M.-J., 2016. Strategic cost management and performance: the case of environmental costs. *British Accounting Review*, 48 (2), 269–282.

Henri, J.-F., and Journeault, M., 2010. Eco-control: the influence of management control systems on environmental and economic performance. *Accounting, Organizations and Society*, 35 (1), 63–80.

Hubbard, G., 2009. Measuring organizational performance: beyond the triple bottom line. *Business Strategy and the Environment*, 18 (3), 177–191.

ICAEW, 2009. *Finance's Role in the Organisation*. London, UK: Institute of Chartered Accountants in England and Wales.

IMA, 2019. *IMA Management Accounting Competency Framework*. Montvale, NJ: Institute of Management Accountants.

Islam, S.M., 2019. A field study of strategy map evolution. *Journal of Management Accounting Research*, 31 (3), 83–98.

Journeault, M., 2016. The influence of the eco-control package on environmental and economic performance: a natural resource-based approach. *Journal of Management Accounting Research*, 28 (2), 149–178.

Kaplan, R.S., 2009. Conceptual foundations of the balanced scorecard. In: C.S. Chapman, A.G. Hopwood, and M.D. Shields, eds. *Handbook of Management Accounting Research*. Volume 3. Oxford, UK: Elsevier, pp. 1253–1269.

Kaplan, R.S., and Norton, D.P., 1992. The balanced scorecard - Measures that drive performance. *Harvard Business Review*, 70 (1), 71–79.

Kaplan, R.S., and Norton, D.P., 1996. *The Balanced Scorecard: Translating Strategy into Action*. Boston, MA: Harvard Business School Press.

Kim, N.K.W., and Matsumura, E.M., 2017. Managerial accounting research in corporate social responsibility: a framework and opportunities for research. In: M. Malina, ed. *Advances in Management Accounting*. Volume 28. Bingley, UK: Emerald Group Publishing Limited, pp. 28–41.

Kunz, J., 2015. Objectivity and subjectivity in performance evaluation and autonomous motivation: an exploratory study. *Management Accounting Research*, 27, 27–46.

Lisi, I.E., 2015. Translating environmental motivations into performance: the role of environmental performance measurement systems. *Management Accounting Research*, 29, 27–44.

Lueg, R., Pedersen, M.M., and Clemmensen, S.N., 2015. The role of corporate sustainability in a low-cost business model - A case study in the Scandinavian fashion industry. *Business Strategy and the Environment*, 24 (5), 344–359.

Lueg, R., and Radlach, R., 2016. Managing sustainable development with management control systems: a literature review. *European Management Journal*, 34 (2), 158–171.

Malmi, T., and Brown, D.A., 2008. Management control systems as a package - Opportunities, challenges and research directions. *Management Accounting Research*, 19 (4), 287–300.

Malmi, T. and Granlund, M., 2009. In search of management accounting theory. *European Accounting Review*, 18 (3), 597–620.

Modell, S., 2014. The societal relevance of management accounting: an introduction to the special issue. *Accounting and Business Research*, 44 (2), 83–103.

Norris, G., and O'Dwyer, B., 2004. Motivating socially responsive decision making: the operation of management controls in a socially responsive organisation. *British Accounting Review*, 36 (2), 173–196.

Otley, D., 2008. Did Kaplan and Johnson get it right? *Accounting, Auditing & Accountability Journal*, 21 (2), 229–239.

Pache, A.-C., and Santos, F., 2013. Inside the hybrid organization: selective coupling as a response to competing institutional logics. *Academy of Management Journal*, 56 (4), 972–1001.

Parker, L.D., and Chung, L.H., 2018. Structuring social and environmental management control and accountability: behind the hotel doors. *Accounting, Auditing & Accountability Journal*, 31 (3), 993–1023.

Parmar, B.L., Keevil, A., and Wicks, A.C., 2019. People and profits: the impact of corporate objectives on employees' need satisfaction at work. *Journal of Business Ethics*, 154 (1), 13–33.

Perego, P., and Hartmann, F., 2009. Aligning performance measurement systems with strategy: the case of environmental strategy. *Abacus*, 45 (4), 397–428.

Pfister, J.A., and Lukka, K., 2019. Interrelation of controls for autonomous motivation: a field study of productivity gains through pressure-induced process innovation. *The Accounting Review*, 94 (3), 345–371.

Pondeville, S., Swaen, V., and De Rongé, Y., 2013. Environmental management control systems: the role of contextual and strategic factors. *Management Accounting Research*, 24 (4), 317–332.

Porter, M.E., and Kramer, M.R., 2006. Strategy and society: the link between competitive advantage and corporate social responsibility. *Harvard Business Review*, 84 (12), 78–92.

Rodrigue, M., Magnan, M., and Boulianne, E., 2013. Stakeholders' influence on environmental strategy and performance indicators: a managerial perspective. *Management Accounting Research*, 24 (4), 301–316.

Ryan, R.M., and Deci, E.L., 2017. *Self-Determination Theory: Basic Psychological Needs in Motivation, Development, and Wellness.* New York, NY: Guilford Publishing.

Sharma, S., 2000. Managerial interpretations and organizational context as predictors of corporate choice of environmental strategy. *Academy of Management Journal*, 43 (3), 681–697.

Soderstrom, K.M., Soderstrom, N.S., and Stewart, C.R., 2017. Sustainability/CSR research in management accounting: a review of the literature. In: M. Malina, ed. *Advances in Management Accounting*. Volume 28. Bingley, UK: Emerald Group Publishing Limited, pp. 42–53.

Sundin, H., and Brown, D.A., 2017. Greening the black box: integrating the environment and management control systems. *Accounting, Auditing & Accountability Journal*, 30 (3), 620–642.

Sundin, H., Granlund, M., and Brown, D.A., 2010. Balancing multiple competing objectives with a balanced scorecard. *European Accounting Review*, 19 (2), 203–246.

Tucker, B.P., and Parker, L.D., 2015. Business as usual? An institutional view of the relationship between management control systems and strategy. *Financial Accountability and Management*, 31 (2), 113–149.

Vallaster, C., Maon, F., Lindgreen, A., and Vanhamme, J., forthcoming. Serving multiple masters: the role of micro-foundations of dynamic capabilities in addressing tensions in for-profit hybrid organizations. *Organization Studies*. https://doi.org/10.1177/0170840619856034

Vansteenkiste, M., Aelterman, N., De Muynck G.-J., Haerens, L., Patall, E., and Reeve, J., 2018. Fostering personal meaning and self-relevance: a self-determination theory perspective on internalization. *Journal of Experimental Education*, 86 (1), 30–49.

Vansteenkiste, M., Ryan, R.M., and Deci, E.L., 2008. Self-determination theory and the explanatory role of psychological needs in human well-being. In: L. Bruni, F. Comim, and M. Pugno, eds. *Capabilities and Happiness*. Oxford, UK: Oxford University Press, pp. 187–223.

Virtanen, T., Tuomaala, M., and Pentti, E., 2013. Energy efficiency complexities: a technical and managerial investigation. *Management Accounting Research*, 24 (4), 401–416.

Vishwanathan, P., van Oosterhout, H.J., Heugens, P.M.A.R., Duran, P., and Van Essen, M., 2020. Strategic CSR: a concept building meta-analysis. *Journal of Management Studies*, 57 (2), 314–350.

Wijethilake, C., Munir, R., and Appuhami, R., 2017. Strategic responses to institutional pressures for sustainability: the role of management control systems. *Accounting, Auditing & Accountability Journal*, 30 (8), 1677–1710.

Wong-On-Wing, B., Guo, L., and Lui, G., 2010. Intrinsic and extrinsic motivation and participation in budgeting: antecedents and consequences. *Behavioral Research in Accounting*, 22 (2), 133–153.

Zimmerman, J.L., 2017. *Accounting for Decision Making and Control*. 9th edn. New York, NY: McGraw-Hill.

15
MATERIALS AND ENERGY ACCOUNTING

Roger Burritt, Katherine Christ and Stefan Schaltegger

Introduction

Environmental management accounting (EMA) is an innovative management accounting approach that covers a large range of tools with the purpose of supporting different actors in environmentally beneficial decision-making in companies. While many different EMA foci and tools have been proposed in the existing literature, material and energy accounting has been the main area of application in corporate practice, guideline development and standardisation for the last two decades.

Materials and energy are becoming of greater interest to business managers for a number of reasons. First, awareness of environmental issues has increased in importance in recent decades such that businesses see these as a dominant risk they face in the years ahead (WEF 2018). Environmental crises and social aspects of the production of some materials are perceived to have a high actual or potential impact and these are increasingly being monitored or even regulated by different stakeholders such as government agencies, local communities, non-government organisations and the finance sector.

Second, anthropocentric global warming is one of the largest environmental problems facing life on Earth and the development of renewable energy sources accompanied by perceived rising costs of energy means that business is becoming ever more mindful of the links between energy, environmental impacts and costs. Initially the focus of environmental concerns was about building awareness of global warming and the need to substitute renewable energy for fossil fuel-based energy. More recently, debate has been about the relative speed at which changes towards a non-fossil fuel economy should take place and it has become more important for business to have an energy policy and monitor relative costs of different energy supplies.

Third, materials and energy use are viewed as important and critically related, interlinked aspects of business operations and have been combined in standards designed to encourage better management of these vital inputs to production. The need for standards to identify separate areas of waste, or "non-product output", is acknowledged in early research which highlights the significance of hidden environmental costs and the need to manage energy and material flows as important, separate business issues in their own right. For instance, ISO 14051 is an environmental management standard which defines Material Flow Cost Accounting (MFCA) as a tool for quantifying the flows and stocks of materials in processes or production lines where materials are defined to include energy and water (ISO 2011). The intention of such a standard is to work towards environmental and financial improvements via efficient use of materials and energy in operations. ISO 14052 extends this intention to supply chains.

Finally, the manner in which some minerals are obtained is causing great concern from economic, social and environmental perspectives (Ali 2014). For example, overconcentration of the supply of rare earth minerals means that these materials, which are critical to the development of high-technology products such as wind turbines, high-efficiency lighting and smart phones, could be used as a bargaining chip to gain a competitive advantage over rivals, and the mining of minerals is hedged about with concerns over social impacts. Furthermore, some materials, known as conflict minerals, are associated with poor labour practices and funding of militia. Procurement and use of these minerals, such as blood diamonds and coltan, could be illegal, be associated with poor labour conditions or forced labour and/or severely damage the reputation of the business (Silva and Schaltegger 2019).

More recently emphasis has been placed on the need to link EMA with overarching societal goals (such as the UN Sustainable Development Goals) and ecological themes such as planetary boundaries (Schaltegger 2018) to guide management in contributing effectively to solving key global ecological problems.

Collectively these concerns suggest the need to manage energy and materials in ways that minimise environmental damage while maximising economic benefit has never been more important. Indeed, since the Brundtland report was published (UNCED 1987), it has been generally accepted that businesses are able in many circumstances to undertake activities that can assist the environment and society while gaining net income and building wealth from improved operations and investments.

The remainder of this chapter deals with materials and energy accounting, which provides necessary information and helps businesses towards better decisions as well as providing information to outside stakeholders about business performance in relation to sustainability.

Framework

In the last 30 years a large number of companies in developed countries and a growing number in developing countries have begun to collect, classify, communicate and use sustainability information (Jamali and Mirshak 2007; Burritt and Schaltegger 2010). Pressures from the public, expressed through the enactment of legislation, industry norms developed through codes of practice and individual moral imperatives have coalesced to bring social and environmental issues alongside conventional economic concerns of business for the investor. In the face of these pressures, the augmented need for management of social and environmental matters alongside economic considerations helps drive the demand for sustainability information, such as that required for materials and energy.

In a fundamental sense, materials and energy accounting is a subset of sustainability accounting, which itself embodies environmental, social and economic accounting and their interactions (see Figure 15.1).

As a subset of sustainability accounting, materials and energy accounting mirrors the characteristics of sustainability accounting, which includes physical and monetary information (horizontal axis in Figure 15.2) and has an internal and an external aspect (vertical axis in Figure 15.2).

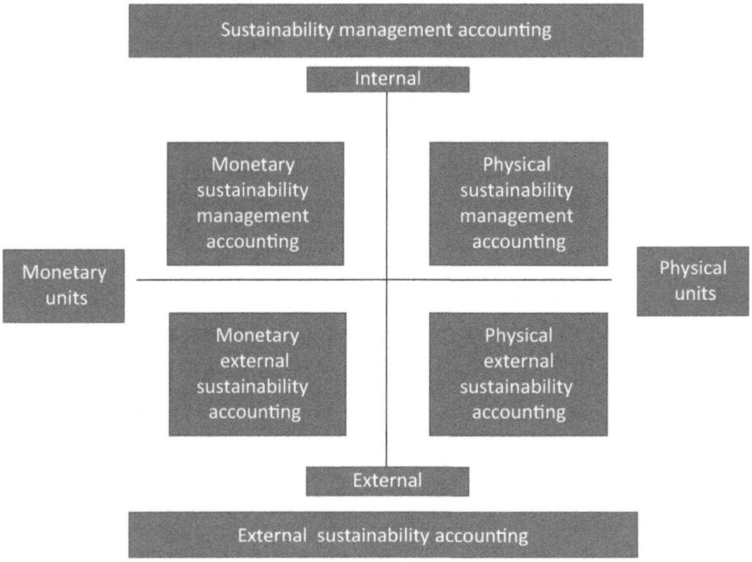

Figure 15.1 Sustainability accounting systems.

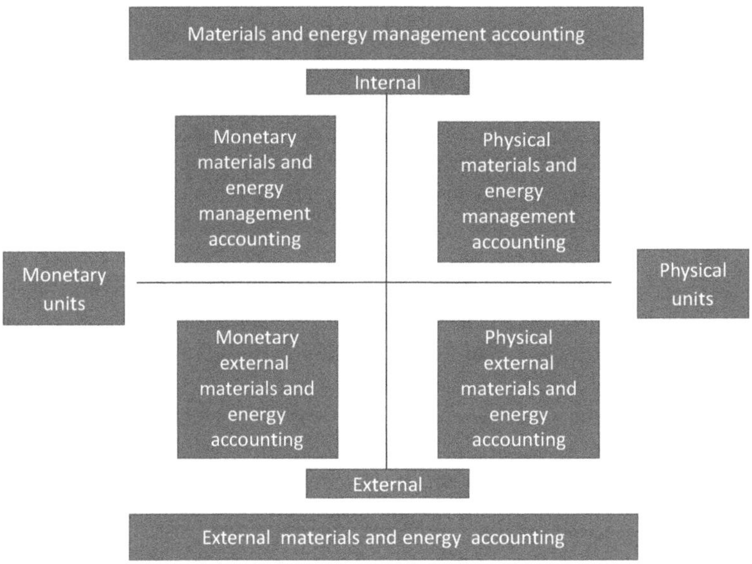

Figure 15.2 Materials and energy accounting systems.

There are two main groups of sustainability impacts related to the activities of corporations. The first group includes sustainability-related impacts on corporate economic position and performance, while the second group includes corporate impacts on sustainability (economic, social and environmental) systems.

Sustainability-related impacts on corporate economic systems are captured by and reflected through monetary sustainability information. Monetary sustainability information addresses the effect of all corporate-related impacts on the past, present or expected future financial position and performance of the corporation and is expressed in monetary units. Examples of monetary sustainability information include measures expressed in terms of expenditure on investment in clean energy production and cost savings from conversion to green energy. Because they are based on the methods of conventional accounting, monetary sustainability accounting systems can be thought of in terms of an extension of conventional accounting, and may include developing, refining and expanding the scope of accounting in monetary units.

Impacts of corporate activities on society and the environment are reflected in physical, social and environmental information. At the corporate level, such physical environmental information includes all past, present and future amounts that have an impact on social and environmental systems. Physical materials and energy information is always expressed in physical units – from the perspective of material and energy accounting this is expected to include measures such as kilograms or joules (e.g. kilograms of material per customer served, or joules of energy used per unit of product).

In aggregate, sustainability accounting can generate information for internal management purposes and for external use by stakeholders, in both monetary and physical terms, with regard to past, present and future impacts (e.g. Burritt and Schaltegger 2001). Any comprehensive system of sustainability accounting needs to address the information needs of the many different types of managers and external stakeholders (see, e.g., for sustainability accounting in Burritt et al. 2002). Similar considerations apply to materials and energy accounting.

Types/categories of materials and energy

Categories of materials

According to ISO 15051, a key international standard for materials and energy flow cost accounting, materials can be divided into two categories: those that become part of a product (e.g. raw materials), and auxiliary materials and intermediate products and materials that do not become part of products (e.g. cleaning solvents and chemical catalysts, which often are referred to as operating materials or "non-product output") (ISO 2011, section 3.10). Hence, materials might be classified as product, non-product output, or both. For example, water is one material which can be part of a product (e.g. bottled wine) and, although used in operations, does not become part of a product (e.g. waste water used to wash bottles in the wine bottling process). Thus, materials like water can be separated in the accounts as a stock of inventory and as flows, in and out, during a period.

While EMA and specific tools of material and energy management accounting have been discussed, applied and even standardised, the question as to whether and exactly how EMA links or could be linked to global ecological issues of sustainability mostly remains unanswered (Schaltegger et al. 2017). Bebbington and Larrinaga (2014) perceived a lack of progress made by social and environmental accounting towards addressing sustainable development and proposed to consider insights from sustainability science (e.g. Kates et al. 2001; Kastenhofer et al. 2011). Most EMA publications focus on intermediate energy and materials issues close to business operations rather than sustainability characteristics of planetary boundaries and the carrying capacity of the Earth. Responding to the call of Winn and Pogutz (2013) and Whiteman et al. (2013), Schaltegger (2018) proposed an explicit consideration of planetary boundaries for the development and for structuring EMA at the corporate level. Referring to the planetary boundary concept by Rockström et al. (2009) and the respective boundary distinctions, this would lead to carbon and greenhouse gas (GHG) accounting (relating to the planetary boundary climate change), water accounting (among other issues also referring to global freshwater use), accounting for chemicals (referring to chemical pollution), accounting for nitrogen (relating to the nitrogen cycle), phosphorus accounting (phosphorus cycle), accounting for acidification (ocean acidification), accounting for biodiversity (biodiversity [loss]), accounting for land use (land use change), accounting for CFCs (chlorofluorocarbons, responsible for stratospheric ozone layer depletion) and accounting for aerosols (atmospheric aerosol loading). As the planetary boundary concept has only more recently gained broader attention, such a structuring of EMA is not corporate practice, so far.

Categories of energy

As with water, energy is another resource that can be classified as a material (e.g. coal as an energy carrier) to be accounted for in that it is an input often associated with production of a good or service. Energy is furthermore viewed as "electricity, fuels, steam, heat, compressed air and other like media" (ISO 2011, section 3.4). If energy is a critical resource, it may be included separately in the chart of accounts; otherwise, it can be included with other materials needed to undertake operations which are traditionally classified as overheads. Although it is easy to perceive energy as being a non-product output, a flow related to operations (e.g. as used for lighting and power in a factory), it might also be stored as a product (e.g. in batteries). Thus, if it is of use to organisational management and stakeholders energy can be recorded separately in the accounts as a stock of inventory with flows, in and out, during a period, and reported.

Furthermore, water and energy can be closely related as with the production of electricity through hydro-electric power and desalination plants. Materials and energy can also be tightly linked as in the case of coal, gas and electricity generation. The interconnected nature of water and energy is sometimes referred to as the water–energy nexus. The water–energy nexus highlights one way in which the types of materials used in operations and production (e.g. water, coal and electricity) can be interrelated with potential impacts for the environment, societies and economies. Furthermore, external events, such as climate change, extreme weather events, energy price shocks, food crises, water crises, etc., beyond the direct control of companies, also highlight the significance of these interdependencies for business risk management of materials (WEF 2019).

As each of these materials (e.g. coal, water and energy) can cause severe disruption to companies or even bring companies, communities and ecosystems down, the critical importance of accounting for the management of materials becomes apparent. Next, links between materials and energy accounting and management are considered.

Materials and energy management accounting

The purpose

Materials and energy management accounting information can be considered relevant to three needs of managers (Simon 1987; Hall 2010):

1. **Attention directing**. Materials and energy accounting information indicates critical impacts and their potential significance to the organisation. It draws the attention of managers to opportunities as well as problems as an analytical tool designed to detect strengths and weaknesses in materials and energy management.

2. **Problem-solving**. Materials and energy accounting provides information about potential alternative courses of action that include consideration of environmental impacts as part of the decision-making process. Such information is an important input to strategic decision-making, leading to improved efficiency. Hence, this toolkit provides information that delivers input to performance measures such as eco-efficiency and eco-effectiveness and can assist with direct and indirect control of the environmental and social consequences of materials and energy use. At a more operational level, certain types of materials (e.g. toxic substances according to the EU chemicals regulations Reach) and certain types of information (quantities of regulated chemicals bought, stored and sold) may be needed, leading to very specific EMA tool development and applications supporting operational managers (e.g. in procurement).
3. **Scorekeeping**. Materials and energy accounting provides information about whether the corporation is moving towards targets established for environmental impact reduction through continuous improvement, value engineering or strategic decisions to change the nature of the business to reduce materials and energy impacts. The scorecard can be used internally, as part of a "balanced scorecard" of performance (Möller and Schaltegger 2005). Alternatively, it can be provided to external parties to help improve their understanding of corporate actions and impacts on the environment, as part of the dialogue with stakeholders. The importance of providing stakeholders with accurate information is their capacity to reduce or destroy the social legitimacy and reputation of a corporation. Materials and energy accounting provides a transparency base for internal and external communication. The toolkit has a close and complementary fit to the set of tools being developed to help promote achievement of the Sustainable Development Goals and to keep within certain planetary boundaries.

As highlighted in Figure 15.2, materials and energy management accounting is concerned with providing management with information to support decision-making and includes both a monetary and a physical aspect.

In essence, materials and energy management accounting is a subsystem of EMA which is a subsystem of sustainability management accounting, which is an extension to conventional management accounting. The move towards introducing greater specificity in accounting systems to help address social and environmental aspects of business activities accompanies growing awareness of the need for focussed attention on critical issues such as the sourcing of electricity in connection with checking global warming and the growing scarcity of certain materials such as unpolluted water. Furthermore, increasing specificity relates to a growing range of actors (e.g. procurement, production, R&D, marketing, sustainability, logistics, etc.) in companies dealing with various aspects of environmental, material and energy topics. Given the wide range of different actors confronted with various sustainability issues and thus in need of different types of information, this spurs the further diversity of material and energy accounting methods (e.g. Schaltegger et al. 2015).

Table 15.1 classifies materials and energy management accounting systems along two dimensions: internal versus external information, and monetary versus physical representation of that information.

Different types of managers rely on and have their performance assessed using physical information, monetary information, or a combination of both. For example, managers in the corporate environmental management department have various goals, including:

- Identifying materials and energy improvement opportunities
- Prioritising materials and energy actions and measures

Table 15.1 Illustrative materials and energy accounting tools

		Materials and energy management accounting			
		Monetary materials and energy management accounting		*Physical materials and energy management accounting*	
		Short-term focus	*Long-term focus*	*Short-term focus*	*Long-term focus*
Past/ present orientated	Routinely generated information	Material flow cost accounting (e.g. variable costing, absorption costing and activity-based costing)	Environmentally induced materials and energy expenditure and revenues	Materials and energy flow accounting (short-term impacts on the environment) product, site, division and company levels)	Materials and energy capital impact accounting
	Ad hoc information	Ex post assessment of relevant materials and energy costing decisions	Materials and energy life cycle (and target) costing Post-investment assessment of individual projects	Ex post assessment of short-term materials and energy impacts (e.g. of a site or product)	Post-investment assessment of physical materials and energy investment appraisal
Future orientated	Routinely generated information	Monetary materials and energy operational budgeting (flows) Monetary materials and energy capital budgeting (stocks)	Materials and energy long-term financial planning	Physical materials and energy budgeting (flows and stocks) (e.g. material and energy flow activity-based budgeting)	Long-term physical materials and energy planning
	Ad hoc information	Relevant materials and energy costing (e.g. special orders, product mix with capacity constraint)	Monetary materials and energy project investment appraisal	Relevant materials and energy impacts (e.g. given short run constraints on activities)	Physical materials and energy investment appraisal

Source: Burritt et al. (2002).

- Differentiating product pricing, mix and development decisions based on materials and energy characteristics
- Transparency about materials and energy relevant corporate activities
- Meeting the claims and information demands of critical stakeholders concerned about materials and energy issues
- Justifying materials and energy protection measures.

Typical styles of information used by different managers are provided in Table 15.2 (based on Schaltegger et al. 2015). All managers also need qualitative information, which is not separately detailed.

Three additional dimensions of materials and energy management accounting tools are important, especially for managers of all business sizes (see Table 15.1):

- Time frame: the chronological orientation of the tool (i.e. past, present, or future)
- Duration: the length of time addressed by the tool (i.e. short term or long term)
- Schedule: the regularity by which the tool gathers information (i.e. ad hoc versus routine).

All these developments play different roles in different industries, countries and times. In summary, they raise awareness and increase the management relevance, leading to a more professional approach in managing materials and energy flows and developing a differentiated information system to support management decisions, which address various goals, including cost-efficiency of production and transactions, resource security, legitimacy, reputation and effective contributions to sustainable development.

The International Organization for Standardization (ISO) has produced an environmental management standard for materials and energy flows. ISO is an independent, non-governmental, international organisation, with a membership of 164 national standards bodies. It develops and sells international standards including those for companies and organisations of all kinds looking to manage their environmental responsibilities. Key ISO materials and energy flow standards include:

- ISO 14051:2011 which provides a general framework for MFCA. Under MFCA, the flows and stocks of materials within an organisation are traced and quantified in physical units (e.g. mass and volume) and the costs associated with those material flows are also evaluated.
- ISO 14052:2017 extends the MFCA environmental management standard to supply chains. In this context, these voluntary standards include energy and water within the definition of materials.
- ISO 50001:2018 addresses Energy Management Systems. It provides a framework for managing energy performance and addressing energy costs, while helping companies reduce their environmental impacts to meet emission reduction targets. The aim of ISO 50001 is for corporations to improve their environmental management systems and the resulting energy performance based on continuous improvement of previous performance which has to be demonstrated. Certification by independent organisations increases the credibility of ISO 50001 information reported to external parties.
- ISO 14064: 2018 Greenhouse gases (GHG). ISO 14064 comes in three parts for organisations, projects and assurance and can be used to quantify, monitor, report and verify GHG emissions, lending the support of a global standard to regulated and voluntary programmes such as emissions trading schemes and public reporting.

Table 15.2 Goals and information foci of different types of managers

Corporate materials and energy management accounting		
Users	*Basic goals*	*Type of information desired*
Top Management	Long-term profitability and survival of company. Securing legal compliance with minimal cost to the corporation. Realisation of all economically beneficial social and environmental protection measures, including materials and energy. Securing the provision of resources from the critical stakeholders.	Highly aggregated financial and strategic (qualitative and quantitative) information on the business materials and energy activities and the company's performance.
Accounting and Finance Department	Identifying and realising cost saving potential. Transparency about materials and energy cost-relevant corporate activities. Transparency about the impact of materials and energy activities on the income statement and/or balance sheet. Reduction of materials and energy-induced risks. Compliance with accounting regulations. Maximisation of company and investor value.	Financial measures about corporate activities (e.g. cost-, income- and balance sheet-related issues, risk assessments, investment decisions, mergers and acquisitions, and so on). Financial information on the value and economic performance of the enterprise.
Environmental Department	Identifying materials and energy improvement opportunities. Prioritising materials and energy actions and measures. Differentiation in product pricing, mix and development decisions in relation to materials and energy issues. Transparency about materials and energy relevant corporate activities. Meeting the claims and information demands of critical stakeholders with an interest in materials and energy issues, including suppliers, to ensure resource provision and access. Justifying the presence of the materials and energy procurement division and addressing protection measures.	Physical measures on material and energy flows and stocks and related processes and products, and their impacts upon the environment.
Health and Safety Department	Safeguarding the safety, health and welfare of employees at work from materials and energy-related accidents and disasters.	Physical measures of health and safety and materials and energy supplies.

(continued)

Table 15.2 Cont.

Corporate materials and energy management accounting		
Users	*Basic goals*	*Type of information desired*
Quality Department	Meeting the materials and energy product requirements of customers at the minimum cost for a given level of product quality.	Information on cost of quality. Physical measures of technical product requirements.
Human Resources Department	Job-related (including materials and energy) concerns of employees. Remuneration, including rewards for good environmental performance. Physical jobs allocated and job conditions monitored.	Information on financial rewards. Physical information on turnover, satisfaction and morale linked with materials and energy impacts.
Legal Department	Ensuring (materials and energy) legal compliance by the company's operations.	Physical measures. Qualitative compliance information.
R & D and Design Department	Development and design of marketable products and services. Reducing (materials and energy) risks of investments. Development of improved production processes.	Strategic information about market demands. Financial information about costs of new products and services. Information on technical feasibility and impacts of newly designed materials and energy products and services.
Corporate Marketing and Public Relations Department	Meeting external information demands of critical stakeholders. Meeting claims and information demands of shareholders, other economic stakeholders (including those interested in materials and energy reports). Developing a green image of the company and its products.	Information about stakeholder claims. Physical and financial information on the company's materials and energy impacts and efforts for pollution reduction and prevention.
Production Management	Task control over operations. Optimising energy and material consumption. Reduction of materials and energy-induced risks.	Information on material and energy flows and process records.
Purchasing Department	Efficient procurement of the inputs for corporate operations. Establishing and securing favourable relationships with suppliers.	Information on quality and materials and energy properties of the goods purchased. Financial information on prices.
Logistics	Efficient organisation, collection, storage, and physical distribution of goods and products.	Physical measures (e.g. on distribution means and storage facilities and related materials and energy impacts).

Table 15.2 Cont.

Corporate materials and energy management accounting		
Users	*Basic goals*	*Type of information desired*
Marketing and Sales Department	Increasing sales and attracting and satisfying buyers. Provision of means by which buyers can purchase the product. Inducing customers to buy the enterprise's products through the tools of the marketing-mix (especially pricing, distribution and communication).	Information on operational market conditions (e.g. pricing, competitor activities, etc.). Information on customer demands.
Disposal and Recycling	Efficient disposal and recycling of wasted or used materials and energy-related products. Minimisation of wastes to be treated, especially hazardous wastes.	Physical measures of the properties of disposable and recyclable goods. Technical information on treatment and recycling options.

The substance of material flow cost accounting

ISO 14051 MFCA presents an independent management accounting tool designed to assist organisations to better understand the potential environmental and financial consequences of their material and energy use practices and seek opportunities to achieve both environmental and financial improvements via changes in those practices. It is particularly focused on short-term, past, routine gathering of information about physical and monetary materials and energy flow accounting reflecting short-term impacts on the environment of products, sites, divisions and companies.

MFCA identifies materials and energy assets in quantity centres which accumulate costs and represent stocks that can be likened to accrual accounting balance sheet items. Emphasis on dividing all costs into product and non-product categories means that product costs are eventually expensed, but as MFCA identifies a larger portion of non-product costs with waste streams, these can lead to different asset values where non-product costs are capitalised.

A key facet of ISO 14051 is the adoption of product costing as the foundation for accounting. All materials, energy and water costs are either traced directly to products or allocated or written off as indirect non-product costs.

Quantity centres. The materials, energy and water quantities and costs are, first, gathered in quantity centres. These are "places" where materials and energy are processed. Each centre can be the responsibility of a designated member of the organisation. The person responsible for each centre is accountable for materials and energy within their realm of responsibility. Quantity centres are selected parts of a process for which inputs and outputs are quantified in physical and monetary units. For example, Christ and Burritt (2017) identified the flows of food (the product) materials and waste (non-product) associated with a restaurant in line with its production steps. Three quantity centres are used for the illustration: storage, preparation and service. Each quantity centre acts as the equivalent of a cost object in traditional cost accounting. In general, the quantity centres represent the products, product groups, departments or divisions that are seen to be responsible for the creation of both economic value added and materials (including energy and water) impact added. These quantity centres should ideally correspond to a company's cost objects because they are used as the basis for compiling economic value added that is then used to calculate eco-efficiency (e.g. Schaltegger and Burritt 2000/2017).

Allocation keys. Allocation of accumulated non-product materials costs is essentially an arbitrary process based on management judgement used to link these overheads with products in order to provide information for decision-making, such as how much waste is to be associated with each unit of product and expensed in the period, and how much will be capitalised. Materials impact added allocation keys describe the relation between the quantity centres and environmental interventions that have occurred. Examples of materials impact added drivers are CO_2 emissions associated with energy used in food preparation in the kitchen, and spoilage volumes of a particular food type.

Materials and energy impact added drivers. These are factors that lead to environmental impacts through materials and energy. Examples of materials and energy impact drivers are CO_2 emissions that are associated with the greenhouse effect or emissions of volatile organic compounds (VOCs) that cause photochemical smog.

Materials and energy assets. Materials purchased and placed in store can go missing or can deteriorate with the costs sometimes being allocated to particular units of good output (e.g. meals in a restaurant) if an absorption costing system is used; otherwise, they may be treated as period costs. As technology develops, energy in the form of electricity is becoming easier to store in batteries and these are a depreciable item. System costs, such as labour costs (e.g. salary of the head chef) and depreciation of machinery (e.g. refrigerators and battery stores), can be the most difficult to assign to products with, as mentioned before, costs allocated based on management judgement. These allocations affect the amounts of product (good output) and non-product (waste) costs and, thus, the way management perceive and manage these costs. ISO 14051 extends the calculations of relevant materials and energy flows to include those associated with downstream aspects of a supply chain.

External materials and energy accounting

The purpose

The main audience for external materials and energy accounting disclosures is external stakeholders with an interest in the business (Schaltegger and Burritt 2000/2017). For example, interest could be because of market-based contractual arrangements as with suppliers providing information about their schedules to a multinational company in order to secure and maintain business. It could also be because of the need for stewardship, for example, a non-government organisation looking for information about production levels at a coal mine where locals in the town are concerned about additional traffic.

External materials and energy accounting mirrors external sustainability accounting inasmuch as it also records information in both monetary and physical terms. Until recently, monetary materials and energy impacts on business were considered to be addressed quite adequately under existing accounting and reporting standards and regulations. However, the increasing number of materials and energy issues has generated substantial financial consequences for companies. Therefore, external "users" of corporate statements have started to influence regulators and standards setting bodies in order to induce them to alter existing, and to create new, granular reporting standards, regulations and guidelines. Three main groups directly influence how corporate management addresses materials and energy issues in reports:

- Regulatory bodies. Conventional financial reporting about materials and energy is guided by regulatory bodies such as the International Accounting Standards Board (IASB) and the Financial Accounting Standards Board (FASB). Both were formed in 1973 to harmonise and improve financial reporting by developing and publishing accounting standards. Materials and energy issues are a subsidiary interest of these bodies. In contrast, two examples of regulatory bodies with a specific materials and energy accounting focus are the European Union's Emissions Trading System (EU ETS) and the Australian Clean Energy Regulator. The EU ETS was launched in 2005 and is the largest international system for trading GHG emission allowances covering over three-quarters of the allowances traded on the international carbon market. Commission Regulation (EU) No 601/2012 of 21 June 2012 lays down rules for the monitoring and reporting of GHG emissions in EU states. The Clean Energy Regulator is established by the Clean Energy Regulator Act 2011 and is an independent statutory authority of the Australian government. Amongst other Acts, it administers the National Greenhouse and Energy Reporting scheme. This provides a national framework for reporting and disseminating company information about greenhouse emissions, and energy production and consumption. Corporations that meet a specified threshold must register under the framework and provide a report each year.
  - Sustainability reporting standard setting bodies. Prominent standard setting bodies in external sustainability reporting include the Global Reporting Initiative (GRI), the US Sustainability Accounting Standards Board (SASB) and the GHG Protocol.
  - Other stakeholders with an interest in materials and energy reporting. These may include professional accounting organisations, industry associations and international initiatives such as the Asian Productivity Organisation (2014).

Regulators have the strongest direct influence on energy and materials disclosures as they create legally enforceable requirements. Other influences are voluntarily adopted through persuasion and potential impact on company reputation from bad practices.

Monetary external materials and energy accounting

Conventional financial accounting and external reporting through annual reports for investors are one major means through which materials and energy accounting information is communicated to external parties. The focus is mainly on monetary aspects of reported issues, with the intention to produce a true and fair view of the financial position and performance of the corporation. In addition, sustainability accounting, often referred to as triple bottom line accounting because it jointly considers environmental, social and economic performances of corporations, provides a second major means through which materials and energy accounting are disclosed to those outside the corporation. Most recently integrated reporting has emerged as a second investor-focused means for reporting on triple bottom line issues, including materials and energy matters of interest.

Issues with conventional financial reporting carry over to monetary external materials and energy accounting when the same conventions and principles are adhered to. For example, these include decisions about whether to capitalise costs as assets.

In practice, there is no definitive answer to the question of whether to capitalise environmental costs as assets, or to write them off against income in the year they are incurred. From an economic perspective, capitalisation of costs should only be allowed if these contribute to additional future economic benefits beyond those originally assessed. These are the incremental benefits that accrue if an alternative course of action is contemplated. However, for example, the costs of, say, cleaning up pollution emanating from coal-fired power generation may qualify as assets if they are absolutely necessary for the company to stay in business. In this case, the expenditure is securing the value of future assets.

A further issue relates to a movement from end-of-pipe improvement to precautionary investment in improvement of materials and energy sourcing. If a firm is using old-style end-of-pipe technology, it is likely to be much easier to isolate the costs of compliance with clean energy management requirements. However, the more a business adopts cleaner production methods, the harder it becomes to identify the compliance costs of energy management. If materials and energy management decisions are integrated with the business-as-usual production process and lead to both improvements in energy sourcing and cost savings, it is not easy to separate materials energy costs from expenditure designed to return a normal commercial profit.

From a materials and energy point of view, on the other hand, capitalisation in the accounts should be favoured if prevention creates future benefits. Furthermore, capitalisation facilitates the write off as an expense over a number of years, and thus enhances long-term thinking.

Physical external materials and energy accounting

The GRI produces the first and most widely adopted global standards for sustainability reporting, which have increased in popularity such that 93% of the world's largest 250 corporations now report on their sustainability performance (KPMG 2017). The GRI is an independent international organisation that, for over 20 years, has pioneered sustainability reporting through the development of universal and topic-specific GRI Sustainability Reporting Standards (GRI Standards) as a free public good. The Europe-based GRI works with policymakers, stock exchanges, regulators and investors to drive transparency and enable effective reporting and improved performance. Materials are addressed in the Global Sustainability Standards Board's GRI 301: Materials 2016. Non-renewable and renewable materials used, recycled and reclaimed form the main disclosure categories. Physical measurement of materials impacts is the focus of this standard, which uses absolute measures such as renewable materials used and non-renewable materials used (301-1), and relative measures such as percent of recycled materials used (301-2) and percent of reclaimed products for each product category (301-3). Energy consumption inside and outside the organisation and its reduction are addressed in GRI 302: Energy 2016. Again, non-renewable and renewable sources of energy disclosures are the focal point. The standards are applicable by an organisation of any size, type, sector or geographic location. There is a close link with GRI 305 Emissions: 2016 as Scope 1 and Scope 2 GHG emissions from non-renewable fuels are the subject of much political controversy and a growing number of businesses are keen to illustrate the actions they are taking to reduce such emissions. Furthermore, Scope 3 energy consumption outside the organisation upstream and downstream in supply chains is also addressed by the "GHG Protocol Corporate Value Chain (Scope 3) Accounting and Reporting Standard" as it is recognised that energy is embodied in goods purchased. The GHG Protocol is a non-governmental organisation–business partnership addressing standardised methods for GHG accounting.

Physical and monetary external materials and energy accounting combined

It should be noted that although the GRI standards have a focus on physical accounting metrics, separate economic measures are suggested in GRI 201, with 201-2 specifically addressing the financial implications for performance and other risks and opportunities caused by climate change. Here the focus is also on absolute and relative measures of performance such as reporting on the capital and operating costs of climate change such as carbon capture and storage, and on relative energy efficiency related to issues such as fuel switching; use of renewable and lower carbon footprint energy and use of carbon offsets.

The US SASB also provides for reporting on monetary and physical aspects of materials and energy. The SASB is a relatively new institution that aims to help businesses identify, manage and report on the sustainability topics that matter most to their investors. SASB has developed standards for 77 industries, which were codified in November 2018. These industry standards relate to financially relevant sustainability issues that affect value of businesses and, hence, investors. Themes within the industry standards are identifiable through a "material map" which identifies, among others, the relevance of energy management (environmental impacts associated with energy consumption in manufacturing); GHG emissions (Scope 1, direct); air quality; water and wastewater management; and waste and hazardous materials management as key areas for disclosure (https://materiality.sasb.org).

The GHG Protocol provides physical standards, guidance, tools and training for business and government to measure and manage seven climate-warming emissions covered by the Kyoto Protocol which, from 1997, commits State Parties to reduce GHG emissions. The GHG Protocol Corporate Accounting and Reporting Standard provides requirements and guidance for companies and other organisations preparing a physical GHG emissions inventory for Scopes 1–3 emissions.

The development of materials and energy accounting leads to a number of challenges and opportunities as outlined next.

Challenges and Opportunities

A first challenge for materials and energy accounting is the presence of multiple competing institutions in the accounting space. This leads to variety in material and energy accounting systems, which need to be harmonised, consolidated, coordinated or linked to reduce costs of material and energy accounting (e.g. Gibassier and Schaltegger 2015, on Danone's consolidation process of their carbon accounting and reporting to become in line with the later developed external GHG Protocol requirements). This situation is recognised by, for example, SASB, which states:

> SASB works alongside and with multiple organisations seeking to advance reporting and corporate disclosure on sustainability issues. SASB complements global initiatives including the Global Reporting Initiative (GRI), the International Integrated Reporting Committee (IIRC), the Task Force on Climate-Related Financial Disclosures (TCFD), the CDP, and others.
>
> *(Working with SASB and other Frameworks; www.sasb.org/standards-overview/sasb-and-others/)*

Nevertheless, there is little sign of convergence between institutions, with the United States largely going its own way, as it has previously with financial reporting. The challenge is how to bring together successful collaborations on best practice standards if critical materials and energy problems such as global warming, resource scarcity and their associated social impacts are to be addressed. Lessons from attempts to achieve the SDGs through SDG 17 could be instructive.

A second challenge is how far to accept the problems of conventional financial accounting, which lies behind financial reporting when looking for a substantive materials and energy accounting. The examples of capitalisation or expensing of costs and allocation keys when using a product costing system illustrate that materials and energy accounting systems are still subject to decisions where management judgement is needed before the accounts can settle on the distribution of income and value generated between time periods. Nonetheless, the problems of financial accounting are legion and long-lived and unlikely to be resolved in the near future. If a financial accounting perspective is adopted, such problems will be forever bundled into materials and energy accounting. Movement towards a sustainability management accounting perspective could change thinking and accounting towards acceptance of information relevant to decision-making and change in management behaviour away from selective disclosure and impression management (greenwash) and incomparable disclosures.

A third challenge is to recognise and develop as appropriate the full spread of materials and energy accounting tools in the toolkit to meet decision-making needs of different managers linking past and future, physical and monetary, short-term and long-term thinking, as well as general and targeted information. Although practice tends to focus on short term, periodic materials and energy accounting, in order to help address longer term sustainability issues accounting needs to provide different types of monetary and physical information to different types of managers for their different purposes.

A final challenge is to establish a programme to demonstrate how EMA links or could be linked to global ecological issues of sustainability and contribute towards the SDGs and planetary boundary solutions.

These challenges also represent opportunities for materials and energy accounting. They range from the broad potential to contribute to resolving some of the largest environmental and social problems facing humanity, such as building awareness of and reducing global warming, as well as engaging different parties in collaborative solutions to materials and energy issues, such as through the integration of suppliers in decision-making and non-government organisations in checking corporation credibility through assurance.

References

Ali, S., 2014. Social and environmental impact of the rare earth industries. *Resources*, 3 (1), 123–134.

Asian Productivity Organization, 2014. *Manual on Material Flow Cost Accounting: ISO 14051*. Tokyo, Japan: Asian Productivity Organization.

Bebbington, J., and Larrinaga, C., 2014. Accounting and sustainable development: An exploration. *Accounting, Organizations and Society*, 39 (6), 395–413.

Burritt, R.L., Hahn, T., and Schaltegger, S., 2002. Towards a comprehensive framework for environmental management accounting—Links between business actors and environmental management accounting tools. *Australian Accounting Review*, 12 (27), 39–50.

Burritt, R., and Schaltegger, S. 2001. Eco-efficiency in corporate budgeting. *Environmental Management and Health*, 12 (2), 158-174.

Burritt, R.L., and Schaltegger, S., 2010. Sustainability accounting and reporting: Fad or trend? *Accounting, Auditing & Accountability Journal*, 23 (7), 829–846.

Christ, K.L., and Burritt, R.L., 2017. Material flow cost accounting for food waste in the restaurant industry. *British Food Journal*, 119 (3), 600–612.

Gibassier, D., and Schaltegger, S., 2015. Carbon management accounting and reporting in practice. A case study on converging emergent approaches. *Sustainability Accounting, Management and Policy Journal*, 6 (3), 340–365.

Hall, M., 2010. Accounting information and managerial work. *Accounting, Organizations and Society*, 35 (3), 301–315.

International Organization for Standardization (ISO), 2011. *ISO14051: Environmental Management: Material Flow Cost Accounting: General Framework*. Geneva, Switzerland: International Organization for Standardization.

Jamali, D., and Mirshak, R., 2007. Corporate social responsibility (CSR): Theory and practice in a developing country context. *Journal of Business Ethics*, 72 (3), 243–262.

Kastenhofer, K., Bechtold, U., and Wilfing H., 2011. Sustaining sustainability science. The role of established inter-disciplines. *Ecological Economics*, 70 (4), 835–843.

Kates, R., Clark, W., Corell, R., Hall, J., Jaeger, C., Lowe, I., McCarthy, J., Schellnhuber, H., Bolin, B., Dickson, N., Faucheux, S., Gallopin, G., Grübler, A., Huntley, B., Jäger, J., Jodha, N., Kasperson, R., Mabogunje, A., Matson, P., Mooney, H., Moore III, B., O'Riordan, T., and Svedin, U., 2001. Sustainability science. *Science*, 292 (5517), 641–642.

KPMG, 2017. *Survey of Corporate Responsibility Reporting 2017*, KPMG. Available from https://home.kpmg/xx/en/home/campaigns/2017/10/survey-of-corporate-responsibility-reporting–2017.html [Accessed 12 June 2019].

Möller, A., and Schaltegger, S., 2005. The sustainability balanced scorecard as a framework for eco-efficiency analysis. *Journal of Industrial Ecology*, 9 (4), 73-83.

Rockström, J., Steffen, W., Noone, K., Persson, A., Chapin, F.S., Lambin, E.F., Lenton, T.M., Scheffer, M., Folke, C., Schellnhuber, H.J., Nykvist, B., de Wit, C.A., Hughes, T., van der Leeuw, S., Rodhe, H., Sorlin, S., Snyder, P.K., Costanza, R., Svedin, U., Falkenmark, M., Karlberg, L., Corell, R.W., Fabry, V.J., Hansen, J., Walker, B., Liverman, D., Richardson, K., Crutzen, P., and Foley, J.A., 2009. A safe operating space for humanity. *Nature*, 461 (7263), 472–475.

Schaltegger, S., 2018. Linking environmental management accounting. A reflection on (missing) links to sustainability and planetary boundaries. *Social and Environmental Accountability Journal*, 38 (1), 19–29. Doi: 10.1080/0969160X.2017.1395351

Schaltegger, S., Álvarez Etxeberria, I., and Ortas, E., 2017. Innovating corporate accounting and reporting for sustainability. Attributes and challenges. *Sustainable Development*, 25 (2), 113–122.

Schaltegger, S., and Burritt, R. 2000. *Contemporary Environmental Accounting*. London: Routledge.

Schaltegger, S., Burritt, R., Zvezdov, D., Hörisch, J., and Tingey-Holyoak, J., 2015. Management roles and sustainability information. Exploring corporate practices. *Australian Accounting Review*, 25 (4), 328–345.

Silva, S., and Schaltegger, S., 2019. Social assessment and management of conflict minerals: A systematic literature review. *Sustainability Accounting, Management and Policy Journal*, 10 (1), 157–182.

Simon, H.A., 1987. Making management decisions: The role of intuition and emotion. *Academy of Management Perspectives*, 1 (1), 57–64.

United Nations World Commission on Environment and Development (UNCED), 1987. *Our Common Future (Brundtland Report)*. Oxford, UK: Oxford University Press.

Whiteman, G., Walker, B., and Perego, P., 2013. Planetary boundaries. Ecological foundations for corporate sustainability. *Journal of Management Studies*, 50, 307–336.

Winn, M.I., and Pogutz, S., 2013. Business, ecosystems, and biodiversity. New horizons for management research. *Organization & Environment*, 26 (2), 203–229.

World Economic Forum (WEF), 2018. *The Global Risks Report 2018*, 13th edn. Geneva, Switzerland: World Economic Forum.

World Economic Forum (WEF), 2019. *The Global Risks Report 2019*, 14th edn. Geneva, Switzerland: World Economic Forum.

16

EXTERNALITIES AND DECISION-MAKING

Nicolas Antheaume and Jan Bebbington

Introduction

Traditional accounting paints a partial picture of organisations' impacts and achievements (Hines 1988), with this partiality having substantive implications for accounting's ability to properly reflect organisational impacts on the natural environment. One way in which this concern has manifested itself is through a concern with how to make externalities (defined below) visible, the use of accounting techniques to achieve that task and how externalities data may affect decision-making. In brief, externalities are impacts (of a social, environmental or economic nature) that arise from the activities of an entity but which are borne by entities beyond the originating entity (Unerman, Bebbington and O'Dwyer 2018). Given this displacement (in time and/or place), these impacts rarely create direct or timely consequences for the originating entity and fall outside the remit of financial reporting, although they may have longer-term financial consequences for the entity. We know that these impacts exist because we face environmental damage from collective organisational activity. This observation also suggests if this data was taken into account, then different decisions and actions would be taken. Providing some mechanism to account for externalities, therefore, is central to policies that aim to address environmental harm.

Environmental reporting and accounting could be seen as an attempt to develop knowledge about externalities (an argument advanced by Unerman et al. 2018 – see also Atkinson 2000). For example, environmental reporting often depicts the impacts arising from organisational operations, such as greenhouse gas emission profiles: these are physical descriptions of externalities. Likewise, management decision-making often seeks to understand the costs and benefits of potential courses of action, including externalities likely to be generated by choices (see Milne 1996). Moreover, more recent interest in carbon, water and biodiversity accounting also arise from concerns with externalities across these physical domains (see Part 5 of this handbook). This chapter, however, focuses on a smaller subset of research (sometimes framed as "full cost accounting") where there is a history of practical experimentation and conceptual debate around how to account for externalities.

This chapter proceeds in three steps. First, we present a short history of work focusing on externalities and decision-making. The key observation from this material is that there has been ongoing and extensive experimentation in this area but little by way of systematic synthesis of this work: this chapter seeks to achieve that synthesis. Second, the chapter will then move to "unpack" the key issues that emerge at each stage of identifying, quantifying and (sometimes) monetising externalities and the various ways in which this data can be incorporated in decision-making processes (by a variety of decision-makers). In particular, the issue of monetisation has generated more discussion than other aspects of full cost accounting and is an issue that goes to the heart of the accounting discipline: how do we appropriately value actions and what are the implications of valuation exercises (see also Chapter 17 of this handbook). The final element in this chapter reviews of what we know about what organisations "do" when they have information about externalities.

A brief history of experimentation

Accounting experiments that seek to identify externalities follow a generic four-step approach (first synthesised by Bebbington, Gray, Hibbitt and Kirk 2001). First, the exercise needs to specify what is going to be subject to the account: this might include a defined activity, a product or the whole organisation. Second, there is a need to specify which externalities are going to be identified: this might be a particular subset of impacts (e.g. social or environmental aspects only or a range of impacts) as well as specifying how many layers of externalities will be identified. Given any impact has its own externalities profile, the problem of infinite regress is ever present in this approach. Third, there is a need to measure externalities in terms of, for example, emissions data or volume of materials used. This step requires either data from management accounting systems or some measure of activity that can be converted (most frequently using standard impact estimates from science or policy) into impacts. The impact pathway method (Friedrich and Bickel 2001), material flow analysis (Brunner and Rechberger 2004) and life cycle analysis (Curran 2012) are often the basis of estimating flows and translating them into impacts (see also chapters 15 and 17 of this handbook). Fourth, accounts translate impacts into some monetary measurement. Here the issue is that there are many different ways to monetise impacts that often create a wide range of figures (for an illustration, see Antheaume 2004). Each of these steps are complex in their own right and various experiments have taken different routes through these core characteristics, generating diverse accounts and insights.

Approaches to accounting for externalities have also evolved over time and Unerman et al. (2018) suggest that there are four phases of experimentation.

The first phase arose in the 1970s and 1980s where research identified the adverse impact of corporate behaviour (though the social audit movement and de-industrialisation/plant closure audits). These experiments provided the first accounts of externalities, even if this language was not used at that time with a focus on social and economic impacts rather than environmental effects (see Corcoran and Leininger 1970; Abt 1977; Seidler 1973; Estes 1976; Harte and Owen 1987; Rubenstein 1994). Besides the work of Abt, few of these proposals developed beyond the conceptual stage (Table 16.1 summarises a sample of this work).

The second phase of work emerged during the 1990s in the form of practical experimentation by organisations. The outcomes of this work were communicated in annual reports (in the case of BSO/Origin from 1990 to 1995) or by research partners: in the case of Ontario Hydro (by the United States Environmental Protection Agency 1996); Manaaki Whenua/Landcare Research (by Bebbington and Gray 2001); and Interface Europe (by Howes 2000). Around the same time, consultants also published externalities accounts: see Bent (2005), Macaulay (1999) and Rubenstein (1994) (and Bebbington et al. 2001 for a summary of these experiments). Table 16.2 provides a brief summary of some of these experiments.

Table 16.1 Accounting for externalities in the 1970s and 1980s – a selection of landmark proposals

Name of approach	*Source*	*Description and comments*
Environmental exchange report	Corcoran & Leininger (1970), enriched by Estes (1976)	Input–output table with data on the exchanges of a corporation with its socio-economic environment. The authors suggest that physical and social data should be included, as well as financial data related to social interest issues. Estes (1976) then suggested that input–output table should be complemented with a report on the social costs and benefits linked to the organization's exchanges with its environment. This proposal considers that it is needed to look beyond the perimeter of financial reports and in order to fully understand the effects of an organization's activity and its physical foundations.
Accruals and deferred liabilities	Beams & Fertig (1971)	Based on existing financial statements, these authors propose a system of accruals and deferred liabilities in order to recognise the social costs for which an organisation is responsible.
Social audit also known as the constituent impact approach	Abt (1977) and experimental implementation from 1971 to 1981.	Publication of mandatory and voluntary expenses which result in an improvement of the well-being of employees and the general public, enhancing product safety and protection of the environment. The account takes the form of a social income statement and balance sheet which show the impacts on the different elements of the company's socio-economic environment. This proposal expresses the social and environmental consequences of an organisation's activity in same monetary terms as the ones which the readers of financial statements are accustomed to. Therefore, they provide an opportunity to combine financial results with social and environmental ones, in order to provide a "full account" of a company's performance.
Social Income Statement	Seidler (1973)	A report of all the costs and benefits to society, linked to the activity of an organisation culminating in a social income statement which presents: - The sum of benefits to society, linked to the activity of the organisation, and for which it earns no revenues. - The sum of costs imposed to society, linked to the activity of an entity, and for which it does not pay any compensation. The difference between the sum of benefits and costs would a net profit/loss for society.

Source: Based on Woodward (1998) and Antheaume (2007).

Table 16.2 Accounting for externalities in the 1990s – a presentation of some landmark experiments

Name of approach	*Source*	*Description and comments*
BSO/Origin	BSO/Origin, Huizing and Dekker (1992)	BSO/Origin (now ATOS), a Dutch consultancy, developed a calculation of the net value added of its activities: defined as personnel costs + depreciation + taxes + net profit (or – loss). Value lost was defined as the cost of the environmental effects caused by the company's operations minus existing expenses aimed at mitigating these effects. Net value added was defined as value added minus value lost. Beyond the calculations, this experiment was also used to argue for a change in tax rules, in order to tax the consumption on non-renewable resources rather than to tax labour.
Ontario Hydro	United States Environmental Protection Agency (1996)	Ontario Hydro (a government owned public utility) developed external cost estimates for its nuclear plants and fossil fuelled stations using a damage function approach (a modelling technique that assesses how much damage is caused by emissions). This translated the physical impact of electricity generation into monetary terms. The aim of this experiment was to combine known internal costs with external costs estimates, to improve decision-making processes.
Accounting for Sustainable Forestry Management	UNCTAD (1994), Rubenstein (1994).	This experiment, based on the case of Kirkland Forest Products, identified the costs of three different operating philosophies, ranging from options where timber production is a primary concern to an option where wood and non-wood values are given equal consideration (with an option between these two also being included). For each option, the costs associated with the approach were compared to the benefits created, including outcomes for the entity and externalities profiles. As could be expected, the most commercial approach generated highest profit but also higher externalities (and vice versa). The key insight from the work was that if you took a time span of 60 years, options that involved less external costs increased the total commercial value of the forest due to increased probability that the concession for the forest would be renewed (an early outworking of "social licence to operate") and to an increase in the total quantity of wood available.
Landcare Research/ Manaaki Whenua	Bebbington and Gray (2001)	In the late 1990s, Landcare Research (a New Zealand research institute) attempted to quantify the gap between its current expenses and the expenses it would have to incur in order to become more sustainable. Remediation costs and potential tax costs were estimated for carbon emissions related to the use of electricity and transport services. A "business-as-unusual" scenario was imagined: the suppression of air travel for all domestic trips and the cost of such a scenario proved to be out of reach. This experiment was useful to understand that the cost of evolving towards sustainability is out of reach of most organisations, even if they are willing to forge the way ahead, unless the rules of the game are changed for everybody, in order to level the playing field.

The third phase of work took place in the 2000s, with entity level experimentation being complemented by project-based externalities modelling. The most sustained work undertaken in this context used the Sustainability Assessment Model (developed in partnership with BP – see Baxter et al. 2004; Bebbington 2007) and extended to the built environment (see Xing et al. 2009) as well as a range of experiments in New Zealand (see Bebbington, Brown and Frame 2007; Frame and Cavanagh 2009; Fraser 2012). During this time, entity-based experimentation also continued (see Lamberton 2000; Casella Stanger, Forum for the Future and Carillion 2002; and Herbohn 2005). Table 16.3 provides more detail on some of this work.

The fourth and final phase of experimentation has tended to focus on physical domains where externalities are experienced: such as carbon (see, e.g., Davies and Dunk 2015) and biodiversity (see Davies 2014). This time period also saw the re-emergence of practice-based initiatives such as PwC's *Total Impact Measurement and Management* tool that seeks to value social, environmental, taxation and economic impacts (see PwC 2013 for an outline of the methodology); PUMA's 2011 Environmental Profit and Loss Account and product-based externalities (A4S 2012); the Crown Estate's "total contribution" methodology; and KPMG's true value methodology – see Hendriksen et al.(2016). These experiments hark back to the earliest experiments in social and environmental accounting documented in Estes (1976). Table 16.3 provides more detail on a sample of this work.

Given the myriad of choices that any account of externalities requires (all of which could be "right" for a particular setting), it should not be surprising that many of these experiments are not directly comparable with each other in terms of the monetary figures generated. That being said, it is possible to synthesise two observations that arise from the combined insight of this work. The first relates to what the experiments might say about (un)sustainability of organisations while the second relates to the connections made to capitals.

In the first instance, many of the experiments have sought to articulate how close to sustainability/how unsustainable current activities are (see, e.g., Rubenstein 1994; Bebbington and Gray 2001; and Bent 2005). In all these instances, "business as usual" was demonstrated as creating substantial externalities profiles. In addition (and BSO/Origin is a case in point), while actions could sometimes be identified for reducing externalities profiles, growth in activity level resulted in a growing externalities profile despite remedial actions being undertaken. The difficulty of eliminating externalities profiles also resulted in some documented hostility to the implications of externalities experiments. This arose where an organisation assumed that the account would provide a flattering picture and where failure to do so was disappointing for them (see Fraser 2012, who documented this and also Figure 16.1). Taken together, these insights suggest that while highlighting unsustainability through an accounting tool may be valuable for those creating the account, it is more difficult to know what can be done on the basis of that information. What is noted, however, is that as the regulatory environment in which organisations operate has and is likely to continue to internalise externalities through a variety of means (climate change externalities being an obvious example – see also Unerman et al. 2018).

Second, since 2000 the concept of capitals has been central to the creation of some models and experiments to account for externalities, with accounts of the impact of an organisation's operations on different categories of capital (this has links with the framing of the Integrated Reporting Initiative – see Chapter 8 of this handbook). Taibi et al. (2020) highlight that assumptions about capital substitution and where you sit on the weak/strong sustainability continuum materially affect how data are calculated and used for decision-making (Bebbington 2007 makes the same point). In contrast, other models (Richard 2012; Richard and Rambaud 2015) treat "capital" as liabilities that that have to be accounted for. Indeed, Faure et al. (2020)

Table 16.3 Accounting for externalities in the 2000s – a presentation of some landmark experiments

Name of approach	*Authors*	*Description and comments*
Sustainability Assessment Model	Baxter et al. (2004); Bebbington (2007); Frame and Cavanagh (2009); Fraser (2012); and Xing et al. (2009).	Taking a project as the unit of analysis, this approach sought to identify economic, environmental and social externalities in monetary terms. The account created a "signature" of impacts across different capital types which were combined in different ways (capital substitution was not assumed for any negative externalities) into an overall "score". Experimental accounts were undertaken for fossil fuel projects, the built environment and local government decision-making processes. The accounts provided valuable input to decision making and strategy processes.
Forum for the Future	Bent (2005) and Taplin et al. (2006).	A British NGO, Forum for the Future, developed tools and guidelines to promote the use of sustainable accounting and applied these in two separate cases (an alcohol producer and a chemical company). For the alcohol producer, their work suggested that the costs incurred to make alcohol are a fraction of the costs imposed to society by the consumption of alcohol. In the chemical company, the costs and benefits of a refrigerant lubricant are compared with one another.
Puma Environmental Profit and Loss Statement	Puma (2011)	With the help of two consultancies (PWC and Trucost), Puma quantified greenhouse gas emissions (in tonnes), water use (volume of water consumed), land use (area of natural land converted); air pollution (tonnes) and waste (tonnes) for its own activities and along supply chain. Each physical quantity was then monetised (based on values identified in the literature) with an estimated externality of €145 million.
Crown Estate Total Contribution Report	Crown Estate (2013 and 2017)	Total contribution is a methodology developed by this organisation in order to measure the impact of its activities on the six capitals on which it depends (financial resources, natural resources, know-how, physical resources, employees, networks). Both positive and negative impacts are taken into account (internal and external appreciation/loss of value). The outcome is total net contribution to the six capitals, of £277 million. Contrary to Puma, the focus is on the idea that organisations create more value than they destroy and that negative and positive values across different capitals can compensate one another.

have proposed a classification of accounting methods that distinguish between those that have an impact on profit only, those which include changes both in the income statement and the balance sheet and those which mimic financial accounts or the financial accounting standardisation process (such as the biological diversity protocol, natural capital statements and accounting for Australia's water – see also Chapter 27).

Figure 16.1 The unflattering effect of externalities accounting

As is apparent from this review, accounting scholars and practitioners have been thinking about and creating accounts of externalities since social and environmental concerns became a part of accounting. This is also an area of ongoing practice and conceptual experimentation. There are two critical aspects of this work that warrant further discussion in this context. First, one element of an "idealised" account of externalities involves translating impacts into monetised amounts. This "step" is not always enacted and is often highly contested (Bebbington et al. 2007; Herbohn 2005; Gasparatos, El-Haram and Horner 2009; Frame and O'Connor 2011; Bebbington and Larrinaga 2014). Second, the question arises as to what action accounts for externalities prompts. Each of these aspects are now considered in turn.

Monetisation issues

Accounting for externalities includes the option for the monetisation of (at least) a subset of impacts: an option that is not always taken. Herbohn (2005) and Davies (2014) explain why they didn't take this step and Antheaume (2004), Bebbington (2007), Gasparatos et al. (2009) and Bebbington and Larrinaga (2014) provide commentary on this aspect. There is an argument that if organisational decision-making will not admit factors other than those that are represented in financial terms, monetisation is necessary (accounting is an exercise in valuation and valuing). At the same time, legitimate concerns exist about the potential dysfunctional effect of adding more monetisation when this narrow way of knowing has created externalities in the first place: there are no easy "answers" to this debate. Three ideas are developed here to exemplify the debate: the source of monetisation data, the concept of monetisation frontier and the link of this work to post-normal science thinking.

Accounting for externalities is sometimes underpinned by a mainstream neo-classical economics view of environmental problems: that the best way to address externalities is to bring more of the environment into the ambit of economic analysis. This includes aspects such as the "polluter pays principle"; the use of taxation to address impacts; and quotas (which can be sold on markets) for the use of environmental resources. These approaches seek to create a market value to environmental goods and services (sometimes conceived of as eco-system services) and thus environmental costs come within the ambit of accounting through these means (carbon taxes are the most well advanced of these techniques). The intellectual "baggage" that comes with this approach leads to concerns. The question is as follows: do we have to accept the theoretical framework proposed by mainstream economists if monetisation is undertaken? Our (cautious) opinion is that it is not necessary. Working on monetisation does not necessarily imply accepting the analysis of mainstream economics. What is necessary, however, is for the framework of the accounting analysis to be clear about wider values. For example, a "strong sustainability" perspective would not see monetisation as a way to uniquely define value but as a way of articulating how much resources have to be allocated by society (and by whom within society) to preserve the resilience of ecosystems and human societies. This framing would need to articulate how resilience is conceptualised, define what actions and programmes are central to resilience, how these actions and programmes are to be evaluated and what allocation of externalities is appropriate (i.e. which economic actors will be held accountable). Such an approach could be linked to Raworth's (2017) conceptualisation of "doughnut economics" to describe approaches that define social foundations and planetary limits as the borders within which a viable economic system is possible. In this case, monetisation serves altogether a different purpose from the one it is assigned in mainstream economics. First, a socially and environmentally viable economy has to be defined, independently from economic considerations. Then, and only then, monetisation is used to establish a monetised estimate for the re-engineered economy.

The second layer of nuance arises from the idea of a "monetization frontier" (Frame and O'Connor 2011) as a way to move beyond the dichotomy that either all or no elements of the environment could be the subject of monetisation. The idea here is that there may be a sense of where the boundaries of "useful" monetisation exist. They suggest that some assets might be more easily included in economic analysis (forests considered for logging, proven reserves of minerals, gas and oil) while other elements might be the subject of debates that do not solely rely on economic analysis (e.g. climate change, health impacts of pollution and biodiversity concerns). There is some evidence of this thinking in some of the accounting experiments, either within the definitions of the bounds of analysis or how critical natural capital is not included in the monetisation process (Bebbington and Gray 2001; Bebbington 2007). Likewise, papers adopting a more post-normal approach also point to this distinction.

Indeed, Bebbington and Larrinaga (2014), in their exploration of how sustainability science motifs might come into accounting, draw on post-normal science thinking to consider accounting for externalities. Post-normal science (see Funtowicz and Ravetz 2003) focuses on the complexity of the systems that humans are seeking to engage within and asserts that there is no unique scientifically justified point of view for measurement (see also Chapter 17 of this handbook). This point is illustrated most clearly in Antheaume (2004) and also infuses Bebbington and Larringa's (2014) argument. In the latter case, the authors argue that an externalities account is the basis for discussion and that different choices with respect to dimensions to be valued and the valuations themselves should be made apparent through dialogic processes (see Bebbington et al. 2007, and Frame and Brown 2008). This chimes with other literature on externalities (see especially Frame and Cavanagh 2009 and Fraser 2012), which highlights that the negotiation of responsibility and accountability is central to the exercise. This consideration directly links to how externalities data are used in decision-making.

Decision-making and externalities

The modelling of externalities profiles (difficult though it is) is only the first step in any accounting for externalities. This section explores possible uses of externalities accounting and the meaning that organisations have attached to these exercises (drawing from Bebbington et al. 2001, as well as Antheaume 2007). It is evident in the various experiments that accounting for externalities feeds a debate on what needs to be changed, who might be responsible for those changes and who should be held accountable for impacts in the meantime.

For example, the attempt by PUMA to take its externalities into account provides impetus for questioning how value chains are organised (in their work, 6% of the external costs was attributed to PUMA as a legal entity while 94% was attributed to suppliers). Thus, this account of externalities tells us that if PUMA sought to reduce its externalities, it would have to cooperate with its suppliers over the long term (Bebbington 2007 also identified that externalities data suggested greater focus on partnerships along value chains). Likewise, a logical extension of these findings would be for PUMA to translate supply chain influence into management control tools which ensure that supply chain work is undertaken. Ultimately, however, PUMA is not currently accountable for supplier impacts.

Complementary insights about the need to change economic systems to address externalities can be found in other works in this area. For example, Bebbington and Gray (2001) highlighted the "business as usual" impediment to action in their case as did Rubenstein (1994). BSO/Origin's experimentation demonstrated that while they used externalities data to reduce impacts, their overall growth in business activities still meant that their overall impact increased over time. This is also where accounting for externalities at the entity level connects to broader policy debates about how externality generating activities are to be regulated and what fiscal tools will be used in this process (it is useful to recall that the early call in the EU's Fifth Action Programme (European Union, 1992) for accounting for externalities was prompted by a concern that processes for internalising externalities might not come to pass).

The final observation in this section relates to how accounting for externalities has the potential to disrupt existing beliefs about the, for example, sustainability credentials of those creating the accounts and, in the process, challenging existing accountability regimes. The extent to which the use of external costs for policy decisions is taken seriously becomes apparent when interest groups adopt counter policy positions, such as the one published in 2017 by the Fédération Internationale de l'Automobile, representing touring clubs, on the internalisation of external costs.[1] This is why not all accounting for externalities work is in the public domain, even if we sometimes catch hints of organisations having undertaken work. Fraser (2012) documents something similar in that the technique he used to create externalities profile (the Sustainability Assessment Model) was accepted as legitimate until it failed to create the "answer" that was sought (see also Figure 16.1). In this case, the account demonstrated that the entities' performance was not in line with espoused sustainability principles. This is why, drawing from Jones and Dugdale (2001) idea of an accounting regime, accounting for externalities can be challenging: externalities profile implies responsibility for impacts and also the need to change activities to avoid creation of the impacts in the first instance.

Conclusion

This chapter has reviewed 50 years of research and experimentations in accounting for externalities. It has explored some of the technical complexities related to full cost accounting as well as examined how such accounts create a "mediating platform" between government authorities, other stakeholders and businesses decision-makers. In this way, full cost accounting constitutes a shared intellectual terrain with work that seeks to understand the functionality of accounting and the impact of organisational practices, as well as deeper questions about monetisation and commensuration. Accounting for externalities has evolved from a "niche" research subject in the 1970s and 1980s to a prominent topic in accounting in academic, business and government circles. It has also progressively gained a degree of freedom from dominant neo-classical economics, from which it evolved, to embrace a plurality of frameworks and perspectives. At the same time, given the variety of experiments, there is relatively little review of this field as a whole (but see Unerman et al. 2018) or of the links between this technique and other environmental accounting and reporting activities.

Note

1 The report is in English and can be downloaded here: www.fiaregion1.com/wp-content/uploads/2017/05/20160713_fia_region_i_policy_position_internalisation_of_external_costs__final.pdf [Accessed 30 May 2020).

References

A4S, 2012. *Future Proofed Decision Making: Integrating Environmental and Social Factors into Strategy, Finance and Operations*. December 2012, London: The Prince's Accounting for Sustainability Project.

Abt, C., 1977. *The Social Audit for Management*. New York: Amacon.

Antheaume, N., 2004. Valuing external costs - from theory to practice: Implications for full cost environmental accounting. *European Accounting Review*, 13(3), 443–464.

Antheaume, N., 2007. Full cost accounting: Adam Smith meets Rachel Carson? In J. Unerman, J. Bebbington, and B. O'Dwyer (Eds.), *Sustainability Accounting and Accountability*. London: Routledge.

Atkinson, G., 2000. Measuring corporate sustainability. *Journal of Environmental Planning and Management*, 43, 235–252.

Baxter, T., Bebbington, J., and Cutteridge, D., 2004. Sustainability assessment model: Modelling economic, resource, environmental and social flows of a project. In A. Henriques and J. Richardson (Eds.), *The Triple Bottom Line: Does It All Add up? Assessing the Sustainability of Business and CSR*. London: Earthscan.

Beams, F.A., and Fertig, P.E., 1971. Pollution control through social cost conversion. *Journal of Accountancy*. November, 37–42.

Bebbington, J., 2007. *Accounting for Sustainable Development Performance*. London: Elsevier.

Bebbington, J., Brown, J., and Frame, B., 2007. Accounting technologies and sustainability assessment models. *Ecological Economics*, 61, 224–236.

Bebbington, J., and Gray, R., 2001. An account of sustainability: Failure, success and a reconceptualisation. *Critical Perspectives on Accounting*, 12(5), 557–605.

Bebbington, J., Gray, R., Hibbitt, C., and Kirk, E., 2001. *Full Cost Accounting: An Agenda for Action*. London: Association of Chartered Certified Accountants.

Bebbington, J., and Larrinaga, C., 2014. Accounting and sustainable development: An exploration. *Accounting, Organizations and Society*, 39(6), 395–413.

Bent, D., 2004. Towards a monetised triple bottom line for an alcohol producer—Using stakeholder dialogue to negotiate a "licence to operate" by constructing an account of social performance. London: Environmental Management Accounting Network.

Brunner, P.H., and Rechberger, H., 2004. *Practical Handbook of Material Flow Analysis*. Boca Raton, FL: Lewis Publishers.

Casella Stanger, Forum for the Future and Carillion, 2002. *Sustainability Accounting in the Construction Industry by Casella Stanger, Forum for the Future, Carillion*. London: Construction Industry Research and Information Association.

Corcoran, A.W., and Leininger, W.E. Jr., 1970. Financial statements, who needs them. *Financial Executive*, August, 34–38.

Crown Estate, 2017. *Total Contribution Report: Everything Is Connected*. London: Crown Estate.

Curran, M.A., 2012. *Life Cycle Assessment Handbook: A Guide for Environmentally Sustainable Products*. Beverly, MA: Scrivener Publishing.

Davies, J., 2014. Full cost accounting: Integrating biodiversity. In M. Jones (Ed.), *Accounting for Biodiversity* (pp. 81–102). London: Routledge.

Davies, J., and Dunk, R., 2015. Flying along the supply chain: Accounting for emissions from student air travel in the higher education sector. *Carbon Management*, 6(5–6), 233–246.

Estes. R., 1976. *Corporate Social Accounting*, New York: John Wiley & Sons.

European Union, 1992, *Fifth Action Programme*, Com (92) 23 final - Vol.I-III, Brussels, 27 March 1992. CB-CO–92–151-EN-C.

Faure, E., Cordano, E., and Taibi, S., 2020. *Quelles connexions entre la comptabilité financière et le non-financier: développement durable et immatériel, état des lieux des représentations en comptabilité financière (Connexions between financial and non-financial accounting: Sustainable development and intangibles, a state of the art of financial accounting representations)*, supervised by Antheaume, N. and Gibassier, D., Multi-Capital Integrated Performance Research Center, Audencia https://fr.calameo.com/read/000137206275898de179e [accessed 30 June, 2020].

Frame, B., and Brown, J., 2008. Developing post-normal technologies for sustainability. *Ecological Economics*, 65(2), 225–241.

Frame, B., and Cavanagh, J., 2009. Experiences of sustainability assessment: An awkward adolescence. *Accounting Forum*, 33, 195–208.

Frame, B., and O'Connor, M., 2011. Integrating valuation and deliberation: The purposes of sustainability assessment. *Environmental Science and Policy*, 14(1), 1–10.

Fraser, M., 2012. Fleshing out an engagement with a social accounting technology. *Accounting, Auditing and Accountability Journal*, 25(3), 508–534.

Friedrich, R., and Bickel P., 2001. Estimation of external costs using the impact-pathway-approach. Results from the ExternE project series. *TA-Datenbank-Nachrichten*, 10(3), pp. 74–82. http://www.externe.info/externe_2006/ [Accessed 1 June 2020].

Funtowicz, S., and Ravetz, J., 2003, *Post Normal Science, Internet Encyclopaedia of Ecological Economics*. International Society for Ecological Economics.

Gasparatos, A., El-Haram, M., and Horner, M., 2009. The argument against a reductionist approach for measuring sustainable development performance and the need for methodological pluralism. *Accounting Forum*, 33, 245–256.

Harte, G., and Owen, D., 1987. Fighting de-industrialisation: The role of local government social audits. *Accounting, Organizations and Society*, 12(2), 123–41.

Hendriksen, B., Weimer, J., and McKenzie, M., 2016. Approaches to quantify value from business to society: Case studies of KPMG's true value methodology. *Sustainability Accounting, Management and Policy Journal*, 7(4), 474–493.

Herbohn, K., 2005. A full cost environmental accounting experiment. *Accounting, Organizations and Society*, 30(6), 519–536.

Hines, R., 1988. Financial accounting: In communicating reality, we construct reality. *Accounting, Organizations and Society*, 13(3), 251–261.

Howes, R., 2000. Corporate environmental accounting: Accounting for environmentally sustainable profits. In J. Proops, and S. Simon (Eds.), *Greening the Accounts, a Volume in the International Library of Ecological Economics*. London: Edward Elgar Publishers.

Huizing, A., and Dekker, C., 1992. Helping to pull or planet out of the red: An environmental report of BSO/Origin. *Accounting, Organizations and Society*, 17(5), 449–558.

Jones, C. and Dugdale, D., 2001. The concept of an accounting regime. *Critical Perspectives on Accounting*, 12(1), 35–63.

Lamberton, G., 2000. Accounting for sustainable development—A case study of city farm. *Critical Perspectives on Accounting*, 11(5), 583–605.

Macaulay, 1999. *Corporate Reporting for Sustainable Development: Agriculture*. Aberdeen: Macaulay Land Use Research Institute.

Milne, M., 1996. On sustainability; the environment and management accounting. *Management Accounting Research*, 7(1), 135–161.

Puma, 2011. *PUMA's Environmental Profit and Loss Account for the year ended 31 december 2010*. Munich: Puma

PwC, 2013. *Measuring and Managing Total Impact: A New Language for Business Decisions*. London: PwC.

Raworth, K., 2017, *Doughnut Economics: Seven Ways to Think Like a 21st-Century Economist*. London: Random House Business.

Richard, J., 2012. *Comptabilité et développement durable.* Paris: Economica.
Richard, J., and Rambaud, A., 2015. The "triple depreciation line" instead of the "triple bottom line": Towards a genuine integrated reporting. *Critical Perspectives on Accounting*, 33, 92–116.
Rubenstein, D.B., 1994. *Environmental Accounting for the Sustainable Corporation—Strategies and Techniques.* Westport: Quorum Books.
Samiolo, R., 2012. Commensuration and styles of reasoning: Venice, cost–benefit, and the defence of place. *Accounting, Organizations and Society*, 37(6), 382–402.
Seidler, L.J., 1973. *Dollar Values in the Social Income Statement.* World, Spring, London: Peat, Marwick, Mitchell & Co., pp. 14, 16, 18–23.
Taïbi, S., Antheaume, N., and Gibassier, D., 2020. Accounting for strong sustainability: An intervention-research based approach. *Sustainability Accounting, Management and Policy Journal,* ahead-of-print.
Taplin, J., Bent, D., and Aeron-Thomas, D., 2006. *Developing a Sustainability Accounting Framework to Inform Strategic Business Decisions: A Case Study from the Chemicals Industry.* London: Forum for the Future.
Unerman, J., Bebbington, J., and O'Dwyer, B., 2018. Corporate reporting and accounting for externalities. *Accounting and Business Research*, 48(5), 497–522.
UNCTAD, 1994. *Accounting for Sustainable Forestry Management, A Case Study.* Geneva: United Nations.
United States Environmental Protection Agency, 1996. *Environmental Accounting Case Studies: Full Cost Accounting for Decision Making at Ontario Hydro.* Washington: United States Environmental Protection Agency.
Woodward, D., 1998. An attempt at the classification of a quarter of a century of (non-critical) corporate social reporting. *International Journal of Accounting and Business Society*, 6(1), 19–66.
Xing, Y., Horner, M., El-Haram, M., and Bebbington, J., 2009. A framework model for assessing sustainability impacts of urban development. *Accounting Forum*, 33 (3), 209–224.

17

DESIGNING ENVIRONMENTAL IMPACT-VALUATION ASSEMBLAGES FOR SUSTAINABLE DECISION-MAKING

Ian Thomson

Setting the scene

The complex process of measurement or valuation of environmental impact involves creating accounts of the consequences of a decision on selected socio-ecological systems. Determining consequences involves a comparison of knowledge of the current nature and driving features within socio-ecological systems as well as the desired outcomes to be attained from the decision. These outcomes are theoretical constructions based on existing data, evidence, assumptions and connections projected forward in time. Paradoxically, the calculation of environmental impacts is designed to prevent them ever happening or to put in place mitigation or restorative measures. Impacts are typically described in terms of impacting on what, impacting on whom, quantification of change, responsibility for the impact, risk and uncertainty, impacting where and when, and legitimacy of impact measurement. Impact-valuation involves multiplying "impact numbers" by "proxy values" derived from selected economic transactions.

There is a plethora of environmental impact measurement methods. Many are covered in this handbook, for example, in chapters on accounting for externalities, carbon accounting, water accounting, biodiversity accounting, material and energy flow accounting and considering animal rights. The problem is that each environmental impact-valuation takes place in a unique time-space configuration that necessitates creating a calculative assemblage or evaluating existing ones. Each environmental impact-valuation is dependent on a series of choices on how to undertake this impact-valuation work. The two challenges of environmental impact-valuation are (1) to know what are the best available practices and (2) how to make informed choices when creating an appropriate calculative space.

Introduction

The premise of this chapter is that accounting could be reimagined and realigned with the rationales of and passionate commitment to sustainability, sustainable governance and sustainability science (Gray 2010; Bebbington and Thomson 2013; Bebbington and Larrinaga 2014). The challenge of developing meaningful environmental impact-valuations lies at the core of sustainability accounting and accountability research and is key to untangling many connected environmental governance, accounting and accountability problems. Central to accounting's future contribution is a capacity to meaningfully measure the consequences and impacts before, during and after any decision. Meaningful environmental impact-valuation measures are critical to holding organisations to account for their past decisions and wider governance and engagement processes.

This chapter provides a framework to evaluate environmental impact-valuation calculative spaces in order to create more sustainable accounting assemblages. This framework borrows and blends from a number of disciplines, including critical accounting studies, sustainability (e.g. Naess 2005), sustainability science (Folke et al. 2010), resilience assessment (Milkoreit et al. 2015), post-normal science (Frame and Brown 2008; Frame and O'Connor 2011) and political projects such as UN Sustainable Development Goals. This chapter will argue that without robust impact-valuation measures, either financial or non-financial, the transformative potential of sustainable governance is diminished.

The purpose of this chapter is not to recommend "the best" technologies, but to present a framework to evaluate impact-valuation methods prior to integration into accounting assemblages. Just as other disciplines naively co-opt accounting logic and techniques, we must avoid the naive co-option of other disciplinary logics or technologies. Some of these techniques, particularly valuation technologies, involve overly simplistic calculative reductions of complex phenomenon that seem destined to repeat the same mistakes that accounting academics are all too aware of.

This handbook is a manifestation of a critically informed engagement with these impact-valuation technologies by the accounting-environmental research community. However, this remains an ongoing challenge. There is a need for positive appreciation of the potential of these techniques as well as their critical evaluation. During these engagements, we should remain vigilant to criticisms as to the impossibility or dangers of environmental impact-valuations (e.g. Hines 1991; Maunders and Burritt 1991; Cooper 1992; Herbohn 2005; Gray 2010).

Pre-study of environmental impacts-valuations

A prestudy into environmental impact-valuations revealed a staggering diversity of measurement techniques, applying methods from artificial intelligence, big data, statistics, satellite imagery, geographic information systems, citizen science, decision science, citizen juries, dialogics, and natural sciences. In addition to quantification methods, environmental impact was valued and made visible through images, art, graffiti, videos, games, confabulations, storytelling and oral testaments.

Searching for "valuing environmental impacts" on Google Scholar came up with 16,900 sources, far too many to review in this chapter. It is enough to state that there is a range of disciplines looking at this problem including economics, development studies, sociology, ecological science, policy studies, climate science, epidemiology, risk, accounting, finance, strategy, geography, ecological philosophy and future studies.

Crudely this domain could be divided into eight categories. These are those seeking or promoting:

- that this can't be done
- that this shouldn't be done

- a single perfect measure or cost
- authoritative multiple-criteria formal decision choice mechanisms
- deliberative multiple criteria models
- mixed, non-integrative quantitative–qualitative methods
- dialogic stakeholder-driven measures and
- alternative environmental art or representation of valuations.

While there was an absence of an authoritative way to measure or value impacts, this prestudy did offer the possibility of technologies that may be appropriable into accounting assemblages. Table 17.1 provides a summary of some these technologies, which complement many others within this handbook.

However, in certain assemblages these technologies may contain incompatible logics, ontological or epistemological contradictions (Mol 1999) that could create dangerous, seductive chimeras wholly inappropriate for sustainable decision-making. It was this observation that led to the consideration of a framework to help make better choices when assembling these technologies for the purposes of sustainable governance, decision-making and accountability.

Assembling environmental impact-valuation assemblages

Any environmental impacts-valuations must be cognisant of the socio-scientific-ecologic-political problems of sustainable development and account for the complex network of challenges and conflicts associated with living within our planetary boundaries. Partial or problematic assumptions of relationships amongst these systems will create problematic impact-valuation.

Even when impacts-valuations are based on "hard", "objective" facts, we have to recognise that these impacts-valuations are unevenly distributed and amplified by structural inequities

Table 17.1 Examples of appropriable environmental impact techniques

Impact Valuation Techniques	Sources and Examples
Multiple criterion decision modelling	Infrastructure Auckland 2004, Frame and O'Connor 2011.
Ecological footprinting	Gallo et al. 2016, Global Footprint Network 2020.
Remote sensing and geographic information systems	Sieber 2006, Brown et al. 2011, Ascui et al. 2018, Denedo et al. 2019, Ecowatch 2020, IMBIE 2020
Sustainable valuation models	Antheaume 2004, Herbohn 2005, Bebbington et al. 2007, Xing et al. 2009, Frame and Cavanagh, 2009.
Product labelling/ environmental profiling	BRE 2008, Cordella et al. 2020, Ecolabel 2020.
SES resilience assessment	Folke et al. 2010, Resilience Alliance 2010.
Environmental impact assessment	UNEP 2004, Carroll et al. 2020, NECR 2020, EPA 2020.
Accounting for biodiversity	Pritchard et al. 2000, Cuckston 2013, 2017, 2019, Natural Capital Alliance 2020.
Sustainable performance frameworks	Russell and Thomson 2009, Allen et al. 2019, Wendling et al. 2018, World Benchmarking Alliance 2020, Futurefit 2020.

or oppressive power dynamics. Environmental impact-valuations cannot be neutral as they are intended to alter our understanding of the past and knowledge of future consequences and aim to draw this new knowledge into organisational decision-making and governance (Unerman and Chapman 2014).

This chapter adapts the analytical approach recommended by Sobkwiak et al. (2020), which builds on Callon's three-stage reflexive framing of a calculable space to understand how socio-technical arrangements create conditions of possibility for meaningful calculations of environmental impact-value (Callon and Law 2005). Any calculative outcome has to be understood as interactions between human calculators, calculative devices and the systems in which they embedded. Any attempt to calculate environmental impact-valuation will require "accountants" to construct a calculative space, extract and appropriate accounts from the calculative spaces of others or become embedded in the calculative spaces of others. However, central to this framework is the recognition of the constitutive agency of those involved in ***choosing*** how measurements are made and used (Callon and Muniesa 2005).

This framework requires consideration of the:

- choices as to how and what things are detached from other systems,
- choices as to the processes of manipulation and transformation, undertaken on detached data and
- choices as to how values are extracted and appropriated into decision processes.

Sobkwiak et al. (2020) argue that understanding environmental accounts as three distinct yet interconnected challenges allows for the evaluation of the messy, multi-organisational, multi-disciplinary calculation processes. Given that any environmental accounting is temporary and incomplete, part of a shifting assemblage, it must be subjected to recurring critical evaluation in order to understand the limitations of any particular assemblage. Similar to the post-normal scientific paradigm (e.g. Frame and Brown 2008), this framework recognises any environmental impact-valuation assemblage as imperfect and constantly in flux due to the interaction of power, politics, epistemologies, paradigms or philosophies in its calculations. However, this does not mean that striving for more meaningful environmental impact-valuations in different decision contexts is without merit or purpose.

The framework in this chapter, which takes the form of a series of propositions, privileges epistemological assumptions that the environment comprises interconnected, uncertain and complex natural resource systems that are governed to deliver long-term sustainable environmental benefits to human well-being in a way that does not compromise system resilience or integrity. Therefore, any choices should be evaluated in relation to their contribution to the future resilience of the socio-ecological systems essential for sustainable development (Resilience Alliance 2010).

Making the wrong choices

Environmental impacts-valuations are calculative outputs of accounting assemblages that attempt to present an intelligible narrative of future consequences of actions that encompass invisible, undetectable phenomena, normally reliant on expert knowledge and scientific methods, perceived through different social norms and values (Callon and Law 2005; Callon and Munesia 2005; Sobkwiak et al. 2020). These impact-valuations need to be considered politically legitimate, interpretable by non-experts and meaningfully appropriated in their everyday decision-making in order to trigger appropriate corrective interventions and governance sanctions.

Problematic impact-valuations allow organisations escape responsibility and associated liabilities for environmental damage, continue to externalise risks and harm to others, and avoid regulations or taxes or other sanctions (Beck 1992; Bebbington and Thomson 2007). There is a clear incentive for those causing environmental damages or those benefitting from this abuse of nature or abuse of power to claim it is impossible to accurately measure or value environmental impact (e.g. Gray 2010). Even when effective measures appear to exist, for example, satellite images of disappearing rainforests (Ecowatch 2020), melting polar ice sheets (IMBIE 2020) these can be insufficient to attribute responsibility or accountability to individuals, communities or organisations.

Overly simplistic or overly complex impact-valuations can also construct false cause–effect consequences or knowledge of the impacts (Frame and Cavanagh 2009). Problematic environmental impact-valuations can falsely label a solution as sustainable, when it merely shifts the problem to another domain or forward in time (Beck 1992; Frame and O'Connor 2011). Environmental impact-valuations, therefore, must make visible and thinkable the sustainable governance of economic, ecological and social life, in particular rendering visible and governable the risks of unsustainable consequences (Bebbington and Thomson 2007; Gray 2010) across systems and generations.

Many others have raised concerns that environmental impact-valuations calculatively captured environmental issues and suppressed fields of visibility, forms of knowledge and techniques of governing considered significant for any sustainable transformations (Hines 1991; Cooper 1992; O'Dwyer 2003). Given the above, it is a logical conclusion that environmental impact-valuations require disciplinary and organisational boundary spanning processes, practices and expertise taking into account uncertainty, the severity of any potential hazards, complex interdependencies and incomplete, contradictory evidence and opinions (Frame and O'Connor 2011).

When evaluating any assemblage of environmental impact-valuations, we need to consider its alignment with sustainable development and whether it will perpetuate or accelerate global or local catastrophes and worsening social injustice (Gray 2010), rather than focus on accuracy or standardisability of measurement protocols. This places responsibility on environmental accountants as to how they choose to calculate impacts-valuations and ensure any impact-valuations take account of legitimate problematisations of past accounting environmental techniques and resistance to solutions promoted in other disciplines.

Environmental detachment – cutting the cord with nature

This stage involves exploring the choices made as to how and what is detached from selected socio-ecological systems prior to manipulation and transformation into an appropriable impact-valuation. For example, if we are interested in governing the water pollution from an industrial plant, then this will trigger a series of questions as to what evidence to collect to measure this impact.

- What is our definition of pollution?
- Where would we look for this information?
- Would we use evidence produced by the company?
- Would we collect our own measures of pollution?
- Would we include non-peer reviewed research?
- Would we use media coverage, anecdotes and oral testimony of local communities?

What is chosen to be detached (or excluded) will shape the calculative possibilities of all subsequent stages. Any detachment choice involves some form of reduction of the complexity of the systems to be measured and privileges different dimensions or impacts. Understanding and critically engaging with the theories or conceptual justification for what gets included/excluded is therefore important. It is critical to recognise that there is a contradiction between the detachment needed for valuation and the holistic nature of socioecological systems. Any detachment involves simplification and reductionism; therefore, all calculative choices should reflect on the extent and implications of this detachment.

Detachment choices must also consider the measurement technologies and the institutions controlling access to those technologies. These could include confidential lab results relating to process safety evaluations; radioactivity levels will require access to Geiger counters and trained operatives; satellite images will depend on access to satellites and so on. Given the political and economic sensitivity of many environmental impacts-valuations, it may not be possible to access the raw data. Instead, detachable information may be restricted to carefully curated and politically edited accounts.

Choices will have to be made as to the acceptability of different data sources, particularly when the detachment is secondary, that is, extracting data from existing calculative spaces such the US Toxic Release Inventory (EPA 2020) or UK Office of National Statistics (Sobkwiak et al. 2020). A number of useful insights into how to make these choices can be found in research into assurance, audit and research design (see chapters 9 and 4 of this handbook, respectively)

Brander (2016, 2017) identified the criticality of the attributional/consequential choice in the design of environmental impact-valuations. Attributional environmental measures use prescribed inventories or lists of impacts to be applied. These often relate to regulations, formal or voluntary governance mechanisms or codes of practice (e.g. UNEP 2004; WBCSD and WRI 2004; BRE 2008; DEFRA 2019; Ecolabel 2020; NECR 2020; EPA 2020). Going down the attributional pathway increases the comparability and consistency of impact-valuations and as such is favoured in formal governance and regulatory settings. However, Brander, in the context of climate change, demonstrated that attributional methods do not capture all critical consequences of a decision, which unintentionally increased rather than decreased carbon emissions. He argues that in most cases choosing a life cycle consequential calculation will improve the chances of selecting more sustainable options. Consequential calculations involve exploring different future scenarios and the construction of decision-specific theories of changes or causal chain maps, rather than applying predetermined inventories.

Consequential detachment is more aligned with the essential attributes from leading sustainability science research (Folke et al. 2010; Milkoreit et al. 2015) and sustainable political programmatic discourses, such as the United Nations' Sustainable Development Goals (UN SDGs), Planetary Boundaries; One Planet Economies (e.g. Allen et al. 2019; Keys et al. 2019). Detached data (in whatever form) should represent what happens in a system and how this affects interconnected systems over relevant action timescales. Measuring the impact of any decision taken anywhere in these interconnected systems requires understanding of what may happen at multiple scales and assumptions as to how the organisation plans to respond to innovations and constraints imposed from these overlapping systems. This also requires consideration of geographic boundaries, regulatory regimes, risks, dependency relationships, stakeholders, level of system coupling and connective vectors as well as culture and conflicts, associated with sustainable governance.

The desired outcome of any environmental impact-valuation is also a critical part of any detachment decision. Without some vision of the future state of socio-ecological systems after the decision, it is difficult to reflect on the quality of any calculative choices made. Imagine you were planning to undertake an environmental impact-valuation of your weekly food shopping. Could you meaningfully undertake this without a preference for specific food scenarios? These

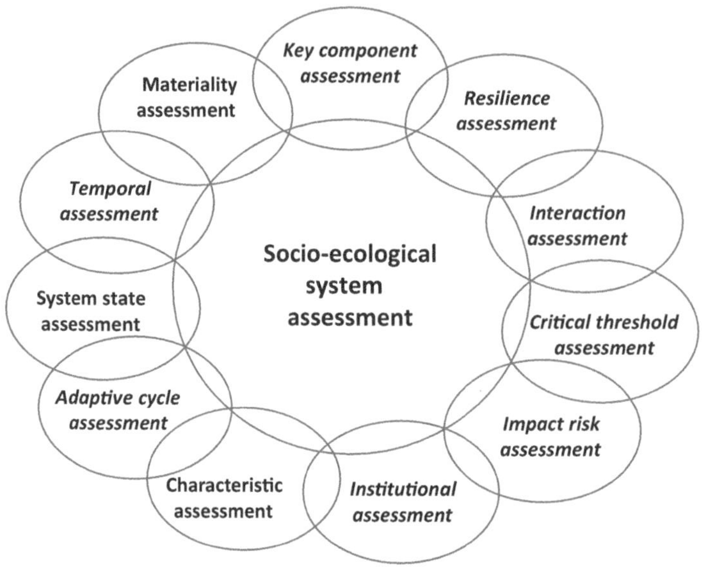

Figure 17.1 Socio-ecological systems assessment. (Source: Authors' construction from Resilience Alliance 2010.)

could include organic, Fairtrade, closed loop, zero carbon, zero waste, zero plastic and slave-free scenarios. These imagined future scenarios shape the detachment processes. Chapter 6 provides a useful distinction for environmental impact-valuation scenarios, classifying them as business-as-usual, adaptive or transformative. Other examples could include legally compliant, socially acceptable, remediative or restorative. Scenarios need to be explicitly considered and made transparent in how they inform detachment choices and other calculative choices.

The Resilience Alliance (2010) developed a comprehensive, consequentialist approach to assessing socio-ecological system that can inform sustainable detachment choices (see Figure 17.1 for key elements of this methodology).

This consequential assessment method helps identify the questions to ask and frames the responses to those questions in order that detachment choices are aligned with adaptive or transformative outcomes. This interdisciplinary approach can be used to evaluate the suitability of detached data that informs all subsequent environmental impact-valuation calculations. Whilst resilience assessment is built on a number of core concepts, it encourages the creation of contextually relevant assemblages of techniques and customising in relation to the data types and sources. It does not rely on a single set of data or techniques and assumes that any limitations of a single impact-valuation can be mitigated through the curation of other methods within the assemblage. For example, the assemblage could include scientific results of tests of river samples, regulatory breach reports, external social audits, media stories, satellite images, photographic evidence, historical maps and accounts, analysis of local myths, school projects, records of local bird watching clubs, interviews with local communities, discussions with local activists and so on.

The following list of questions is designed to help with data detachment choices:

- What are the outcome, desired scenarios or system configurations?
- What are the relevant disciplines and measurement techniques?

- To what extent is this an attributional or consequential set of techniques?
- What stages of the impact life cycle are included?
- How reliable are individual sources and their collective impact?
- How representative are the views/objectives included?
- How does the data reflect the interest of marginalised systems or communities?
- What systems are included/excluded?
- What is the time frame?
- Does it incorporate risks, uncertainties or system thresholds?
- Does it reflect power, conflicts and governance structures?
- What are the theories of system dynamics and change?
- Does it reflect the interconnections between different systems?
- Does it allow for the evaluation of current and future system states?
- Are there any methodological biases?

Manipulation and transformation – messing around with messy data

The second stage of environmental impact-valuation involves the manipulation and transformation of that which has been detached from socio-ecological systems. Impact-valuation work has now shifted from measuring things like "river", "forest" or "coastline" to processing the data gathered about "river", "forest" or "coastline". This involves manipulating and transforming the data into measurements that should be decision relevant; commensurable; culturally appropriate; aligned with laws, rules and regulations; compliant with disciplinary norms and socially acceptable. Central to this stage are transformation algorithms or protocols. Understanding the cumulative impact of these algorithms or protocols is critical to evaluating the meaningfulness of any environmental measurement assemblage.

Transformation algorithms or protocols often unintentionally exclude "non-compliant" or "non-legitimated" source material. This exclusion could include any qualitative data, "opinions", unknown sources or provenance and/or elements of pollution not subject to regulatory control. Chapters 7, 8 and 10 of this handbook demonstrate how exclusion protocols embedded in the financial reporting transformation algorithms result in manipulated representations of businesses. When evaluating any impact-valuations technique (or assemblage) it is important to identify potential bias, problematic exclusions or representational distortions in the transformation processes.

Throughout the handbook, examples are provided of how transformation problems or exclusions are often problematically black boxed. For example, current UK Financial Reporting guidance on how to transform attributional data on carbon emissions into financial reporting disclosures contains a number of exclusions (Ascui and Lovell 2011; Brander 2016, 2017; DEFRA 2019; see also Chapter 26). These "carbon emissions", which are proxies for business's contribution to global warming, are limited to scope 1 and 2 emissions (WBCSD and WRI 2004). The exclusion of scope 3 was the result of a choice to align reported carbon disclosures with the UK's carbon reduction commitment and international climate change conventions.[1] However, this choice results in carbon emissions embedded in purchased goods, assets, fuel, waste, travel, leased assets, product use and end-of-life being excluded from mandated financial disclosures.

These scope 1 and 2 carbon emissions are restricted to a scientific politically determined set of greenhouse gases (GHG) and do not include all global warming gases. A further exclusion relates to the cocktail of chemicals emitted with these GHG that damages human health, buildings and ecosystems. Choosing only to measure GHG volumes also excludes consideration of the inequitable social and geographic distribution of the harms of global warming.

The current UK manipulation and transformation of company actions into 'financial-reporting-carbon-emissions' is appropriate in the context of UK regulations to reduce carbon emissions. However, these exclusions make this measure inappropriate for other carbon-related decisions (Brander 2016, 2017). Excluding the full life cycle consequences, social impact and associated air pollution when calculating a climate change impact potentially allows short-term low-carbon, but socially unsustainable, options to be inappropriately evaluated as sustainable. However, this process resulted from a ***choice*** of a range of options as to how to detach and transform carbon emissions. This range of options includes life cycle carbon consequential methods that are aligned with sustainable outcomes, governance and system resilience (Brander 2017).

As discussed earlier, single-dimensional impact transformation algorithms or protocols are unlikely to provide useful insights into the multidimensional challenges associated with sustainable transformation or adaptation. Algorithms or protocols associated with multiple criterion models are more suitable to sustainable challenges as they enable interdimensional trade-offs or intersectional deliberative processes that are more visible, transparent and democratic (Frame and O'Connor 2011). Who is invited and when they participate in these processes will change the impact-valuations (Brown et al. 2011; Frame and O'Connor 2011; Denedo et al. 2018). Generally speaking, the less representative and the later participants are involved, the more likely the measure will contain bias or privilege the powerful.

There is an epistemic bias in environmental accounting to transform uncertain, future estimates of complex, multidimensional data into a single normalised figure, as either a score or financial value. This tendency can be problematic if it results in an oversimplification of complex chains of impacts or designed to minimise dissent or force consensus, particularly in relation to controversial topics. This tendency should also be recognised as a choice privileged in accounting calculations and there are many other ways to transform and manipulate data. These involve reporting ranges, contingent values, scenario outcomes, disaggregated data or profiles.

Bebbington et al. 2007 (see also Frame and Brown 2008; Frame and Cavanagh 2009; Xing et al. 2009; Fraser 2012) provide an example of a multidimensional consequential calculative assemblage that produces profiles of the positive and negative externalities associated with different activities. This approach allows greater transparency of the complexity of impacts and the possibility of more nuanced commensuration and decision-making.

Figure 17.2 represents two such profiles (framed as "signatures") which otherwise could have been represented by single numbers (e.g. the net sum of the total impacts above and below the line – or some variant thereof) with an attendant loss of information of the distribution of values across social, environmental, resources and economic dimensions. This approach to data decomposition and presentation, therefore, enhances the possibilities that the distribution of impacts can be brought into decision processes. It should be noted that each "stack" of impacts are themselves composites of multiple other values and this visual presentation of impact-values provides greater informational content and is less dependent on protocols/algorithms designed for informational reductionism.

To sum up this section, in addition to evaluating detachment choices there is a need to evaluate transformation and manipulation choices, in particular exclusions and potentially distorting calculative reductionism. However, there are calculative transformation protocols and algorithms that are more dialogic, transparent, inclusive, multidimensional, multidisciplinary, culturally sensitive and aligned to sustainability sciences. If choices are made to incorporate these protocols or algorithms in environmental impact-valuation assemblages, then the lower the probability of privileged, problematic impact-valuations (Bebbington and Thomson 2007; Frame and O'Connor 2011).

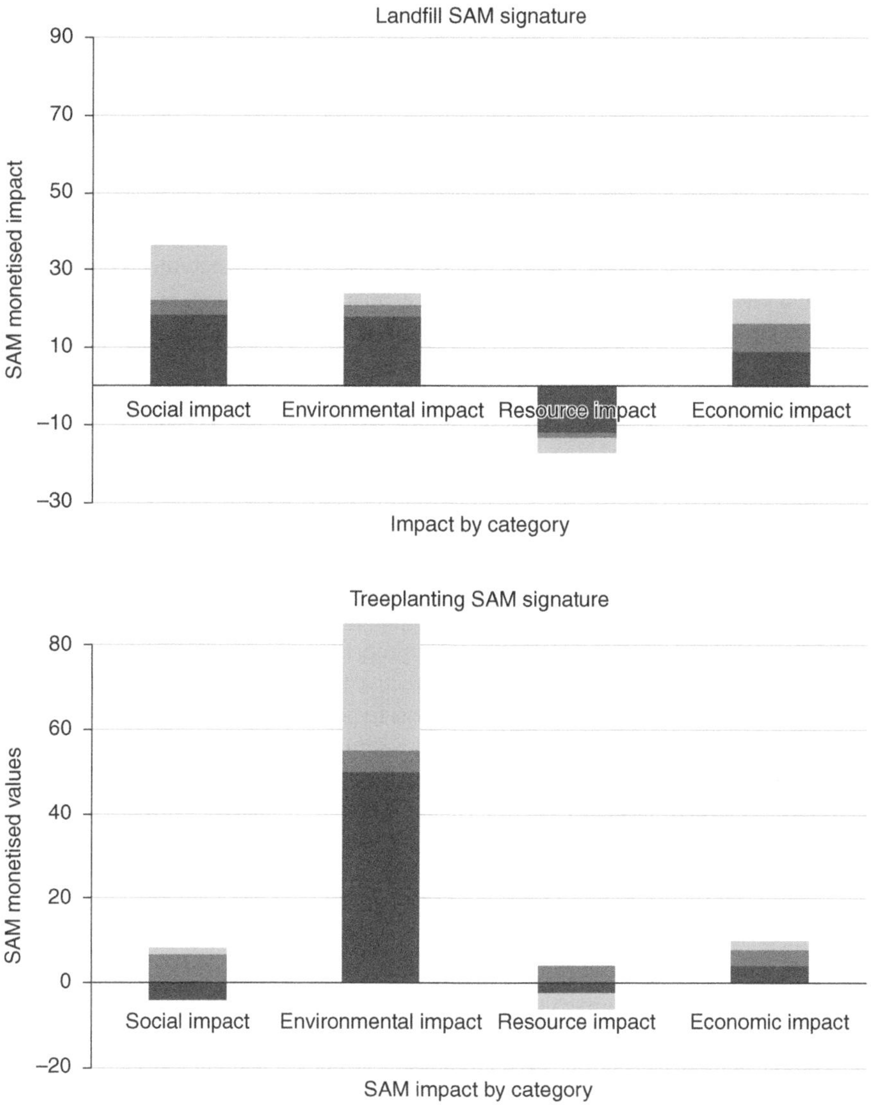

Figure 17.2 Examples of the output of the Sustainability Assessment Model. (Source: Provided by Jan Bebbington.)

In addition to the questions in detachment sections (many of which are applicable here), there are also some specific questions to inform the choice of environmental impact-valuations manipulation and transformation protocols or algorithms.

- What detached data is excluded?
- Are there any (sub)systems excluded in the impact-valuation?
- Are the impact-values co-produced with communities, non-expert or natural system advocates?

- How transparent, auditable, justifiable, understandable or accountable are the calculations?
- Are there any methodological or disciplinary bias in how data is transformed or manipulated?
- How is intragenerational and intergenerational equity taken into account?
- Are there risks of political interference?
- How are critical thresholds, adaptive capacity or systemic risks incorporated in the process?
- What information content is lost in calculative reductions or data visualisations?
- What is the logic underpinning the choice of impact-valuation results (e.g. point estimates, profiles or contingent values).
- How does the process deal with uncertainties, multiple scenarios or contradictory outcomes?
- How well does the assemblage deal with limitations in individual techniques?
- What underlying theories are used to justify transformation protocols?

Extraction and appropriation – pulling the right rabbit from the right hat

The third stage is shaped by choices as to what to extract from the impact-valuations created by the manipulation and transformation stages for input into decision processes (Callon and Muniesa 2005). Extracting and appropriating inappropriate impact-valuations into other decision-making models could trigger ineffective corrective interventions, increasing the risk of environmental harm or allowing problematic behaviours to persist (Russell and Thomson 2009).

There are two important consequences of this observation. First, the detachment, manipulation and transformation processes should be informed by an understanding of the decisions that need to be taken as part of sustainable governance. These stages need to consider the likely consequences of any numbers extracted in different decision contexts. For example, a "low willingness to pay" number for anthropocentrically unattractive keystone species, such as wasps or weevils, could result in decisions that reduce their population size below critical thresholds collapsing whole eco-systems.

Second, caution must be taken when extracting a value from one context and appropriating into decision processes without knowledge of potential limitations accruing from prior detachment, manipulations and transformation choices. An example would be investors assuming the amortised value of capitalised R&D in waste reduction technology is a measure of the innovative capacity of a business in relation to the environment. Without knowing how that figure is calculated (e.g. what is included/excluded; internal accounting transformation protocols; national accounting standards; professional disciplinary norms; regulatory implications; debt covenants; tax write-off potential; income smoothing choices; historic knowledge of investor reactions), this number should not be naively appropriated in a decision to "green" an investment portfolio.

It is important to remember that any environmental impact-valuation emerges from a complex sequence of diverse calculative practices, which cannot transcend any underlying limitations (Mol 1999; Callon and Muniesa 2005). Choices made at the detachment, manipulation and transformation stages *will* affect the usability of the impact measures.

Choices made as to how any impact-valuations are extracted are also important, particularly if that extraction is partial or ignores methodological or other known limitations. For example, the biodiversity value of a tropical forest (Cuckston 2013) could be an aggregation of separate values for:

- purification and regulation of water flows
- regulation of climate
- provision of food, fuel and fibres
- biological control of pests and disease
- prevention of soil erosion
- maintenance of soil fertility
- regulation of air quality
- oxygen production
- cultural services
- spiritual experience
- inspiration for art
- tourism.

However, the availability of these impact-valuations does not require any data users to extract all of these values. Choices will need to be made as to which values to extract and are appropriate based on different logics to that which informed the calculation of that number. For instance, to what extent is it valid to include a value that only aggregates *cultural services, spiritual experience, inspiration for art, and for tourism* for inclusion in a cost–benefit analysis for a forest conservation project? However, the existence of separate values, rather than reducing a forest's eco-system benefits to a single number, does enhance the possibility for more sustainable extraction and appropriation.

The more the detachment, manipulation and transformation stages embrace the attributes identified earlier, the greater the potential for meaningful extraction and appropriation. This potential will be enhanced, if extraction and appropriation is undertaken in a similar transparent, inclusive fashion. This will not remove the possibility of problematic decisions arising from structurally unsustainable decision processes or governance regimes, but incorporating these attributes into impact-valuation assemblages will reduce these risks.

Key questions for evaluating extraction choices include the following:

- How do values reflect complexity, adaptive capacity or uncertainty?
- How do they take into account different scenarios, power imbalances or time scales?
- What detached and transformed data is excluded?
- Do the extracted values obscure contradictory or contested measures?
- Do the extracted values help decision-makers learn about the problem and enable inclusive dialogue?
- Is the extraction process transparent, justifiable and accountable?
- How representative of the range of results are any extracted values?
- Are users able to apply their preferences, values, risk thresholds, outcomes or extraction protocols and decision rules?

Conclusion

We exist in a time of apparently unresolvable social and environmental problems. Unlocking them is a challenge and if environmental accounting is to play a meaningful role in this process, then researchers need to build capacity to evaluate, problematise and engage in designing environmental impact-valuation assemblages appropriate for sustainable transformation. This includes an understanding of what is allowing unsustainable practices to persist and why certain decision-makers are unable or unwilling to imagine sustainable solutions. Environmental impact-valuations have to consider where different unsustainable drivers come from, how they collide, interlock and intersect, in order for more effective targeted interventions and sustainable solutions. This requires a more holistic and inclusive measurement of decision consequences. This chapter has presented a framework with which to interrogate how any environmental impact-valuation is calculated in order to avoid known pitfalls and build in attributes that have been found to increase the chances of more sustainable governance and decision-making.

Note

1 These conventions only apply to scopes 1 and 2 ostensibly to avoid double counting of carbon emissions.

References

Allen, C., Metternicht, G., and Wiedmann, T., 2019. Prioritising SDG targets: Assessing baselines, gaps and interlinkages. *Sustainability Science,* 14, 421–438.

Ascui, F, Haward, M., and Lovell, H., 2018. Salmon, sensors, and translation: The agency of Big Data in environmental governance. *Environment and Planning D: Society and Space*, 36, 905–925

Ascui, F., and Lovell, H., 2011. As frames collide: Making sense of carbon accounting. *Accounting, Auditing and Accountability Journal*, 24(8), 978–999.

Antheaume, N., 2004. Valuing external costs - from theory to practice: Implications for full cost environmental accounting. *European Accounting Review*, 13(3), 443–464.

Bebbington, J., Brown, J., and Frame, B. 2007. Accounting technologies and sustainability assessment models. *Ecological Economics*, 61, 224–236.

Bebbington, J., and Larrinaga C., 2014. Accounting and sustainable development: An exploration. *Accounting, Organizations and Society*, 39, 395–413.

Bebbington, J., and Thomson, I., 2007. Social and environmental accounting, auditing and reporting: A potential source of organizational risk governance? *Environment and Planning C,* 25(1), 38–55.

Bebbington, J., and Thomson, I., 2013. Theorising sustainable management accounting. *Management Accounting Research*, 24(4), 277–284.

Beck, U., 1992. *Risk Society: Towards a New Modernity*. London: Sage.

Brander, M., 2016. Transposing lessons between different forms of consequential greenhouse gas accounting: lessons for consequential life cycle assessment, project-level accounting, and policy-level accounting. *Journal of Cleaner Production,* 112, 4247–4256.

Brander, M., 2017. Comparative analysis of attributional corporate greenhouse gas accounting, consequential life cycle assessment, and project/policy level accounting: A bioenergy case study. *Journal of Cleaner Production*, 167, 1401–1414.

BRE., 2008. *Global Methodology for Environmental Profiles of Construction Products*. available at: www.bre.co.uk.

Brown, G., Montag, J., and Lyon, K., 2011. Public participation GIS: A method for identifying eco-system services. *Society and Natural Resources*, 24, 633–651.

Callon, M., and Law, J., 2005. On qualculation, agency, and otherness. *Environment and Planning D: Society and Space,* 23(5), 717–733.

Callon, M., and Muniesa, F., 2005. Peripheral visions: Economic markets as calculative devices. *Organization Studies*, 26(8), 1229–1250.

Carroll, B., et al., 2020. *Environmental Impact Assessment Handbook: A practical Guide for Planners, Developers and Communities.* London: ICE Publishing.

Cooper, C., 1992. The non and nom of accounting for (m)other Nature. *Accounting, Auditing and Accountability Journal*, 6(3), 16–39.

Cordella, M., et al., 2020. Improving material efficiency in the life cycle of products: A review of EU Ecolabel criteria. *International Journal of Life Cycle Assessment*, 25, 921–935

Cuckston, T., 2013. Bringing tropical forest biodiversity conservation into financial accounting calculation. *Accounting, Auditing and Accountability Journal*, 26 (5), 688–714.

Cuckston, T., 2017. Ecology-centred accounting for biodiversity in the production of a blanket bog. *Accounting, Auditing and Accountability Journal*, 30(7), 1537–1567.

Cuckston, T., 2019. Seeking an ecologically defensible calculation of net loss/gain of biodiversity. *Accounting, Auditing and Accountability Journal*, 32 (5), 1358–1383.
DEFRA., 2019. *Environmental Reporting Guidelines: Including Streamlined Energy and Carbon Reporting and Greenhouse Gas Reporting*. London, UK; HMSO.
Denedo, M., Thomson, I., and Yonekura, A., 2018. Accountability, maps and inter-generational equity: Evaluating the Nigerian Oil Spill Monitor. *Public Money and Management*, 38(5), 355–364.
Ecolabel., 2020. https://ec.europa.eu/environment/ecolabel/.
Ecowatch., 2020. www.ecowatch.com/6-striking-aerial-images-show-how-deforestation-has-altered-the-earth–1882004620.html.
EPA., 2020. *Toxic Release Inventory*. www.epa.gov/toxics-release-inventory-tri-program/find-understand-and-use-tri.
Folke, C., et al., 2010. Resilience thinking: Integrating resilience, adaptability and transformability. *Ecology and Society*, 15(4), 20.
Frame, B., and Brown, J., 2008. Developing post-normal technologies for sustainability. *Ecological Economics*, 65(2), 225–241.
Frame, B., and Cavanagh, J., 2009. Experiences of sustainability assessment: An awkward adolescence. *Accounting Forum*, 33, 195–208.
Frame, B., and O'Connor, M., 2011. Integrating valuation and deliberation: The purposes of sustainability assessment. *Environment Science and Policy*, 14(1), 1–10.
Fraser, M., 2012. Fleshing out an engagement with a social accounting technology. *Accounting, Auditing and Accountability Journal*, 25(3), 508–534.
Futurefit., 2020. *Methodology Guide*. https://futurefitbusiness.org/benchmark-documents/.
Gallo, A. et al., 2016. Questioning the ecological footprint. *Ecological Indicators*, 69, 224–232.
Global Footprint Network, 2020. www.footprintnetwork.org/.
Gray, R., 2010. Is accounting for sustainability actually accounting for sustainability and how would we know? *Accounting, Organizations and Society*, 35(1), 47–62.
Herbohn, K., 2005. A full cost environmental accounting experiment. *Accounting Organizations and Society*, 30(6), 519–536.
Hines, R., 1991. On valuing nature. *Accounting, Auditing and Accountability Journal*, 4(3), 27–29.
IMBIE., 2020. http://imbie.org/data-downloads/.
Infrastructure Auckland., 2004. *Manual for MCE*, Auckland, NZ; Infrastructure Auckland.
Keys, P., et al., 2019. Anthropocene risk. *Nature Sustainability*, 2, 667–673.
Maunders, K., and Burritt, R., 1991. Accounting and ecological crisis. *Accounting, Auditing and Accountability Journal*, 4(3), 9–26.
Milkoreit, M., et al., 2015. Resilience scientists as change-makers—Growing the middle ground between science and advocacy? *Environmental Science and Policy*, 5(3), 87 – 95.
Mol, A., 1999. Ontological politics. A word and some questions. *The Sociological Review*, 47(1), 74–89.
Naess, A., 2005. *The Selected Works of Arne Naess*. Dordrecht: Springer.
Natural Capital Alliance., 2020. Natural capital protocols. available at https://naturalcapitalcoalition.org/natural-capital-protocol/.
NECR., 2020. *ESIA and SEA for Sustainable Hydropower Development*. Utrecht, NL: The Netherlands Commission for Environmental Assessment.
O'Dwyer, B., 2003. Conceptions of corporate social responsibility: The nature of managerial capture. *Accounting, Auditing and Accountability Journal*, 16(4), 523–557.
Pritchard, L., Folke, C., and Gunderson, L., 2000. Valuation of ecosystem services in institutional context. *Ecosystems*, 3(1), 36–40.
Resilience Alliance., 2010. *Assessing Resilience in Social-Ecological Systems: Workbook for Practitioners*. www.resalliance.org/resilience-assessment.
Russell, S., and Thomson, I., 2009. Analysing the role of sustainable development indicators in accounting for and constructing a Sustainable Scotland. *Accounting Forum*, 33(3), 225–244.
Sieber, R., 2006. Public participation geographic information systems. *Annals of the Association of American Geographers*, 96(3), 491–507.
Sobkwiak, M., Thomson, I., and Cuckson, T., 2020. Framing sustainable development challenges: Accounting for SDG–15 in the UK. *Accounting, Auditing and Accountability Journal, 33(7), 1671-1703.*
UNEP., 2004. *Environmental Impact Assessment and Strategic Environmental Assessment: Towards an Integrated Approach*. https://unep.ch/etu/publications/textONUBr.pdf.

Unerman, J., and Chapman, C., 2014. Academic contributions to enhancing accounting for sustainable development. *Accounting, Organizations and Society*, 39(6), 385–394.
WBCSD and WRI., 2004. *The Greenhouse Gas Protocol: A Corporate Accounting and Reporting Standard: Revised Edition*, WBCSD and WRI, USA.
Wendling, L., et al., 2018. Nature-based solution and smart city assessment schemes against the Sustainable Development Goal Indicator Framework. *Frontiers in Environmental Science,* 6, 69.
World Benchmarking Alliance., 2020. www.worldbenchmarkingalliance.org/.
Xing, Y., et al., 2009. A framework model for assessing sustainability impacts of urban development. *Accounting Forum*, 33(3), 209–224.

18
ACCOUNTING FOR CIRCULARITY

Lucy Wishart and Nicolas Antheaume

Introduction

Every year humans dispose of over 2 billion (bn) tonnes of solid waste and the World Bank estimates that by 2050 this will increase to over 3.4 bn tonnes (Kaza et al. 2018). Our current economic system is worryingly linear: with resources following a "take, make, use, dispose" model. Haas et al. (2015) analysed global material flows, waste production and recycling to investigate the circularity (or linearity) of the current global economy. They found that just 6.6% of the raw materials processed worldwide are recycled, despite the fact that access to raw materials is becoming more difficult.

Increased circularity will require a radical transformation of our economic systems with more efficient recycling and waste management processes, but also with a shift in production methods and increased employment of eco-design strategies (Haas et al. 2015). The circular economy (CE) has emerged as an idea which encapsulates many sustainable resource management objectives from zero waste to cradle-to-cradle design and from cleaner production to reducing consumption (Corvellec et al. 2020). A popular definition of CE, but by no means the only one, is that promoted by the Ellen McArthur Foundation (EMF) (a think tank established in 2012 that is influential in shaping policy and business discourse in the CE). EMF describes the CE as:

> [A]n industrial system that is restorative or regenerative by intention and design. It replaces the "end-of-life" concept with restoration, shifts towards the use of renewable energy, eliminates the use of toxic chemicals, which impair reuse, and aims for the elimination of waste through the superior design of materials, products, systems, and, within this, business models.
>
> *(Ellen McArthur Foundation 2013, p. 7)*

The above definition indicates a clear emphasis on the need of closed-loops of material use.

Within academic literature there has been a growing interest in the idea of a CE (Geissdoerfer et al. 2017; Kirchherr et al. 2017; Korhonen et al. 2018; Prieto-Sandoval et al. 2018). However, there is no singular definition of the concept (Geissdoerfer et al. 2017; Korhonen et al. 2018): in their review, Kirchherr et al. (2017) identified 114 definitions of CE used across academic literature and policy documents. As a consequence, a number of studies have tried to make sense of how the CE is used in scholarship: Boldrini and Antheaume (2019a) identified 15 reviews of literature on the subject, with only one study published before 2016. There has been a notable lack of attention paid to the idea within organisation and accountancy (Murray et al. 2017; Swensson and Funck 2019). In this chapter we offer some clarity on the concept of the CE and how it might present consequences within the field of accounting.

In the second section of this chapter we give a review of academic literature on CE proposing a short history of the concept, as well as an overview of current achievements and challenges in the transition to a CE. In the third section we consider accounting for the transition to a CE, using existing literature to identify potential consequences for the accounting field and highlighting current gaps in understanding. In the final section we explore a case study which relates to the application of CE.

The concept of circular economy

In order to explore the consequences of adopting a CE goal for the field of accounting it is first important to understand what the concept means. The variety of definitions and ideas associated with the CE makes this no easy task and so in this section we focus closely on the organisational requirements of businesses. We give a short history and a summary of the main concepts associated with a CE, and then begin to imagine what a transition towards a CE requires, allowing us to focus on exploring particular business models for the CE and identifying the limitations of the current literature, and which leads us to suggest perspectives for future research.

A short history of the circular economy

The history of the CE is complex; the concept has multiple affiliations. Its use within various fields and sources means that there is no singular definition of the term "CE" within academic or policy sources, although a number of recent papers have tried to clarify what is meant by the term (Geissdoerfer et al. 2017; Kirchherr et al. 2017; Ghisellini et al. 2016). These papers show that CE research is grounded in eco-efficiency literature as well as in more radical limits-to-growth debates found in transformational sustainability studies (Kalmykova et al. 2018).

For some, CE is closely associated with the ideas of Industrial Ecology which emerged in the 1970s inspired by the Club of Rome's report on the limits of growth (Meadows et al. 1972). Industrial Ecology is a field of study which is inspired by the cyclical operations of natural ecosystems, and considers the flows of materials and energy in order to create closed-loop systems between economic actors. Industrial Ecology has created concepts such as "industrial metabolism", an idea which encourages analysis of the inefficiencies of flows of matter and energy (Ayres 1989); "regenerative design" which promotes the need to extend the concept of regeneration beyond agriculture to other materials within geographically defined communities (Lyle 1996) and "cradle to cradle" which highlights the importance of manufacturers to take responsibility for the full life cycle of their product (Braungart and McDonough 2002). Stahel (2006) described the CE as a generic framework in which a number of concepts such as eco-efficiency, closed-loop and product-service systems are "nested".

Its industrial ecology roots have meant that the CE concept is often depicted as a technical idea focused on improving material efficiencies, primarily through recycling (Kirchherr et al. 2017; Ghisellini et al. 2016). However, some have criticised this depiction of the CE, arguing that it focuses too heavily on recycling, failing to adequately address waste reduction and lacking a consideration of the radical societal transformations also required for a CE (Kalmykova et al. 2018; Hobson 2016; Camacho-Otero et al. 2018; Korhonen et al. 2018). Some critical scholars have questioned whether the emphasis of the technical elements of the CE undermines its possibility as a strong sustainability concept, promoting transformational change towards a more ecologically friendly society (Schröder et al. 2019).

Organising the transition to a circular economy

Moving to a CE implies refusing a linear approach in which resources are extracted from the environment, transformed, used, disposed of and returned, as waste, to the environment. Instead, the CE encourages limiting the extraction of new resources and extending the life of existing resources within the economy. Moreover, CE goals are met by adopting a system of preference which prioritises reducing, reusing, repairing over recycling (commonly referred to as the waste hierarchy) in order to reduce the overall environmental impact of the CE. For example, using the waste hierarchy model, a return system for glass bottles will be preferred to a recycling scheme. With a return system, consumers take bottles back to retailers, manufacturers pick up the empty bottles as they come and deliver full ones. The bottles are washed and reused. Only broken bottles are recycled. A CE scheme by which consumers dispose of their glass bottles directly to recycling centres presents an extra cost in terms of energy, and so under the waste hierarchy is considered a second-best solution only.

CE objectives can therefore be achieved by neither consumers nor producers alone, and CE policies are found across multiple scales. Kirchherr et al. (2017; p. 225) maintained that CE must operate at "micro level (products, companies, consumers), meso level (eco-industrial parks) and macro level (region, nation and beyond)" which will require multiple stakeholder engagement including with citizens (Hobson 2016) and wider communities.

At a macro-systems level, policy changes are needed to reorient the structure of the economy towards sustainable production and consumption (Ghisellini et al. 2016; Su et al. 2013). At the moment CE strategies are implemented across various directions – economic systems change (cities, regions and states) and change within specific sectors (material and product) such as electronics or agriculture (Kalmykova et al. 2018). Prieto-Sandoval et al. (2018) argue that both approaches are important, as CE collaboration between organisations is dependent on both geography and common vision.

At a meso-systems level, a transition to the CE implies an increase in diversity of stakeholders involved in organisational practices as well as in the setting up of new forms of governance. According to Acquier et al. (2011), this systems transformation entails transaction costs (setting up a relationship, negotiating, implication of not-for-profit stakeholders, new political and cost-calculation approaches).

At a micro-level, within individual organisations the principles of CE are often translated into business models (Bocken et al. 2016). The transition to a CE will require a systemic shift in business approaches (Frishammar and Parida 2019) as "revaluing waste as a resource requires actions across more than one firm" (Perey et al. 2018, p. 632) and so these new business models inevitably require cooperation.

Business models for the circular economy: a need for cooperation

Cooperation amongst organisations can help overcome some of the technical difficulties associated with the CE through knowledge sharing (Prieto-Sandoval et al. 2018) as well as helping individual companies respond to broader market demands (ibid) and increasing transparency: a necessity for CE system (Pauliuk 2018).

However, despite a need for organisational collaboration within a CE, cooperation cannot be achieved without consideration for the current, competitive, economic context. Stakeholders may be more likely to be in a situation of competition and strategies will vary depending on the position of each stakeholder within the supply chain and production system (Kalmykova et al. 2018).

Cooperation may be easier when organisations are not in direct competition with one another. Industrial ecoparks – where resources are shared and waste is recycled across industries – are a classic example of such situations. The most cited example, with over 40 years of operations, is perhaps Kalundborg[1] (Ehrenfeld and Gertler 1997). Although the generalisation to other contexts, such as those envisaged by industrial ecology thinking, may be difficult (ibid), this case illustrates that local authorities and communities, not just businesses play an important role in facilitating connexions and making things happen.

More research is needed and calls have been made to better understand barriers to CE in relation to particular business models (Kirchherr et al. 2018; Lahti et al. 2018). There is also a recognised need in the CE literature for further consideration of business models/businesses which address strong sustainability and slower forms of consumption (Geissdoerfer et al. 2017).

Limitations and perspectives for future research on the circular economy

Until now, a major focus of the CE literature has been on technical elements of a transition towards a closed-loop system (Camacho-Otero et al. 2018; Korhonen et al. 2018) with an emphasis on recycling (Kirchherr et al. 2017; Ghisellini et al. 2016); and yet, barriers to CE have been found to be technical but also cultural, regulatory and market-based (Kirchherr et al. 2018). Furthermore, existing CE scholarship tends to consider the role of governments and business (Geissdoerfer et al. 2017): undermining CE's potential as a paradigm shifting concept and breaking with the predominant idea that a truly sustainable CE requires cross-board systems change (Perey et al. 2018; Kirchherr et al. 2018) which must include a diversity of perspectives on the concept from a wide variety of stakeholders (Millar et al. 2019).

This technical focus draws attention to the depiction of critical CE visions. Questions have been raised within literature on the beneficiaries of the CE and whether the concept is a sustainability or economic goal (Kirchherr et al. 2017; Korhonen et al. 2018). Although many argue that the concept does have inherent links to sustainability (Kirchherr et al. 2017; Hobson 2016), more work is needed to integrate social issues and organisational perspectives within CE understanding (Camacho-Otero et al. 2018; Murray et al. 2017; Geissdoerfer et al. 2017; Korhonen et al. 2018; Millar et al. 2019). In particular, critical perspectives are lacking on such issues as power (Valenzuela and Böhm 2017; Hobson and Lynch 2016; Camacho-Otero et al. 2018) and responsibility (Camacho-Otero et al. 2018; Hobson 2016; Murray et al. 2017), particularly in relation to organisations and operations at meso levels (Camacho-Otero et al. 2018; Murray et al. 2017; Korhonen et al. 2018; Pauliuk 2018).

Linking these critical perspectives to research on how to implement CE strategies raises questions about how to evaluate CE with further consideration needed of what are the units of analysis and at what level this evaluation occurs (Korhonen et al. 2018). Despite the recognition that CE is still a concept with unclear boundaries, multiple definitions and subject to debate, there is still an importance of specific measures to account for progress towards CE.

This leads us to investigate the roles accounting can play in the transition to a CE.

Accounting for a circular economy

Whilst the CE has yet to be fully explored within the accounting field, current literature seems to encourage the use of accounting practices to facilitate the transition towards the CE. Some researchers suggest that one framework should be able to embrace and monitor all the characteristics of CE (Elia et al. 2017; Iacovidou et al. 2017). Proposals have emerged for frameworks, typologies or lists of indicators which encompass a wide range of measurements (Pauliuk 2018; Moraga et al. 2019; Sassanelli et al. 2019; Saidani et al. 2019). We offer a brief discussion of some of these proposals, identify limitations with current approaches and suggest how accountancy research could be used to establish a deeper transition towards the CE.

Identifying indicators and existing standards for CE

In practice, an accounting standard (BS 8001:2017) for the CE already exists but as Pauliuk (2018) notes, within this framework organisations are left responsible for choosing appropriate CE indicators and very little guidance is provided on monitoring the implementation of a CE strategy. Pauliuk (2018) suggests extending the scope of BS 8001:2017 by developing a dashboard which uses a number of indicators ensuring a focus on the environmental dimensions of a CE.

In their review of CE performance assessment at the organisational level, Sassanelli et al. (2019) identified Life Cycle Assessment (LCA) as the most frequently used tool (15/45 articles). Within these studies a stronger focus was placed on environmental impacts than on economic dimensions, with social elements of the CE rarely considered, with the exception of Iacovidou et al. (2017). As a consequence, Sassanelli et al. (2019) argued literature on circularity assessment currently predominantly considers indicators linked to material flows. Furthermore, only half of performance assessments encompass the whole cycle, with a third focusing solely on the beginning of life and a fifth on the end of life (ibid).

In another study, Moraga et al. (2019) explicitly considered the questions of "what" and "how" to measure in their categorisations of CE indicators. Through these questions they proposed an inventory of existing indicators which again focus on materials and products. More radical CE strategies (refuse, rethink, reduce and so on) and social indicators are not considered. From Morago et al.'s (2019) inventory it is not clear what accounting techniques can be used to address the economic growth and social equity elements of CE, thus rendering the idea of a technical term for managing material flows (Millar et al. 2019).

Saidani et al. (2019) propose a CE taxonomy based on the needs of users. The end result is an application which supports the search for appropriate indicators by asking questions on the scale of measurement, the type of circularity performance, the usages and the purposes envisioned, the types of circularity loops. The focus once again is primarily on environmental dimensions, and less on economic considerations, with attention being paid to product design, industrial processes, logistics, material flows and energy. No consideration is given to social elements of a CE.

The classifications and typologies of indicators, such as the very small selection presented in Table 18.1, are relevant to accounting for circularity. They are useful for the identification of gaps in what is currently measured, for proposing future frameworks, as well as for the creation of guidelines and conventions. However, these classifications also, in turn, shape understandings of the CE concept and, as for financial accounting, its reality (Hines 1988). Thus, scrutiny of the underlying methodologies is important.

Table 18.1 A selection of indicators related to the circular economy (selected from Iacovidou et al. 2017)

CE strategy	*Metric*	*Description*	*Unit*
Avoid	Avoided carbon emissions	Savings accruing from reductions in quantity and quality of primary materials, based on the sum of avoided unit inputs (in kg), multiplied by the process-specific input emission-factor (e.g. $kgCO_2e/kg$).	tCO_2e
Remanufacture	Remanufacturability	Potential to restore a component/product to like-new condition through measuring, disassembly, cleaning, inspection and sorting, part repair/ refurbishment/ replacement, reassembly and final testing, on a weight or item basis.	% weight or item
Recover	Weight recovery (product recovered)	Measured based on the difference between the mass of the product and the sum of material waste as output from recovery process x, divided by the mass of the product.	% weight
Recycle	Technical recyclability	Proportion of the material, or component made of only one material collected for recycling that will be recycled for producing high-quality recycled MCPs.	% weight

Methodological limitations

So far most of the research on accounting for circularity has been based on reviews of literature. Studies have focused on defining typologies and frameworks, on identifying which indicators correspond to which levels (micro, meso and macro) and to which needs. The measurement of physical flows, and their interpretation in terms of environmental impact, is given a lot of consideration. However, even for physical flows, data is lacking and research is underdeveloped (Kalmykova et al. 2018). A number of techniques presented in other chapters of this book could possibly be used to account for circularity (carbon accounting, materials accounting, energy accounting, externalities, etc.).

The current literature on accounting for circularity also does not address such issues as cooperation, transaction costs, innovation, new approaches to cost calculation, capabilities and power relationships within networks, and strong sustainability. We suggest that an alternative methodology for considering accounting practices within the CE is the use of individual case studies, the results of which have wider implications than the case itself.

Expanding research possibilities using case studies

Limited examples of using case studies to understand CE and accountancy exist. Swensson and Funck (2019) presented three different organisations and examined the implications of their CE practices for management control. They concluded that a CE culture and new cultural controls must be present in organisations in order for management control to focus on circularity. They also showed how strategic planning and action plans change in order to meet CE objectives. Budgets adapt, new performance measurements appear (mostly non-financial ones), as well as (sometimes), reward and compensation systems. More attention is being paid to the early design phase of a product or service, which has a strong impact on future possibilities to prolong the life, and promote the reuse or recycling of materials. Also, the imperatives of CE make management control focus on the long-term effect of decisions. For example, in the field of procurement, life extension strategies for equipment lead to consider maintenance, usage as well as end-of-life costs, rather than just acquisition costs. These evolutions may affect the whole management accounting package used by the organisation.

Taking a measurement-oriented perspective, Lonca et al. (2019) conducted a case study on used tires and questioned the idea that material circularity is consistent with environmental efficiency. In the context of Brazil, they compared the re-treading and re-grooving of tires to the baseline scenario of buying new tires. The results are complicated; while re-treading tires improves material circularity, the tires are less efficient and lead vehicles to consume more fuel. Although environmental impacts of tires may be reduced at a micro-level by repurposing, on a macro scale, the consequences of this act of circularity are mixed. The paper also suggests that circularity and the reduction of environmental and health impacts will not always align. As a result, the challenge for experts seeking to develop an accounting framework for the CE is that it must be designed with a systemic view in mind. There is a need for an extended framework which would include environmental, economic and social indicators at different scales; and a way to view these outcomes as a whole, in order to avoid cherry-picking (Pauliuk 2018, p. 91) by companies and also to support transformational systems change.

We found that almost no accounting scholars have published on accounting for circularity. We believe that there is room for accountants to take part in this debate and we argue that case studies, the conclusions of which have wider implications than the case itself, are a sensible methodology to provide helpful contributions to the conversation of accounting for CE. With this in mind, in the next section we present a case study on an agricultural cooperative in France from which we can draw lessons on accounting for the CE.

Case study: innovation in horticultural farming

Our case study concerns SMART[2], an inter-organisational research and development (R&D) project involving a manufacturer of agricultural plastic films with horticultural farmers, and including five other partners (two professional bodies, a technical centre, a school of engineering in agronomy and a university). For further details on the project, see Antheaume and Boldrini (2017) and Boldrini and Antheaume (2019b). The SMART project is based near the city of Nantes, in the North West of France, in the department of *Loire Atlantique*, known for horticultural farming. The study took place between 2014 and 2018. One of us (Antheaume) participated in the project as an academic observer to evaluate environmental and economic benefits. In the following section we explain the socio-economic and material context for circularity, analyse the resource consequences of the project and explore the role of accounting in facilitating the results.

The context: plastic circularity and farming in the Loire Valley

Horticultural farming in *Loire Atlantique* is a highly mechanised "industry". The main produce are the vegetable Lamb's Lettuce and the flower, Lily of the Valley[3]. Tractors are used for sowing, laying and dismantling tunnels, harvesting and ploughing. Crops are grown on mounded rows with plastic polyethylene films being essential inputs. They are stretched over tunnel arches so as to protect seedlings and young shoots from bad weather and diseases, and accelerate the plant growth. Once dismantled, the plastic films are collected by *Adivalor*, a national organisation which is funded through a tax on agricultural plastics. The used films are "downcycled" in order to make garbage bags and tarpaulins.

Farmers are subject to intense pressure from the retail industry with no firm commitment over the long, or even the medium, term. As a consequence, they have organised themselves in cooperatives, allowing them to share equipment and to increase their bargaining power with suppliers. Plastic film manufacturers are thus under intense pressure from their farming customers; however, they have very little bargaining power with their suppliers of plastic pellet (major international petrochemical companies). It is worth mentioning that representatives of neither the retailing nor petrochemical industry were part of the project.

The case study followed a project, the aim of which was to conceive a new and local business relationship where the farmers return the used films directly to the original manufacturer, who then "isocycles"[4] the film and delivers it back to the farmers, thus bypassing *Adivalor*. The manufacturer would become both a supplier of plastics and a collector of used plastics. Although a simple idea in theory, only a guaranteed level of activity over three years would ensure sufficient revenues to make the initial investment worthwhile. The SMART project received funding from the region of *Pays de la Loire* in order to finance an experimental phase, for a period of four years.

Boldrini and Antheaume contributed to the project by considering the costs and environmental impacts of films' lifecycle for 1 km of mounded rows, for one harvest (approximately 1,000 m or 57 kg of film). See Figure 18.1 for the boundaries of the analysis. The baseline scenario was made up of two linear sequences (a+a), as represented in Figure 18.1, which was compared to a linear sequence + a recycling loop (a+b), in which the films contain 50% of isocycled plastic films.

The analysis: performance of the circular system

From a material perspective, the baseline scenario used more virgin plastic (114 kg) in comparison with the alternative circular scenario (85.5 kg of plastic). However, the environmental impacts of both scenarios were then evaluated using LCA and secondary data from the ecoinvent database. This process involved estimating the physical material flows of the system, and interpreted them in terms of impacts on the environment. Standardized end-point indicators were used for impacts on human health, on the natural environment as well as for depletion of

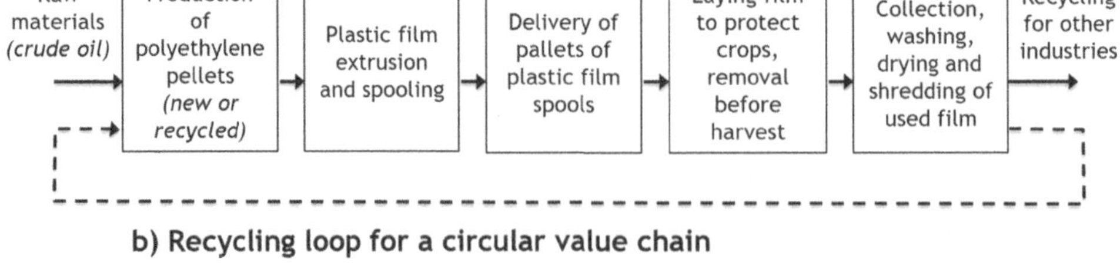

Figure 18.1 Boundaries of the study (based on Boldrini and Antheaume 2019b).

natural resources (JRC-IES 2010). Compared to the baseline scenario, the alternative circular scenario scored better on the three indicators.

Analysis published elsewhere (Antheaume and Boldrini 2017) considers the impacts of transport, comparing two baseline scenarios with two alternative circular scenarios. The first baseline scenario assumed the farmers would work with the local plastic film manufacturer, involved in the experiment. The second baseline scenario assumed the manufacturer was the main competitor, located 700 km away. The same process was conducted with the alternative scenario (local manufacturer and main competitor). The best scenario (the one with the least kilometres travelled) was the alternative scenario with the local manufacturer. The second best scenario was the baseline scenario with the local manufacturer. Scenarios with the main competitor came third (baseline) and fourth (alternative). As a result, the closer the farmers are to the manufacturer, the lower transport costs and emissions will be. For a circular economy scheme to bring environmental benefits and economic gains, geographical proximity seems to be an important criterion.

Finally, manufacturing costs were analysed. The plastic material included in a roll of film represented half the cost of the roll. For the alternative circular scenario to provide economic benefits, any saving in reusing the plastic materials would need to outweigh the cost of collecting, sorting, washing and shredding the waste before turning it into plastic pellets. There was no difference in costs between plastic pellets made from 100% of raw materials and plastic pellets with recycled content. With economies of scale there are perspectives for reducing the cost of plastic pellets for example by using the equipment at full capacity, rather than for small quantities and by continuously improving collecting, cleaning and shredding processes.

However, one should be aware of the limitations of this work. Most of the data used for SMART was secondary data from databases used by LCA software solutions. The results in terms of environmental performance can be interpreted as an average based on data extracted from the literature. It would be a mistake to interpret the result as a "true and fair" view of horticultural farming from *Loire Atlantique*, in France. By comparison, despite concerns for confidentiality, economic data proved relatively easy to collect, from the farmers, the cooperatives and the plastic film manufacturer. Societal data had no role within the project, reflecting what has been identified in the literature.

Discussion: accounting for CE

Despite limitations in the quality of the data, the analysis showed the potential for a convergence between economic and environmental gains. Even though the project was able to demonstrate the existence of gains it proved impossible for the parties involved to move from an experimental phase to a full implementation of the project. The researchers involved in the process observed a number of political, organisational, cultural and legal obstacles which stood in the way of a transition towards a CE. We present them and discuss their implications for accounting.

Firstly, not all the relevant stakeholders were involved in SMART. For example, the involvement of key retailers was missing. Would committed retailers have accepted long-term commitments with the farmers? In turn, might have this encouraged the farmers to take long-term commitments with the plastic film manufacturer? Cooperation, which was presented as necessary ingredient earlier on, was not present. Constraints at the level of each organisation (micro level) were too strong for inter-organisational cooperation to emerge (meso level).

Policy changes enacted by government (macro level) would have been needed to facilitate the emergence of cooperation, beyond the experimental phase. Indeed, as discussed earlier, a multi-level perspective is needed to move forward.

For example, a more radical change, more in line with the waste management hierarchy presented in the first section, would require the design of re-usable plastic tunnels. The films would be thicker in order to ensure durability and require more labour to install and uninstall. The films would not be recycled after each use, but once every two years. A careful design of the film might thus save raw materials, create agricultural jobs, save transport, optimise recycling and rely less on tractors that consume fossil fuels. Compared to this radical change, recycling used films is probably better than landfilling but it is not optimal. It may consume more water, non-renewable materials and energy than a labour-intensive solution. Actually, some 30 years ago, re-usable films were found in horticultural farming. However, in order to respond to evolving policy and economic incentives, it became necessary to "industrialise" processes, to rely less on labour and re-usable products, and to produce more crops.

As a consequence, accounting for circularity can never be complete if it does not take into account a larger picture. This is why, as discussed earlier, the focus of accounting for CE should not just be technical, but integrate social issues, organisational perspectives and critical perspectives with issues of power and responsibility.

Conclusion

Despite data limitations, in the case of SMART, it proved possible to measure the impacts of a CE project that had already been designed which, if implemented, would have been a marginal improvement to the existing situation. Even if this small improvement was demonstrated and proven, there were too many obstacles for it to be implemented. Accounting on its own was not enough to provoke change. Also, the scope of this project was such that it did not explore and assess alternative solutions to recycling. Even if we know that more labour-intensive alternatives might have been better from an environmental and social point of view, they are probably not within reach given current economic conditions.

Reflecting on this case, it is possible to suggest that an accounting framework for the CE should not just measure the costs, environmental impacts and social impacts of a given CE project. It should also help evaluate the relevance of projects and help shape policy. However, if we consider that accounting for the CE should "show the way forward", then issues of cooperation and inclusion of all stakeholders are major ones to be considered. There is more to accounting for the CE than developing indicators. Current research is dominated by environmental indicators that are derived from well-known methods such as LCA and MFA, but which implicitly narrow down accounting for the CE to a technical subject. However, the lack of research on social indicators related to the circular economy should be an encouragement for accountants to make proposals.

Finally, an accounting framework for the transition to a CE should start from the founding principle that no one organisation can become circular on its own. Thus, it should focus on how an organisation contributes to common objectives, at micro, meso and macro levels. It should thus clearly identify the value created by each organisation as distinct from the value created at the level of system. Common value created is not the sum of individual values and value creation at the level of one organisation should not be allowed if it is done at the expense of common value.

Notes

1 www.symbiosis.dk/en/, accessed on 24 June 2020.
2 SMART stands for *Sustainability, Material, Agreement, Recycling, Together.*
3 Of the 60,000 tonnes of Lamb's Lettuce produced in Europe, 50% comes from this region. Eighty per cent of the French production of Lilly of the valley, a flower sold on Labour Day, comes from this region. Farmers from this region are also the number one producer in France for radish, cucumber and early leeks.
4 "isocycle": neologism meaning same function, same value or same quality after second use or recycling.

References

Acquier, A., Daudigeos, T. and Valiorgue, B., 2011. Responsabiliser les chaînes de valeur éclatées, Enjeux et limites. *Revue française de gestion*, 215, 167–183.

Antheaume, N. and Boldrini, J.C., 2017. La convergence entre gain économique et gain écologique en économie circulaire. *L'expérimentation d'une innovation environnementale dans le maraîchage nantais.* Available from: https://hal.archives-ouvertes.fr/hal–01460080/document, [Accessed 10 February 2020].

Ayres, R.U., 1989. Industrial metabolism: theory and policy. In: Ayres, R.U. and Simonis, U.K. (Eds.), *Industrial Metabolism: Restructuring for Sustainable Development.* Tokyo: United Nations University Press.

Bocken, N.P. et al., 2016. Product design and business model strategies for a circular economy. *Journal of Industrial and Production Engineering*, 33(5), 308–320.

Boldrini, J.C. and Antheaume, N., 2019a. Une transition vers quelle économie circulaire? A transition to which circular economy? *Technologie et Innovation, Techonology and Innovation*, 19(4), Open Science, Available from: www.openscience.fr/Une-transition-vers-quelle-economie-circulaire, [Accessed 3 February 2020].

Boldrini, J.C. and Antheaume, N., 2019b. Visualizing the connection and the alignment between business models in a circular economy. A circular framework based on the RCOV model. *28th congress of the Association for International Management and Strategy (AIMS)*, Dakar, Sénégal.

Braungart, M. and McDonough, W., 2002. *Cradle to cradle. Remaking the way we make things.* New York: North Point Press.

Camacho-Otero, J., Boks, C. and Pettersen, I., 2018. Consumption in the circular economy: a literature review. *Sustainability*, 10(8), 2758.

Corvellec, H., et al., 2020. Introduction to the special issue on the contested realities of the circular economy. *Culture and Organization*, 26, 97–102.

Ehrenfeld, J. and Gertler, N., 1997. Industrial ecology in practice: the evolution of interdependence at Kalundborg. *Journal of Industrial Ecology*, 1, 67–79.

Elia, V., Grazia Gnoni, M. and Tornese, F., 2017. Measuring circular economy strategies through index methods: a critical analysis. *Journal of Cleaner Production*, 142, 2741–2751.

Ellen McArthur Foundation, 2013. *Towards the Circular Economy Vol 1 [Report].* Available from: www.ellenmacarthurfoundation.org/assets/downloads/publications/Ellen-MacArthur-Foundation-Towards-the-Circular-Economy-vol.1.pdf [Accessed 3 February 2020].

Frishammar, J. and Parida, V., 2019. Circular business model transformation: a roadmap for incumbent firms. *California Management Review*, 61(2), 5–29. https://doi.org/10.1177/0008125618811926 [Accessed 20 June 2020].

Geissdoerfer, M. et al., 2017. The Circular Economy– a new sustainability paradigm?. *Journal of Cleaner Production*, 143, 757–768.

Ghisellini, P., Cialani, C. and Ulgiati, S., 2016. A review on circular economy: the expected transition to a balanced interplay of environmental and economic systems. *Journal of Cleaner Production*, 114, 11–32.

Haas, W. et al., 2015. How circular is the global economy? An assessment of material flows, waste production, and recycling in the European Union and the world in 2005. *Journal of Industrial Ecology*, 19, 765–777.

Hines, R., 1988. Financial accounting: in communicating reality, we construct reality. *Accounting, Organizations and Society*, 13(3), 251–261.

Hobson, K., 2016. Closing the loop or squaring the circle? Locating generative spaces for the circular economy. *Progress In Human Geography*, 40(1), 88–104.

Hobson, K. and Lynch, N., 2016. Diversifying and de-growing the circular economy: radical social transformation in a resource-scarce world. *Futures*, 82, 15–25.

Iacovidou, E. et al., 2017. Metrics for optimising the multi-dimensional value of resources recovered from waste in a circular economy: a critical review. *Journal of Cleaner Production*, 166, 910–938.

JRC-IES, 2010. *ILCD Handbook, International Reference Life Cycle Data System,* European Commission, EUR 24586 EN – 2010, Available from: https://eplca.jrc.ec.europa.eu/uploads/ILCD-Handbook-LCIA-Framework-Requirements-ONLINE-March-2010-ISBN-fin-v1.0-EN.pdf, [Accessed 10 February 2020].

Kalmykova, Y., Sadagopan, M. and Rosado, L., 2018. Circular economy–From review of theories and practices to development of implementation tools. *Resources, conservation and recycling*, 135, 190–201.

Kaza, S. et al. 2018. *What a Waste 2.0: A Global Snapshot of Solid Waste Management to 2050,* Urban Development, Washington, DC: World Bank. Available from: https://openknowledge.worldbank.org/handle/10986/30317 [Accessed 20 June 2020].

Kirchherr, J., Reike, D. and Hekkert, M., 2017. Conceptualising the circular economy: an analysis of 114 definitions. *Resources Conservation and Recycling,* 127, 221–232.

Kirchherr, J. et al., 2018. Barriers to the circular economy: evidence from the European Union. *Ecological Economics,* 150, 264–272.

Korhonen, J. et al., 2018. Circular economy as an essentially contested concept. *Journal of Cleaner Production*, 175, 544–552.

Lahti, T., Wincent, J. and Parida, V. 2018. A definition and theoretical review of the circular economy, value creation and sustainable business models: where are we now and where should research move in the future. *Sustainability,* 10, Available from: https://helda.helsinki.fi/dhanken/bitstream/handle/123456789/195391/Lahti_et_al._2018_.pdf?sequence=1&isAllowed=y, [Accessed 3 February 2020].

Lonca, G., Bernard, S. and Margni, M., 2019. A versatile approach to assess circularity: the case of decoupling. *Journal of Cleaner Production*, 240, 118–174.

Lyle, J.T., 1996. *Regenerative Design for Sustainable Development.* Hoboken, NJ: John Wiley & Sons.

Meadows, D.H. et al., 1972. *The Limits to Growth: A Report for the Club of Rome's Project on the Predicament of Mankind.* Washington, DC: Potomac Associates.

Millar, N., McLaughlin, E. and Börger, T., 2019. The circular economy: swings and roundabouts?. *Ecological Economics*, 158, 11–19.

Moraga, G. et al., 2019. Circular economy indicators: what do they measure? *Resources Conservation and Recycling*, 146, 452–461.

Murray, A., Skene, K. and Haynes, K., 2017. The circular economy: an interdisciplinary exploration of the concept and application in a global context. *Journal of Business Ethics*, 140(3), 369–380.

Pauliuk, S., 2018. Critical appraisal of the circular economy standard bs 8001:2017 and a dashboard of quantitative system indicators for its implementation in organisations. *Resources Conservation and Recycling*, 129, 81–92.

Perey, R. et al., 2018. The place of waste: changing business value for the circular economy. *Business Strategy and the Environment*, 27(5), 631–642.

Prieto-Sandoval, V., Jaca, C. and Ormazabal, M., 2018. Towards a consensus on the circular economy. *Journal of Cleaner Production,* 179, 605–615.

Saidani, M. et al., 2019. A taxonomy of circular economy indicators. *Journal of Cleaner Production*, 207, 542–559.

Sassanelli, C. et al., 2019. Circular economy performance assessment methods: a systematic literature review. *Journal of Cleaner Production*, 229, 440–453.

Schröder, P. et al., 2019. Degrowth within – aligning circular economy and strong sustainability narratives. *Resources Conservation and Recycling*, 146, 190–191.

Stahel, W., 2006. *The Performance Economy,* 1st edn. London: Palgrave-MacMillan.

Su, B. et al., 2013. A review of the circular economy in China: moving from rhetoric to implementation. *Journal of Cleaner Production*, 42, 215–227.

Swensson, N. and Funck, E.K., 2019. Management control in a circular economy. Exploring and theorizing the adaptation of management control to circular business models. *Journal of Cleaner Production,* 233, 390–398. https://doi.org/10.1016/j.jclepro.2019.06.089.

Valenzuela, F. and Böhm, S., 2017. Against wasted politics: a critique of the circular economy. *Ephemera: Theory & Politics in Organization*, 17(1), 23–60.

PART 4

Global and local perspectives

19

AFRICA, FROM THE PAST TO THE PRESENT

Moving the critical environmental accounting research on Africa forward

Mercy Denedo and Osamuyimen Egbon

Introduction

This chapter focuses on environmental accounting in Africa, home to 54 sovereign countries with vast socio-economic resources, mineral reserves, rich histories, cultural diversity and ecosystems upon which the rest of the world depends (North African countries were excluded from this chapter as they are discussed in Chapter 22). Africa possesses "54% of the world's platinum, 21% of gold, 40% of chrome, 28% of manganese, 51% of vanadium, 60% of cobalt, and 78% of diamonds" (Tuokuu et al. 2019, p.923). Edwards et al. (2014) claimed that less than 5% of the minerals in Africa have been discovered, suggesting massive growth potential. However, this wealth and potential has been plundered by a history of violent, exploitative colonisation and a history of exploitation that continues to this day.

Many African countries have been branded as unsustainable rentier states (Adams et al. 2019; Idemudia 2012) as governments across Africa have focused on economic growth at the expense of social or environmental outcomes when negotiating deals with multinational corporations (MNCs) (Rwabizambuga 2007). These negotiations have provided MNCs generous, but unaccountable, incentives and lax regulations to attract foreign investments that have resulted in widespread pollution, social inequities and environmental degradation across the continent.

Africa has suffered enormous environmental degradation from natural resource exploitation, including indiscriminate deforestation in a region blessed with globally important tropical rainforests and ecosystems. This enormous and unaccounted biodiversity loss has been exacerbated by civil unrest, conflicts, unsustainable agriculture, lack of energy infrastructure, weak governance and poorly policed enforcement (Acheampong et al. 2019; Nartey 2018). Emerging environmental accounting research has yet to systematically explore all of the environmental problems and risks facing Africa and Africans.

Problems remain as to how to define the costs and benefits from extractive activities, oftentimes, interconnected with contentious debates amplified by corruption and weak governance (see Lauwo et al. 2019). Substantive problems such as climate change, human rights violations, destruction of ecosystems, mass poverty, political ideological struggles, armed conflicts, corruption and mismanagement of revenue, ineffective governance and poor accountability practices have been associated with negative consequences for Africa and Africans. Increasingly, civil society organisations are pressuring MNCs to adopt internationally recognised best practices to do no harm across their African supply chains (Lauwo et al. 2019; Ruggie 2013). However, civil society's effort towards compelling corporations to voluntarily adopt global best practices often falls short of robust and effective public policies and governance to achieve environmental sustainability.

In this chapter, we reflect on the trends and gaps in accounting research publications on Africa. We provide an overview that highlights the connections between governance, accountability, and social and environmental issues within this continent. The chapter provides a context for what we need to know in order to set the scene for future environmental accounting research on Africa aligned with a sustainable vision for the continent.

Literature review

Environmental accounting in Africa remains underexplored (Tauringana 2019; Tilt 2018) and, in common with the rest of social and environmental accounting (SEA) research, largely absent in mainstream North American accounting journals (Parker 2011). At the same time, it is encouraging that mainstream and interdisciplinary accounting journals are increasingly giving attention to SEA research on Africa. However, we argue that the level of accounting research publications on Africa is too low relative to the unacceptable degree of social and environmental harm evident in Africa and the continent's importance to the rest of the world. There is an urgent need for a more comprehensive understanding of accounting and its role in exploiting Africa's natural resources, destructive environmental practices, creation of endemic poverty and perpetuating human rights abuses.

There is evidence of a growing body of African environmental accounting research, building from isolated publications from the late 1990s in a more coherent research field. The growing recognition of the importance of Africa can be seen in special issues of accounting journals, notably *Critical Perspectives on Accounting* in 2010 and *Accounting, Auditing and Accountability Journal* in 2017 (there is also a new special issue of accounting on Africa in *Critical Perspectives on Accounting*). However, environmental accounting did not feature significantly on these special issues, other than in Denedo et al. (2017).

Several non-accounting journals are increasingly publishing environmental accounting research on Africa. These include *Social Responsibility Journal, Corporate Social Responsibility and Environmental Management, Resource Policy, Journal of Business Ethics, Business & Society, Marine Policy, The Extractive Industries and Society: An International Journal, Futures, Journal of Cleaner Production, World Development, Land Use Policy*, and *Sustainable Development*. Despite this growth in the volume of published studies, there remain significant gaps. For example, the majority of environmental accounting publications report on practices in South Africa, with a predominance of studies concerned with integrated reporting. There is limited coverage on Africa's Francophone countries (Elad 2001; Lassou et al. 2019), with most studies limited to English language disclosures of corporations in South Africa, Tanzania, Nigeria and Ghana. It is worth noting that Africa has a high level of linguistic diversity with over 1,500 identifiable languages spoken; therefore, this narrowing of perspective will mean that a number of perspectives are lost.

Environmental accounting research in Africa has been dominated by publications reporting on quantity measures, rather than on the quality of disclosures in corporate reports (see Coetzee and van Staden 2011; de Villiers and Alexander 2014; Disu and Gray 1998). Since the 1990s, there has been a significant growth in corporate environmental reporting practice, leading to a number of studies that have explored possible motivations behind these changes. For example,

Alstine (2009) explored internal, external and global factors that affected environmental reporting by MNCs in South Africa. With integrated reporting mandatory in South Africa, studies have also explored the impact of mandatory and voluntary reporting initiatives in South Africa (Atkins and Maroun 2015; Wachira et al. 2020). Unlike conventional financial statements, social and environmental reports are voluntary without requirements for independent assurance, thus creating a credibility deficit.

Increasing demands for social, environmental and sustainability disclosures has implications for companies publishing reports and their contents. However, research on the quality of disclosures is limited. There are, however, a number of critical commentaries labelling these reports as largely symbolic, produced to legitimise corporate operations (see de Villiers and Barnard 2000; de Villiers and van Staden 2006).

Some studies have attempted to examine the impact of regulations and independent assurance on social, environmental and sustainability reports. For example, Ackers (2009) showed that corporate disclosures in South Africa are comparable to corporate disclosures in developed countries due to stringent regulations governing corporate disclosures in South Africa. South African reporting regulations are more developed than other African countries. For example, King III and IV Reports made it mandatory for listed companies on the Johannesburg Stock Exchange to disclose sustainability-related information in the form of independently assured integrated reports (Marx and Dyk 2011). While combined assurance is a core element of sustainability reporting in King III and IV Reports (Prinsloo and Maroun, 2020), research on other African countries has not examined the impact of regulations and independent assurance on environmental or sustainability reporting.

Within the African environmental accounting research literature, there is an emerging discourse on problematic accountability and power relations relating to environmental sustainability disclosures. The desire and capacity of MNCs and governments to account and behave responsibly are subject to ongoing public debate, and thus need greater attention from environmental accounting scholars (see Denedo et al. 2017, 2018; Lauwo et al. 2019). Recently, studies have begun to explore the motivation of small and medium-sized enterprises (SMEs) for engaging in environmental practices, including environmental management systems. Hamman et al.'s (2017) study suggests that in South Africa managers' personal conviction drives the adoption of proactive environmental behaviour. Amankwah et al. (2019) explored the relationship between a proactive strategy for integrating environmental issues into operations, entrepreneurial orientations and performance of SMEs in Ghana. While these findings are encouraging, researchers have yet to explore how widespread or representative these observed practices are, or their impact on accounting.

The mining sector has increasingly received research attention in Africa. This has included the role of MNCs as well as studies examining the accounting for environmental impacts of artisanal mining (see Hilson et al. 2007, 2019; Siwale and Siwale 2017). While the exploitation of natural resources has led to increased revenues with potential to promote social and economic development in Africa, it has come with a barrage of (avoidable and unavoidable) negative environmental impacts (see UNECA 2011). Incidents of serious negative environmental impacts associated with extractive industries have drawn attention to these industries, including environmental reporting research. Much of this research (from within and outside the accounting discipline) has problematised the absence of accountability associated with human rights abuses (Denedo et al. 2017, 2019; Lauwo et al. 2016, 2020), environmental pollution, and poor governance (see Egbon et al. 2018; Egbon and Mgbame 2020; Hassan and Kouhy 2013; Khalid et al. 2019).

Sadly, the consequences of extractive industries in Africa under-represented in the research literature also include disease, corruption, governance failures, ecosystem destruction, river and wetlands pollution, extinction, deforestation, child and forced labour, armed conflicts, dilapidated infrastructure and land grabbing. Paradoxically, this research reveals that countries with abundant natural resources suffer from the resource curse and are worse off than non-extractive countries in Africa (Owusu 2018; Wegenast and Schneider 2017). The environmental, social and governance externalities of "profitable" extractive industries are often absent in discourses promoting African socio-economic growth or corporate accounting. Neither do these accounts represent the divergence of interests among stakeholders suffering from unacceptable corporate practices nor inequitable government policies (see Denedo et al. 2017, 2019; Lauwo et al. 2020).

A common theme of this research is that governments and MNCs have ignored the broader social, human rights and environmental interests of stakeholders, including local communities. For instance, governments of Nigeria, Ghana, South Africa, Tanzania, Zambia and the Democratic Republic of Congo (DRC) have been criticised for profiting from extraction of crude oil, cobalt, copper and gold at the expense of the local people and ecosystems (see Human Rights Watch 2015; Khalid et al. 2019; Lauwo and Otusanya 2014; Sanderson 2019). Rather than seeking to be open and accountable, companies operating within Africa and particularly within the extractive sectors have strived to gain, maintain and repair their legitimacy and reputation through increased, but problematic, corporate social reporting practices (see Egbon et al. 2018; Idemudie et al. 2020; Nwoke 2019; Phiri et al. 2019; Pupovac and Moerman 2017). For example, Khalid et al. (2019) criticised site-specific social, environmental and ethical reporting by mining companies in Ghana as being inaccurate and insincere. Similarly, Phiri et al. (2019) examined the interactions of key stakeholders and their impacts on corporate social and environmental practices in the Zambian copper mining sector. The diverse socio-economic-ecological networks of problems associated with corporations in Africa, for example, poor regulation and governance, weak public sector management, accountability and corruption, are seen to influence environmental management and reporting.

There is an emerging body of research that has examined the importance of non-governmental organisations (NGOs) in driving humanitarian discourses, sustainable development and accountability reform (see Agyemang et al. 2017; Awio et al. 2011; Goddard and Assad 2006). For example, Denedo et al. (2017) reported on counter accounting as part of the international NGOs' engagement with the MNCs in the Nigerian oil industry in relation to the poor environmental practices and ecosystem degradation. Collectively, these NGO studies provide important insights on the roles of NGOs in accounting for environmental damage and/or mitigation in Africa. For instance, Lauwo and Otusanya (2014) revealed that Tanzania is still ravaged by poverty and unemployment despite decades of profitable extractive activities by MNCs. Lauwo et al. (2016) explored how advocacy NGOs provided marginalised stakeholders in Tanzania a voice to resist environmental and human rights violations stemming from resource extraction. Similarly, Denedo et al. (2019) reported on alternative accounting engagements by local advocacy NGOs in problematising human rights violations, regulatory inadequacies, unsustainable environmental practices and the marginalisation of the local communities in Nigeria's Niger Delta region. Such engagement was necessitated by the negative environmental impacts of oil operations in Nigeria by both the Nigerian government and the MNCs. Finally, there is also an emerging body of ecological accounting research that includes accounting for loss of biodiversity and extinction of (un)threatened species and critical ecosystems in Africa (Denedo et al. 2017, 2018, 2019; Elad 2001; Hassan et al. 2020; Maroun and Atkins 2018; Wachira and Wang'ombe 2019).

Relative to more developed countries, SEA research and practices in Africa is still in its infancy. Accounting researchers are yet to fully engage with all possible ways to address Africa's urgent social, economic or environmental problems. There is insufficient practice-relevant environmental accounting research that has focused on sustainability, conservation and emancipation of the voiceless and powerless groups in Africa (Khalid et al. 2019; Phiri et al. 2019). The question facing the SEA community is how (or whether) environmental accounting developments could address the problems that plague Africa. For example, could more accountability and transparency from African governments in relation to mineral development contracts and foreign direct investment clauses lead to intragenerational and intergenerational equity or more sustainable growth or development?

Would greater accountability across all levels, states and nations on the integration of extractive policies with sustainable development lead to transformative socio-economic growth and development (Edward et al. 2014; Gupta and Vegelin 2016)? It is argued that there is a need to fundamentally reform the lack of accountability in African countries in relation to revenue collection and distribution, effectiveness of poverty alleviation and employment policies, impact of environmental conservation policies, infrastructural development, oppression, marginalisation and social capacity building efforts.

The literature review also identified a number of gaps, including indigenous peoples' rights, environmental rights, land rights, social conflicts, workers' rights, child labour, modern slavery, access to education and healthcare, and public information rights. Although most of these issues touch upon issues of social justice, they are connected to unsustainable environmental practices and environmental injustices. For example, the denial of human rights to a clean environment, good health, arable land and unpolluted water resources, and means of subsistence, has often emanated from bad environmental practices.

The way forward

The above literature review identified an emerging body of environmental accounting research that needs to evolve if it is to systematically address the environmental risks (and the drivers of these risks) faced by Africa and Africans. Environmental accounting researchers have begun to consider the global and local implications of the Sustainable Development Goals (SDGs – see Bebbington and Unerman 2018). This section will explore some of the implications of the SDGs for the future development of environmental accounting research in Africa.

The SDGs have social, economic and environmental implications pivotal to socio-economic developments through an equitable, inclusive accountability and effective governance systems to eradicate poverty, social exclusion and environmental degradation in order for people to live sustainably. The SDGs have substantive human rights ramifications for African governments and all stakeholders at the local, national and regional levels due to their ambitious and people-centric focus on sustainability (Gupta and Vegelin 2016; UN 2015). Given the degree of environmental degradation, human rights violation, deforestation, biodiversity and extinction of threatened species caused by actions and inactions of corporations, individuals and governments, research is required to not only provide evidence of these problems but also to provide practical and policy solutions underpinned by the SDGs framework.

There appears to be a strong political will to implement, monitor, track and report on the SDGs across Africa. For instance, Kenyan, Ghanaian and Nigerian governments published SDGs baseline reports to map out aspects of their economy that require urgent attention (see Ghana 2017; Kenya 2017; Nigeria 2017; Nigeria 2020). Alongside these SDG baseline reports, accounting research can help in articulating measures to address environmental pollution problems affecting intragenerational and intergenerational sustainable development in Africa. Previous research shows that African governments had embraced ambitious initiatives and frameworks, without any meaningful corresponding implementation on the ground (see Denedo et al. 2017; Lauwo and Otusanya 2014). Critical environmental accounting literature recognises accounting as a powerful technology that could be harnessed to address existing sustainability problems through enhanced monitoring and evaluations (Contrafatto et al. 2015; Gray et al. 2014).

While there is a need for more conceptual discussion on effective mechanisms of accountability and governance in Africa, there is also a need for field-based qualitative approaches to explore social and environmental issues integral to the SDGs and sustainability beyond 2030 in Africa. For instance, there is an urgent need to explore sustainable management and multi-stakeholder's engagement strategies to prevent the loss of biodiversity and the extinction of endangered species (SDG 14 and 15). Due to potential problems with secondary data sets (see Atkins et al. 2018; Hassan et al. 2020), there is a need for studies to collect primary data on biodiversity loss and endangered species extinction from a multi-stakeholder lens, in order to account effectively for SDG 15 in Africa.

Despite the rising global research interest in accounting for water, there remains a dearth of accounting for safe drinking water in Africa despite the unsustainable environmental practices that pollute many sources of drinking water. SDG 6 has targets to assure accessible, affordable and safe drinking water (UN 2015), which are being adopted by many African countries (see, for instance, Ghana 2017; Kenya 2017; Nigeria 2017). However, setting water targets is insufficient in themselves without effective governance and accountability frameworks deliberately designed to achieve them (Odume and Slaughter 2017; WaterAid 2014). We encourage practice-relevant field-based accounting studies on governance and accountability strategies to ensure safe water for all in Africa. As highlighted in the SDGs framework (SDG 16, 17), diverse stakeholders have a role to play in the supply of safe drinking and affordable water regardless of where people are located. With high poverty levels (SDG 1) in African countries, access to water by local communities close to mining and extractive sites is problematic (SDG 12) due to ineffective governance mechanisms (SDG 16) for the provision of safe water (SDG 6).

In addition, limited research has been conducted on critical environmental issues, such as non-degradable products (plastics), biodiversity extinction, deforestation and afforestation, climate change and their implications for accounting in Africa (SDGs 11, 12, 13). With high levels of poverty and poor hygiene in many cities, towns and villages in Africa, there is widespread poor waste disposal and management infrastructure, especially for non-degradable items (e.g. plastics). Recent media revelations suggest that the production and usage of plastics and the attendant environmental pollution constitute risks to human, terrestrial and aquatic life (SDG 14, 15) in addition to their contribution to global greenhouse gas emissions. For example, in Nigeria and Ghana, sachet water (water is packaged in 500 ml polythene bags which are heat-sealed on either end) is a cheap source of drinking water, but the sachets are indiscriminately disposed of leading to environmental hazards and blockage to public drains (Odume and Slaughter 2017; Water Aid 2014). In developed nations, consumer behaviour towards the use of plastics is rapidly changing due to regulations banning or restricting plastic usage to protect biodiversity and the environment. The impacts of poor plastics management on biodiversity and the environment have been under-researched in Africa. In pursuit of environmental integrity in Africa, more research needs to be conducted to explore waste management, safe water provision and waste management regulations.

In relation to deforestation, limited accounting studies have explored deforestation and its environmental implications. This is despite accounting's potential to contribute to this genre of research. Deforestation is closely connected with climate change and environmental imbalance caused by biodiversity extinction (Acheampong et al. 2019; Elad 2001). Such studies could be linked to the United Nations Reducing Emissions from Deforestation and Forest Degradation (REDD) programme (Cuckston 2018) and the Paris Agreement on Climate Change (SDG 13, 15). Recently, some African countries, particularly Ethiopia, have been engaging in vigorous afforestation strategies aimed at planting millions of trees. It would be interesting to explore and evaluate the accounting for these environmental projects in different African countries.

Climate change and environmental crises have had detrimental impacts on communities and cities in Africa (SDGs 10, 11 and 13). For instance, Oxfam (2019) and Eckstein et al. (2020) revealed that African countries experienced the deadliest and costliest weather-related catastrophes in 2019. They are increasingly experiencing drought due to rising temperatures, leading to greater food insecurity (SDG 2) and poverty (SDG 1) (Oxfam 2019; UNEP 2020). In March 2019, Cyclone Idai swept through Mozambique, Malawi and Zimbabwe, destroying towns and villages with over 100 people killed and hundreds of thousands more displaced (Oxfam 2019). Shortly afterwards, Cyclone Kenneth dealt another blow to Mozambique, leading to lack of food, water, healthcare and power infrastructure accompanied by massive damage to the built environment (Maclean 2019). In Nigeria, erosion has swallowed homes, roads and farmland, and the economic damage is estimated at $100 million (approximately £80 million) every year, resulting in enormous loss in agricultural products (Unah 2020). Since 2018, swarms of gigantic locusts have been devastating crops, pastureland, vegetation and landscape in East Africa, resulting in threat to food security of 25 million East Africans, wildlife and livestock (Gilliland 2020; UNEP 2020). Accounting for the social and environmental implications of climate change, governance and the responses of NGOs and public–private sectors to these disasters are yet to be fully explored, particularly when there are potential conflicts with uncoordinated projects. For instance, in Malawi, communities are planting trees and digging drainage to handle stormwater run-off, while NGOs are supporting farmers to improve agricultural productivity to ensure food sustainability (World Vision 2019).

As discussed earlier, most environmental accounting publications have concentrated on large companies, especially MNCs. While these studies have shed light on corporate environmental practices and their social implications for human rights violations involving labour, host communities and supply chains, research efforts are also needed in public sector organisations and third sector organisations. Investigations into the environmental practices and accountability of the public sector in Africa are important especially as the public sector in these countries plays a dominant role in local economic systems. Moreover, there is an emerging research interest in sustainability reporting in higher education institutions (HEIs) in Africa, particularly in South Africa (see Calitz and Zietsman 2018). We expect more empirical research on the sustainability practices and sustainability reporting of African HEIs (SDG 4), especially in the areas of energy efficiency/wastage (SDG 7), and water and waste management. Future research could explore whether public sector organisations are more "environmentally friendly" than their private sector counterparts. We also encourage studies on private businesses that seek to meaningfully report their environmental practices to local or indigenous communities.

Moreover, individuals and institutions, other than MNCs, engage in business activities without regard for the environmental consequences. For instance, small-scale artisanal mining has been gaining momentum despite the environmental and health risk associated with such practices (see Hilson et al. 2007, 2019; Siwale and Siwale 2017). The prevalence and environmental impacts of these non-MNC institutions, often unique to Africa, would merit environmental accounting research attention. Furthermore, future environmental studies should capture and evaluate the nature of the environmental accounting issues around mineral extraction (e.g. coal, limestone, iron ore, diamond, tin, bronzite, cobalt, bitumen, copper and aluminium) across all African countries (see Amnesty International 2016; Milos 2015).

In addition, there is potential for accounting research to reflect ongoing concerns in the academia and institutional investment arenas on the prevalence of modern slavery, child labour and worker rights in Africa. Government institutions dealing with child labour and child protection are weak, under-resourced and under-funded in Africa (SDGs 3, 4 and 10). There is a need for enhanced accountability to facilitate sustainable investments and supply chain interventions (SDGs 8, 9 and 12). Studies have indicated that children are often enslaved or employed in cocoa plantations in Africa and exposed to chemicals, leading to high mortality rate. Children are used to mine cobalt, copper, diamond, tantalum, tin, gold and lead in DRC, Nigeria and Ghana (see Amnesty International 2016; Human Rights Watch 2015; Sanderson 2019). In 2010, the world's worst lead poisoning incident was linked to artisanal gold mining in Zamfara State of Nigeria. This led to the death of approximately 400–500 children, unaccounted death of animals and neurological damage to thousands of children (Human Rights Watch 2011; Medecins Sans Frontieres 2012).

We encourage future social and environmental accounting researchers to contribute to the policy and practice debates on the elimination of child labour and modern slavery in Africa. Future accounting research could build on the UN Business and Human Rights Guiding Principles, which require corporations to do no harm by adopting effective due diligence procedures across their supply chains and for governments to protect the fundamental rights of their citizens (Ruggie 2013). We proposed an evidence-based research that goes beyond voluntary corporate disclosures on the elimination of conflict minerals and child labour (see Islam and van Staden 2018) to a practice-based accounting research that could articulate measures to eliminate child labour and modern slavery in Africa.

Conclusion

This chapter has highlighted some key social, environmental and governance issues and their implications for accountability and environmental accounting in Africa. The chapter captured the centrality of natural resources to Africa and how these resources affect social, economic, environmental, political, governance, accountability, social justice and sustainability issues in Africa. Given the prevalence of resource curse in Africa, this chapter has reflected on and identified the direction for future social and environmental accounting research required on this continent to address the urgent set of social and environmental issues if Africa is to become environmentally sustainable while meeting its SDGs.

References

Acheampong, E.O., Macgregor, C.J., Sloan, S. and Sayer, J., 2019. Deforestation is driven by agricultural expansion in Ghana's forest reserves. *Scientific African*, 5, 1–11.

Ackers, B., 2009. Corporate social responsibility assurance: How do South African publicly listed companies compare? *Meditari Accountancy Research*, 17 (2), 1–17.

Adams, D., Ullah, S., Akhtar, P., Adams, K. and Saidi, S., 2019. The role of country-level institutional factors in escaping the natural resource curse: Insights from Ghana. *Resources Policy*, 61, 433–440.

Agyemang, G., O'Dwyer, B., Unerman, J. and Awumbila, M., 2017. Seeking "conversations for accountability" mediating the impact of non-governmental organisation (NGO) upward accountability processes. *Accounting, Auditing and Accountability Journal*, 30 (5), 982–1007.

Alstine, J.V., 2009. Governance from below: Contesting corporate environmentalism in Durban, South Africa. *Business Strategy and the Environment*, 18, 108–121.

Amankwah-Amoah, J., Danso, A. and Adomako, S., 2019. Entrepreneurial orientation, environmental sustainability and new venture performance: Does stakeholder integration matter? *Business Strategy and the Environment*, 28, 79–87.

Amnesty International, 2016. *"This is what we die for". Human rights abuses in the Democratic Republic of the Congo power. The global trade in cobalt* [Online]. Amnesty International. Available from: www.amnesty.org/download/Documents/AFR6231832016ENGLISH.PDF [Accessed 24 June 2020].

Atkins, J. and Maroun, W., 2015. Integrated reporting in South Africa in 2012, perspectives from South African institutional investors. *Accounting, Auditing and Accountability Journal*, 23 (2), 197–221.

Atkins, J., Maroun, W., Atkins, B.C. and Barone, E., 2018. From the big five to the big four: Exploring extinction accounting for the rhinoceros. *Accounting, Auditing and Accountability Journal,* 31 (2), 674–702.

Awio, G., Northcott, D. and Lawrence, S., 2011. Social capital and accountability in grassroots NGOs: The case of the Ugandan community-led HIV/AIDS Initiative. *Accounting Auditing and Accountability Journal,* 24 (1), 63–92.

Bebbington, J. and Unerman, J., 2018. Achieving the United Nations Sustainable Development Goals: An enabling role for accounting research. *Accounting, Auditing and Accountability Journal,* 31 (1), 2–24.

Calitz, A.P. and Zietsman, J.F., 2018. An adapted framework for environmental sustainability reporting using mobile technologies. *The African Journal of Information Systems*, 10 (3), 174–190.

Coetzee, C.M. and van Staden, C.J., 2011. Disclosure responses to mining accidents: South African evidence. *Accounting Forum*, 35 (4), 232–246.

Contrafatto, M., Thomson, I. and Monk, E., 2015. Peru, mountains and los ninos: Dialogic action, accounting and sustainable transformation. *Critical Perspectives on Accounting,* 33, 117–136.

Cuckston, T., 2018. Creating financial value for tropical forests by disentangling people from nature. *Accounting Forum*, 42 (3), 219–234.

de Villiars, C.J. and Barnard, P., 2000. Environmental reporting in South Africa from 1994 to 1999: A research note. *Meditari Accountancy Research,* 8, 15–23.

de Villiars, C.J. and van Staden, C.J., 2006. Can less environmental disclosure have a legitimising effect? Evidence from Africa. *Accounting, Organizations and Society*, 31, 763–781.

de Villiers, C. and Alexander, D., 2014. The institutionalisation of corporate social responsibility reporting. *British Accounting Review,* 46, 198–212.

Denedo, M., Thomson, I. and Yonekura, A., 2017. International advocacy NGOs, counter accounting, accountability and engagement. *Accounting, Auditing and Accountability Journal,* 30 (6), 1309–1343.

Denedo, M., Thomson, I. and Yonekura, A., 2018. Accountability, maps and intergenerational equity: Evaluating the Nigerian Oil Spill Monitor. *Public Money and Management,* 38 (5), 355–364.

Denedo, M., Thomson, I. and Yonekura, A., 2019. Ecological damage, human rights and oil: Local advocacy NGOs dialogic action and alternative accounting practices. *Accounting Forum*, 43 (1), 85–112.

Disu, A. and Gray, R., 1998. An exploration of social reporting and MNCs in Nigeria. *Social and Environmental Accountability Journal*, 18 (2), 13–15.

Eckstein, D., Kunzel, V., Schafer, L. and Winges, M., 2019. *Global Climate Index 2020. Who suffers most from extreme weather events? Weather-related loss events in 2018 and 1999 to 2018* [Online]. Germanwatch. Available from: www.germanwatch.org/en/17307 [Accessed 19 June 2020].

Edwards, D.P., Sloan, S., Weng, L., Dirks, P., Sayer, J. and Laurence, W.F., 2014. Mining and the African environment. *Conservation Letters,* 7 (3), 302–311.

Egbon, O., Idemudia, U. and Amaeshi, K., 2018. Shell Nigeria's Global Memorandum of Understanding and corporate-community accountability relations. *Accounting, Auditing and Accountability Journal,* 31 (1), 51–74.

Egbon, O. and Mgbame, O.C., 2020. 'Examining the accounts of oil spills crises in Nigeria through sensegiving and defensive behaviours. *Accounting, Auditing & Accountability Journal*, 33(8), 2053–2076.

Elad, C., 2001. Auditing and governance in the forestry industry: Between protest and professionalism. *Critical Perspectives on Accounting*, 12, 647–671.

Ghana, 2017. *The Sustainable Development Goals (SDGs) in Ghana. Why they matter & How we can help* [Online]. Available from: www.undp.org/content/dam/unct/ghana/docs/SDGs/UNCT-GH-SDGs-in-Ghana-Avocacy-Messages–2017.pdf [Accessed 16 September 2019].

Gilliland, H.C., 2020. *Gigantic new locust swarms hit East Africa* [Online]. National Geographic. Available from: www.nationalgeographic.co.uk/environment-and-conservation/2020/05/gigantic-new-locust-swarms-hit-east-africa [Accessed 28 June 2020].

Goddard, A. and Assad, M.J., 2006. Accounting and navigating legitimacy in Tanzanian NGOs. *Accounting Auditing and Accountability Journal,* 30 (5), 982–1007.

Gray, R., Brennan, A. and Malpas, J., 2014. New accounts: Towards a reframing of social accounting. *Accounting Forum,* 38 (4), 258–273.

Gupta, J. and Vegelin, C., 2016. Sustainable development goals and inclusive development. *International Environmental Agreements: Politics, Law and Economics,* 16, 433–488.

Hamann, R., Smith, J., Tashman, P. and Marshall, R.S., 2017. Why do SMEs go green? An analysis of wine firms in South Africa. *Business and Society*, 56 (1), 23–56.

Hassan, A. and Kouhy, R., 2013. Gas flaring in Nigeria: Analysis of changes in its consequent carbon emission and reporting. *Accounting Forum,* 37 (2), 124–134.

Hassan, A.M., Roberts, L. and Atkins, J., 2020. Exploring factors relating to extinction disclosures: What motivates companies to report on biodiversity and species protection? *Business Strategy and the Environment,* 29, 1419–1436.
Hilson, G., Gumandakoye, H. and Diallo, P., 2019. Formalizing artisanal mining "spaces" in rural sub-Saharan Africa: The case of Niger. *Land Use Policy,* 80, 259–268.
Hilson, G., Yakovleva, N. and Banchirigah, S.M., 2007. "To move or not to move": Reflections on the resettlement of artisanal miners in the western region of Ghana. *African Affairs,* 106 (424), 413–436.
Human Rights Watch., 2011. *A Heavy Price: Lead poisoning and gold mining in Nigeria's Zamfara State* [Online]. Human Right Watch. Available from: www.hrw.org/sites/default/files/related_material/Nigeria_0212.pdf [Accessed 16 September 2019].
Human Rights Watch., 2015. *Precious Metal, Cheap Labor, Child Labor and Corporate Responsibility in Ghana's Artisanal Gold Mines* [Online]. Humans Rights Watch. Available from: www.hrw.org/sites/default/files/report_pdf/ghana0515_forinsertltr2_0.pdf [Accessed 24 September 2019].
Idemudia, U., 2012. The resource curse and the decentralization of oil revenue: The case of Nigeria. *Journal of Cleaner Production,* 35, 183–193.
Idemudia, U., Kwakyewah, C. and Muthuri, J., 2020. Mining, the Environment, and Human Rights in Ghana: An Area of Limited Statehood Perspective. *Business Strategy and the Environment,* 29(7), 2919–2926.
Institute of Directors., 2009. *King Report on Corporate Governance for South Africa 2009* [Online]. Institute of Directors, SA. Available from: https://cdn.ymaws.com/www.iodsa.co.za/resource/resmgr/king_iii/King_Report_on_Governance_fo.pdf [Accessed 21 June 2020].
Islam, M.A. and van Staden, C.J., 2018. Social movement NGOs and the comprehensiveness of conflict mineral disclosures: Evidence from global companies. *Accounting Organizations and Society,* 65, 1–19.
Kenya., 2017. *Implementation of the Agenda 2030 for Sustainable Development in Kenya* [Online]. Ministry of Devolution and Planning, Available from: https://sustainabledevelopment.un.org/content/documents/15689Kenya.pdf [Accessed 16 September 2019].
Khalid, S., Atkins, J. and Barone, E., 2019. Sartrean bad-faith? Site-specific social, ethical and environmental disclosures by multinational mining companies. *Accounting, Auditing and Accountability Journal,* 32 (1), 55–74.
Lassou, P., Hopper, T., Tsamenyi, M. and Murinde, V., 2019. Varieties of neo-colonialism: Government accounting reforms in Anglophone and Francophone Africa – Benin and Ghana compared. *Critical Perspectives on Accounting,* 65, 1–22.
Lauwo, S. and Otusanya, O.J., 2014. Corporate accountability and human rights disclosures: A case study of Barrick Gold Mine in Tanzania. *Accounting Forum,* 38 (2), 91–108.
Lauwo, S.G., Otusanya, O.J. and Bakre, O., 2016. Corporate social responsibility reporting in the mining sector of Tanzania: (Lack of) government regulatory controls and NGO activism. *Accounting, Auditing and Accountability Journal,* 29 (6), 1038–1074.
Lauwo, S., Kyriacou, O. and Otusanya, O.J., 2020. When sorry is not an option: CSR reporting and "face work" in a stigmatised industry – A case study of Barrick (Acacia) goldmine in Tanzania. *Critical Perspectives on Accounting,* 71, 102099.
Maclean, R., 2019. *Cyclone Kenneth: UN says Mozambique may need another huge aid effort* [Online]. *The Guardian,* Available from: www.theguardian.com/world/2019/apr/25/cyclone-kenneth-mozambique-hit-by-strongest-storm-ever. [Accessed 19 June 2020].
Maroun, W. and Atkins, J., 2018. Integrated extinction accounting and accountability: Building an ark. *Accounting, Auditing and Accountability Journal,* 31 (3), 750–786.
Marx, B. and van Dyk, V., 2011. Sustainability reporting and assurance: An analysis of assurance practices in South Africa. *Meditari Accountancy Research,* 19 (1/2), 39–55.
Medecins Sans Frontieres., 2012. *Lead Poisoning Crisis in Zamfara State, Northern Nigeria* [Online]. Available from: www.doctorswithoutborders.org/news-stories/briefing-document/lead-poisoning-crisis-zamfara-state-northern-nigeria [Accessed 16 September 2019].
Milos, C., 2015. *Bitumen in Nigeria. Weighing the true costs of extraction* [Online] Heinrich Böll Stiftung. Available from: https://ng.boell.org/sites/default/files/bitumen_in_nigeria.pdf [Accessed 24 June 2020].
Nartey, E., 2018. Determinants of carbon management accounting adoption in Ghanaian firms. *Meditari Accountancy Research,* 26 (1), 88–121.
Nigeria., 2017. *Nigeria: Sustainable Development Goals (SDGs) Indicators Baseline Report 2016* [Online]. Available from: https://reliefweb.int/report/nigeria/nigeria-sdgs-baseline-indicators-report–2016 [Accessed 14 September 2019].

Nigeria., 2020. *Nigeria: Integration of the SDGs into National Development Planning: A second voluntary national review*. Abuja: The Office of the Senior Special Assistant to the President on SDGs (OSSAP-SDGs).

Nwoke, U., 2019. (In)Effective Business Responsibility Engagements in Areas of Limited Statehood: Nigeria's Oil Sector as a Case Study. *Business & Society*, Ahead-of-print.

Odume, N. and Slaughter, A., 2017. *How Nigeria is wasting its rich water resources* [Online]. Conversation. Available from: http://theconversation.com/how-nigeria-is-wasting-its-rich-water-resources–83110 [Accessed 3 March 2019].

Owusu, B., 2018. "Doomed by the 'Resource Curse?' Fish and Oil Conflicts in the Western Gulf of Guinea, Ghana. *Development,* 61, 149–159.

Oxfam., 2019. *Forced from home, climate-fuelled displacement* [Online]. *Oxfam*. Available from: www.oxfam.org/en/research/forced-home-climate-fuelled-displacement [Accessed 19 June 2020].

Parker, L., 2011. Building bridges to the future: Mapping the territory for developing social and environmental accountability. *Social and Environmental Accountability Journal,* 31 (1), 7–24.

Phiri, O., Mantzari, E. and Gleadle, P., 2019. Stakeholder interactions and corporate social responsibility (CSR) practices: Evidence from the Zambian copper mining sector. *Accounting, Auditing and Accountability Journal,* 32 (1), 26–54.

Prinsloo, A. and Maroun, W., 2020. An exploratory study on the components and quality of combined assurance in an integrated or a sustainability reporting setting. *Sustainability Accounting, Management and Policy Journal,* 12(1), 1-29.

Pupovac, S. and Moerman, L., 2017. Hybrid accounts: Shell's letter to Mr and Mrs shareholder. *Accounting, Auditing and Accountability Journal,* 30(5), 1184–1201.

Ruggie, J.G., 2013. *Just Business, Multinational Corporations and Human Rights*. New York: W.W. Norton & Company.

Rwabizambuga, A., 2007. Negotiating corporate social responsibility policies and practices in developing countries: an examination of the experiences from the Nigerian oil sector. *Business and Society Review,* 112 (3), 407–430.

Sanderson, H., 2019. *Congo, child labour and your electric car* [Online]. Financial Times. Available from: www.ft.com/content/c6909812–9ce4–11e9–9c06-a4640c9feebb [Accessed 23 September 2019].

Siwale, A. and Siwale, T., 2017. Has the promise of formalizing artisanal and small-scale mining (ASM) failed? The case of Zambia. *The Extractive Industries and Society,* 4, 191–201.

Tauringana, V., 2019. *Environmental reporting and management in Africa*. Advances in Environmental Accounting & Management (Vol. 8). Bingley, UK: Emerald Publishing Limited.

Tilt, C.A., 2018. Making social and environmental accounting research relevant in developing countries: A matter of context? *Social and Environmental Accounting Journal,* 38 (2), 145–150.

Tuokuu, F.X.D., Idemudia, U., Gruber, J.S. and Kayira, J., 2019. Identifying and clarifying environmental policy best practices for the mining industry – A systematic review. *Journal of Cleaner Production,* 22, 922–933.

Unah, L., 2020. *Erosion crisis swallows homes and livelihoods in Nigeria* [Online]. Climate Home News. Available from: www.climatechangenews.com/2020/01/20/erosion-crisis-swallows-homes-livelihoods-nigeria/ [Accessed 13 July 2020].

UNECA., 2011. *Minerals and Africa's Development: The International Study Group Report on Africa's Mineral Regimes*. Addis Ababa. Ethiopia: United Nations Economic Commission for Africa.

UNEP., 2020. *Locust swarms and climate change* [Online]. United Nations Environment Programme. Available from: www.unenvironment.org/news-and-stories/story/locust-swarms-and-climate-change [Accessed 28 June 2020].

United Nations, 2015. *Transforming our world: The 2030 Agenda for Sustainable Development - A/RES/70/1* [Online]. United Nations (UN) Sustainable Development Knowledge Platform. Available from: https://sustainabledevelopment.un.org/post2015/transformingourworld [Accessed 30 August 2019].

Wachira, M.M., Berndt, T. and Romero, C.M., 2020. The adoption of international sustainability and integrated reporting guidelines within a mandatory reporting framework: Lessons from South Africa. *Social Responsibility Journal,* 16 (5), 613–629.

WaterAid Nigeria, 2014. *Mairuwa: The WaterAid Nigeria newsletter*. Abuja: WaterAid Nigeria.

Wegenast, T. and Schneider, G., 2017. Ownership matters: Natural resources property rights and social conflict in sub-Saharan Africa. *Political Geography,* 61, 110–122.

World Vision, 2019. *2019 Cyclone Idai: Facts, FAQs, and how to help* [Online]. World Vision. Available from: www.worldvision.org/disaster-relief-news-stories/2019-cyclone-idai-facts [Accessed 19 June 2020].

20
ENVIRONMENTAL ACCOUNTING AND REPORTING PRACTICES IN ASIAN COUNTRIES

Tiffany Cheng-Han Leung

Introduction

The Asia Pacific region covers a large geographical area with abundant natural resources. However, this region is expanding at an accelerating rate due to rapid economic development, population growth and being the world's manufacturing hub. This has resulted in overconsumption of and increasing demand for non-renewable resources. The impacts of climate change, greenhouse gas (GHG) emissions and biodiversity degradation have become visible in the Asia Pacific region (Lee 2014). Multi-national and local companies in this region have faced significant environmental pressures and resource constraints, such as water scarcity, soil erosion and severe biodiversity loss, which lead to increase raw material costs, energy costs and environmental costs (Lee and Schaltegger 2018).

Taking this context into account, companies in the Asia Pacific region increasingly pay attention to their environmental impacts and risks in their business operation. Approximately 37% of the Global 250 companies are from the Asia Pacific region and 78% of the largest 100 companies in the Asia Pacific region report on social and environmental information in their annual reports and stand-alone sustainability reports (KPMG 2017). Governments, investor pressures and local stock exchange requirements in this region play important roles in increasing environmental reporting incidence over the past decade (KPMG 2017). Companies in the Asia Pacific region are attempting to be more accountable, transparent and responsible with regard to environmental performance so that investors can evaluate non-financial information in corporate reports more closely (Noronha et al. 2015; Leung and Snell 2017; Solovida and Latan 2017; Leung 2019).

A growing number of studies on environmental accounting in Asian countries have been conducted in the past decades (Rahman et al. 2010; Herzig et al. 2012; Zhao and Patten 2016) and companies in Asian countries have made significant progress in providing environmental related information in corporate reports and in developing the environmental performance systems and accessing ecological impacts (Herzig et al. 2012). Most of environmental accounting studies among Asian countries tend to examine single or one specific country rather than multiple countries (Williams and Pei 1999; Thompson 2002; Herzig et al. 2012; Leung and

Gray 2016). Thus, the objective of this chapter is to provide a general overview of the recent development and observation of environmental accounting and reporting practices among five Asian countries.

The rationale of choosing these countries is threefold. First, Mainland China, Singapore and Malaysia were chosen because of the presence of environmental reporting regulations, driven by both government and local stock exchanges (KPMG 2017). Second, Hong Kong, a special administrative region in China, is included in this study because it is s one of the leading international financial centres and has environmental reporting standards on par with international reporting practices (Ng and Leung 2020). Third, Japan is selected in this study for historical and contextual reasons. Japan was the first Asian country to experience serious environmental pollution between 1950s and 1970s, which they addressed through strict environmental protection regulations. Japan also experienced a substantial change in environmental policies after the Kyoto Protocol in 1997 (Saka and Oshika 2014; Yook et al. 2017). Thus, the environmental reporting regulation in Japan is strongly driven by government and draws from this historical background (KPMG 2017).

This chapter is structured as follows. After the introduction, the next section provides a literature review on environmental accounting and reporting practices in Mainland China, Hong Kong, Japan, Singapore and Malaysia. This is followed by a discussion about the incidence of corporate reporting, drivers of environmental reporting regulations and quality of environmental reporting. Lastly, some concluding comments are made.

Environmental accounting and reporting practices in Asian countries

Mainland China

Despite the remarkable industrial development and economic growth over the past three decades, China has faced a number of environmental challenges and problems. China is one of the world's largest energy consumers, with around 20% of global energy consumption in 2018 due to its heavy reliance on fossil fuel and coal (International Energy Agency 2018). The World Bank (2013) estimates the cost of environmental degradation in China as being more than 10% of its gross domestic product (GDP), including the costs of air pollution (6.5%), water pollution (2.1%) and soil degradation (1.1%).

Prior to 2006, the level of environmental reporting in Chinese language studies tended to be low (or absent), which was in line with the findings in English language studies (Yang et al. 2015). There are three main factors to explain this phenomenon: (i) a lack of a transparent information disclosure environment, (ii) absence of accounting skills to report environmental related information and (iii) any reporting being seen as having potential negative economic and political impacts on Chinese companies (Yang et al. 2015).

In 2006, the Ministry of Finance, the State Environmental Protection Administration of China required companies to disclose social and environmental information on their reports (Noronha et al. 2013). Subsequently, the Shanghai Stock Exchange (SSE) required companies listed abroad to issue annual Corporate Social Responsibility (CSR) reports in 2009, while the Shenzhen Stock Exchange (SZSE) required companies listed in the SZSE 100 Index to follow *Social Responsibility Guidelines for Listed Companies* in 2009 (Yu and Rowe 2017). The Chinese government and the domestic stock exchange requirements are major factors contributing to the substantial growth of stand-alone CSR reports in China: such reporting is a mandatory practice (Rowe and Guthrie 2010; Yin and Zhang 2012; Yu and Rowe 2017).

More importantly, the Chinese government has established regulations for environmental protection, including environmental reporting to local government (He and Loftus 2014). For example, the Prevention and Control of Air Pollution Act requires companies to disclose their carbon emissions and environmental management efforts. Government authorities have the right to such environmental information in order to evaluate their environmental performance (He and Loftus 2014). Some local governments collaborated with the World Bank's InfoDev Program and the Ministry for Environmental Protection to enforce environmental regulations, namely, "China Green Watch Program" which deploys a colour-coded system to rate companies' environmental performance (He and Loftus 2014). Pertinently, the Chinese government has taken a major step to launch "Green Securities Policy", which is the revised Environmental Protection Law, in 1 January 2015 and to require companies to disclose pollution data with local government agencies being responsible for disseminating this information to the public (Hong Kong Exchanges and Clearing Limited 2015).

While these environmental regulations and guidelines are prevalent in China, the extent of environmental accounting and reporting is still in its infancy (Yang et al. 2015; Zhao and Patten 2016; Yu and Rowe 2017). The empirical environmental accounting research tends to focus on environmental performance in polluting industries and environmental assurance (Yang et al. 2015). Environmental sensitive companies appear to voluntarily disclose environmental information in order to maintain their legitimacy in the eyes of the public (Yu and Rowe 2017). In addition, peer pressures from salient stakeholders to embrace environmental reporting practices are mainly driven by the prevalence of a collectivist approach and the deep-rooted face (Mianzi) culture (i.e. to avoid embarrassment or saving face culture) (Yu and Rowe 2017).

Hong Kong

Hong Kong, the special administrative region of Mainland China, has positioned itself as the global financial centre, supporting capital raising and cross-border financial functions (Chan and Welford 2005). Hong Kong focuses on the service industry rather than the energy-intensive industry. GHG emission mainly comes from the building sector (Lai 2014). The Environmental Protection Department and the Electrical and Mechanical Services Department issued the Guideline to Account for and Report on Greenhouse Gas Emissions and Removals for Building in 2008 (Lai 2014). This guideline focuses on commercial, residential buildings, and institutional buildings and highly relies on self-assessment and voluntary reporting practices at that time (Lai 2014).

Several environmental reporting studies have investigated reporting among Hong Kong companies from 1990 to 2005. The results show that the level of environmental reporting among Hong Kong listed companies is fairly low during the observed period (Lynn 1992; Ho et al. 1994; Jaggi and Zhao 1996; Gao et al. 2005). These listed companies tend to disclose social rather than environmental information in their reports (Williams and Pei 1999; Xiao et al. 2005). Prior to 2010, Hong Kong listed companies tend to provide insufficient information for investors in relation to corporate environmental risk, performance and management (Chan and Welford 2005).

The Hong Kong Exchanges and Clearing Limited (HKEX) released a consultation paper for the Environmental, Social and Governance Reporting Guide in 2011 (the ESG Guide). However, Bloomberg's study shows that over 50% of 330 sample issuers did not report or disclose any ESG-related issues in 2014 (Hong Kong Exchanges and Clearing Limited 2015). After the public consultation closed, all Hong Kong listed companies were required (in 2017) to publish an annual ESG report to improve the non-financial information and improve risk management (specifically, issuers were required to report "General Disclosures" and Key Performance Indicators – see Hong Kong Exchanges and Clearing Limited 2015).

Given ESG is a relatively new area in Hong Kong in recent years, only 37% of business leaders have integrated ESG issues into their strategic planning (KPMG 2018). Hong Kong Exchanges and Clearing Limited (2018) published a review of listed companies' ESG reports and found that 77% of companies were in full compliance of each environmental aspect in the ESG guide and 39% of companies published stand-alone ESG reports. Some companies show excellent reporting in terms of detailed environmental information and clarity on providing comprehensive description on environmental policies, giving explanations under the "Comply or Explain" provisions and conducting materiality assessment through stakeholder engagement process. In contrast, others appeared to adopt a "box-ticking" approach with short and simple statement without further explanations or lengthy narratives (Hong Kong Exchanges and Clearing Limited 2018).

There are three major barriers for business managers in Hong Kong to address ESG issues: (i) limited knowledge and expertise, (ii) weak association between ESG issues and their impact on the business and (iii) limited expected short-term or immediate return of ESG to business operations (KPMG 2018). Currently, Hong Kong Stock Exchange was ranked the 24th out of 45 global stock exchanges of measuring sustainability disclosure in 2017 (Corporate Knights 2018). Regional counterparts, namely, Bursa Malaysia (BM, known as the Kuala Lumpur Stock Exchange) and Singapore Exchange (SGX), were ranked the 15th and 16th, respectively, suggesting that Hong Kong has some distance to travel yet (Financial Services Development Council 2018).

Japan

Japan experienced serious environmental pollution between 1950s and 1970s and these problems were addressed by strict environmental protection regulations and the new technological development of pollution control (Saka and Oshika 2014). Thus, Japanese companies are the top-ranking list in global carbon efficiency (Saka and Oshika 2014) and Japan has the second highest corporate reporting rate (social and environmental information) in the world, with 99% of the largest 100 listed companies in Japan (KPMG 2017).

Yamagami and Kokubu (1991) and Fukukawa and Moon (2004) are two early works to examine the extent and nature of environmental disclosure in 1985 and 2002. A number of more recent studies have examined various environmental accounting research topics, such as carbon management disclosure, environmental assurance and environmental conservation costs (Saka and Oshika 2014; Ali et al. 2015; Haider and Kokubu 2015; Yook et al. 2017).

The Japanese government and the Japan Business Federation (Keidanren) play important roles and influence on the development of environmental reporting practices (Ali et al. 2015). There are three main environmental regulations in Japan. First, the Japanese government revised the law in relation to climate change for the Kyoto Protocol in 2002 and implemented in 2005 (Sueyoshi and Goto 2010). Japan's Ministry of Environment issued the Environmental Accounting Guidelines in 2005 and other measures (Law No. 77 of 2004 Japan) and Environmental Reporting Guidelines in 2012 to promote environmental reporting practices with numerical data (Yook et al. 2017; Fitriasari and Kawahara 2018). However, even though Japanese firms disclose environmental information in their reports, it tends not to be comparable with other Japanese firms (Yook et al. 2017).

Second, the mandatory GHG accounting and reporting system of the Ministry of Environment was introduced in 2006 (Nishitani and Kokubu 2012; Yook et al. 2017). These regulations apply to business operators with a minimum of 21 employees or more, with total energy consumption of 1,500 kw of energy per year or above, and/or with more than 3,000 metric tons of equivalent of carbon dioxide each year. This means that these companies are obliged to report their GHG emissions to the government every year (Lai 2014; Saka and Oshika 2014; Fitriasari and Kawahara 2018). The Environmental Consideration Law stipulates that large firms should also disclose environmental information, initiatives and performance (Yook et al. 2017).

Third, the Rational Use of Energy Act (Act No. 49 of 1979) was initiated by the Ministry of Economy, Trade and Industry to promote energy management and energy efficient usage in factories (Fitriasari and Kawahara 2018). The amendment of the law in 2008 requires all firms to improve energy conservation (and to endeavour to improve energy efficiency more than 1% of the annual energy consumption) with quantitative disclosures required in their reports (Fitriasari and Kawahara 2018). This act is intended to monitor particular emitters, including specified freight and passenger carriers, consigners and air carriers (Lai 2014).

Singapore

The awareness level of environmental protection in the government and companies in Singapore is high. In 2005, around 93% of 44 sampled Singapore companies were accredited with the ISO 14001 – environmental management system certification (Chung and Parker 2010; Batra 2013). These accredited companies in Singapore and Malaysia are often the regional headquarters of multinational corporations (MNCs) that operate across Southeast Asia and they are responding to pressure from parent companies to standardise environmental performance and reporting practices (Thompson 2002).

ACCA (2002) showed that 14% of listed companies in Singapore and 23% of government-linked companies (GLCs) disclose environmental information in their annual reports. Rahman et al. (2010) showed that 30% of listed companies in Singapore disclose environmental information in their annual reports. 87% of the sample companies tend to disclose general environmental information, while 13% of companies report narrative disclosure with monetary quantification (Rahman et al. 2010). The trend of environmental reporting among Singapore companies is growing but is still in a low level when compared to other Asian countries, such as Japan, Malaysia and Thailand (Rahman et al. 2010; Batra 2013).

There is a regulatory framework for the environmental management in Singapore which is governed by (i) codes of practices and standards and (ii) legislation such as Government Acts, Rules and Regulations (Batra 2013, p. 76). Codes of practices and standards for environmental management were established by authorities, such as the National Environment Agency, Standards, Productivity and Innovation Board (SPRING Singapore) and PUB Singapore National Water Agency (World Business Council for Sustainable Development [WBCSD] 2018). The SGX issued voluntary sustainability reporting guideline for listed companies in June 2011. In relation to this guideline, the role of corporate governance has been identified as crucial in responding to investor concerns of environmental and social issues. The SGX has issued rules and guidance to require companies to publish the mandatory sustainability reporting in 2016 on a comply or explain basis (WBCSD 2018).

WBCSD (2018) showed that there is a rapid increase in environmental reporting provisions for companies based in Singapore after the new legislation to require companies to disclose key environmental related information, such as water usage, GHG emissions and energy consumption strategies. Over 90% of companies disclose environmental issues and the top three environmental areas are environmental incidents, waste treatment and effluent (WBCSD 2018).

From 2019, the Singapore government will impose a carbon tax to minimise GHG emission and SGX-listed companies need to embrace it into their corporate strategies and risk management (WBCSD 2018). Importantly, Singapore is the first country in Southeast Asia to introduce a carbon price (WBCSD 2018). Furthermore, issuance of green products, such as green bonds, and green financing continues to grow in the next few years.

Malaysia

In 2001, 367 Malaysian companies had been accredited with the ISO 14001 as these accredited companies are major suppliers to secure their supply contracts with MNCs (Thompson 2002). Malaysia has no statutory requirements for local companies to report environmental information prior to 2006 (Smith et al. 2007). However, there are three main institutions or agencies, namely, the Malaysian Accounting Standard Board (MASB) under the Financial Reporting Act 1997, the Malaysian Code on Corporate Governance (MCCG), and the Association of Chartered Certified Accountant's (ACCA) Environmental Reporting Guidelines that (in combination) created guidelines in order to promote local Malaysian companies to disclose environmental related information (Smith et al. 2007; Buniamin 2010).

There are three main environmental reporting standards in Malaysia. First, Paragraph 10 of MASB 1 – FRSs 101 – *Presentation of Financial Statements* –encourages local companies to provide supplementary environmental information in their reports to enhance investors' decision-making. Furthermore, MASB 20 – FRS 137 – *Provisions, Contingent Liabilities and Contingent Assets* – was issued in 2001 that helps companies to identify the contingent environmental liabilities and assets (but MASB 20 does not provide clear explanation about what types of liability that companies should report – Smith et al. 2007; Buniamin 2010; Batra 2013). Second, the Finance Committee on Corporate Governance of the Securities Commission initiated the MCCG in 2000 that established the guidelines or practices to help the board of directors who not only seek financial information but also environmental information (Buniamin 2010). Third, the ACCA with the collaboration of the Malaysian Department of Environment published *Environmental Reporting Guidelines for Malaysian Companies* in 2003, which provides a general overview of companies' environmental performance over the last decade (Buniamin 2010). Prior to 2003, the Department of Environment also established the Environmental Quality Act in 1974 (Section 37) requiring companies to disclose environmental information and Section 33A of the Act mandated the environmental audit and Section 34A indicated to disclose environmental impact from prescribed labelling (Smith et al. 2007; Nor et al. 2016).

In 2006, Bursa Malaysia launched the CSR Framework and Guideline for Malaysian public listed companies to encourage to report CSR information in their annual reports and became mandatory requirement in 2007 (Esa and Ghazali 2012; Fatima et al. 2016). However, the level of social and environmental reporting among Malaysian listed companies is fairly low (Sumiani et al. 2007; Buniamin 2010; Othman et al. 2011; Batra 2013; Sundarasen et al. 2016). In particular, key environmental disclosure includes water reporting, hazardous waste management and ecosystem management (Anas et al. 2015; Fatima et al. 2016). These environmental issues have been addressed in Bursa Malaysia's Sustainability Portal in 2010 (Fatima et al. 2016).

In 2015, Bursa Malaysia issued the new Sustainability Amendments to the Main Market Listing Requirements and ACE Market Listing Requirement, which upgraded the obligation to require listed issuers to disclose statement of material economic, environmental and social (EES) risks and opportunities from voluntary to "comply or explain" in their annual reports that replaced the existing statement of the CSR (Sustainable Stock Exchanges Initiative 2019). This new guideline provides guidance on governance, materiality and stakeholder engagement for companies (WBCSD 2018).

Discussion

Corporate reporting rate

According to KPMG reports (2013, 2015, 2017), Japan consistently has the highest reporting rate with 99% of the largest 100 listed companies in Japan, which is also the second highest of global reporting rate and the highest rate of reporting among Asian countries. While the reporting rate in Malaysia in 2011 was only 2% of the largest 100 listed companies, it rapidly increased to 97% in 2017 due to the new regulation and obligation of EES risks and opportunities in 2015. Currently, Malaysia ranks the fourth of global reporting rate and the second among Asian countries. The reporting rate in Singapore has doubled from 2011 to 2017. The reporting rate in China (including Hong Kong) has also continued to grow from 59% of the largest 100 listed companies in 2011 to 75% in 2017 (KPMG 2015, 2017). Overall, the corporate reporting rate among five Asian countries is higher than the global average with above 72% (KPMG 2017).

Drivers of environmental reporting regulations

Environmental consciousness is growing among Asian countries over the past few years. New environmental regulations, investor pressures and local stock exchange requirements play important roles in increasing corporate environmental reporting rates for five Asian countries (KPMG 2017). The level of environmental disclosure appears to be affected by both global concerns (i.e. climate change and SDGs) and national concerns (i.e. government and stock exchange regulations). The presence of environmental reporting regulations in China, Singapore and Malaysia is mainly driven by the local government and local stock exchanges in recent years (see Table 20.1). More pertinently, Bursa Malaysia and Singapore Stock Exchange were ranked the 15th and 16th out of 45 global stock exchanges of measuring sustainability disclosure in 2017 (Corporate Knights 2018).

Hong Kong reporting is mainly driven by the local exchange rather than the government. The implementation of environmental reporting in Hong Kong tends to have gone through an open consultation with HKEX and an ongoing stakeholder dialogue for 4 years (Ng and Leung 2020). However, Hong Kong was ranked 24th in global stock exchanges of measuring sustainability disclosure that indicates a warning signal to Hong Kong's global competitiveness and is lagging behind Bursa Malaysia and Singapore Stock Exchange (Corporate Knights 2018) (see Table 20.1).

China is driven by both the Chinese government and two stock exchanges, namely, the SSE and SZSE, which required companies to follow and issue CSR reports in 2009. The SSE was ranked 26th and SZSE was ranked 37th in global stock exchanges of measuring sustainability disclosure and the results show that the existence of CSR reporting policies is not well defined and combined with weak enforcement, which means that reporting practices in China are not as strong as elsewhere in Asia (Corporate Knights 2018). By contrast, Japan is mainly driven by the local government rather than the local stock exchange (KPMG 2017). According to Corporate Knights (2018), Japan has fallen from third in 2013 to 36th in 2017 of global stock exchanges of measuring sustainability disclosure due to weakness in the disclosure timeliness.

Table 20.1 Comparison of environmental reporting practices in five Asian countries

Country	*China*	*Hong Kong*	*Japan*	*Singapore*	*Malaysia*
Corporate reporting rates in 2011	59%	N/A	98%	42%	2%
Corporate reporting rates in 2017	75%	N/A	99%	84%	97%
Quality of environmental report	Low	Low	Medium	Low	Low
Quality of carbon reporting	10%	N/A	58%	N/A	N/A
Government	Mandatory	No	Mandatory	Mandatory	Mandatory
Stock exchange requirement	Yes, 2006 (SSE) 2008 (SZSE)	Yes, 2017	No	Yes, 2016	Yes, 2015
Global stock exchanges of measuring sustainability disclosure	27th (SSE) 37th (SZSE)	24th	36th	16th	15th

Source: KPMG 2013, 2015, 2017; Corporate Knights 2018.

Quality of environmental reporting

The quality of environmental reporting varies across countries with different regulatory systems and institutional environments. Larger companies tend to provide better quality environmental information than smaller companies (Buniamin 2010; Sulaiman et al. 2014). In particular, larger companies in Japan (with scores of 55 out of 100 in quality of environmental disclosure) are the highest among five Asian countries (KPMG 2013). Several environmental accounting studies indicate that the quality of environmental disclosure in China (excluding Hong Kong), Singapore and Malaysia tends to be low with descriptive and general statements as companies appear to provide insufficient balanced disclosure (including positive and negative news), inadequate quantitative environmental information and low standardised environmental performance indicators (Chung and Parker 2010; Guan and Yu 2011; Yu and Rowe 2017; Fatima et al. 2018). These findings could be useful for regulators and organisations to better understand how to establish effective policies and environmental standards to promote environmental reporting practices that could fit the political, institutional and cultural settings in the Asian contexts (Yu and Rowe 2017; Lee and Schaltegger 2018).

Regarding the quality of carbon reporting, around 27% of Japanese companies are more likely to disclose carbon reduction targets with long-term timelines of 15 years or more, which is above the global average of 14% (KPMG 2015). Japanese companies score 58% in the quality of carbon emission reporting, which is above the global average carbon reporting score of 51% (KPMG 2015). By contrast, Chinese companies score only 10% in the quality of carbon emission reporting, which shows that Chinese companies tend not to publish specific targets for carbon reduction, while European countries, such as Germany, France and the United Kingdom, are more likely to do so (KPMG 2015).

Conclusion

This chapter provides a general overview of the recent developments in environmental accounting and reporting practices among five Asian countries, namely, Mainland China, Hong Kong, Japan, Singapore and Malaysia. A number of observations can be made on the basis of this material.

First, the presence of coercive pressure from the local government and local stock exchange requirements in these countries has driven disclosure of environmental information. Second, third-party independent assurance of environmental information has become standard practices among Global 250 companies (KPMG 2017) despite not being legally mandated. Managers could consider external assurance to enhance investors or other stakeholders to increase confidence in the quality of environmental reporting and encourage the progress of internal environmental performance as key performance indicators. Third, the independent third-party assurance rate of carbon reporting information in Mainland China, Hong Kong, Singapore and Malaysia is still lagging behind the global average assurance rate of 62%, except for Japan that has a score of 65% (KPMG 2015). Ironically, China is one of the largest carbon emission countries, but the independent third-party assurance rate for carbon data and the quality of carbon reporting are merely 9% and 10%, respectively. Governments and regulatory authorities in these countries may need to take further actions or provide incentive schemes, such as tax reduction, to increase the carbon reporting rate.

This study has three main limitations and provides some suggestions for future research. First, it provides a brief overview of environmental accounting and reporting practices in the Asian context. However, this study has been still confined to five Asian countries. The extent and nature of environmental issues can vary across countries, regulatory systems and institutional environments due to different political, social and technological factors. More detailed research is needed on the environmental accounting and reporting practices by comparing differences and similarities among the developed and less developed Asian economies.

Second, this chapter has been confined to the literature review across five countries on this topic. The presence of environmental reporting regulation is primarily driven by the local government and the local stock exchange in recent years (see Table 20.1). Further empirical research and longitudinal studies could examine whether the extent, quality and assurance of environmental accounting and reporting practices in Asian countries could change over time. In addition, recent studies have advocated about the use of reflexivity by corporations in environmental accounting to promote evidence-based performance evaluations of progress made and ongoing attempts to redesign environmental accounting practices (Solomon et al. 2013; Leung and Snell 2019). Future research could explore this area in great details.

Third, this chapter has been limited to environmental reporting practices. Further research could focus on environmental governance (e.g. environmental committee, environmentally aware directors and environmental incentives in executive compensation) to understand the role and impact of boards, audit and compensation committees on the quality of environmental reporting (Mallin et al. 2013; Rodrigue et al. 2013).

References

Ali, M., Haider, M. B. and Islam, M.T., 2015. Revisiting corporate social disclosure in Japan. In: C, Noronha, ed., *Corporate Social Disclosure: Critical Perspectives in China and Japan*. Hampshire: Palgrave Macmillan, pp. 201–235.

Anas, A., Rashid, H. M. A. and Annuar, H. A., 2015. The effect of award on CSR disclosures in annual reports of Malaysian PLCs. *Social Responsibility Journal*, 11(4), 831–851.

Association of Chartered Certified Accountants, 2002. *The State of Corporate Environmental Reporting in Singapore*. Singapore: ACCA.
Batra, G. S., 2013. Environmental management and environmental disclosures: A comparison of corporate practices across Malaysia, Singapore and India. *South Asian Journal of Management*, 20(1), 62–96.
Buniamin, S., 2010. The quantity and quality of environmental reporting in annual report of publish listed companies in Malaysia. *Issues in Social and Environmental Accounting*, 4(2), 115–135.
Chan, J. C. H. and Welford, R., 2005. Assessing corporate environmental risk in China: An evaluation of reporting activities of Hong Kong listed enterprises. *Corporate Social Responsibility and Environmental Management*, 12, 88–104.
Chung, L. H. and Parker, L. D., 2010. Managing social and environmental action and accountability in the hospitality industry: A Singapore perspective. *Accounting Forum*, 34, 46–53.
Corporate Knights, 2018. *Measuring Sustainability Disclosure: Ranking the Worlds' Stock Exchanges*. Toronto: Corporate Knights.
Esa, E. and Ghazali, N. A. M., 2012. Corporate social responsibility and corporate governance in Malaysian government-linked companies. *Corporate Governance*, 12(3), 292–305.
Fatima, A. H., Abdullah, N. and Sulaiman, M., 2015. Environmental disclosure quality: Examining the impact of the stock exchange of Malaysia's listing requirements. *Social Responsibility Journal*, 11(4), 904–922.
Financial Services Development Council, 2018. *Environmental, Social and Governance (ESG) Strategy for Hong Kong*. Hong Kong: Financial Services Development Council.
Fitriasari, D. and Kawahara, N., 2018. Japan investment and Indonesia sustainability reporting: An isomorphism perspective. *Social Responsibility Journal,* 14 (4), 859–874.
Fukukawa, K. and Moon, J., 2004. A Japanese mode of corporate social responsibility: A study of website reporting. *Journal of Corporate Citizenship*, 14, 45–59.
Gao, S. S., Heravi, S. and Xiao, J. Z., 2005. Determinants of corporate social and environmental reporting in Hong Kong: A research note. *Accounting Forum*, 29, 233–242.
Guan, Z. and Yu, Z., 2011. A study of corporate social responsibility reports in China. *The China Nonprofit Review*, 3 (2), 171–193.
Jaggi, B., and Zhao, R., 1996. Environmental performance and reporting: Perceptions of managers and accounting professionals in Hong Kong. *The International Journal of Accounting*, 31(3), 333–346.
Haider, M. B. and Kokubu, K., 2015. Assurance and third-party comment on sustainability reporting in Japan: A descriptive study. *International Journal of Environment and Sustainable Development*, 14(3), 207–230.
He, C. and Loftus, J., 2014. Does environmental reporting reflect environmental performance? Evidence from China? *Pacific Accounting Review*, 26(1/2), 134–154.
Herzig, C., Viere, T., Schaltegger, S. and Burritt, R., 2012. *Environmental Management Accounting: Cases of South-East Asian Companies*. New York: Routledge.
Ho, S., Ng, P. and Ng, A., 1994. A study of environmental reporting in Hong Kong. *Hong Kong Accountant*, 5(1), 62–65.
Hong Kong Exchanges and Clearing Limited, 2015. *Consultation Paper: Review of the Environmental, Social and Governance Reporting Guide*. Hong Kong: Hong Kong Exchanges and Clearing Limited.
Hong Kong Exchanges and Clearing Limited, 2018. *Analysis of Environmental, Social and Governance Practice Disclosure in 2016/2017*. Hong Kong: Hong Kong Exchanges and Clearing Limited.
International Energy Agency, 2018. *Global Energy and CO2 Status Report 2017*. France: International Energy Agency.
KPMG, 2013. *KPMG International Survey of Corporate Social Reporting 2013*. Netherlands: KPMG.
KPMG, 2015. *KPMG International Survey of Corporate Social Reporting 2015*. Netherlands: KPMG.
KPMG, 2017. *KPMG International Survey of Corporate Social Reporting 2017*. Netherlands: KPMG.
KPMG, 2018. ESG: *A View from the Top: The KPMG, CLP and HKICS Survey on Environmental, Social and Governance (ESG)*. Hong Kong: KPMG.
Lai, J. H. K., 2014. Mandatory reporting of greenhouse gas emissions from buildings: Stakeholders' opinions in Hong Kong. *Energy Policy*, 75, 278–288.
Lee, K. H., 2014. Globalization, green management and climate change in the Asia-Pacific economy. *Journal of Asia Pacific Business*, 15(2), 101–104.
Lee, K. H. and Schaltegger, S., 2018. Asia Pacific perspectives on accounting for sustainability: An introduction. In: K. H. Lee and S. Schaltegger, ed., *Accounting for Sustainability: Asia Pacific Perspectives*. New York and London: Springer, pp. 1–8.

Leung, T. C. H., 2019. Legitimacy-seeking strategies in the gambling industry: The case of responsible gambling. *Sustainability Accounting, Management and Policy Journal*, 10(1), 97–125.
Leung, T. C. H. and Gray R., 2016. Social responsibility disclosure in the international gambling industry: A research note. *Meditari Accountancy Research*, 24(1), 73–90.
Leung, T. C. H. and Snell, R. S., 2017. Attraction or distraction? Corporate social responsibility in Macao's gambling industry. *Journal of Business Ethics*, 145(3), 637–658.
Leung, T. C. H. and Snell, R. S., 2019. Strategies for social and environmental disclosure: The case of multinational gambling companies. *Journal of Business Ethics*, doi.org/10.1007/s10551-019-04190-z.
Lynn, M., 1992. A note on corporate social disclosure in Hong Kong. *The British Accounting Review*, 2(2), 105–110.
Mallin, C., Michelon, G. and Raggi, C., 2012. Monitoring intensity and stakeholders' orientation: How does governance affect social and environmental disclosure? *Journal of Business Ethics*, 114, 29–43.
Ng, A. W. and Leung, T. C. H., 2020. Relevance of social environmental accounting to a global financial centre under one country two systems: Engaging stakeholders for sustainability and climate change. *Social and Environmental Accounting Journal*. doi.org/10.1080/0969160X.2020.1776625
Nishitani, K. and Kokubu, K., 2012. Why does the reduction of greenhouse gas emissions enhance firm value? The case of Japanese manufacturing firms. *Business Strategy and the Environment*, 21(8), 517–529.
Nor, N. M., Bahari, N. A. S., Adnan, N. A., Kamal, S. M. Q. A. S. and Ali, I. M., 2016. The effects of environmental disclosure on financial performance in Malaysia. *Porcedia Economics and Finance*, 35, 117–126.
Noronha, C., Tou, S., Cynthia, M. I. and Guan, J. J., 2013. Corporate social responsibility reporting in China: An overview and comparison with major trends. *Corporate Social Responsibility and Environmental Management*, 29(1), 29–42.
Noronha, C., Leung, T. C. H., and Lei, O., 2015. Corporate social responsibility disclosure in Chinese railway companies: Corporate response after a major train accident. *Sustainability Accounting, Management and Policy Journal*, 6 (4), 446–476.
Othman, S., Darus, F. and Arshad, R., 2011. The influence of coercive isomorphism on corporate social responsibility reporting and reputation. *Social Responsibility Journal*, 7(1), 119–135.
Rahman, S. A. B. A., Yusoff, R. B. and Mohamed, W. N. B. W., 2010. Environmental disclosure and financial performance: An empirical study of Malaysia, Thailand and Singapore. *Social and Environmental Accounting Journal*, 29 (2), 46–58.
Rodrigue, M., Magnan, M. and Cho, C. H., 2013. Is environmental governance substantive or symbolic? An empirical investigation. *Journal of Business Ethics*, 114, 107–129.
Rowe, A. L. and Guthrie, J., 2010. The Chinese government's formal institutional influence on corporate environmental management. *Public Management Review*, 12(4), 511–529.
Saka, C. and Oshika, T., 2014. Disclosure effects, carbon emissions and corporate value. *Sustainability Accounting, Management and Policy Journal*, 5(1), 22–45.
Smith, M., Yahya, K. and Amiruddin, A. M., 2007. Environmental disclosure and performance reporting in Malaysia. *Asian Review of Accounting*, 15(2), 185–199.
Solomon, J. F., Solomon, A., Joseph, N. L. and Norton, S. D., 2013. Impression management, myth creation and fabrication in private social and environmental reporting: Insights from Erving Goffman. *Accounting, Organizations and Society*, 38(3), 195–213.
Solovida, G. T. and Latan, H., 2017. Linking environmental strategy to environmental performance: Mediation role of environmental management accounting. *Sustainability Accounting, Management and Policy Journal*, 8(5), pp. 596–619.
Sueyoshi, T. and Goto, M., 2010. Measurement of a link Measurement of a linkage among environmental, operational, and financial performance in Japanese manufacturing firms: A use of data envelopment analysis with strong complementary slackness condition. *European Journal of Operational Research*, 207, 1742–1753.
Sulaiman, M., Abdullah, N. and Fatima, A. H., 2014. Determinants of environmental reporting quality in Malaysia. *International Journal of Economics, Management and Accounting*, 22, (1), 63–90.
Sumiani, Y., Haslinda, Y. and Lehman, G., 2007. Environmental reporting in a developing country: A case study on status and implementation in Malaysia. *Journal of Cleaner Production*, 12, 895–901.
Sundarasen, S. D., Je-Yen, T. and Rajangam, N., 2016. Board composition and corporate social responsibility in an emerging market. *Corporate Governance: The International Journal of Business in Society*, 16(1), 35–53.
Sustainable Stock Exchanges Initiative, 2019. *Bursa Malaysia (Malaysian Exchange)*. [online]. Available from: www.sseinitiative.org/data/myx/ [Accessed 20 May 2019].
The World Bank, 2013. *China Overview*. Washington: The World Bank.

The World Business Council for Sustainable Development (WBCSD), 2018. *The Reporting Exchange: Corporate and Sustainability Reporting in Singapore and Southeast Asia*. Geneva: The World Business Council for Sustainable Development.

Thompson, P., 2002. *Corporate Environmental Reporting in Singapore and Malaysia: Progress and Prospects*. Research Paper Series. UK: Nottingham University Business School.

Williams, S. M. and Pei, C. A. H. W., 1999. Corporate social disclosures by listed companies on their websites: An international comparison. *The International Journal of Accounting*, 34(4), 389–419.

Xiao, J. Z., Gao, S. S., Heravi, S. and Cheung, Y. C. Q., 2005. The impact of social and economic development on corporate social and environmental disclosure in Hong Kong and the UK. *Advances in International Accounting*, 18, 219–243.

Yamagami, T. and Kokubu, K., 1991. A note on corporate social disclosure in Japan. *Accounting, Auditing and Accountability Journal*, 4(4), 32–39.

Yang, H. H., Craig, R. and Farley, A., 2015. A review of Chinese and English language studies on corporate environmental reporting in China. *Critical Perspectives on Accounting*, 28, 30–48.

Yin, J. and Zhang, Y., 2012. Institutional dynamics and corporate social responsibility (CSR) in an emerging country context: Evidence from China. *Journal of Business Ethics*, 111(2), 301–316.

Yook, K. H., Song, H., Patten, D. M. and Kim, I. W., 2017. The disclosure of environmental conservation costs and its relation to eco-efficiency: Evidence from Japan. *Sustainability Accounting, Management and Policy Journal*, 8(1), 2–42.

Yu, S. and Rowe, A. L., 2017. Emerging phenomenon of corporate social and environmental reporting in China, *Sustainability Accounting, Management and Policy Journal*, 8(3), 386–415.

Zhao, N. and Patten, D. M., 2016. An exploratory analysis of managerial perceptions of social and environmental reporting in China: Evidence from state-owned enterprises in Beijing. *Sustainability Accounting, Management and Policy Journal*, 7(1), 80–98.

21
EUROPE

Thomas Riise Johansen

Introduction

Debates surrounding industrial democracy, stakeholder value added and similar issues in the 1970s fuelled an interest in research on social reporting (e.g. Ullmann 1979; Purdy 1981). Similarly, "environmentalism" (Gray 1992; Owen et al. 1997) and the influential Brundtland report (UNWCED 1987) revitalised social and environmental accounting research in the 1990s, with a growing interest in accounting for the environment. This interest has sustained until now, and for the past two decades or so attention has been given to both social and environmental reporting, including what is associated with the umbrella term "sustainability reporting". A difference between social reporting and environmental reporting is that the latter has been subjected to more extensive regulatory experiments, and this is particularly the case in a European context. The purpose of this chapter is thus to present environmental reporting regulations in Europe, to review research on these regulations and to outline related research opportunities.

Mandated environmental disclosures

Environmental disclosures in the annual report

About 20 years ago, several European countries began to mandate disclosure of environmental information in the management commentary section of the annual report. In most cases, this was a response to the 2001 recommendation from the European Commission (EC 2001a) that recommended environmental disclosure in the annual report. Spain pre-empted the 2001 recommendation with an environmental reporting standard in 1998 that required companies to disclose how environmental matters impacted their financial position (Larrinaga et al. 2002; Criado-Jiménez et al. 2008; Bebbington et al. 2012). Around 2001, Denmark, Finland, France, Norway, Portugal, Sweden and the United Kingdom (UK) added requirements for reporting on environmental impacts (Nyquist 2003; Hibbitt and Collison 2004; da Silva Monteiro and Aibar Guzmán 2010; Chelli et al. 2014, 2018; Fallan 2016), but in most cases, the details of how to report, including which impacts to report, were not specified.

One exception was the "New Economic Regulations" (NER) in France which required listed companies to report on 25 specified environmental indicators from 2002 onwards (Chelli et al. 2014, 2018). The Grenelle II regulation replaced NER starting in 2012 and represented an even more ambitious approach to mandatory reporting, expanding the NER requirements and also mandating larger, unlisted companies to report on environmental impacts. France can be seen as one of the most active countries in terms of mandating environmental reporting, not only due to its national initiatives but also for its role as a strong proponent for tough regulation at the European level (Kinderman 2020).

In 2003 the European Union (EU) amended its accounting directive (2003/51/EC) so that it included an overall requirement for large companies to disclose environmental matters in the management commentary. Accordingly, around 2005–2006 and after member state implementation of the Directive, all EU countries had such environmental reporting requirements in place.

In addition to France, some countries later expanded requirements for reporting on environmental matters as part of wider non-financial reporting. Denmark mandated reporting on Corporate Social Responsibility (CSR) policies, but on a "report-or-explain" basis from 2009 onwards (DBA 2013). The UK introduced a requirement in 2013 for companies to include a "strategic report" in the annual report which contained a section about impacts on the environment (HM Government 2019). That regulation also included a requirement for listed companies to disclose annual greenhouse gas emissions (Hummel and Rötzel 2019). In 2018, the UK further mandated reporting on energy use and greenhouse gas emissions in a new report, "the Energy and Carbon report", obliging inclusion of more information than just emissions (HM Government 2019).

Mandatory stand-alone environmental reports

Denmark was the first country to require organisations to prepare stand-alone environmental reports. The Danish stand-alone green accounts became mandatory in 1996 and many companies, including even small- and medium-sized companies, were subject to the regulation. The regulation on green accounts was clearly promising in terms of advancing environmental reporting and companies largely complied with the regulation from the beginning (Bebbington and Thy 1999). It was revised after some years, and the revisions included, among other things, a requirement for environmental authorities to augment the environmental report with a statement indicating whether the information contained in the report corresponded with the information the authority had gathered as part of its oversight responsibility for that particular company (Holgaard and Jørgensen 2005). As such, it appeared that this initiative had elements of what Owen et al. (1997) referred to as an administrative reform (mandating environmental reporting) and an institutional reform (motivating environmental protection agencies [EPAs] to use the information). Nevertheless, the Danish government later abolished mandatory green accounts on the stated grounds that there was no need for such accounts anymore as there were other reporting requirements, including the disclosure requirements as part of the "Pollutant Release and Transfer Register" (PRTR), that took over the role of the green accounts (Miljøstyrelsen 2014). See section "Other forms environmental accounting and reporting in the EU regulation" for comments on the PRTR.

In the Netherlands, a limited number of companies (reported to be about 250 companies) were categorised to have "serious adverse effects" on the environment and were required to prepare environmental reports starting in 1999 (Hibbitt and Collison 2004; Rahim 2013). The mandatory reporting contained detailed reporting requirements to the environmental protection authorities as well as a less ambitious overview or summary available to the public.

In 2011 the Sustainable Economy Law (SEL) in Spain mandated sustainability reports for large companies (Luque-Vilchez and Larrinaga 2016). Seemingly this is one of the most ambitious attempts to regulate environmental reporting, but subsequent empirical work has shown that few companies responded to this regulation.

Starting in 2008, more than 50 state-owned companies in Sweden have been required to prepare a GRI-based sustainability report (Borglund et al. 2010). A similar requirement for state owned companies was adopted in Spain in 2011 as part of the SEL (Larrinaga et al. 2018; Garcia-Torea et al. 2019) and was in the same year included in the state ownership policy of the Finnish government (PMO 2011).

EU initiatives in environmental accounting and reporting

The EU has a long history of initiatives directed at the environment, CSR and sustainability. Although in essence an environmental quality management system, the rather innovative Eco-Management and Audit Scheme (EMAS) (see more details below) developed by the EU in the 1990s contained some external reporting and generally pushed the environmental agenda forward (Power 1997; Hibbitt and Collison 2004).

The environmental reporting agenda was later driven by both the European Parliament and the Commission. Voices within the European Parliament have in particular for the past 15 years pushed for mandatory sustainability reporting. The different Directorates-General (DGs) within the European Commission – in particular DG Environment, DG Enterprise and DG internal market – have also been active, albeit less ambitious, and have over the years attempted to intervene through various means in the debate over environmental and sustainability reporting. Examples include workshops, consultations, recommendations and mandatory regulation (e.g. EC 2001b, 2009, 2010, 2017a). The following focuses on the initiatives related to mandatory environmental reporting regulation.

EU regulation on environmental disclosures in the annual report

As mentioned above, the EU recommendation from 2001 encouraged several countries to adopt environmental reporting requirements for annual reports. In that year the European Commission further published a green paper in which it was discussed whether large companies should prepare sustainability reports (EC 2001b). In the first instance, the subsequent accounting directive was only amended to include a simple disclosure requirement on environmental and employee matters in the management commentary section of the annual report. That change appeared in 2003 and there were no changes to EU regulations regarding environmental disclosures until 2014 despite the ambitions in 2001 about sustainability reporting, and despite pressure for more regulation put forward by the European Parliament and outside stakeholders. Some of the reasons for this stagnation were reported to be significant disagreements within the Commission and because of a prevalent concern about the administrative burden for businesses (Kinderman 2013; Johansen 2016).

The EU then adopted additional changes to the accounting directive in 2014. After a lengthy regulatory process (see, e.g., Johansen 2016; Monciardini 2016), it was legislated that large public interest companies were required to prepare non-financial reporting, including social and environmental reporting, for their annual reports. This regulation was more ambitious than the 2003 amendments, but it still contained a great deal of flexibility.

Although this regulatory instrument is a matter for member states to implement, the European Commission has demonstrated an interest in further supporting the preparation of non-financial reporting through the publication of non-binding guidelines on non-financial reporting and on climate-related information (EC 2017a, 2019).

Other forms of environmental accounting and reporting in the EU regulation

There are other environmental measurement and reporting requirements (to authorities) within the EU regulation. An initiative that includes publicly available information is the European Pollutant Release and Transfer Register (E-PRTR). The E-PRTR is a register of data from industrial facilities on emissions into air, land and water as well as waste management (transfers of waste). As its legal backing is a regulation and not a directive (EU 2006), it has direct effect in member states and is not part of member state implementation processes. It covers data from about 30,000 facilities in EU member states, as well as facilities in Iceland, Lichtenstein and Norway. Thus, the reporting unit (facility) is different from the environmental reporting in annual reports or stand-alone reports (entity level), and each company could potentially have a range of facilities to report on.

The European EMAS is an environmental management standard, which seeks to evaluate, report on and improve environmental management systems. The EMAS includes an environmental report (the EMAS report), and it is possible for companies to obtain an EMAS certification. The regulation on EMAS was introduced in 1993, its current version is from 2009 (EU 2009) and its appendices and guidelines are still being updated, reflecting an important initiative that has managed to gain a foothold.

Empirical research in the European region

A considerable body of empirical research has focused on environmental reporting in the European region. France, Italy, the Nordic countries, Spain and the UK have particularly been used as empirical settings for a range of studies, whereas studies originating in an Eastern European context are scarce (see, e.g., Fifka 2011). The intention here is not to conduct a general review of this empirical research, but to address those studies that intend to analyse and inform regulatory interventions in environmental reporting.

As evident from the previous sections, European countries have adopted a variety of environmental reporting regulations. These represent interesting settings for research. This section outlines some of the studies that have focused on unique European contexts.

The extent to which organisations respond to mandatory reporting requirements

The introduction of mandatory environmental reporting has sparked interest in investigations into whether regulatory instruments are successful in raising information levels, as well as the quality of information in those areas they intend to regulate. The results are mixed.

There is a great deal of evidence that mandatory requirements lead companies to report more on the environment (Bebbington and Thy 1999; Llena et al. 2007; Criado-Jiménez et al. 2008; Borglund et al. 2010; DBA 2013; Chelli et al. 2014; Costa and Agostini 2016; Hummel and Rötzel 2019). It is notable and surprising that there are a few exceptions to this. Most noteworthy in this regard are the findings from Spain. Researchers have found that relatively few companies comply with the Spanish law from 1998 that required environmental information in annual reports (Larrinaga et al. 2002; Garcia-Torea et al. 2019). In the Spanish context, researchers also found that the mandated sustainability reports in 2011 initially had no effect on the number of reports being prepared in Spain as a limited number of private companies (Luque-Vilchez and Larrinaga 2016) and public sector organisations (Larrinaga et al. 2018) complied with the sustainability report requirement.

While prior research generally documents that mandatory reporting increases the quantity of environmental information, there is less conclusive evidence about the quality of the information. In a Spanish context, Criado-Jiménez et al. (2008) found that the quality is improved to a lesser extent or not at all. The observed problem is, for example, that organisations tend to emphasise good and positive performance while placing less emphasis on the matters that may show the organisation in an unfavourable light (see also Llena et al. 2007). Luque-Vilchez and Larrinaga (2016) also found limited improvement in the quality of information in response to the Spanish regulation, inferring this development to the absence of institutional reform (Owen et al. 1997). Similar results appear in Costa and Agostini (2016), in which environmental reporting practices for Italian listed firms are analysed. The authors of that study concluded that the Italian environmental reporting regulation has no noteworthy effect on the completeness of information.

Chelli et al. (2018) are more positive and found that the French environmental reporting regulations (NER and Grenelle II) lead to more environmental reporting and that government-backed regulation is more effective in doing so than stock exchange regulation. Chelli et al. (2014) focused on the impact of NER in France and found that companies subjected to the regulation disclose more environmental information and seemingly also improve the quality of information. That study spanned 10 years and is one of the few that took advantage of the fact that environmental reporting regulation has been in place in France for many years. This allowed Chelli et al. (2014) to demonstrate that mandatory reporting has a lasting effect beyond the effects immediately seen after NER's introduction. A similar study by Chauvey et al. (2015) regarding CSR disclosure did not find any significant improvements in the quality of disclosures, however.

The effects of mandatory reporting on voluntary reporting

Mandatory regulation is linked to voluntary reporting as it may condition opportunities for wider environmental reporting and, indeed, some regulators view their regulatory instruments as having this purpose. From this perspective, mandatory reporting may inspire or encourage companies to report voluntarily. It may also be discerned that companies are forced to do so when responses to disclosure requirements raise the stakeholder's appetite for environmental reporting. Thus, the question is: does mandatory environmental reporting facilitate more voluntary reporting?

Answering this question is not without problems due to the blurred line between mandatory and voluntary reporting. Several regulatory instruments across Europe contain either rather narrow or vaguely specified disclosure requirements, potentially making compliance an undemanding exercise and potentially meaningless without supplementary voluntary reporting. In addition, management often has a great deal of discretion in responding to mandatory environmental reporting, which makes it further difficult to distinguish between mandatory and voluntary reporting (Schneider et al. 2018).

Although there may be a problem in distinguishing between mandatory and voluntary disclosure, some researchers have pursued this interrelation. Chelli et al. (2018) found that the French environmental reporting regulations (NER and Crenelle II) tend to prompt more voluntary reporting based on the GRI guidelines. The share of sustainability reporters among the largest companies also suggests that the existence of environmental disclosure regulation prompts (voluntary) sustainability reporting. This is visible when comparing the share of reporters in Denmark, France, the UK and Germany, where the uptake of reporting in those first three countries has increased over a 10-year period, whereas it has stagnated in Germany (Kinderman 2020).

Other effects of mandatory reporting

Regulation may improve the publicly available information about the environmental impacts of organisations, at least when it comes to the quantity of information. However, this does not necessarily imply that it induces a positive impact on the environment, nor does it necessarily imply that this information becomes part of accountability processes involving stakeholders as users of information.

There have been few studies that seek to address these matters in the European region.

Jackson et al. (2020) included a number of European countries in a study of whether disclosures have effects on CSR. While they found that reporting organisations initiate more CSR activities than non-reporting organisations, there is no evidence of the impact on CSR behaviour or performance. In the context of state-owned companies in Sweden, however, Borglund et al. (2010) found little impact on either sustainability activities or behaviour.

In terms of quantitatively associating environmental information with user reactions, there has been little research in the European region (see also Hassel et al. 2005).

Research on regulatory processes

A small number of studies have focused on the regulatory processes, or standardisation processes, that precede, or otherwise impact environmental reporting regulation.

As noted above, Spain has had environmental reporting for years, but a limited number of companies have complied with the regulation. The normativity of this reporting environment has been studied (Bebbington et al. 2012; Luque-Vilchez and Larrinaga 2016) and rather detailed accounts of regulatory processes have appeared in previous research (Luque-Vilchez and Larrinaga 2016; Garcia-Torea et al. 2019).

Kinderman (2013, 2019) has provided useful accounts of the EU regulatory process pertaining to CSR and disclosure regulation (see also Monciardini 2016). Kinderman (2020) demonstrated how and why the EU regulation from 2014 on non-financial reporting was weakened in the regulatory process. He also provided a better understanding of how and why country-level representatives and international stakeholder groups interact and attempt to intervene in this process. Among other things, this work demonstrates that cost concerns are central to non-financial reporting regulation and that EU regulation is greatly influenced by the existing reporting regulations in its member states. Kinderman's work suggests that Denmark, France and the UK all sought to "sell" their regulation in order to make it mandatory across Europe and that the interplay between countries in the regulatory process greatly reflects what countries already had in place in terms of reporting regulation.

These analyses further illustrate how fragile, and symbolic, attempts to form environmental reporting regulation can be. It is clear that the preference for regulation changed after the financial crisis in 2008–2009. In the period up to the crisis, the dominant view was that there was less need for mandatory reporting as companies were motivated by the "business case" and therefore reported voluntarily (Kinderman 2020). The combination of three factors was however conditioning environmental reporting regulation: a political climate in favour of "hard law", a commissioner from France and the European Parliament that pushed for stringent reporting regulation. Despite these conditions strongly in favour of stricter and mandatory environmental reporting regulation, the final regulation was rather weak. As such, this work demonstrates that support for regulation can be fragile and that some actors are part of these processes for other and sometimes symbolic reasons (Kinderman 2013, 2020; Johansen 2016; Monciardini 2016).

With regard to EU regulation, there has been some further research addressing how EU regulation is implemented in member states. Subsequent reviews showed that with few exceptions, the regulation has been implemented rather similarly across Europe (GRI et al. 2018). Some countries only made minor adjustments and, indeed, one purpose of the regulation was to facilitate an "upward regulatory harmonization" (Kinderman 2020). This was, for example, the case for France and the UK, both of which already had similar regulations in place (Aureli et al. 2019). Other countries had to adopt considerable changes to existing disclosure regulation. These countries included Italy and Eastern European countries (GRI et al. 2018; Aureli et al. 2019).

Opportunities for future research

Empirical research in the European area has predominantly focused on if, what and how much environmental information is reported. Yet, in coming to conclusions about the desirability of mandating environment reporting, such research must be supplemented by other foci. This includes studies that closely consider the institutional context within which organisations report on the environment as well as studies that seek to further inform policymaking. In this section, three lines of research are suggested that will offer great opportunities for future environmental reporting research conducted in the European region.

The institutional context of environmental reporting

Many studies adopt content analysis to study the effects of regulation on environmental reporting. It seems important to move this research more in the direction of being attentive to the institutional contexts. Even though disclosure requirements appear similar across European countries, the institutional contexts for disclosure differ. This provides an opportunity for research that develops an understanding of how regulation functions in particular institutional settings (Johansen 2016).

This line of research could be conducted as single-country studies. Opportunities seem particularly promising in some European countries, including Germany and those states in Eastern Europe that are scarcely researched, and in which the national setting could be of interest for international research. Environmental reporting research addressing institutional contexts could however preferably be done as multi-country studies; it is notable that the few studies of this kind have been viewed as having provided significant contributions (Bebbington et al. 2012; Chelli et al. 2018).

There has been some research on the role of monitoring, enforcing and sanctioning non-compliance with environmental reporting regulation (Costa and Agostini 2016; Fallan 2016; Luque-Vilchez and Larrinaga 2016), but there is a need for further research in this area (Chelli et al. 2018). Such oversight should generally be expected to have a positive impact on the extent of, and in particular the quality of, compliance with reporting regulation, but there are also scholars who suggest that normativity (i.e. uptake and quality of environmental reporting) can be achieved in regimes without sanctioning non-compliance (Chelli et al. 2014, 2018) and even in purely voluntary regimes (Bebbington et al. 2012).

Research focusing on other disclosures has, however, shown that enforcement styles impact reporting practice, for example, in terms of whether and how the reporting entity comes to see disclosure requirements as meaningful (Johansen and Plenborg 2018). As Bebbington et al. (2012) have forcefully argued, the success of mandatory reporting depends on whether reporting organisations perceive requirements as legitimate. So, it would be highly interesting to see more research that addresses the role of monitoring, enforcement and sanctioning of environmental reporting. It seems that some countries already offer a context in which such interrelations could be explored. For example, a survey across the financial reporting enforcement regimes in Europe suggests that the disclosures in the management commentary are subject to enforcement in many countries, and in several countries have actually led to enforcement decisions (CBS and EY 2014). On the other hand, environmental reporting regulations are rarely detailed and prescriptive, which makes reporting enforcement different from, for example, enforcing International Financial Reporting Standards (IFRS) disclosures. This could however call for other roles for authorities, including a role in providing encouragement, guidance and setting out routes towards best-practice reporting.

EU regulation

There also appears to be interesting research opportunities surrounding the EU regulation from 2014 on non-financial reporting. As this initiative led to rather similar regulations across Europe (GRI et al. 2018), it would be fruitful to compare how companies in multiple countries respond to the regulation. This could also expose the implications of different institutional contexts. As part of this, it is possible to examine whether it matters if new reporting regulation gradually builds on previous regulation, or if the regulation potentially alters existing reporting practices to a great extent. Such a study would relate to the argument made by Bebbington et al. (2012) that the nature of the reporting practices that existed before the regulatory intervention is important for the normativity of such an intervention (see also Luque-Vilchez and Larrinaga 2016).

In addition to the above-mentioned rationales for multi-country studies in Europe, it is worth noting that considerable differences in viewpoints were observed across countries in the EU regulatory process leading up to the 2014 regulation (Kinderman 2013, 2020; Monciardini 2016), and it could be interesting to investigate whether these differences are reflected in reporting practices. Kinderman (2020), for example, suggested that the 2014 regulation was considerably shaped by the European Council during intense debates between the governments of Germany, France and the UK. Germany was clearly an opponent of tough regulation, France preferred regulation that was demanding, while the UK stood in the middle and sought to ensure that the regulation was as similar as possible to the existing UK regulation. In addition to the study of how these debates are reflected in reporting practices, research could also seek to further understand how and why they were implicated in regulatory processes at the EU and at the member-state levels. In this regard, and as discussed above, it is noteworthy that the EU regulation ended up rather weak although the regulatory environment has arguably never been more susceptible to environmental reporting regulation than in the years preceding the 2014 EU regulation.

Finally, there is also plenty of room for policymakers to draw more on academics, both in terms of empirical research and involving academics in policymaking. Garcia-Torea et al. (2019) provided specific examples of how researchers participated in the Spanish implementation of the 2014 EU regulation on non-financial information in a way that served to make the regulation more strict and increased the number of companies subjected to the regulation.

In addition to the EU regulation on non-financial reporting, there is also space for research examining the interrelations between environmental management systems and environmental reporting. The EMAS regulation has a long tradition and also contains an element of reporting. Although it has some similarities with ISA 14001, the EMAS is rather unique from an international perspective and research could examine the potential of linking management systems with external reporting and the extent to which this linking drives reporting quality and environmental performance.

Other forms of environmental reporting

The third line of research opportunities could go beyond the traditional reporting model where accounts are aggregated to the highest level and reported to stakeholders at this level. This model is known from financial reporting where the financial statements aggregate information from all legal entities in a group and report to investors and other stakeholders presumably interested in group-level information. However, while group environmental reporting may have merit, there may also be relevant environmental reporting that differs in two related ways.

First, environmental reporting research could be more attentive to reporting at the level of industrial facilities. Given that environmental permits for industrial activities are granted at the facility level and that different EPAs typically are assigned with the responsibility of overseeing environmental impacts of facilities, there is significant external reporting of environmental indicators from this level. It would be interesting to see research that addresses these forms of reporting and which adopts site-level focus. There are valuable opportunities for such research in the European region. For example, the European Pollutant Release and Transfer Register (E-PRTR) has not been studied by accounting researchers even though the register seemingly contains a lot of data on externally reported emissions from industrial facilities in Europe. The European Commission has conducted an evaluation of the PRTR (EC 2017b), in which the EC argues that the register is effective, but there has been no research to challenge such claims or critically evaluate whether such accounts are useful for observing, comparing and responding to environmental impacts. This should certainly be of interest to accounting researchers as such information on environmental impacts at the facility level may be stronger, and more present and relevant for accountability processes than entity-level accounts.

Second, as EPAs and similar stakeholder groups relate to companies at the facility level and would be less interested in group-level reporting, it would be interesting to see research focusing on users of environmental reporting at the facility level. Such research could examine the role of environmental accounting information in holding companies to account for environmental impacts. This should include the role of EPAs, how these authorities form a view of environmental impacts caused by companies, whether they enforce environmental information as well as what defines the role of environmental indicators in the oversight of companies by these authorities. Research along these lines would address the intersection between administrative and institutional reforms (Owen et al. 1997), which have been argued to be necessary if environmental accounting and reporting should make a difference (Larrinaga et al. 2002; Bebbington 2013).

Conclusion

Compared to other regions, countries within the European region have generally showcased many examples of environmental reporting regulation from the early 1990s (Hibbitt and Collison 2004) up to today. This chapter has sought to identify country- and EU-level regulations and has reviewed research that has investigated these regulations. This demonstrates that the European region offers plenty of opportunities for research on environmental reporting regulations. Suggestions for future research include research that carefully addresses the institutional context of reporting, research on EU initiatives and research that focuses on site-level reporting and accountability processes.

References

Aureli, S., Magnaghi, E., and Salvatori, F., 2019. The role of existing regulation and discretion in harmonising non-financial disclosure. *Accounting in Europe*, 16 (3), 290–312.

Bebbington, J., 2013. As a matter of policy. *Social and Environmental Accountability Journal*, 33 (1), 1–4.

Bebbington, J., Kirk, E.A., and Larrinaga, C., 2012. The production of normativity: A comparison of reporting regimes in Spain and the UK. *Accounting, Organizations and Society*, 37 (2), 78–94.

Bebbington, J., and Thy, C., 1999. Compulsory environmental reporting in Denmark: An evaluation. *Social and Environmental Accountability Journal*, 19 (2), 2–4.

Borglund, T., Frostenson, M., and Windell, K., 2010. *Increasing responsibility through transparency? A study of the consequences of new guidelines for sustainability reporting by Swedish state-owned companies.* Stockholm: Regeringskansliet.

CBS and EY, 2014. *Financial reporting enforcement: A study of enforcement activities in 17 European countries.* Copenhagen: Ernst & Young.

Chauvey, J.N., Giordano-Spring, S., Cho, C.H., and Patten, D.M., 2015. The normativity and legitimacy of CSR disclosure: Evidence from France. *Journal of Business Ethics*, 130 (4), 789–803.

Chelli, M., Durocher, S., and Fortin, A., 2018. Normativity in environmental reporting: A comparison of three regimes. *Journal of Business Ethics*, 149 (2), 285–311.

Chelli, M., Durocher, S., and Richard, J., 2014. France's new economic regulations: Insights from institutional legitimacy theory. *Accounting, Auditing & Accountability Journal*, 27 (2), 283–316.

Costa, E., and Agostini, M., 2016. Mandatory disclosure about environmental and employee matters in the reports of Italian listed corporate groups. *Social and Environmental Accountability Journal*, 36 (1), 10–33.

Criado-Jiménez, I., Fernández-Chulián, M., Larrinaga-González, C., and Husillos-Carqués, F.J., 2008. Compliance with mandatory environmental reporting in financial statements: The case of Spain (2001–2003). *Journal of Business Ethics*, 79 (3), 245–262.

da Silva Monteiro, S.M., and Aibar Guzmán, B., 2010. The influence of the Portuguese environmental accounting standard on the environmental disclosures in the annual reports of large companies operating in Portugal: A first view (2002–2004). *Management of Environmental Quality: An International Journal*, 21 (4), 414–435.

DBA, 2013. *Corporate social responsibility and reporting in Denmark: Impact of the third year subject to legal requirements for reporting on CSR in the Danish Financial Statements Act.* Copenhagen: Danish Business Agency.

EC, 2001a. *Commission recommendation of 30 May 2001 on the recognition, measurement and disclosure of environmental issues in the annual accounts and annual reports of companies.* Brussels: European Commission.

EC, 2001b. *Promoting a European framework for corporate social responsibility.* Green Paper, European Commission.

EC, 2009. *European workshops on the disclosure of environmental, social and governance information: Five workshops in 2009 and 2010.* Brussels: European Commission.

EC, 2010. *Public consultation of disclosure of non-financial information by companies.* Brussels: European Commission.

EC, 2017a. *Communication from the Commission: Guidelines on non-financial reporting.* Brussels: European Commission.

EC, 2017b. *REFIT evaluation of Regulation (EC) No 166/2006 concerning the establishment of a European Pollutant Release and Transfer Register.* Brussels: European Commission.

EC, 2019. *Communication from the Commission: Guidelines on non-financial reporting: Supplement on reporting climate-related information.* Brussels: European Commission.

EU, 2006. *Regulation (EC) No 166/2006 concerning the establishment of a European Pollutant Release and Transfer Register (E-PRTR).* Brussels: European Union.

EU, 2009. *Regulation (EC) No 1221/2009 of the European Parliament and of the Council of 25 November 2009.* Brussels: European Union.

Fallan, E., 2016. Environmental reporting regulations and reporting practices. *Social and Environmental Accountability Journal*, 36 (1), 34–55.

Fifka, M.S., 2011. Corporate responsibility reporting and its determinants in comparative perspective–A review of the empirical literature and a meta-analysis. *Business Strategy and the Environment*, 22 (1), 1–35.

Garcia-Torea, N., Larrinaga, C., and Luque-Vílchez, M., 2019. Academic engagement in policy-making and social and environmental reporting. *Sustainability Accounting, Management and Policy Journal*, 11 (2), 281–290.

Gray, R., 1992. Accounting and environmentalism: An exploration of the challenge of gently accounting for accountability, transparency and sustainability. *Accounting, Organizations and Society*, 17 (5), 399–425.

GRI, CSR Europe, and Accountancy Europe, 2018. *Member State Implementation of Directive 2014/95/EU: A comprehensive overview of how member states are implementing the EU Directive on Non-financial and Diversity Information*. Amsterdam and Brussels: GRI, CSR Europe and Accountancy Europe.

Hassel, L., Nilsson, H., and Nyquist, S., 2005. The value relevance of environmental performance. *European Accounting Review*, 14 (1), 41–61.

Hibbitt, C., and Collison, D., 2004. Corporate environmental disclosure and reporting developments in Europe. *Social and Environmental Accountability Journal*, 24 (1), 1–11.

Holgaard, J.E., and Jørgensen, T.H., 2005. A decade of mandatory environmental reporting in Denmark. *European Environment*, 15 (6), 362–373.

HM Government, 2019. *Environmental Reporting Guidelines: Including Streamlined Energy and Carbon Reporting Guidance*. London: HM Government.

Hummel, K., and Rötzel, P., 2019. Mandating the sustainability disclosure in annual reports—Evidence from the United Kingdom. *Schmalenbach Business Review*, 71 (2), 205–247.

Jackson, G., Bartosch, J., Avetisyan, E., Kinderman, D., and Knudsen, J.S., 2020. Mandatory non-financial disclosure and its influence on CSR: An international comparison. *Journal of Business Ethics*, 162 (2), 323–342.

Johansen, T.R., 2016. EU regulation of corporate social and environmental reporting, 36 (1), 1–9.

Johansen, T.R., and Plenborg, T., 2018. Company responses to demands for annual report changes. *Accounting, Auditing & Accountability Journal*, 31 (6), 1593–1617.

Kinderman, D., 2013. Corporate social responsibility in the EU, 1993–2013: Institutional ambiguity, economic crises, business legitimacy and bureaucratic politics. *Journal of Common Market Studies*, 51 (4), 701–720.

Kinderman, D., 2020. The challenges of upward regulatory harmonization: The case of sustainability reporting in the European Union. *Regulation & Governance*, 14 (4), 674–697.

Larrinaga, C., Carrasco, F., Correa, C., Llena, F., and Moneva, J., 2002. Accountability and accounting regulation: The case of the Spanish environmental disclosure standard. *European Accounting Review*, 11 (4), 723–740.

Larrinaga, C., Luque-Vilchez, M., and Fernández, R., 2018. Sustainability accounting regulation in Spanish public sector organizations. *Public Money & Management*, 38 (5), 345–354.

Llena, F., Moneva, J.M., and Hernandez, B., 2007. Environmental disclosures and compulsory accounting standards: The case of Spanish annual reports. *Business Strategy and the Environment*, 16 (1), 50–63.

Luque-Vilchez, M., and Larrinaga, C., 2016. Reporting models do not translate well: Failing to regulate CSR reporting in Spain. *Social and Environmental Accountability Journal*, 36 (1), 56–75.

Miljøstyrelsen, 2014. *Evaluering af grønne regnskaber: En undersøgelse af de grønne regnskabers effekt og vurdering af fremtidige muligheder for miljørapportering*. Copenhagen: Miljøstyrelsen.

Monciardini, D., 2016. The "Coalition of the Unlikely" driving the EU regulatory process of non-financial reporting. *Social and Environmental Accountability Journal*, 36 (1), 76–89.

Nyquist, S., 2003. The legislation of environmental disclosures in three Nordic countries – A comparison. *Business Strategy and the Environment*, 12 (1), 12–25.

Owen, D.L., Gray, R., and Bebbington, J., 1997. Green accounting: Cosmetic irrelevance or radical agenda for change. *Asia-Pacific Journal of Accounting*, 4 (2), 175–198.

PMO, 2011. *Government resolution on state ownership policy 3 November 2011*. Helsinki: Prime Minister's Office.

Power, M., 1997. *The Audit Society*. Oxford: Oxford University Press.

Purdy, D.E., 1981. The provision of financial information to employees: A study of the reporting practices of some large public companies in the United Kingdom. *Accounting, Organizations and Society*, 6 (4), 327–338.

Rahim, M.M., 2013. Legal regulation of corporate social responsibility. A meta-regulation approach of law for raising CSR in a weak economy. Berlin: Springer.

Schneider, T., Michelon, G., and Paananen, M., 2018. Environmental and social matters in mandatory corporate reporting: An academic note. *Accounting Perspectives*, 17 (2), 275–305.

Ullmann, A.A., 1979. Corporate social reporting: Political interests and conflicts in Germany. *Accounting, Organizations and Society*, 4 (1/2), 123–133.

UNWCED, 1987. *Our Common Future*. Oxford: United Nations World Commission on Environment and Development and Oxford University Press.

22

ENVIRONMENTAL ACCOUNTING AND REPORTING

Evidence from the MENA region

Radhi Al-Hamadeen

Introduction and overview of the region

This chapter focuses on environmental accounting and reporting (EAR) in the Middle East and North Africa (MENA) region. Like other countries of the world, the Sustainable Development Goals (SDGs) form the backdrop of regional developmental priorities and these goals resonate with business in the region. Likewise, environmental reporting is undertaken by large companies in the region. For example, KPMG (2017) noted that reporting in the MENA region sits at 52% of large companies (for comparison, other regions have a higher incidence: Americas, 83%; Asia Pacific, 78%; and Europe, 77%). Of concern in this context is an apparent decline in reporting in the region, from 61% in 2011 to 54% and 53% in 2013 and 2015, respectively).[1] This sits in contrast to the challenges that face the region and the widespread belief that "environmental and social issues such as climate change, water scarcity and human rights will increasingly be seen as financial rather than non-financial issues" (KPMG 2017, p. 7). These issues, and others, are central to the region.

The MENA region (which also corresponds to the Greater Middle East – see World Bank 2014) covers a surface of over 15 million square kilometres and contains some 6% of the world's population of which half live in cities (IMF 2020). The region contains abundant human and natural resources and accounts for a large share of the world's petroleum production and exports (IMF 2020). In addition, the region has, on average, a reasonable standard of living in international terms, with countries in the region varying substantially in terms of resources, economic and geographical size, population and standards of living (IMF 2020). In terms of economic ties and intra-regional relations, the region suffers from weak intra-regional interaction, limited trade of goods and services, and lack of integration of capital markets, which have been all negatively impacted by the geo-political conflicts in some parts of the MENA region (IMF 2020). At the same time, it could be argued that the MENA region shares many common developmental challenges, has similar demographics, environmental similarities and some points of shared culture (Word Bank 2020a; UNICEF 2019).

O'Sullivan et al. (2012) emphasised that the Arab Spring (specifically after 2010) brought to light key challenges in the MENA region that already existed. These multi-level challenges (economic, social, and political) have significantly impacted the region and the people's quality of life. These challenges include, for example (O'Sullivan et al. 2012, p. 2):

- High levels of unemployment (in particular among youth generation)
- Pervasive corruption and lack of accountability and transparency
- Large public sectors with state-owned enterprises that "crowd out" the development of private sector and investment, which in turn decreases enterprise creation
- High dependence, for some countries in the region, on fuel and food imports, hence generating extensive exposure to commodity price volatility
- Additionally, the region faces serious environmental challenges such as water scarcity, loss of biodiversity, air pollution, inadequate waste management, declining marine resources and degradation of coastal ecosystems (Abumoghli and Goncalves, 2020).

According to O'Sullivan et al. (2012), these challenges, which are both "structural and interconnected", can be faced and addressed only through precise coordinated and comprehensive strategy that would involve all of the governments, civil society, the private sector, and the international community.

The OECD (2018) emphasises that almost two-thirds of MENA nations are dependent on natural resources; economic diversification (production, export and government revenue) is thus a major developmental challenge. Although MENA's exports and imports of goods account only for 4% of the world trade and 15% of trade of developing countries (IMF 2020), the current estimates indicate that 79.4% of the world's proven oil reserves are located in Organization of the Petroleum Exporting Countries (OPEC) member countries, with the bulk of OPEC oil reserves being in the Middle East (64.5% of the OPEC total and 51.2% of the world's oil reserves – see OPEC 2020). In this context, it can be said that the oil-industry-related activities (including exploration, development, and exportation) create particular environmental challenges. This is also evident in the CO_2 emissions ratio (metric tons per capita) for the MENA region (see Table 22.1).

The Work Bank (2007) classifies countries in the region by reference to the availability of oil resources and population size with three country types emerging:

- **Group I: Resource-rich, labour-abundant** countries. This group represents producers and exporters of oil and gas and have large home country populations, which

Table 22.1 Key demographical, economic, and environmental characteristics of MENA region

Aspect | Indicator	*MENA*		*The World*	
	2015	*2020*	*2015*	*2020*
Population growth rate (%)	1.88	1.73	1.17	1.08
Real GDP growth (%)	1.90	−4.00	3.50	−3.00
Inflation (average consumer prices) (%)	4.20	7.60	2.80	3.00
CO_2 emissions (metric tons per capita) *	6.22	-	4.98	-

Source: Adapted from International Monetary Fund (IMF 2020). *Adapted from World Bank (2020b).

represent almost the totality of their residents. This group includes Algeria, Iraq, Syria, and Yemen.

- **Group II: Resource-rich, labour-importing** countries. This group represents producers and exporters of oil and gas and have large number of foreign or expatriate residents, who represent a significant percentage of the total population of some countries (or even the majority in some cases). This group comprises Libya and the Gulf Cooperation Council (GCC) countries (Bahrain, Kuwait, Oman, Qatar, Saudi Arabia, and the United Arab Emirates [UAE]).
- **Group III: Resource-poor** countries. This group represents small producers or importers of oil and gas. These countries include Djibouti, Egypt, Jordan, Lebanon, Mauritania, Morocco, Tunisia, and Palestine.

For the purpose of this chapter, and based on World Bank (2007) classification (indicated above), the MENA region is divided into three categories as follows:

- Levant countries: Jordan, Lebanon, Syria, and Palestine
- GCC countries and Iraq: Bahrain, Iraq, Kuwait, Qatar, Saudi Arabia, UAE, and Oman
- North Africa (Arab countries): Algeria, Egypt, Libya, Morocco, and Tunisia.

This chapter now moves to provide an overview of the recent development of EAR practices among different countries in the MENA region, that is, Levant countries, GCC (plus Iraq) and North Africa. Finally, the chapter concludes with a discussion and conclusion.

Environmental accounting and reporting practices in the MENA region

Environmental challenges in the MENA region

Abumoghli and Goncalves (2020) emphasised that the MENA countries share common environmental challenges and "trans-boundary conflicts" that threaten the long-term stability of the region. In a report issued by the United Nations Environmental Program (UNEP), Abumoghli and Goncalves (2020) identified the crucial environmental challenges of water scarcity, loss of biodiversity, arable land depletion, air pollution, inadequate waste management, declining marine resources, and degradation of coastal ecosystems. In this regard, it has been argued that the "future development scenarios are expected to exacerbate these challenges, especially given that MENA is one of the regions that is most vulnerable to the impacts of climate change" (IPCC 2013 in Abumoghli and Goncalves 2020, p. 2). Sakmar et al. (2011) emphasised that while many of the MENA region's economic challenges have been widely explored and analysed, the environmental challenges, in particular, are rarely taken into consideration in the process of formulating economic policies in the region. In addition, and according to Carbon Dioxide Information Analysis Center (CDIAC 2016 in the World Bank 2020b), oil and gas producing countries generate the most environmental pollution in the region (specifically Algeria, Kuwait, and Saudi Arabia). Analysis now turns to how EAR has developed in this region.

Trends of environmental accounting and reporting research in the MENA region

Choi and Meek (2014) stated that, in general, corporate disclosures in developing countries are less extensive and less credible than disclosures from developed countries. One of the key reasons for this is the absence of monitoring techniques and enforcement of disclosure requirements. In the same context, accounting literature suggests that in comparison with the developed countries, less attention has been given to investigating EAR practices in the developing countries (Suwaidan et al. 2004; Ismail and Ibrahim 2009; Luo et al. 2013; Al-Hamadeen and Badran 2014).

Research on EAR in the MENA region can be classified according to the geographical scope (national and regional) and thematic interest of the research. The national studies focus on a specific country (see, e.g., Suwaidan et al. 2004; Aladwan 2018; Gerged et al. 2018; Abdull Razak et al. 2019; Rabi 2019), whereas the regional ones give focus to a group of countries within the region, for example, GCC, MENA, and North Africa (see, e.g., Sakmar et al. 2011; Eljayash et al. 2012; Eljayash 2015; Hawkamah 2014; Khalifa and Hammad 2014; Akrout and Ben Othman 2016; Gerged et al. 2018; Kilincarslan et al. 2020).

According to thematic interest of the research, literature on EAR in the MENA region can be classified into four thematic clusters that influence the EAR practice. These include investigating the ownership structure (Habbash 2015; Akrout and Ben Othman 2016; Al Amosh and Mansor 2020); examining the reporting companies' characteristics (Ismail and Ibrahim 2009, Eljayash et al. 2012; Al-Hamadeen and Badran 2014; Elshabasy 2018; Gerged et al. 2020); investigating the national contextual determinants (Ahmad and Gao 2005; Al-Ajmi et al. 2015; Al-Nimer 2015; Bani-Khalid and Kouhy 2017; Aladwan 2018); and governance attributes and board of directors' characteristics (Aboud and Diab 2018; Rabi 2019; Arayssi et al. 2020; Kilincarslan et al. 2020). Table 22.2 illustrates the key and sub-thematic research ideas on EAR in the MENA region.

Table 22.2 shows the factors that each of the thematic aspects encompasses. The reader is referred to the above-mentioned studies to see how each of these sub-factors affects EAR practices.

Practices of environmental accounting and reporting in Levant countries

Jordan

In recent years, considerable effort has been made by public and private parties in addressing environmental issues with three developments emerging. These include (1) the establishment

Table 22.2 Key and sub-thematic research ideas on EAR in the MENA region

Thematic research aspect	*Sub-themes covered*
Ownership structure	State ownership; Institutional ownership; Foreign ownership; Managerial ownership; Family ownership
Characteristics of the reporting companies	Business sector; Firm size, Profitability; Firm leverage; Firm value, Firm age, Audit firm size; Business culture
National contextual determinants	Regulatory reform; Political conditions, Legal system, Cultural values; Economic development; Country's Internet penetration, Stock market liquidity
Governance attributes and board of directors' characteristics	CG codes; Role duality; Board independence; Board ownership; Board size; Audit committee effectiveness; ESG index; BOD structure; Female board participation

of the Ministry of Environment in 2006 (under the provisional Environmental Protection Law No. [1] of 2003), (2) using the permanent *Environment Protection Law* (№. 52 of 2006), and (3) the establishment of the Royal Administration for Environmental Protection (Environment Police/Rangers) in 2006. Additionally, on the unofficial level, many civil associations and non-governmental organisations have been established, such as Jordan Environment Society in 1988; Association for Energy, Water & Environment in 2009; and the Jordanian Climate Change & Environmental Protection Society in 2015. These organisations play an important role in raising public awareness and community involvement on the environmental related issues.

In Jordan, there is no generally accepted framework for accounting and disclosing environmental information. However, national legislation emphasises the necessity of protecting the environment especially in areas governed by the *Environment Protection Act* (2006).[2] Nevertheless, the Act did not require business entities to disclose information about their commitment to environmental protection (e.g. the environmental protection-related expenditures). Furthermore, the Jordanian business-related regulations (i.e. Companies Law, Securities Law, and Commercial Law) do not oblige companies to issue periodic reports on their environmental performance. However, the Jordanian Securities Law No. 23 of 1997 requires the publicly listed companies to disclose their contributions to serving the environment and the local community.

Within the Jordanian business environment, limited studies have been conducted in the area of EAR. The earlier wave of research was conducted during the years 1990–2010 (see, e.g., Sha'shaa 1991; Al-Hamadeen 2002; Suwaidan et al. 2004; Ismail and Ibrahim 2009). Although research in this area is still not well established, there is a noticeable increase of research from 2010 onwards that addresses this issue (see, e.g., Al-Hamadeen and Badran 2014; Al-Nimer 2015; Bani-Khalid and Kouhy 2017; Aladwan 2018; Joudeh et al. 2018; Rabi 2019; Al-Amosh and Mansor 2020).

When it comes to business sectors, attention was given in the majority of these studies to investigate practices of the publicly listed "industrial" companies with a special focus on environment-sensitive industries: namely, mining and extraction, chemicals, and pharmaceuticals (see, e.g., Sha'shaa 1991; Suwaidan et al. 2004; Al-Nimer 2015; Aladwan 2018; Joudeh et al. 2018; Rabi 2019). Other studies have investigated EAR practices implemented by the largest Jordanian businesses in three different sectors (i.e. industrial, financial, and services – see, e.g., Ismail and Ibrahim 2009; Barakat et al. 2011; and Al-Hamadeen and Badran 2014).

When it comes to improvements in the Jordanian companies' practice of EAR, previous studies indicate that although there was an increase in the companies' disclosures, more information about their non-financial performance over the years is still needed (Barakat et al. 2011; Aladwan 2018). Moreover, these studies show that environment is still the weakest among all other sustainability-related disclosed issues (Ismail and Ibrahim 2009; Barakat et al. 2011; Al-Hamadeen and Badran 2014). Among all investigated factors, ownership structure, governance, size, and sector (predominantly industrial) are associated with disclosing more environmental related information (Ismail and Ibrahim 2009; Rabi 2019). Nevertheless, it has been suggested that the Jordanian companies are committed to EAR practices as part of sustainable development (Aladwan 2018). Notably, these companies also consider the cultural values, economic development, political conditions, and legal system as significant factors for explaining the level of "corporate environmental reporting" (Bani-Khalid and Kouhy 2017).

Lebanon and Syria

In Lebanon and Syria, the political scene conditions all other aspects. Lebanon suffered heavily from the civil war in the 1970s and 1980s, and it still suffering from the consequences of that conflict. At the same time, Lebanon faces a number of environmental threats, including solid waste management, air and water pollution, risks associated with climate change, and shortage of water supply. Jadam (2010) stated that increased population, public awareness and lifestyle, political indecision, and inadequate legislation are the most important reasons for increasing environmental challenges in Lebanon. According to a study conducted by the World Bank in 2004 on the state of environmental degradation in Lebanon, the cost of degradation caused by pollution from illegal dumping and waste burning was estimated at $10 million per year, and was still rising (Jadam 2010).

In Syria, and since the outbreak of the Arab Spring in 2011 which, in turn, has been transformed into a civil war, the environmental challenges have increased dramatically. According to Zwijnenburg and Te Pas (2015), Syria has major environmental issues, such as desertification, deforestation, soil erosion, coastal pollution, water pollution from the dumping of raw sewage and wastes from petroleum refining, and inadequate supplies of potable water.

To the best of the author's knowledge, and based on the publicly available literature, no evidence has been provided within the accounting, finance, and business disciplines to describe, examine, or critique business practices in the area of EAR in Lebanon and Syria. Therefore, it is exceptionally difficult to infer or judge the corporate practices around EAR in this part of the MENA region.

Palestine

Since 1948, Palestine has faced two challenges: the Israeli occupation and internal division that in turn have further weakened the state and its legal system (Barakat et al. 2011). Economic stability, investments flows, business environment, and legislation of business practices have all been negatively impacted by these challenges.

Within the Palestinian context, a very limited attention has been given to explore EAR practices (see, Barakat et al. 2011; Alkababji 2014; Ahmed 2019) and it is difficult to build a clear image about EAR practices. In general, it is believed that information disclosed about environmental practices is minimal due to weaknesses in reporting and accounting practices of Palestinian companies. Alkababji (2014) who examined 48 corporate annual reports that were listed on the Palestine Exchange (PEX) in 2012 asserted that the disclosed environmental performance indicators were "on average" less common than social performance indicators. According to Ahmed (2019), the low level and quality of EAR is caused by factors, such as lack of public awareness, absence of regulations, lack of training programs, lack of environmental accounting and disclosure programmes, difficulties with measuring environmental costs, and lack of accountability and transparency. These shortcomings arise because most of the companies were unlikely to disclose information about any environmental damage. Therefore, recommendations have been frequently released to encourage the Palestinian universities to help business entities to adapt to the EAR practices (Ahmed 2019).

Given the additional political complexities that occupation brings, while companies might be willing to develop EAR practices, the instability in the area as well as business restrictions makes it hard for these companies to develop such practices. This means that Palestine is a special case with regard to EAR since the impediments there are different from other Arab countries in the MENA region.

Practices of environmental accounting and reporting in GCC countries and Iraq

In comparison with other places in the MENA region, GCC countries have been given considerable attention by EAR researchers during the last two decades. Most of the studies have focused on the whole region (i.e. GCC countries as a part of the MENA) rather than on individual country (see, e.g., Akrout and Ben Othman 2016; Eljayash 2017; Arayssi et al. 2020). Attention in this part of the chapter will be given to explore EAR practices in GCC countries and Iraq.

Kuwait

Kuwait is a wealthy "petroleum-based" economy. Globally, the Kuwaiti dinar is the highest valued unit of currency, and the country is the fourth richest in the world per capita (World Bank 2020a). The country has an active capital market with a mixture of large businesses being listed (mainly non-petroleum industries and financial services). During the last decade, practices of EAR have significantly developed within the Kuwaiti business environment. Regulations have played a key role in this regard through addressing environmental violations and enforcing environmental compliance in the country. The most influential environmental "business-based" regulations are the following: (1) Act No. 210 of 2001 Public Authority for Environment, which was established to preserve the environment from pollution caused by the companies' operations; (2) the Environmental Protection Law No. 42 of 2014 which provides guidelines to improve the environmental management and accounting in Kuwait; and (3) the Environmental and Social Impact Assessment System, which requires listed firms to voluntarily disclose the assessment of the impact of their economic activities on the environment and society. Requirements of these environmental regulations increase the costs of compliance especially on environmentally sensitive firms in Kuwait (Gerged et al. 2018).

Saudi Arabia

Saudi Arabia economy is the largest in the MENA region (World Bank 2020a).[3] The country is part of the G20 group of countries, and it is the largest exporter of petroleum products and the second largest oil reserves holder in the world (US$33 trillion). Saudi Arabia holds 25% of the world's oil reserves (Anthony 2019). The industrial sector (incorporating oil and gas) in Saudi Arabia is considered the biggest contributor to the national economy (representing 60% of the total gross domestic product [GDP]).

Prior to mid-1990s, environmental regulations did not exist in Saudi Arabia, but in recent years, the country has focused more on the environmentalism. Three main developments have recently taken place (Abdull Razak et al. 2019):

- Establishing nine new environmental laws, passed in 2012 by the government
- In 2014, a Royal Decree demanded that all companies have five years to meet the new environmental standards relating to air, water and noise pollution
- All the business projects are required to fit into the Saudi's *Plan for International Development,* which, in turn, advises companies to meet the international benchmark standards (such as the GRI) as part of Presidency of Meteorology and Environment's environmental plan.

Regardless, a study in 2018 of energy and materials consumption by publicly listed companies found that the level of environmental disclosure is still low, with a slight improvement in disclosure of environmental compliance with the GRI benchmark (in 26% of the targeted companies), emissions disclosure (20.6%), with the least disclosed information being related to biodiversity and waste (Abdull Razak et al. 2019).

Literature indicates that environmental reporting has improved following the application of Saudi Corporate Governance Code (SCG-2006) in 2007. Habbash (2015) found that, on average and during the period 2006–2011, reporting incidence has increased to 30% of companies governed by the code, which is more than double the 14.61% found by Al Janadi et al. (2013). It has also been found that state and institutional ownership, firm profitability and industry sensitivity were the key factors that positively influence reporting incidence, while the degree of Board of Directors independence, family ownership and firm size were not significant determinants of this type of reporting (Habbash 2015).

United Arab Emirates

According to the World Bank (2020a), the economy of the UAE is the second largest in the MENA region (after Saudi Arabia), with GDP of US$414 billion (AED 1.52 trillion) in 2018. The country has been successfully diversifying its economy, particularly in Dubai where tourism, real estate and other supportive services have grown significantly in recent years. Other emirates (namely, Abu Dhabi) still remain heavily reliant on revenues from petroleum and natural gas (World Bank, 2020a).

In 2008, Abu Dhabi Sustainability Group (ADSG) was founded by the Environment Agency-Abu Dhabi (EAD),[4] with an objective of raising sustainability awareness among the companies, as it promotes transparency and encourages companies to report on their sustainability practices. Among their significant achievements, ADSG issues an annual report that reviews companies' management of sustainability and also provides recommendations for the future. The sustainability disclosure focuses mainly on environmental and energy disclosure items.

Further to the ADSG initiative (2008), the Abu Dhabi Securities Exchange (ADX) recently released the *Environmental, Social and Governance (ESG) Disclosure Guidance for Listed Companies*. ADX (2019) stated that it has developed this disclosure guidance to generally support the listed companies' sustainability reporting journey, and to support the voluntary disclosure of ESG information in particular.[5] Given the fact that the two above indicated initiatives (i.e. ADSG and ADX ESG Code) have recently been launched, no evidence has yet been provided by the literature on their value to the sustainability/environmental reporters.

Among very limited studies available from the UAE, Nobanee and Ellili (2016) investigated the sustainability reporting (including environmental) of the UAE banking sector. All listed banks in the country's financial markets during the period 2003–2013 were analysed. The results indicated that the overall level of sustainability disclosure (including environmental) is at a low level. Interestingly, results of that study revealed that the degree of the corporate sustainability disclosure of the conventional banks is higher than the Islamic banks (Nobanee and Ellili 2016). It has been concluded from this study that the sustainability disclosure significantly and positively affects the banking performance of the conventional banks while no significant effect was noted on the performance of the Islamic banks.

Other GCC countries

According to some studies, practices of EAR in other GCC countries (i.e. Bahrain, Oman, and Qatar) are not different from those practices observed in other countries in the region, that is, the level is low (Naser et al. 2006; Eljayash et al. 2012). Naser et al. (2006) conducted a study in Qatar regarding environmental disclosure produced by the listed companies in Doha Securities Market (DSM). The results indicated that there are variations in corporate environmental disclosure in the sampled companies associated with firm characteristics (such as size and business risk). It has also been noted that some national oil and gas large businesses (in Qatar, Saudi Arabia, and UAE) had provided a quality of environmental disclosure higher than similar businesses in other countries. In addition, Jahmani (2014) examined the publicly listed companies in Bahrain Bourse in 2012 and found that 57% of the sampled listed companies provided social and environmental information in their annual reports and their websites. It has been concluded that banks and insurance companies were the most frequent disclosers, while the least disclosure was made by service-based companies (e.g. hotels and tourism sector) as well as the industrial sector.

In the GCC context, it should be indicated that at present there is no generally accepted set of standards or benchmarks proposed for the purpose of preparation of environmental (or sustainability) reporting.

Iraq

The economy of Iraq heavily relies on the oil industry. According to OPEC (2020), oil is responsible for over 65% of the Iraqi GDP, and it is the main element in the country's export income. Oil provides almost 90% of the governmental revenue.[6] In terms of environmental challenges facing Iraq, Price (2018) asserted that Iraq faces serious environmental problems. These involve poor water quality, air pollution, soil salinity, conflict pollution to the deterioration of key ecosystems, climate change impacts, and threat of water shortages.

There is a limited amount of research related to EAR practices in Iraq. It could be argued that this is caused by the unstable political situation, internal conflict, and the "brain drain" from the country related to these factors. In those studies that have been undertaken into voluntary disclosure (including environmental information), low levels of corporate disclosure have been found. In general, Iraqi companies tend to disclose the mandatory requirements in their annual reports rather than voluntary information (Almagtome et al. 2017). According to the previous studies, firms operating in environmentally sensitive industries tend to disclose more voluntary information than other companies. In terms of the sector of the reporting companies, literature has indicated that banking, tourism and manufacturing industry took the first three ranks, respectively, while the last rank was for financial investment industry. Low levels of disclosure by oil and refining companies have also been documented (Thabit and Jasim 2016). Furthermore, in a cross-regional analysis it has been found that Iraqi companies' corporate voluntary disclosure is low in comparison to other developing countries, such as Iran, Egypt, Jordan, Bangladesh, and Malaysia (Almagtome et al. 2017).

Practices of environmental accounting and reporting in North Africa (Arab countries)

In this section, literature related to Arab countries in North Africa will be examined as a whole because the majority of the research produced in this sub-region of MENA was comparative in nature (usually, comparing practices of business entities in Egypt, Libya, and Tunisia). The North Africa "Arab countries" have been significantly impacted by the Arab Spring (started in 2010). Egypt, Tunisia, and Libya have witnessed a change in the governance system due to popular revolutions in 2011 that became known as "revolutions of the Arab Spring" (Eljayash 2015). According to the literature, in the last two decades, the importance of environmental activities and issues has increased, especially in environmentally sensitive industries within the region (Eljayash 2015).

Despite the increasing trend in researching EAR practices in this region, it is ultimately noted that attention on this area of research is still weak in comparison to other regions in the world. In terms of environmental concerns facing these countries, these are the same as others in the MENA region and include desertification, soil erosion, water pollution, air pollution, and waste management (Abumoghli and Goncalves 2020).

The oil and gas industry is the most frequently investigated sector among other business industries (see, e.g., Eljayash et al. 2012; Eljayash 2015). Empirically, it has been shown that environmental disclosure in annual reports has increased in national oil and gas companies. It has been also noted that EAR is found more frequently in Egypt than in the firms in Libya and Tunisia. Likewise, the quality of EAR has increased in the three countries, with the largest increase arising in Egypt (Eljayash 2015). In comparison with other countries in the MENA region, literature suggests that the EAR produced by oil and gas firms in Egypt, Libya, and Tunisia, for instance, is less than other companies operating in the region. Moreover, even though the quantity of EAR slightly improved in the oil and gas companies in Egypt, Tunisia, and Libya, the environmental information is more descriptive than quantitative (e.g. less quantitative key performance indicators [KPIs] are disclosed).

Within the Egyptian context, and for reform purposes, Aboud and Diab (2018) provided feedback to regulators and standard-setters in the developing countries, and more specifically the Egyptian regulators, on the benefits associated with the introduction of a sustainability index (i.e. Standard & Poor's EGX ESG index).[7] This feedback clarifies how the government's efforts to promote ESG benefited businesses (namely, publicly traded firms; see Aboud and Diab 2018).

In the Libyan context, very limited studies have been conducted on EAR. Elmogla et al. (2015) examined a sample of 270 annual reports from 54 companies (both public and private) from different business sectors for the years 2001–2005 and found that the Libyan companies generally disclose some information related to social responsibility (including environmental information) but at a low level in comparison to developed countries and only on certain topics, and this situation changed little over the five-year period under investigation.

In the Tunisian context, literature suggests that industrial firms with higher sensitivity to environment tend to provide more disclosure (which includes environmental information) than industrial firms that are less environmentally sensitive (Eljayash 2015). This finding is supported by Belhaj and Damak-Ayadi (2011), who reported that of 500 largest Tunisian firms only 53 published environmental information in their annual reports or even on their websites. Chakroun and Matoussi (2012) noted that Tunisian non-financial businesses tend to disclose more mandatory information, and these businesses (non-financial) also tend to disclose voluntary information closely linked to mandatory disclosure. This may raise concerns about the importance of the process of mandating disclosure of important environmental concerns.

Discussion and conclusion

This section presents key findings as well as identifying ideas for potential future research on the area of EAR in the MENA region. Despite the extent of the environmental threats facing this region, the MENA region has less EAR practice and research than other parts of the world

(Habbash 2015; KPMG 2015, 2017). From the author's perspective, the factors behind this weakness could include the following:

- Regional causes, represented by instability, political conflicts, and weak intra-regional ties
- Poor practices of EAR by the reporting business entities due to absence of public accountability and transparency, incomplete/absence of regulations, absence of regional-based benchmark/standards that simulate the nature of the region and its culture, and premature of organisational culture
- Weaknesses in the research and educational infrastructure, including lack of specialised databases and research centres, absence of academic enthusiasm to conduct empirical and theoretical research in this area, lack of the EAR topic on the accounting curricula within the educational institutions
- Absence of the public interest in general, due to prioritising other societal needs such as fighting poverty, jobs creation and fighting unemployment, and inefficient and weak role of media, and
- Finally, the lack of accounting research into these factors in MENA published environmental accounting research.

These factors can also be transformed with the aim of changing societal values and culture (including business values) towards educating society in environmental issues and improving practices of EAR premised on increasing demands of citizens for corporate accountability.

In terms of the thematic research aspects covered by the literature, which to some extent pointed out the key determinants of EAR practice in the region, this chapter identified four main thematic areas investigated. These include ownership structure, characteristics of the reporting companies, national contextual determinants, and governance attributes and board of directors' characteristics. These aspects have also been examined in academic literature in other regions of the world; thus, they have been re-examined employing the same methodologies in the MENA region. In this context, it has been noticed, for example, that more literature has been produced in Egypt, Jordan, and Saudi Arabia in comparison to other countries in the region. This can be referred to political stability, capacities of the educational institutions, and motivation of the researchers.

Given the importance of the MENA region, where 51% of the world's oil and gas reserves are located (OPEC 2020), the oil and gas industry along with other related industrial sectors is the most examined among all other businesses. However, environmental reporting produced by these businesses is still lagging behind similar businesses in the developed countries. In the same context, it has been concluded that there is a difference between the reporting companies and even between the MENA countries in the quality and quantity of ER (Gerged et al. 2018). In this regard, it has been suggested that innovation can be spread quickly and in "a consistent manner due the cultural similarities and economic connections across the region, especially if they take place in leading countries such as Egypt and Saudi Arabia" (Gerged et al. 2018, p. 583).

In parallel with the improved levels of practising EAR by the reporting companies, it has been observed that research in this area has been excessively improved. However, and from the author's point of view, the following aspects/factors/dimensions were missed or considered as "under researched" by the EAR research conducted in the MENA region:

- Employing well-developed different theoretical frameworks to empirically examining the business practices of EAR
- Investigating stand-alone environmental/CSR/sustainability reporting practices

- Examining web-based (online) environmental/CSR/sustainability reporting practices
- Exploring stakeholders' role/engagement in EAR practices, and investigating their perspectives on these practices
- Examining the impact of the international generally accepted benchmark/standards over the EAR practices in the MENA region (e.g. GRI and the SDGs)
- Investigating value-added of the regionally based developed ESG codes/indices (e.g. ADX ESG Disclosure Guidance, and Standard & Poor's EGX ESG index)
- Environmental management accounting and assurance practices and
- Critically examining why EAR is a weak research area in the MENA region.

It can be concluded that the above research shortcomings are areas of future research in the area of EAR in the MENA region.

Notes

1 The base of this comparison is 4,900 N100 companies where the MENA region represents 8% of the regional sample.
2 Under this fundamental regulation (*Environment Protection Law* No. 52, 2006 – provisionally issued in 2003) and for the purpose of providing a practical framework for controlling resources as well as managing the environmental impact of entities, the Jordanian government issued in 2005 the following supplement environmental related implementation rules relating to: Environmental Impact Assessment; Air Protection; Soil Protection; Protecting the Environment from Pollution in Emergency Situations; Natural Reserves and National Parks; Management of Solid Waste; and Management of Hazardous Materials, their Moving and Circulation.
3 In 2016, the Saudi government launched its *Saudi Vision 2030,* which aims to reduce dependency on oil, and thus diversify its non-oil revenue and other economic resources.
4 The Environment Agency-Abu Dhabi (EAD) is a governmental agency established in 1996 in Abu Dhabi, UAE. In its mission, the agency is committed to protecting and managing biodiversity, providing a clean environment and promoting sustainable development in the Emirate of Abu Dhabi. Further details are provided on their website (www.ead.gov.ae/en).
5 ADX (2019) confirmed that this voluntary guidance provides ADX's listed companies with 31 ESG indicators that are considered essential to report in alignment with the recommendations of the Sustainable Stock Exchanges Initiative and the World Federation of Exchanges. According to the ADX, the indicators are also mapped against Global Reporting Initiative (GRI) indicators and the Sustainable Development Goals for companies willing to adopt more detailed sustainability reporting standards that go beyond the proposed framework (ADX 2019).
6 According to OPEC (2020), petroleum industry constitutes 97% of the Iraqi exports, with a value of US$80.02 billion in 2019.
7 Standard & Poor's EGX ESG: Standard & Poor's – Egyptian Stock Exchange Environment, Social and Governance.

References

Abdull Razak, R., Al Hujaili, R., and Al Ahmedi, R., 2019. Environmental disclosure practices of Saudi companies according to the new GRI standards. *5th Asia Pacific Conference on Contemporary Research (APCCR 2019)*, Adelaide, South Australia, pp. 9–13.

Aboud, A., and Diab, A., 2018. The impact of social, environmental and corporate governance disclosures on firm value: Evidence from Egypt. *Journal of Accounting in Emerging Economies*, 8(4): 442–458.

Abu Dhabi Securities Exchange (ADX)., 2019. *Environmental, Social and Governance (ESG) Disclosure Guidance for Listed Companies*, Abu Dhabi Securities Exchange, Abu Dhabi, UAE.

Abumoghli, I., and Goncalves, A., 2020. *Environmental Challenges in the MENA Region*. United Nations Environment Programme (UNEP).

Ahmed, N. S., 2019. Environmental accounting disclosures: The case of manufacturing listed companies in Palestine Securities Exchange. *International Journal of Business, Economics and Law*, 18(5): 15–21.

Ahmed, N. S., and Gao, S. S., 2005. Corporate environmental reporting in Libya: A study of absence. *Social and Environmental Accountability Journal*, 25(1): 11–14.
Akrout, M. M., and Ben Othman, H., 2016. Ownership structure and environmental disclosure in the MENA emerging countries. *Corporate Ownership & Control,* Summer, Continued – 2, 13(4): 381–388.
Aladwan, M., 2018. Undertaking of environmental accounting responsibility to achieve sustainable development: Evidence from Jordanian chemical, and mining companies. *International Journal of Managerial and Financial Accounting*, 10(1): 48–64.
Al-Ajmi, M., Al-Mutairi, A., and Al-Duwaila, N., 2015. Corporate social disclosure practices in Kuwait. *International Journal of Economics and Finance*, 7(9): 244–254.
Al Amosh, H., and Mansor, N., 2020. The implications of ownership structure on the environmental disclosure in Jordan. *International Journal of Academic Research in Business and Social Sciences*, 10(3): 330–346.
Al-Hamadeen, R., 2002. *Social Responsibility Accounting in the Jordanian Hotel Corporations: An Empirical Study*. Unpublished Master's Thesis, Al al-Bayt University, Al Mafraq, Jordan.
Al-Hamadeen, R., and Badran, S., 2014. Nature and determinants of CSR disclosure: Experience of the Jordanian public shareholding companies. *European Journal of Business and Management*, 6(13): 18–34.
Al-Janadi, Y., Abdul Rahman, R., and Binti Omar, N., 2013. Corporate governance mechanisms and voluntary disclosure in Saudi Arabia. *Research Journal of Finance and Accounting*, 4(4): 25–35.
Alkababji, M., 2014. Voluntary disclosure on corporate social responsibility: A study on the annual reports of Palestinian corporations. *European Journal of Accounting Auditing and Finance Research*, 2(4): 59–82.
Almagtome, A., Almusawi, I., and Aureaar, K., 2017. Challenges of corporate voluntary disclosures through the annual reports: Evidence from Iraq. *World Applied Sciences Journal,* 35(10): 2093–2100.
Al-Nimer, M., 2015. Perceptions of environmental accounting in the Jordanian pharmaceutical industries (applications and disclosure). *International Journal of Business and Management*, 10(2): 73–80.
Anthony, C., 2019. Which 10 countries have the most natural resources? [online] Available from: www.investopedia.com/articles/markets-economy/090516/10-countries-most-natural-resources.asp [Accessed 10 August 2020].
Arayssi, M., Jizi, M., and Tabaja, H.H., 2020. The impact of board composition on the level of ESG disclosures in GCC countries. *Sustainability Accounting, Management and Policy Journal*, 11(1): 137–161.
Bani Khalid, T., and Kouhy, R., 2017. Impact of national contextual factors on corporate social and environmental disclosure (CSED): The perceptions of Jordanian stakeholders. *International Review of Management and Business Research*, 6(2): 556–578.
Barakat, F. S., López Pérez, M.V., and Rodríguez Ariza, L., 2011. *Corporate Social Responsibility Disclosure (CSRD) Determinants of Listed Companies in Palestine (PXE) and Jordan (ASE)*. Unpublished Research Paper, University of Granada, Spain.
Belhaj, M., and Damak-Ayadi, S., 2011. Financial performance, environmental performance and environmental disclosure: The case of Tunisian firms. *Afro-Asian Journal of Finance and Accounting*, 2(3): 248–269.
Chakroun, R., and Matoussi, H., 2012. Determinants of the extent of voluntary disclosure in the annual reports of the Tunisian firms. *Accounting and Managerial Information Systems*, 11(3): 335–370.
Choi, F. D., and Meek, G. K., 2014. *International Accounting*, 7th Edition (International version). Essex: Pearson Education.
Eljayash, K. M., 2015. Documentation of environmental disclosure practices in the oil companies in the countries of the Arab Spring – Some evidences from Egypt, Libya and Tunisia. *Journal of Economics, Business and Management*, 3(10): 954–960.
Eljayash, K., 2017. Environmental disclosure studies in Middle East and Northern Africa in shadow of theoretical context. World Journal of Entrepreneurship. *Management and Sustainable Development*, 13(4): 334–349.
Eljayash, K. M., James, K., and Kong, E., 2012. The quantity and quality of environmental disclosure in annual reports of national oil and gas companies in Middle East and North Africa. *International Journal of Economics and Finance*, 4(10): 201–217.
Elmogla, M., Cowton, C. J., and Downs, Y., 2015. Corporate social reporting in Libya: A research note. *Social Responsibility Journal*, (11)4: 923–932.
Elshabasy, Y., 2018. The impact of corporate characteristics on environmental information disclosure: An empirical study on the listed firms in Egypt. *Journal of Business and Retail Management Research (JBRMR)*, 12(2): 232–241.
Gerged, A., Beddewela, E. S., and Cowton C. J., 2020. Is corporate environmental disclosure associated with firm value? A multi country study of Gulf Cooperation Council firms. *Business Strategy and the Environment*. In press, 1–19.

Gerged, A., Cowton C. J, and Beddewela, E. S., 2018. Towards sustainable development in the Arab Middle East and North Africa region: A longitudinal analysis of environmental disclosure in corporate annual reports. *Business Strategy and the Environment*, 27(4): 572–587.

Habbash, M., 2015. Corporate governance. Ownership, company structure and environmental disclosure: Evidence from Saudi Arabia. *Journal of Governance and Regulation*, Continued – 4, 4(4): 460–470.

Hawkamah, 2014. *Environmental, Social & Corporate Governance Practices in the MENA Region 2007-2012: Review of the S&P/Hawkamah Pan Arab ESG Index*. Hawkamah – The Institute of Corporate Governance & EY.

International Monetary Fund (IMF)., 2020. *World Economic Outlook (April 2020)*. [Online] Available from: www.imf.org/external/datamapper/NGDP_RPCH@WEO/OEMDC/WEOWORLD/MEQ [Accessed 02 August 2020].

Ismail, K. N., and Ibrahim, A., 2009. Social and environmental disclosure in the annual reports of Jordanian companies. *Issues in Social and Environmental Accounting*, 2(2): 198–210.

Jadam, J., 2010. *State and Trends of the Lebanese Environment – Chapter 8: Solid Waste*, edited by Rita Stephan, ECODIT, Lebanon.

Joudeh, A. M., Almubaideen, H. I., and Alroud, S. F., 2018. Environmental disclosure in the annual reports of the Jordanian mining and extraction companies. *Journal of Economics, Finance and Accounting*, 5(1): 18–25.

Khalifa, H. M., and Hammad, S. M., 2014. Problems with the application of environmental accounting in Middle East. *International Journal of Business and Social Science*, [Special Issue – March], 5(4): 181–191.

Kilincarslan, E., Elmagrhi, M. H., and Li, Z., 2020. Impact of governance structures on environmental disclosures in the Middle East and Africa. Forthcoming in *Corporate Governance: The International Journal of Business in Society* – Accepted on 17 April 2020.

KPMG, 2015. *KPMG International Survey of Corporate Social Reporting 2015*. Netherlands: KPMG.

KPMG, 2017. *KPMG International Survey of Corporate Social Reporting 2017*. Netherlands: KPMG.

Luo, L., Tang, Q., and Lan, Y., 2013. Comparison of propensity for carbon disclosure between developing and developed countries: A resource constraint perspective. *Accounting Research Journal*, 26(1): 6–34.

Naser, K., Al-Hussaini, A., Al-Kwari, D., and Nuseibeh, R., 2006. Determinants of corporate social disclosure in developing countries: The case of Qatar. *Advances in International Accounting*, 19: 1–23.

Nobanee, H., and Ellili, N., 2016. Corporate sustainability disclosure in annual reports: Evidence from UAE banks: Islamic versus conventional. *Renewable and Sustainable Energy Reviews*, 55 (March): 1336–1341.

OECD, 2018. *Trends in Trade and Investment Policies in the MENA Region*. MENA-OECD Working Group on Investment and Trade – (MENA-OECD Competitiveness Programme), 27–28 November 2018, Dead Sea, Jordan.

OPEC, 2020. OPEC Annual Statistical Bulletin 2020, [Online]. Available from: www.opec.org/opec_web/en/data_graphs/330.htm [Accessed 06 July 2020].

O'Sullivan, A., Rey, M., and Mendez, J., 2012. *Opportunities and Challenges in the MENA Region*. OECD Middle East and North Africa Region Regional Economic Update.

Price, R.A., 2018. *Environmental Risks in Iraq*. K4D Helpdesk Report. Brighton, Institute of Development Studies, UK.

Rabi, A. M., 2019. Board characteristics and environmental disclosure: Evidence from Jordan. *International Journal of Business and Management*, 14(2): 57–65.

Sakmar, S. L., Wackernagel, M., Galli, A., and Moore, D., 2011. *Sustainable Development and Environmental Challenges in the MENA Region; Accounting for the Environment in the 21st Century*. Working Paper 592, Economic Research Forum, Egypt.

Sha'shaa, M. H., 1991. *Application of Social Responsibility Accounting in the Jordanian Public Shareholding Industrial Company*. Unpublished Master's Thesis, University of Jordan, Amman, Jordan.

Suwaidan, M., Al-Omari, A., and Haddad, R. H., 2004. Social responsibility disclosure and corporate characteristics: The case of Jordanian industrial companies. *International Journal of Accounting Auditing and Performance Evaluation*, 1(4): 432–447.

Thabit, T. H., and Jasim, Y., 2016. *The Role of Environmental Accounting Disclosure to Reduce Harmful Emissions of Oil Refining Companies*. Unpublished Research Paper, Cihan University, Erbil, Iraq.

UNICEF, 2019. *The State of the World's Children 2019: Children, Food and Nutrition: Growing Well in a Changing World*. The United Nations Children's Fund (UNICEF), October 2019.

World Bank, 2007. *Middle East and North Africa Region: 2007 Economic Developments and Prospects. Job Creation in an Era of High Growth*. Washington DC: World Bank.

World Bank, 2014. *World Bank Definition: MENA*. Worldbank.org. Archived from the original on 29 October 2014. [Online]. Available from: https://en.wikipedia.org/wiki/MENA [Accessed 5 August 2020].
World Bank, 2020a. *World Bank Country and Lending Groups*. [Online] Available from: https://datahelpdesk.worldbank.org/knowledgebase/articles/906519-world-bank-country-and-lending-groups [Accessed 20 July 2020].
World Bank, 2020b. *Co2 Emissions, Carbon Dioxide Information Analysis Center, Environmental Sciences Division*, Tennessee, United States. [Online] Available from: https://data.worldbank.org/indicator/EN.ATM.CO2E.PC?name_desc=false/ [Accessed 5 August 2020].
Zwijnenburg, W., and Te Pas, K., 2015. *Amidst the Debris: A Desktop Study on the Environmental and Public Health Impact of Syria's Conflict*, edited by Weir, D., and van der Zeijden, W. Netherlands: Pax for Peace.

23
THE NORTH AMERICAN ENVIRONMENTAL ACCOUNTING RESEARCH LANDSCAPE

Stacy L. Chavez and Andrea M. Romi

Introduction

North America (NA) provides a unique and dynamic landscape for environmental accounting research (EAR), particularly with respect to Canada and the United States of America (USA). In a region plagued with an ever-growing carbon footprint, a focus on unyielding growth and consumption, continuously increasing income inequality, and a portion of the population which formally denies the existence of climate change altogether, research on environmental accounting (EA) is distinctive. Over the last several decades, NA has experienced an explosion of EAR. Most research focuses on reporting mechanisms from an archival perspective in combination with positive and negative consequences, voluntary versus mandatory incentives, assurance, markets, value relevance, reliability, greenwashing, the use of performance metrics, etc. These studies tend to focus on legitimacy theory (e.g., Mobus 2005; Magness 2006; Cho et al. 2011; Cho et al. 2012a; Cho et al. 2015; Cho and Patten 2007; Peters and Romi 2014; Clarkson et al. 2008; Chen et al. 2008; Rodrigue et al. 2013; Thorne et al. 2014; Elayan 2019; Buhr 1998; Cormier and Gordon 2001; Iyer and Lulseged 2013; Freedman and Stagliano 2008), but also stakeholder theory (e.g., Clarkson et al. 2008), disclosure theory (e.g., Mahoney et al. 2013; Griffin et al. 2017; Clarkson et al. 2008), agency theory (e.g., Buhr 2001; Mallin et al. 2013), and economic theory (e.g., Peters and Romi 2014; Buhr 1998), or a combination thereof.

The NA region is certainly not uniform, with many unique continental aspects. Within Canada, for example, researchers have focused on mining and indigenous groups (Horn 2019). Within the USA, on the other hand, oil spills, B-corps[1], Superfund sites, and voluntary carbon markets, including the defunct Chicago Climate Exchange (Griffin 2013; EDF 2019), have provided unique research opportunities. While less examined, Mexico also provides a unique setting to investigate air pollution, the lack of clean water, deforestation, and the effects on the environment from Mexico's insourcing of manufacturing from other countries. Each of these countries also deal with different governing structures, potentially influencing their environmental policies. While we outline the long history of EAR within NA in this chapter, there are many issues unresolved, providing us an opportunity to discuss limitations and possible avenues for future work.

The NA continent lies in the Western hemisphere, between the Arctic Circle and the Tropic of Cancer, and encompasses Canada, the USA, Mexico, Greenland, and the Caribbean Islands, terminating at the southern tip of Central America. A region of this size sustains a variety of ecosystems, terrain, climate, and cultural diversity, all potentially influenced by climate change. NA is surrounded on the east by the Atlantic Ocean and on the west by the Pacific Ocean, making the region particularly susceptible to severe oceanic storms. The West Coast and Hawaiian Islands lie along the Pacific Rim, or the Ring of Fire, highly sensitive to earthquakes and volcano eruptions. A large swath of the US Midwest, with expansive agricultural responsibilities, comprises the severe weather path known as "tornado alley." The far northern regions also experience climate change effects, both on the Canadian permafrost and on icebergs in the Arctic Sea between Canada and Greenland. One far-reaching environmental concern connecting the entire NA region is the ever-deteriorating Monarch butterfly migration, from Mexico, through the USA, and into Canada. The Monarch parallels other declining pollinator populations, such as the honeybee, which provide the natural pollination imperative to sustain the global food supply. Pollinator decline from human-induced habitat loss, disease, pesticides, climate change, etc., foreshadows the potential consequences to civilization from ignoring environmental concerns.

Environmental context shaping accounting

While some researchers adopt a global perspective, in the North American context, we find that EAR almost exclusively takes place in a US or Canadian setting. As such, this chapter focuses on the research issues in these countries. Both governments have environmental regulations in place, motivating EAR examining disclosures related to firm-specific environmental performance (EP). Table 23.1 provides a summary of the NA environmental regulatory agencies and regulations commonly discussed in the literature.[2]

NA EAR addresses various issues and observes a relationship between some industries and greater environmental degradation, based solely on industry-specific operations (Patten 1991). For example, Cho and Patten (2007) describe firms in the oil exploration (SIC 13), pulp and paper (SIC 26), chemical and allied products (SIC 28), petroleum refining (SIC 29), and metals (SIC 33) as environmentally sensitive industries (ESI) where firms are likely to exhibit unique behaviors with respect to both EP and disclosures. Although two of these industries (oil and gas, pulp and paper) dominate the research, other industries, such as mining, power plants (electricity), and chemical plants, stimulate greater variety in research topic areas, including disclosure (e.g., Cormier and Gordon 2001; Freedman and Stagliano 2008; Magness 2006; Buhr 1998), firm value (e.g., Hughes 2000; Joshi et al. 2001), eco-efficiency (e.g., Burnett and Hansen 2008; Henri and Journeault 2010), and biodiversity (Schneider and Andreaus 2018).

With respect to non-weather-related environmental disasters, perhaps the most commonly recognized relates to oil, with approximately 44 recorded oil spill disasters since 1969 (NOAA 2019). Most notable among them was the 1989 Exxon Valdez disaster, which resulted in the leakage of approximately 11 million gallons of crude oil (NOAA 1989). The 2010 Deepwater Horizon disaster is possibly the most "famous" spill, contributing to its central role in a Hollywood movie. The rig exploded during a drilling procedure, resulting in 11 deaths and oil spillage of approximately 168 million gallons into the Gulf of Mexico (NOAA 2010).

Oil tankers are not the only source of environmental concern. Many oil pipelines crisscross the continent, which threaten not only the land, but also waterways sourcing drinking water and crop irrigation. In 2015, the Nexen pipeline in Alberta, Canada, began leaking a mixture

Table 23.1 Overview of regulatory environment

North American Environmental Regulatory Agencies	
Carbon Disclosure Project (CDP)	Sustainability Accounting Standards Board (SASB)
Federal Energy Regulatory Commission (FERC)	United States Environmental Protection Agency (EPA)
International Accounting Standards Board (IASB)	United States Financial Accounting Standards Board (FASB)
North American Free Trade Agreement (NAFTA)	United States Securities and Exchange Commission (SEC)
North American Environmental Acts/Agreements	
Name	*Description (citation)*
Canadian Environmental Protection Act (CEPA)	Aims to prevent pollution and protect the environment and human health (Canada 1999)
The Clean Air Act (CAA)	Aims to solve the problem of air pollution through science and technology (EPA 1970)
Comprehensive Environmental Response, Compensation, and Liability Act (CERCLA) – also known as the Superfund	Allows the EPA to identify potentially responsible parties (PRP) that contribute to contamination of an environmental site, thus holding them liable for the cleanup and transaction costs (EPA 1980)
Dodd Frank Act (in response to the 2008 financial crisis)	Enacts regulation on the financial industry and swaps market to protect consumers, as well as requiring responsible minerals sourcing (CFTC 2010)
Emergency Planning and Community Right to Know Act (EPCRA)	Helps communities plan for chemical emergencies, as well as reporting on hazardous substances (EPA 1986)
National Environmental Policy Act (NEPA)	This act aims to declare a national policy to protect the environment through harmony between humans and their environment (EPA 1969)
Toxic Release Inventory (TRI)	Database containing details of chemical transfers by most manufacturing facilities; falls under the EPCRA (EPA 1986)

of approximately 31,000 gallons of bitumen oil, sand, and water in the largest land spillage on record (Gaworecki 2015). While pipelines are a major source of employment, they are also a hotly contested environmental and political issue. For instance, the US Native Americans and Canada's First Nations heavily protested the Keystone XL project, concerned about the environment, damage to sacred sites, and the health of indigenous peoples.

According to the World Wildlife Fund, the pulp and paper industry, commonly associated with deforestation and air pollution, is responsible for consumption of 40% of industrial wood traded throughout the world (WWF 2019). Deforestation, while benefiting many industries within NA, is a topic often discussed in relation to the Amazon Rainforest in South America, and as such has not been examined in the NA accounting literature. NA EAR, however, has focused on the pulp and paper industry, and how air and water pollution relate to firm disclosures (e.g., Spicer 1978; Clarkson et al. 2004; Shane and Spicer 1983; Cho et al. 2006; Clarkson et al. 2008) and firm value (e.g., Clarkson et al. 2004; Freedman and Jaggi 1992).

Despite the environmental impacts of these industries, very little accounting research examines the actual impacts of these disasters (e.g., biodiversity damage, increased water contamination, and long-term health costs). Instead, research to date in the petroleum industry primarily focuses on firm-specific disclosures (e.g., Mobus 2005; Cho et al. 2006; Clarkson et al. 2008; Herremans et al. 2009) and level of commitment to social responsibility (e.g., Mobus 2005; Schneider et al. 2017; Cho et al. 2018; Herremans et al. 2009). Other research considers the value impact of disclosure by external parties (e.g., Shane and Spicer 1983) and the choice of accounting treatment for environmental liabilities related to abatement regulation (e.g., Schneider et al. 2017).

Accounting research outline

Disclosure emerges as the dominant topic in the NA EA literature. Both voluntary and mandatory environmental disclosures (EDs) exist in various locations, including financial statements, stand-alone reports, integrated reports, firm-specific websites, etc. Disclosures help accounting researchers examine firm environmental behavior with respect to a myriad of topics, such as accountability, investor interest, and governance.

The primary source of environmental information for external parties is voluntary disclosure. External stakeholders without access to internal firm-specific environmental information must rely on firm disclosures to evaluate potential decisions. Research often examines investor interest in firm-specific environmental actions by examining the market reaction to, or a change in firm value associated with, an environmental event or disclosure. For example, Blacconiere and Patten (1994) examined the market response for all US firms in the chemical industry after the Union Carbide chemical leak in Bhopal, India. All chemical industry firms experienced a negative stock market reaction following the leak, yet firms with more extensive ED prior to the leak experienced less of a negative reaction, providing initial evidence that investors interpret extensive disclosures as a sign of proactive environmental strategy within firms. Clarkson et al. (2013) also established investor interest in environmental activities for US polluting industries, finding that investors incorporate environmental information into decision-making, with respect to both performance and disclosures.

In addition to the these studies, EA literature has also examined investor perceptions of disclosures based on the type of investor (e.g., Epstein and Freedman 1994; Dilla et al. 2019), the environmental strategy of the firm (e.g., Spicer 1978; Clarkson et al. 2004; Shane and Spicer 1983; Reitenga 2000), the ranking of the firm by third-party agencies (e.g., Cordeiro and Tewari 2015), firm responses to regulation or regulatory pressure (e.g., Elayan 2019; Patten and Nance 1998), overall firm-specific ED (e.g., Anderson and Frankle 1980; Griffin and Sun 2013; Griffin et al. 2017), and the quality of a firm's ED (e.g., Cho et al. 2015; Guidry and Patten 2010). The direction of investor reaction resulting from these studies is mixed, while some find no reaction at all.

Political forces and the media also play a particularly important role as external stakeholders, pressuring firms into desired behaviors. Greater attention to poor EP is likely to result in increased negative attention, influencing the firm's bottom line through boycotts, negative market reactions, higher employee turnover, etc. Cho et al. (2006) examined the possibility that worse environmentally performing firms might spend more on political activities than better performing firms as a way to influence policy and decrease political risk. They found that poor environmentally performing firms in US ESI spent more on political donations to manage political exposure and that political donations and ED were complementary strategies to manage public policy pressures.

In addition to greater amounts of information to influence public perceptions, firms often disclose different types of information in different outlets. For example, Villiers and van Staden (2011) examined 120 NA firms, based on EP and experience with environmental crises, to determine the extent of ED in their annual reports and websites. They found that EP influenced managers' ED decisions. Firms with bad performance disclosed greater amounts of environmental information in their annual reports, which represented management's attempt to reduce information asymmetry for investors. Additionally, firms facing an environmental crisis reported more environmental information on their websites, where they could expedite the communication process toward investors and attempt to reduce political costs (Villiers and van Staden 2011, p. 521).

Another potential factor influencing environmental issues is that of strong governance, although these results remains largely mixed. Rupley et al. (2012) examined the relationship between strong boards (i.e., independence, gender diversity, proportion of board members serving on more than one board, chief executive officer [CEO] not a director, and Corporate Social Responsibility [CSR] committee), the tone of environmental media coverage, and ED and found a positive relationship. These findings demonstrate that firms facing negative media attention will attempt to change perceptions through higher quality and quantity of ED. Similarly, Peters and Romi (2014) suggested that strong environmental governance mechanisms, such as environmental committees, chief sustainability officers, and board environmental expertise, influence the quantity and quality of ED. Rodrigue et al. (2013), on the other hand, found that environmental governance is largely symbolic, employed by the board to protect the firm's reputation and reduce regulatory risk, ultimately having no impact on EP.

Additional literature in the political and public pressure arena includes investigations of the disclosure strategies to influence policy (e.g., Cho et al. 2012a), the amount or types of disclosures in response to facing greater public pressures overall (e.g., Cormier and Gordon 2001; Thorne et al. 2014; Li et al. 1997; Herremans et al. 2009), ED levels when firms are targeted specifically based on a differentiating characteristic (e.g., Freedman and Stagliano 2002; Dawkins and Fraas 2011), and ED levels when a firm faces a negative environmental event (e.g., Magness 2006; Darrell and Schwartz 1997). Many of these papers found increasing disclosures in response to additional public or political pressures, supporting legitimacy theory as the prominent theory in ED literature within NA.

As one of the most pervasive motivations suggested for ED results in accounting academic literature, legitimacy focuses on a firm's attempt to act in way that aligns the firm's objectives and actions with that of society's expectations (Dowling and Pfeffer 1975; Lindblom 1994; Suchman 1995). Much of the EA literature suggests that firm disclosures often do not match true performance, also known as "ceremonial conformity" (Meyer and Rowan 1977). Other papers focus on similar behavior but refer to it as "greenwashing" (e.g., Berrone et al. 2017; Walker and Wan 2012) or impression management (e.g., Talbot and Boiral 2015; Diouf and Boiral 2017; Lee and Sweeney 2015; Chen et al. 2014).

Prior to Patten (2002), many studies found no significant relationship between a firm's EP and ED. Patten (2002) examined US firm-specific toxic release and found a negative relationship between EP and disclosures, supporting Patten's (2002) assertion that firms with poor EP, facing threats to their legitimacy, will attempt to counter this threat by providing more environmental information. Additionally, Patten (2002) found that firms operating in non-ESIs provide greater levels of disclosure in response to greater toxic releases, indicating that firms in ESIs already face greater exposure to the social/political environment, where preexisting expectations of poor EP negate firm benefits from additional disclosures.

Contending that all disclosure channels are not equally efficient or effective in reaching legitimacy goals and that different channels might serve as complements or substitutes to one another, Aerts and Cormier (2009) investigated the impact of a firm's environmental communication efforts on media legitimacy. The authors found, in Canadian and US firms, that the extent and quality of economic-based segments of ED in the annual report, and reactive press releases, positively affected the environmental legitimacy of the firm. Additionally, inclusion in an ESI negatively affected this positive relationship between annual report disclosures and legitimacy. Moreover, proactive press releases did not interfere with the effectiveness of annual report ED, suggesting complementary roles between press releases and annual report disclosures. Overall, these findings provided further evidence of the legitimizing role of ED.

While Patten (2002) found a negative association between EP and ED, the literature renders mixed results over time. Cho and Patten (2007) addressed these mixed results and argued that they are a product of a failure to consider management's motivation for ED, leading to issues with the disclosure metrics used in studies, where some disclosures were used as legitimizing tools, and others not. Attempting to isolate the legitimizing nature of disclosures, these authors focused on non-litigation-related environmental information, while also differentiating between monetary and non-monetary information. Overall, the authors provided additional evidence that corporations appear to use financial report ED as a legitimizing tool, and that there are differences in legitimizing behaviors depending on the type of ED examined. Other EA disclosure research focused on legitimacy includes those examining legitimacy tactics after an event or increased media attention (e.g., Buhr 1998; Patten 1992; Neu et al. 1998), the influence of external factors on legitimizing behavior (e.g., Cho et al. 2012b; Cho et al. 2011), and the difference in legitimizing tactics based on different aspects of ED (e.g., Patten 2005; Clarkson et al. 2008).

Not surprisingly, given all the regulatory bodies and regulations within NA, there is a large body of EAR focused on the effects of regulation. For example, Cho et al. (2008) examined how firms operating in an ESI influenced politicians during the passage of ED legislation proposing additional mandatory disclosures for firms in ESIs. The results suggested that the chemical and petroleum industry made significantly higher PAC contributions to members of Congress who held influential positions in the passage of the environmental amendment. Additionally, those congressional members receiving more campaign funds from the chemical and petroleum industry were more likely to vote against the amendment.

While some papers examine corporate strategy to avoid additional disclosure requirements, other papers examine corporate strategy to influence particular regulations (e.g., Cho et al. 2018), strategic responses after regulation (e.g., Patten 1998; Hughes 2000), the lack of disclosure pertaining to newly passed regulation (e.g., Buhr and Freedman 2001), the inconsistency in different types of disclosures (e.g., Freedman and Stagliano 2008), and the levels of disclosure around regulation (e.g., Alciatore et al. 2004; Patten and Trompeter 2003).

Each regulation passed results in newly mandated disclosure requirements. As such, another area of EAR within NA focuses on the determinates and/or consequences of mandated ED. Patten and Freedman (2008) evaluated and discussed the Government Accountability Office (GAO) report about the state of affairs regarding corporate ED. The authors suggested that the GAO did not make good use of their thorough data collection and that, in fact, the level and quality of corporate ED at the time were inadequate. Furthermore, they felt the GAO report should have examined the status of ED with a broader group of stakeholders in mind, beyond that of just investors. Finally, they concluded the Securities and Exchange Commission's (SEC) monitoring and enforcement capabilities were lacking and that many firms were not complying with ED requirements. Peters and Romi (2013) supported these findings by examining the frequency and consequences of reporting mandated EPA environmental sanctions. The authors found a 72% non-compliance rate with the mandatory disclosures due to inadequate SEC monitoring and enforcement, in combination with a significant negative stock market reaction for firms choosing to comply and disclose required sanction information.

Additional papers in the mandatory environmental accounting literature stream examine the influence of mandatory disclosures on subsequent performance (e.g., Mobus 2005), the differences in reporting behavior in reaction to regulations between different countries (e.g., Chelli et al. 2018; Buhr and Freedman 2001), and reporting changes after the initial passage of an environmental regulation (e.g., Sankara et al. 2019).

While most NA disclosure papers focus on the relationship between EP and ED (e.g., Clarkson et al. 2008; Al-Tuwaijri et al. 2004; Wiseman 1982; Hughes et al. 2001), disclosures serve to influence other factors as well. Two unique areas include assurance, where the level of disclosure and industry participation influence the choice to obtain report assurance (e.g., Cho et al. 2014), and religion, where the religious and social norms of a community influence the types of ED (e.g., Griffin and Sun 2018). Despite all this research, there remain concerns about ED measurement. Some suggest that, in addition to quantity, the type and nature of ED should be considered as these characteristics would likely influence results (e.g., Cho et al. 2010; Plumlee et al. 2015).

Although disclosure continues to be an important topic, research also focuses on broader topics such as the economic result of environmental initiatives, the influence of regulation on environmental actions, etc. With respect to economic consequences, Johnston (2012) examined the influence of differing R&D components on future earnings volatility and found that environmental R&D is considered less risky than other R&D projects. In another study, Bouslah et al. (2010) analyzed the relationship between the adoption of forest environmental certification and the financial performance of firms. Relying on a sample of 160 third-party certifications in Canada and the USA made by 42 public firms, they found that certification did not have a short-term impact on financial performance but did have a long-term negative impact on financial performance. This negative result was attributed solely to industry-led certification, as opposed to certification by non-governmental organizations (NGOs). Other studies examining effects of EP include the positive influence of eco-efficiency on firm-specific financial performance (e.g., Henri and Journeault 2010; Burnett and Hansen 2008; Sinkin et al. 2008; Clarkson et al. 2011), the trade-off between the low cost of hydropower and the high cost to human rights and biodiversity (Schneider and Andreaus 2018), the charity donation behavior of firms with worse EP (e.g., Chen et al. 2008), the decreasing risk associated with firms with better EP (e.g., Cai et al. 2016), and the influence of managerial ability on improving EP (e.g., Sun 2017). Prior literature also examines the response of investors to EP based on issues such as the level of pollution (e.g., Cormier and Magnan 1997) and third-party performance scores (e.g., Cai and He 2014), as well as the impact of EP on executive compensation (e.g., Campbell et al. 2007).

NA EA literature extensively examines the relationship between regulation and environmental activities. For example, Johnston (2005) examines the influence of regulatory and voluntary environmental capital expenditures on future abnormal earnings, stock prices, and stock returns. While regulatory capital expenditures were negatively associated with financial performance (i.e., future abnormal earnings and negative market price), the voluntary capital expenditures were positively associated with future abnormal earnings, indicating different valuations for the regulatory and voluntary nature of environmental capital expenditures.

In a Canadian setting, Schneider et al. (2017) focused on the reporting diversity of environmental liabilities in response to changing regulation. When Canada changed to International Financial Reporting Standards (IFRS), they required a lower discount rate, rendering higher liabilities. Examining a sample of publicly traded ESI firms, which should have higher liabilities, the authors found a strategic choice by management to hide larger environmental liabilities, where approximately one-third of firms chose a higher discount rate. Other papers focusing on regulation include examinations of regulatory compliance (e.g., Mishra et al. 1997), firm-specific strategy in response to regulation (e.g., Johnston and Rock 2005), the financial consequences of regulation (e.g., Freedman and Jaggi 1992), and management's understanding and efficient use of EA metrics (e.g., Joshi et al. 2001).

Conclusion

Throughout the literature, a common set of limitations is reported. First, there is often a lack of generalizability. Since many of these studies focus on one industry or a similar set of industries, it is difficult to argue that the results will hold true for other industries. Often, this focus also results in a limited sample size. Furthermore, much of the NA literature relies on archival-based research from large databases of public companies, with fewer focused on in-depth case studies, interviews, or smaller private firms, which may garner additional EA insights. Additionally, the research stream to date has relied almost exclusively on legitimacy theory; we encourage expansion into other theories, including those from other disciplines, not yet introduced to the accounting field. Finally, NA research concentrates on Canada and the USA, often excluding Mexico's large and important economy. We argue that there is much to learn from the areas of Mexico, Latin America, the Caribbean islands, and Greenland. Additional topics to consider for NA research might be the influence of drastic administrative shifts, the new and emerging cannabis industry, growing income inequality, and recent extreme weather events. With so many possibilities, it is our hope that current and future researchers will expand their horizons and explore new and exciting areas of EA.

Notes

1 See Romi et al. (2018), Hiller (2012), André (2012), and B-Lab (2019).
2 The regulatory context is always in a state of flux, particularly with changes in administration.

References

Aerts, W. and Cormier, D. 2009. Media legitimacy and corporate environmental communication. *Accounting, Organizations and Society,* 34(1), 1–27.

Al-Tuwaijri, S. A., Christensen, T. E. and Hughes, K. E. 2004. The relations among environmental disclosure, environmental performance, and economic performance: A simultaneous equations approach. *Accounting, Organizations and Society,* 29(5), 447–471.

Alciatore, M., Dee, C. C. and Easton, P. 2004. Changes in environmental regulation and reporting: The case of the petroleum industry from 1989 to 1998. *Journal of Accounting and Public Policy,* 23(4), 295–304.

André, R. 2012. Assessing the accountability of the benefit corporation: Will this new gray sector organization enhance corporate social responsibility? *Journal of Business Ethics,* 110(1), 133–150.

Anderson, J. C. and Frankle, A. W. 1980. Voluntary social reporting: An iso-beta portfolio analysis. *The Accounting Review,* 55(3), 467.

B-Lab, 2019. *Certified B Corporation* [online]. B Lab. Available from: https://bcorporation.net/ [Accessed 10 October 2019].

Berrone, P., Fosfuri, A. and Gelabert, L. 2017. Does greenwashing pay off? Understanding the relationship between environmental actions and environmental legitimacy. *Journal of Business Ethics,* 144(2), 363–379.

Blacconiere, W. G. and Patten, D. M. 1994. Environmental disclosures, regulatory costs, and changes in firm value. *Journal of Accounting and Economics,* 18(3), 357–377.

Bouslah, K. et al. 2010. The impact of forest certification on firm financial performance in Canada and the U.S. *Journal of Business Ethics,* 96(4), 551–572.

Buhr, N. 1998. Environmental performance, legislation and annual report disclosure: The case of acid rain and Falconbridge. *Accounting, Auditing & Accountability Journal,* 11(2), 163–190.

Buhr, N. 2001. Corporate silence: Environmental disclosure and the North American Free Trade Agreement. *Critical Perspectives on Accounting,* 12(4), 405–421.

Buhr, N. and Freedman, M. 2001. Culture, institutional factors and differences in environmental disclosure between Canada and the United States. *Critical Perspectives on Accounting,* 12(3), 293–322.

Burnett, R. D. and Hansen, D. R. 2008. Ecoefficiency: Defining a role for environmental cost management. *Accounting, Organizations and Society,* 33(6), 551–581.

Cai, L., Cui, J. and Jo, H. 2016. Corporate environmental responsibility and firm risk. *Journal of Business Ethics,* 139(3), 563–594.

Cai, L. and He, C. 2014. Corporate environmental responsibility and equity prices. *Journal of Business Ethics,* 125(4), 617–635.

Campbell, K. et al. 2007. Executive compensation and non-financial risk: An empirical examination. *Journal of Accounting and Public Policy,* 26(4), 436–462.

Canada, 1999. *Overview of Canadian Environmental Protection Act (CEPA)* [online]. Government of Canada. Available from: www.canada.ca/en/environment-climate-change/services/canadian-environmental-protection-act-registry/general-information/overview.html [Accessed 17 September 2019].

CFTC, 2010. *Dodd-Frank Act* [online]. United States Commodity Futures Trading Commission. Available from: www.cftc.gov/LawRegulation/DoddFrankAct/index.htm [Accessed 17 September 2019].

Chelli, M., Durocher, S. and Fortin, A. 2018. Normativity in environmental reporting: A comparison of three regimes. *Journal of Business Ethics,* 149(2), 285–311.

Chen, J. C., Cho, C. H. and Patten, D. M. 2014. Initiating disclosure of environmental liability information: An empirical analysis of firm choice. *Journal of Business Ethics,* 125(4), 681–692.

Chen, J. C., Patten, D. M. and Roberts, R. W. 2008. Corporate charitable contributions: A corporate social performance or legitimacy strategy? *Journal of Business Ethics,* 82(1), 131–144.

Cho, C. et al. 2018. The frontstage and backstage of corporate sustainability reporting: Evidence from the Arctic National Wildlife Refuge Bill. *Journal of Business Ethics,* 152(3), 865–886.

Cho, C. H., Chen, J. C. and Roberts, R. W. 2008. The politics of environmental disclosure regulation in the chemical and petroleum industries: Evidence from the Emergency Planning and Community Right-to-Know Act of 1986. *Critical Perspectives on Accounting,* 19(4), 450–465.

Cho, C. H., Freedman, M. and Patten, D. M. 2012a. Corporate disclosure of environmental capital expenditures. *Accounting, Auditing & Accountability Journal,* 25(3), 486–507.

Cho, C. H., et al. 2012b. Do actions speak louder than words? An empirical investigation of corporate environmental reputation. *Accounting, Organizations and Society,* 37(1), 14–25.

Cho, C. H., et al. 2011. Astroturfing global warming: It isn't always greener on the other side of the fence. *Journal of Business Ethics,* 104(4), 571–587.

Cho, C. H. et al. 2014. CSR report assurance in the USA: An empirical investigation of determinants and effects. *Sustainability Accounting, Management and Policy Journal,* 5(2), 130–148.

Cho, C. H., et al. 2015. CSR disclosure: The more things change…? *Accounting, Auditing & Accountability Journal,* 28(1), 14–35.

Cho, C. H. and Patten, D. M. 2007. The role of environmental disclosures as tools of legitimacy: A research note. *Accounting, Organizations and Society,* 32(7), 639–647.

Cho, C. H., Patten, D. M. and Roberts, R. W. 2006. Corporate political strategy: An examination of the relation between political expenditures, environmental performance, and environmental disclosure. *Journal of Business Ethics,* 67(2), 139–154.

Cho, C. H., Roberts, R. W. and Patten, D. M. 2010. The language of US corporate environmental disclosure. *Accounting, Organizations and Society,* 35(4), 431–443.

Clarkson, P. M., et al. 2013. The relevance of environmental disclosures: Are such disclosures incrementally informative? *Journal of Accounting and Public Policy,* 32(5), 410–431.

Clarkson, P. M., Li, Y. and Richardson, G. D. 2004. The market valuation of environmental capital expenditures by pulp and paper companies. *The Accounting Review,* 79(2), 329–353.

Clarkson, P. M. et al. 2008. Revisiting the relation between environmental performance and environmental disclosure: An empirical analysis. *Accounting, Organizations and Society,* 33(4), 303–327.

Clarkson, P. M. et al. 2011. Does it really pay to be green? Determinants and consequences of proactive environmental strategies. *Journal of Accounting and Public Policy,* 30(2), 122–144.

Cordeiro, J. J. and Tewari, M. 2015. Firm characteristics, industry context, and investor reactions to environmental CSR: A stakeholder theory approach. *Journal of Business Ethics,* 130(4), 833–849.

Cormier, D. and Gordon, I. M. 2001. An examination of social and environmental reporting strategies. *Accounting, Auditing & Accountability Journal,* 14(5), 587–616.

Cormier, D. and Magnan, M. 1997. Investors' assessment of implicit environmental liabilities: An empirical investigation. *Journal of Accounting and Public Policy,* 16(2), 215–241.

Darrell, W. and Schwartz, B. N. 1997. Environmental disclosures and public policy pressure. *Journal of Accounting and Public Policy,* 16(2), 125–154.

Dawkins, C. and Fraas, J. 2011. Coming clean: The impact of environmental performance and visibility on corporate climate change disclosure. *Journal of Business Ethics,* 100(2), 303–322.

de Villiers, C. and van Staden, C. J. 2011. Where firms choose to disclose voluntary environmental information. *Journal of Accounting and Public Policy,* 30(6), 504–525.

Dilla, W. et al. 2019. Do environmental responsibility views influence investors' use of environmental performance and assurance information? *Sustainability Accounting, Management and Policy Journal,* 10(3), 476–497.

Diouf, D. and Boiral, O. 2017. The quality of sustainability reports and impression management. *Accounting, Auditing & Accountability Journal,* 30(3), 643–667.

Dowling, J. and Pfeffer, J. 1975. Organizational legitimacy: Social values and organizational behavior. *Pacific Sociological Review,* 18(1), 122–136.

EDF, 2019. *How Cap and Trade Works* [online]. Environmental Defense Fund. Available from: www.edf.org/climate/how-cap-and-trade-works [Accessed 17 September 2019].

Elayan, F. A., Brown, K., Li, J. et al. 2019. The market response to mandatory conflict mineral disclosures. *Journal of Business Ethics,* 1–30. DOI: 10.1007/s10551-019-04283-9

EPA, 1969. *National Environmental Policy Act (NEPA)* [online]. United States Environmental Protection Agency. Available from: https://ceq.doe.gov/ [Accessed 17 September 2019].

EPA, 1970. *The Clean Air Act (CAA)* [online]. United States Environmental Protection Agency. Available from: www.epa.gov/clean-air-act-overview [Accessed 17 September 2019].

EPA, 1980. *Superfund: CERCLA Overview* [online]. United States Environmental Protection Agency. Available from: www.epa.gov/superfund/superfund-cercla-overview [Accessed 17 September 2019].

EPA, 1986. *Emergency Planning and Community Right-to-Know Act (EPCRA)* [online]. United States Environmental Protection Agency. Available from: www.epa.gov/epcra [Accessed 17 September 2019].

Epstein, M. J. and Freedman, M. 1994. Social disclosure and the individual investor. *Accounting, Auditing & Accountability Journal,* 7(4), 94.

Freedman, M. and Jaggi, B. 1992. An investigation of the long-run relationship between pollution performance and economic performance: The case of pulp and paper firms. *Critical Perspectives on Accounting,* 3(4), 315–336.

Freedman, M. and Stagliano, A. J. 2002. Environmental disclosure by companies involved in initial public offerings. *Accounting, Auditing & Accountability Journal,* 15(1), 94–105.

Freedman, M. and Stagliano, A. J. 2008. Environmental disclosures: Electric utilities and Phase 2 of the Clean Air Act. *Critical Perspectives on Accounting,* 19(4), 466–486.

Gaworecki, M. 2015. *Nexen's Brand New, Double-Layered Pipeline Just Ruptured, Causing One of the Biggest Oil Spills Ever in Alberta* [online]. DESMOG. Available from: www.desmogblog.com/2015/07/17/nexen-brand-new-pipeline-ruptured-causing-one-biggest-oil-spills-ever-alberta [Accessed 17 September 2019].

Griffin, P. A. 2013. Cap-and-trade emission allowances and US companies' balance sheets. *Sustainability Accounting, Management and Policy Journal,* 4(1), 7–31.

Griffin, P. A., Lont, D. H. and Sun, E. Y. 2017. The relevance to investors of greenhouse gas emission disclosures. *Contemporary Accounting Research,* 34(2), 1265–1297.

Griffin, P. A. and Sun, E. Y. 2018. Voluntary corporate social responsibility disclosure and religion. *Sustainability Accounting, Management and Policy Journal,* 9(1), 63–94.

Griffin, P. A. and Sun, Y. 2013. Going green: Market reaction to CSRwire news releases. *Journal of Accounting and Public Policy,* 32(2), 93–113.
Guidry, R. P. and Patten, D. M. 2010. Market reactions to the first-time issuance of corporate sustainability reports: Evidence that quality matters. *Sustainability Accounting, Management and Policy Journal,* 1(1), 33–50.
Henri, J.-F. and Journeault, M. 2010. Eco-control: The influence of management control systems on environmental and economic performance. *Accounting, Organizations and Society,* 35(1), 63–80.
Herremans, I. M., Herschovis, M. S. and Bertels, S. 2009. Leaders and laggards: The influence of competing logics on corporate environmental action. *Journal of Business Ethics,* 89(3), 449–472.
Hiller, J. S. 2012. The benefit corporation and corporate social responsibility. *Journal of Business Ethics,* 118(2), 1–15.
Horn, S. 2019. *As Indigenous Peoples Protest, California Approves Global Cap-and-Trade Plan* [online]. Sacramento, CA: The Real News Network. Available from: https://therealnews.com/columns/as-indigenous-peoples-protest-california-approves-global-cap-and-trade-plan [Accessed 10 November 2019].
Hughes, K. E., II. 2000. The value relevance of nonfinancial measures of air pollution in the electric utility industry. *The Accounting Review,* 75(2), 209–228.
Hughes, S. B., Anderson, A. and Golden, S. 2001. Corporate environmental disclosures: Are they useful in determining environmental performance? *Journal of Accounting and Public Policy,* 20(3), 217–240.
Iyer, V. and Lulseged, A. 2013. Does family status impact US firms' sustainability reporting? *Sustainability Accounting, Management and Policy Journal,* 4(2), 163–189.
Johnston, D. 2005. An investigation of regulatory and voluntary environmental capital expenditures. *Journal of Accounting and Public Policy,* 24(3), 175–206.
Johnston, D. 2012. Environmental R&D and the uncertainty of future earnings. *Journal of Accounting and Public Policy,* 31(6), 593–609.
Johnston, D. and Rock, S. 2005. Earnings management to minimize Superfund clean-up and transaction costs. *Contemporary Accounting Research,* 22(3), 617–642.
Joshi, S., Krishnan, R. and Lave, L. 2001. Estimating the hidden costs of environmental regulation. *The Accounting Review,* 76(2), 171–198.
Lee, W. E. and Sweeney, J. T. 2015. Use of discretionary environmental accounting narratives to influence stakeholders: The case of jurors' award assessments. *Journal of Business Ethics,* 129(3), 673–688.
Li, Y., Richardson, G. D. and Thornton, D. B. 1997. Corporate disclosure of environmental liability information: Theory and evidence. *Contemporary Accounting Research,* 14(3), 435–474.
Lindblom, C. K., 1994. The implications of organizational legitimacy for corporate social performance and disclosure. *Critical Perspectives on Accounting Conference.* New York.
Magness, V. 2006. Strategic posture, financial performance and environmental disclosure: An empirical test of legitimacy theory. *Accounting, Auditing & Accountability Journal,* 19(4), 540.
Mahoney, L. S. et al. 2013. A research note on standalone corporate social responsibility reports: Signaling or greenwashing? *Critical Perspectives on Accounting,* 24(4), 350–359.
Mallin, C., Michelon, G. and Raggi, D. 2013. Monitoring intensity and stakeholders' orientation: How does governance affect social and environmental disclosure? *Journal of Business Ethics,* 114(1), 29–43.
Meyer, J. W. and Rowan, B. 1977. Institutionalized organizations: Formal structure as myth and ceremony. *American Journal of Sociology,* 83(2), 340–363.
Mishra, B. K., Paul Newman, D. and Stinson, C. H. 1997. Environmental regulations and incentives for compliance audits. *Journal of Accounting and Public Policy,* 16(2), 187–214.
Mobus, J. L. 2005. Mandatory environmental disclosures in a legitimacy theory context. *Accounting, Auditing & Accountability Journal,* 18(4), 492–517.
Neu, D., Warsame, H. and Pedwell, K. 1998. Managing public impressions: Environmental disclosures in annual reports. *Accounting, Organizations and Society,* 23(3), 265–282.
NOAA, 1989. *T/V Exxon Valdez* [online]. National Oceanic and Atmospheric Administration. Available from: https://incidentnews.noaa.gov/incident/6683 [Accessed 17 September 2019].
NOAA, 2010. *Deepwater Horizon* [online]. National Oceanic and Atmospheric Administration. Available from: https://incidentnews.noaa.gov/incident/8220#! [Accessed 17 September 2019].
NOAA, 2019. *Largest Oil Spills Affecting U.S. Waters since 1969* [online]. National Oceanic and Atmospheric Administration. Available from: https://response.restoration.noaa.gov/oil-and-chemical-spills/oil-spills/largest-oil-spills-affecting-us-waters–1969.html [Accessed 17 September 2019].

Patten, D. M. 1991. Exposure, legitimacy, and social disclosure. *Journal of Accounting and Public Policy*, 10(4), 297–308.
Patten, D. M. 1992. Intra-industry environmental disclosures in response to the Alaskan oil spill: A note on legitimacy theory. *Accounting, Organizations and Society*, 17(5), 471–475.
Patten, D. M. 1998. The impact of the EPA's TRI disclosure program on state environmental and natural resource expenditures. *Journal of Accounting and Public Policy*, 17(4), 367–382.
Patten, D. M. 2002. The relation between environmental performance and environmental disclosure: A research note. *Accounting, Organizations and Society*, 27(8), 763–773.
Patten, D. M. 2005. The accuracy of financial report projections of future environmental capital expenditures: A research note. *Accounting, Organizations and Society*, 30(5), 457–468.
Patten, D. M. and Freedman, M. 2008. The GAO investigation of corporate environmental disclosure: An opportunity missed. *Critical Perspectives on Accounting*, 19(4), 435–449.
Patten, D. M. and Nance, J. R. 1998. Regulatory cost effects in a good news environment: The intra-industry reaction to the Alaskan oil spill. *Journal of Accounting and Public Policy*, 17(4), 409–429.
Patten, D. M. and Trompeter, G. 2003. Corporate responses to political costs: An examination of the relation between environmental disclosure and earnings management. *Journal of Accounting and Public Policy*, 22(1), 83–94.
Peters, G. F. and Romi, A. M. 2013. Discretionary compliance with mandatory environmental disclosures: Evidence from SEC filings. *Journal of Accounting and Public Policy*, 32(4), 213–236.
Peters, G. F. and Romi, A. M. 2014. Does the voluntary adoption of corporate governance mechanisms improve environmental risk disclosures? Evidence from greenhouse gas emission accounting. *Journal of Business Ethics*, 125(4), 637–666.
Plumlee, M. et al. 2015. Voluntary environmental disclosure quality and firm value: Further evidence. *Journal of Accounting and Public Policy*, 34(4), 336–361.
Reitenga, A. L. 2000. Environmental regulation, capital intensity, and cross-sectional variation in market returns. *Journal of Accounting and Public Policy*, 19(2), 189–198.
Rodrigue, M., Magnan, M. and Cho, C. H. 2013. Is environmental governance substantive or symbolic? An empirical investigation. *Journal of Business Ethics*, 114(1), 107–129.
Romi, A., Cook, K. A. and Dixon-Fowler, H. R. 2018. The influence of social responsibility on employee productivity and sales growth. *Sustainability Accounting, Management and Policy Journal*, 9(4), 392–421.
Rupley, K. H., Brown, D. and Marshall, R. S. 2012. Governance, media and the quality of environmental disclosure. *Journal of Accounting and Public Policy*, 31(6), 610–640.
Sankara, J., Patten, D. M. and Lindberg, D. L. 2019. Mandated social disclosure. *Sustainability Accounting, Management and Policy Journal*, 10(1), 208–228.
Schneider, T. and Andreaus, M. 2018. A dam tale. *Sustainability Accounting, Management and Policy Journal*, 9(5), 685–712.
Schneider, T., Michelon, G. and Maier, M. 2017. Environmental liabilities and diversity in practice under international financial reporting standards. *Accounting, Auditing & Accountability Journal*, 30(2), 378–403.
Shane, P. B. and Spicer, B. H. 1983. Market response to environmental information produced outside the firm. *The Accounting Review*, 58(3), 521.
Sinkin, C., Wright, C. J. and Burnett, R. D. 2008. Eco-efficiency and firm value. *Journal of Accounting and Public Policy*, 27(2), 167–176.
Spicer, B. H. 1978. Investors, corporate social performance and information disclosure: An empirical study. *The Accounting Review*, 53(1), 94.
Suchman, M. C. 1995. Managing legitimacy - Strategic and institutional approaches. *The Academy of Management Review*, 20(3), 571–610. Retrieved from https://www-proquest-com.lib-e2.lib.ttu.edu/scholarly-journals/managing-legitimacy-strategic-institutional/docview/210941848/se-2?accountid=7098
Sun, L. 2017. Managerial ability and chemical releases. *Sustainability Accounting, Management and Policy Journal*, 8(3), 281–306.
Talbot, D. and Boiral, O. 2015. Strategies for climate change and impression management: A case study among Canada's large industrial emitters. *Journal of Business Ethics*, 132(2), 329–346.
Thorne, L., Mahoney, L. S. and Manetti, G. 2014. Motivations for issuing standalone CSR reports: A survey of Canadian firms. *Accounting, Auditing & Accountability Journal*, 27(4), 686–714.

Walker, K. and Wan, F. 2012. The harm of symbolic actions and green-washing: Corporate actions and communications on environmental performance and their financial implications. *Journal of Business Ethics,* 109(2), 227–242.
Wiseman, J. 1982. An evaluation of environmental disclosures made in corporate annual reports. *Accounting, Organizations and Society,* 7(1), 53–63.
WWF, 2019. *Pulp and Paper* [online]. World Wildlife Fund. Available from: www.worldwildlife.org/industries/pulp-and-paper [Accessed 17 September 2019].

24
THE PACIFIC REGION

Matthew Scobie, Matthew Sorola and Glenn Finau

Introduction

There is an urgent need to address social and environmental issues across many regions of the world, but social and environmental impacts are particularly acute in the Pacific region (Mimura 1999; Intergovernmental Panel on Climate Change 2018; Ministry of Foreign Affairs and Trade 2018). We define the Pacific region broadly, a vast geographical area made up of a great number of sovereign nations and cultures within these nations. This includes larger nations like Australia and Aotearoa New Zealand, but also the Small Island Developing States (SIDS) of the Pacific. Rather than being connected by a landmass, this region is connected by an ocean, with genealogies of pre- and post-colonial relations (Hau'ofa 2008). This reality of being connected by an ocean, which has sustained these relations, but is currently threatening them, not only illustrates the unique setting within which environmental accounting research takes place across the Pacific, but it also highlights the urgency that underpins it.

In this chapter, we provide a snapshot of published works relating to environmental accounting and reporting issues to demonstrate the past, present and potential future of the discipline in the Pacific region. We categorise our review into a simplified conceptual framework that recognises Indigenous perspectives and mainstream perspectives which can conflict, coerce or complement one another. We argue that sustainability, in its relation to social and environmental issues, has been defined in this mainstream perspective, and distributed to the Indigenous perspective *from above*, where this concept has existed in different forms across different cultures in our region since time immemorial. We therefore advocate for future research which embraces Indigenous perspectives *from below* to confront these global issues as an empowering approach rather than a deficit or colonial approach. Although social and environmental concerns are devastating our region today, there are solutions emerging from these – often marginalised – perspectives which imagine alternative futures. While the functionality of this chapter is to provide an overview of existing social and environmental accounting research in the Pacific region, we hope that it will also enable future researchers to engage with these solutions in respectful and generative ways so that we can imagine and create these alternative futures together.

Contextualising the Pacific region

Years of exploration, migration and colonisation across the Pacific has led to a variety of unique cultures, many of which are grounded in intimate relationships with land and water (Ravuvu 1983; Hau'ofa 2008). These relationships have been constrained by the forces of capitalist-colonialism (Teaiwa 2005). However, it is these relationships that can lead individuals and collectives within these communities to engage with, resist or create alternatives to social and environmental exploitation and degradation (Govan 2009). These pressures impact on both the extrinsic (social, environmental and economic livelihoods) and intrinsic (identity, language and sense-making) relationships these communities share with the world, that is, their culture as a mode of production within a mode of life (Coulthard 2014). This culture as a mode of life, and its adaptation through colonial-capitalist pressures, is crucial to understand how environmental accounting and reporting has developed across the region. It illustrates how culture may impact to who, for what and how environmental accountability has, is or can be practised. And it presents alternatives.

The Pacific region is diverse and environmental accounting and reporting is a complex research area that is interdisciplinary in nature (Bebbington et al. 1999). Environmental accounting research lies at the intersection of organisational reporting and environmental science, two fields that can complement or conflict with one another (Gray and Bebbington 2000). This complexity is especially challenging for the developing economies of the Pacific where, from tourism to mining, the well-being of the environment is intimately tied with the economic prosperity of the region (Milne 1992; Emberson-Bain 1994). That which gives can also take away. Many of the countries that have capitalised on their environmental resources, as well as those that have not, are also poised to be dramatically impacted by the effects of the climate crisis. From small island nations like Tuvalu, where rising sea levels have already reclaimed islands into the sea (Mortreux and Barnett 2009), to larger countries like Australia where extended droughts, fires and heatwaves stand to make it uninhabitable in the near future (CSIRO 2015), the Pacific region is uniquely embedded within, and impacted by, the environment.

Despite having a rich Indigenous history, any understanding of the Pacific region must recognise the pervasive impact that Anglo-American knowledge systems, from colonialism to neoliberalism, have across the region (Smith 1999). Years of imperialism and neo/settler-colonialism laid much of the groundwork needed for these systems to take root, leading to the disenfranchisement of many of the voices that did not align with a narrowly defined and largely imposed economic agenda (Hau'ofa 2008). Many of the economies that have developed across the Pacific region are prone to the same kinds of problematic tensions that have historically prioritised business interests over those of the environment (Teaiwa 2005). It is difficult to separate economic considerations from an understanding of environmental accounting and reporting in the Pacific region. While the relative size of economies can be useful in determining which countries have the economic and financial clout to lead in its development, it can also help understand how some countries are motivated to align themselves through adoption and may be marginalised from the process. Australia is the largest economy in the region, followed by New Zealand and Papua New Guinea based on gross domestic product (World Bank n.d.). The economic power of Australia is important in the context of environmental accounting and reporting, as it affords its institutions regional dominance and enables them to drive much of the regulatory dialogue (Tarte 2014).

While the relative size of economies helps understand one aspect of the relationship between countries around the Pacific region, it is also important to consider the type of economic output that supports these positions. For example, while Australia may lead regulatory and disclosure regulation in the region, its relative financial positioning does not reflect its economy's reliance on industries that have a direct impact on the environment. These industries are largely extractive (Mudd 2010). In turn, this means meaningful environmental accounting and reporting poses a direct risk to the economic prosperity of these countries under their current economic structures. Commercial fishing operations, mining, agriculture and even tourism all have environmental impacts, but they also represent major economic drivers within countries across the Pacific region. Any understanding of environmental accounting and reporting must recognise that it represents a direct challenge to the status quo of these industries. Finally, a key to understanding environmental accounting and reporting around the Pacific region is the capacity of different countries to measure and disclose such information. Access to environmental information varies from country to county, as the quality of information captured relies on the measurement systems and data collection techniques that are used in its development.

Zooming in on Australia, Aotearoa New Zealand and Pacific SIDS

It would be unwise to attempt to provide a catch-all systematic literature review in this short chapter. Instead, here we provide readers with a snapshot of historical and contemporary trends in environmental accounting and reporting research in the region. The literature review is organised geographically with a focus on Australia, Aotearoa New Zealand and the SIDS of the Pacific. This results in a disproportionate focus on Australia and New Zealand; however, given these two countries host a disproportionately large number of universities and accounting researchers, this bias is unavoidable. We seek to counter this bias by exploring the scant SIDS Pacific literature in more detail. We argue that the Pacific region punches above its weight in terms of environmental accounting and reporting research, but the diversity of the region and urgency of the issues warrant a considerable escalation of research activities that recognise alternative perspectives as potential solutions.

Australia dominates much of the regulatory development taking place around environmental accounting and reporting in the Pacific region. Not only is there a relatively high output of environmental accounting and reporting among organisations, including those in the public sector and local government, but prior literature has also focused on the motivations underpinning their decision to report. Australia is a unique site for this kind of research given that a large portion of the country's economic output comes from environmentally harmful industries, which reflects some of the focus on motivations in prior research. The colonial history of Australia is also unique, as can be seen in the role accounting has played within – and against – Indigenous communities and their intersection with economic interests.

From a national perspective, efforts to develop environmental accounting and reporting are readily apparent. Van Dijk et al. (2014) discussed the context within which organisations operate and their capacity to capture the environmental information needed to assess their impact, providing a high-level sense of the direction in which the country is heading. More specifically, Gibson and O'Donovan (2007) discussed how environmental accounting and reporting has developed within Australia, noting an increase in both the volume of information produced and the number of reporting organisations. These increases appear to signal proactive measures on the part of organisations to address their social and environmental impact. However, while quantitative research like Lee (2017) has helped identify the strong correlation between firm size, quality and quantity of disclosure, others posit this increase has more to do with an exercise in corporate messaging (Clarkson et al. 2011).

Concerns around the motivations of environmentally harmful organisations choosing to produce environmental accounting and reporting are understandable (see, e.g., Deegan and

Blomquist 2006; Higgins et al. 2015). The process of legitimisation within organisational efforts to develop environmental accounting and reporting in O'Donovan (2002) has been a long-standing concern. Although the uptake of environmental accounting and reporting in Australia has been followed for some time now, researchers have long been concerned with the quality of disclosures being made and the interests around which "best practices" are being established (Haque and Deegan 2010). For example, Higgins et al. (2015) explored the role of lobby groups within the Australian minerals industry and discussed how their involvement facilitates opposition to the development of disclosure regulation.

Many of the same concerns regarding environmental accounting and reporting in the private sector can also be found in research on public sector and local government organisations. Williams et al. (2011) provided a useful introduction to this literature and discuss government reporting practices that are both relatively new and under-resourced, while Farneti and Guthrie (2009) explored the motivations behind public sector environmental accounting and reporting. Although these discussions are focused on the Australian context, the work of Guthrie and Farneti (2008) helps illustrate efforts to align reporting with international organisations like the Global Reporting Initiative.

The influence of international organisations on environmental accounting and reporting is substantial (Guthrie and Farneti 2008; Lee 2017), but within Australia, there lies a potential to transform environmental accounting and reporting. Indigenous peoples often appear in Australian accounting literature to illustrate the use of accounting as a weapon of dispossession (Chew and Greer 1997; Gibson 2000; Greer and McNicholas 2017). Of concern here is that these efforts are frequently motivated by an intention to raise the economic status of these communities, but in doing so, they can also create new forms of cultural assimilation (Rkein and Norris 2012; Dang et al. 2016). However, in articulating the impact of accounting technologies on Indigenous communities and their incorporation into the accounting profession (Lombardi and Cooper 2015; Lombardi 2016), it is important to consider how their perspectives can enrich the preparation and communication of social and environmental accounting (Chew and Greer 1997; Greer and Patel 2000). For example, Greer and Patel (2000) used a "Yin and Yang" framework to explore cultural differences in Australia (cf. Hines 1992). In doing so, they explored Indigenous values that could help inform a new approach to environmental accounting. Evans and Jacobs (2010) explored the core differences that may constitute an alternative Indigenous approach in their discussion of the clash between "economic rationality" and values rooted in community and the environment. Evans and Jacobs (2010) reconceptualised Australian cultural identity, and in doing so, they articulated a framework for evaluating environmental accounting and reporting that may hold potential for future research. Finally, although their focus is on management, Bodle et al. (2018) articulated the factors that lead to successful Indigenous businesses. In the context of environmental accounting and reporting, the economic and social values identified by these authors are not constrained by a narrowly defined economic rationalisation, and as such, may help inform a new way to approach core issues like the valuation of intangible assets.

The lengthy history of environmental accounting and reporting in Australia is reflected in its high reporting output relative to the rest of the region. With an economy dominated by environmentally harmful industries, researchers have problematised the quality of reporting, and these concerns have informed research into the motivations that underpin the decision to report. While much of this research focused on private sector organisations, there is some engagement with the public sector. Finally, research around the role of accounting in Indigenous communities illustrates its potential to inform new approaches to environmental accounting and reporting. As a tool that can both enrich and dispossess, accounting has a problematic history from the perspective of Indigenous communities. However, these shortcomings have led to new ways in which to approach the use of environmental accounting and reporting that are not constrained by an economic rationale.

In Aotearoa New Zealand, environmental accounting and reporting research can be broadly categorised into three overlapping perspectives. These are based on different methodologies and assumptions about knowledge and its relation to the world. One stream of literature *measures* a number of different relationships between specified variables within environmental accounting and reporting practices (Hackston and Milne 1996; Lemon and Cahan 1997; Cahan et al. 2016; Dodds and van Staden 2016). Because of the small number of voluntary reporters and listed companies (Dodds and van Staden 2016), studies from New Zealand working within these assumptions tend to conduct multi-country or comparative studies (e.g. Cahan et al. 2016), or use novel methodological approaches to compensate for smaller sample sizes (e.g. Dodds and van Staden 2016). These approaches tend to replicate or advance other studies, through assumptions embedded within the scientific method, to investigate quantitative relationships between variables that can be used as evidence for some broader qualitative relationship. For example, Hackston and Milne (1996) provided a contemporary description of the social and environmental reporting practices of New Zealand companies, discussed some potential determinants of these disclosure practices and critically examined different techniques of disclosure measurement. Dodds and van Staden (2016) investigated the motivations for voluntary social and environmental reporting by matching survey responses with content analysis of reports. Ultimately, the authors concluded that community concerns and shareholder rights are the most important factors influencing an organisation's decision to voluntarily report (Dodds and van Staden 2016).

Another strand of research *interprets* the social and environmental disclosures of New Zealand organisations through different theoretical lenses (see, e.g., Milne et al. 2006; Milne et al. 2009; Schneider et al. 2012; Tregidga et al. 2013; Samkin et al. 2014). These studies explore the qualitative and visual disclosures within reports to theorise how and why these are the way they are in addition to the wider social and environmental implications of this. Milne et al. (2009) critically examined the language and other visual presentations of sustainable development in annual and voluntary reports and found that although organisational language suggests that businesses are "doing" sustainability, interpreted through a broader lens, these communications reveal an economic and instrumental approach to the natural environment. Tregidga et al. (2013) investigated the representations of sustainable development through a discourse analysis of organisations within the New Zealand Business Council for Sustainable Development. They engaged with a number of different themes within reporting which construct sustainable development as accommodating current organisations and systems of organising (Tregidga et al. 2013). Samkin et al. (2014) longitudinally examined the biodiversity disclosures of a New Zealand conservation organisation through a deep ecology perspective. In turn, this perspective enables the authors to develop a framework that can be used as both an assessment and a guide for biodiversity reporting (Samkin et al. 2014).

Another strand of research *conceptualises, imagines or critiques* the role of environmental accounting and reporting in society (see, e.g., Mataira 1994; Gallhofer et al. 2000; Bebbington et al. 2007; Brown 2009; Craig et al. 2012; Tregidga et al. 2018). These studies engaged with environmental accounting and reporting through a plurality of perspectives to conceptualise relations between accounting and the environment in different ways, imagined a more enabling role for environmental accounting or critiqued existing or potential frameworks. Bebbington et al. (2007) argued for a dialogic accounting which recognises different perspectives in engagement. They emphasised the benefits that can accrue to all parties through committed dialogic engagement. Brown and co-authors (Brown 2009; Dillard and Brown 2012) extended this approach by linking dialogic engagement with theories of agonistic democracy to take "ideological conflicts seriously" (Brown 2009, p. 313). Brown (2009), for example, developed a framework for a critical dialogic approach with eight motifs aimed at broadening out accounting to pluralise dialogue.

Several authors explored environmental accounting and reporting practices through a Māori (Indigenous) lens (Mataira 1994; Gallhofer et al. 2000; McNicholas and Barrett 2005; Craig et al. 2012). Mataira (1994) argued that accountability in Māori society can be understood as "based on the norms, obligations, laws and traditions in the way Māori people continue to organise themselves, primarily as hapū (sub-tribes) and iwi (tribes), in pursuit of sovereignty" (p. 33). Gallhofer et al. (2000) explored the potential for principles underlying Indigenous cultures to contribute to developing an environmental accounting. For example, the Māori concept of *whakapapa* (a structured genealogical relationship between all things) emphasises an understanding of the interrelatedness of all things which brings to attention the limitations of corporate conceptualisations of an account and the organisational boundaries of accounts. McNicholas and Barrett (2005) advocated methodological approaches in accounting research which recognise the relationship between research and the self-determination of marginalised voices. Craig et al. (2012) explored the Māori concept of *taonga* (treasure). They engaged directly with Indigenous knowledge and knowledge keepers to provide an alternative perspective on asset valuation through the concept of *taonga*, which emphasises guardianship over ownership, collective over individual rights and intergenerational obligations (Craig et al. 2012). Despite this, Tregidga et al. (2018) argued that dominant business-case articulations of sustainable development need to be interrogated, critiqued and resisted and alternatives need to be imagined within and outside of the academy to move beyond the status quo.

Environmental accounting and reporting research in the SIDS of the Pacific is sparse, sporadic and has been relatively static over recent years. Sharma and An (2018) provided a comprehensive review of accounting and accountability issues in one of the most developed SIDS of the Pacific – Fiji. They found that 46.8% of papers relate to financial reporting and accountability, 29.8% relate to new public management and only 12.7% relate to sustainability accounting. Finau (2020) extended this literature review out to other SIDS of the Pacific. Finau (2020) identified 67 papers and classified these into three common themes: (i) accounting, colonialism and culture, (ii) accounting and the public sector and (iii) social and environmental accounting research. Of these papers, only 15 papers relate to social and environmental accounting research (22%), the lowest percentage of the three categories. The vast majority of environmental accounting and reporting in the Pacific is based in Fiji. This dominance is primarily due to Fiji being, arguably, the most "developed" SIDS of the Pacific (Finau 2020). We therefore argue for a need to use this base to develop alternative methodological and theoretical approaches across the diversity that is the Pacific.

Early environmental accounting and reporting research focused on in-depth case studies of the pioneering environmental reporting practices of particular entities in the Pacific Islands. Lodhia (1999) examined the Fiji Sugar Corporation and argued that environmental accounting practices adopted by the company serve to legitimise the company's operations rather than to extend stewardship to their stakeholders. Lodhia (2000) conducted a content analysis of corporate annual reports of public companies in Fiji and found that social and environmental disclosures are only made by a few companies, and those that comply only provide minimal disclosures. Lodhia's earlier studies focused on reporting practices by publicly listed companies in Fiji, but later studies examined legislation aimed at encouraging sustainability in Fiji and the implication of this legislation for companies and the accounting profession (Lodhia 2001). Lodhia (2003) extended his earlier work by exploring accountants' perspectives towards environmental accounting and reporting in Fiji and found that Fijian organisations do not generally consider accountants as playing a role in environmental reporting, and as a consequence, accountants are generally apathetic towards environmental accounting and reporting in Fiji. Lodhia's work on social and environmental accounting research on the Pacific has generally been qualitative in nature. Some of his papers have also incorporated quantitative data, such as content analysis of annual reports of publicly listed companies in Fiji. These studies are important in understanding the history and evolution of environmental accounting and reporting practices by companies, government organisations and accountants in Fiji.

Building on the work of Lodhia, Rika (2009) investigated the motivation of Fiji's Office of the Auditor-General to commence environmental audits of Fijian government entities. Rika (2009) employed a case study approach and drew on institutional theory to argue that the motivation was based on pressure from regional audit bodies in the Pacific and supranational organisations such as the United Nations (UN) that perceived environmental auditing as a means to accomplish the UN's Millennium Development Goals.

While accounting studies in Fiji provide important insights into environmental accounting and reporting in the Pacific, more research on other Pacific SIDS that have their own particularities, challenges and experiences with respect to environmental accounting is required (Finau 2020). To date, there have been no peer-reviewed articles in accounting journals that examine environmental accounting and reporting in other Pacific Island economies. This review also highlights the sporadic nature of these publications. Lodhia's last study on environmental accounting in Fiji was in 2003; Rika's (2009) study emerged six years later and since that period there has been relatively scant literature published.

Recently however, Sharma et al. (2017) and Perkiss and Moerman (2018) investigated implications of the climate crisis for the Pacific. Sharma et al. (2017) explored the potential of accountants to contribute towards facilitating mitigation and adaptation to the climate crisis for SIDS in the Pacific. Perkiss and Moerman (2018) focused on the moral dimensions of the climate crisis and the alternative accounts created by Pacific Island peoples displaced by sea level rise. Both papers examined the Pacific region as a whole instead of individual economies in their analysis because the climate crisis affects all SIDS in the Pacific. These studies have reinvigorated environmental accounting research in the Pacific by focusing on our most pressing issue – the climate crisis. They have examined this using novel methodological and theoretical perspectives and provide a solid foundation for the future of environmental accounting and reporting research in the Pacific. This future requires an urgent response that examines present and future implications of the climate crisis, the greatest existential threat to the Pacific. Accounting researchers have a role to play in focusing on the region as a whole, with local particularities, and imagining the potential for new accounting(s) to enable Pacific Island economies to respond, together, to this existential climate crisis.

This brief review has highlighted the relative scarcity, sporadic and static nature of the literature on environmental accounting and reporting based on the SIDS of the Pacific. Existing studies have tended to focus on Fiji, and these adopt similar methodologies, the most common being the case study and content analysis methods. These papers are largely descriptive and do not engage deeply with theoretical frameworks. Those that employ theories from the management and organisational sociology literature draw on legitimacy, stakeholder or institutional theory, rather than building theory grounded in Pacific perspectives. There has also been a lack of research that seeks to push the boundaries of existing knowledge, but we believe this is set to change and we explore this in the next section.

Discussion

This chapter has provided a brief historical and contemporary snapshot of the environmental accounting and reporting literature in the Pacific Region. This region has punched above its weight in terms of environmental accounting and reporting research, including that which measures, interprets and imagines alternatives. However, because of the dominance of two countries in this region – Australia and Aotearoa New Zealand – and anglo-settler perspectives within them, we argue that there are two general absences within this literature that future research can address. Firstly, there are novel empirical fields of research which require urgent attention, for example, the climate crisis and related social and ecological consequences (e.g. climate migration/refugees, sea-level rise, ocean acidification) (Intergovernmental Panel on Climate Change 2018; Ministry of Foreign Affairs and Trade 2018). Secondly, there are novel Indigenous perspectives and experiences which we believe can provide alternative solutions to these looming crises.

These absences suggest a more fundamental shortcoming in research within the region, which stems from a top-down approach where researchers define the problem, methods, empirics and theory within the disciplinary parameters they deem necessary. This is in contrast to affected communities determining research needs within their own perspectives and researchers supporting those. Co-created research projects can be locally grounded but globally aware, and we see no reason why international collaborations cannot join the dots to move from particular problems and solutions to universal problems and solutions, or indeed, pluriversal problems and solutions (Mbembe 2016). Our call then is to embrace research practices *led from below with support from above* which we suggest will result in alternative perspectives of environmental accounting and reporting grounded in community and Indigenous thought. This approach holds the potential for alternative solutions to the wicked problems of the world, urgently unfolding across the Pacific Region.

There is very little time left to address the climate crisis on a level that would protect many of these island nations (Intergovernmental Panel on Climate Change 2018). If researchers continue to focus on publicly available external accounts because they are easier to access, and engage with these through conventional methods, we risk rearranging (or even just counting) the deckchairs on the Titanic rather than steering clear of the iceberg. Should reporting alone be seen as the solution, or is something else needed at state level (e.g. regulatory enforcement) or community level (e.g. alternative practices of accounting and reporting)? We argue here that the value of reporting cannot be based on generic, imposed measures of performance but should instead be co-constructed within the communities and nations that they are being implemented within. While there is a global push towards homogeneity, we assert the need for particular pushes towards heterogeneity that reflect the local needs, aspirations, knowledge and common sense of communities. These perspectives can emerge together from below into a pluriversal perspective, which respects the particularities of grounded knowledge in a universal way. This embraces the plurality of the dialogic accounting project emerging within environmental accounting and reporting research in the theoretical, empirical and methodological bases of our research.

In this chapter, we have provided a brief historical and contemporary context of the Pacific region. We have asserted the importance of recognising the history of imperialism and colonialism in the region and its effect on contemporary environmental accounting and reporting. Within this we acknowledge that there are Indigenous perspectives that have largely been marginalised by these structures which hold the potential to (re)build a better world. Researchers who seek to engage with the Pacific region must acknowledge this and work with communities of interest to co-create alternatives to environmental accounting and reporting. This will benefit the research and the researchers. Climate change, ocean acidification, social upheaval, biodiversity collapse and other issues affecting and affected by environmental accounting and reporting are not intellectual curiosities in our region but threatening realities (Intergovernmental Panel on Climate Change 2018). If environmental accounting and reporting research is to contribute to a better world, then environmental accounting and reporting researchers need to stop, look and listen to communities of interest who are experiencing these lived realities, and who may hold solutions to them.

References

Bebbington, J., Brown, J., Frame, B., and Thomson, I., 2007. Theorizing engagement: the potential of a critical dialogic approach. *Accounting, Auditing & Accountability Journal*, 20 (3), 356–381.

Bebbington, J., Gray, R., and Owen, D., 1999. Seeing the wood for the trees: taking the pulse of social and environmental accounting. *Accounting, Auditing & Accountability Journal*, 12 (1), 47–52.

Bodle, K., Brimble, M., Weaven, S., Frazer, L., and Blue, L., 2018. Critical success factors in managing sustainable indigenous businesses in Australia. *Pacific Accounting Review*, 30 (1), 35–51.

Brown, J., 2009. Democracy, sustainability and dialogic accounting technologies: taking pluralism seriously. *Critical Perspectives on Accounting*, 20 (3), 313–342.

Cahan, S., de Villiers, C., Jeter, D., Naiker, V., and van Staden, C. J., 2016. Are CSR disclosures value relevant? Cross-country evidence. *European Accounting Review*, 25 (3), 579–611.

Chew, A., and Greer, S., 1997. Contrasting world views on accounting: accountability and Aboriginal culture. *Accounting, Auditing & Accountability Journal*, 10 (3), 276–298.

Clarkson, P. M., Overell, M. B., and Chapple, L., 2011. Environmental reporting and its relation to corporate environmental performance. *Abacus*, 47 (1), 27–60.

Commonwealth Scientific and Industrial Research Organisation, 2015. Climate Change in Australia Technical Report. Available from: www.climatechangeinaustralia.gov.au/en/publications-library/technical-report/ [Accessed 23 December 2019].

Coulthard, G., 2014. *Red Skin, White Masks.* Minneapolis, MN: University of Minnesota Press.

Craig, R., Taonui, R., and Wild, S., 2012. The concept of taonga in Māori culture: insights for accounting. *Accounting, Auditing & Accountability Journal*, 25 (6), 1025–1047.

Dang, T. K. A., Vitartas, P., Ambrose, K., and Millar, H., 2016. Improving the participation and engagement of Aboriginal and Torres Strait Islander students in business education. *Journal of Higher Education Policy and Management*, 38 (1), 19–38.

de Villiers, C., and Hsiao, P.-C., 2018. A review of accounting research in Australasia. *Accounting & Finance*, 58 (4), 993–1026.

Deegan, C., and Blomquist, C., 2006. Stakeholder influence on corporate reporting: An exploration of the interaction between WWF-Australia and the Australian minerals industry. *Accounting, Organizations and Society*, 31 (4–5), 343–372.

Dillard, J., and Brown, J., 2012. Agonistic pluralism and imagining CSEAR into the future. *Social and Environmental Accountability Journal*, 32 (1), 3–16.

Dodds, S., and van Staden, C., 2016. Motivations for corporate social and environmental reporting: New Zealand evidence. *Sustainability, Accounting, Management, and Policy Journal*, 7 (3), 449–472.

Emberson-Bain, A., 1994. Mining development in the Pacific: are we sustaining the unsustainable? In Harcourt W. (ed.), *Feminist Perspectives on Sustainable Development.* London: Zed Books.

Evans, S., and Jacobs, K., 2010. Accounting: an un-Australian activity? *Qualitative Research in Accounting & Management*, 7 (3), 378–394.

Farneti, F., and Guthrie, J., 2009. Sustainability reporting by Australian public sector organisations: why they report. *Accounting Forum*, 33 (2), 89–98.

Finau, G., 2020. Imagining the future of social and environmental accounting research for Pacific small island developing states. *Social and Environmental Accountability Journal*, 40 (1), in press.

Frost, G., 2007. The introduction of mandatory environmental reporting guidelines: Australian evidence. *Abacus*, 43 (2), 190–216.

Gallhofer, S., Gibson, K., Haslam, J., McNicholas, P., and Takiari, B., 2000. Developing environmental accounting: insights from Indigenous cultures. *Accounting, Auditing & Accountability Journal*, 13 (3), 381–409.

Gibson, K., 2000. Accounting as a tool for Aboriginal dispossession: then and now. *Accounting, Auditing & Accountability Journal*, 13 (3), 289–306.
Gibson, K., and O'Donovan, G., 2007. Corporate governance and environmental reporting: an Australian study. *Corporate Governance*, 15 (5), 944–956.
Govan, H., 2009. Achieving the potential of locally managed marine areas in the South Pacific. *SPC Traditional Marine Resource Management*, 25 (July), 16–25.
Gray, R., and Bebbington, J., 2000. Environmental accounting, managerialism and sustainability: is the planet safe in the hands of business and accounting? *Advances in Environmental Accounting & Management*, 1 (1), 1–44.
Greer, S., and McNicholas, P., 2017. Accounting for "moral betterment": pastoral power and indentured Aboriginal apprenticeship programs in New South Wales. *Accounting, Auditing & Accountability Journal*, 30 (8), 1843–1866.
Greer, S., and Patel, C., 2000. The issue of Australian Indigenous world-views and accounting. *Accounting, Auditing & Accountability Journal*, 13 (3), 307–329.
Guthrie, J., and Farneti, F., 2008. GRI sustainability reporting by Australian public sector organizations. *Public Money and Management*, 28 (6), 361–366.
Hackston, D., and Milne, M. J., 1996. Some determinants of social and environmental disclosures in New Zealand companies. *Accounting, Auditing & Accountability Journal*, 9 (1), 77–108.
Haque, S., and Deegan, C., 2010. Corporate climate change-related governance practices and related disclosures: evidence from Australia. *Australian Accounting Review*, 20 (4), 317–333.
Hau'ofa, E., 2008. *We Are the Ocean*. Honolulu, HI: University of Hawai'i Press.
Higgins, C., Milne, M. J., and Van Gramberg, B., 2015. The uptake of sustainability reporting in Australia. *Journal of Business Ethics*, 129 (2), 445–468.
Hines, R., 1992. Accounting: filling the negative space. *Accounting, Organizations and Society*, 17 (3–4), 313–341.
Intergovernmental Panel on Climate Change, 2018. *Special report: global warming of 1.5 °c.* Available from: www.ipcc.ch/sr15/ [Accessed 18 December 2019].
Lee, K. H., 2017. Does size matter? Evaluating corporate environmental disclosure in the Australian mining and metal industry: a combined approach of quantity and quality measurement. *Business Strategy and the Environment*, 26 (2), 209–223.
Lemon, A., and Cahan, S., 1997. Environmental legislation and environmental disclosures: some evidence from New Zealand. *Asian Review of Accounting*, 5 (1), 78–105.
Lodhia, S., 1999. Environmental accounting in Fiji: an extended case study of the Fiji Sugar Corporation. *Journal of Pacific Studies*, 20 (2000), 15–18.
Lodhia, S., 2000. Social and environmental reporting in Fiji: a review of recent corporate annual reports. *Social and Environmental Accountability Journal*, 20 (1), 15–18.
Lodhia, S., 2001. The accounting implications of the sustainable development bill. *Social and Environmental Accountability Journal*, 21 (1), 8–11.
Lodhia, S., 2003. Accountants' responses to the environmental agenda in a developing nation: an initial and exploratory study on Fiji. *Critical Perspectives on Accounting*, 14 (7), 715–737.
Lombardi, L., 2016. Disempowerment and empowerment of accounting: an Indigenous accounting context. *Accounting, Auditing & Accountability Journal*, 29 (8), 1320–1341.
Lombardi, L., and Cooper, B. J., 2015. Aboriginal and Torres Strait Islander people in the accounting profession–an exploratory study. *Australian Accounting Review*, 25 (1), 84–99.
Mataira, K., 1994. Accountability in Māori society. *Accountants' Journal*, 1994 (February), 32–33.
Mbembe, A. J., 2016. Decolonizing the university: new directions. *Arts & Humanities in Higher Education*, 15 (1), 29–45.
McNicholas, P., and Barrett, M., 2005. Answering the emancipatory call: an emerging research approach "on the margins" of accounting. *Critical Perspectives on Accounting*, 16 (4), 391–414.
Milne, M. J., Kearins, K., and Walton, S., 2006. Creating adventures in wonderland: the journey metaphor and environmental sustainability. *Organization*, 13 (6), 801–839.
Milne, M. J., Tregidga, H. and Walton, S., 2009. Words not actions! The ideological role of sustainable development reporting. *Accounting, Auditing & Accountability Journal, 22* (8), 1211–1257.
Milne, S., 1992. Tourism and development in South Pacific microstates. *Annals of Tourism Research*, 19 (2), 191–212.
Mimura, N., 1999. Vulnerability of island countries in the South Pacific to sea level rise and climate change. *Climate Research*, 12 (2–3), 137–143.

Ministry of Foreign Affairs and Trade, 2018. *Pacific Climate Change-Related Displacement and Migration: A New Zealand Action Plan*. Available from: www.mfat.govt.nz/assets/Uploads/Redacted-Cabinet-Paper-Pacific-climate-migration-2-May-2018.pdf [Accessed 20 December 2019].

Mortreux, C., and Barnett, J., 2009. Climate change, migration and adaptation in Funafuti, Tuvalu. *Journal of Global Environmental Change*, 19 (1), 105–112.

Mudd, G. M., 2010. The environmental sustainability of mining in Australia: key mega-trends and looming constraints. *Resources Policy*, 35 (2), 98–115.

O'Donovan, G., 2002. Environmental disclosures in the annual report: extending the applicability and predictive power of legitimacy theory. *Accounting, Auditing & Accountability Journal*, 15 (3), 344–371.

Perkiss, S., and Moerman, L., 2018. A dispute in the making: a critical examination of displacement, climate change and the Pacific Islands. *Accounting, Auditing & Accountability Journal*, 31 (1), 166–192.

Ravuvu, A., 1983. Vaka i Taukei: the Fijian way of life. Suva: Institute of Pacific Studies of the University of the South Pacific.

Rkein, H. I., and Norris, G., 2012. Barriers to accounting: Australian indigenous students' experience. *Social and Environmental Accountability Journal*, 32 (2), 95–107.

Samkin, G., Schneider, A., and Tappin, D., 2014. Developing a reporting and evaluation framework for biodiversity. *Accounting, Auditing & Accountability Journal*, 27 (3), 527–556.

Schneider, A., Samkin, G., and Pitu, E., 2012. Incorporating indigenous values in corporate social responsibility reports. *Journal of New Business Ideas & Trends*, 10 (2), 19–38.

Sharma, U., and An, Y., 2018. Accounting and accountability in Fiji: a review and synthesis. *Australian Accounting Review*, 28 (3), 421–427.

Sharma, U., Botes, V., Foo, D., Karan, R., and Nandan, R., 2017. Climate change accounting: the challenge of uncertainty in Pacific Islands. *International Journal of Critical Accounting*, 9 (5), 393–405.

Smith, L. T., 1999. *Decolonizing Methodologies: Research and Indigenous Peoples*. Dunedin, New Zealand: University of Otago Press.

Tarte, S., 2014. Regionalism and changing regional order in the Pacific Islands. *Asia & the Pacific Policy Studies*, 1 (2), 312–324.

Teaiwa, K., 2005. Our sea of phosphate: the diaspora of Ocean Island. In Harvey, G. & Thompson, C. (eds.), *Indigenous Diasporas and Dislocations*. Aldershot: Ashgate, 69–91.

Tregidga, H., Kearins, K., and Milne, M. J., 2013. The politics of knowing "organizational sustainable development". *Organization & Environment*, 26 (1), 102–129.

Tregidga, H., Milne, M. J., and Kearins, K., 2018. Ramping up resistance: corporate sustainable development and academic research. *Business & Society*, 57 (2), 292–334.

van Dijk, A., Mount, R., Gibbons, P., Vardon, M., and Canadell, P., 2014. Environmental reporting and accounting in Australia: progress, prospects and research priorities. *Science of the Total Environment*, 473–474, 338–349.

Williams, B., Wilmshurst, T., and Clift, R., 2011. Sustainability reporting by local government in Australia: current and future prospects. *Accounting Forum*, 35 (3), 176–186.

World Bank, n.d. *The World Bank DataBank*. Available from: https://data.worldbank.org [Accessed 18 December 2019].

25
TOWARDS AN ACCOUNTING OF SOCIO-ENVIRONMENTAL CONFLICTS IN SOUTH AMERICA

Mauricio Gómez-Villegas

Introduction

Although environmental accounting in South America has been reasonably well received from a corporate, professional and academic perspective, its achievements continue to be tied to the modern project, which, to some extent, is colonial in nature and strongly informed by an economic rationality (Santos 2014; Escobar 2014). The reproduction of a financial logic, using "best" corporate practices for measuring and reporting, and the adoption of global guidelines and standards are found in the region. Likewise, the South American academic community has replicated mainstream theories, instruments, and methodologies for research, from its focus on *business case* reasoning and, to a lesser extent, *stakeholder-accountability* approaches (Brown and Fraser 2006; de Lima Voss et al. 2017). A type of normative research prevails among experts and most empirical work focuses on reports, disregarding their correspondence with actions, results and organizational sustainability.

In contrast to some other regions better covered by environmental accounting research (EAR), South America is facing deep socio-environmental conflicts (Martínez-Alier 2009; Scheidel et al. 2020) with financial and commercial globalization leading to "extractivism" throughout the subcontinent (Helwege 2015). Extractivism can be understood as an economic model that is based on the exploitation and appropriation of natural resources for exportation (Gudynas 2012; Escobar 2014). Although communities, institutions and productive structures in Latin American countries are heterogeneous, the intensive re-primarization of economies is a common element. Macroeconomic data show that mining and hydrocarbon exploitation, monocultures, and extensive livestock breeding are the primary source of products offered by this region to international markets (Oxfam 2016). Such a dynamic threatens tropical biodiversity not only in terms of natural resources but also threatens the ethnic and cultural diversity. In the region, the Western development imperative is in conflict, not only with the "balance of nature" but also with the self-determination and subsistence of indigenous and hybrid cultures resulting from colonization (Gudynas 2012; Escobar 2014). Inequity is one of the endemic problems of the region that has not been overcome through the ideals of "developmentalism", which further encourages the destruction of the environment. This is the basis for the socio-environmental conflicts faced by the region. Therefore, sustainable development is even more paradoxical and contradictory in the Global South than in the Global North (Escobar 2000, 2014; Leff 2004).

However, within this controversial context, interdisciplinary academic studies that seek to understand and show the complexity of social and environmental conflicts and their impact on the various ways of life and social structures in this region are emerging. For this reason, I propose that the future of socio-environmental accounting research (SEAR) in South America, from a critical perspective, will likely focus on exposing and providing accounts of this type of conflict (Martínez and Gómez-Villegas 2015; Quinche-Martín and Cabrera-Narváez 2020). Accounting research on socio-environmental conflicts not only requires commitment to interdisciplinary work (Larrinaga et al. 2019), but also intercultural dialogue and the translation of other kinds of knowledge (Leff 2004; Santos 2014). This will enable a de-colonization from the predominant "environmental accounting for development" approach.

Therefore, the purpose of this chapter is to introduce a critical assessment of the evolution of EAR in South America, suggesting the need for an accounting of socio-environmental conflicts that explains the biodiversity of the region from a decolonial perspective. In this sense, this chapter seeks to establish a connection between decolonial thinking and SEAR. For this purpose, arguments about the decoloniality of development are first presented. Subsequently, a general assessment of SEAR in the region is introduced. Then I argue the need and importance of an accounting approach to socio-environmental conflicts. The last section offers some brief conclusions.

Decolonializing development

Colonialism can be understood as the set of political and military domination structures and processes used to guarantee the exploitation of the colonies' resources and labor. Overcoming these structures and processes is characterized as decolonialization (Castro-Gómez 2005; Grosfoguel 2007). A philosophical, cultural, and political current known as post-colonialism emerged during the 20th century, hand in hand with African and Asian countries becoming independent. Postcolonialism[1] states that certain colonial power–knowledge relations may persist in the subjectivities, institutions, and structures of the former "colonies", even after formal political independence processes (Castro-Gómez 2005).

Despite the importance of post-colonialism in explaining and understanding the persistence of colonial forms following independence processes, this perspective fails to problematize capitalist modernity as a unity that reproduces hierarchies (Castro-Gómez 2005; Santos 2014). Hence, a tradition of thinkers[2] who argue that modernity expanded by reproducing hierarchies, that is, people (through racial and ethnic superiority), ways of life (through dichotomies such as metropolis-colony or center-periphery), and knowledge (through the idea of superiority and universality of Western scientific knowledge and European culture), emerged in Latin America. The establishment of such hierarchies is called the coloniality of power (Grosfoguel 2007). This concept is vital for South America, as it recognizes its socio-historical context and problematizes specific power–knowledge relationships that are distinctive from those contexts in which postcolonial theory emerged. The modernity/coloniality perspective emphasizes the limitations of Eurocentric critical thinking to understand the contradictions and social dynamics that affect emancipation in Latin America (Grosfoguel 2007; Santos 2014). Thus, decoloniality is concerned not only about the visibility and rupture of the discourses and mechanisms that extend economic exploitation, but also about the deconstruction of a struggle against the forms of subalternity that produce new forms of dominance (Castro-Gómez 2005; Grosfoguel 2007).

Mainstream discussion of development requires decolonization. For example, the adjectives and categories "developed", "underdeveloped" or "developing" are examples of hierarchies that subordinate territories, populations, and individuals (Escobar 2014). The very notion of development became a concept that allows reproducing structures of epistemic, axiological, sociological, and psychological domination over others and over nature. Consequently, the category does not refer to a "neutral" description of the evolution of societies or living beings. Rather, it has been operationalized as a "horizon of meaning" that underlies a particular idea of history and a direction of life, both with pretensions of universality and ascending progress (Escobar 2000, 2014). Development assumes that nature and people are resources, that is, means to an end of upward progress and accumulation. This way of thinking does not recognize other cosmogonies and perceptions of reality existing in the Global South (Ángel-Maya 2015). When development becomes contradictory or its promises are not fulfilled, adjectives like "human development", "participatory development" or "sustainable development" appear, limiting our capacity to imagine other nouns (Leff 2004; Santos 2014).

Decolonizing development is essential to identify the possibilities of SEAR in South America. Although such an aim exceeds the objectives of this chapter, I draw attention to its social and academic importance and argue that decolonizing development is important for three reasons. First, because the emergence and evolution of EAR in the region are related to the social, political, and academic relevance that the concept of sustainable development has gained (Araujo 1995; Donaire 1995; Pahlen and Fronti 2004; Mantilla 2006; de Lima Voss et al. 2017; Martínez and Sánchez 2019), which is similar in many parts of the world (Bebbington 2001; Parker 2011; Bebbington and Larrinaga 2014). Second, because an exploration of the academic literature on environmental accounting in South America calls into question the dominant view that primarily values international publication as a measure of the development of a field or an academic community (Bajo Canales et al. 2009; Gómez-Morales 2018). Third, because the self-proclaimed "developed" countries continue to externalize the negative impacts of their form of social and productive organization, which is evidenced in the reprimarization, export extractivism and socio-environmental conflicts that such processes generate in South America (Gudynas 2012; Helwege 2015; Suescun et al. 2015). Likewise, there are few resources in SEAR addressing this situation (Larrinaga et al. 2019).

An overview of socio-environmental accounting research in South America

It is convenient to differentiate the academic processes and dynamics in the accounting field in South America between Spanish-speaking countries and Brazil.[3] The social, political, economic, and demographic conditions, and the education, science, and technology policies implemented in Brazil explain its relative advantage in the region (Schwartzman 1991). These differences in the Brazilian accounting academia have become apparent in a greater number of master's and PhD programmes, scientific journals, and academic associations (Macias 2018), which generate effects on EAR.

In Brazil, the academic discussion on social and environmental accounting dates back to 1970 (Calixto 2005), but formally began in the early 1990s with publications in national accounting journals (Grzebieluckas et al. 2012). There are also highly referenced books on environmental accounting edited in Brazil, for example, Donaire (1995) and Ferreira (2003). Similarly, the sources that promoted the field of socio-environmental accounting in Spanish-speaking countries are books edited since the mid-1990s. In Colombia, the publication by Araujo (1995) was relevant; in Argentina, the works by Fronti and Wainstein (2000), and the compilation by Pahlen and Fronti (2004) are relevant. The Spanish translation of *Accounting for the environment*, entitled

Contabilidad y Auditoría Ambiental (Gray et al. 1999) was also significant for these countries. The growth of EAR began in the late 1990s and early 2000s, as evidenced by the increasing number of articles published in national academic journals in this period (Calixto 2005; Grzebieluckas et al. 2012; de Lima Voss et al. 2017; Rodríguez and Valdés 2018; Martínez and Sánchez 2019).

Although there were earlier local and national initiatives, the first conferences on environmental accounting that sought to bring Latin American researchers together were promoted by the Center for Social and Environmental Accounting Research at St. Andrews University, and were called CSEAR South America.[4] Five conferences were held under this name – all of them in Brazil.[5] The conference began a transformation and regional autonomy process in 2015 by taking the name *Conferência Sulamericana de Contabilidade Ambiental* (CSCS – South American Accounting Conference for Sustainability); the sixth conference was held in 2019 under this name (Universidade Federal de Santa Catarina). A review of the papers presented in the six versions of the conference shows that it has mainly been a national space for Brazilian researchers. As far as is known, the first and only international compendium made to collect contributions in the field of SEAR in the region is *Advances in Environmental Accounting & Management No 6: Social and Environmental Accounting in Brazil* (Freire 2017).

There are several SEAR groups, centers, networks, and initiatives beyond Brazil, with permanent activities and published results. This is the case of Universidad de Buenos Aires (Pahlen and Fronti 2004; Fronti and Wainstein 2000; García-Fronti 2012; Rodríguez 2012; Fronti and García-Fronti 2013), Universidad Nacional de La Plata (Geba et al. 2010); Universidad Nacional de Colombia (Ariza 2000, 2007; Gómez-Villegas 2004, 2009; Gómez et al. 2012; Martínez and Gómez-Villegas 2015; Quinche-Martín and Cabrera-Narváez 2020), and Universidad del Quindío, Colombia (Mejía et al. 2010; Mejía 2014; Mejía and Ceballos 2016).

To get an overview of SEAR in the region, we explored the articles published on indexed journals in two leading regional databases, emphasizing our interest in advancing the decoloniality of academic "development" or "worthwhile" research (Gómez-Morales 2018). The low visibility or participation of Latin American academics in international accounting publications does not mean that research in the region is nonexistent. The databases selected emerge precisely due to "the need to increase the visibility and reach of Latin American scientific literature, underrepresented in the main international indexes" (Bojo-Canales et al. 2009, p. 50). These databases are Scientific Electronic Library Online (SciELO, https://scielo.org) and Red de Revistas Científicas de América Latina y el Caribe, España y Portugal (Redalyc, www.redalyc.org).

The search was limited to articles in Spanish and Portuguese using the terms [(contabilidad AND ambiental/contabilidad AND socioambiental) and (contabilidade AND ambiental/contabilidade AND socioambiental)]. As a result, in the SciELO repository, 50 articles in Spanish and 47 in Portuguese were found. After filtering for repeated documents and exclusively selecting the journals dedicated to Accounting, Management, Business and Finance, Economics, Social Sciences, and Interdisciplinary Journals, 57 articles were obtained in both languages, published between 2001 and 2019, with 68% of these articles being published in the last decade. Most of the articles were published in Brazilian (24) and Colombian (19) journals. The journals with the most papers published are *Revista Contabilidade & Finanças* (Brazil), with 11 papers; *Cuadernos de Contabilidad* (Colombia), 7 papers; and *Revista Facultad de Ciencias Económicas: Investigación y Reflexión* (Colombia), 4 papers. The journals *Contaduría y Administración* (Mexico) and *Revista Científica General José María Córdova* (Colombia) have three papers each. The other journals have published just one paper.

Under equivalent search criteria, a total of 52 papers were published and indexed in Redalyc database between 2005 and 2019. Of these, 29 were written in Portuguese and 23 in Spanish. The distribution of journals within this field by country of origin is as follows: Brazil (30), Colombia (10), Mexico (5), Venezuela (4), Argentina (2), and Peru (1). Most of the articles in this bibliographic database were published in the following journals: *Enfoque Reflexão Contábil* (Brazil), with 8 papers; *Revista Catarinense da Ciência Contábil* (Brazil), 8 papers; and *Revista de Gestão Ambiental e Sustentabilidade* (Brazil), 5 papers. The remaining journals have published one or two contributions. In addition, Redalyc has indexed two journals also included in ScieELO: *Revista Científica General José María Córdova* (Colombia) and *Revista Científica Visión de Futuro* (Cuba).

By searching on the Web of Science (WOS) using the terms [("Environmental Accounting" AND "Latin America" AND "Socio-environmental Accounting")], and limiting this search to publications in economics, business and finance, and interdisciplinary social sciences, a total of 20 articles were found. The review of the abstract shows that only one of them is related to socio-environmental accounting and was published in *Revista de Ciencias Sociales* (Venezuela). The same search on SCOPUS showed four articles; of these, only the work by Zacari and Perera-Aldama (2020), published in *Social and Environmental Accountability Journal* (UK), is related to our field.

These results reinforce the need for a decolonial approach to SEAR in South America. The dominant academic practices demand using the two indexing databases with impact measurement (WOS and Scopus) as the primary source for literature reviews. These practices actively produce invisibility, a kind of epistemicide[6] (Santos 2014), mostly excluding research not published in English (Boussbaa and Brown 2017; Gómez-Morales 2018). This can distort the understanding of the state of academic fields in the Global South. My argument does not imply an underestimation of the necessary interaction of the South American community with the international academia, nor a defense of "parochialism"; on the contrary, I seek to make this "invisibility" apparent, which could be overcome, among other forms, through mutual recognition as contemporaries, promoting intercultural translation and dialogue of knowledge (Leff 2004; Santos 2014). I value the invitation to participate in this handbook because I think that it fits in such a perspective.

As a result of the exploration, previous literature reviews were identified, especially in Brazil and Colombia (Calixto 2005; Cunha and Porte 2011; Grzebieluckas et al. 2012; de Lima Voss et al. 2017; Linares and Suárez-Rico 2017; Rodríguez and Valdés 2018; Martínez and Sánchez 2019), which, together with the data presented, show the dynamism of SEAR in both countries. As in other regions of the world, environmental accounting built upon and continue to evolve alongside social issues (Gómez-Villegas 2009; Parker 2011; Larrinaga et al. 2019). A precedent for social reports in the region was the Social Balance Sheet, which was used – although not widely spread – by some companies since the late 1980s (Araujo 1995; Cunha and Porte 2011).

De Lima Voss et al. (2017) reviewed 352 articles published in Brazil from 1989 to 2016. From the perspective of Laclau and Mouffe, the authors argue that research on the field reflects a weak version of sustainability, with a focus on economic growth and preponderance of framing of the issues in line with how Northern countries view the crisis: the business case approach (Brown and Fraser 2006) prevails in SEAR in Brazil. The representation of environmental variables in financial statements, cost systems, and other reports seeks to represent the effects felt on corporate profits, business risks and the needs of owners and investors. Positivist methodologies prevail in the research, and there is little discussion about theoretical stances, with an economic perspective of the relevance of the information dominating. Nevertheless, some research reflects an institutionalist vision of legitimacy theory (Cunha and Porte 2011; de Lima Voss et al. 2017).

Turning to literature from Colombia, Martínez and Sánchez (2019) reviewed ten accounting journals with the most celebrated academic tradition in Colombia and identified 56 articles published from 1996 to 2015 and classified them according to their alignment with strong and weak visions of sustainable development. Similarly, Rodríguez and Valdéz (2018) studied the evolution of the concept of environmental accounting in the articles published from 1981 to 2017 in nine Colombian journals, characterizing authors, theories, subjects, methodologies, and types of research on 77 papers.

Many of the papers identified by Martínez and Sánchez (2019) and Rodríguez and Valdés (2018) focus on the recognition of environmental expenses, assets, and liabilities, following the conventional logic for corporate financial accounting. There are also papers addressing the cost structures required for environmental cost management systems. Environmental auditing has received less attention from a financial and compliance perspective. Following the effective date of the International Financial Reporting Standards (IFRS) in Colombia, several papers have sought to relate these standards with the recognition of liabilities, contingencies, and other items in financial statements. With the increased dissemination of non-financial reports and sustainability reports,[7] several papers have studied the disclosure of these reports. They also study the relationship between social and integrated reports and value creation (Correa-García et al. 2016; Zacari and Perera-Aldama 2020). All these papers take on the vision of weak sustainability (Bebbington 2001) and are based on studying reports or perceptions without considering their relation with organizational practices. Although most papers adopt a business case perspective, some studies assume a stakeholder-accountability approach (Brown and Fraser 2006), such as Rueda (2002), or others that propose a tri-dimensional accounting theory (Mejía 2014; Mejía and Ceballos 2016). While most functionalist papers point out difficulties in accounting measurement and valuation of environmental dimensions, few concrete interdisciplinary efforts are identified to address such obstacles.

There are also normative and conceptual papers of the relationship between accounting, and the limits of growth, the contradictions of sustainable development, the visibility of hidden costs, links to ecology, ecological debt, ecological justice, and the ontological and epistemological changes needed for sustainability (Sarmiento 2003; Gómez 2004, 2009; Quinche 2008; Ariza 2007; Carbal 2011; Arias 2017; Martínez and Sánchez 2019; de Lima Voss et al. 2017). Some papers are inspired by Latin American philosophers and socio-environmental thinkers with strong political ties to social movements in the region, such as Augusto Ángel-Maya, Enrique Leff, Arturo Escobar, and Eduardo Gudynas, among others. Similarly, empirical research, mostly with qualitative methodologies or fieldwork methods, is emerging (Martínez and Gómez-Villegas 2015; Lemos and Rodríguez 2016; Quinche-Martín and Cabrera-Narváez 2020). This research often adopts a strong sustainability[8] approach. Legitimacy theory and various critical theories (e.g., political ecology) are also being explored through SEAR. Other topics less represented include environmental macro-accounting (Gómez et al. 2012) as well as the accounting aspects of clean development mechanisms (Fronti and García-Fronti 2013).

This outlook shows that SEAR has experienced significant progress, taking up conventional and, to a lesser extent, heterodox perspectives to study the dynamics of socio-environmental accounting in the region. Despite this, considering the dimension and the type of impacts caused by socio-environmental conflicts in South America, the participation of accounting in such conflictive arena is decisive (Georgakopoulos and Thomson 2008).

Toward an accounting of socio-environmental conflicts

There are different approaches to define socio-environmental conflicts (Napadensky and Azocar 2016). Political ecology (Martínez-Alier 2009) argues the existence of an ecological dimension (due to human impact on natural systems) and a distributive dimension (due to the social patterns of access to the benefits of transformation and appropriation of nature). Thus, we can define a socio-environmental conflict as "a confrontation between diverse actors, derived from the existence of varied interests around the appropriation, management, use and sustainability of natural resources" (Martínez and Gómez-Villegas 2015, p. 286). These conflicts are also critically determined by the nature of "development" being pursued.

The "mainstream" conception of development, even with the adjective "sustainable" (Santos 2014; Escobar 2014), promotes a globalized social metabolism that increases the consumption of materials and energy, expanding extractivism and generation of waste in the countries of the Global South. This implies power relations in the conception and use of nature, which not only cause tensions between the North and the South but also within Southern countries' communities, where extractivism is expanding (Oxfam 2016). For instance, during the last decades, even under the Latin-American "progressive" governments of Argentina, Ecuador, and Venezuela, extractivist policies were intensified, causing socio-environmental conflicts in different territories (Gudynas 2012; Escobar 2014; Cáceres 2015). This implies that extractivism is not only associated with conservative governments, but may be enduring the policies promoted by governments that could initially be considered as progressive and, for example, more receptive to the interests of nature and indigenous communities.

Socio-environmental conflicts are more evident in hydrocarbon extraction and mining, the extensive production of agrofuels, the expansion of livestock and agriculture for export, the extraction of new minerals, the creation of hydroelectric energy and alternative energy projects that modify the use and access to the territories, among others (Bebbington et al. 2008; Helwege 2015; Cáceres 2015; Bebbington et al. 2018; Scheider et al. 2020).

Indigenous communities persist in South America whose understanding of the territory and its relationship with nature do not seek Western patterns of development nor the "valorization" for the market (Gudynas 2012; Escobar 2014). Likewise, the socio-cultural hybridization of Latin Americans may require different forms of understanding and action beyond the Eurocentric model of "well-being". The projects of *Buen Vivir* (good living) in the Andean region are proof of this (Escobar 2000; Bebbington et al. 2008; Gudynas 2012).

Although research on the limitations of socio-environmental information of corporations involved in some of these activities is emerging in the region (Suescun et al. 2015; Yokovleva and Vazquez-Brust 2012; Déniz et al. 2019; Quinche-Martín and Cabrera-Narváez 2020), understanding conflicts from a de-coloniality of development perspective must be problematized, alongside examining the role that socio-environmental accounting could play. Therefore, we take up Gray's (2019) call to understand that there are many different ways in which human beings give and receive accounts. Deforestation in the Amazon, the decline of biodiversity, structural inequality, violence against communities, and the systematic murder of environmental and human rights activists, among others, are manifestations of socio-environmental conflicts (Scheidel et al. 2020) that corporate information and SEAR are not making visible. Social movements and the citizenry are immersed in such conflicts; they claim alternative ways to give meaning to their interactions and counterbalance the "naturalization" and hegemony of development as a desirable life horizon for all social formations.

This project of accounting for socio-environmental conflicts implies going beyond interdisciplinarity (overcoming the "blind" spots of Western science) to recognize South

Americans (in all their diversity and within their historical-contextual problems) as contemporaries, with their forms of knowledge that also support the granting rights to nature. Some emerging studies are making visible the importance of the indigenous worldviews that grant rights to nature for the sustainability (Macpherson 2019; Barret et al. 2020). This requires accepting and promoting a dialogue of knowledge recognizing other forms of thinking and living beyond the productive and calculative Western modern subject (Leff 2004; Escobar 2014).

Conclusion

This overview shows that the history of SEAR in South America spans almost 30 years. A review of the literature in this period shows that it has a pronounced national origin and scope, although they draw on sources and arguments from the leading international research perspectives in the field. The developments in Brazil, Colombia, and Argentina are the most significant. Some of the characteristics of regional research on socio-environmental accounting, the leading journals, and their approaches were identified in this chapter. The emergence and evolution of research have been strongly related to the concept of sustainable development with a functionalist and managerialist view of socio-environmental accounting prevailing (mostly with a business case vision) aligned with a *weak sustainability* perspective. However, some research with a critical emphasis close to *strong sustainability approach* is also emerging.

Of the many future possibilities for this field of research in the region, we have highlighted the need for a decolonial approach to development, promoting the accounting research of socio-environmental conflicts. Despite the institutionalization of the SDGs in the Global North, South America is facing the exacerbation of extractivism with a significant impact on its natural and social systems. Incorporating this perspective within environmental accounting is crucial because it can change the approach to environmental and social issues by reimagining the interaction of both dimensions, that is, its concern is to build another meaning for the hyphen in 'socio-environmental', creating other forms of visibility as to where accounting must act.

Notes

1 Some influential authors of the postcolonial theory are Edward Said, Gayatri Spivak, and Frantz Fanon.

2 The most representative authors are Aníbal Quijano, Enrique Dussel, Edgardo Lander, Walter Mignolo, Ramón Grosfoguel, Arturo Escobar, and Santiago Castro-Gómez. They are known as the Modernity/Coloniality collective (Castro-Gómez 2005). Some of these authors are known for their contribution and participation in the social and ecologist movements in the region.

3 Of course, there are also significant differences between Spanish-speaking countries; however, in this chapter I make this distinction due to the significant difference in Brazil's situation compared with the other South American countries.

4 www.csearsouthamerica.net/events/index.php/csca/index/schedConfs/archive

5 2009 (Universidade Federal do Rio de Janeiro), 2011 (Universidade São Paulo), 2013 (Universidade Federal do Pará), 2015 (Universidade Federal da Bahia), and 2017 (Universidade de Brasília).

6 From the sociology of absences, an epistemicide (epistemological homicide) is the invalidation, the annulment of experiences and knowledge (realities), promoted by modifications in language, categories, archetypes, and conceptual frameworks, as well as by the transformation of known subjectivities (Santos 2014).

7 Under the principles, guides, and standards of the Global Reporting Initiative (GRI).

8 In Spanish, the same English word "Sustainability" can have two semantic distinctions: "Sostenibilidad" and "Sustentabilidad." Latin American thinkers have shown how each of these concepts is based on different socioecological rationales (Leff 2004). "Sustentabilidad" is closely related to strong sustainability.

References

Ángel-Maya, A., 2015. *La fragilidad Ambiental de la cultura. Historia y medio ambiente.* Segunda Edición. Universidad Nacional de Colombia. www.augustoangelmaya.org/images/obra/fragilidad_ambiental_de_la_cultura.pdf.

Araujo, J., 1995. *La contabilidad social. La contabilidad del recurso humano, el balance social y la contabilidad ambiental.* Medellín. Centro Colombiano de Investigaciones Contables. Editorial Implicar.

Arias, J. D., 2017. Ecología Política: Desafíos de la Contabilidad frente a la Justicia Ambiental. *En-Contexto Revista de Investigación en Administración, Contabilidad, Economía y Sociedad,* 5(6), 303–326.

Ariza, E. D., 2000. Una perspectiva para captar la inserción contable en la problemática medio ambiental. *Revista Internacional Legis de Contabilidad y Auditoria,* (4), 161–191.

Ariza, E. D., 2007. Luces y sombras en el poder constitutivo de la contabilidad ambiental. *Revista Facultad de Ciencias Económicas: Investigación y Reflexión,* XV (2), 45–60. www.redalyc.org/pdf/909/90915204.pdf

Barrett, M., Watene, K., and McNicholas, P., 2020. Legal personality in Aotearoa New Zealand: an example of integrated thinking on sustainable development. *Accounting, Auditing & Accountability Journal,* ahead-of-print. https://doi.org/10.1108/AAAJ–01–2019–3819

Bebbington, A., Fash, B., and Rogan, J., 2018. Socio-environmental conflict, political settlements, and mining governance: a cross-border comparison, El Salvador and Honduras. *Latin American Perspectives,* 4, 84–106. https://doi.org/10.1177/0094582X18813567

Bebbington, A., Humphreys Bebbington, D., Bury, J., Lingan, J., Muñoz, J. P., and Scurrah, M., 2008. Mining and social movements: struggles over livelihood and rural territorial development in the Andes. *World Development,* 36 (12), 2888–2905. https://doi.org/10.1016/j.worlddev.2007.11.016

Bebbington, J., 2001. Sustainable development: a review of the international development, business and accounting literature. *Accounting Forum,* 25(2), 128–157.

Bebbington, J., and Larrinaga, C., 2014. Accounting and sustainable development: an exploration. *Accounting, Organizations and Society,* 39, 395–413.

Bojo-Canales, C., Fraga-Medín, C., Hernández-Villegas, S., and Primo-Peña, E., 2009. SciELO: un proyecto cooperativo para la difusión de la ciencia. *Revista Española de Sanidad Penitenciaria,* 11(2), 49–56.

Boussebaa, M., and Brown, A., 2017. Englishization, identity regulation and imperialism. *Organization Studies,* 38(19), 7–29.

Brown, J., and Fraser, M., 2006. Approaches and perspectives in social and environmental accounting: An overview of the conceptual landscape. *Business Strategy and the Environment,* 15(2), 103–117.

Cáceres, D., 2015. Accumulation by dispossession and socio-environmental conflicts caused by the expansion of agribusiness in Argentina. *Journal of Agrarian Change,* 15(1), 116–147.

Calixto, L., 2005. Análise da pesquisa sobre contabilidade ambiental no Brasil. *Revista Brasileira de Contabilidade,* 154, 22–35.

Carbal, A., 2011. Una redefinición de la contabilidad socioambiental a partir del paradigma de la complejidad: consideraciones teóricas básicas. *Lúmina,* 12, 280–299.

Castro-Gómez, S., 2005. *La poscolonialidad explicada a los niños.* Popayá. Editorial Universidad del Cauca e Instituto Pensar - Pontificia Universidad Javeriana.

Correa-García, J., Hernández-Espinal, M., Vásquez-Arango, L., and Soto-Restrepo, Y., 2016. Reportes integrados y generación de valor en empresas colombianas incluidas en el Índice de Sostenibilidad Dow Jones. *Cuadernos de Contabilidad,* 17(43), 73–108. https://dx.doi.org/10.11144/Javeriana.cc17–43.rig

Cunha, D., and Porte, M., 2011. Pesquisa científica em contabilidade ambiental: análise dos trabalhos publicados em periódicos nacionais de 2005 a 2010. *II CSEAR Conference South America. A sustentabilidade em discussao.* Ribeirao

de Lima Voss, B., Carter, D.B., and Salotti, B. M., 2017. Hegemonies, politics, and the Brazilian Academy in Social and Environmental Accounting: a post-structural note. *Advances in Environmental Accounting & Management: Social and Environmental Accounting in Brazil* (Advances in Environmental Accounting & Management, Vol. 6), Bingley: Emerald Publishing Limited, pp. 3–68. https://doi.org/10.1108/S1479–359820160000006001

Déniz, J. J., Verona, M. C., and de la Rosa, M. E., 2019. Materialidad de los impactos sociales en la memoria de sostenibilidad. El caso del sector eólico y los pueblos indígenas en Oaxaca, México. *Revista Española de Financiación y Contabilidad,* 48 (4), 492–524. https://doi.org/10.1080/02102412.2018.1511157

Donaire, D., 1995. *Gestão Ambiental na Empresa.* São Paulo. Editorial Atlas.

Escobar, A., 2000. El Lugar de la Naturaleza y la Naturaleza del Lugar: ¿Globalización o Postdesarrollo? (pp. 113–143). En E. Lander (Comp.), *La Colonialidad del Saber: Eurocentrismo y Saberes Coloniales. Perspectivas Latinoamericanas.* Buenos Aires, Argentina: Consejo Latinoamericano de Ciencias Sociales (CLACSO).

Escobar, A., 2014. *La invención del desarrollo.* Popayán. Cuarta edición. Editorial Universidad del Cauca.

Ferreira, A.C. de S., 2003. *Contabilidade ambiental: uma informação para o desenvolvimento sustentável.* Sao Paulo. Atlas.

Freire, F.d.S., 2017. Guest Editorial: Introduction to the Special Issue. *Advances in Environmental Accounting & Management: Social and Environmental Accounting in Brazil* (Advances in Environmental Accounting & Management, Vol. 6, Emerald Publishing Limited, pp. 9–11. https://doi.org/10.1108/S1479-359820160000006004

Fronti, L., and García-Fronti, I., 2013. Viabilidad y cuestiones contables de los proyectos de mecanismo de desarrollo limpio en Argentina. *Visión de futuro*, 10(17), 30–48.

Fronti, L., and Wainstein, M., 2000. *Contabilidad y Auditoría Ambiental.* Buenos Aires. Ediciones Macchi.

García-Fronti, I., 2012. Problemas de contabilidad social y ambiental: algunas reflexiones sobre la necesidad de un abordaje interdisciplinario. *Contaduría de la Universidad de Antioquia,* 60, 209–218.

Geba, N., Fernández, L., and Bifaretti, M., 2010. Marco conceptual para la especialidad contable socio-ambiental. *Actualidad Contable Faces*, 13(20), 49–60.

Georgakopoulos, G., and Thomson, I., 2008. Social reporting, engagements, controversies and conflict in an arena context. *Accounting, Auditing & Accountability Journal*, 21(8), 1116–1143. https://doi.org/10.1108/09513570810918788

Gómez-Morales, Y., 2018. Abuso de las medidas y medidas abusivas. Crítica al pensamiento bibliométrico hegemónico. *Anuario Colombiano de Historia Social y de la Cultura*, 45, 1, pp. 269–290.

Gómez-Villegas, M., 2004. Avances de la contabilidad medio ambiental empresarial: evaluación y posturas críticas. *Revista Internacional Legis de Contabilidad y Auditoria*, 18, 87–120.

Gómez-Villegas, M., 2009. Tensiones, posibilidades y riesgos de la contabilidad medioambiental empresarial. (Una síntesis de su evolución). *Revista de Contaduría Universidad de Antioquia*, 54, 55–78.

Gómez, J., Niño, C., and Rojas, J. C., 2012. La información de las cuentas satélite de ambiente emitida en Colombia (1995-2010): una revisión crítica. *Revista Facultad de Ciencias Económicas: Investigación y Reflexión*, XX(1), 143–169.

Gray, R., 2019. Towards an ecological accounting: tensions and possibilities in social and environmental accounting. Chapter 4. In: Birkin, F. and Polesie, T. (Eds.), *Intrinsic Capability. Implementing intrinsic Sustainable Development for an Ecological Civilisation.* London. World Scientific Press.

Gray, R., Bebbington, J., and Walters, D., 1999. *Contabilidad y auditoría ambiental.* Bogotá: Ecoe Ediciones.

Grosfoguel, R., 2007. The epistemic decolonial turn. Beyond political-economy paradigms. *Cultural Studies*, 21(2–3), 221–223.

Grzebieluckas, C., Campos, L. M., and Selig, P., 2012. Contabilidade e custos ambientais: um levantamento da produção científica no período de 1996 a 2007. *Production*, 22(2), 322–332. https://doi.org/10.1590/S0103-65132011005000054

Gudynas, E., 2012. Debates sobre el desarrollo y sus alternativas en América Latina: Una breve guía heterodoxa. En: Lang, M., & Moktanu, D. (Eds.), *Más allá del Desarrollo. Grupo permanente de trabajo sobre alternativas al desarrollo.* Fundación Rosa Luxemburg/Abya Yala – Universidad Politécnica Salesiana.

Helwege, A., 2015. Challenges with resolving mining conflicts in Latin America. *The Extractive Industries and Society*, 2(1), 73–84.

Larrinaga, C., Moneva, J. M., and Ortas, E., 2019. Veinticinco años de Contabilidad Social y Medioambiental en España: pasado, presente y futuro. *Revista Española de Financiación y Contabilidad*, 48(4), 387–405. https://doi.org/10.1080/02102412.2019.1632020

Leff, E., 2004. Racionalidad ambiental y diálogo de saberes: significancia y sentido en la construcción de un futuro sustentable. *Polis*, 7, http://journals.openedition.org/polis/6232

Lemos, J. E., Rodríguez, J. A., 2016. Propuesta de diseño de costos ambientales para el proceso productivo del ácido cítrico de la empresa Ramo de alimentos de la ciudad de Palmira (valle). *Contexto,* 5, 183–196.

Linares, M. C., and Suárez-Rico, Y. M., 2017. Los costos ambientales: un análisis de la producción científica en el periodo 1977–2016 y una revisión de herramientas y teorías subyacentes. *Criterio Libre*, 15(27), 89–114.

Macías, H., 2018. Introducción a la investigación contable en Brasil. *Revista Activos*, 16(30), 155–186.

Macpherson, E., 2019. Rivers as Subjects and Indigenous Water Rights in Colombia. In: *Indigenous Water Rights in Law and Regulation: Lessons from Comparative Experience* (Cambridge Studies in Law and Society, pp. 131–160). Cambridge: Cambridge University Press. doi:10.1017/9781108611091.006

Mantilla, E., 2006. La contabilidad ambiental en el desarrollo sostenible. *Revista Legis de Contabilidad y Auditoría,* 25, 133–160.
Martínez-Alier, J., 2009. El ecologismo de los pobres: conflictos ambientales y lenguajes de valoración. Barcelona: Icaria.
Martínez-Pulido, V. A., and Gómez-Villegas, M., 2015. La contabilidad y los conflictos ambientales en el sistema financiero: estudio de caso en el sector bancario argentino. *Cuadernos de Contabilidad,* 16(41). https://doi.org/10.11144/Javeriana.cc16-41.ccas
Martínez, M. R., and Sánchez, A., 2019. Una mirada a la contabilidad ambiental en Colombia desde las perspectivas del desarrollo sostenible. *Revista Facultad De Ciencias Económicas,* 27(1), 87–106. https://doi.org/10.18359/rfce.3196
Mejía, E., 2014. Biocontabilidad: haciia una definición de una nueva disciplina contable. *Lúmina,* 15, 116–129.
Mejía, E., and Ceballos, O., 2016. Medición contable de la sustentabilidad organizacional desde la Teoría Tridimensional de la Contabilidad. *Rev. Cient. Gen. José María Córdova,* 14(18), 215–243.
Mejía, E., Montilla, O., and Montes., C., 2010. Análisis de los métodos de medición de las cuentas ambientales en el modelo contable financiero y concepciones alternativas. *Entramado,* 6(2), 106–128.
Napadensky, A., and Azocar, R., 2016. Espacios globales y espacios locales: en busca de nuevos enfoques a los conflictos ambientales. Panorámica sobre Sudamérica y Chile, 2010–2015. *Revista de Estudios Sociales,* 61, 28–43. https://dx.doi.org/10.7440/res61.2017.03
Oxfam, 2016. *Unearthed: land, power and inequality in Latin America.* Oxfam International. www-cdn.oxfam.org/s3fs-public/file_attachments/bp-land-power-inequality-latin-america-301116-en.pdf
Pahlen, R., and Fronti, L., 2004. *Contabilidad social y ambiental.* Buenos Aires. Ediciones Macchi.
Parker, L., 2011. Twenty-one years of social and environmental accountability research: a coming of age. *Accounting Forum,* 35, 1–10.
Quinche-Martín, F., and Cabrera-Narváez, A., 2020. Exploring the potential links between social and environmental accounting and political ecology. *Social and Environmental Accountability Journal,* 40(1), 53–74. https://doi.org/10.1080/0969160X.2020.1730214
Quinche, F., 2008. Una evaluación crítica de la contabilidad ambiental empresarial. *Revista Facultad de Ciencias Económicas: Investigación y Reflexión,* 16(1), 197–216.
Rodríguez, M. C., 2012. Contabilidad y responsabilidad social: un camino por recorrer. *Contabilidad y Auditoría,* 18, 63–74.
Rodríguez, D., and Valdés, P., 2018. Balance de las publicaciones que abordan el concepto de contabilidad ambiental en revistas contables colombianas. *Revista Visión Contable,* (17), 26–79. https://doi.org/10.24142/rvc.n17a2
Rueda, G., 2002. Desarrollo alternativo y contabilidad: una aproximación. *Revista Internacional Legis de Contabilidad y Auditoria,* 9(1), 11–128.
Santos B. de Sousa, 2014. *Epistemologies of the South: Justice against Epistemicide.* Boulder, CO: Paradigm Publishers.
Sarmiento, H., 2003. Hacia una línea de investigación en contabilidad y medio ambiente. *Lúmina,* 4, 93–99.
Scheidel, A., del Bene, D., Liu, J., Navas, G., Mingorría, S., Demaria, F., Avila, S., Roy B., Ertör, I., Temper, L., and Martínez-Alier, J., 2020. Environmental conflicts and defenders: a global overview. *Global Environmental Change,* 63, 102104. https://doi.org/10.1016/j.gloenvcha.2020.102104
Schwartzman, S., 1991. *A Space for Science. The development of the Scientific Community in Brazil.* University Park: The Pennsylvania State University Press.
Suescun, M.C., Lindsay, N., du Monceau, M., 2015. Corporate social responsibility and extractives industries in Latin America and the Caribbean: Perspectives from the ground. *The Extractive Industries and Society,* 2(1), 93–103.
Yakovleva, N., and Vazquez-Brust, D., 2012. Stakeholder perspectives on CSR of mining MNCs in Argentina. *Journal of Business Ethics,* 106(2), 191–211.
Zacari, A., and Perera-Aldama, L., 2020. Building from scratch: an auto-ethnographic approach for the development of a social reporting model. *Social and Environmental Accountability Journal.* https://doi.org/10.1080/0969160X.2020.1765825

PART 5

Thematic topics in environmental accounting

26
CARBON

Robert Charnock, Matthew Brander and Thomas Schneider

Introduction

Momentum is building in the global effort to tackle climate change and it continues to rise on the agendas of business, finance, civil society, and government with accounting being implicated in this process. A pressing need thus emerges for accounting research that builds on scholarly insights to address the looming challenges of climate action. This chapter provides an overview of research related to carbon accounting, including natural science, technical, and social science research. In each area we describe prominent themes within these research domains and illustrate work undertaken. We also describe the research methods that tend to be used and the theoretical framings employed, and outline possible avenues for future research.

We begin by discussing how definitions of carbon accounting do not remain fixed in this rapidly evolving space. This chapter then reviews the scholarship "doing" carbon accounting and engaging in technical debate. It proceeds to also review scholarship "about" carbon accounting, which centres on its relationship with climate action, regulatory, and governance issues as well as the direction in which carbon accounting is evolving. We then set out promising avenues for research and theoretical development before concluding that climate change remains a pressing and crucial site that is primed for insights from accounting academics.

Ever-shifting definitions

Stechemesser and Guenther (2012) propose the following definition of carbon accounting:

> Carbon accounting comprises the recognition, the non-monetary and monetary evaluation and the monitoring of greenhouse gas emissions on all levels of the value chain and the recognition, evaluation and monitoring of the effects of these emissions on the carbon cycle of ecosystems.
>
> *(Stechemesser and Guenther 2012, p. 35)*

However, any attempt at a comprehensive definition may be doomed to failure as the diversity of practices that can be considered as "carbon accounting" is just too great and continues to grow. For instance, the definition above does not include estimating *changes* in emissions caused by actions or decisions, which is a major field of carbon accounting practice. It also only mentions *emissions*, and not *removals* (i.e. the removal of greenhouse gases (GHGs) from the atmosphere). Ascui and Lovell (2011) offer a more open-ended approach by enumerating practices that can be subsumed under the title "carbon accounting". This approach illustrates the way carbon accounting operates at different levels, from global and national inventories down to corporate or product-level assessments, and for different purposes, such as compliance, research, marketing, and risk management. The authors emphasise that their listings are not intended to be comprehensive and that further types of "carbon accounting" can be added.

Given the diversity of practices that can be called "carbon accounting", we also take an open-ended approach to discussing "carbon accounting" research. As a result, if the reader sees something we have included and thinks "but that's not carbon accounting", it means we've reached the fuzzy edges of how the term is used. A final introductory point is that we use "carbon accounting" interchangeably with "greenhouse gas accounting", and arguably the latter is a more accurate term as many GHGs don't actually contain carbon. Nevertheless, "carbon accounting" is a helpful and ubiquitous shorthand.

Technical and natural science research

We distinguish between research that is *about* carbon accounting (i.e. where some form of carbon accounting practice is the research object) and research that is *doing* some form of carbon accounting (i.e. the research employs a carbon accounting method or engages with carbon accounting practices). Although much research discussed in this chapter (and book) is *about* carbon (and environmental) accounting, we also emphasise the importance of the latter variety. This section therefore offers an overview of research *doing* carbon accounting.

One area of research that *does* carbon accounting falls within the natural sciences, particularly geosciences, climate science, and ecology. Research in this area covers issues such as the global carbon cycle. For example, Liu et al. (2010) explore the magnitude of CO_2 removals from the atmosphere by aquatic organisms. Here the researchers are *doing* carbon accounting, rather than studying carbon accounting as a (social) research object.

A major research theme within this field is understanding the Earth's response to increasing levels of GHG emissions, and the related concept of "carbon budgets". Rogelj et al. (2016), who reviewed a number of such estimates and methods, concluded that the remaining budget from 2015, if the temperate increase is to be kept below 2°C, is 590–1,240 $GtCO_2$-equivalent to between 15 and 30 years of emissions at current levels. There is also often a *normative* element to this research (i.e. how to do carbon accounting better). The authors also argue that there *should be* greater consistency in the carbon budget methods used by the different working groups of the Intergovernmental Panel on Climate Change (IPCC). Although this kind of normative element is not always present within the natural science carbon accounting literature, our point is that this type of research is not solely descriptive or calculative.

Another field of research, that is *doing* carbon accounting, can be characterised as the "technical" literature, which employs some form of numerical method to calculate GHG emissions. A prominent example is the *life cycle assessment* (LCA) literature, which calculates GHG emissions (and other forms of environmental impact) across different stages of a product's life cycle. For example, Eide (2002) studies the environmental impacts from industrial milk production, including agricultural emissions, processing, consumption, and the waste management of packaging, and reports figures in the range of 500–600 $kgCO_2e$ per 1,000 L of milk (see also Chapter 17 of this handbook on materials and energy accounting).

These studies often apply a carbon accounting method to derive a numerical answer. However, normative method development remains an important theme within this field, especially in studies that apply carbon accounting methods to demonstrate a broader methodological point. For instance, Thomassen et al. (2008) demonstrate the way different forms of LCA give different results for milk production. In contrast, Ekvall et al. (2005) is an example of a conceptual study, with the authors suggesting that different forms of LCA align with either consequential or deontological ethical perspectives, and are therefore appropriate for different purposes.

A focal topic for method development, *par excellence*, is bioenergy. Searchinger et al.'s (2008) seminal study of US biofuel policy uses an economic model to project that demand for US corn ethanol will increase global agricultural commodity prices, and increase GHG emissions from indirect land use change. This paper sparked considerable debate not only within academia, but also within governments, on the appropriate use of different carbon accounting methods.

A noteworthy feature of the "technical" carbon accounting literature is its focus on LCA. There are many other methods used in practice – such as corporate GHG inventory accounting, project-level accounting, national GHG inventories – but relatively few academic studies use these methods. It appears to be a contingent feature of the research landscape that there is a large and highly active academic community for LCA, with dedicated journals and conferences, but little comparable activity focused on applying and developing other carbon accounting methods.

A final observation on what we have described as the "scientific" or "technical" carbon accounting literature is that it tends not to be "theorised". That is, there is less need to enrich insights through theorisations of the empirical material. This is notably different from the academic research that treats carbon accounting as a social research object, which tends to use theory to make sense of carbon accounting practice and climate governance.

Research "about" carbon accounting

The research *about* carbon accounting largely focusses on *corporate* carbon accounting and disclosure, with less attention directed to national-level governance and accounting (e.g. Harris and Symons 2013; McGlade and Ekins 2015; Charnock and Hoskin 2020), product-level accounting and labelling (e.g. Ormond and Goodman 2015), and personal carbon accounts (e.g. Lövbrand and Stripple 2011). The following is an overview of some of the key themes and approaches within this extensive literature.

Corporate carbon disclosure

In the broadest sense, almost all corporate environmental disclosure literature includes carbon accounting, as carbon features in environmental disclosure and disclosure scores. Hahn et al.'s (2015) review of carbon disclosure studies, from 2005 to 2013, shows a marked increase in the number of publications, comprising a number of sub-themes (e.g. voluntary versus mandatory disclosure, real versus market effects) and research methods (e.g. regression analysis, content analysis, interview-based, field study and survey).

The work on carbon disclosure uses data such as sustainability reports, CDP (formerly the Carbon Disclosure Project) annual survey results, and/or mandatory company reports. Carbon disclosure requirements are becoming increasingly prevalent, via securities regulation and an array of laws that especially target large emitters (Schneider et al. 2018). The sheer volume of work on disclosure is a function of carbon reporting providing a new data source, combined with global warming becoming recognised as a material issue. For voluntary disclosures, the determinants of disclosure are typically studied (Luo et al. 2012). Furthermore, CDP provides a large set of scope 1 and scope 2 emissions[1] data, which can be incorporated into research as "hard" data.

Theorisation is a central feature of disclosure research. This aims to enable and enrich explanations of the social phenomenon being studied, such as the amount and purpose of disclosure. The prevalence of legitimacy theory has arguably made it a theme unto itself (cf. Ascui 2014). It implies that the more a firm pollutes, the more it discloses. Thus, the argument goes, more voluntary disclosure is harmful because disclosure is being used for the obfuscation of actual performance (Patten 2020). Stakeholder theory enjoys similar prominence, focusing on firm-specific responses to actual stakeholder demands (Fernando and Lawrence 2014; Roberts 1992). Although the seminal work in this area plays an important role in the literature, applications of these two theories have, at times, been rather vague and unreflective. We consider these instances of what Guthrie and Parker (2017) call *theoretical engorgement*. This is where researchers are compelled to insert a theoretical framework into research papers, even when this does not aid the sensemaking process or enrich research insights. As a result, we would warn emerging scholars embarking on yet another disclosure-based study to avoid taking legitimacy and stakeholder theory for granted. Rather, one must thoroughly and critically engage with the conceptual underpinnings of carbon disclosure research, focussing on building a theoretical contribution and justifying its value to academia, practice and policy.

Nevertheless, the main debate in carbon disclosure literature is between these two perspectives, as exemplified by Wei and Schaltegger (2017). They found that if a firm reports more under CDP, as reflected in disclosure score changes, there will be a decrease in carbon emission intensity in following years. So even if a firm starts reporting for obfuscation reasons, that reporting triggers real action because it pays more attention to the activity.

The disclosure literature also investigates the assurance of carbon disclosures. Again, sustainability assurance literature does encompass carbon disclosure audit, and the practice is comparably dominated by the big four auditing firms (KPMG 2017). However, carbon audit can be mapped more directly into the scientific or technical aspects of carbon accounting. These particularly relate to "hard" targets set by the firm or regulators. Green, Taylor, and Wu (2017, p. 31) state that "there is a clear and defined set of disclosures of measurable parameters", arguing that this implies more similarities with a financial audit.

There has also been a substantial rise in regulatory guidance on carbon disclosure, both regarding environmental risk and disclosure (e.g. CSA 2019; BIS 2020), and specifically on carbon disclosure (e.g. SEC 2010). With both the regulatory and real effects of climate change becoming manifest, carbon accounting is now a material item for investors and thus falls under the continuous disclosure regulations underlying all major stock exchanges, or is specifically mandated by securities regulations (Bebbington et al. 2020; Schneider et al. 2018). In many ways, this renders the literature on carbon disclosure moot, particularly the work on voluntary disclosure of GHG emissions. Increasingly, carbon accounting practice (including in the CDP questionnaire) and research centres on addressing climate risk (and opportunity). This represents yet another expansion of what carbon accounting is. Indeed, the next section, focused on carbon management, sheds light on the surging interest in climate risk.

Carbon management

Climate risk and carbon management accounting

Climate risk has recently attracted increasing attention within academic research *about* carbon accounting. Since the landmark 2015 Paris Agreement on climate change, governments and practitioners have become increasingly concerned about the physical, market and regulatory risks that climate change could pose to business and finance.

These risks are not entirely new to social and environmental scholarship. By the mid-1990s a range of primarily qualitative studies – drawing on interviews, case studies and documentary analyses – were already highlighting the litigation risks of environmental disasters (Coulson and Dixon 1995) and how climate change could be factored into risk management practice. However, there is renewed interest in this space, across academia, industry and policymaking. Where physical risks arise through the impacts of climate change, the market and regulatory risks are now seen as stemming from the prospect of a "carbon-constrained future" (Bebbington and Larrinaga-González 2008) and a global transition away from fossil fuels.

Bebbington et al. (2020) provided a recent example by exposing the (in)adequacy of current reporting practices within the fossil fuel sector. The study is based on the concepts of *unburnable carbon* and *stranded assets* that question whether existing fossil fuel resources can be burned if climate change goals are to be met. The authors used a multi-methods approach, combining a survey of accounting disclosure rules for fossil fuel resources, accounting disclosures made by fossil fuel firms, and stock market participants' views on stranded asset risk.

The paper also exemplifies the value of theorisation in this rapidly evolving space, employing Miller and Power's (2013) framework on the four roles of accounting to develop insights into how these ideas could become part of corporate reporting. In this manner, the paper provides a foundation for valuable theoretical development, which may be especially insightful for making sense of shifting climate risk perceptions and regulatory agendas, as well as proposing climate-related applications for existing accounting techniques.

A different perspective, however, is the managerialist approach. This sets aside questions of disclosure and centres instead on changes in management practices (Kumarasiri and Jubb 2016) ranging from mixed-methods case studies that help highlight the more carbon-intensive aspects of production (Cadez and Guilding 2017) to benchmarking approaches that identify supply chain hot spots (Acquaye et al. 2014). These management-oriented studies also offer insight into both the interplay between national policies, corporate strategies and carbon management accounting (Bui and Fowler 2019) and the emergence and development of new practice. This is exemplified by Gibassier and Schaltegger's (2015) 12-month participant observation, which explores the parallel emergence of multiple carbon management accounting practices. The common theme, however, is the ongoing evolution of management accounting as it is called on to operationalise carbon control.

Emissions trading schemes and the accounting treatment of emission rights

Emissions trading schemes (ETSs), a mainstay of climate change mitigation, first came to prominence during the United States' Acid Rain Programme (Burtraw et al. 2005). Braun shows how this earlier experience was pivotal to the European Union's interest in the mechanism, following its failed attempt to implement a carbon tax (Braun 2009). These schemes have attracted considerable interest among accounting scholars interested in the sociology of markets, with scholars investigating ETSs through lenses of (in)commensurability (MacKenzie 2009; Lovell et al. 2013) and experimentation (Callon 2009).

Such studies are also exemplars of how theorisation within carbon accounting can problematise prevailing economic theories and unearth the rationales and ideologies that underpin climate governance. As Unerman and Chapman state:

> [G]reater theoretical sophistication can play a vital role in the provision of robust evidence and understandings upon which existing practices can be evaluated and critiqued, and new and sounder practices developed.
>
> *(2014, p. 386)*

For example, the question of how to account for emission rights has remained a heated subject since Bebbington and Larrinaga-González (2008) rekindled a debate on accounting problems associated with earlier sulphur dioxide trading schemes. This has prompted considerable effort to problematise ETS-related accounting treatments, from demonstrating how different treatments advance either a market imperative or a regulation and compliance notion (Mete et al. 2010), to arguing that emission rights are a financialisation of the atmosphere and that market-based solutions are inappropriate for a problem caused by markets (McNicholas and Windsor 2011).

With the proliferation of carbon markets around the world, these debates and accounting treatments are far from settled. Indeed the Chinese experience in transitioning from regional schemes to a national scheme appears especially noteworthy (Jotzo et al. 2018). Moreover, theoretical insights into the financialisation of climate change and their problematisation of market-based approaches have become an especially pressing topic since the Paris Agreement was forged and opened up new possibilities for climate governance.

Emergent directions for research projects

As discussed above, carbon accounting encompasses a diverse range and ever-evolving set of practices. Researchers therefore need to constantly look for emergent practices that either require testing and development (via natural scientific or technical research), or need explaining, problematising, and critiquing (via social and political science research). The following sections set out currently emergent areas that we identified, at the time of writing, as important and pressing areas for research.

International climate governance

When the Paris Agreement was reached in December 2015 it marked a fundamental shift in climate governance towards a decentralised "pledge and review" system (Charnock and Hoskin 2020; Falkner 2016). This raises significant and pressing questions, such as how nations are held accountable for their pledges, how to ensure financial flows are consistent with the Paris goals, and whether carbon accounting methods for national GHG inventories are fit for purpose.

These debates – and related work on the transparency of international flows of climate finance, technology and information (Weikmans and Roberts 2019) – have largely emerged outside of the accounting discipline. Yet there is much potential for accounting insights to inform these debates, especially by drawing on our rich vein of scholarship on accountability (Archel et al. 2011; Roberts 1991) and transparency (Gray 1992; Radcliffe et al. 2017). Indeed, there is also a growing need for the social sciences to engage with bodies such as the IPCC, whose highly influential synthesis reports are now looking beyond the natural sciences (Charnock and Thomson 2019). Now more than ever these bodies require insight into the suitability and effectiveness of different policy approaches to specific aspects of the climate agenda and region-specific impacts and risks.

Science-based target setting

An interesting area for further research, below the level of national governments, is the response of "non-state actors" – for example, regional governments, non-governmental organisations (NGOs), corporations, and public bodies – to the imperative for climate change mitigation (Bebbington and Harrison 2017). An increasingly prevalent framing is the concept and practice of "science-based target" setting (CDP et al. 2015), which involves setting sector- or company-level reduction targets that are consistent with the global goals of the Paris Agreement. Such initiatives deserve scrutiny from both the technical and social science research communities. For the former, there are crucial questions such as "are the proposed target-setting methods genuinely aligned with below 2°C pathways?" and for the latter there are questions such as 'how do voluntary initiatives, such as science-based targets, shape organisational activity and influence regulatory agendas?".

Negative emissions technologies

Negative emissions technologies (NETs) are technologies that remove GHGs from the atmosphere, such as bioenergy with carbon capture and storage (BECCS), afforestation, and direct air capture and storage. Such technologies will be required to achieve targets such as the UK government's pledge to achieve net zero emissions by 2050 (UK Parliament 2008), and also for dealing with an emissions "overshoot" if warming exceeds 2°C (Smith et al. 2015). These technologies pose distinct accounting challenges, such as how to support NETs within existing incentive mechanisms, and how to allocate responsibility for historic contributions to cumulative emissions. We see the limited academic engagement in these matters as highly problematic and the topics as a key priority requiring urgent attention.

The avenues outlined above are only three of the emergent issues that warrant and would benefit from scholarly insight. There are, of course, many other valuable lines of inquiry. To name a few: shadow pricing and internal carbon pricing, carbon taxes, production and consumption-based accounting, financial accounting for carbon-based assets and liabilities, project-level accounting, marginal abatement costs, and the standardisation of carbon accounting practices. However, we must now turn to potential directions for theoretical development that may help our sensemaking on thematic challenges cutting across the carbon accounting agenda.

Emergent directions for theoretical development

As noted earlier in this chapter, the explicit use or development of theory does not appear to be a prominent or necessary feature of the academic research that *does* carbon accounting. However, within the literature *about* carbon accounting, and *about* sustainable development accounting more generally, there are calls for greater theoretical development (Unerman and Chapman 2014). We reiterate these calls by identifying thematic challenges where theoretical development may advance our efforts to make sense of, problematise, and inform action.

Larrinaga (2014) identifies a recurrent theme in the literature *about* carbon accounting: these are emergent and deeply contested practices. Following the spirit of early studies of accounting change (Hopwood 1983), we suggest that this theme is central to our contextual understanding of carbon accounting as a rapidly evolving and ever-expanding field. Here, Moore and McPhail (2016) offer an insightful approach to analysing levels of change. They demonstrate how strong structuration theory can be applied to grapple with the interplay between macro-, meso-, and micro-levels of change. Furthermore, their theoretical analysis offers much-needed nuance to the homogeneity of institutional analyses, allowing them to begin unveiling the complex and reflexive interplay between multiple structuration processes and active agency. So, their study provides one approach for scholars interested in exploring dynamics across levels and sectors, through which carbon accounting practices may (or may not) coalesce over time.

Similarly, longitudinal studies of how carbon accounting emerges and evolves is especially suited to theoretical development. For example, Le Breton and Aggeri's (2019) work on *Bilan Carbon* – a French GHG accounting tool – draws on the Foucauldian concept of a strategic *dispositif* to analyse how the tool was created and disseminated. This focuses their analysis both on tracing the emergence of a network and on the intentionality in how elements were brought together when faced with responding to an emergency such as climate change.

However, there is still considerable scope and further need for theoretical development in this domain. Considering the overhaul seen in climate governance with the transition from the Kyoto Protocol to the Paris Agreement (Falkner 2016), certain thematic challenges have come to the fore. The shift towards a decentred version of climate governance further emphasises the importance of investigating interactions between a diverse range of state, private, and civil society actors. This will be pivotal for creating a dynamic through which the ambition of national pledges can be increased to a point aligned with limiting warming to well below 2°C. Here, decentred regulation scholars (Black 2008) can offer valuable conceptual insight into new forms of polycentric governance. This also adds to the challenge of coordinating efforts across multiple actors, an issue that has been the subject of much theoretical insight through notions of boundary objects (Bowker et al. 2016), mediating instruments (Miller and O'Leary 2007), and meta-governance (Charnock and Hoskin 2020).

Additional challenges are becoming immanent at the organisational level, adding to interest in dynamics between accounting and organisational action on climate change. Fortunately, decades of scholarly insights provide a remarkable foundation. For example, integrating carbon metrics into remuneration could draw valuable conceptual insights from performance management scholarship (Chenhall, Hall, and Smith 2013). Similarly, we should develop conceptual insights on how to operationalise the low-carbon transition through CAPEX decisions – mitigating locked-in emissions and the stranding of assets – from a wealth of extant studies (Larrinaga-Gonzalez and Bebbington 2001; Cushen 2013).

Conclusion

This chapter has reviewed key themes running through carbon accounting scholarship and has also introduced the reader to emergent themes that warrant further academic scrutiny. We have described a number of different types of research related to carbon accounting (i.e. natural science, "technical", and social science research), and have emphasised that these areas are interconnected. For example, the natural science research on carbon budgets is used in more economics-focused research on stranded assets (McGlade and Ekins 2015) that is relevant to corporate-level analysis (see Bebbington et al. 2020). Alternatively, social science research may treat natural science or "technical" research as research objects, asking questions about the underlying assumptions and social processes that shape carbon accounting practice (Ascui and Lovell 2012). Of course, given the breadth and shifting nature of carbon accounting research, there are a range of relevant issues that warrant further research but to which this chapter was not able to dedicate sufficient time.[2]

Yet this chapter has also highlighted the extent to which theorisation on carbon issues has and can continue to offer insights. Reiterating Guthrie and Parker's (2017) arguments, carbon accounting scholarship may have, at times, engaged in *theory engorgement*, the inclusion of theoretical frameworks without due consideration of their applicability and the value this brings to the study. Similarly, we have emphasised that theorisation is not relevant to all types of research, and may even be an unhelpful distraction within applied studies. We do hope, however, to have illuminated the potential for theorisation within studies *about* carbon accounting, especially in problematising the utopian neoliberal impulses of financialisation and economisation and, in doing so, in opening up spaces for rethinking the vectors of possibility along which carbon accounting continues to evolve (Unerman and Chapman 2014).

To close, across the growing bodies of scholarship we described, there remains a pressing need for further academic insights on the linkages between carbon and accounting. Given the pressing nature of climate change, academic focus on the effectiveness of policies and practices in catalysing and directing climate action is essential. What is more is that civil society, businesses, financial organisations, and government agencies are grasping their increasingly important role in climate governance, which will continue to drive and reshape carbon accounting practices for decades to come. Considered as a whole, the linkages between climate change and accounting are set to remain a crucial site for scholarly attention, with the potential for highly impactful research projects and profound theoretical developments on the shifting landscape of what we call carbon accounting.

Notes

1 Scope 1 emissions are those from sources owned or controlled by the firm; scope 2 are emissions from purchased electricity, heating and cooling; and scope 3 are upstream and downstream indirect emissions. There is little evidence of a critical mass of scope 3 emissions being disclosed (Bebbington et al. 2020).

2 For instance, there appears to be considerable value in furthering our knowledge and understanding of standardisation, scenario planning and stress testing, development finance, climate change adaptation, operationalising and aligning action with the Paris Agreement, as well as project-level and policy-level carbon accounting.

References

Acquaye, A., Genovese, A., Barrett, J., Koh, S.C.L., 2014. Benchmarking carbon emissions performance in supply chains. *Supply Chain Management: An International Journal* 19, 306–321.

Archel, P., Husillos, J., Spence, C., 2011. The institutionalisation of unaccountability: Loading the dice of corporate social responsibility discourse. *Accounting, Organizations and Society* 36, 327–343.

Ascui, F., 2014. A review of carbon accounting in the social and environmental accounting literature: What can it contribute to the debate? *Social and Environmental Accountability Journal* 34, 6–28.

Ascui, F., Lovell, H., 2011. As frames collide: Making sense of carbon accounting. *Accounting, Auditing and Accountability Journal* 24, 978–999.

Ascui, F., Lovell, H., 2012. Carbon accounting and the construction of competence. *Journal of Cleaner Production* 36, 48–59.

Bebbington, J., Harrison, J., 2017. Global climate change responsiveness in the USA: An estimation of population coverage and implications for environmental accountants. *Social and Environmental Accountability Journal* 37, 137–143.

Bebbington, J., Larrinaga-González, C., 2008. Carbon trading: Accounting and reporting issues. *European Accounting Review* 17, 697–717.

Bebbington, J., Schneider, T., Stevenson, L., Fox, A., 2020. Fossil fuel reserves and resources reporting and unburnable carbon: Investigating conflicting accounts. *Critical Perspectives on Accounting* 66, 102083.

BIS, 2020. *The Green Swan: Central Banking and Financial Stability in the Age of Climate Change*. Bank of International Settlements. Basel, Switzerland.

Black, J., 2008. Constructing and contesting legitimacy and accountability in polycentric regulatory regimes. *Regulation and Governance* 2, 137–164.

Bowker, G.C., Timmermans, S., Clarke, A.E., Balka, E., 2016. *Boundary Objects and Beyond: Working with Leigh Star*. MIT Press, Cambridge, MA.

Braun, M., 2009. The evolution of emissions trading in the European Union – The role of policy networks, knowledge and policy entrepreneurs. *Accounting, Organizations and Society* 34, 469–487.

Bui, B., Fowler, C.J., 2019. Strategic responses to changing climate change policies: The role played by carbon accounting. *Australian Accounting Review* 29, 360–375.

Burtraw, D., Evans, D.A., Krupnick, A., Palmer, K., Toth, R., 2005. Economics of pollution trading for SO2 and Nox. *Annual Review of Environment and Resources* 30, 253–289.

Cadez, S., Guilding, C., 2017. Examining distinct carbon cost structures and climate change abatement strategies in CO_2 polluting firms. *Accounting, Auditing and Accountability Journal* 30, 1041–1064.

Callon, M., 2009. Civilizing markets: Carbon trading between in vitro and in vivo experiments. *Accounting, Organizations and Society* 34, 535–548.

CDP, UN Global Compact, WRI, WWF, 2015. *Science-Based Target Setting Manual: Driving Ambitious Corporate Climate Action*. Science Based Targets Initiative, London, UK. Available at https://sciencebasedtargets.org/resources/files/SBTi-manual.pdf

Charnock, R., Hoskin, K.W., 2020. SDG 13 and the entwining of climate and sustainability metagovernance: An archaeological-genealogical analysis of goals-based climate governance. *Accounting, Auditing and Accountability Journal* 33, 1731-1759.

Charnock, R., Thomson, I., 2019. A pressing need to engage with the Intergovernmental Panel on Climate Change: The role of SEA scholars in syntheses of social science climate research. *Social and Environmental Accountability Journal* 39, 192–199.

Chenhall, R.H., Hall, M., Smith, D., 2013. Performance measurement, modes of evaluation and the development of compromising accounts. *Accounting, Organizations and Society* 38, 268–287.

Coulson, A., Dixon, R., 1995. Environmental risk and management strategy. *International Journal of Bank Marketing* 13, 22–29.

CSA, 2019. *Reporting of Climate Change Related Risks*. Canadian Securities Administrators. CSA Staff Notice 51–358.

Cushen, J., 2013. Financialization in the workplace: Hegemonic narratives, performative interventions and the angry knowledge worker. *Accounting, Organizations and Society* 38, 314–331.

Eide, M.H., 2002. Life cycle assessment (LCA) of industrial milk production. *International Journal of Life Cycle Assessment* 7, 115–126.

Ekvall, T., Tillman, A.-M., Molander, S., 2005. Normative ethics and methodology for life cycle assessment. *Journal of Cleaner Production* 13, 1225–1234.

Falkner, R., 2016. The Paris Agreement and the new logic of international climate politics. *International Affairs* 92, 1107–1125.

Fernando, S., Lawrence, S., 2014. A theoretical framework for CSR practices: Integrating legitimacy theory, stakeholder theory and institutional theory. *Journal of Theoretical Accounting Research* 10, 149–178.

Gibassier, D., Schaltegger, S., 2015. Carbon management accounting and reporting in practice: A case study on converging emergent approaches. *Sustainability Accounting, Management and Policy Journal* 6, 340–365.

Gray, R., 1992. Accounting and environmentalism: An exploration of the challenge of gently accounting for accountability, transparency and sustainability. *Accounting, Organizations and Society* 17, 399–425.

Green, W., Taylor, S., Wu, J., 2017. Determinants of greenhouse gas assurance provider choice. *Meditari Accountancy Research* 25, 114–135.

Guthrie, J., Parker, L.D., 2017. Reflections and projections: 30 years of the interdisciplinary accounting, auditing and accountability search for a fairer society. *Accounting, Auditing and Accountability Journal* 30, 2–17.

Hahn, R., Reimsbach, D., Schiemann, F., 2015. Organizations, climate change, and transparency: Reviewing the literature on carbon disclosure. *Organization and Environment* 28, 80–102.

Harris, P., Symons, J., 2013. Norm conflict in climate governance: Greenhouse gas accounting and the problem of consumption. *Global Environmental Politics* 13, 9–29.

Hopwood, A.G., 1983. On trying to study accounting in the contexts in which it operates. *Accounting, Organizations and Society* 8, 287–305.

IPCC, 2006. *IPCC Guidelines for National Greenhouse Gas Inventories*. Intergovernmental Panel on Climate Change, IGES, Japan.

IPCC, 2019. *Overview of 2019 Refinement to the 2006 IPCC Guidelines for National Greenhouse Gas Inventories*. Kyoto, Japan.

Jotzo, F., Karplus, V., Grubb, M., Löschel, A., Neuhoff, K., Wu, L., Teng, F., 2018. China's emissions trading takes steps towards big ambitions. *Nature Climate Change* 8, 265.

Kolk, A., Levy, D., 2001. Winds of change: Corporate strategy, climate change and oil multinationals. *European Management Journal* 19, 501–509.

KPMG, 2017. The road ahead: The KPMG survey of corporate responsibility reporting 2017. Zurich: KPMG International. Retrieved November 20, 2018.

Kumarasiri, J., Jubb, C., 2016. Carbon emission risks and management accounting: Australian evidence. *Accounting Research Journal* 29, 137–153.

Larrinaga, C., 2014. Carbon accounting and carbon governance. *Social and Environmental Accountability Journal* 34, 1–5.

Larrinaga-Gonzalez, C., Bebbington, J., 2001. Accounting change or institutional appropriation?—A case study of the implementation of environmental accounting. *Critical Perspectives on Accounting* 12, 269–292.

Le Breton, M., Aggeri, F., 2019. The emergence of carbon accounting: How instruments and *dispositifs* interact in new practice creation. *Sustainability Accounting, Management and Policy Journal* 11, 505–522.

Liu, Z., Dreybrodt, W., Wang, H., 2010. A new direction in effective accounting for the atmospheric CO_2 budget: Considering the combined action of carbonate dissolution, the global water cycle and photosynthetic uptake of DIC by aquatic organisms. *Earth-Science Reviews* 99, 162–172.

Lövbrand, E., Stripple, J., 2011. Making climate change governable: Accounting for carbon as sinks, credits and personal budgets. *Critical Policy Studies* 5, 187–200.

Lovell, H., Bebbington, J., Larrinaga, C., de Aguiar, T.R.S., 2013. Putting carbon markets into practice: A case study of financial accounting in Europe. *Environment and Planning C: Government and Policy* 31, 741–757.

Luo, L., Lan, Y., Tang, Q., 2012. Corporate incentives to disclose carbon information: Evidence from the CDP Global 500 report. *Journal of International Financial Management and Accounting* 23, 93–120.

MacKenzie, D., 2009. Making things the same: Gases, emission rights and the politics of carbon markets. *Accounting, Organizations and Society* 34, 440–455.

McGlade, C., Ekins, P., 2015. The geographical distribution of fossil fuels unused when limiting global warming to 2°C. *Nature* 517, 187–190.

McNicholas, P., Windsor, C., 2011. Can the financialised atmosphere be effectively regulated and accounted for? *Accounting, Auditing and Accountability Journal* 24, 1071–1096.

Mete, P., Dick, C., Moerman, L., 2010. Creating institutional meaning: Accounting and taxation law perspectives of carbon permits. *Critical Perspectives on Accounting* 21, 619–630.

Miller, P., O'Leary, T., 2007. Mediating instruments and making markets: Capital budgeting, science and the economy. *Accounting, Organizations and Society* 32, 701–734.

Miller, P., Power, M., 2013. Accounting, organizing, and economizing: Connecting accounting research and organization theory. *The Academy of Management Annals* 7, 557–605.

Moore, D.R.J., McPhail, K., 2016. Strong structuration and carbon accounting: A position-practice perspective of policy development at the macro, industry and organizational levels. *Accounting, Auditing and Accountability Journal* 29, 1204–1233.

Ormond, J., Goodman, M.K., 2015. A new regime of carbon counting: The practices and politics of accounting for everyday carbon through CO2e. *Global Environmental Change* 34, 119–131.

Patten, D.M., 2020. Seeking legitimacy. *Sustainability Accounting, Management and Policy Journal* 16, ahead of print.

Radcliffe, V.S., Spence, C., Stein, M., 2017. The impotence of accountability: The relationship between greater transparency and corporate reform. *Contemporary Accounting Research* 34, 622–657.

Roberts, J., 1991. The possibilities of accountability. *Accounting, Organizations and Society* 16, 355–368.

Roberts, R., 1992. Determinants of corporate social responsibility disclosure: An application of stakeholder theory. *Accounting, Organizations and Society* 17, 595–612.

Rogelj, J., Schaeffer, M., Friedlingstein, P., Gillett, N.P., Van Vuuren, D.P., Riahi, K., Allen, M., Knutti, R., 2016. Differences between carbon budget estimates unravelled. *Nature Climate Change* 6, 245–252.

Royal Society, Royal Academy of Engineering, 2018. *Greenhouse Gas Removal*. London: Royal Society and Royal Academy of Engineering.

Schneider, T., Michelon, G., Paananen, M., 2018. Environmental and social matters in mandatory corporate reporting: An academic note. *Accounting Perspectives* 17, 275–305.

Searchinger, T., Heimlich, R., Houghton, R., Dong, F., Elobeid, A., Fabiosa, J., Tokgoz, S., Hayes, D., Yu, T.-H., 2008. Use of U.S. croplands for biofuels increases greenhouse gases through emissions from land-use change. *Science* 319, 1238–1240.

Securities and Exchange Commission, 2010. Commission guidance regarding disclosure related to climate change, Final Rule 6290. Securities and Exchange Commission. Washington DC, USA.

Smith, P., Davis, S.J., Creutzig, F., Fuss, S., Minx, J., Gabrielle, B., Kato, E., Jackson, R.B., Cowie, A., Kriegler, E., van Vuuren, D.P., Rogelj, J., Ciais, P., Milne, J., Canadell, J.G., McCollum, D., Peters, G., Andrew, R., Krey, V., Shrestha, G., Friedlingstein, P., Gasser, T., Grübler, A., Heidug, W.K., Jonas, M., Jones, C.D., Kraxner, F., Littleton, E., Lowe, J., Moreira, J.R., Nakicenovic, N., Obersteiner, M., Patwardhan, A., Rogner, M., Rubin, E., Sharifi, A., Torvanger, A., Yamagata, Y., Edmonds, J., Yongsung, C., 2015. Biophysical and economic limits to negative CO_2 emissions. *Nature Climate Change* 6, 42.

Stechemesser, K., Guenther, E., 2012. Carbon accounting: A systematic literature review. *Journal of Cleaner Production* 36, 17–38.

Thomassen, M.A., Dalgaard, R., Heijungs, R., Boer, I., 2008. Attributional and consequential LCA of milk production. *The International Journal of Life Cycle Assessment* 13, 339–349.

UK Parliament, 2008. *Climate Change Act 2008*. London, UK.

Unerman, J., Chapman, C., 2014. Academic contributions to enhancing accounting for sustainable development. *Accounting, Organizations and Society* 39, 385–394.

Wei, Q., Schaltegger, S., 2017. Revisiting carbon disclosure and performance: Legitimacy and management views. *The British Accounting Review* 49, 365–379.

Weikmans, R., Roberts, J.T., 2019. The international climate finance accounting muddle: Is there hope on the horizon? *Climate and Development* 11, 97–111.

27
WATER

Shona Russell

Introduction

Water – a crucial constituent of any society (Bijker 2012:625) or socio-ecological systems – has garnered less attention amongst accounting scholarship than climate change (Chapter 26) and biodiversity loss (Chapter 28). As a major challenge in the Anthropocene, water scarcity, flooding and ongoing debates about rights to water sit alongside concerns about "clean water and sanitation for all" (UN SDG 6) and sustainable water management. This chapter reviews water-related accounting research by identifying and discussing prominent themes, theoretical framings and approaches to research, issues being addressed and concludes by outlining future research areas.

Water has attracted the attention of many across the social sciences. Insights from anthropology and geography have enriched understanding of how water is embedded in social, cultural and political domains (Orlove and Caton 2010); theorised the material and symbolic dimensions of water (Linton and Budds 2014); and emphasised the politics of water (Bakker 2012). Science and technology studies attend to the multiple ontologies of water (Barnes and Alatout 2012) and see water and societies as intertwined. Accounting scholarship must engage with such debates and assumptions about and configurations of the relationships between water and society. These ways of thinking about water effect and are affected by accounting and accountability for the provision of water and sanitation services; the use and management of water by organisations; and the governance of water and freshwater ecosystems. By explicitly considering what is water (an ontological question) and how water can be understood and represented (an epistemological question), accounting scholarship may provide deeper and more critical analysis of existing arrangements and generate important recommendations that enhance accounting's contributions to more sustainable ways of living and organising.

To orientate ourselves to the scope and scale of water issues around the world, we first explore two recently published United Nations World Water Development Reports (UNWWDR). Second, common themes in water-related accounting research are reviewed and future research areas are identified. Third, we discuss the need to consider perspectives on water–society relations ensuring that future research supports more socially and ecologically sustainable ways of managing water before bringing the chapter to a conclusion.

Water in our world

While water is integral to everyday lives, the scale and scope of challenges vary around the world and are featured prominently in both the Millennium Development Goals and Sustainable Development Goals. Key insights from the two most recent UNWWDR (WWAP 2019, 2020) provide a context in which to examine water accounting scholarship in the next section. The reports, from the UNESCO World Water Assessment Programme (WWAP), provide authoritative and comprehensive overviews of global water use and projections for future pressures demonstrating water's importance to global and regional socio-economic development regions. Since its first publication in 2003, subsequent reports examined important connections between water and energy (WWAP 2014), jobs (WWAP 2016), wastewater (WWAP 2017), inclusion (WWAP 2019) and climate change (WWAP 2020). With each report drawing on various global databases and experts.

Global water demand has increased by 600% over the past 100 years (Wada et al. 2016). Growth in global water use is a result of increasing population, economic development and changing consumption patterns. While progress has been made in terms of access to clean water and sanitation, 2.1 billion people continue to lack access to safe, readily available water at home, and 4.5 billion people lack safely managed sanitation in 2015 (WWAP 2020). Inequalities remain within and between countries, between genders and persist between the richest and the poorest. For example, almost half of people drinking water from unprotected sources live in sub-Saharan Africa (WHO/UNICEF 2017), where the burden of collecting water lies mainly on women and girls, many of whom spend more than 30 minutes on each trip to collect water (UNICEF/WHO 2019). Lack of access to safe water and sanitation is associated with poor health and living conditions, malnutrition and lack of opportunities for education and employment. Water stress, including insufficient access to water and sanitation services, has also been associated with social unrest, conflict, violence and, increasingly, in human displacement and migration (Miletto et al. 2017).

Climate change will aggravate challenges concerning availability, quantity and quality in existing water-stressed regions, and generate water stress in areas where water resources are currently abundant (WWAP 2020). Water resource management will be further complicated by increasing the frequency and magnitude of extreme climate events, including heat waves and storm surges; adverse impacts on water quality due to higher temperatures or higher pollutant concentrations during drought; degradation of ecosystems leading to loss of biodiversity; diminished provision of water-related ecosystem services; and demand for water for agriculture, fisheries and recreation (WWAP 2020).

Contemporary responses to these water challenges are shaped by a collective of international, national and regional policy frameworks. For example, accounting scholars may need to attend to frameworks including the 2030 Sustainable Development Agenda (Bebbington and Unerman, 2018), focusing on water through UN SDG 6 "Ensure availability and sustainable management of water and sanitation for all"; the Paris Agreement where water is not explicitly mentioned but recognised to be essential to all mitigation and adaptation strategies (WWAP 2020); and the Sendai Framework for Disaster Risk Reduction (UNDRR 2015) where water is relevant to all priorities for action. These international frameworks inform much of the work of the public and private sectors and as such shape the understanding and possibilities of enacting water accounting and accountability.

These reports and policy frameworks map a range of water challenges that have considerable potential for future accounting research projects. By taking a problem-centred approach to research (Bebbington & Larrinaga 2014), promising areas for accounting scholarship emerge at the intersection of water, other environmental, societal and economic concerns, and governing institutions. Regarding the challenges listed in Table 27.1, accounting scholars could:

- Investigate financing and investment in water infrastructure (new and existing) as part efforts to meet SDG 6 and adapt to climate change (SDG 13)
- Examine and design accounting and accountability systems to support conservation of freshwater ecosystems as part of climate mitigation
- Examine and evaluate generation and use science-based targets to guide responses to water challenges (Pacific Institute 2017).

Table 27.1 Challenges emerging from trends in the world's water resources

Challenges	*Supplementary information to support future research projects*
Water equity, availability & demand	• Water use has been increasing worldwide by approximately 1% per year since the 1980s and is expected to continue to increase at a similar rate until 2050, which is an increase of 20–30% above current levels of water use. • Globally, agriculture (including irrigation, livestock and aquaculture) uses most water (69% of annual water withdrawals); industry (including power generation) accounts for 19% and households (12%).
Water quality	• Worldwide over 80% of wastewater returns to the environment without treatment. • Several water-related diseases, for example, cholera, remain widespread across developing countries, where only a small fraction of domestic and urban wastewater is treated before being released into the environment. • Nutrient loadings remain a prevalent form of water pollution and agriculture remains the main source of nutrient emissions. • In the future, rapidly growing cities in developing countries are projected to be major sources of nutrient emissions, especially where households lack adequate wastewater treatment systems.
Water-related disasters and extreme events	• About 90% of natural disasters are water-related. Floods accounted for 43% of all documented natural disasters, affecting 2.3 billion people, killing 157,000 more and causing US$662 billion in damage between 1995 and 2015. • Droughts accounted for 5% of natural disasters, affecting 1.1 billion people, killing 22,000 more and causing US$100 billion in damage over the same period.
Water supply and sanitation	• In 2015, 181 countries had achieved over 75% coverage with at least basic drinking water services and the global population using at least basic drinking water services has increased to 89% from 81% between 2000 and 2015. About three out of ten people did not use a safely managed drinking water service in 2015. • The number of people affected or killed by inadequate water and sanitation outnumbers challenges presented by climate change.
Water infrastructure	- Significant investment in water infrastructure is required. Global estimates range from US$6.7 trillion by 2030 to US$22.6 trillion by 2050. - To achieve the WASH component of SDG 6 by 2030, it is estimated that capital investment needs to triple (to reach US$1.7 trillion), and operating and maintenance costs will be commensurately higher. - The Food and Agriculture Organization has projected that an estimated US$960 billion of capital investment is needed to expand and improve irrigation until 2050 in 93 developing countries, compared to the 2005–2007 levels of investment.

(continued)

Table 27.1 Cont.

Challenges	*Supplementary information to support future research projects*
Freshwater ecosystems	- Over the past 100 years, it is estimated that half of the world's natural wetlands have been lost and with this a significant number of freshwater species. - The loss rate of wetlands is three times higher than that of forests - Wetlands, including peatlands, accommodate the largest carbon stocks amongst terrestrial ecosystems and store twice as much carbon as forests. - Climate-induced harmful algae blooms are increasing due to warmer water temperatures and climate change is severely affecting efforts to control such blooms. - Many lakes and estuaries around the world, which provide drinking water for millions of people and support ecosystem services, already have toxic, food web-altering, hypoxia-generating blooms of harmful cyanobacteria. - Poor water quality due to eutrophication (mostly from poor sanitation and poor nutrient management) is one of the most widespread problems affecting available water supplies, fisheries and recreational activities. For example, the estimated cost of damage caused by eutrophication in the United States of America (USA) alone is approximately US$2.2 billion annually.

Source: Adapted from WWAP2019, 2020.

The two most recent reports have identified several key water challenges that are relevant to accounting research. These are water equity, availability and demand; water quality; water-related disasters and extreme events; water supply and sanitation, water infrastructure; and freshwater ecosystems. Having outlined global water challenges to identify potential research areas, we now turn to a literature review that identifies what and how water has been considered in accounting scholarship.

Tracing the contours of water accounting scholarship

"Water" is an emerging topic for environmental accounting scholars, with published studies on issues of quality, quantity, access, rights and water use, sustainable resource management, company and industry management (Kurland and Zell 2010) that touch upon all of the themes outlined in the UN reports. A review of accounting-related research published from 2010 onwards identified four streams that concern:

i) The *provision of water and sanitation services*
ii) *Water governance*, most notably Australia's General Purpose Water Accounting
iii) *Organisations and water management* incorporating disclosures and management accounting, and
iv) *Water resource management,* addressing water issues, including freshwater ecosystems and impacts from social and commercial practices.

Each stream of work is discussed before outlining future research areas.

Provision of water and sanitation services

The provision of water and sanitation services by water utilities (including state suppliers, local governments and corporatised publicly owned companies) is a primary site for accounting research reflecting a long-term interest in this sector. This can be traced back to accounting studies of UK water privatisation (Ogden 1997; Shaoul 1997). Unsurprisingly, water utilities are common institutions selected to explore water accounting and reporting. For example, recent work has explored institutionalisation of sustainable and environmental management (accounting) in water organisations in Australia (Ferdous et al. 2019; Moore 2013), the diffusion and decline of voluntary environmental reporting by municipal water utilities in Finland (Vinnari and Laine 2013) and the role of accounting in moral legitimation processes connected to water sustainability in an Italian water utility (Passetti and Rinaldi (2020). The early accounting privatisation studies (e.g. Shaoul 1997) have been extended to consider the inclusion of social and environmental concerns in water infrastructure (Kennedy 2011; McDonald-Kerr 2017); the mobilisation of accounting concepts in politicised debates of water sector reform (Jollands and Quinn 2017) and sustainable water management (Cashman 2011; Egan and Agyemang 2019).

In this stream, case studies (single or comparative) are a common research design offering in-depth insights into the contexts and histories that shaped the provision and regulation of water and wastewater services in particular sites and over time. For example, Egan and Agyemang's (2019) study of sustainable urban water management in Ghana between 2005 and 2017 offers important insights into the impact of changing configurations of agencies and other institutions involved in sustainable development initiatives. Similarly, Jollands and Quinn's (2017) longitudinal study of the mobilisation of accounting concepts in the reform of Ireland's water sector, through the lens of actor-network theory, highlighted the persistent influence of accounting on the delivery of this important public service.

Recent work from political ecology demonstrates the value of attending to artefacts, such as smart meters, in the continued reconfiguration of responsibilities and accountability amongst water utilities and consumers (Loftus et al. 2016). Inspired by such work and continuing work informed by actor-network theory (Jollands and Quinn 2017) and performativity (Egan 2014), future research could explore the reflexive impacts of artefacts, technologies, institutional reconfigurations, accounting practices, concepts and ideologies to further enrich our understanding of their consequences on the performing of water and sanitation services.

If accounting scholarship is to contribute to the achievement of SDG 6, then much needs to be done, particularly concerning investments in sustainable water supply and accounting information systems in areas of multiple deprivation (see Truslove et al. 2020), and the less palatable, but critically important, issue of sanitation and wastewater.

Water governance

The second stream examines the contributions and consequences of accounting in water governance spanning voluntary and regulatory institutions, where water accounting systems provide information to users to inform and evaluate decisions (Chalmers et al. 2012a,b). Different theoretical approaches and research designs have been used in this stream. For example, underpinned by a rights to information framework, Hazelton (2013) differentiated types of accounts regarding the scale, entity and use of water information as part of designing water governance systems. These included national water accounts to reflect the stocks and flows of water in particular countries; catchment-based reports that provide information to stakeholders regarding water quality, allocation and use; corporate accounts that disclose aspects of their use and impacts on water and associated freshwater ecosystems; and accounts of water associated with individual products or services.

The development and implementation of Australia's General Purpose Water Accounting System have garnered much research scrutiny. Studies have covered the initial proposed institutional arrangements (Chalmers et al. 2012b); the contribution of the accounting discipline (Chalmers et al. 2012a); potential and actual use and understanding of accounts and accounting systems by stakeholders, at different levels (site and catchment) including groundwater (Leong et al. 2014; Tello and Hazelton 2018). While formal water accounting systems associated with regulatory systems have emerged in practice, the research findings to date suggest that further work is required to understand how they can contribute to the sustainable management of surface and groundwater.

Voluntary initiatives concerning disclosure or stewardship standards have attracted less attention. One notable exception is Mundle et al.'s (2017) study of the Alliance of Water Stewardship and associated meta-governance frameworks that guide future multi-stakeholder partnerships. Another more prominent initiative, the Global Reporting Initiative (GRI 2018), also shapes water governance and organisational disclosure, most recently through the GRI 303: Water and Effluents 2018 Standard. While most GRI-related works concern comparing disclosures against these standards (see the next section), future research could investigate the processes by which any new accounting and accountability standards, regulatory and voluntary, are negotiated, finalised and applied (see, e.g., Hewawithana 2019). This would enrich the understanding of the design and operation of water governance, the appropriate role of water accounting and accountability, as well as identifying possible areas for change. If accounting research is to contribute to future sustainable water governance outcomes, it is important to understand how organisations are responding to and perhaps shaping existing governance initiatives as well as the impacts of doing so. The next section will discuss research that has examined water management, accounting and reporting by organisations.

Organisations and water management

There's growing interest in organisational accounts of water management spanning external (reporting) and internal (management accounting) interests. Reflecting water management as a nascent research area, there is a need for conceptual papers that debate and establish the need for water-related accounting and disclosures. This research stream is dominated by assumptions that "water" accounting information, including external disclosure, is important for decision-making. This assumption echoes the conceptual underpinnings of water governance and the proliferation of water accounting guidelines and standards. For example, Christ and Burritt's (2017b) conceptual framework accounts for the water issues arising within organisations, primarily corporations, in water-intensive industries to understand water impacts, dependencies and how to integrate such understandings into existing accounting systems. Despite the recognition of water crises, associated impacts and wealth of guidance available to businesses, the authors observe a lack of water accounting by corporations.

Reflecting trends in carbon and biodiversity research, much research in this stream draws on secondary data to assess the level and quality of water-related disclosure often regarding reporting standards with a focus on multi-national companies in specific countries (Gibassier 2018) or events. See, for example, Burritt and Christ's (2018) study on water risk associated with the failure of the Samarco dam in Brazil. Many of these studies suggest that disclosures are of poor quality and call for improvements in water disclosures within operations and across supply chains (Linneman et al. 2015; Christ and Burritt 2017a). Other disclosure works examine the performance of industries including agriculture (Tashakor et al. 2019), food and beverage

(Egan 2015) or mining (Burritt and Christ 2018) reflecting their high exposure to water-related concerns.

Management accounting studies include individual (Christ 2014) or industry-wide case studies (Egan 2015). These studies have considered the need and contribution of environmental management tools to support water management within organisations. In-depth case studies provide important insights into the efforts required to design and embed water accounting systems and support organisational transformation for sustainability (Ferdous et al. 2019), the contribution of accountants (Egan 2017) and the role of existing knowledge systems (Tingey-Holyoak and Pisaniello 2019).

Future work could examine organisational and sectoral efforts to translate regulatory and voluntary frameworks into practice. While much of the work above focuses on Australia, studies from other jurisdictions and industries would broaden our understanding of water-related dependencies and impacts across the world, as well as the regulatory contexts in which organisations operate. Recognising that the primary industries are commonly high water users, it may be useful to investigate their water use analysed by particular catchments and the materiality to these ecosystems following similar work in marine ecosystems (see Österblom et al. 2015). Additional approaches to data collection may need to be developed recognising the limited amount of water disclosures. Public sector bodies may be charged with monitoring water use and impacts, or privately-owned company could be shaping water use and management around the world, without having to disclose this information. As ever, a deep understanding of the particular contexts in which organisations are operating is imperative as part of investigations of organisations and water management.

Finally, a noticeable feature of recent conceptual or reviews of water management accounting is the assertion of the need for monetisation of corporate water accounting information to provide a common metric upon which to base decisions (Burritt and Christ 2017). Monetisation raises questions about how knowledge is constructed, meaning is created and water is valued linking back to Hines's (1991) mediation on the value of nature (in this case, water). Undoubtedly, such debates about the multiple values of water will continue to percolate water accounting research and should be welcomed in light of concerns that economic value on water could crowd out other ways of accounting for and relating to water and in doing so detract from possible ways to contribute to water sustainability (Passetti and Rinaldi 2020).

Water resource management

A fourth stream concerns accounting and accountability in connection with natural disasters, infrastructure and management of lakes and rivers. While garnering less attention than other streams, this collection of work demonstrates rich opportunities to enliven and enrich understanding of past, contemporary and future accounting and accountability to support water resource management. Natural disasters, experienced or expected, have sparked a series of studies concerning flood events in Italy and Australia (Lai et al. 2014; Sciulli 2018), investment in flood infrastructure and the use of cost–benefit analysis (Samiolo 2012); Hurricane Katrina in the United States (Baker 2014) as well as historical analysis of the impact of drought in 1930s America (Walker 2014). Studies here draw on qualitative data and narrative analysis to understand breakdowns in accountability (Baker 2014), the facilitative (Walker 2014) and socialising effects of accounting (Lai et al 2014; Sciulli 2018).

Given predicted increases in water-related natural disasters and recognition that water is the primary medium through which climate change is experienced (UNDRR 2015; WWAP 2020), traditional accounting and accountability systems are likely to be found wanting in post-recovery phases. However, this research has illustrated opportunities for alternative accounting and accountability to be engaged in dialogues in these contexts. These studies illustrate the diverse and differential temporal, spatial and socio-political impacts of drought and floods where the former can be "long-term and pernicious" (Walker 2014:606) and the latter happen over shorter periods with varying consequences for those affected (Baker 2014). As such, further work could centre on historical and contemporary cases, thereby informing the design and development of adaptive and anticipatory accounting and accountability systems rather than traditional forms of accounting that look to the past (see Chapter 6 on environmental accounting and 21st-century sustainability governance).

Rivers and freshwater ecosystems perhaps surprisingly feature in the accounting literature. Rivers provided a metaphor for Hines' (1988) discussion of financial accounting's ability to construct and communicate reality. This observation resonates with more recent debates about catchments. Just as Hines challenged the boundaries and concreteness of organisations, the same applies to catchments. It is often assumed that catchments are objectively defined by science and a static geographic entity around which to organise water resource management and associated responsibilities. However, catchments themselves are boundary objects and where those boundaries lie and how they change is politically, culturally and scientifically determined (Cohen 2012). The interplay between science, politics and culture produces new configurations of entities and what is to be accounted for and what is to be discarded or that which is supposed to be within or outside the responsibilities of those producing or receiving accounts. Thus, if practices and systems of accounting and accountability are to be designed around catchments, as well as organisations, it is pertinent to be aware of the political, cultural, ecological and social implications (Hines 1988).

Rivers and their catchments provide empirical sites in which to examine accounting. Recent work has evaluated accounting the building of dams for hydro-electricity (Hrasky and Jones 2016), access to water rights in Canada (Schneider and Andreaus 2018) and river restoration in Scotland (Dey and Russell 2014). Collectively these studies illustrate water's importance to connected socio-ecological systems and the need for analytical approaches that take account of the multiplicity of human and non-human actors involved in the management and governance of water. While many studies focus on particular individual actors or industries, studies of accounting and water resource management may benefit from the arena framework to illuminate the web of responsibilities associated with the management and governance of water (see Georgakopolous and Thomson 2008). Finally, responsibilities for rivers remain with regulatory authorities or collaborative initiatives; thus, those interested in accountability for such freshwater systems should focus on organisations such as catchment management bodies attending to their institutional history and how that is shaping accountability as it is enacted today and in the future – for example, Duncan's (2017) examination of water management reforms in Aotearoa, New Zealand.

Surveying the landscape of water scholarship

This literature review has identified an array of different motivations for water accounting scholarship. These include drought, water scarcity, flooding, climate change, innovation and experimentation in policy and practice amongst public, private and civil society. The studies reviewed above signal broad agreement that water merits sustained attention from accounting scholars and practitioners. Issues of water rights and water sustainability to date have garnered less interest amongst the accounting community compared to the provision of water and sanitation and organisational management of water. However, as outlined above, further work is still required to support efforts to ensure access to clean water and sanitation, in line with SDG 6, and the impacts of climate change on water infrastructure, including flooding.

Theoretical interests and methodological approaches vary across the studies yet share a common position that accounting is seen as a social and institutional practice that enacts and produces certain ways of organising, accounting and accountability relationships (Miller and Power 2013). Against this backdrop, various theoretical perspectives can be identified in the studies reviewed, including institutional theory to investigate changes to management accounting (Ferdous et al. 2019) or stakeholder theory to analysis water-related disclosures in Japan (Burritt et al. 2016); performativity to understand organisational change (Egan 2014) and orders of worth to establish moral legitimacy (Passetti and Rinaldi 2020). Such perspectives will likely continue to inform theorisation of accounts, accounting and accountability in years to come. Fewer studies draw upon primary fieldwork or qualitative data. To date, research has been dominated by desk-based research exploring secondary data in the form of documents, policies and corporate reports. Building on the emergent insights from the body of works in Australia, Europe and North America, future research could turn to other contexts where water-related issues are particularly acute, such as the provision of water and sanitation in sub-Saharan Africa (Egan and Agyemang 2019; Truslove et al. 2020).

While many studies cite the need to contribute to sustainable water resource management, questions arise as to their actual and potential contribution to sustainability science and practice. Disclosure studies firmly anchored in existing streams of accounting scholarship have their place as do in-depth investigations of particular empirical sites and case studies that enrich and enliven theorisation of accounts, accounting and accountability. Efforts to encourage further water disclosure need to sit alongside in-depth investigations of the efforts of managers, professionals and others and the technologies that shape water management in organisations (Egan 2015) and wider governance arrangements and aspirations for sustainability.

Conclusion

Drought, flood, access to clean drinking water and sanitation and degradation of freshwater ecosystems continue to present challenges around the world. Evidently, accounting scholars are beginning to attend to these concerns (Bebbington and Unerman 2018) focusing on primary industries and water utilities through studies of disclosure and management accounting, engaging with water governance and examining the role of accounting profession in addressing water-related concerns. Global water trends extend beyond these themes and identify a series of promising areas for future research, including flooding and investment in water infrastructure.

Increasingly, scholars recommend interdisciplinary and transdisciplinary research to further enhance water accounting practice and frameworks (Christ and Burritt 2018) echoing a problem-centred sustainability science approach (Bebbington and Larrinaga 2014). Future scholarship should follow this stream, perhaps addressing the global water trends and challenges outlined and responding to gaps identified above. Reflecting the multidisciplinary nature of water issues, others could document and examine the experiences of collaboration and contribution to policy and practice, which in turn may include consideration of the ontological and epistemological assumptions that inform how research issues are formulated, research approaches are undertaken and recommendations are made.

The studies reviewed illustrate that water and associated industries or events have provided a backdrop to deepen theoretical and empirical understanding of accounting and accountability (see, e.g., Baker 2014). In other cases, water has been treated as a resource or externality to be managed, demonstrating a seemingly common perspective of "modern water", which is distinct from society (Linton 2014). Only some studies have recognised the social and cultural dimensions of water or considered the ontological and epistemological perspectives of water–society relations (see Jollands and Quinn 2017; Passetti and Rinaldi 2020). Future research could extend the view that accounting, as a productive force, to consider how accounting shapes and is shaped by water–society relations (Linton and Budds 2014). By explicitly considering multiple perspectives on what water is (ontology) and how it is represented (epistemology) (Yates et al. 2017), future analysis may be sharper and richer, understanding of the politics of water may be enhanced, and be able to offer innovative contributions to theorising and practising accounting and accountability for water. To do so requires engagement with water scholarship in fields of anthropology, geography and science-technology studies, as well as engineering and law. This review of contemporary research is intended to inspire, provoke and inform future work. To conclude, water merits sustained attention. Accounting scholars have much to offer and to learn.

References

Baker, C., 2014. Breakdowns of accountability in the face of natural disasters: The case of Hurricane Katrina. *Critical Perspectives on Accounting,* 25(7), 620–632.

Bakker, K., 2012. Water: Political, biopolitical, material. *Social Studies of Science*, 42(4), 616–623.

Barnes, J,. and Alatout, S., 2012. Water worlds: Introduction to the special issue of social studies of science. *Social Studies of Science*, 42(4), 483–488.

Bebbington, J., and Larrinaga, C., 2014. Accounting and sustainable development: An exploration. *Accounting, Organizations and Society,* 39(6), 395–413.

Bebbington, J., and Unerman, J., 2018. Achieving the United Nations Sustainable Development Goals: An enabling role of accounting research. *Accounting, Auditing & Accountability Journal,* 31(1), 2–24.

Bijker, W., 2012. Do we live in water cultures? A methodological commentary. *Social Studies of Science,* 42(4), 624–627.

Burritt, R., and Christ, K., 2017. The need for monetary information within corporate water accounting. *Journal of Environmental Management,* 201, 72–81.

Burritt, R., and Christ, K., 2018. Water risk in mining: Analysis of the Samarco dam failure. *Journal of Cleaner Production,* 178, 196–205.

Burritt, R., Christ, K., and Omori, A., 2016. Drivers of corporate water-related disclosure: Evidence from Japan. *Journal of Cleaner Production,* 129, 65–74.

Cashman, A., 2011. Our water supply is being managed like a rumshop: Water governance in Barbados. *Social and Environmental Accountability Journal*, 31(2), 155–165.

Chalmers, K., Godfrey, J., and Lynch, B., 2012a. Regulatory theory insights into the past, present and future of general purpose water accounting standard setting. *Accounting, Auditing & Accountability Journal,* 25(6), 1001–1024.

Chalmers, K., Godfrey, J., and Potter, B., 2012b. Discipline-informed approaches to water accounting. *Australian Accounting Review,* 22(3), 275–285.

Christ, K., 2014. Water management accounting and the wine supply chain: Empirical evidence from Australia. *The British Accounting Review,* 46(4), 379–396.

Christ, K., and Burritt, R., 2017a. Supply chain-oriented corporate water accounting: A research agenda. *Sustainability Accounting, Management and Policy Journal,* 8(2), 216–242.

Christ, K., and Burritt, R., 2017b. Water management accounting: A framework for corporate practice. *Journal of Cleaner Production*, 152, 379–386.

Christ, K., and Burritt, R., 2018. The role for transdisciplinarity in water accounting by business: Reflections and opportunities. *Australasian Journal of Environmental Management*, 25(3), 1–19.

Cohen, A., 2012. Rescaling environmental governance: Watersheds as boundary objects at the intersection of science, neoliberalism, and participation. *Environment and Planning A: Economy and Space*, 44(9), 2207–2224.

Dey, C., and Russell, S., 2014. Who speaks for the river? Exploring biodiversity accounting using an arena approach. In: Jones, M. (ed.), *Accounting for Biodiversity*. London: Routledge, pp. 245–266.

Duncan, R., 2017. Rescaling knowledge and governance and enrolling the future in New Zealand: A co-production analysis of Canterbury's water management reforms to regulate diffuse pollution. *Society & Natural Resources*, 30(4), 436–452.

Egan, M., 2014. Making water count: Water accountability change within an Australian university. *Accounting, Auditing & Accountability Journal,* 27(2), 259–282.

Egan, M., 2015. Driving water management change where economic incentive is limited. *Journal of Business Ethics* 132, 73–90.

Egan, M., 2017. Utilising accounting and accountants in the management of water efficiency: Utilising accounting and accountants in the management of water efficiency. *Australian Accounting Review,* 28(3), 356–373.

Egan, M., and Agyemang, G., 2019. Progress towards sustainable urban water management in Ghana. *Sustainability Accounting, Management and Policy Journal,* 10(2), 235–259.

Ferdous, M., Adams, C., and Boyce, G., 2019. Institutional drivers of environmental management accounting adoption in public sector water organisations. *Accounting, Auditing & Accountability Journal,* 32(4), 984–1012.

Georgakopoulos, G., and Thomson, I., 2008. Social reporting, engagements, controversies and conflict in an arena context. *Accounting Auditing & Accountability Journal*, 21(8), 1116–1143.

Gibassier, D., 2018. Corporate water accounting, where do we stand? The international water accounting field and French organizations. *Sustainabilty Accounting (Advances in Environmental Accounting & Management)*,Vol. 7, 31–65.

Global Reporting Initiative, 2018. *GRI 303: Water and Effluents* www.globalreporting.org/standards/media/1909/gri-303-water-and-effluents-2018.pdf.

Hazelton, J., 2013. Accounting as a human right: The case of water information. *Accounting, Auditing & Accountability Journal*, 26(2), 267–311.

Hewawithana, D., 2019. *"New" accounting for water: Lessons learnt in accountability, user engagement and innovation from the Australian experience.* PhD Thesis. Macquarie University.

Hines, R., 1988. Financial accounting: In communicating reality, we construct reality. *Accounting, Organizations and Society,* 13(3), 251–261.

Hines, R., 1991. On valuing nature. *Accounting, Auditing & Accountability Journal* 4(3), 27–29.

Hrasky, S., and Jones, M., 2016. Lake Pedder: Accounting, environmental decision-making, nature and impression management. *Accounting Forum*, 40(4), 285–299.

Jiménez, A., et al., 2020. Unpacking water governance: A framework for practitioners. *Water,* 12(3), 827.

Jollands, S., and Quinn, M., 2017. Politicising the sustaining of water supply in Ireland – The role of accounting concepts. *Accounting, Auditing & Accountability Journal,* 30(1), 164–190.

Kennedy, S., 2011. Stakeholder management for sustainable development implementation: The case of a sustainable urban drainage system. *Social and Environmental Accountability Journal*, 31(2), 139–153.

Kurland, N., and Zell, D., 2010. Water and business: A taxonomy and review of the research. *Organization & Environment*, 23(3), 316–353.

Lai, A., Leoni, G., and Stacchezzini, R., 2014. The socializing effects of accounting in flood recovery. *Critical Perspectives on Accounting,* 25(7), 579–603.

Leong, S., Hazelton, J., Taplin, R., Timms, W., and Laurence, D., 2014. Mine site-level water reporting in the Macquarie and Lachlan catchments: A study of voluntary and mandatory disclosures and their value for community decision-making. *Journal of Cleaner Production,* 84, 94–106.

Linneman, M., Hoekstra, A., and Berkhout, W., 2015. Ranking water transparency of Dutch stock-listed companies. *Sustainability,* 7(4), 4341–4359.

Linton, J., 2014. Modern water and its discontents: a history of hydrosocial renewal. *WIREs Water,* 1(1): 111–120.

Linton, J., and Budds, J., 2014. The hydrosocial cycle: Defining and mobilizing a relational-dialectical approach to water. *Geoforum*, 57, 170–180.

Loftus, A., March, H., and Nash, F., 2016. Water infrastructure and the making of financial subjects in the South East of England. *Water Alternatives*, 9(2), 319–335.

McDonald-Kerr, L., 2017. Water, water, everywhere sustainability accounting. *Management and Policy Journal,* 8(1), 43–76.

Miletto, M., Caretta, M.A., Burchi, F.M., and Zanlucchi, G., 2017. *Migration and its interdependencies with water scarcity, gender and youth employment.* World Water Assessment Programme. Paris, UNESCO.

Miller, P., and Power, M., 2013. Accounting, organizing, and economizing: Connecting accounting research and organization theory. *The Academy of Management Annals*, 7(1), 557–605.

Moore, D.R., 2013. Sustainability, institutionalization and the duality of structure: Contradiction and unintended consequences in the political context of an Australian water business. *Management Accounting Research*, 24(4), 366–386.

Mundle, L., Beisheim, M., and Berger, L., 2017. How private meta-governance helps standard-setting partnerships deliver. *Sustainability Accounting, Management and Policy Journal*, 8(5), 525–546.

Ogden, S., 1997. Accounting for organizational performance: The construction of the customer in the privatized water industry. *Accounting, Organizations and Society*, 22(6), 529–556.

Orlove, B., and Caton, S., 2010. Water sustainability: Anthropological approaches and prospects. *Annual Review of Anthropology*, 39(1), 401–415.

Österblom, H. et al., 2015. Transnational corporations as 'keystone actors' in marine ecosystems. *Plos One*, 10(5), 0127533.

Pacific Institute., 2017. Exploring the case for corporate context-based water targets. https://ceowatermandate.org/files/context-based-targets.pdf.

Passetti, E., and Rinaldi, L., 2020. Micro-processes of justification and critique in a water sustainability controversy: Examining the establishment of moral legitimacy through accounting. *The British Accounting Review*, 52(3), 1–23.

Samiolo, R., 2012. Commensuration and styles of reasoning: Venice, cost-benefit, and the defence of place. *Accounting, Organizations and Society*, 37(6), 382–402.

Schneider, T., and Andreaus, M., 2018. A dam tale: Using institutional logics in a case study on water rights in the Canadian coastal mountains. *Sustainability Accounting, Management and Policy Journal*, 9(5), 685–712.

Sciulli, N., 2018. Weathering the storm: Accountability implications for flood relief and recovery from a local government perspective. *Financial Accountability & Management*, 34(1), 30–44.

Shaoul, J., 1997. The power of accounting: Reflecting on water privatization? *Accounting, Auditing & Accountability Journal*, 10(3), 382–405.

Tashakor, S., Appuhami, R., and Munir, R., 2019. Environmental management accounting practices in Australian cotton farming. *Accounting, Auditing & Accountability Journal*, 32(4), 1175–1202.

Tello, E., and Hazelton, J., 2018. The challenges and opportunities of implementing general purpose groundwater accounting in Australia. *Australasian Journal of Environmental Management*, 25(3), 285–301.

Tingey-Holyoak, J., and Pisaniello, J., 2019. Water accounting knowledge pathways. *Pacific Accounting Review*, 31(2), 258–274.

Truslove, J., Coulson, A., Mblame, E., and Kalin, R., 2020. Barriers to handpump serviceability in Malawi: Life-cycle costing for sustainable service delivery. *Environmental Science: Water Research and Technology*, 2020(6), 2138–2152.

UNDRR., 2015. *Sendai Framework for disaster risk reduction*. Available at www.undrr.org/publication/sendai-framework-disaster-risk-reduction–2015–2030.

UNICEF/WHO., 2019. *Progress on household drinking water, sanitation and hygiene 2000-2017. Special focus on inequalities*. New York: UNICEF and World Health Organization.

Vinnari, E., and Laine, M., 2013. Just a passing fad? The diffusion and decline of environmental reporting in the Finnish water sector. *Accounting, Auditing & Accountability Journal*, 26(7), 1107–1134.

Wada, Y., Flörke, M., Hanasaki, N., Eisner, S., Fischer, G., Tramberend, S., Satoh, Y., van Vliet, M. T. H., Yillia, P., Ringler, C., Burek, P., and Wiberg, D., 2016. Modeling global water use for the 21st century: the Water Futures and Solutions (WFaS) initiative and its approaches, *Geoscientific Model Development*, 9, 175–222, https://doi.org/10.5194/gmd-9-175-2016.

Walker, S., 2014. Drought, resettlement and accounting. *Critical Perspectives on Accounting*, 25(7), 604–619.

WHO/UNICEF., 2017. *Progress on Drinking Water, Sanitation and Hygiene: 2017 Update and SDG Baselines*. Geneva/New York: WHO/UNICEF. www.unicef.org/publications/index_96611.htm.

WWAP., 2014. *The United Nations World Water Development Report 2014: Water and Energy*. Paris: UNESCO.

WWAP., 2016. *The United Nations World Water Development Report 2016: Water and Jobs*. Paris: UNESCO.

WWAP., 2017. *The United Nations World Water Development Report 2017. Wastewater: The Untapped Resource*. Paris: UNESCO.

WWAP., 2019. *The United Nations World Water Development Report 2019: Leaving No One Behind*. Paris: UNESCO.

WWAP., 2020. *The United Nations World Water Development Report 2020: Water and Climate Change*. Paris: UNESCO.

Yates, J., Harris, L., and Wilson, N., 2017. Multiple ontologies of water: Politics, conflict and implications for governance. *Environment and Planning D: Society and Space*, 35(5), 797–815.

28
BIODIVERSITY

Jan Bebbington, Thomas Cuckston and Clément Feger

Introduction

Our current best estimate of the number of eukaryotic species comprising Earth's biological diversity stands at 8.7 million (Mora, Tittensor, Adl, Simpson, and Worm 2011). Species interact in myriad ways, within different kinds of terrestrial and marine habitats, to form complex ecological systems (Begon, Townsend, and Harper 2006). The United Nations (1992, p. 1), given the vital importance of these ecological systems for "maintaining [the] life sustaining systems of the biosphere", recognises that "conservation of biological diversity is a common concern of humankind". Despite this collective sentiment, however, biologists warn that humanity's ongoing impacts upon the natural environment are causing losses of biodiversity at a rate equivalent to a mass extinction event (Ceballos et al. 2015). There remains a fundamental problem that, even if human societies collectively agree that Earth's biodiversity should be conserved, it is very difficult to translate this into effective action at the level of governments, organisations and individuals (Cuckston 2018a, 2018b). In this chapter, we review the emerging stream of research in accounting for biodiversity, which explores possible roles that accounting might play in creating conditions in which it becomes possible to achieve some form of sustainable development that conserves the biodiversity of the planet.

This chapter is structured as follows: first we examine the global picture of biodiversity loss through an analysis of what Gray and Owen (this volume) call an *account of nature*, the WWF Living Planet Report; next, we evaluate intergovernmental initiatives to establish global governance and accountability frameworks for biodiversity; then we review research into organisation-level mechanisms of accounting for the biodiversity impacts of production activities and the uses of accounting in the organising of conservation activities; finally, we suggest some possible future directions for accounting research that might help enable ecologically and socially sustainable ways of organising and managing Earth's biosphere.

An account of nature

WWF's Living Planet Report is a biennial publication, described as a "comprehensive study of trends in global biodiversity and the health of the planet" (WWF 2019). These trends are tracked quantitatively, principally via a global indicator that it calls the *Living Planet*

Index. This indicator is a measure of wildlife population abundance, calculated using time-series data for 4,005 species of mammals, birds, reptiles, amphibians and fish from different biomes around the planet. The headline result is a stark representation of the scale of Earth's biodiversity loss.

> The global index, calculated using available data for all species and regions, shows an overall decline of 60% in the population sizes of vertebrates between 1970 and 2014.
> *(WWF 2018, p. 90)*

Using the same database of species, the Living Planet Report also documents the principal threats that are driving wildlife population declines. These are shown to vary across taxonomic groups and across geographic regions, but habitat degradation/destruction (mostly from conversion of land to agriculture) and species overexploitation (especially unsustainable fishing) together account for two-thirds of recorded threats. These are seen to result from "exploding human population and economic growth" (WWF 2018, p. 22), with rapidly accelerating demands for food, water and energy. Economic development has generated dramatic improvements in quality of life for a great many people. However, these advances in our well-being are only made possible by the life-supporting resources provided by functioning ecological systems.

> All our economic activity ultimately depends on nature. It's estimated that, globally, nature provides services worth around US$125 trillion a year.
> *(WWF 2018, p. 11)*

Given this fundamental entanglement of the fates of human societies and Earth's biodiversity, it might be assumed that humanity should have a strong collective motivation to act, identifying and instigating some much needed "major changes to production, supply and consumption activities" (WWF 2018, p. 28). On the contrary, the kind of international collaboration needed to achieve this has, thus far, been lacking.

> The extinction of a multitude of species on Earth seems not to have captured the imagination, or attention, of the world's leaders enough to catalyse the change necessary.
> *(WWF 2018, p. 10)*

Yet the Living Planet Report, and other such *accounts of nature* (cf. Russell, Milne, and Dey 2017), perhaps offers cause for hope. These are accounts that portray both biodiversity's immense value to human societies and economies, and the full extent of the impact that humanity's current ways of organising its societies and economies is having on this biodiversity. Is it possible that, in rendering these realities visible and comprehensible, these accounts might help propel us to seek new ways of organising that allow us to conserve Earth's biodiversity? Can we turn this awareness of our predicament into a vision for a better future and a viable plan to pursue it?

> [W]hat the world requires is bold and well-defined goals and a credible set of actions to restore the abundance of nature to levels that enable both people and nature to thrive.
> *(WWF 2018, p. 110)*

In the next section we will review the existing international governance and accountability frameworks for biodiversity and consider the mechanisms that are meant to compel action by governments and corporations.

International governance and accountability frameworks

Accounting and reporting activities are social artefacts that arise from particular governance contexts within which demands for accountability emerge, based on responsibility being assigned for actions and/or impacts. Taking this perspective, this section will outline the source(s) of responsibility for organisational biodiversity impacts.

At the global level of resolution, the *United Nations Convention on Biodiversity Diversity* provides an overarching source of normativity (see Bebbington, Kirk, and Larrinaga-Gonzalez 2012) that shapes the context in which organisations operate. A key carrier of normativity in this context includes the *Aichi Targets* (for a summary, see Table 28.1). These goals are addressed to national governments and, through them, provide a point of connection between organisations and the biodiversity outcomes sought. In particular, the goals provide a coherent framework for any organisation to reflect upon their biodiversity and ecosystem services interactions.

Inter-governmental agreements create commitments that are the responsibility of state actors to implement and actions by states will directly affect organisations in the countries in which they operate. Examples of such cascades of requirements include legal and regulatory provisions covering resource extraction, such as the:

- Granting of resource extraction permits, rules for harvesting processes and requirements for remediation after corporate activities,
- Pollution control, in order to protect biodiversity and the functionality of ecosystems (including point source and diffuse pollution), and
- Regulation of competing demands for resources (e.g., by setting areas beyond use for conservation).

In this way, the regulatory environment encompasses both conservation concerns and the impact of productive sectors.

A more recent overarching inter-governmental attempt to define the goals towards which global society (including organisations) needs to address themselves can be found in the *Sustainable Development Goals* – SDGs (for an accounting-based introduction, see Bebbington

Table 28.1 Strategic goals for biodiversity (see www.cbd.int/sp/targets/ for more detail on specific targets under each goal)

Address underlying causes of biodiversity loss (and mainstream biodiversity across government and society)
Reduce direct pressures on biodiversity and promote sustainable use (across a number of production sectors and including the crossover impacts of climate change on biodiversity)
Protect and enhance biodiversity by safeguarding ecosystems, species and genetic diversity.
Enhance the benefits that flow from biodiversity and ecosystem services.
Enhancing implementation through participatory planning, knowledge management and capacity building.

and Unerman 2018)). While all the goals interact with and are inter-dependent on each other, four main goals are at the heart of the organisation–biodiversity nexus, namely:

- Responsible Consumption and Production (Goal 12),
- Climate Action (Goal 13),
- Life Below Water (Goal 14), and
- Life on Land (Goal 15).

Responses to the imperatives of the SDGs will also affect the accountability context of organisational activities.

By their nature, the effects of these sources of normativity will vary according to what biodiversity and/or ecosystem service is affected as well what standards are applied. It is also the case that some organisational activities take place in areas that are beyond state jurisdiction, notably in ocean ecosystems. In this context, non-state actors (such as Regional Fisheries Management Organisations) exert influence on organisational responsibilities. There is an ongoing process to address marine biodiversity of areas beyond national jurisdiction – see www.un.org/bbnj/.

In order for organisations to navigate this context (as well as to address biodiversity well), there are also a myriad of voluntary initiatives and guidelines to support companies across an array of industries. Bebbington, Larrinaga, Russell and Stevenson (2015) describe some of these including the *Business and Biodiversity Offsetting Programme*, *Natural Value Initiative* and the *Corporate Ecosystem Services Review*. In addition, product certifications (such as those provided by the *Marine Stewardship Council* and the *Forest Stewardship Council*) create a private voluntary regulatory space for organisations to address biodiversity responsibilities. As previously noted in this chapter, translating protection of biodiversity and ecosystems services to organisational levels is non-trivial and it is to this topic that attention now turns.

Organisational level accounting for biodiversity

Recently, accounting as both a field of critical research and a space for innovation has turned to the issue of biodiversity conservation. This dynamic has been fuelled by confidence in the fact that accounting has real potential to contribute to the improvement, enforcement and operationalisation of the above-mentioned complex systems of accountabilities that are instrumental to biodiversity conservation. We will now review the main research areas that have been explored by accounting for biodiversity research, at the organisational level and beyond. We will do so by following the triple movement that has so far characterised the development of the field (Feger 2016, chap. 2; Feger and Mermet 2017): *extension* of the historical accountability perimeter of organisations to biodiversity and natural capital; *decentring* from the corporation to study accounts produced in the context of wider biodiversity governance programmes and market mechanisms; and actively *re-centring* accounting research on organized action at the ecosystem-management level to put it at the service of conservation strategies.

At the organisational level, business and biodiversity issues have been increasingly framed as a problem of managing firms' interdependencies with biodiversity and ecosystem services (i.e. the benefits that humans receive from nature), also often conceptualised as "natural capital" (Bishop 2012; van den Burg and Bogaardt 2014). In that perspective, a new family of tools and accounting devices has flourished in the past decade, designed specifically to support managers from different industrial sectors to better identify and reduce the impacts of their activities on biodiversity and ecosystems and/or assess the value that various ecosystem services bring to their organisation in biophysical or monetary terms. Examples include biodiversity life cycle assessment tools (Zhang, Singh, and Bakshi 2010), full cost accounting methods applied to biodiversity issues and used to measure hidden costs associated with ecosystem degradation (Davies 2014), and a large spectrum of *ad hoc* qualitative and quantitative decision-support tools, frameworks and guidelines designed to analyse risks and opportunities associated with organisations' interdependences with ecosystems (e.g. NCC 2016; Waage and Kester 2015). Other authors have also proposed methods to account for costs and revenues associated with the use of ecosystem services by organisations along their supply chains, and integrate them directly into their existing management accounting systems (Houdet and Germaneau 2014).

Staying at the organisational level, another strand of accounting for biodiversity research, well in line with social and environmental accounting's main research orientation since its early development, focuses not on the managerial level of decision-making but rather on how organisations (could) develop forms of biodiversity reporting, enabling them to be accountable to external stakeholders regarding their impacts on ecosystems and their commitments to reduce them. Pioneering research on this topic has been the development of a methodology based on structured inventory of fauna, flora and critical habitats under the stewardship of a given organisation (Jones 1996).This approach privileges the intrinsic value of nature rather than an ecosystem services philosophy, often considered as being too anthropocentric (Barter 2015; Jones and Solomon 2013). Biodiversity reporting does not solely concern private organisations and similar research has studied biodiversity reporting in public sector organisations such as the Government of Bangladesh, Australian regional authorities or the United Kingdom (UK) local councils (Gaia and Jones 2017; Siddiqui 2013; Raar 2014).

One important challenge when it comes to organisational disclosure is the need for standardisation, or at least for a gradual convergence of the proposed frameworks and indicators that would allow comparability between organisations under a shared narrative. This is particularly difficult for topics as complex and heterogeneous as biodiversity and ecosystem services (Kareiva et al. 2015). Organisations such as the *Global Reporting Initiative*, for instance, have been proposing indicators on biodiversity (e.g. regarding land management, proximity of activities to protected areas, etc.) as well as on ecosystem services (GRI 2016, 2011, 2007). Other proposals have been put forward such as using indicators developed as part of national and international biodiversity assessment and governance programmes (Thomson, 2014) or frameworks based on species extinction metrics (Atkins and Maroun 2018). With the constant improvement of conservation science and data sets, initiatives to develop corporate-level "biodiversity footprint" tools and synthetic biodiversity indicators based on scientific modelling are now increasing (Lammerant, Müller, and Kisielewicz 2018).

However, recent critical studies of current reporting practices of Swedish, Danish, British, German as well as Top-fortune companies have put into perspective the effectiveness of this biodiversity reporting. They showed that information levels on this subject are still very low in the Sustainable Development/Corporate Social Responsibility (CSR) reports of big companies (with the exception of highly exposed sectors such as mining) (Boiral 2016; Van Liempd and Busch 2013; Rimmel and Jonäll 2013; Samkin, Schneider, and Tappin 2014; Adler, Mansi, and Pandey 2018; Adler et al. 2017). These studies reflect the progress that is yet to be made in moving towards more specific and quantifiable forms of reporting that would allow satisfactory assessment of firms' responsibilities and commitments on biodiversity (Addison, Bull, and Milner-Gulland 2018).

In the past two decades, research on accounting for biodiversity has pioneered the decentring of the social and environmental accounting agenda beyond the "obsession of the corporation" towards new accounting entities and "new accounts" (Gray, Brennan, and Malpas, 2014). Decentring from the organisational level as the main accounting entity, part of biodiversity accounting research has turned to the critical study of accounting practices emerging along with the development of new biodiversity governance schemes and market mechanisms involving multiple organisations.

Cuckston (2013), for instance, analyses how biodiversity conservation is integrated through financial calculations into the construction of new "goods" in emerging carbon markets such as the *Reducing Emissions from Deforestation and forest Degradation* mechanism (REDD). The same author shows how the creation of value for nature under such schemes entails the alienation of people from nature (Cuckston 2018c). In his study of reporting practices under REDD in Kalimantan (Borneo), Khan (2014) proposes the development of a "multi-faceted framework of biodiversity reporting and disclosure" model that would make it possible to account for the impacts of multiple organisations on the area's ecosystems (companies in the palm oil supply chain, environmental non-governmental organisations (NGOs), local administrations that finance conservation projects, the Indonesian government, etc.).

New forms of "accounts" are also being developed as part of environmental certifications, be it on terrestrial (Eden 2008) or marine ecosystems (Bear and Eden 2008). Borsato et al. (2014) showed, for instance, how the LIFE® Certification programme has assessed biodiversity impacts of many companies in Brazil and has developed a rating system of their biodiversity-friendly voluntary actions that creates new forms of accountabilities for companies as well as incentives to act. Elad (2014) studied the Forest Stewardship Council programme and its methods for certifying logging companies in the Congo Basin, and shows how biodiversity monitoring and reporting audits based on fauna/flora inventories are conducted to help ensure a form of control of the quality of forest management by companies.

Turning to biodiversity offsetting mechanisms, Tregidga (2013) and Sullivan and Hannis (2017) provided critical analysis of methods used to create "biodiversity credits", and questioned whether biodiversity quantification methods based on financial accounting logics can really lead to better ecosystem protection. Cuckston (2019) studied another type of offsetting mechanism developed by the New South Wales authorities (Australia) based rather on biophysical units, highlighting how more *ecocentric* alternatives exist to progress towards reconciling economic development and biodiversity conservation goals.

Explicitly breaking with an accounting entity approach centred on an organisation, a government authority, a well-bounded protected area or a biodiversity governance or market mechanism, Dey and Russell (2014) adopted a system-level conceptualisation of the accounting entity encompassing both the ecosystem itself (a river and its catchments) and the stakeholders operating around it. They analysed how these various actors produce and exchange a variety of accounts around this entity as they pursue diverging courses of action: environmental reports produced by the company in charge of a dam structure; "external accounts" produced by public regulatory actors or associations and citizens concerned by the quality of the river and its salmon, etc. Feger and Mermet (2017) and Cuckston (2017) adopted similar approaches when, respectively, re-centring their analytical lens on West Vancouver Island coastal ecosystems and the way natural capital scientists attempt to re-negotiate its future with multiple stakeholders, and on a degraded blanket bog habitat and the works undertaken to restore it.

Developing such an ecosystem-centred or "accounting for the management of ecosystems" perspective is now crucial, since when it comes to obtaining measurable ecological performance at the ecosystem level, conservation practitioners (scientists, NGOs, etc.) often have to act in deeply strategic contexts where the way they produce and/or demand biodiversity accounts is in fact only one dimension of the wider collective organised action dynamics that require special attention and in-depth analysis (Feger and Mermet 2017). With several decades of critical studies on the intricate links between accounts design and use, on the one hand, and the details of organising decisions and actions in a diversity of organisational contexts, on the other hand, accounting research is now well-equipped to be put at the service of conservation practitioners' actions, strategies and goals (Cuckston 2018a; Feger and Mermet 2017). In that perspective, the foundations for a fruitful interdisciplinary dialogue have now been laid out, between accounting researchers motivated by obtaining results on the biodiversity front and conservation scientists well aware of the limitations of their multiple information tools in creating expected changes (Feger et al. 2019. This dialogue now needs to be pursued and enriched with more empirical case studies, constructive critical reflexivity and theoretical developments at the crossroads of accounting and biodiversity conservation, to contribute to a wider agenda of accounting *for* sustainable development (*Ibid*; Bebbington and Larrinaga 2014).

In the final section, we reflect on some possible future directions for accounting research aimed at advancing society's capacity for pursuing forms of sustainable development that conserve biodiversity.

Future directions

The vast extent to which humanity has come to reshape Earth's biosphere has led geologists to coin the term "Anthropocene" to describe the current era, in which human society and nature are inseparably entwined (see Crutzen 2002). Returning to the WWF's Living Planet Report, the challenge of biodiversity loss is characterised here in terms of how humanity can find a way of continuing to pursue its economic development whilst, in its own interests, conserving nature and sustaining healthy ecological systems. Is it possible that human society and nature can find a sustainable form of co-existence?

> It is not known whether a stable Anthropocene state will come to exist. It certainly isn't stable now.
>
> *(WWF 2018)*

The *Anthropocene* concept renders biodiversity loss into an organisational challenge, inviting us to seek out ways to organise and manage the biosphere to enable sustainable development that conserves biodiversity (Bebbington et al. 2019; Cuckston 2017). It is a basic premise in the study of accounting as a social practice that accounting constitutes what Miller and Power (2013, p. 587) call a "productive force", driving and shaping processes of organising by rending different forms of action thinkable and possible. As such, accounting research offers the potential for valuable insights into how this kind of organising of Earth's biosphere might be pursued.

A recent survey of 9,264 conservationists, seeking to gauge areas of consensus and disagreement on the future of conservation and on "fundamental questions regarding why, what and how to conserve", enabled Sandbrook et al. (2019, p. 316) to identify three "dimensions of conservation thinking". These are people-centred conservation, science-led ecocentrism, and conservation through capitalism. We suggest that accounting research can potentially contribute to thinking within each of these dimensions.

People-centred conservation relates to the role of human participants and stakeholders in conservation work. This is essentially the ethical dimension of conservation thinking, concerned with the effects of conservation on people (especially those living in poverty) and with how to ensure that conservation work has the support of those impacted by it. A key question for community-based conservation, which aims to engage and benefit local people, ensuring fair and just access to natural resources, is how to encourage and enable people to accept responsibility for conserving the biodiversity around them and to act in ways conducive to its protection. The accounting academe has studied, in numerous contexts, how the calculative devices of accounting work to invent and shape particular calculating selves, capable of being organised and managed (Miller 2001; Vollmer 2019). It may be that insights generated from this kind of research can provide a basis for studies of how various calculative devices can/should be deployed in organising and managing community-based conservation initiatives.

Science-led ecocentrism is a dimension of conservation thinking concerned with how the work of conserving species and ecosystems is informed and guided by the biological sciences. A key question for science-led conservation is how ecological principles and knowledge can be deployed in the management of protected areas, including areas subject to the so-called sustainable management practices. The accounting academe has studied, in numerous contexts, how codified knowledge – especially economics – comes to be embodied within, and performed by, the calculative devices of accounting (Hopwood 1992; Skaerbaek and Tryggestad 2010). It may be that insights from this kind of research can provide a basis for studies of how the biological sciences can/should be operationalised within various calculative devices used to organise and manage different kinds of protected areas.

Conservation through capitalism relates to the role of corporations, economic metaphors and market-based approaches. This is the dimension of conservation thinking that has so far attracted the most attention from accounting scholars. A fundamental question for the conservation movement is how, if at all, the capitalist economic model can be shifted to make it less ecologically destructive and more capable of reconciliation with conservation objectives. Much accounting research has been highly pessimistic about the prospects of such a shift (Gray and Milne 2018). Yet, emerging work in accounting for sustainable development holds out the promise of an enabling role for accounting practice and research in addressing the ecological and social challenges facing humanity (Bebbington and Larrinaga 2014; Bebbington and Unerman 2018). Might it be that this mode of accounting research can provide insights into how production landscapes and ocean spaces can/should be organised and managed by corporations and through market mechanisms in ways that make these less hostile to wildlife and more supportive of ecological processes?

In the era of the Anthropocene, accounting research has a potentially pivotal role to play in envisaging a future where Earth's biosphere is organised and managed in ways that are ecologically and socially sustainable.

References

Addison, P., Bull, J., and Milner-Gulland, E., 2018. Using conservation science to advance corporate biodiversity accountability. *Conservation Biology*, 33 (2), 307–328.

Adler, R., Mansi M., and Pandey, R., 2018. Biodiversity and threatened species reporting by the top Fortune Global companies. *Accounting, Auditing and Accountability Journal,* 31 (3), 787–825.

Adler, R., Mansi, M., Pandey, R., and Stringer, C., 2017. United Nations decade on biodiversity: A study of the reporting practices of the Australian mining industry. *Accounting, Auditing and Accountability Journal,* 30 (8), 1711–1745.

Atkins, J., and Maroun, W., 2018. Integrated extinction accounting and accountability: Building an ark. *Accounting, Auditing and Accountability Journal,* 31 (3), 750–786.

Barter, N., 2015. Natural capital: Dollars and cents/dollars and sense. *Sustainability Accounting, Management and Policy Journal,* 6 (3), 366–373.

Bear, C., and Eden, S., 2008. Making space for fish: The regional, network and fluid spaces of fisheries certification. *Social and Cultural Geography,* 9 (5), 487–504.

Bebbington, J., Kirk, E., and Larrinaga-Gonzalez, C., 2012. The production of normativity: A comparison of reporting regimes in Spain and the UK. *Accounting, Organizations and Society,* 37 (2), 78–94.

Bebbington, J., and Larrinaga, C., 2014. Accounting and sustainable development: An exploration. *Accounting, Organizations and Society,* 39 (6), 395–413.

Bebbington, J., Larrinaga, C., Russell, S., and Stevenson, L., 2015. Organizational, management and accounting perspectives on biodiversity. In: A. Gasparatos and K. Willis, eds. *Biodiversity in the Green Economy*. London: Routledge, pp. 213–239.

Bebbington, J., Österblom, H., Crona, B., Jouffray, J., Larrinaga, C., Russell, S., and Scholtens, B., 2019. Accounting and accountability in the Anthropocene. *Accounting, Auditing and Accountability Journal*, In Press. https://doi.org/10.1108/AAAJ-11-2018-3745

Bebbington, J., and Unerman, J., 2018. Achieving the United Nations Sustainable Development Goals: An enabling role for accounting research. *Accounting, Auditing and Accountability Journal*, 31 (1), 2–24.

Begon, M., Townsend, C., and Harper, J., 2006. *Ecology: From Individuals to Ecosystems*. Oxford: Blackwell.

Bishop, J., ed., 2012. *The economics of ecosystems and biodiversity in business and enterprise*. London and New York: Earthscan.

Boiral, O., 2016. Accounting for the unaccountable: Biodiversity reporting and impression management. *Journal of Business Ethics*, 135 (4), 751–768.

Borsato, R., Filho, J.T.M., Milano, M.S., Salzmann, A.M., Brasil, B., Alexandre, M.A., De Lourdes Da Silva Nunes, M., Borges, C., and Posonski, M., 2014. Biodiversity accountability in Brazil: The role of LIFE certification. In: M.J. Jones, ed. *Accounting for Biodiversity*. Oxon: Routledge, pp. 172–188.

Ceballos, G., Ehrlich, P., Barnosky, A., Garcia, A., Pringle, R., and Palmer, T., 2015. Accelerated modern human-induced species losses: Entering the sixth mass extinction. *Science Advances*, 1 (5), e1400253.

Crutzen, P., 2002. Geology of mankind. *Nature*, 415, 23.

Cuckston, T., 2013. Bringing tropical forest biodiversity conservation into financial accounting calculation. *Accounting, Auditing and Accountability Journal*, 26 (5), 688–714.

Cuckston, T., 2017. Ecology-centred accounting for biodiversity in the production of a blanket bog. *Accounting, Auditing and Accountability Journal*, 30 (7), 1537–1567.

Cuckston, T., 2018a. Making accounting for biodiversity research a force for conservation. *Social and Environmental Accountability Journal*, 38 (3), 218–226.

Cuckston, T., 2018b. Making extinction calculable. *Accounting, Auditing and Accountability Journal*, 31 (3), 849–874.

Cuckston, T., 2018c. Creating financial value for tropical forests by disentangling people from nature. *Accounting Forum*, 42 (3), 219–234.

Cuckston, T., 2019. Seeking an ecologically defensible calculation of net loss/gain of biodiversity. *Accounting, Auditing and Accountability Journal*, 32 (5), 1358–1383.

Davies, J., 2014. Full cost accounting - Integrating biodiversity. In: M.J. Jones, ed. *Accounting for Biodiversity*. Oxon: Routledge, pp. 81–102.

Dey, C., and Russell, S., 2014. Who speaks for the river? Exploring biodiversity accounting using an arena approach. In: M.J. Jones, ed. *Accounting for Biodiversity*. Oxon: Routledge, pp. 245–266.

Eden, S., 2008. Being fieldworthy: Environmental knowledge practices and the space of the field in forest certification. *Environment and Planning D: Society and Space*, 26 (6), 1018–1035.

Elad, C., 2014. Forest certification and biodiversity accounting in the Congo basin countries. In: M.J. Jones, ed. *Accounting for Biodiversity*. Oxon: Routledge, pp. 189–211.

Feger, C., 2016. Nouvelles comptabilités au service des écosystèmes. Une recherche engagée auprès d'une entreprise du secteur de l'environnement. *Sciences de gestion*. Paris: AgroParisTech. https://pastel.archives-ouvertes.fr/tel-01563379/document

Feger, C., and Mermet, L., 2017. A blueprint towards accounting for the management of ecosystems. *Accounting, Auditing and Accountability Journal*, 30 (7), 1511–1536.

Feger, C., Mermet, L., Vira, B., Addison, P., Barker, R., Birkin, F., Burns, J., Cooper, S., Couvet, D., Cuckston, T., Daily, G., Dey, C., Gallagher, L., Hails, R., Jollands, S., Mace, G., Mckenzie, E., Milne, M., Quattrone, P., Rambaud, A., Russell, S., Santamaria, M., & Sutherland, W., 2019. Four priorities for new links between conservation science and accounting research. *Conservation Biology*, 33(4), 972–975. doi: https://doi.org/10.1111/cobi.13254

Gaia, S., and Jones, M.J., 2017. UK local councils reporting of biodiversity values: A stakeholder perspective. *Accounting, Auditing and Accountability Journal*, 30 (7), 1614–1638.

Gray, R., Brennan, A., and Malpas, J., 2014. New accounts: Towards a reframing of social accounting. *Accounting Forum*, 38 (4), 258–273.

Gray, R., and Milne, M., 2018. Perhaps the Dodo should have accounted for human beings? Accounts of humanity and (its) extinction. *Accounting, Auditing and Accountability Journal*, 31 (3), 826–848.

GRI, 2007. *Biodiversity: A GRI Reporting Resource*. Amsterdam: Global Reporting Initiative.

GRI, 2011. *Approach for reporting on ecosystem services. Incorporating ecosystem services into an organization's performance disclosure.* Global Reporting Initiative. www.globalreporting.org/resourcelibrary/Approach-for-reporting-on-ecosystem-services.pdf.

GRI, 2016. *GRI 304: Biodiversity.* Amsterdam: Global Reporting Initiative.

Hopwood, A., 1992. Accounting calculation and the shifting sphere of the economic. *The European Accounting Review,* 1, 125–143.

Houdet, J., and Germaneau, C., 2014. Accounting for biodiversity and ecosystem services from an EMA perspective: Towards a standardised biodiversity footprint methodology. In: M.J. Jones, ed. *Accounting for Biodiversity.* Oxon: Routledge, pp. 62–80.

Jones, M.J., 1996. Accounting for biodiversity: A pilot study. *British Accounting Review,* 28 (4), 281–303.

Jones, M.J., and Solomon, J.F., 2013. Problematising accounting for biodiversity. *Accounting, Auditing and Accountability Journal,* 26 (5), 668–687.

Kareiva, P., McNally, B., McCormick, S., Miller, T., and Ruckelshaus, M., 2015. Improving global environmental management with standard corporate reporting. *Proceedings of the National Academy of Sciences of the United States of America,* 112 (24), 7375–7382.

Khan, T., 2014. Kalimantan's biodiversity: Developing accounting models to prevent its economic destruction. *Accounting, Auditing and Accountability Journal,* 27 (1), 150–182.

Lammerant, J., Müller, L., and Kisielewicz, J., 2018. *Biodiversity accounting approaches for businesses. Discussion paper for EU Business and Biodiversity Platform.* Draft report.

Miller, P., 2001. Governing by numbers: Why calculative practices matter. *Social Research,* 68 (2), 379–396.

Miller, P., and Power, M., 2013. Accounting, organizing, and economizing: Connecting accounting research and organization theory. *The Academy of Management Annals,* 7 (1), 557–605.

Mora, C., Tittensor, D., Adl, S., Simpson, A., and Worm, B., 2011. How many species are there on Earth and in the ocean? *PLOS Biology,* 9 (8), e1001127.

NCC, 2016. *Natural Capital Protocol.* Natural Capital Coalition. www.naturalcapitalcoalition.org/protocol.

Raar, J., 2014. Biodiversity and regional authorities: A common-pool resources and accounting perspective. In: M.J. Jones, ed. *Accounting for Biodiversity.* Oxon: Routledge, pp. 103–123.

Rimmel, G., and Jonäll, K., 2013. Biodiversity reporting in Sweden: Corporate disclosure and preparers' views. *Accounting, Auditing and Accountability Journal,* 26 (5), 746–778.

Russell, S., Milne, M., and Dey, C., 2017. Accounts of nature and the nature of accounts: Critical reflections on environmental accounting and propositions for ecologically informed accounting. *Accounting, Auditing and Accountability Journal,* 30 (7), 1426–1458.

Samkin, G., Schneider, A., and Tappin, D., 2014. Developing a reporting and evaluation framework for biodiversity. *Accounting, Auditing and Accountability Journal,* 27 (3), 527–562.

Sandbrook, C., Fisher, J., Holmes, G., Luque-Lora, R., and Keane, A., 2019. The global conservation movement is diverse but not divided. *Nature Sustainability,* 2, 316–323.

Siddiqui, J., 2013. Mainstreaming biodiversity accounting: Potential implications for a developing economy. *Accounting, Auditing and Accountability Journal,* 26 (5), 779–805.

Skaerbaek, P., and Tryggestad, K., 2010. The role of accounting devices in performing corporate strategy. *Accounting, Organizations and Society,* 35 (1), 108–124.

Sullivan, S., and Hannis, M., 2017. "Mathematics maybe, but not money": On balance sheets, numbers and nature in ecological accounting. *Accounting, Auditing and Accountability Journal,* 30 (7), 1459–1480.

Thomson, I., 2014. Biodiversity, International Conventions, Government Strategy and Indicators: The Case of the UK. In: M.J. Jones, ed. *Accounting for Biodiversity.* Oxon: Routledge, pp. 149–171.

Tregidga, H., 2013. Biodiversity offsetting: Problematisation of an emerging governance regime. *Accounting, Auditing and Accountability Journal,* 26 (5), 806–832.

UN, 1992. *Convention on Biological Diversity.* New York: United Nations.

van den Burg, S.W.K., and Bogaardt, M.J., 2014. Business and biodiversity: A frame analysis. *Ecosystem Services,* 8, 178–184.

Van Liempd, D., and Busch, J., 2013. Biodiversity reporting in Denmark. *Accounting, Auditing and Accountability Journal,* 26 (5), 833–872.

Vollmer, H., 2019. Accounting for tacit coordination: The passing of accounts and the broader case for accounting theory. *Accounting, Organizations and Society,* 73, 15–34.

Waage, S., and Kester, C., 2015. Making the invisible visible: Analytical tools for assessing business impacts and dependencies upon ecosystem services. BSR. www.bsr.org/reports/BSR_Analytical_Tools_for_Ecosystem_Services_2015.pdf.

WWF, 2018. *Living Planet Report - 2018: Aiming higher.* Gland, Switzerland: WWF.
WWF, 2019. *What Is the Living Planet Report?* Retrieved from wwf.panda.org/knowledge_hub/all_publications/living_planet_report_2018/.
Zhang, Y.I., Singh, S., and Bakshi, B.R., 2010. Accounting for ecosystem services in life cycle assessment, Part II: Toward an ecologically based LCA. *Environmental Science and Technology*, 44 (7), 2624–2631.

29
ACCOUNTING FOR ANIMAL RIGHTS

Eija Vinnari and Markus Vinnari

Introduction

An unprecedented number of non-human animals, both domesticated and wild ones, are currently adversely affected by human activities. According to estimates, there are at least 21 billion chicken, 1.485 billion cattle and 1.169 billion sheep in the world (Cawthorn and Hoffman 2014). Of these individuals, more than 65 billion are slaughtered annually for food production purposes (Allievi et al. 2015). In turn, the exponential increase of both human beings and farmed animals[1] has resulted in severe habitat loss and hence a decline in wild animal populations (Barnosky 2008; Machovina et al. 2015; Ripple et al. 2014, 2015). Human activity is driving wild animal species' extinction at such a pace that authoritative experts have labelled this phenomenon as "biological annihilation" (Ceballos et al. 2017).

The widespread concern over wild species' extinction has given rise to biodiversity accounting[2], a set of practices whereby different types of organisations attempt to account for endangered species, with varying success (Jones 2014; Jones and Solomon 2013; Rimmel and Jonäll 2013; see also chapter 28 by Bebbington, Cuckston and Feger in the present book). Meanwhile, public concerns over the treatment of farmed animals have prompted meat and dairy companies to develop policies, systems and processes for managing animal welfare, including accounting and reporting on associated performance. To accelerate the adoption of such practices, systems for assessing companies' animal welfare performance have also emerged, such as the Business Benchmark on Farm Animal Welfare (BBFAW) launched in 2012 (see McLaren and Appleyard 2019).

In this chapter, we consider accounting for both wild animals and farmed animals. However, we are not interested in accounting for animal *welfare* but accounting for animal *rights*. The notions of animal welfare and animal rights have different moral philosophical roots, with radically different implications for contemporary societies' treatment of non-human animals. Animal welfare is often associated with a utilitarian view (e.g. Singer 1975), which approves of humans using other animals as long as their interests are given equal consideration to those of humans, and such use increases the overall well-being. Animal welfarists therefore advocate "compassionate" treatment of non-human animals and "humane" methods of killing them. In contrast, those defending animal rights have presented views which consider it morally wrong to abuse or kill non-human animals (Regan 1985). The ultimate goal of animal rights advocates is therefore to radically decrease or even abolish all use of non-human animals for food, clothing, science, entertainment and sports (e.g. Cochrane 2012; Francione 2010). Although such a goal has sometimes been derided as utopian (e.g. Mepham 2006), the constant advances in scientific knowledge regarding non-human animals' cognitive abilities and emotional intelligence have made the case for their equal consideration even more compelling (e.g. Rachels 1990; Aaltola 2012).

The purpose of this chapter is thus to explore how to account for animal rights. This is a less-than-straightforward task for various reasons. First, it signifies a commitment to a radical agenda of social change where the aim is to considerably decrease the use of non-human animals by human beings. This implies the need to conceive of a framework for conceptualising the transition. Moreover, as such a major change will inevitably take place over an extended period, the framework needs to incorporate a step-wise approach towards the ultimate goal. Second, if we wish to account for societal progress towards this aim, it is clear that indicators measuring animal welfare will soon prove inadequate. This presents us with the challenge of accounting for society-level change that might be more difficult to observe and measure than, say, transport times from farms to slaughterhouses. Third, as this is, at least to our knowledge, the first attempt to outline what accounting for animal rights might look like, this chapter is necessarily explorative and forward-looking. The ideas and indicators presented herein are tentative and illustrative; we leave it to future research to refine and elaborate on them.

In addition to the societal goal of advancing animal rights, this chapter is hoped to contribute to the fundamental themes of environmental accounting research. Many of the early works in this vein focused on how accounting and accountability systems could be harnessed for the purpose of establishing rights, responsibilities and accountability in relation to the natural environment (for a selection of such articles, see Gray et al. 2010). Our study extends previous work by proposing how accounting could be mobilised in establishing rights for non-human animals, an actor group largely neglected in prior accounting research (Dillard and Vinnari 2017). Furthermore, our proposal could be considered a challenge to the social contract basis upon which environmental accounting is founded. Can the notion of social constituent (Ramanathan 1976) be extended to include also non-human animals and if so, with what implications[3]?

This chapter proceeds as follows. We begin by reviewing seminal contributions to the debate on the moral value of non-human animals and the political implications thereof. These issues have mainly been debated in the field of animal ethics, but also to some extent in political philosophy. In reviewing this literature, we point out the different ways in which animal rights has been theorised and how these result in different normative views regarding the extent to which animal use is considered acceptable. Subsequently, building on the goals presented in the animal ethics/political philosophy literature, we develop a hierarchical framework for conceptualising a step-wise process towards the achievement of animal rights. The framework begins from acknowledging the existence of non-human animals and ends up with them being completely liberated in the sense intended by the abolitionist animal rights scholars. We also provide examples of qualitative and quantitative indicators that could be utilised at each step of the hierarchy. Finally, we discuss questions related to the operationalisation of the framework and associated accounting measures, including what kind of institutional arrangements would be required to support such a transition; who would collect, collate and report the data; as well as who would utilise the data and to what effect.

Perspectives on the moral worth of non-human animals

In this section we introduce ideas concerning the moral worth of non-human animals as presented in animal ethics, an interdisciplinary field of study comprising contributions from political scientists, legal studies scholars, philosophers, zoologists and social scientists. Due to the vastness of this established field of inquiry, we must necessarily confine our review to discussing the key contributions to the debate concerning animal rights.

The debate around animal welfare and animal rights is an old one and it has taken different forms during past centuries (Walters and Portmess 1999). In its modern form the debate can be said to have begun when Singer (1975) published a book which not only contained graphic photos of animals used in scientific and agricultural practices, but also further developed a philosophical framework explaining why such instances of animal use were morally unacceptable. The key concept in Singer's (1975) argumentation is sentience, in other words an individual's capacity to experience the world, to feel pain and pleasure. He argued that it is sentience – as opposed to, for instance, race, rationality, gender, or level of intelligence, which provides the basis for the moral equality of all human individuals. This is because the ability to suffer endows us with morally significant interests in how our lives turn out. Since many non-human animals are also sentient, Singer (1975) continued, for the sake of consistency we should extend moral equality to such animals. Importantly, abiding by this principle would not imply equal *treatment* of humans and non-human animals but giving the latter's interests equal *consideration* when making decisions and designing actions. Although this proposal might sound radical, Singer embedded it in a utilitarian philosophical framework that holds in highest value the maximisation of society's aggregate utility. In other words, the framework permits the use and even the killing of non-human animals provided that their interests have been duly considered and that such activities increase overall satisfaction of interests. Because of these allowances, Singer (1975) has often been interpreted to promote improving non-human animals' welfare instead of granting them rights.

Singer's (1975) ideas gave rise to a wave of responses which criticised his utilitarian approach for allowing the subjugation of non-human animals by humans[4]. One of the most vocal critics was Regan (1984), who put forth the philosophical case for animal rights, specifically moral rights that go beyond equal consideration of non-human animals' interests alongside those of human beings. Drawing on Kantian deontological reasoning, Regan (1984) posited that sentient animals are subjects-of-a-life, in other words beings that have desires, beliefs, interests in their own fates and a sense of themselves over time. Because of this subjectivity, such animals possess inherent value that is distinct from their instrumental value to human beings, and this in turn implies that they possess the basic right to be treated respectfully. Hence, Regan (1984) concluded that sentient animals should never be treated as mere means to achieve aggregate benefits for human societies but as ends-in-themselves. When discussing the practical implication of his rights-based position, Regan (1984) explicitly referred to the need to dissolve the modern animal industry. This line of thinking has been elaborated by Regan's followers, such as legal philosopher Francione (1995), according to whom the basic right of non-human animals is not to be treated as the property of others. He also posits that the acknowledgement of such animals' right to be treated respectfully implies that they should not be used at all in agriculture, science, entertainment or sports (Francione 1996); this position is referred to as abolitionism (Francione 2010).

A more recent version of animal rights theory has been developed by Cochrane (2012, 2014), who considers his interest-based approach to cover the middle ground between Singer's (1975) utilitarian ideas and Regan's (1984) deontological ones. In contrast to Regan (1984), Cochrane

(2012, 2014) argues that most sentient animals cannot be considered as ends-in-themselves because they are not autonomous agents in the Kantian sense – in other words, they are not capable of framing, revising and pursuing their own conception of the good. Therefore, he claims that most sentient animals do not have an interest in liberty, but they do have an interest in not being made to suffer and not being killed. These two interests give rise to the *prima facie* rights of not being made to suffer and not being killed. After a thorough examination of a variety of modern-day contexts where animals are used, Cochrane (2012) concludes that the application of the interest-based approach would spell an end to a number of practices, including most forms of animal experimentation; industrial agriculture and the raising of animals for their flesh; breeding species that suffer because of bodily features; keeping great apes and cetaceans in captivity; using animals in circuses; baiting, fishing, hunting and arranged animal fights; environmental actions such as routine deforestation and other forms of habitat destruction as well as greenhouse gas emissions; and cultural practices that involve animal suffering and/or death. Permissible but regulated activities would include genetic engineering of animals, keeping of companion animals, zoos and animal racing – but only on condition that they do not inflict suffering or death upon the animals. Cochrane (2014) further argues that ensuring the fulfilment of non-human animals' interest-based rights requires the political representation of such animals by human beings, for instance, through the establishment of a committee comprising members elected by a citizen assembly.

Another recent version of animal rights theory has been proposed by Donaldson and Kymlicka (2011), whose work pledges allegiance to the rights-based approach developed by Regan (1984) and elaborated by Francione (1996). However, these authors are concerned that the "classical" rights-based approach alienates potential advocates of animal rights by focusing only on the universal negative rights of non-human animals, that is, the right not to be exploited, be made to suffer or killed. According to Donaldson and Kymlicka (2011), classical animal rights theorists' vision of a world where domesticated animals as a category have been abolished, leaving only wild animals that live undisturbed by human beings, is unrealistic as it ignores the myriad relationships where humans and non-human animals necessarily coexist and interact and prevents consideration of what non-exploitative relations between them might be like. Thus, Donaldson and Kymlicka (2011) argue that the classical animal rights theory needs to be elaborated to cover not only negative universal rights but also positive relational rights, and this can be achieved by drawing on political theory. More specifically, Donaldson and Kymlicka (2011) propose that due to their proximity to human beings, domesticated animals could be conceived of as political agents and, consequently, human beings' co-citizens, whose interests regarding issues that affect them should be actively solicited and taken into consideration in political decision-making. Wild animals in turn could be compared to the citizens of foreign nations, sovereign beings whose lives should not be infringed upon by human beings. Like Cochrane (2014), Donaldson and Kymlicka (2011) perceive it necessary to establish a body comprised of human beings genuinely willing to pursue non-human animals' interests.

As the preceding review of animal ethics literature indicates, the moral worth of animals can be conceptualised in different ways, with different political implications. We can place the main approaches along a continuum from Singer's (1975) utilitarian, welfarist views via Cochrane (2012, 2014) as well as Donaldson and Kymlicka (2011) to Regan's (1984) and Francione's (1996) deontological, abolitionist stance. In the following section, we utilise this continuum as the basis for developing a framework for characterising progress towards the attainment of animal rights.

Accounting for progress towards animal rights

Our proposed framework for conceptualising progress towards the attainment of animal rights is presented in Table 29.1. In the case of human beings, it is relatively widely accepted that individuals' needs can be placed in a hierarchical order, such as in Maslow's (1954) hierarchy of needs. Correspondingly, our framework begins from the acknowledgement of non-human animals and proceeds via the fulfilment of their basic needs and basic rights to the fulfilment of their advanced rights. The level of basic needs corresponds roughly to the utilitarian or welfarist position, whereas the level of advanced rights reflects the abolitionist goals of the deontological interpretation of animal rights. The intermediate level of basic rights corresponds to animal rights views that perceive the abolitionist stance as either unnecessary (Cochrane 2012) or unrealistic (Donaldson and Kymlicka 2011). Following Donaldson and Kymlicka (2011), our framework considers two distinct groups of non-human animals[5]: wild animals and domesticated ones, the latter including not only farmed animals but also laboratory animals and companion animals.

The indicators that we propose for each level of the framework are a selection of contemporary examples complemented with some of our own ideas. One source of inspiration in this respect is the Animal Protection Index (API), which is a composite of several indicators compiled by a group of non-governmental animal protection organisations led by World Animal Protection[6]. The API is promoted as a simple comprehensive tool with which to chart different nation states' progress in animal protection. However, in our view, some of the API indicators evaluate very basic issues (e.g. acknowledgement of animal sentience in national legislation) whereas others could be considered to assess more advanced aspects (e.g. a ban on zoos in national legislation). Therefore, we found it more meaningful to distribute selected API indicators among the different levels of our framework. Moreover, due to its focus on nation states, the API appears to focus mainly on legislation and policy, whereas we considered it useful to complement such measures with those related to corporations.

To elaborate on the various levels of the hierarchy, a very elementary (level 1) target is for non-human animals to be acknowledged in existential terms. One does not need to go very far back in history to find locations where the existence of certain groups of human individuals and their needs was denied or ignored and therefore considered irrelevant for policymaking.[7] Likewise, the existence of non-human animals' needs is still ignored in several jurisdictions throughout the world. A rather self-evident indicator for this level would be the acknowledgement of both domesticated and wild animals' sentience in national legislation or policy as well as corporate social responsibility (CSR) policies, processes and reporting.

After the target of being acknowledged has been met, the next step up in the hierarchy (level 2) would be the satisfaction of basic needs. This goal is underpinned by welfarist views which approve of non-human animals being used for human purposes as long as the animals are treated "compassionately" and attempts are made to minimise their suffering. In the case of domesticated animals, an adequate level of welfare has been defined in the form of the widely spread five freedoms, which were originally developed by Britain's Farm Animal Welfare Council in 1965. These include freedom from thirst and hunger, discomfort, pain, fear and stress as well as the freedom to express natural behaviour. Since animal welfare has been deemed an acceptable goal in several Western countries, a variety of quantitative animal welfare indicators have already been developed (for an overview, see Sandøe et al. 2019). The extent to which firms in the animal industry publicly disclose information on their performance in this respect is assessed by the Business Benchmark on Farm Animal Welfare. In addition, there are also qualitative indicators developed by the API, which can be considered to measure progress towards

Table 29.1 Hierarchical approach to accounting for animal rights

	Domesticated animals	*Wild animals*
Level 4	**Advanced rights**	
	Goal: Abolishment of all use by humans	**Goal:** Sovereignty
	Measures of progress towards goal: 1. A ban on all the remaining uses of non-human animals for human purposes 2. Number of non-human animals used for food and as companions	**Measures of progress towards goal:** 1. Legislation granting sovereignty to wild animals 2. Share of land area dedicated mainly to non-human animals
Level 3	**Basic rights**	
	Goal: Right not to be made to suffer; right not to be killed by humans	**Goal:** Right not to be made to suffer; right not be killed purposefully by humans
	Measures of progress towards goal: 1. The establishment of dedicated animal rights body within government 2. Legislation granting citizenship to domesticated animals 3. A ban on: i) animal experiments that induce suffering and/or death of the animals ii) industrial farming and the raising of animals for their flesh iii) breeding certain species iv) animal fights v) cultural practices that induce suffering and/or death of animals 4. Number of animals used/killed in categories 3i–ii 5. Decrease in use of animal-originated foodstuffs in local and national government canteens, cafeterias and restaurants (e.g. in percentage terms) 6. Decrease in corporate use of animals (e.g. in kilograms) 7. Increase in corporate use of non-animal materials (e.g. number of animal-free products in portfolio; investments in R&D; number of patents)	**Measures of progress towards goal:** 1. The establishment of dedicated animal rights body within government 2. A ban on: i) fur farming ii) the use of wild animals in circuses iii) recreational hunting and fishing iv) keeping specific animal species in zoos* v) routine deforestation and other forms of habitat destruction vi) greenhouse gas emissions and other forms of pollution 3. Number of animals used/killed in categories 2i–iv 4. Biodiversity accounting indicators currently in use (e.g. IUCN Red List) 5. Decrease in corporate land use because of wild animals 6. Decrease in corporate activities affecting wild animals (e.g. use of palm oil which has a detrimental effect on the habitats of orangutans)
Level 2	**Basic needs**	
	Goal: Five freedoms (freedom from hunger, discomfort, pain, fear; freedom to express natural behaviour)	**Goal:** Freedom from excessive harm inflicted by humans
	Measures of progress towards goal: 1. Animal protection laws that prohibit causing animal suffering either by a deliberate act of cruelty or by a failure to act*	**Measures of progress towards goal:** 1. Animal protection laws that prohibit causing animal suffering either by a deliberate act of cruelty or by a failure to act*

(continued)

Table 29.1 Cont.

	Domesticated animals	*Wild animals*
	2. Rules and regulations pertaining to the welfare of (i) companion animals, (ii) working animals and (iii) animals used in science** 3. The establishment of a dedicated animal welfare body or bodies within government* 4. Business Benchmark on Farm Animal Welfare (BBFAW) 5. Animal welfare indicators currently in use	2. Rules and regulations pertaining to the welfare of captive wild animals (in zoos, circuses, etc.)** 3. Laws restricting land use because of possible harm to wild animals 4. The welfare needs of captive wild animals are recognised in corporate social responsibility policies, processes and reporting
Level 1	**Acknowledgement**	
	Goal: To be considered as individuals with interests relevant to policy-making **Measures of progress towards goal:** 1. Animal sentience is formally recognised in legislation and/or policy* 2. Animal sentience is recognised in corporate social responsibility policies, processes and reporting	**Goal:** To be considered as individuals with interests relevant to policy-making **Measures of progress towards goal:** 1. Animal sentience is formally recognised in legislation and/or policy* 2. Animal sentience is recognised in corporate social responsibility policies, processes and reporting.

* Indicator taken as such from Animal Protection Index (API).

** Indicator modified from an API indicator.

the goal of meeting non-human animals' basic needs. These include the existence of animal protection laws that prohibit causing animal suffering; the existence of rules and regulations pertaining to the welfare of companion animals, working animals and animals used in scientific experiments; as well as the existence of a dedicated animal welfare body within government.

As concerns wild animals, the welfarist goal related to satisfaction of basic needs translates in our framework to freedom from excessive harm inflicted by human beings. We suggest that appropriate measures for tracking progress towards this aim would include the same API indicator as for domesticated animals, namely, the existence of animal protection laws that prohibit causing animal suffering. Likewise, a pertinent API indicator is the existence of rules and regulations related to the welfare of wild animals kept in circuses, zoos or other institutionalised forms of captivity. Other suggested indicators include the existence of laws restricting land use on the grounds of possible harm inflicted on wild animals as well as the recognition of the basic needs of captive wild animals in CSR policies, processes and reporting.

The third-level target in our framework is the attainment of basic rights, in other words non-human animals' right not to be made to suffer and the right not to be killed by humans (Cochrane 2012). This target is remarkably more ambitious and radical than the welfarist goals that are gaining traction at least in several European countries. In the case of domestic animals, progress towards the attainment of basic rights could be measured by advances in legislation, such as the establishment of a dedicated animal rights body within government and the introduction of laws granting citizenship to such animals. Additional qualitative measures include laws banning animal experiments that induce suffering and/or the death of the animals; industrial farming and raising animals for their flesh; breeding species that suffer; and animal fights as well as cultural practices such as rituals that induce suffering and/or death of the animals. Quantitative indicators in turn could include estimates of the number of animals used or killed in each of the preceding activities. Alongside these, it might be informative to measure decreases in the use of animal-originated foodstuffs in government canteens and cafeterias. Corresponding indicators for companies could include decrease in the use of animal-derived materials, measured, for instance, in kilograms, or increase in the use of non-animal-derived materials (e.g. share of animal-free products in portfolio; investments in associated research and development activities as well as number of associated patents).

The basic rights of wild animals would include the same targets as for domesticated animals, namely, the right not to be made to suffer and the right not to be killed by humans. Likewise, a measure for the third-level goal would be the establishment of a dedicated animal rights body within government. Other qualitative indicators would include a ban on fur farming, the use of wild animals in circuses, recreational hunting and fishing, keeping of great apes and cetaceans in zoos; as well as forms of habitat destruction, greenhouse gas emissions and pollution. Quantitative indicators in turn would include estimating the number of non-human animals used or killed in each of the preceding activities. We also consider individual wild animal's right not to be killed by humans to cover the right not to become extinct. Therefore, we suggest that progress towards this right should be measured with biodiversity/extinction accounting indicators that have already developed, such as the Red List compiled and updated by the International Union for the Conservation of Species (IUCN). In terms of corporate indicators, possible examples include decrease in corporate land use because of potential harm inflicted on wild animals as well as decrease in corporate activities that affect wild animals. For instance, the logging associated with the sourcing of palm oil from Southeast Asia has been found to reduce the habitats of orangutans.

Finally, the highest level target in the framework is the achievement of advanced rights, derived from the deontological interpretation of animal rights which advocates the abolishment of all use of domesticated animals by human beings and all human interference with wild animals' lives. Since many forms of animal use have already been banned on a lower level of the hierarchy, all that remains to be banned on the highest level are some forms of using animals for food (e.g. free-range egg and dairy production) and as companions. Progress towards this goal can be measured by the number of chickens, cows and pets. For wild animals, advanced rights entail sovereignty granted through legislation. An example of a quantitative measure would be the share of land dedicated completely to these animals without fear of human infringement or invasion.

Conclusion

In this chapter, we have tried to tackle the question of how to account for animal rights. In doing so, we first reviewed literature in animal ethics, particularly the debate concerning the moral value of non-human animals and the political implications thereof. Based on these theoretical ideas, we then proposed a hierarchical framework that outlines a phased approach towards the attainment of animal rights, beginning from the acknowledgement of animal sentience, proceeding through basic needs and basic rights to advanced rights. We also suggested some qualitative and quantitative indicators that could be utilised to account for the progress. Some of the indicators were derived from the API and others were our own ideas.

A point briefly mentioned in the preceding section is worth emphasising, namely, the alignment of nature conservation targets and animal rights. Conserving large tracts of land from deforestation and other forms of destruction is beneficial for the diversity of both plant and animal species. It thus makes sense for ecological conservationists and animal rights proponents to join forces.

Few remaining questions are, "who would apply the framework developed in this chapter?" "Who would collect, compile and report the data, and to what effect?" "Which kind of institutional arrangements would be required to frame and support such activities?" Starting from existing entities, one obvious candidate to collect the data could be the group of non-governmental animal protection organisations that developed the API. At least the political and legislative indicators included in our framework would be compatible with the API's scope of measuring progress in nation states. As concerns the indicators related to corporate progress, in the first instance these could be picked up voluntarily by frontrunner companies from which they would diffuse to other organisations. It is noteworthy that some industries (e.g. production and pharmaceuticals) would be more implicated by this theme than others, and might not readily disclose their performance information. However, if voluntary action was considered insufficient, institutional arrangements could be put in place. Progressive governments could, for instance, stipulate the inclusion of such indicators in corporate reports. Moving from existing entities to those envisioned in the framework, data required to measure progress towards animal rights could also be compiled by animal welfare or animal rights bodies established within government. These bodies might also be tasked with the reconciliation of the conflicts of interest that are bound to arise between non-human animals and human beings as well as between different species of non-human animals. At some point time might also be ripe for a transnational animal rights body (Cochrane 2014), which could track global progress.

As a final thought, we acknowledge that sometimes well-intended attempts to account for those near and dear to us might paradoxically end up distancing them from us (Hines 1991). This is why the development of qualitative indicators alongside quantitative ones is of paramount importance.

Acknowledgements

A previous version of this chapter was presented at the Responsible Management (RESPMAN) research seminar, Tampere University, in December 2019. The authors gratefully acknowledge the comments received from the seminar participants. Markus Vinnari wishes to thank the Academy of Finland for supporting this research as part of a funded project on "Politics, practices and the transformative potential of sustainable diets (POPRASUS)", research grant 296702. Eija Vinnari wishes to thank the Academy of Finland for supporting this research as part of a funded project on "Constructing accountability in business–stakeholder relationships: the role of CSR communication", research grant 324215.

Notes

1 To put things into perspective, the biomass of farmed animals is already double the human biomass and 20 times the biomass of wild megafauna (Bar-On et al. 2018), and this development is expected to continue during the next decades.

2 Sometimes also referred to as "extinction accounting" (Cuckston 2018; Weir 2018)

3 For a discussion on critical dialogic accountability systems involving non-human constituents, see Dillard and Vinnari (2019).

4 Singer (1975) was also criticised by those who considered his work too radical and dangerous. However, reviewing such arguments is beyond the scope and space limitations of this chapter.
5 Donaldson and Kymlicka (2011) also consider a third group, liminal animals, with which they refer to rats, bats, city foxes and other wild animals that have voluntarily come to live among human beings. However, for the sake of simplicity, we have chosen not to place liminals in a separate category in our framework.
6 https://api.worldanimalprotection.org/
7 In some cultures, this can be still the case for women, certain societal classes (e.g. untouchables in India) or sexual minorities.

References

Aaltola, E., 2012. *Animal Suffering: Philosophy and Culture*. Basingstone: Palgrave MacMillan.

Allievi, F., Vinnari, M. and Luukkanen, J., 2015. Meat consumption and production-analysis of efficiency, sufficiency and consistency of global trends. *Journal of Cleaner Production*, 92 (1), 142–151.

Barnosky, A., 2008. Megafauna biomass tradeoff as a driver of quaternary and future extinctions. *PNAS*, 105 (suppl. 1), 11543–11548.

Bar-On, Y.M., Phillips, R. and Milo, R., 2018. The biomass distribution on Earth. *PNAS*, 115 (25), 6506–6511.

Cochrane, A., 2012. *Animal Rights without Liberation*. New York, NY: Columbia University Press.

Cochrane, A., 2014. *Sentientist Politics: A Theory of Global Inter-Species Justice*. Oxford: Oxford University Press.

Cawthorn, D. and Hoffman, L., 2014. The role of traditional and non-traditional meat animals in feeding a growing and evolving world. *Animal Frontiers*, 4 (4), 6–12.

Ceballos, G., Ehrlich, P.R. and Dirzo, R., 2017. Biological annihilation via the ongoing sixth mass extinction signaled by vertebrate population losses and declines. *PNAS*, 114 (30), E6089–E6096.

Cuckston T., 2018. Making extinction calculable. *Accounting, Auditing and Accountability Journal*, 31 (3), 849–874.

Dillard, J. and Vinnari, E., 2017. A case study of critique: Critical perspectives on critical accounting. *Critical Perspectives on Accounting*, 43, 88–109.

Dillard, J. and Vinnari, E., 2019. Critical dialogical accountability: From accounting-based accountability to accountability-based accounting. *Critical Perspectives on Accounting*, 62, 16–38.

Donaldson, S. and Kymlicka, W., 2011. *Zoopolis: A Political Theory of Animal Rights*. Oxford: Oxford University Press.

Francione, G., 1996. *Rain without Thunder: The Ideology of the Animal Rights Movement*. Philadelphia: Temple University Press.

Francione, G., 2010. The abolition of animal exploitation. In: G. Francione and R. Garner, eds. *The Animal Rights Debate. Abolition or Regulation?* New York, NY: Columbia University Press, pp. 1–103.

Gray, R., Bebbington, J. and Gray, S., eds., 2010. *Social and Environmental Accounting. Volume 1. Laying Foundations*. London: Sage.

Hines, R., 1991. On valuing nature. *Accounting, Auditing & Accountability Journal*, 4 (3), 27–29.

Jones, M., ed., 2014. *Accounting for Biodiversity*. London: Routledge.

Jones, M.J. and Solomon, J.F., 2013. Problematising accounting for biodiversity. *Accounting, Auditing & Accountability Journal*, 26 (5), 668–687.

Machovina, B., Feeley, K., and Ripple, W., 2015. Biodiversity conservation: The key is reducing meat consumption. *Science of the Total Environment*, 536, 419–431.

Maslow, A., 1954. *Motivation and Personality*. New York, NY: Harper.

McLaren, J. and Appleyard, T., 2019. Improving accountability for farm animal welfare: The performative role of a benchmark device. *Accounting, Auditing and Accountability Journal*. In press. https://doi.org/10.1108/AAAJ-06-2017-2955

Mepham, T. B., 2006. The ethical matrix as a decision-making tool with specific reference to animal sentience. In: J. Turner and J. D'Silva, eds. *Animals, Ethics and Trade*. London: Earthscan, pp. 134–145.

Rachels, J., 1990. *Created from Animals—The Moral Implications of Darwinism*. Oxford: Oxford University Press.

Ramanathan, K.V., 1976. Toward a theory of social accounting. *The Accounting Review*, 51 (3), 516–528.

Rimmel, G. and Jonäll, K., 2013. Biodiversity reporting in Sweden: Corporate disclosure and preparers' views. *Accounting, Auditing & Accountability Journal*, 26 (5), 746–778.

Ripple, W. J. et al., 2014. Status and ecological effects of the world's largest carnivores. *Science*, 343 (6167), 1241484.

Ripple, W.J. et al., 2015. Collapse of the world's largest herbivores. *Science Advances*, 1 (4), 1–12.

Sandøe, P. et al., 2019. Benchmarking farm animal welfare – Ethical considerations when developing a tool for cross-country comparison. In: E. Vinnari and M. Vinnari, M., eds. *Sustainable Governance and Management of the Food System: Ethical Perspectives*. Wageningen: Wageningen Academic Press.

Singer, P., 1975. *Animal Liberation: A New Ethics for Our Treatment of Animals*. London: HarperCollins.

Walters, K. and Portmess, L., 1999. *Ethical Vegetarianism - From Pythagoras to Peter Singer*. Albany, NY: State University of New York Press.

Weir, K., 2018. The purposes, promises and compromises of extinction accounting in the UK public sector. *Accounting, Auditing & Accountability Journal*, 31 (3), 875–899.

INDEX

Note: Page numbers in **bold** indicate tables, and in *italic* indicate figures.

abolitionism 390
Aboud, A. 309
Abrahamson, E. 36
Abt, C. 225, **226**
Abu Dhabi 307; Environmental Agency 307, 311n4; Securities Exchange (ADX) 307, 311, 311n5; Sustainability Group (ADSG) 307
Abumoghli, I. 302
Academy of Management 8
AccountAbility 133, 134n3; 1000 Assurance Standard (AA1000AS) 130, **131**, 134n3
accountability: Africa 265–272; Asia 276; biodiversity 379–382; carbon 358; environmental impact-valuation assemblages 237, 240; environmental reporting 112–113, 115, 119–120; externalities 231–232; foundations of environmental accounting 20–22, 24; future of environmental accounting 11–12; Middle East and North Africa 301, 305, 310; New Zealand 333; norm development in environmental reporting 144–145; Pacific region 329, 333; strategic environmental management accounting 185; sustainability governance 87; sustainability report assurance 128, 133; theorising environmental accounting and reporting 30; water 367, 370–373
Accountancy Europe (earlier Fédération des Experts Comptables Européens) 8, 69, 75
Accounting, Auditing and Accountability Journal 8, 18, **19**, 31, 266
Accounting for Sustainability Project (A4S) 69, 74–75
Accounting for Sustainable Forestry Management **227**
Accounting Forum 8
Accounting, Organizations and Society 8, 18
accounting profession: assurance services 119; championing of environmental accounting 7–8; ecological literacy of future accountants 8–11; foundations of environmental accounting 17–18, 20, 22; future of environmental accounting 23; Integrated Reporting (<IR>) initiative 116; norm development in environmental reporting 147; strategic environmental management accounting 185–186; sustainability report assurance 125, 128–132; thought leadership 65–75, 99; *see also* "Big Four" accountancy/professional service firms
accruals and deferred liabilities **226**
accuracy, environmental reporting **113**, 114
Ackers, B. 267
Acquier, A. 253
action research 34
actor network theory (ANT) 35
Adams, C. **19**, 32–33, 34, 39n4, 85
Adams, R. 18, 22, 69
Adivalor 258
administrative environmental controls 196
Aerts, W. 320
afforestation 270–271, 359
Africa 265–272, 366, 373; *see also* Middle East and North Africa; *specific countries*
agency theory 33, 195, 315
Aggeri, F. 360
Agostini, M. 292
Agyemang, G. 369
Ahmed, N. S. 305
Aichi Targets **379**, 379
"Aiming for A" Coalition 152, 160
Alawatage, C. 38

Algeria 302
Al Janadi, Y. 307
Alkababji, M. 305
Alliance of Water Stewardship 370
Alstine, J. V. 267
altruism 196
Amankwah-Amoah, J. 267
Amel-Zadeh, A. 172
American Accounting Association (AAA) 8, 95–96
American Institute of Certified Public Accountants 76n1
Ammar, S. 85
An, Y. 333
analysis, suitable objects of 11, 12
Andrew, J. 21
Ángel-Maya, A. 344
Animal Protection Index (API) 392, 394–396
animal rights 388–389, 395–396; accounting for progress towards 392–395, **393–394**; moral worth of non-human animals 390–391
animal welfare 388, 390, 392, 396
annual general meetings (AGMs) 151, 153, 155–160
annual reports 288–291, 319–320, 333
Antheaume, N. 230–231, 252, 257–259
Anthropocene 5, 7, 13, 23–24; biodiversity 383–384; sustainability governance 78–81, 87; water 365
Aotearoa New Zealand *see* New Zealand
Arab Spring 301, 305, 309
Araujo, J. 341
Archel, P. 31, 37, 144
Argentina 341, 343, 345–346
Arjaliès, D.-L. 34, 185
armed conflicts, Africa 265, 268
Ascui, F. 354
Asia 276–277, 284; corporate reporting rate 282; drivers of environmental reporting regulations 282, **283**; environmental reporting practice 109; quality of environmental reporting 283; *see also specific countries*
Asian Productivity Organisation 219
Asia Pacific Interdisciplinary Perspectives on Accounting (APIRA) 8
Association of Chartered Certified Accountants (ACCA): ecological literacy 9; environmental reporting awards 69, 146; Environmental Reporting Guidelines 281; foundations of environmental accounting 18; public interest remit 68; Singapore 280; size 76n1; thought leadership 69, 72, 75, 99
Association of International Certified Public Accountants (AICPA) 68, 72, 76n1
assurance, environmental reporting 119–120, 125–126; accounting profession and standards 130–132; Africa 267; Asia 284; carbon accounting 356; current practice and future development 133–134; financial markets 171; market and provider types 128–130; materiality assessment 132–133; norm development 146; North America 315, 321; overview *127*; rationales and purposes 126–128
Atkins, B. 50
Atkins, J. 50, 189
Attfield, R. 21
attributional detachment, environmental impact-valuation assemblages 241
audit 119–120; *see also* assurance, environmental reporting
Australia 328–332, 335; biodiversity 381–382; Clean Energy Regulator 219; corporate governance 85; environmental reporting practice 109; General Purpose Water Accounting System 370; National Greenhouse and Energy Reporting scheme 219; stakeholder engagement 37; water 369–371, 373

Bahrain 302, 308
Balakrishnan, R. 198
balance, environmental reporting **113**, 114
balanced scorecard 182, 188; eco-controls 197, 199–200; materials and energy accounting 212
Ball, A. 34, 39n2, 201
Banerjee, S. B. 183
Bangladesh 308, 381
Bansal, P. 183
Barrett, M. 21, 333
Battaglia, M. 186
Baxter, T. **229**
Beams, F. A. **226**
Bebbington, J. 5, 10, 13, **19**, 30, 32–34, 36–38, 39n3, 50, 66, 80–81, 87–88, 103–104, 137–138, 144–146, 210, **227**, **229**, 230–232, 244, 295, 332, 357–358, 380
Belhaj, M. 309
benchmarking 189
Bennett, M. 37–38
Benston, G. 98
Bent, D. 225, **229**
Berthelot, S. 168
Bhabha, H. 38
"Big Four" accountancy/professional service firms: relative size 67, **67**; sustainability report assurance 129, 133; thought leadership 67–72, 75; *see also* Deloitte; EY; KPMG; PwC
Bilan Carbon 360
biodiversity 377; Africa 265, 268–270; animal rights 388, 395; Asia 276; future directions 383–384; international governance and accountability frameworks 379–380; Middle East and North Africa 301–302, 307; nature, account of 377–379; North America 318; organisational level accounting for 380–383;

Pacific region 336; South America 339–340, 345; strategic goal for **379**; water 366
bioenergy 355
bioenergy with carbon capture and storage (BECCS) 359
biosphere stewardship 12, 24–25, 86–87
Blacconiere, W. G. 318
blood diamonds 208
Bloomberg 168
boards of directors: Middle East and North Africa 303, **303**, 307, 310; North America 319; Saudi Arabia 307; shareholder activism 151, 157, 159; sustainability governance 82, 84–85
Bodle, K. 331
Boiral, O. 116, 172
Bojo-Canales, C. 342
Boldrini, J. C. 252, 257–259
Bolthanski, L. 36
Bonacchi, M. 186
Boo, E. F. 132
Borglund, T. 293
Borneo 382
boundaries, environmental reporting 112–113
Bourdieu, P. 36
Bouslah, K. 321
Bouten, L. 33–34
BP 228; corporate governance 85; Deepwater Horizon disaster 85, 167, 316; financial markets 167; shareholder activism 160
Brander, M. 241
Braun, M. 357
Brazil: biodiversity 382; circular economy 257; research overview 341–344, 346; Samarco dam 370
Bristol-Meyers 188
British Accounting Review 8
Brown, D. A. 194, 197
Brown, J. 37–38, 333
Brundtland report 18, 208, 288
BS 8001 255
BSO/Origin 225, **227**, 228, 232
Buccina, S. 101
Buhovac, A. R. 200
Buhr, N. 31
Burns, J. 201
Burritt, R. L. 98, 217, 370
Bursa Malaysia (BM) 279, 281–282
Busco, C. 39, 182
Business and Biodiversity Offsetting Programme 380
Business & Society 266
Business Benchmark on Farm Animal Welfare (BBFAW) 388, 392

Cadez, S. 187
Callicott, J. 21
Callon, M. 239
Canada: biodiversity 382; environmental accounting research 315–317, 320–322; Environmental Protection Act (CEPA) **317**; financial accounting and reporting 99; regulatory environment **317**; shareholder activism 152; water 372
Canadian Institute of Chartered Accountants 99
capabilities approach 24
capital expenditure tools, environmental 188–189
capitalisation of costs 219–220, 222
Caputo, F. 182, 185
carbon accounting 353, 360–361; definitions 353–354; emergent directions for research 358–359; emergent directions for theoretical development 359–360; emissions trading schemes and emission rights 357–358; international climate governance 358; negative emissions technologies 359; research about 355–358; research doing 354–355; science-based target setting 359
carbon budgets 354
Carbon Dioxide Information Analysis Center (CDIAC) 302
carbon disclosure 355–356
Carbon Disclosure Project *see* CDP
carbon emissions: China 278, 283–284; environmental impact-valuation assemblages 241, 243–244; Europe 283; financial markets 168, 170–171; Hong Kong 284; Japan 283–284; Malaysia 284; Middle East and North Africa 301, **301**; narrative disclosures 168; Singapore 284; *see also* greenhouse gas emissions
carbon management 356–357
carbon taxes 231, 281, 357
Caribbean islands 322
Carlsson-Wall, M. 199
Carney, M. 165, 173
carriers (norm development) 143–144, **143**
carrying capacity of the Earth 210
Carson, R. xxi, 18
Cavanagh, J. **229**
CCLA Investment Management 160
CDP (formerly Carbon Disclosure Project) 114, 355–356; financial accounting and reporting 103; materials and energy accounting 221; shareholder activism 155, 160; sustainability governance 87
Center for Social and Environmental Accounting Research (CSEAR) 4, 8, 342; foundations of environmental accounting 18, **19**
Ceres Investor Network 152
certification bodies: biodiversity 380, 382; North America 321; sustainability report assurance 125, 133
Chaffin, B. C. 86–88
Chakroun, R. 309
Chan, C. C. 171

change, theory of 52, 63n7
Channuntapipat, C. 128, 132–133
Chapman, C. 29, 357–358
Chartered Institute of Management Accountants (CIMA) 72, 76n1
Chauvey, J. N. 292
Chelli, M. 189, 292
chemical industry 318, 320
Chevron 159–160
Chicago Climate Exchange 315
Chief Value Officers 185–186, 190
child labour 268–269, 271–272
China 277–278, 282–284, **283**, 358
Chipotle 153
Cho, C. 32, 316, 318, 320
Choi, F. D. 302
Christ, K. L. 217, 370
Christensen, H. B. 117, 119, 169
Chung, L. H. 183–184, 200
circular economy (CE) 251–252, 260; accounting for a 255–256; business models 253–254; case studies 256–260; history 252–253; indicators 255, **256**; limitations and future research 254; standards 255; transition, organising the 253
clarity, environmental reporting **113**
Clarkson, P. M. 170, 318
climate change: Africa 265, 270–271; Asia 276, 279, 282; carbon accounting 353–354, 356–61; denial 315; environmental impact-valuation assemblages 241, 243–244; externalities 228; financial accounting and reporting 101–103, **102**; financial markets 165, 170, 173–174, **173**; Japan 279; materials and energy accounting 207, 221–222; Middle East and North Africa 300, 302, 305, 308; North America 315–316; Pacific region 329, 334–336; shareholder activism 159–161; strategic environmental management accounting 182; water 366–367, **368**, 371, 373
climate governance 358, 360
closed-loop systems 252, 254
Clune, C. 36
Cochrane, A. 390–391
cognitive integration of sustainability into strategy 185–186
collaboration theory 32
Collison, D. 9
Colombia 341–344, 346
coloniality of power 340
coltan 208
Common Good Balance Sheet 88
comparability, environmental reporting **96**, **113**
Conferência Sulamericana de Contabilidade Ambiental (CSCS) 342
conflict minerals 208
Congo 382
consequential detachment, environmental impact-valuation assemblages 241–242
conservation 383–384, 396
constituent impact approach (social audit) 225, **226**
contingency theory 32–33
Contrafatto, M. 11, 34, 201
Convention on Biological Diversity 80
Cooper, S. 37
Corcoran, A. W. **226**
Cormier, D. 167, 320
Corporate Ecosystem Services Review 380
corporate governance: enlightened 83–85, **83–84**; Malaysia 281; Middle East and North Africa 303–304, **303**, 307, 310; North America 319; pristine 82–83, **83–84**; Saudi Arabia 307; shareholder activism 159; Singapore 280; sustainability governance 81–85, **83**, 87–89; sustainability report assurance 128; transformative **83–84**, 87–89
Corporate Knights 282
corporate social reporting *see* social accounting
corporate social responsibility (CSR): animal rights 392, 394; biodiversity 381; China 277, 282; Denmark 289; eco-controls 198; environmental reporting frameworks 116–117; Europe 290, 293; financial markets 169; foundations of environmental accounting 20; France 292; Malaysia 282; Middle East and North Africa 310–311; social contract theory 24; sustainability governance 81–83, 85–86
Corporate Social Responsibility and Environmental Management 266
corruption 265, 267–268, 301
Costa, E. 292
counter accounting 120, 268
cradle to cradle 252
Craig, R. 34, 333
creative representation of project 50–52, *51*
Criado-Jiménez, I. 292
Critical Perspectives on Accounting (CPA) 8, 266
Crown Estate 228, **229**
Crutzen, N. 190
Cuckston, T. 382
Cuellar, B. 170
cultural environmental controls 197, 200
cybernetic environmental controls 195
cyclones 271
Cziraki, P. 159

Damak-Ayadi, S. 309
Danone 184–185, 189, 221
Davies, J. 230
Davis, G. F. 154
decision-making: eco-controls 194–195; externalities 224–225, 232; materials and energy accounting 212, 222; product

footprinting 188; strategic environmental management accounting 184, 188; water accounting 370
decision usefulness theory 30–31
decolonialisation, South America 340–341
decommissioning costs 99, 101
Deegan, C. 9, 31
Deepwater Horizon disaster 85, 167, 316
deforestation: Africa 265, 268–271; animal rights 396; Middle East and North Africa 305; North America 315, 317; South America 345
de-industrialisation/plant closure audits 225
Dekker, C. **227**
De Lima Voss, B. 343
Deloitte: size 67, **67**; thought leadership 70–71, 73; *see also* "Big Four" accountancy/professional service firms
Democratic Republic of Congo (DRC) 268, 272
Denedo, M. 268
Denmark: biodiversity 381; environmental reporting 288–289, 293; green accounts 289; norm development in environmental reporting 139, **141**; Pollutant Release and Transfer Register (PRTR) 289
depth-hermeneutic framework 38–39
desertification 305, 309
De Villiers, C. 33, 319
Dey, C. 50, 382
Dhaliwal, D. S. 169
Diab, A. 309
dialogic theory 37
dialogue (shareholder activism) 153–155, 161
diamonds, blood 208
Dierkes, M. 98
Diouf, D. 116, 172
direct air capture and storage 359
discourse theory 32, 38–39, 315
divestment (shareholder activism) 154, 161–162
Djibouti 302
Dodds, S. 332
domain pre-study 49–50, 52; environmental impacts-valuations 237–238
Dominican Sisters of Caldwell 152
Dominion Energy 159
Donaire, D. 341
Donaldson, S. 391–392, 397n5
"doughnut economics" 231
droughts 366, **367**, 372–373; Africa 271; Australia 329
Dubai 307
Dugdale, D. 232
Duncan, R. 372
Durden, C. 200
Dutta, S. K. 184

East Africa 271
Eastern Europe 291, 294; *see also specific countries*
Eckstein, D. 271
eco-controls 194, 201–202; beyond organisational boundaries 197; multiple objectives 198–201; subsystems 198–199, *198*, *200*; types 194–197
eco-efficiency 252
ecological literacy 8–13
Eco-Management and Audit Scheme (EMAS) 142, 145, 197, 290–291, 296
economic theory 30–31, 315
ecosystem degradation/loss: Africa 265, 267–268; biodiversity 380–381; Middle East and North Africa 301–302, 308; water 366
Ecuador 345
Edwards, D. P. 265
Egan, M. 35, 36, 189, 369
Egypt 302, 308–310
Ehnert, I. 138
Eide, M. H. 354
Ekvall, T. 355
Elad, C. 382
Ellen McArthur Foundation (EMF) 251
Ellili, N. 307
Elmogla, M. 309
Elsayed, N. 85
emissions *see* carbon emissions; greenhouse gas emissions
emissions rights 101–103, **102**, 358
emissions trading schemes (ETSs) 357–358; European Union 102, 219, 357
energy: categories of 211; consumption 277, 280–281, 289; efficiency 271; management systems 214; *see also* materials and energy accounting
entrepreneurs, institutional (norm development) 143–144, **143**, *146*
environmental accounting: foundations 3–4, 17–25, 69; future 11–13, 23–25; privileges and biases 4; problem arena 5–7; processes 32–33; regulation *see* regulation of environmental accounting and reporting; resources and retrospectives **19**; role in organisational level change 33–35; stakeholder engagement 37–38; strategic environmental management accounting 182, 189–190
Environmental and Sustainability Management Accounting Network (EMAN) 8
environmental capital expenditure tools 188–189
environmental committees 84–85
environmental consultancy firms 125, 133
environmental ethics 21
environmental exchange report **226**
environmental governance 319
environmental impact-valuation assemblages 236–237, 247–248; appropriable techniques **238**; assembling 238–239; detachment choices

240–243; extraction and appropriation 246–247; manipulation and transformation 243–246; pre-study 237–238; wrong choices 239–240
environmental management accounting (EMA) 207–212, 222; *see also* materials and energy accounting
environmental management systems (EMS) 183–184
environmental officers 84–85
environmental performance indicators (EPIs) 195, 197, 199
environmental planning controls 194
environmental reporting 108–109, 120–121; assurance 119–120, 125–134; background to current practice 109–110; characteristics 112–114, **113**; counter accounting 120; emergence 30; externalities 224; field-level change 35–36; forms 110–112; frameworks 114–119, **114**; integrated 110–112, 114–118; language, role of 38–39; norms *see* norms in environmental reporting; processes 32–33; reasons for 30–32; regulation *see* regulation of environmental accounting and reporting; social media 111, 117–118; stakeholder engagement 37–38; stand-alone 110–112, 114–118; talk vs action 118–119; web-based disclosure 111, 117–118
Environmental Reporting Awards (ACCA) 69, 146
environmental reward and compensation controls 195–196
environmental rights 269
Environmental, Social and Governance Reporting Guide (ESG Guide) 278–279
epistemic communities (norm development) 143, **143**
Epstein, M. J. 6, 184, 188, 200
Equator Principles 144–145
Ernst and Young *see* EY
Escobar, A. 344
Estes, R. **226**, 228
Ethiopia 271
Europe 288, 296–297; effects of mandatory reporting 292–293; future research 294–296; mandated environmental disclosures 288–290; regulatory processes 293–294; response to mandatory reporting 291–292; shareholder activism 152, 159–161; water 373; *see also* European Union; *specific countries*
European Accounting Review 8
European Pollutant Release and Transfer Register (E-PRTR) 291, 296
European Union (EU): climate-related disclosures 174; Eco-Management and Audit Scheme (EMAS) 142, 145, 197, 290–291, 296; Emissions Trading Scheme (ETS) 102, 219, 357; externalities 232; Fifth Action Programme 232; foundations of environmental accounting 18; initiatives in environmental accounting and reporting 290–291; mandated environmental disclosures 289; norm development in environmental reporting 139, **140**, 143, 145, 147; Reach chemicals regulations 212; regulatory processes 293–297; shareholder activism 159; sustainability governance 80, 82; Sustainable Finance Initiative 172; *see also specific countries*
Evans, S. 331
executional cost management 187
external accounting (counter accounting) 120, 268
externalities 224–225, 232–233; decision-making 224–225, 232; environmental impact-valuation assemblages 244; experimentation history 225–30, **226–227**, **229**, *230*; limits of financial accounting and reporting 98; monetisation issues 230–231; strategic environmental cost management 187
extinctions: Africa 268–270; animal rights 388, 395; biosphere integrity 79
extractive industries *see* mining and extractive industries
Extractive Industries and Society, The 266
extractivism 339, 345–346
extrinsic motivation 195–196, **195**, 201
ExxonMobil 151, 156–161
Exxon Valdez disaster 316
EY: size **67**; thought leadership 71; *see also* "Big Four" accountancy/professional service firms

faithful information (IASB Conceptual Framework) **96**
Farneti, F. 331
Farooq, M. 33
Faure, E. 228–229
Fédération des Experts Comptables Européens (FEE, later Accountancy Europe) 8
Fédération Internationale de l'Automobile 232
Feger, C. 382
Ferguson, A. 129
Ferguson, J. 11, 38–39
Fernando, S. 38
Ferreira, A. C. de S. 341
Fertig, P. E. **226**
field-level change in environmental reporting, theorising 35–36
field theory 34
Fiji 333–334
Fiji Sugar Corporation 333
financial accounting and reporting 95, 103–104; audit 119–120; environmental disclosure 99–101, **100**, 168; focus and purpose 95–98; integrated reports 110–112, 114–118; key financial statements **97**; limits 98; materials and

energy accounting 219, 222; novel issues 101–103; regulatory frameworks 109
Financial Accounting Standard Board (FASB) 99, 219
financial markets 165–166, 174–175; characteristics of environmental disclosures 167–170; effects and use of environmental information 170–171; experimental research and survey studies 171–172; North America 318; recent institutional developments 172–174; theoretical views 166–167
Financial Reporting Council (FRC) 96
Financial Stability Board 173
Finau, G. 333
Finland 288, 290, 369
fires 329
floods 365, **367**, 371–373
Folke, C. 12, 81, 86, 88
Food and Agriculture Organization **367**
food system 79–80, 271
forced labour 268–269, 271–272
forest environmental certification 321
Forest Stewardship Council 380, 382
Forum for the Future **229**
Frame, B. **229**
France: *Bilan Carbon* 360; carbon emissions 283; circular economy 257–260, *258*; Corporate Duty of Vigilance Law 80; environmental reporting practice 109, 288–289, 291–295; financial accounting and reporting 101; Grenelle II regulation 289, 292; horticultural farming 257–260, *258*; New Economic Regulations (NER) 288–289, 292; norm development in environmental reporting 139, **140**; social accounting 6; strategic environmental management accounting 185
Francione, G. 390–391
Fraser, M. **229**, 232
Freedman, M. 320
Freire, P. 10, 37
Fronti, L. 341
Fukukawa, K. 279
full cost accounting 34, 187–188, 381; *see also* externalities
Funck, E. K. 256
Future Fit 49
Futures 266

Gallhofer, S. 39n5, 333
García-Sánchez, I.-M. 129
Garcia-Torea, N. 295
Gardiner, S. 21
Gasparatos, A. 230
Gendron, Y. 189
Georg, S. 35
Georgakopoulos, G. 50
Gerged, A. 310
Germany: biodiversity 381; carbon emissions 283; environmental reporting 293–295; Green Party (Die Grünen) 18; social accounting 6
Gerten, D. 79
Ghana 266–268; child labour 272; Sustainable Development Goals 269; water 270, 369
Gibassier, D. 357
Gibson, K. 330
Gindis, D. 11
Gish, E. 151
globalisation 7
Global Reporting Initiative (GRI) 6–7, 114–119, **114**, **142**; Australia 331; biodiversity 381; Colombia 346n7; financial markets 174; foundations of environmental accounting 22; France 292; materials and energy accounting 219–221; Middle East and North Africa 306–307, 311, 311n5; norm development in environmental reporting 138, 142, 144–145, 147; Saudi Arabia 306–307; Sweden 290; United Arab Emirates 311n5; water 370
global warming *see* climate change
Goffman, E. 37
Gómez-Villegas, M. 345
Goncalves, A. 302
Gond, J. P. 181–182, 185–186
Goranova, M. 151
governance: African countries 265–271; biodiversity 379–382; climate 358, 360; environmental 319; North African countries 309; water 369–370, 373; *see also* corporate governance; sustainability governance
governmentality theory 35
governments, and norm development in environmental reporting 138–139, **143**, 144, 147
Gramsci, A. 32
Gray, R. 3–4, 6–7, 9, 11, 17–18, **19**, 19–23, 30–34, 39, 69, 95, **227**, 232, 342, 345
Gray, S. **19**
Green, W. 356
greenhouse gas emissions: Africa 270; Asia 276, 278, 280–281; environmental impact-valuation assemblages 243; EU Emissions Trading System 102, 219, 357; financial markets 168, 170–171; Hong Kong 278; ISO 14064 214; Japan 280; materials and energy accounting 214, 219–221; narrative disclosures 168; Singapore 280–281; UK 289; *see also* carbon accounting; carbon emissions
Greenhouse Gas Protocol **142**; materials and energy accounting 219, 221
Greenland 316, 322
greenwashing 109, 118, 222; North America 315, 319
Greer, S. 331
Gudynas, E. 344

Guenther, E. 353
Guidry, R. P. 169
Guilding, C. 187
Gulf Cooperation Council (GCC) 302–303, 306–308
Guthrie, J. 4, 17, **19**, 31, 331, 356, 360

Haas, W. 251
Habbash, M. 307
Habermas, J. 32, 37
Hackston, D. 332
Hahn, R. 355
Hail, L. 117
Hamman, R. 267
Hannis, M. 382
Harmann, F. 184
Hazelton, J. 34–35, 369
heatwaves 329, 366
Heflin, F. 167
hegemony theory 38
Henri, J. F. 182, 187, 201
Herbohn, K. 230
Higgins, C. 33, 172, 331
higher education institutions, Africa 271
Hines, R. D. 98, 371–372
Hoezée, S. 33–34
Holm, C. 171
Hong Kong 277–279, 282, **283**, 284
Hong Kong Exchanges and Clearing Limited (HKEX) 278–279, 282
Hopwood, A. G. 82
Huizing, A. **227**
human rights: Africa 265–269; Middle East and North Africa 300; South America 345
Humphrey, C. 35
hybrid organisations, eco-controls 199–201, *200*
hydraulic fracturing 156–158, **157**
hydro-electricity dams 372

Iacovidou, E. 255
Iceland 291
ideal speech situation 37–38
impact pathways 225
impression management *see* greenwashing
Imtiaz Ferdous, M. 33
India 318
Indigenous peoples: Africa 269; North America 317; Pacific region 328–333, 335; South America 339, 345–346
Indonesia 126
industrial ecology 252, 254
industrial ecoparks 254
industrial metabolism 252
informal controls, strategic environmental management accounting 187
innovation: eco-controls 198; strategic environmental management accounting 184–185
Institute of Chartered Accountants in England and Wales (ICAEW): ecological literacy 9; public interest remit 68, 73; size 76n1; thought leadership 72–74, 76n2, 99
Institute of Chartered Accountants of India (ICAI) 72, 76n1
Institute of Social and Ethical Accountability **142**
institutional entrepreneurs (norm development) 143–144, **143**, *146*
institutional investors 151–152
institutional theory 32–34, 334, 373
instrumental stakeholder theory 32
Integrated Reporting (<IR>) 114–119, **114**; externalities 228; financial markets 172
integrated reports 110–112, 114–118; Africa 266–267; assurance 133; materials and energy accounting 219; theorising 35–36
integration of sustainability into strategy 185–186
Interdisciplinary Perspectives on Accounting (IPA) 8
Interface Europe 225
Interfaith Center on Corporate Responsibility 152
intergenerational equity 190, 269
Intergovernmental Panel on Climate Change (IPCC) 18, 354, 358
International Accounting Standards (IAS) **100**, **102**
International Accounting Standards Board (IASB): Conceptual Framework 96–98, **96**, 101, 103; emissions rights 102; materials and energy accounting 219; norm development in environmental reporting 138, 142; reporting entity defined 96–97
International Auditing and Assurance Standards Board (IAASB) 133, 134nn1–2
International Federation of Accountants (IFAC): Chief Value Officers 190; IAASB 134n2; public interest remit 68
International Financial Reporting Interpretation Committee: IFRIC 3 (Emissions rights) 102–103, **102**
International Financial Reporting Standards (IFRS) **100**, 295; Canada 322; Colombia 344; financial markets' response to adoption of 170
International Geosphere-Biosphere Programme 18
International Integrated Reporting Council (IIRC) 111, **142**; Chief Value Officers 190; Integrated Reporting *see* Integrated Reporting (<IR>) ; materials and energy accounting 221; merger plans with the SASB 121n3
International Organization for Standardization (ISO) 214; ISO 14001 188, 197, 280–281; ISO 14051 207–208, 214, 217–218; ISO 14052

208, 214; ISO 14064 214; ISO 15051 210; ISO 26000 **142**; ISO 50001 214
International Standard on Assurance Engagement 3000 (ISAE3000) 130, **131**, 134nn1–2
International Union for the Conservation of Species (IUCN), Red List 395
intragenerational equity 269
intrinsic motivation 195–196, **195**, 201
Iran 308
Iraq 302, 308
Ireland 369
Islam, M. 32
isocycling 258, 261n3
Israel 126, 305
Italy 291–292, 294; water 369, 371

Jackson, G. 293
Jacob, K. 88
Jacobs, K. 36, 331
Jadam, J. 305
Japan 277, 279–280, 282–284, **283**; Integrated Reporting (<IR>) initiative 116; water 373
Japan Business Federation (Keidanren) 279
Jensen, J. S. 88
Jensen, M. C. 82–83, 85
Johannesburg Stock Exchange 267
Johnston, D. 321
Johnstone, L. 182, 189–190
Jollands, S. 369
Jones, C. 232
Jones, M. J. 126, 128
Jordan 302–304, 308, 310
Jordan Environment Society 304
Jordanian Climate Change & Environmental Protection Society 304
Jouffray, J.-B. 87
Journal of Business Ethics 11–12, 266
Journal of Cleaner Production 266
journals 46, 54
Journeault, M. 198–199, 201
Justesen, L. 35
justice 80

Kaplan, R. S. 197
Kaur, A. 37
Kazakhstan 126
Kenya 269
key performance indicators (KPIs) 199
Khalid, S. 268
Khan, T. 382
Kinderman, D. 293, 295
King, B. G. 154
King, L. 151
King, M. 190
Kirchherr, J. 251, 253
Kirkland Forest Products **227**
Kokubu, K. 279
KPMG: Middle East and North Africa 300; size 67, **67** surveys of environmental reporting practices 121n1, 126, 128, 132, 142; sustainability report assurance 126, 132; thought leadership 70–72; true value methodology 228; *see also* "Big Four" accountancy/professional service firms
Kuala Lumpur Stock Exchange (Bursa Malaysia, BM) 279, 281–282
Kuwait 302, 306
Kymlicka, W. 391–392, 397n5
Kyoto Protocol: carbon accounting 360; GHG Protocol 221; Japan 277, 279

Labelle, R. 169–170
Laclau, E. 32, 38
Lade, S. J. 79
Laine, M. 11, 36, 38
Landcare Research, Manaaki Whenua 34, 225, **227**
land rights 269
Land Use Policy 266
Larrinaga, C. 11, 13, **19**, 30, 34, 81, 87, 146, 210, 230–231, 292, 359, 380
Larrinaga-Gonzalez, C. 33, 358
Latan, H. 183
Latin America *see* South America
Laughlin, R. 4, **19**, 33–34
Lauwo, S. 268
Lave, C. 47
Lebanon 302, 305
Le Breton, M. 360
Lee, K. H. 330
Leff, E. 344
legitimacy theory 31–33; carbon accounting 356; financial markets 166–167; North America 315, 319–320, 322; Pacific region 331, 333–334; South America 344
Lehman, C. 20
Lehman, G. 30
Leininger, W. E. Jr **226**
Leone, E. L. 182, 184, 187–188, 190
Leong, S. 34–35
Leopold, A. xxi, 21
Leuz, C. 117
Levant countries 302–305
levers of control (LOC) framework 34
Levin, K. 23
Levy, D. L. 144
Lewin, K. 34
Libya 302, 309
Lichtenstein 291
Liesen, A. 171
LIFE® Certification programme 382
life cycle assessment (LCA) 188: carbon accounting 354–355; circular economy 255, 259–260; externalities 225

limits-to-growth debates 252
Lindblom, C. 31
Liu, Z. 354
Locke, J. 35
locusts 271
Lodhia, S. 36–37, 333–334
Logsdon, J. 155
Lonca, G. 257
loose coupling theory 33
L'Oréal 182
Lovell, H. 354
Low, K.-Y. 132
Luque-Vílchez, M. 146, 292

Macaulay 225
Magnan, M. 167
mainstream investors, shareholder activism 152–153, 161
Mäkelä, H. 115
Malawi 271
Malaysia 277, 280–284, **283**, 308; sustainability report assurance 126
Malaysian Accounting Standard Board (MASB) 281
Malaysian Code on Corporate Governance (MCCG) 281
Malmi, T. 194, 197
Manaaki Whenua/Landcare Research 225, **227**
management accounting: biodiversity 381; carbon 356–357; circular economy 256–257; eco-controls 202; strategic 181–182; water 371; *see also* strategic environmental management accounting
Management Accounting Research 34
Mansell, S. 11
Māori people 333
March, J. 47
marine biodiversity 380
Marine Policy 266
Marine Stewardship Council 380
Martin, P. R. 171
Martínez, M. R. 344
Martínez-Ferrero, J. 129
Martínez-Pulido, V. A. 345
Maslow, A. 392
Mataira, K. 333
material flow analysis 225
material flow cost accounting (MFCA) 208, 214, 217–218
materiality, environmental reporting 112–113, 119; assurance 132–133; financial markets 174; Global Reporting Initiative 115; Sustainability Accounting Standards Board 117
materials, categories of 210–211
materials and energy accounting 207–208; challenges and opportunities 221–222; external 218–221; framework 208–210, *209*; managers' requirements 214, **215–217**; material flow cost accounting 208, 214, 217–218; purpose 211–214; tools **213**, 214; types/categories of materials and energy 210–211
Mathews, M. R. **19**, 69
Matoussi, H. 309
Matthews, R. 4, 17
Maunders, K. 4, 17, **19**, 98
Mauritania 302
McNicholas, P. 21, 34, 333
McPhail, K. 359–360
Medawar, C. 120
media 320
Medley, P. 69
Meek, G. K. 302
Mermet, L. 382
methodising 46–47, **47**, 62; building method bundles 53–55, **54**; creative representation of project 50–52, *51*; example of method bundle, pathways and contingencies 57–62, *58*, **59–61**; multi-perspective bundle evaluation 55–57, **55–56**; pre-study of domain 49–50; purpose and imagination 47–49, *49*; reasons for 47; scoping process 52, **53**; summary sheet 55–57, **55–56**; useful research method texts 64
Mexico 315–316, 322, 343
Michelon, G. 32, 159
Middle East and North Africa (MENA) 300–302, 309–311; demographical, economic and environmental characteristics **301**; environmental challenges 302; Gulf Cooperation Council countries 306–308; Levant countries 303–305; North Africa (Arab countries) 308–309; research trends 302–303, **303**; *see also specific countries*
Millennium Development Goals 334, 366
Miller, P. 104, 357, 383
Millington, A. 126
Milne, M. J. 38, 171, 201, 332
minerals: Africa 265, 269, 271–272; Australia 331; conflict 208; materials and energy accounting 208
mine-safety performance 169
mining and extractive industries 208: Africa 267–272; biodiversity 379, 381; Pacific region 330; *see also* mining
Mir, M. Z. 186
mission statements 197
Modernity/Coloniality collective 346n2
modern slavery 268–269, 271–272
Moerman, L. 334
Moneva, J. M. 170
Monarch butterfly migration 316
monetisation: externalities 225, 230–231; water management 371
Moon, J. 279
Moore, D. R. J. 34, 359–360

Moraga, G. 255
Morocco 302
Mörth, U. 142
Moser, D. V. 171
motivational psychology 195, 201
Mouffe, C. 32, 38
Mozambique 271
multinational corporations (MNCs): Africa 265–268, 271; Asia 276, 280–281; sustainability governance 81–82; water management 370
Mundle, L. 370
Mundy, J. 34, 185

narrative environmental disclosures 168–169
Naser, K. 308
Natural Capital Coalition 72–73
Natural Value Initiative 380
negative emissions technologies (NETs) 359
Neimark, M. 20
neo-classical economics: externalities 230; financial markets 166, 170; limits of financial accounting 98
neo-institutional theory 33–37
Netherlands 116, 289
Neu, D. 31
New Zealand 328–330, 332–333, 335; Business Council for Sustainable Development 332; externalities experimentation 228; language in environmental reporting 38; water 372
Nigeria: child labour 272; erosion 271; literature review 266, 268; sustainability report assurance 126; Sustainable Development Goals 269; water 270
Nobanee, H. 307
Nordic countries 291; *see also specific countries*
norms in environmental reporting 36, 137–139; authority 144–145; dynamics 145–146, *146*; future 146–147; hard and soft law 139–143; main standards **142**; state and non-state actors 143–144, **143**
Norris, G. 184, 187, 199
North Africa *see* Middle East and North Africa
North America: decision usefulness theory 31; environmental accounting research 315–322; foundations of environmental accounting 22; regulatory environment **317**; water 373; *see also specific countries*
Norway 288, 291
nuclear power plants, decommissioning costs 99
Nussbaum, M. 24

ocean acidification 336
O'Donovan, G. 330–331
O'Dwyer, B. 31–32, 35–36, 66, 144, 184, 187, 199
oil and gas industry: corporate governance 85; decommissioning costs 99; financial markets 167, 170; litigation costs 101; Middle East and North Africa 301–302, 305–310; Nigeria 268; North America 316–318, 320; oil spill disasters 85, 167, 316; shareholder activism 156–158, 160–161
Olam 185
Oman 302, 308
One Planet Economies 241
Ontario Hydro 225, **227**
Organisation for Economic Co-operation and Development (OECD) 301
organisations: biodiversity 380–383; change, theorising the role of environmental accounting in 33–35; integration of sustainability into strategy 185; norm development in environmental reporting 143–144, **143**; water management 370–371
Organization of Petroleum Exporting Countries (OPEC) 301, 308
Origin/BSO 225, **227**, 228, 232
Orsted 185
O'Sullivan, A. 301
O'Sullivan, N. 32, 35, 144
Österblom, H. 80–81, 86
Otusanya, O. J. 268
Owen, D. 4, 17, **19**, 22, 37, 289
Oxfam 271; Donut 49

Pacific region 18, 328–336; *see also specific countries*
Pahlen, R. 341
Palestine 302, 305
Palestine Exchange (PEX) 305
palm oil 395
Papua New Guinea 329
Paris Agreement: Africa 270; carbon accounting 356, 358–360, 361n2; financial markets 165, 172; PwC's work 72; water 366
Parker, L. D. 4, 17, **19**, 31, 183–184, 187, 200, 356, 360
Parmar, B. L. 196
Pasternak, A. 11
Patagonia 186
Patel, C. 331
Patten, D. M. 22, 31, 169, 171, 316, 318–320
Pauliuk, S. 255
Peirce, C. 57
Perego, P. 184
Perera-Aldama, L. 343
Perey, R. 253
Perkiss, S. 334
Peru 343
Peters, G. F. 169, 319, 321
Phiri, O. 268
planetary boundaries 7; environmental impact-valuation assemblages 241; environmental management accounting 208, 210–212, 222; foundations of environmental accounting

23–24; methodising 49; strategic environmental management accounting 190; sustainability governance 78–79, 85–87
planned behaviour theory 39n2
plant closure audits 225
Plumlee, M. 170
Pogutz, S. 210
political economy theory 31
pollinator decline 316
polluter pays principle 231
pollution: Africa 267–270; biodiversity 379; China 277–278; control and abatement 168; Europe 291; Japan 279; Mexico 315; Middle East and North Africa 301–302, 305, 308–309; North America 315, 317–318, 321
Pondeville, S. 186
Portugal 288
post-colonialism 38, 340
post-normal science 231, 239
poverty: Africa 265–266, 268–271; Middle East and North Africa 310
Power, D. 128
Power, M. 104, 357, 383
Preston, L. E. 98
pre-study of domain 49–50, 52; environmental impacts-valuations 237–238
Price, R. A. 308
Prieto-Sandoval, V. 253
Procter & Gamble (P&G) 182, 186–187
product footprinting 188
product life cycle assessment 188
product-service systems 252
Product Sustainability Assessment Tool 188
professional accounting and research partners 7–8
professional accounting bodies: public interest remit 68–69, 73; thought leadership 68–70, 72–75
proposals for discussion (shareholder activism) 153–154
prudent information (IASB Conceptual Framework) 96
pulp and paper industry 317–318
PUMA 228, **229**, 232
Pündrich, G. 129
Puroila, J. 115
PwC: externalities 228, **229**; size **67**; thought leadership 72; *Total Impact Measurement and Management* tool 228; *see also* "Big Four" accountancy/professional service firms

Qatar 302, 308
Qian, W. 33
quality of life 300–301
Quattrone, P. 182
Quinn, M. 369
quotas 231

Rahaman, A. S. 32, 186
Rahman, S. A. B. A. 280
Ranciere, J. 38
ratings/rankings 189
Rawls, J. **20**, 186
Raworth, K. 79, 231
recycling *see* circular economy
Red List, International Union for the Conservation of Species 395
Reducing Emissions from Deforestation and Forest Degradation (REDD) programme 270, 382
Regan, T. 390–391
regenerative design 252
regime theory 32
Regional Fisheries Management Organisations 380
regulation of environmental accounting and reporting 119, 137–139; animal rights 394–395; Asia 277–82, **283**, 284; authority 144–145; biodiversity 379–380, 382; carbon accounting 356; Europe 139, **140–141**, 288–294; financial markets 169, 174–175; future 146–147; hard and soft law 139–143; main standards **142**; materials and energy accounting 219; Middle East and North Africa 304–310; norm development in environmental reporting 143–144, **143**; North America 316, **317**, 318–322; Pacific region 329–331, 335; state and non-state actors 143–144, **143**; water 369–372
relevant information (IASB Conceptual Framework) **96**, 101
reliability, environmental reporting **113**; Global Reporting Initiative 116
religious issues 151–152, 154, 321
Renaud, A. 184–185
Renneboog, L. 159
reputation: eco-controls 198, 201; environmental reporting 118; financial accounting and reporting 101; North America 319; risk management 32; sustainability governance 85; sustainability report assurance 129
research and development (R&D) 321
Resilience Alliance 242
resilience assessment framework 57–59, *58*, **59–61**
Resource Policy 266
Riccaboni, A. 182, 184, 187–188, 190
Rikhardsson, P. 171
Rinaldi, L. 35, 81, 186
rivers and catchments 372
Rivière-Giordano, G. 171
Roberts, R. 22, 31
Rockström, J. 7, 78–79, 210
Rodrigue, M. 32, 34, 85, 159, 186, 319
Rodríguez, D. 344
Rogelj, J. 354

Rolston, H. 21
Romi, A. M. 169, 319, 321
Roth, K. 183
Rowbottom, N. 35
Roy, M. 184
Royal Dutch Shell 37, 160
Rubenstein, D. B. 225, **227**, 232
Rueda, G. 344
Rupley, K. H. 319
Russell, S. **19**, 36, 50, 380, 382
Ryan, L. V. 151

safe operating space 79–82, 85–86, 88
Saidani, M. 255
Sakmar, S. L. 302
Samkin, G. 332
Sánchez, A. 344
Sandbrook, C. 383
Sandel, S. 21
Sassanelli, C. 255
Saudi Arabia 302, 306–308, 310
Schaltegger, S. 11, 189, 210, 356–357
Schneider, T. E. 168
Science-Based Targets Initiative 13; carbon 359; water 367
scoping process 52, **53**
SeaBOS 50, 86
seafood production industry 86
sea levels, rising 329, 334
Searchinger, T. 355
Securities and Exchange Commission (SEC) 320–321: financial accounting and reporting 99; financial markets and environmental information 169; shareholder activism 155, 157, 160–161
Seidler, L. J. **226**
self-determination theory 195–196, **195**
Sen, A. 24
Sendai Framework for Disaster Risk Reduction 366
Serafeim, G. 172
Shanghai Stock Exchange (SSE) 277, 282
shareholder activism 151, 161–162; actors 152–153; examples 155–161; history 151–152; outcomes 155; tactics 153–154
shareholder value: eco-controls 199, 201; sustainability governance 83, 85–86, 88
Sharma, U. 333–334
Shell 37, 160
Shenzhen Stock Exchange (SZSE) 277, 282
Simmonds, K. 181
Simnett, R. 130
Simons, R. 182
Singapore 277, 280–284, **283**; sustainability report assurance 126
Singapore Exchange (SGX) 279–282
Singer, P. 390–391, 397n4
Slack, R. 172
slavery, modern 268–269, 271–272
small and medium-sized enterprises (SMEs): Africa 267; Denmark 289
Small Islands Developing States (SIDS), Pacific 328, 330, 333–334
SMART project 257–260
Sobkwiak, M. 239
social accounting 6; debates 17; resources and retrospectives **19**
Social Accounting Monitor 4
Social and Environmental Accountability Journal 4, 8, **19**
social and political theory 30–31
social audit 225, **226**
Social Balance Sheet 343
social contract theory 30; animal rights 389; foundations of environmental accounting 20; future of environmental accounting 24
social dimensions of environmental change 6–7
social income statement **226**
socially responsible investment (SRI) firms 152–153
social media environmental reports 111, 117–118
social movement theory 32, 36; shareholder activism 154
Social Responsibility Journal 266
socio-ecological systems 7, *242*
socio-ideological control 197
sociology of worth framework 36
sociopolitical theory 167
soil degradation: China 277; Middle East and North Africa 305, 308–309
Solomon, J. F. 37, 126, 128
Solovida, G. T. 183
Solvay 182
South Africa 266–268; corporate governance 85; Integrated Reporting (<IR>) initiative 116; sustainability reporting 271
South America 322, 339–340, 346; decolonising development 340–341; environmental reporting practice 109; research overview 341–344; socio-environmental conflicts 345–346; *see also specific countries*
Southeast Asia 395
Spain 288, 290–293, 295; norm development in environmental reporting 36, 138–139, **141**, 144, 146; social accounting 6; stakeholder engagement 37
special interest groups, shareholder activism 152, 161
Spence, C. 32, 35, 38
Sri Lanka 184
Stahel, W. 252

stakeholder engagement: social media environmental reports 111; sustainability report assurance 129; theorising 37–38; web-based environmental reports 111
stakeholder inclusiveness, environmental reporting **113**
stakeholder interactions, strategic environmental management accounting 186–187
stakeholder theory 31–32; carbon accounting 356; foundations of environmental accounting 20; North America 315; Pacific region 334; shareholder activism 154; sustainability governance 82; water 373
stand-alone environmental reports 110–112, 114–118; Europe 289–290
Standard & Poor's EGX ESG index 309, 311
Statement of Financial Performance **97**
Statement of Financial Position **97**
Stechemesser, K. 353
Steffen, W. 80
Stevenson, L. 380
stewardship: biodiversity 381; future of environmental accounting 12, 24–25; materials and energy accounting 218; water 370
storm surges 366
strategic environmental cost management 187
strategic environmental management accounting (SEMA) 181–183, 190, 194; environmental accountant as strategic business partner for the environment 189–190; key questions 183–185; links to environmental strategy 185–187; tools 187–189
strategic management accounting (SMA) 181–182
strategy, emergence and implementation of 183–184
strategy maps 199
structural cost management 187
structuration theory 31–32, 34
Stubbs, W. 172
substance over form (IASB Conceptual Framework) 96
Sullivan, S. 382
sulphur dioxide trading schemes 358
Sundin, H. 200
"super wicked" problems 23
SustainAbility 189
sustainability accounting: materials and energy accounting 208–210, *209*, 212, 219, 222; strategic environmental management accounting 186, 190
Sustainability Accounting Standards Board (SASB) 114–119, **114**, **142**; financial markets 174; materials and energy accounting 219, 221; merger plans with the IIRC 121n3
Sustainability Assessment Model 228, **229**, 232; output examples *245*
sustainability balanced scorecard 182, 188
sustainability governance 78–89; adaptive **83–84**, 85–87, 89; environmental impact-valuation assemblages 237, 239–241, 244, 246; transformative **83–84**, 87–89
sustainability report assurance *see* assurance, environmental reporting
sustainability variance 184
Sustainable Development 266
Sustainable Development Goals (SDGs) 7, 23; accounting profession, thought leadership 70, 72–73; Africa 269–272; Asia 282; benchmarking 189; biodiversity 379–380; environmental impact-valuation assemblages 237, 241; environmental management accounting 208, 212, 221–222; financial markets 172, 175; methodising 48–49, *49*; Middle East and North Africa 300, 311, 311n5; sustainability governance 80, 87; United Arab Emirates 311n5; water 365–367, **367**, 369, 373
Sustainable Fashion initiative 71
Sustainable Finance Initiative 172
Sustainable Stock Exchanges Initiative 311n5
Swedberg, R. 47, 50, 57
Sweden 288, 291, 293; biodiversity 381; norm development in environmental reporting 139, **141**
Swensson, N. 256
Syria 302, 305
systems theory 30; complex adaptive 23; general 19–20, 23
Szilagyi, P. G. 159

Taibi, S. 228
Tanzania 266, 268
Taplin, J. **229**
Task Force on Climate-related Financial Disclosures (TCFD) 114; financial accounting and reporting 103; financial markets 173–174, **173**; KPMG's work 71; materials and energy accounting 221; strategic environmental management accounting 182; sustainability governance 87
taxes 231; carbon 231, 281, 357
Taylor, S. 356
technical integration of sustainability into strategy 185
Te Pas, K. 305
Terziovski, M. 128
Thailand 280
theorising 29, 39; carbon accounting 356–357; emergence of environmental reporting 30; field-level change in environmental reporting 35–36; *how* of environmental accounting and reporting 32–33; role of environmental accounting in organisational level change 33–35; role of language in environmental reporting 38–39; stakeholder engagement

around environmental reporting 37–38; *why* of environmental reporting 30–32
theory of change 52, 63n7
Thevenot, L. 36
Thomassen, M. A. 355
Thompson, A. 21
Thompson, T. A. 154
Thomson, I. 5, 10, **19**, 34–35, 37–38, 50, 88
Thoradeniya, P. 39n2
thought leadership, accounting profession 65–75, 99
timeless information (IASB Conceptual Framework) **96**
timeliness, environmental reporting **113**
Tinker, A. M. 20, 98
transparency: Africa 269; Asia 276–277; carbon accounting 358; China 277; environmental reporting 120; financial accounting and reporting 101; foundations of environmental accounting 20, 22; future of environmental accounting 12; materials and energy accounting 212; Middle East and North Africa 301, 305, 307, 310; norm development in environmental reporting 139, 146; shareholder activism 155, 157–158; sustainability governance 87; sustainability report assurance 128, 133
Tregidga, H. 38, 332–333, 382
Trillium Asset Management 153
triple bottom line accounting *see* sustainability accounting
Trucost **229**
Tsalavoutas, I. 172
Tunisia 302, 309
Tuokuu, F. X. D. 265
Tuvalu 329
Tweedie, D. 36, 189

Ullmann, A. E. 31
unburnable carbon 103–104
understandable information (IASB Conceptual Framework) **96**
unemployment: Africa 268; Middle East and North Africa 301, 310
Unerman, J. 13, 29, 37–38, 66, 174, 225, 357–358
UNESCO World Water Assessment Programme (WWAP) 366
Union Carbide 318
United Arab Emirates (UAE) 126, 302, 307–308
United Kingdom (UK): biodiversity 381; carbon emissions 243–244, 283; environmental reporting practice 109, 288–289, 291, 293–295; Farm Animal Welfare Council 392; financial accounting and reporting 96; foundations of environmental accounting 22; general election (2019) 73; Green Party 73; Modern Slavery Act 80; negative emissions technologies 359; norm development in environmental reporting 36, 138–139, **141**, 146; Office of National Statistics 241; *Pearce Report* 18; rewilding project 58–62, **59–61**; shareholder activism 160; social accounting 6; stakeholder engagement 37; sustainability report assurance 126; university accounting courses 17; water 369, 372
United Nations (UN): biodiversity 377, 379; Business and Human Rights Guiding Principles 272; *Convention on Biological Diversity* 379; environmental management accounting defined 181; Environmental Programme (UNEP) 302; Intergovernmental Panel on Climate Change (IPCC) 18, 354, 358; Millennium Development Goals 334, 366; *Millennium Ecosystem Assessment* xxi; Reducing Emissions from Deforestation and Forest Degradation (REDD) programme 270, 382; SDGs *see* Sustainable Development Goals; World Water Development Reports (WWDR) 365–366, 368
United Nations Conference for Trade and Development (UNCTAD): externalities **227**; financial accounting and reporting 99, **100**; International Standards of Accounting and Reporting 8
United States of America (USA): Acid Rain Programme 357; biofuel policy 355; civil rights movement 18; Clean Air Act (CAA) 18, **317**; Dodd Frank Act 169, **317**; Emergency Planning and Community Right to Know Act (EPCRA) **317**; Energy Policy Act 156; environmental accounting research 315–322; Environmental Protection Agency (EPA) 156, 225, **227**; environmental reporting frameworks 117; financial accounting and reporting 99, 101; financial markets 169; Generally Accepted Accounting Principles (GAAP) 101; Government Accountability Office (GAO) 320; Hurricane Katrina 371; materials and energy accounting 221; National Environmental Policy Act (NEPA) **317**; regulatory environment **317**; Safe Drinking Water Act 156; shareholder activism 151–153, 155–161; Superfund 99, **317**; Toxic Release Inventory (TRI) 241, **317**
Universidad de Buenos Aires 342
Universidad del Quindío, Colombia 342
Universidad Nacional de Colombia 342
Universidad Nacional de La Plata 342
US Mine Safety and Health 169

Valdés, P. 344
Value Reporting Foundation 121n3
Van Bommel, K. 36
Van Buren, H. III 155
Van Dijk, A. 330
van Staden, C. 32, 319, 332
Venezuela 343, 345

verifiable information (IASB Conceptual Framework) **96**
verification *see* assurance, environmental reporting
Vesty, G. M. 184, 189
Vinnari, E. 36
Vishwanathan, P. 198

Wainstein, M. 341
Wallace, D. 22, 167
waste hierarchy 253
waste management: Africa 270–271; Middle East and North Africa 301–302, 305, 307, 309; *see also* circular economy
Watene, K. 21
water 365–368, 373–374; Africa 270–271; challenges 366–367, **367–368**, 368; governance 369–370, 373; management, and organisations 370–371; Mexico 315; Middle East and North Africa 300–302, 305, 308–309; North America 315, 317–318; provision of water and sanitation services 368–369; resource management 371–372; scholarship 368–373; Singapore 280
water–energy nexus 211
web-based environmental reports 111, 117–118
Wegener, M. 169–170
Wei, Q. 356
Weick, K. 29, 39
Whiteman, G. 210
"wicked" problems: future of environmental accounting 23; methodising 54; Pacific region 335; sustainability governance 86
wildfires 329
Wijethilake, C. 183–184
Williams, B. 331
Winn, M. I. 210
Wisner, P. S. 188
Wong, R. 126
workers' rights 268, 272
World Animal Protection 392
World Bank 301–302, 305, 307; InfoDev Program 278
World Benchmarking Alliance 13, 87, 189
World Business Council for Sustainable Development (WBCSD) **142**, 280; KPMG's work 71–72
World Development 266
World Economic Forum 72
World Federation of Exchanges 311n5
World Wildlife Fund (WWF): *Living Planet Reports* xxi, 377–378, 383; pulp and paper industry 317
Wu, J. 356

Xing, Y. **229**

Yamagami, T. 279
Yemen 302

Zacari, A. 343
Zambia 268
Zimbabwe 271
Zvedov, D. 189
Zwijnenburg, W. 305

For Product Safety Concerns and Information please contact our
EU representative GPSR@taylorandfrancis.com Taylor & Francis
Verlag GmbH, Kaufingerstraße 24, 80331 München, Germany